STO

W9-DFF-719

11·5·79

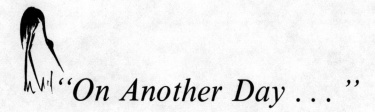

"On Another Day ..."

TALES TOLD AMONG THE NKUNDO OF ZAÏRE

"On Another Day..."

TALES TOLD AMONG THE NKUNDO OF ZAÏRE

BY MABEL H. ROSS AND BARBARA K. WALKER

With a Foreword by Daniel J. Crowley

ARCHON BOOKS / 1979

Library of Congress Cataloging in Publication Data

Main entry under title:

"On another day ... "

    Collected folktales translated from Lonkundo, Flemish, and French.
    "Adaptations ... of five of the tales ... appeared in the March 1975 issue of *Instructor*."
    Bibliography: p.
    Includes index.
    1. Tales, Nkundo. I. Ross, Mabel H., 1909– II.
Walker, Barbara K., 1921–
GR357.82.N57052   398.2'09675'1   78-6860
ISBN 0-208-01699-6

Adaptations by Mabel Ross and Barbara K. Walker of five of the tales in the present volume—Tales 13, 14, 27, 36, and 41—appeared in the March 1975 issue of *Instructor* under the title "Folktales from Zaïre."

Dedicated to our husbands,
John E. Ross and Warren S. Walker

Contents

Foreword

SURROUNDED BY FILE CABINETS containing copies of some 12,000 African folktale texts taken from published sources, and knowing that another 3,000 to 5,000 could easily be found in recently published books, older books not yet processed by me, public and private archives such as Biebuyck's 800 Nyanga tales, and other unpublished sources, I must ask myself, "Does the world really need a collection of 95 Nkundo tales?"

In 1964 in his enlightening survey of African folklore, Bascom[1] demonstrated that, despite preconceptions to the contrary, Zaïre (ex-Belgian Congo and Congo Kinshasa) is exceedingly well represented in the published sources. Limiting himself largely to major collections of over 50 tales each, Bascom cites a total of 1,099 tale texts from Zaïre, of which an astonishing 446, or nearly half, were published in their original language as well as in translation in a European language, and are thus available for close analysis of stylistic and linguistic features otherwise impossible. He adds that "within the last ten years ... more verbal art has been published for the Nkundo of the Congo than for any other African group; the works of Boelaert, van Goethem, Hulstaert, and de Rop include major collections of proverbs, riddles, and tales (including the largest collection of dilemma tales), two versions of a long epic poem, and a unique collection of formal greetings, all with text and translations." Of these, 88 Nkundo texts (including the 46 dilemma tales) have been published in Lonkundo and, of all difficult languages, Flemish,

9

and another 10 or so may lurk unidentified in mixed collections by
Stappers, Mamet, de Bouveignes, and Badibanga. Now we are faced
with 95 more, mercifully in English, as well as the 25 texts published
by Cobble and those 42 still only in Lonkundo in the *Bekolo Bèmò*
. . . reader cited by Walker but not by Bascom (18 of the 60 are
translated here), for an estimated grand total of 254 Nkundo tales
in print, nearly one quarter of the Zaïre total. An impressive amount
of documentation on the verbal art of a small and rather obscure
people in far-off Central Africa, but what forever for? What use can
ever be made of them?

That small and elite group of zealots who actually read forewords
know full well that every rhetorical question posed therein is sure to
be answered, if you will pardon the expression, in spades. So let me
begin by stating categorically that every carefully collected text is a
valuable artifact *sui generis*, or such is the faith of the folklorist.
As students of narrative performances and the texts they produce,
we can never have too much raw material for our analyses, whether
literary, ethnological, diffusionistic, linguistic, statistical, psycho-
logical, structural, or whatever other approaches or methods have
been or one day will be tried on them. Even more, we value the
stories in their own right, for the aesthetic impact they have on their
intended audiences, and for the cultural values they propagate so
subtly. In this view, we non-Nkundo are lucky to have a chance to
enjoy these stories, so carefully collected, translated, and mounted
for our appreciation. And by the very number of their published
tales, the Nkundo have become the most important people in Zaïre
for folklorists.

The collection and study of African narrative began long ago,
the first known published collection being *Fables Sénégalaises
Recueillies de l'Oulof*, 43 Wolof tales translated into French verse
by le Bon Roger, French Commandant of Senegal, in 1828. Such
an early collection, and by so unlikely a collector, suggests that the
importance of African folklore was apparent even to the earliest
colonialists, and indeed, a collection of proverbs was published in a
Wolof grammar by Dard two years previously.[2] And this was just
the beginning. As European administrators, traders, and missionaries
spread through the continent, more and more tale collections were
published. Inevitably the distribution was highly uneven, with many
areas such as Mauritania, the Gambia, Guinea Bissau, Congo
Brazzaville, and Centrafrique ill-reported, but with some 1,207
texts published from a single ethnic group alone, the Hausa of
Nigeria.

The central problem is that we have too many tales and not enough analyses. These vast riches do not readily lend themselves to any scholarly analysis beyond content, and indeed were all too often collected without any such analysis in mind. Linguists collected tales as samples of language usage, teachers as a means of inculcating local languages, missionaries to study local values and beliefs, African elites in pursuit of vindication against colonialism, diffusionists in search of distribution patterns on which to base migration theories, litterateurs and journalists looking for "authentic" themes, and the writers of children's books in need of fresh sources to patronize, bowdlerize, and prettify. Alas, the quality was equally uneven, varying from the most erudite and detailed texts analyzed for linguistic purposes through pedestrian translations and slapdash journalistic rewrites to enigmatic plot summaries that omit all that is valuable and meaningful in the stories. Very very few of these myriad collectors were interested in the tales for their own sake or for what value they might have to scholars with interests different from their own. Worst of all, they ignored all the facts surrounding the texts themselves: the storytellers, their age, class, and training, and the circumstances of collection, not to mention the relationship between the narrator and his audience, or between his tales and the cultural values they reflect. Because of this unevenness in distribution and in quality, the total published body of African tale texts can be used for only one kind of analysis, that of their *content*, since their forms and styles are all too often dissipated through translation, rewriting and editing. But alas, as yet only a few limited attempts have been made to work out an African Tale Type Index containing all available bibliographic references for every tale that occurs more than once in African tradition, thereby allowing the kinds of textual and diffusionistic studies of content that have proven so useful in European folklore research since the publication of the Aarne-Thompson Type Index.[3] The list of Types and Motifs for these tales in the appendix is a rare and important development in the study of African narration. Until Africa has such a basic reference work, we cannot even begin to solve the most obvious problems of our discipline, the nature of tale creation and dissemination, and what relationship, if any, these have with language, religion, geography, culture, or other factors. Oft attempted, the task is so laborious that only a well-financed multidisciplinary team of scholars can ever hope to accomplish it. But until we do, we will always be a bit amateurish, and unable to attack the more challenging problems of style and function that confront us.[4]

But if all texts are valuable in their own right and for their use in literary or distribution studies or other kinds of content analysis, this particular study is outstanding in the high quality of its collection and presentation. Because of the enlightened approach of the collector, Mabel H. Ross, these texts are impeccable, without editing or "correcting" of any kind, and when it is suspected that the informants have been a little more explicit about difficult local history, terms, or concepts than they would have been with an all-Nkundo audience, such "asides" are carefully demoted to verbatim footnotes. Since the collecting took place in five different contexts ranging from the traditional village setting to a solitary narrator performing into his own tape recorder, some observations of contextual influences can be made in the manner of the contemporary performance-oriented school of folklorists.

The most serious criticism that can be leveled against this collection is that it is of necessity almost entirely in translation, with no original texts in Lonkundo except the eighteen from *Bekolo Bemo* ... by which to check the degree of closeness to original idioms, forms of expression, or other stylistic or linguistic conformations. No matter how meticulously collected, texts in African languages are forever incomprehensible to everyone outside the culture, and translation inevitably destroys much of the narrative style and flavor. At the same time, in these Nkundo texts, length and cost war against the inclusion of the original texts in Lonkundo. Considering the few bilinguals capable of evaluating the quality of the translation, and the existence of over half (148 to 254) of all Nkundo texts already available in the original language, their omission here is acceptable. The multilingual team of translators is just about as efficient as possible under the circumstances. At the same time, no translation, no matter how sensitive, can ever carry all the nuances of the original language—one has only to visualize how Shakespeare's Prince Hamlet would sound if he really did speak his lines in Danish, or how Eliza Doolittle comes through in Viennese German. Unless we learn Lonkundo, we can never hope to appreciate all the facets of these narrations, no matter how carefully the translators have sought to preserve linguistic and stylistic effects. The scholarly world awaits the insights of the African folklorists now in training abroad. Their bilingual skills and cross-cultural experiences make them the exegetes of the future.

The care taken with the translations is also evident in the completeness of the documentation of the circumstances of the telling: the name, age, and background of the narrators, the audience rapport and method of collection, the use of gestures, and such stylistic devices as rhyme, songs, repetition, and onomatopoeia. Short of learning Lonkundo and then watching a narrator in person or on film, this is as close as we can get to the tales of an exotic society. The extensive ethnographic notes appended to every tale also help illuminate the implications of the plot and the meaning of some of the terms, beliefs, and actions of the characters. As an infinitely curious and questioning ethnographer, I value the positioning of the notes close to the text, although I admit they may disturb the narrative continuity for more casual readers. Certainly they bring the stories to life for me, adding point and fleshing out the storytelling events.

Just as with translation, nothing can replace the actual singing of the songs in the many *cante fables* in this collection, but at least they are translated as expressions set apart from the prose texts, and not merely omitted as in too many collections. In some future ideal world, a tape or disc of the songs will be fitted into an envelope attached to the back cover of publications such as this, but then one would want samples of the original narrative as well, or, better yet, sound films of the complete event with dubbed English subtitles as in an Italian film.

Perhaps the most exciting aspect of this study beyond the fine texts themselves is the right-mindedness and completeness of their analysis by Barbara K. Walker. Her choice of titles based on values or actions rather than on mere characters, her inclusion of all tales collected, even not especially artistic texts, and her ample discussion of variants both in space and in time are models of rational presentation. Although it may raise a few eyebrows among the Nkundo, her arrangement of the tales according to the four Aarne-Thompson divisions is acceptable in lieu of a local Nkundo concept of their proper order, and her indication of types and motifs both previously identified in the available indexes and identified here for the first time will be greeted with cheers by that small and aging band of unreconstructed diffusionists who know the effort it cost and the stimulus it will give to basic comparative content analysis in the future. Her discussions of diffusion patterns too are scrupulously based on the data at hand, and strictly limited by area. Her interest in aesthetics, in citing the distinguishing techniques of each narrator and the responses he produced in his audiences, will please scholars from the many disciplines now concerned with "communication." Finally, the publication of an "original" tale text, so very rare in the annals of the folk, must be heralded even though one suspects that the narrator is not quite as unfettered by tradition as he thinks himself to be. Proof that even the creative act is limited by the culture in which it occurs only serves to encourage further study of the nature of tradition and innovation.

Storytelling is one of the very few universal practices of mankind over the last twenty millenia or so. Narrative is important to mankind, for entertainment, for education, for projecting dreams and experiencing aggression, and some day we will know better how to comprehend the deeper meanings these stories hold. In the meantime, these Nkundo tales are ours for the reading, courtesy of their narrators, collector, and analyst.

University of California   DANIEL J. CROWLEY
Davis, California

1. William R. Bascom, "Folklore Research in Africa," *Journal of American Folklore*, 77/303 (January–March 1964), 12–31.

2. M. le Bon Roger, *Fables Sénégalaises Recueillies de l'Oulof* (Paris: Nepvue, Firmin Didot, Ponthieu, 1828); J. Dard, *Grammaire Wolofe* ([n.p.]: l'Imprimerie Royale, 1826), both cited by Bascom, above.

3. Stith Thompson, *The Types of the Folktale: A Classification and Bibliography*, Antti Aarne's *Verzeichnis der Märchentypen* (FF Communications No. 3) translated and enlarged. FF Communications No. 184, second revision (Helsinki: Suomalainen Tiedeakatemia, Academia Scientiarum Fennica, 1961).

4. Daniel J. Crowley, "A Tale Type Index for Africa," *Research in African Literatures*, I/1 (1970), 50–52.

Acknowledgments

A WORK OF THIS SCOPE cannot be completed without the help of many people, not least of these "the fathers" from whose rich oral repertories our Nkundo storytellers drew their own treasuries of tales. The present narrators, of course, deserve our deepest thanks for their willingness to share with those outside their own culture the narratives mirroring their values, their customs, and their oral history; all of these narrators have been identified in "Sites and Circumstances of Narration." Our thanks go also to those missionaries who opened their homes to Mrs. Ross during the collecting of these tales and who provided transportation, background information, encouragement, and access to a wide range of narrators. Included among Mrs. Ross's host families were Don and Barbara Angle of Bóléngé, Ron and Clela Anderson of Boende, Robert and Jane Williams of Mbandaka, and Mary Hitchings of Tondo. We are grateful also to President Mobutu Sese Seko and to his personal physician, Dr. William Close, for numerous courtesies extended during the period of tale collecting.

Without the help of such translation aides as Bokunge Jacques, Tata Manga, and Pierre Sangana, the transliterations of the taped Lonkundo tales would have lacked the richness of Lonkundo diction offered here. For their patience and persistence we are truly grateful. Gratitude is expressed, too, to Clayton and Ethel Terry, of Indianapolis, who aided Mrs. Ross most graciously during the period spent there in working with Pierre Sangana.

We want especially to thank Robert Stewart, of the Peace Corps, who recorded for this volume a memorable evening storytelling session at Bonga-Iteli and who has maintained a lively interest in this project from its beginning; the quotations from Bob's letter concerning his Bonga-Iteli visit have been included with his permission. Our appreciation goes, too, to Dorothy Parker, still in the mission field in Zaïre, for the continuing encouragement of the Nkundo themselves to record and preserve the tales they know and value.

Any scholarly study of field-collected narratives owes a debt beyond measure to the scholars and to the scholarly works that have blazed the trail. The indexes of types and of motifs, both those published and those available only through microxerography, have been of inestimable help to us; our indebtedness to the indexers has been indicated in the individual source citations for all type and motif entries throughout the volume. Among the scores of Africanists —some Europeans and some Americans—whose works have influenced our own, we wish especially to credit Hulstaert, de Rop, Rattray, Torrend, Bascom, Crowley, and the Herskovitses. Our dependence upon these and many other researchers in the field of African verbal art is readily apparent throughout the present work.

Special thanks go, too, to our indefatigable translators of the Flemish volumes, Dr. Tinco E. A. van Hylckama and Francien Muijen Wright, who expanded our research horizons immensely by their labors. Their good-tempered handling of these works has added decided dimension to our own efforts.

Words are inadequate to express our appreciation to Barbara Geyer, experienced and dedicated cartographer, for her contribution of the map prepared especially for this volume. The map clarifies the locations of all narration sites, of the homes of storytellers narrating while away from home, and of Monieka, scene of the compilation of *Bekolo Bémó Bendemba Ba-Nkundo* and of *Wembi, the Singer of Stories*. The use, form, and spelling of all geographic names are in accordance with the *United States Board on Geographic Names Gazetteer No. 80, Republic of the Congo (Leopoldville) 1964, Gazetteer No. 61, Republic of the Congo (Brazzaville) 1962*, and *Gazetteer Supplement, Asia and Africa, 1972*, with the exception of the use and spelling of "Besenge" instead of "Bensenge." Other materials relied upon in the compilation of the map have been the *Times Atlas of the World, Comprehensive Edition, 1975*, and the *International Map of the World (United Nations) at 1:1,000,000*, Sheet SA 34, Inongo, Series 1301, Edition 3—AMS, 1960.

For aid and encouragement in the present project, we are indebted also to Dan Crowley, who has consistently buttressed our intentions; to George Griffin, who saw this manuscript in its earliest stages; to Botsang Mosienyane, of Botswana, Reatile S. Mochebelele and Edwin Seitlheko, of Lesotho, and Joseph K. Kibera, of Kenya, for sharing tales still current in the oral traditions of their respective countries; to Jo Carr, lay missionary in Rhodesia (then the Federation of Rhodesia and Nyasaland) from 1952–1957, for invaluable insights into that area and its oral traditions; to numerous librarians all over the United States who made possible our use of books and articles we could not otherwise have obtained; and to the entire staff at The Shoe String Press, without whose forbearance and splendid workmanship this study would not now be in the hands of its readers.

M.H.R. and B.K.W.

General Introduction

THE GENERAL INTRODUCTION *has been presented in two signed sections. Mabel H. Ross first sets Zaïre in geographical and historical perspective, introduces the Nkundo (the Zaïrian tribe among whom her major field collecting was done), details Nkundo life style, customs, values, and diction, cites the cultural changes evidenced by the Nkundo over a twenty-five-year period (1950–1975), describes the techniques used in collecting and preserving the narratives reflecting the Nkundo as a people, and states her purpose in making these tales available. Barbara K. Walker then describes the method selected for the handling of the Ross collection and of variants of the field-collected tales translated from Lonkundo, Flemish, and French, defines and distinguishes among the sources and scholarly tools used, clarifies the organizational plan for the present volume, and evaluates the field tapes, indicating at relevant points the contributions of this study to the field of African verbal-art research. Additional contributions of the study are cited in the introductions to the four subdivisions of the tales and in the notes, eliminating the need for an Afterword.*

Aids to users of the volume include a map prepared specifically for this study, a pronunciation guide to Lonkundo (the language of the Nkundo), descriptions of the sites and circumstances of the collecting and of the personal characteristics and storytelling techniques of the narrators, introductions to the four subdivisions of the narrative materials, notes, a selected bibliography, and an index.

B. K. W.

19

ZAÏRE (until 1960 known to most Westerners as the Belgian Congo) is located in the heart of Africa, straddling the equator. About one-third the size of the United States, it has a population of approximately twenty-two million. Except that it lacks true desert areas, the country offers as many different kinds of terrain as can be found elsewhere at that latitude; rivers are everywhere, threading grasslands, swamps, dense forests, and agricultural areas producing palm fruit, cotton, rubber, sugar cane, and coffee. The country's political history —from the early tribal kingdoms and empires, through exploration and colonization by the Portuguese, followed by establishment of the Congo Free State under Belgium's King Léopold II and its subsequent annexation as the Belgian Congo in 1908, with continued Belgian development of the colony's vast natural resources— culminated on June 30, 1960, in the achievement of independence from colonial rule. Renamed first The Republic of the Congo and then The Democratic Republic of the Congo, in 1971 it assumed the title The Republic of Zaïre.

The Nkundo, or Mongo-Nkundo, one of many Bantu-language-speaking groups, live in the central part of Zaïre known as the Cuvette, within Équateur Province. Much of this area is rain forest with some commercial agriculture—chiefly palm fruit and cotton— immense stretches of swamp land, and almost no known mineral wealth. The field collecting for this volume was done in a large rain forest interlaced with swamps and rivers; the temperature there ranges normally from about 65 degrees to 92 degrees Fahrenheit. In this particular portion of Zaïre, travel poses problems for the field collector as well as for the Nkundo themselves. Canoes are commonly used in the swamps and on the rivers, and paths wind through the forest for those traveling by bicycle or on foot. One traveling by bicycle must carry his bicycle and other equipment on his head or shoulders when he wades the swamps. River boats, introduced during the era of Belgian control, afford scheduled though decidedly uncomfortable transportation on the major waterways.

Because they live in forest and swamp areas, economically the Nkundo are poor, a factor which causes other peoples of Zaïre to consider them inferior; despite this stigma, many Nkundo have attained important positions in their country both politically and financially. Their location in a forest area, with the adaptations necessary to that habitat, has determined the chief distinguishing characteristics of the Nkundo, whose neighbors live in entirely different geographical settings: grassy savannas, rolling grasslands, rugged mountains, shrub-covered uplands, and coastal lowlands, each producing its distinctive living and occupational pattern, domestic structure, and local tongue.

The forest about them is in continuous biotic production, so the Nkundo feel a less pressing need of preparing for the future or of amassing a supply of material goods than do those tribal groups living in areas where food and shelter are less readily available. Also, the extended-family pattern of living prevalent among the Nkundo ensures care and protection for those unable to provide for themselves in times of misfortune. This combination of factors has contributed to the supposition that the Nkundo are by nature irresponsible, even lazy. Those who have lived and worked among them have found the Nkundo, on the contrary, ready to assume the obligations established within their tradition, intensely loyal to and supportive of their families and friends, and concerned with the maintenance of sound reputations among their peers. Long-standing social disapproval of theft, of murder, and of false accusation—quite apart from legislated law and order—prompt them to be honest and deserving of community approbation.

As is true with most other Zaïrian peoples, the Nkundo live in villages—usually small ones, since each centers around an extended-family group—stretching along a path, a road, or a waterway. These villages are surrounded by patches of cleared places in the forest where the women plant their gardens. On the outskirts of many Nkundo villages live the *elinga*, year-round specialists in fishing, and the Batswa, the semipygmy peoples who have for centuries been the slaves of the Nkundo. Differentiated only by their occupational specialty, the fisher people are a part of the Nkundo community; the Batswa, segregated for many generations by marriage tabus, are regarded almost as animals, rather than as people, and their presence is tolerated only for the services they can render.

Apart from the menial labor performed by the Batswa, the work in and about the Nkundo community is divided along strictly sexual lines, with the men expected to hunt, fish in the larger waterways, clear the land for the women's gardens, gather palm fruit, collect and erect the supporting poles and prepare the heavy *ndele* thatch for the houses, protect the women and children, make canoes, and assume leadership of the household and of the village. To the women is assigned the work proper to women in that culture: the bearing and nurture of children, the cultivating of the gardens, the gathering of swamp and forest foods other than meat and palm fruit, the preparing of food and of condiments, the tying together and mudding of the house walls, the care of the house and the surrounding grounds, the washing of clothes for family members at home and in hospital care, and the fetching of water for household use. As is shown in the tales in the Ross collection, the women also do limited types of fishing—chiefly in the swamps—and occasionally accompany their husbands on extended hunting or fishing expeditions to cook for them and to prepare and preserve the game caught. At an early age, the children are taught their respective roles in the community, and undertake whatever work they are old enough and strong enough to do. Cultural expectations of each of these groups are confirmed and strengthened by the secret societies to which, according to their ages, they belong, affording peer-group support lacking in some Zaïrian tribes, including the Bolia.

Since sources of protein are scarce in the Cuvette, both hunting and fishing are essential concerns of the men; a good hunter is especially respected. For the securing of large animals, pits are dug and covered with branches in the paths of the desired prey, usually wild pigs, leopards, and elephants; traps for birds and monkeys are set in the trees. Often, huge nets are spread over open areas by a group of hunters who then frighten such animals as antelopes, rats, tortoises, and porcupines into the nets by the making of loud noises. At times, the men of a village build a long, leaf-covered fence with traps at intervals along it; then they drive various animals toward the fence by means of pounding noises, catching the prey as they dodge into the traps in their effort to pass through the fence. Bows and arrows and spears are also used by hunters in the rain forest. From early childhood, boys learn to set traps for birds and rats near their village and are always ready to be included in a hunting trip into the forest. Since no hunt has been completed until the products of the hunt have been shared, the division of the spoils is observed, with the partition of each kind of animal following a prescribed pattern; the most elaborate pattern follows the killing of an elephant. First, the hunter must *sésa njòku* (literally, "bless or *greet* the elephant"). Since it is such a large animal, he must go into great detail in telling how he killed it, beginning with the tracing of his ancestry, since traits of his ancestors led to his being able to kill the elephant. After the lengthy telling of this story, he cuts off the elephant's tail, which by rights belongs to him; then others can help with the cutting and dividing. The village chief receives a prescribed part, as do the elders of the village. The hunter's family must also have a share. A smaller catch does not require as extensive a ceremony, but the ceremony must still follow the traditional pattern.

Fishing is done by the men largely during the dry season, when hunting becomes more difficult because of the animals' consequently increased range and when the rivers are more likely to be contained within their banks. Huge woven traps placed at intervals in deeper portions of the river enable the Nkundo to secure some of the larger types of fish. In shallow places in the river, the spearing of fish is common. Long lines with hooks lowered into the water are often used for securing bait for larger fish. Fish of all sizes and varieties are captured in nets. Sometimes a fisherman manages to capture a crocodile, either by spearing him or by catching him asleep on the river bank with his mouth wide open; in the latter case, after propping the crocodile's mouth open with a stick, the fisherman ties the crocodile's jaws very tightly in that position and then loops the crocodile's tail, tying it to the animal's body; he can thus safely drag the live crocodile to a place where he can cut up and share the meat, a delicacy with more the flavor of fowl than of fish.

Since the packets of meat or fish must be carried long distances from the hunting or fishing site, they are wrapped in large, strong leaves (the *nkongo* is a favorite choice, and readily accessible) or in palm fronds; a package, or *boteta*, made of palm fronds is usable for carrying items as widely varied as wild honey—found in the forest—and live chickens (since the container can be dipped occasionally into a stream or into a pool in the swamp to cool it, this method eliminates the need for refrigeration). Food packets requiring tying can be secured by cord made from *ngòji*, a vine readily available.

Swidden agriculture, practiced among the Nkundo, requires the clearing of large trees and much brush from the land; this is considered men's work. Machetes and occasionally axes are used in cutting the forest growth; the usable wood is removed from the site, and then the scraps and the brush are burned, producing an ash that enriches the soil for gardening. Trees and tree limbs that are straight and of the thickness of a man's arm are especially sought for use in house construction. After they have been pointed at the end, these posts are driven into the ground to form the uprights for the house—again, properly the work of the men, as is the making of the thatch for the roof, for which a wide, durable type of palm frond, *ndele*, is used.

Gathering of the palm fruit, a difficult and taxing chore reserved for the men, requires the climbing of the palm-tree trunk to the point where the branches begin and where the clusters of palm fruit needed in food preparation are to be found. Two methods of climbing the palm tree are in use in the Cuvette: the bamboo ladder and the *bolango*, or climbing belt. Among the Nkundo, the bamboo ladder

is slightly more popular than is the *bolango*. The ladder consists of
a long stalk of bamboo, with its joints or nodes serving as rungs for
the barefooted climber; leaned against the tree trunk, it functions
as a sturdy and dependable means of ascent and descent. Instead of
a bamboo ladder, all of the Ubangi and many of the Nkundo use
a climbing belt made of unslit *ngòji* or some other durable, flexible,
wide vine; the belt is wrapped around the tree and then around the
hips of the climber, allowing him to lean back on it and move it
up one side of the tree while he walks up the other side. The climber's
dependence on the climbing belt is illustrated in several of the tales
in the Ross collection.

The work of Nkundo women is steady, unremitting, and arduous.
The care of the home, unaided by cleaning implements other than
rough brooms, the gardening, by means of very crude tools, the
preparation of the one meal of the day—served after dark, following
the gathering of ingredients from garden and forest, preparation of
flour and even of salt by hand, and cooking over an open fire—and
the incessant carrying of water for all household uses, often long
distances, in jars or buckets balanced on their heads would seem
sufficiently onerous. But concurrent with this labor is the responsibility for one or more small children, the youngest tied to the
mother's back by her *ifuta*, or overskirt, except when nursing, and
the toddlers in the care of still older children supervised by the mother.

In general, the women's time is divided between food cultivating
and gathering and work at the home site. Planted, hoed, cultivated,
harvested, and carried home by the women from their forest gardens
are usually manioc or cassava, corn, and sweet potatoes; beneath
the plantains and bananas in the gardens behind the houses are
normally peppers, beans, and eggplants. Supplementing these starchy
foods are edible roots dug in the forest, an asparaguslike vegetable
(*bieya*) found in the swampy areas, various wild fruits (*nsabu*, a
cylindrical deep-purple fruit requiring heating and seasoning, and
etofi, which can be eaten raw), and caterpillars, found tucked in the
crevices of trees and carried home as a toothsome treat for the
husband. Once these foods have been gathered, the lengthy, toilsome
process of food preparation begins. The manioc roots must have
been soaked in water for at least a week before they can be used;
the leaf of the manioc does not require soaking, but is instead
pounded, cooked, and served with palm-oil sauce. Plantains, a
bananalike fruit, may be cooked by steaming (wrapped in leaves) or
by baking, may be pounded into dough and then made into bread
or cakes, or may be prepared with a seasoning of palm sauce. After

the overlapping leaves of the *bieya* have been removed and the stalks have been thoroughly washed, this delicacy is steamed to tenderness. Equally carefully treated are the caterpillars: first blanched to remove the fur, they are then fried to a crisp and delicious state. The meat and fish brought home by the husband are usually either fried in palm oil or steamed in palm sauce. The inclusion of much hot pepper relieves this starchy diet of its deadly monotony, since more often than not, the meal lacks such embellishments as meat or fish, *bieya*, caterpillars, and forest fruits; the only foods of which the family can be certain are the products of the woman's garden. Food preparation occurs in the woman's kitchen, close behind the house and with easy access to the home garden.

The home of the Nkundo, the scene of most of the family activities when the members are not at work, is a rectangular structure supported by poles pounded into the earth and tied together by strips of *ngòji*; these tying strips are close enough together so that the women, aided by the children, can mud the walls thus made, securing the family against the evening chill and the heavy rain. The thatched *ndele* roof, put on by the men before the floor can be prepared, is unbroken by any openings for the escape of smoke, so the rafters and inside walls of the house are black and shiny from the smoke of the household fire; no house can be truly "homey" until it has been thoroughly darkened by the fire. The most satisfactory floor is one made of ant-hill clay, clay brought largely by the children and then pounded down by all the family members to make a firm, smooth floor. Both the floor and the fenced front yard are swept clean by homemade brooms, removing the litter caused by windblown leaves as well as by the droppings of the scrawny chickens, goats, dogs, and occasionally pigs regarded as domestic property (and readily identifiable by their respective owners) but not the specific responsibility of any given family member and dependent for their food on whatever scraps might be foraged in their yard or in someone else's.

The carrying of water from the nearest river, swamp, or spring, work delegated to the women and girls, is a never-ending task; apart from clothes-washing and bathing, done at the water source, all home water needs are supplied by what has been hauled. Since dangers accompany any solitary foray from home, two or more women tend to go together to the same water source, affording them a welcome opportunity to talk and thus lighten the deadening character of their labors. In view of the difficulty involved in providing water, an Nkundo traveler or visitor carries his own water gourd with him; unless there is an excellent spring near his home, he fills the gourd with water that has been boiled. The gourd he carries has been prepared first by thorough drying and then by cleaning on the inside by the repeated shaking of very hard seeds dropped within it; it is corked with a leaf folded many times. (Incidents associated with water-fetching or water supply occur frequently in the Ross-collected tales.) Supplementing water as a beverage— particularly at feasts—are corn liquor and palm wine.

Whether engaged in feasting or in everyday labor, the Nkundo —except for very small children—wear some form of clothing, however improvised and scanty it may be. The Nkundo man is most often attired in shorts and shirt or in trousers and shirt, as is customary among the Western men whom he has seen. The Nkundo woman, however, tends to rely on the colorful and utilitarian blouse and two wraparound skirts traditional among her people. The underskirt is firmly tied in place; the outer skirt, or *ifuta*, may be wrapped about her shoulders or over her head for protection against rain or cold, may be tied at her back to carry an infant snugly and safely or at her hips to support a somewhat older small child, or—as in several of the Ross field tales—may be tucked in at her waist to conceal valuable belongings or weapons on her person, ensuring their safety and hers.

Ownership in an Nkundo village, where the people live largely in the open and share in all the activities of life, is rarely private. A few items do belong to an individual and must be firmly guarded: one's drinking gourd, one's knife or machete, one's scarring needle, or other special tool of some sort; many of the oral narratives teach respect for private ownership of such articles. However, the land on which the houses are built is generally the property of a few people, the *bamongesi*, those people—or their descendants—who originally settled that particular village site. The *bamongesi* must be consulted concerning any new home sites, any garden sites, hunting and fishing rights, and any other uses of the surrounding area. When a village is quite small, everyone in it may be a member of the *bamongesi*, but in a larger village only a few men or women, or both, are left to make such decisions. Often these and other matters are discussed and settled by palaver in a special village structure, the *botumba*, centrally located and roofed but not walled; this meeting place also houses trials for lawbreakers and palavers concerning domestic and local disputes, and serves as a refuge for any man wishing to escape the surveillance of his wife or wives.

In the old Nkundo culture, polygyny was· the accepted way of

life, and a man's wealth was determined by the number of wives
he possessed. Since the women made the gardens, cooked the food,
and did most of the heavy work of the household, it was not only
advantageous to the man to have several wives, but it was also
helpful for the wives to be able to share the work. Polygyny also
held some advantage for the newborn, for in a polygynistic household,
the husband does not cohabit with the new mother for two years
after the birth of her baby, thus ensuring her continued lactation
during that period—the mother's milk furnishes the child's only
food until he is two years old, at which time he is transferred to
the family diet. With the development of large-scale agriculture, of
industrialization, and of urban living, however, polygyny is becoming
increasingly unpopular. In the changing culture, one wife is all most
men can afford to obtain and to support. For, despite the fact that
Nkundo women are attaining greater freedom and are gradually
entering into many new activities both socially and economically,
the practice of the payment of bridewealth persists: bridewealth—
traditionally in the form of iron or copper bars, iron or copper
anklets and neck pieces, and other items of equal value—is still
passed from the groom's family to the bride's family as compensation
for the bride; this bridewealth is held in reserve for a brother of
the bride wishing to secure a wife for himself. The worth of a woman
as a potential wife is determined by a variety of factors, primary
among them the matter of fertility: a woman who has demonstrated
her ability to have a child possesses decided value; the child born
before wedlock normally belongs not to the new husband but to
the father of the bride, and no social criticism is brought to bear
upon such premarital pregnancies. Initially, an "educated" woman
was worth less to a prospective husband than was one who had not
gone to school; increasingly, the value of having a reasonably well-
educated wife has become apparent to the Nkundo, and the amount
of the woman's formal schooling has begun to enhance her worth as
a bride. A woman's general health, her strength, her willingness to
work, and her acceptance by her own community are among other
factors considered by the prospective groom's family; since the
expenditure for a wife is the heaviest one incurred during the lifetime
of most Nkundo males, a debt whose payment is more often than
not extended over a period of many years, the importance of a wise
choice is evident. On those occasions where divorce occurs, the
bridewealth—or at least a substantial portion of it—is returned to
the groom's family if the official palaver determines that the fault
in the matter lies with the wife; if the fault lies with the husband,

considerable difficulty attends the recovery of any part of the bride-wealth.

Children, the eagerly anticipated fruit of any Nkundo marriage, are an important part of Nkundo culture. From birth they are surrounded by the extended family and loved and nurtured by it. A child has many "parents" in the village, and grows up expecting them to help him in all he undertakes to do. Likewise, he will respect and care for his elders as he grows older. There are no "orphans" in such a society, nor are there any "childless" marriages. Education of the children has long been shared by both natural parents, although the wife does more teaching of the girls and the husband of the boys. History and the tribal and family traditions have been left to the elders, who have passed these traditions along most often in the form of tales, myths, and legends; the formal schooling introduced with Westernization has supplemented but not replaced the traditional oral instruction. Most Nkundo children learn to read and write, and many continue their education at schools far removed from their homes, an expense that has tended to prompt the Nkundo to limit the size of their families in order to make possible the financing of their children's higher education.

French is the educational and political language of Zaïre; almost all Nkundo children attend classes taught entirely in French, beginning with the first grade. The lingua franca of the country—an artificial language, Lingala—can be used almost anywhere in either the cities or the back country, leaving the truly native language of the people a threatened art. How many years, or perhaps generations, will a language such as Lonkundo continue in common use? Its tonal character, posing decided difficulties for the non-African, has no echoes either in French or in Lingala, and as the tendency toward Westernization accelerates, fewer and fewer Nkundo will trouble to maintain the language unless the importance of its function as a carrier of the oral tradition can be convincingly demonstrated. Even the *lokole*, the talking drum, for centuries the means of Nkundo long-distance communication as well as the summons to work, to school, to meetings, or to special events within the village, will fall out of use, since it depends on the tonal qualities of the Lonkundo.

The Nkundo are naturally responsive to tone and are decidedly musical. Their traditional instruments—developed largely for rhythm rather than for melody—and the songs and chants available for every occasion have been commended in a number of studies, among them de Rop's *De gesproken woordkunst van de Nkundó* (1956). A sense of rhythm is expressed even by the small child as he plays in the village street; lacking another instrument, he keeps time by patting his arms, legs, thighs, stomach, or buttocks, producing not only rhythm but pitch differences. As he matures, every step he takes has rhythm; paddling a canoe is lightened by a chant, and almost all other work is accompanied by some kind of song. Although none of the Ross-collected tales incorporated the use of any musical instrument other than the voice, the Nkundo in furnishing music for dancing do employ various handmade flutelike instruments, rattles, bells (similar to those affixed to hunting dogs), a wooden xylophone, a guitarlike stringed instrument, and a portable "thumb piano" consisting of a hollow wooden base to which the ends of reed or metal strips of varying thicknesses are attached (the free ends of the strips are plucked by the thumbs of the player). The singing and chanting in the *cante fables* are described at length in the notes for the tales concerned; the samples from Bonga-Iteli are especially rich in this respect.

Though the rhythm in the lives of the Nkundo continues to lighten their labors and brighten their nights, what facets of Nkundo life have changed during the third quarter of the twentieth century? And what elements of the culture—like their response to rhythm— have remained stable despite outward pressures? The most apparent changes, both economically and culturally, are those brought about by contact with Westerners, with the accompanying desires created for foreign products. In the aftermath of political change, much of the control formerly vested in the local chiefs has passed into the hands of a new élite class. As more and more young people benefit from higher education far from home, they tend to lose the deep respect formerly held for their elders, who have not had such worldly experiences. And women, both married and single, have found in urban areas freedoms that would have been impossible under their former village circumstances. Still, changes in the subtler and most basic aspects of Nkundo life have proceeded so slowly that they can scarcely be marked: most tribal customs have withstood the inroads of Westernization; the value system has been little altered; substantially the same tabus are still observed.

As do other Bantu-language peoples, the Nkundo believe in one all-superior god who is so far away that he has little or no interest in man's daily round. Of more immediate concern to the Nkundo as an individual are the supernatural beings and creatures with exceptional power and ability who dwell in every object or place he sees or encounters. The *bokalo* (spirit, or shade) who has dominion over a spring, a river, a swamp, a forest, or a whirlpool must be propitiated if one is to travel safely through its domain, and any tabus associated with it must be strictly observed. The *eloko* (plural, *biloko*), a carnivorous ogre with a preference for human flesh, must be avoided or outwitted. Aiding the Nkundo in their unceasing defense against these ogres is the *itòji*, a small bird adept at devising schemes for defeating the huge but slow-thinking monsters. The Nkundo's reliance on the *itòji* is second only to his dependence on the *nkanga*, or witch doctor, holder still of a significant role in Nkundo life despite the introduction of Western medications and surgery.

Fortunately, tenaciously maintaining its hold in the face of Westernization is the Nkundo practice of storytelling: a moonlit evening in the Cuvette is not meant for sleeping but for singing and dancing and for sharing the tales of the fathers and the grandfathers, carriers of the Nkundo value system, of the tongue of the ancestors, and of tribal history. Nearly a quarter of a century's service among the Nkundo had afforded me countless opportunities to sit in on entire evenings of tale-telling, totally caught up in the storytelling situation, complete with chanting, gesticulating narrator and eagerly participating Nkundo audience, furnishing handclapping, choral responses, and rhythmic swaying. Such memorable experiences over a period of many years prepared the ground for field collecting. Determined to accumulate and preserve such tales, I equipped myself with dependable battery-operated tape recorders and polyester tape, secured both transportation and housing throughout various portions of the Cuvette, and set forth to elicit, record, and document those narratives still central to the lives of the Nkundo. Convinced themselves of the worth of their own oral tradition, more than enough narrators crowded around the tape recorders to provide an adequate sampling of current Nkundo folk narrative. With tapes in hand, only patience and persistence were required to move the tales from Old Lonkundo (the tongue of most of the tale-tellers) into a modern Lonkundo—here, the help of such men as Bokunge Jacques and Pierre Sangana was indispensable—that could be transcribed into English without loss of the nuances, the flavorful locutions, the ideophones, and the onomatopoeia present in any accomplished narration.

Certain terms and sounds in Lonkundo are earmarks of that language and are found as regularly in oral narrative as in everyday conversation among the Nkundo. A tale told without these earmarks lacks the winning way that sets these narratives apart from all other African folktales and marks them as mirrors of Nkundo culture. A sampling of these terms and sounds suggests the richness and variety of Lonkundo diction. Action in Lonkundo does not appear final until it has been overemphasized: a person asleep or very ill may be "dead," but his life has not terminated until he is "dead dead" (expressed either with the word *ci* after the verb for "to die" or the word for "finished" placed before it); the word "*ci*" is used to make positive assertion about an act or to indicate its correctness. Use of a negative expression is preferred to use of a positive expression; for example, one says "not a little" instead of "much" and "not a little while" rather than "soon." To "go together as friends" describes an extra-familial friendship tie, usually between males, carrying its own obligations and benefits; chief among these are hospitality, the exchange of gifts, and help in time of trouble. A culture uncorrupted by "civilization" centers its life about the hearth or fire; thus the Lonkundo term for "to establish a home" is "to light a fire." The fire, considered the heart of the home, normally is kept burning at all times and provides coals for the hunter's fire in his temporary shelter in the forest.

Other Lonkundo words commonly used both in conversation and in storytelling include "*Nko jŏi*," "*nyĕ*," and "*Mo!*" "*Nko jŏi*" literally means "No word," but is better translated by a shrug of the shoulders indicating "I have no complaint," "All right," "No matter," or "Let it go." "*Nyĕ*" is used for emphasis, with the negative meaning "never" or "not at all" and with the affirmative meaning "completely," "totally," or "absolutely." "*Mo!*" is commonly used to express surprise, disgust, or wonder.

Lonkundo has a greeting for every occasion; if no greeting is prestructured, one can easily be supplied out of the current circumstance. All greetings must be answered with "*O*," or "Yes," even before the greeting is returned. The early-morning greeting is "Are you awake?" After that hour is past, one asks "Are you there?" To the person going on a journey, one admonishes "Go well," with the response being "Stay well." When one person meets another on the path, the one of lower prestige says to the one of greater prestige (as determined by age, affluence, or some other factor) "*Losako*" (meaning "Proverb"). The more prestigious person responds by stating the proverb by which he is currently most influenced. Greetings are then exchanged. If the questioner has not understood the significance of the proverb, he is free to ask for further information about it.

In common use and expressive of the dramatic spirit of the Nkundo are many ideophones and onomatopoetical words. *Ikao-ikao* and *cwa-cwa* represent steady movement by foot along the path, and *lomo-lomo* the panting and shortness of breath following one's running fast. *Kao-kao* is often used by the storyteller to suggest cutting or chopping with an axe, and *tee-tee-tee* or *ti-i-i* or *te-e-e* indicates that an activity goes on and on until it is at last finished. *Pao-pao* duplicates the sound of thunder and *ao-ao* the sound of gulping. These and many other sounds enrich the tales of every accomplished Nkundo narrator and echo the culture out of which that narrative repertory has grown.

To provide an increased understanding of the many-dimensioned Nkundo, including a sense of the flavor of their culture, has been my primary purpose for the preparation of this book. It is hoped that those who meet the Nkundo herein will recognize the dignity and worth of this gracious and hospitable tribal group. Too often in the past, the continent of Africa—particularly that portion known as Zaïre—has been termed "dark"; perhaps this mirror, the folk narrative, will reflect the "light" that has always been present there, quite undimmed by the cliché that for far too long has closed the door on a vital oral art and the culture which nourishes it.

M. H. R.

My INITIAL PURPOSE in preparing an annotated collection of Nkundo oral narratives had been a conservative one: to establish representative samples of Zaïrian verbal art in their own cultural milieu in an effort to preserve the language, the tales which showed that language at work creatively, and the culture mirrored in those tales. But an Nkundo-centered study could not be of maximum service in the complex field of African verbal-art research unless it were to be set within a larger framework, chronologically, geographically, and culturally.

How did the Ross sampling compare with the range of tales available among the Nkundo—say—twenty-five years ago? What tales appeared to be in a state of flux, moving from myth toward *märchen*, from dilemma tale toward *pourquoi*, or, indeed, moving out of the oral tradition entirely? What had happened to Lonkundo diction in the process of the Nkundo tales' translation into non-African languages? Had the Nkundo value system been as clearly evidenced in the tales captured in print as it had in the narratives preserved on tape in the Ross collection? What indications could be furnished of the diffusion of tales, even within Zaïre? Where did these tales fit in the immense continental oral tradition of which they were undeniably a part? All these questions had to be considered, and conclusions about them must be drawn in the course of the study.

It seemed sensible to explore first whatever tales had been published in the Nkundo's own language. Fortunately, Mrs. Ross had preserved a copy of a paperbound Lonkundo school reader, *Bekolo Bėmỏ Bendemba Ba-Nkundo* (1957), compiled by three mission-school teachers from folktales current in the Nkundo oral tradition of the late 1940s and early 1950s. Use of this reader was short lived: the book fell victim to the introduction of French as the language of public instruction. Nonetheless, it might well, in its brief tenure, have influenced one or more of the narrators encountered by Mrs. Ross, and the degree of such influence needed to be determined. The possibility of indebtedness could be pursued only through close examination of the book, using as a check against content Alice Cobble's *Wembi, the Singer of Stories* (1959), the only English-language volume of Nkundo-based tales to be found. *Bekolo Bėmỏ* ... proved sufficiently relevant to the question of tales still maintained in the oral tradition of the 1970s to warrant translation and inclusion of more than a dozen stories, largely as variants of the narratives Mrs. Ross had collected in the field. In each instance, these tales have been fully identified; the degree to which each of the school-text versions bears resemblance to the Ross-collected tale should be readily apparent. Admittedly, in terms of oral-tradition preservation, twenty-five years seemed a short time, but in the light of the stressful events occurring in Zaïre during the period, that particular quarter-century was especially valuable to study for the effect of cultural changes on tales transmitted by word of mouth.

For her work with *Bekolo Bėmỏ* ..., as had been true in her transliteration of the tape-recorded tales, Mrs. Ross enlisted the aid of several multilingual Nkundo, with varying levels of formal education, but all fully committed to the significance of the work at hand: an entirely literal translation of the school text, preserving whatever nuances of Lonkundo diction might be present. Of special concern to both of us in subsequent analysis of these translations was the relatively minimal use of ideophones and onomatopoeia and of such characteristic Lonkundo locutions as "not a little" for "much" or "very" and "Make me live" for "Help me" or "Save me." These expressions, as well as greeting customs and formulaic and ritualistic patterns of speech, were furnished less frequently in the school-text tales than they tended to occur in the taped tellings, perhaps a consequence either of an effort to shorten the tales for young readers or of incomplete recognition of their significance in oral literature as a reflection of the culture. The reader is left to draw his own conclusions as to the degree of service done to Lonkundo narrative style and diction in these Lonkundo-to-Lonkundo treatments.

If marked stylistic changes had been noted in a transition from oral to written Lonkundo, changes might also be expected in translations from Lonkundo to Flemish and from Lonkundo to French; a representative sampling of Flemish and French translations must thus be examined. Whatever their limitations (notably in the area of documentation: in few instances had the collectors-translators supplied identifications of the narrators, the sites of narration, or the dates of collection), these European-printed European-language compilations could certainly widen the "net"—especially for myths, tales involving animism, and other narratives some storytellers might feel reluctant to record for a white woman missionary—as well as provide a basis for comparison in the handling of Lonkundo or other Bantu-language-group diction. Several of these translations afforded an invaluable bonus: a parallel-text treatment of the tales, with the Lonkundo text and the French or Flemish translation on facing pages. (It must be noted that in one volume, *Rechtspraakfabels van de Nkundó* [1954], Hulstaert undertook to "correct" the Lonkundo text as well as the Flemish translation—de Rop had done the Flemish transliterations and annotations—so one cannot be certain that the Lonkundo stands as the Nkundo informant initially furnished it.) Mrs. Ross and her multilingual team undertook the translation of the Lonkundo; two different Dutch-Flemish specialists worked with me on the Flemish versions. Samples of the paired texts have been provided as variants of dilemma tales in part 4 of the present volume; translated passages from another work by de Rop (. . . *woordkunst . . .*) may be found at other points where they extended my own understanding and appreciation of Nkundo culture.

Since French translations have been both more numerous and more accessible than have the Flemish volumes, I have examined and compared a number of the French-language collections. In most of these volumes, the translator had not furnished the African-language version at all. For the texts in the Luba language provided by Stappers in his *Textes Luba: Contes d'Animaux* (1962) and the texts from the Bolia tongue furnished by Mamet in *Le Langage des Bolia* (1960) no help was available for transliteration into English, so the French translations were examined in the light of the comments made in the introductory materials, aided by the collector's familiarity with Lonkundo locution. (Two of the tales in the Mamet volume Nkundo in origin, translated into Bolia from the Lonkundo, have been commented upon in the notes for Tale 2.) The de Bouveignes [a pseudonym for Léon Guébels] collections, of which I read several —representing the oral literatures of several peoples, largely the Luba of Shaba Province (formerly Katanga Province), and close enough in geographical and tribal ties to be useful for the study of diffusion— offered versions only in French, a French which had a delightful flavor but which carried within it no readily discernible variations in diction indicating the origins of the tales (the dramatis personae— the rabbit, for instance—provided some clues as to locale). No tales carried consistently the earmarks of Lonkundo diction assiduously sought. De Bouveignes himself declared (p. 5) in the preface to his *Entendu dans la Brousse: Contes Congolaises* (1938), one of three collections of presumably Baluba tales that he had published, that he had engaged in "transposing them [the tales] into French." Later in the preface (pp. 5–6), he clarified "transposing":

2066119

> He [the storyteller] has voice inflections, interrogations, abridgments which make his story a mimed story, a little dramatic work. We do not have all these resources in the printed story, which forces us to translate, out of context . . . to make an appeal to that which, in our written language, plays the same role as the gesture and the physiognomy in the spoken story.

Having read several of de Bouveignes' transpositions, I became increasingly aware of the length to which a translator might stray from authentic diction—say, of Lonkundo—and still, to all appearances, be telling an Nkundo tale.

Especially illuminating in this study was the single volume of oral narratives compiled and translated into French by a black Zaïrian. Badibanga, born in Luluabourg, had translated into French (apparently for children, though there was no suggestion of condescension in the tone or content) a fine collection of tales he had heard in his youth; the book, *L'Éléphant Qui Marche sur des Oeufs* (1931), does not provide the text in Lulua, but Lulua diction and narrative style have, according to the preface, been faithfully conveyed in the French. The difference between the direct, flavorsome style used by Badibanga and the dancing, polished prose of de Bouveignes (with the preciousness evident in the foreword of his *Sur des Levres*

Congolaises: Contes [no date]) furnished a challenge to examine closely the fidelity in content, as well as in diction, of each tale to what appeared to be the "traditional" form presented in the other available sources. Stappers' dedicated handling of diction and style as well as of content in his French translation of Luba tales (frequent footnotes called attention to stylistic differences detected between Luba and other tongues) and Mamet's unmannered French in his painstakingly annotated translation of tales from the Bolia (incorporated in his study of the language of the Bolia) offered evidence that Zaïrian tales could be presented effectively in French in straightforward fashion without loss of dignity or flavor; the tales enhanced themselves.

Is such close and critical examination of various translations a kind of "nit-picking"? No. Unquestionably, there is a need for translation of Nkundo and other Zaïrian tales from the relatively "arcane" Lonkundo and other little-known Bantu languages into a tongue of greater currency, such as French or English, both to make these tales more accessible and to open up to readers the mores and value systems of the Nkundo and their neighbors. On the other hand, a considerable disservice is rendered both to the Nkundo and to their culture if the translator disregards the fact that Nkundo tales are oral *literature*, and that—as is true of any other literature, oral or written—that literature has a distinctive flavor meriting preservation in its own right and with its own time-tested turns of phrase.

Quite apart from its usefulness in the determination of fidelity to oral literature as literature, this examination of printed works from cultures largely outside the Nkundo area aided us in probing the question of diffusion of oral narrative. These supplementary sources confirmed what Mrs. Ross had already discovered in her field collecting both at Tondo and in areas influenced by the Ubangi: travelers, students, family and tribal visitors, missionaries, traders, and even hospital patients were busily engaged in communicating the favorite tales from their own repertories to residents of the towns and villages they visited, and in turn were bringing back tales that, once they had been adapted to the Nkundo setting, might well become a part of the Nkundo oral tradition. The key factor in such diffusion, in Mrs. Ross's experience, appeared to be that of language: the tales exchanged were likely not to be told in Lonkundo, because of its limited currency, but either in Lingala or in Bangala (if the range were northward) or Lontumba (if the range were southward); retold in Lonkundo, the tales would tend then to acquire the turns of phrase that would make them pleasing to an Nkundo audience.

Such exchanges presupposed a degree of bilingualism sufficiently common to permit limited cultural exchanges, including that of communicating at least the kernel of a good tale. Wherever we have been confident of instances of diffusion, these have been cited in the notes for the tales concerned.

In support of observations on diffusion, we have either reproduced or summarized a number of variants—some drawn from the school text *Bekolo Bèmò* . . . , some from the various translations cited, and still others from the store of oral narratives in the repertories of university students from Botswana, Swaziland, Lesotho, Rhodesia, and Nigeria—to encourage comparison of the tales in the Ross field collection with similar narratives from an earlier period or from another geographical location. No variant has been offered or cited in the present volume that has not borne some internal evidence of Nkundolike cultural patterns and of some elements of the Nkundo value system, since such variants seemed the likeliest candidates for diffusion. Shortage of space rather than a paucity of materials served to limit the number of variants presented. Since Lonkundo is less accessible to scholars than is either French or Flemish, the bulk of the variants have been transliterated from that local tongue; mention and/or summaries of numerous variants available in other languages have been provided in the notes, permitting useful content and stylistic analyses for a broader application of the Nkundo findings.

It would be presumptuous to assume that such a work as the present study could ever be "finished." We have been constantly bedeviled by motifs and types found under the unlikeliest of headings in the various indexes used. Aarne-Thompson's *Types of the Folktale* (1961), Thompson's *Motif Index* (second edition [1955–1958]), Clarke's unpublished "A Motif-Index of the Folktales of Culture-Area V West Africa" (1958), Arewa's unpublished "A Classification of the Folktales of the Northern East African Cattle Area" (1966), and Lambrecht's unpublished "A Tale Type Index for Central Africa" (1967) have been indispensable in the quest. Klipple's unpublished "African Folk Tales with Foreign Analogues" (1938), a two-volume, trail-blazing, thorough work which first whetted my own appetite for the study of African oral narrative, has furnished a significant additional source unparalleled in its usefulness for this particular project, despite its early date of compilation, because it includes a wealth of variants not found in later studies yet essential in an informed approach to African tales in the international setting of man's verbal art. Full-length studies such as Rattray's *Akan-*

Ashanti Folk-Tales (1930), Postma's *Tales from the Basotho* (1974), the Herskovitses' *Dahomean Narrative* (1958), and Bascom's *African Dilemma Tales* (1975) have been beacons. The scholarly articles by Bascom, Crowley, and others citing weaknesses and omissions in existing folktale collections have sharpened our perceptions and have widened our sights in the matter of details deserving of inclusion. Perhaps the criticisms brought to bear against the present volume will stimulate others to expand the investigation of oral art, if not among the Nkundo, then at least among some other Central African tribes so that appreciation of the folk literature as yet unmined in that portion of the continent may be deepened.

To make the present materials accessible in a form with which scholars and most laymen are reasonably familiar, the text proper has been subdivided basically according to the four major groupings in the Aarne-Thompson *Types of the Folktale*; each of the four parts has its own Introduction. Wherever feasible, the tales within each part have been arranged in "clusters" according to the values they emphasize in the Nkundo value system, with these clusters noted in the introductory portion. In instances where one or more versions of a tale have been supplied, the Ross field-collected form or forms precede variants derived from other sources.

Certain other points about the volume's organizational scheme require comment here.

(1) A formal headnote precedes each tale collected by Mrs. Ross; this headnote furnishes the narrator's name and occasionally other personal details, the location at which the tale was tape recorded, and the date on which the recording was made. An equally precise headnote identifies each variant (from whatever source) for which an English translation has been furnished. In a handful of instances, narrators have shared with Mrs. Ross bits of Nkundo oral history which have seemed to belong among the notes rather than as oral narratives; these items, too, have been provided with full headnotes, although they have not been numbered as have the tales in the text.

(2) The notes for all tales have been entered directly after the tales concerned, with these materials indexed in the volume Index.

(3) Within any given note, the order of information is as follows:

   (a) General introductory comments on the tale.

   (b) Relationship of the tale to others in the present volume and citation of variants in reasonably available collections but not given in this text.

   (c) Identification, insofar as is possible, of the tale type and of the major motifs. To avoid confusion among the several type indexes, with differing type numbers, the surname of the indexer (Aarne-Thompson, Klipple, Arewa, Lambrecht) is provided preceding the type number. The sources for established motif numbers are indicated by the use of the surname initial of the indexer preceding the motif number (*T*, for Thompson [second edition], and *C*, for Clarke); *new* motif numbers, by the surname initial of the scholar whose index first cites the motif as new (*K*, for Klipple [new detail noted]; *C*, for Clarke; *A*, for Arewa; *L*, for Lambrecht; ∗∗ following the motif number, for Ross/Walker). The motif numbers have been listed, in general, in the order of their occurrence in the tale text, a system admittedly more feasible for single tales than for tales with variants and for clusters.

(d) Footnotes (keyed to the footnote numbers in the tale text) furnishing information of literary, ethnological, or other interest to the reader, including in situ observations of the narrator's actions and intonations, intergroup exchange and argument, choral response, and other performance details preserved on the tape but not present in the text.

Several other matters affecting the physical appearance of this book require explanation. As is true in many other situations where a nonnative investigator (whether missionary, linguist, anthropologist, administrator, sociologist, or folklorist) has entered a group to elicit information about a culture quite different from his own, the problem arises as to how to handle the various bits of data furnished as "asides" in an effort to aid the investigator toward a fuller appreciation of what he is seeing or feeling or smelling or hearing. Unquestionably, every such item is grist to the mill. When the focus of interest is the oral narrative, however, and such bits are inserted in the course of the telling of a tale, they are included on the tape very much as if they were customary elements of the tale. On playback of the tape for the gratification of the narrator and for whatever additions and criticisms may be offered by narrator or audience, a heated discussion may well ensue as to whether such informational material really "belongs" in the tale. Quite obviously, an Nkundo telling a hunting tale to an all-Nkundo audience would not interrupt the narrative to explain the construction and function of an *nganda*, since in this hunting and fishing culture the temporary hut is a familiar structure. Likewise, the Nkundo storyteller would not need to identify for his tribesmen an *nsolo* as an eggplant, or to explain that a wooden knife in the rain forest sinks rather than floats when it is thrown into the river to propitiate the river spirit. Out of courtesy for Mrs. Ross, such information was provided precisely when it was most needed: at the relevant point in the narrative. The Ross/Walker-agreed objective had been to provide a verbatim translation of all narratives; out of fairness to the reader, and in the interest of preserving the narratives' wholeness as literature, a superior number has been placed in the tale text at each point where nonnarrative material interrupted the flow of a tale, and the matching note at the end of the tale provides a verbatim translation of the information furnished at that point by the narrator. There is thus available a translation of the entire narration, complete with interruptive notes, but the interpolated comments have been separated from the tale itself in an effort to reproduce the piece of oral literature as nearly as possible as it would have been told in the absence of Mrs. Ross.

For the readers' convenience, though at the appreciable expense of narrative flavor, English rather than Nkundo terminology has been employed in the tales themselves with the exception of initial use of Nkundo proper names and uniform inclusion of Lonkundo ideophones and onomatopoetic expressions. Identification of various Lonkundo terms, traditional greetings, ideophones, and instances of onomatopoeia occurring frequently in the tales has been furnished by Mrs. Ross in her portion of the General Introduction; identification of such items used only occasionally has been provided in the notes.

Titling the tales posed a decided challenge. In only a few instances did the storyteller provide a title for a narrative; in these instances, the titles presented more problems than they solved. Bomponge Joseph's title "The Parable of the Antelope and the Leopard" (for Tale 33) employed the term "parable" in a sense that would have served merely to confuse an English-speaking reader; "A Parable of Cain and Abel," attached by Bongonda Michele to Tale 72, was an outright misnomer, since neither rivalry nor fratricide entered the tale at any stage. As is true of oral narratives in any culture, these tales do not require titles; when they appear in print, as "set-pieces," the interest of the tale-as-literature, of the casual reader, and of the scholar is customarily served by the furnishing of an apt title. What determines the aptness of a title for an oral narrative preserved in print? The soundest title appears to be one indicating the object or relationship or deed or value or personal characteristic prompting the narrator to choose that particular tale to tell. A great many tales stress the Nkundo's concern with fidelity in friendship (usually male–male friendship); this stress is evidenced both in tales of true friendship, where the relationship is preserved, and in those of false friendship, where the relationship is broken through betrayal, deceit, or some other cause. Numerous tales emphasize the strength of blood ties: sibling-to-sibling and parent-to-child; ties between husband and wife or wives rank as considerably less strong, with much mistrust obvious between mates. Many narratives include encounters (and occasionally marriages) of mortals with supernatural beings; the *eloko*, or ogre, is alive and well in the forests entered by the Nkundo, despite the "whistling-in-the-dark" tales titled "The Last of the Ogres," and every stream, lake, swamp, and forest has its animating spirit to be feared, propitiated, bargained with, or cheated. The right of ownership and the regulations regarding sharing, the penalties attached to greed and to theft, the squabbles between co-wives, the interminable palavers to settle disputes of one kind or another—these and countless other subjects inform Nkundo tales, and, through these tales, instruct the listeners in the many faceted value system preserved by means of the oral tradition. Clues to the "teaching" are furnished in the tale title and occasionally in a terminal proverb or proverbs. In instances where one or more variants appear to offer the same emphasis as that of the field tale, the field-tale title has been retained, followed by (Variant I), (Variant II). In those instances in which two tales seem almost close enough to be variants one of the other but in which the focus of one narrator differed from that of the other, separate titles have been assigned and the two have been treated as individual tales. Guidance in the decisions concerning the tales in the Ross collection has come from the narrators themselves and from multilingual Nkundo translators in conference with Mrs. Ross; decisions on the assignment of titles for tales outside that field collection have been made jointly by us in terms of evidence within the tales themselves. In cases where the collector-translator had assigned a title to the tale, that title and page references have been furnished in the notes so that readers of Flemish, French, or Lonkundo can locate the tale in the volume from which the variant was drawn. To facilitate cross-reference, the tales and variants have been numbered consecutively throughout this study; cross-referencing will utilize the number rather than the title of the tale or variant.

This exploration of Nkundo oral art was enriched by the variety among participating narrators, both in terms of competence as raconteurs and in terms of age, sex, formal education, social position, and exposure to cultures outside their own. Response of the storytellers to use of the tape recorder was enthusiastic. The tales were gathered through five different means: (1) narrator recording Zaïrian stories in English on his own recorder with no live audience but himself [Sam, in Tondo]; (2) narrators recording in Lonkundo solely with Mrs. Ross as audience; (3) narrators recording in Lonkundo with Mrs. Ross and four or five others listening; (4) narrators recording in Lonkundo in a daytime outdoor village setting with Mrs. Ross and a varying come-and-go audience; (5) narrator recording in a dialect of Lonkundo in a traditional evening story-telling situation, with a large continuous audience [Bob Stewart, Mrs. Ross's "deputy," recording Mpanga Iyende's dramatic narratives in Bonga-Iteli]. Full accounts of the storytelling circumstances are furnished in the section entitled "Sites and Circumstances of Narration."

What identifies a narrator as "competent"? For the purpose of this study, "competence" in a narrator has been defined in terms of the following benchmarks: (1) selection of a tale appropriate to his own cultural patterns and to the needs and expectations of his audience; (2) control of story content, including a strong beginning, middle, and end; (3) subordination of details to the central theme; (4) clear differentiation of characters; (5) command of the nuances of the Lonkundo language; (6) ability to arouse response from the audience; (7) recognition that the tale originated prior to his own time and had value both of itself and to the preservation of his culture; (8) memory and consistency in handling of names, places, and events. An "excellent" narrator surpasses a "competent" narrator in several respects: he is able to improvise, investing what would otherwise be a routine telling with sufficient flavor and appeal so that the tale is certain to be relished and retold; he "reads" his audience skillfully and by use of intonation, pregnant pause, mime, and vocal mimicry brings the tale home to his hearers; he is able to utilize interruptions and distractions as signals for need of variation of his storytelling technique. Among the narrators represented in this volume were several who were excellent as well as many who were competent tale-tellers, not only willing but eager to record their narratives on tape.

The field tapes on which this study has been based open an inviting window on the art of field collecting as well as on Nkundo folk narrative itself. Clearly through her quarter-century's work among the Nkundo, Mrs. Ross had won the trust and the confidence of those among whom she sought tales, a decided advantage for a field collector, if not imperative. Too, the narrators felt certain of her concern for the responsible handling and preservation of the tales, and of her respect for the culture which the tales mirrored: they could safely share with her their traits and their traditions. At only one or two points in the entire set of narratives is there even a hint of stiffness or strangeness, of dictation trauma, or of withholding of information because of the collector's color, sex, age, religious commitment, or national origin. Only at points in the telling where a non-Nkundo might benefit from supplementary information was any concession made to her role as collector: she was just one more Nkundo listener. Responses were free and open; audience participation was vociferous and uninhibited. Observation of Mrs. Ross's field techniques prompted Bob Stewart, a Peace Corps teacher, to tape a tale-telling session at Bonga-Iteli; her contagious enthusiasm moved Lontomba Samuel to tell tales to a live audience envisioned beyond the tape recorder in his solitary room: his inflections, his intonations, his imitations of animal sounds, his inclusion of internal rhyme and ideophones and onomatopoeia—all these elements of dramatic narration confirm on tape his rekindled conviction of the value of Nkundo verbal art and the importance of sharing the wealth of his own neighboring oral tradition with others. Quite without understanding the Lonkundo words, but yielding oneself entirely to the fervor and flavor of the storytelling and the response it aroused in the audience, one can sense from the tapes in the Ross collection the outstanding contribution made by Nkundo tale-telling to the African oral tradition.

With the treasury of African folk literature still barely tapped, any conclusion as to whether a given tale is "good" or "poor" is clearly premature. Included, therefore, are all of the oral accounts Mrs. Ross collected; the judgment of their worth is left open to determination by scholars assessing the entire range of African verbal art.

B. K. W.

Pronunciation Guide to Lonkundo

a as in "f*a*ther"
e as the *a* in "r*a*te"
e̦ as in "s*e*t"
i as the double *e* in "f*ee*t"
o as in "g*o*"

o̦ as the *aw* in "r*aw*"
u as the double *o* in "b*oo*t"
c as in "mar*ch*"
f (pronounced with the lips closed)
s (always soft)

NOTE: Every vowel either marks the end of a syllable or, if it follows a syllable already ended by a vowel, constitutes a syllable by itself:

Nza-ko-mba   Nso-i   Nsa-o-la

Sites and Circumstances of Narration

AWARE THAT FULLER UNDERSTANDING and appreciation of any form of verbal art can be gained by an acquaintance with the site and circumstances of its presentation, we have furnished here such information as will aid the reader in placing these samples of Nkundo oral narrative in situational perspective. For the convenience of those pursuing special areas of inquiry, we have arranged all available data on each site (except for Monieka) in the following order:

(1) Identification of the city, town, or village itself, with brief comments about it;

(2) The chief sources for informants at that site;

(3) A list of the informants tape-recorded there, with the tales they told (the tales are identified by number);

(4) Personal information acquired or inferred about the narrators, including age, formal education, employment, and so forth;

(5) Details of the recording situation: setting, audience, language or dialect used, interruptive sounds;

(6) Evidences of narrative techniques used by each storyteller;

(7) Opportunities for further field work at that site.

Accepting the risk of wide variations in paragraph length, we have provided within a single paragraph all the details pertinent to the item being discussed: for example, all of the aspects of the recording situation for a given location—no matter how many

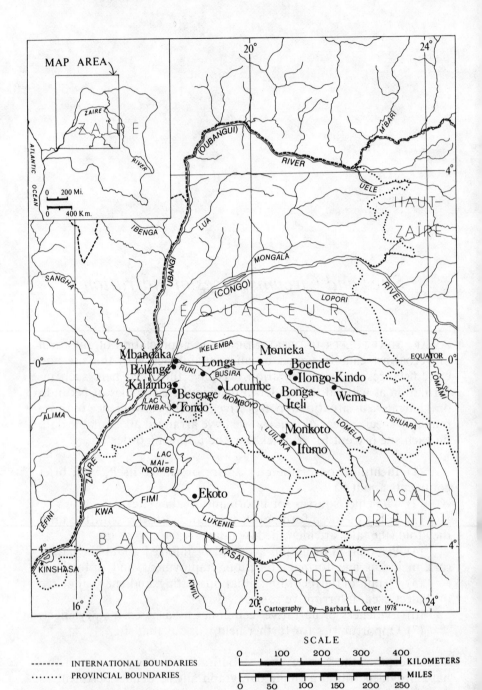

SCALE

0   100   200   300   400   **KILOMETERS**

0   50   100   150   200   250   **MILES**

-------- INTERNATIONAL BOUNDARIES

········ PROVINCIAL BOUNDARIES

Province of Équateur, Republic of Zaïre, and surrounding area

narrators are involved—are included in the same paragraph. Use of the map in conjunction with these materials will strengthen the identification of the tales with their geographic reference points as well as open opportunities for consideration of folktale diffusion.

Arranged alphabetically, the narrative sites with accompanying data follow.

BOENDE

Boende, a small city, is located on the Tshuapa River, a tributary of the Ruki River system. During the period of colonial government, it became a center for local and regional officials, and the French terms for some of those officials have persisted in some of the folk narratives (see Tale 56); in every part of that government center, police are in evidence. Made initially eye-appealing by the Belgians, Boende has been attractively maintained by the successive Nkundo officials. At the time Mrs. Ross collected narratives there, Boende offered the advantages of an excellent secondary school and a large hospital (the latter operated as a cooperative project by the Catholic Church, the Protestants, and the Zaïrian government), both of which have induced many rural families to settle in this city. Fortunately, Boende has retained its traditional welcome and appreciation of strangers.

Assured by the missionary family living in Boende that able informants were abundant in that city, Mrs. Ross spent two weeks there during her field collecting. Excellent contacts with narrators were afforded through three employees at the secondary school— Tata Itofi and Tata Manga, part-time workers, and Robert Stewart, a full-time Peace Corps teacher. Through these three men, Mrs. Ross secured narrators not only in Boende but also in Ilongo-Kindo and in Bonga-Iteli.

Tata Manga told six tales himself: two animal narratives, both involving false friendships (Tales 16 and 19), a cautionary tale (Tale 5), two marital-relationship narratives (Tales 73 and 79), and a portion of the Nkundo oral epic (Tale 69); Tale 73 offered a humorous ending—uncommon among the Ross-collected tales—and Tale 79 afforded a decidedly grisly series of episodes, indications of this narrator's wide storytelling range. Tata Itofi told only one story (Tale 87), the single cumulative tale encountered by Mrs. Ross in her field collecting. Ikwa Isilombe, a friend recruited by Tata Manga, provided five narratives, including a courtship *cante fable* (Tale 52), two didactic tales concerning parent-child relationships (Tales 55 and 58), and two versions of the same ogre tale (Tales 67 and 68); the last two narratives provide an excellent opportunity for observing the .Nkundo narrator's freedom to explore a basic tale and to improve upon his own initial version of that tale. Two female narrators also furnished tales in Boende for Mrs. Ross: Bofaya Efalaiso's single narrative (Tale 32), an animal tale, dealt with the problem of the impossible restitution of a lost object; both of Bolumbu Elakankoi's stories (Tales 48 and 56) reflected the significance attached by the Nkundo to names, as well as the obligations attendant upon extra-familial friendships and upon bridewealth arrangements. Curiously, all three tales told by the women included grisly elements: murder (Tale 32), cannibalism (Tale 48), and live burial (Tale 56).

All of the narrators used in Boende were past fifty years of age; they differed considerably, however, in their formal schooling, their personal situations, and their prompting for recording the tales, in addition to the obvious difference in sex. Tata Manga, in his late fifties when he told these tales, had spent many years teaching at the elementary-school level. He had had considerably more than the minimal education required for lower-elementary teaching (seven years of school, with the last two years devoted partly to teacher training)—perhaps as many as eleven years of formal schooling—but this professional training had neither reduced his attachment to the oral tradition nor stiffened his narrative style. At the time of the tale-telling, he was partially retired, working only during the mornings in the office at the secondary school. Tata Itofi [Nyamaseko] had for most of his life been a teacher in a small village near Wema; on retire-ment, he had moved to Boende, and was both occupying himself and supplementing his retirement income by teaching afternoon classes for the wives of the young men attending the secondary school there. Ikwa Isilombe, a retired elder living in Boende, had apparently received little exposure to formal schooling; his freedom from other obligations allowed him to sit in on storytelling sessions and to furnish several narratives from his own repertory. Tata Itofi located Bofaya Efalaiso, an elderly woman living with her daughter not far from the secondary school in Boende. In common with most Nkundo women her age, Bofaya had received little or no formal education; her husband, a fisherman, had been dead for a number of years, and she had finally left her home village, Ekoto, to live in Boende. Bolumbu Elakankoi, a woman probably in her late fifties at the time Mrs. Ross recorded her, was accidentally discovered by

Tata Itofi in his search for an old woman reputed to be an excellent storyteller; the extent of Bolumbu's formal education was not revealed. Bolumbu had come from her home in Wema to visit her daughter in Boende, and she willingly acceded to Mrs. Ross's request that she tell a tale.

Tata Manga brought a group of Lonkundo-speaking elderly men to the church-owned house where the missionary lived. The storytelling sessions that ensued were lively ones, filled with interruptions and additions from the narrator's peers (comments usually grandly ignored by the storyteller) and embellished by choral responses and percussive sounds. Mrs. Ross was well aware of Tata Manga's eagerness to tell tales himself, but she was also cognizant of her need for his aid in translating the tales told by the others. By the time Tata Manga had met her need for the transcriptions, most of his peers had gone home for dinner, leaving him only a small, constantly changing audience consisting of those who had other business in the missionary home: household workmen, Nkundo teachers who had come to the missionary for help in their teaching, occasional Nkundo elders seeking diversion, and a Peace Corps teacher or two with little comprehension of Lonkundo, the language in which all the tales were being told. The come-and-go audience in no way reduced Tata Manga's enthusiasm in his storytelling; his conviction that he was thus preserving the tales of "the fathers" outweighed the inconvenience of his not having a continuous, participating audience and prompted him to use even greater artistry in order to preserve the flavor of the tales he cherished. The noises of arrivals and departures in the missionary home—itself amply protected from external traffic sounds by its location well away from the road—distracted neither the storytellers nor their audience from the business at hand; a rooster's crowing likewise attracted no notice, though it seems intrusive on the tape. During the telling of Tata Itofi's cumulative tale, response from the listeners was especially marked at the conclusion of each new bargain; at these times, the delighted laughter of the listeners made it difficult for the narrator to complete his songs and still be heard. The telling of Ikwa Isilombe's first narrative (Tale 52) occurred in the back part of the sanctuary, with the members of the audience varying widely in age; from the surprise ending, the narrator reaped both laughter and applause. His rendering (at the missionary's home) of Tale 68 was received with clapping, laughter, and choral participation, in distinct contrast to the grumbling and dispute among the elders during his telling of Tale 67. Response to the other Ikwa Isilombe tales (Tales 55 and 58) was

relatively restrained, though the choice of the name for the "special
knife" (Tale 58) roused appreciative laughter. Extraneous sounds
marred the delivery of all three tales told by the female informants:
passing vehicles on the busy street, the coming and going of women
and children, the crying of babies, the crowing of roosters, and the
babble of voices within and outside of the audience resulted in a high
noise level that made communication difficult and greatly reduced
the degree of audience response to the narratives themselves. Neither
Bofaya Efalaiso nor Bolumbu Elakankoi appeared distracted by
these sounds—both were totally involved in their storytelling—but
Mrs. Ross found it exceptionally difficult to follow the narrative line
in the midst of so much confusion, especially in view of Bofaya
Efalaiso's slurred speech. (Fortunately, through repeated listenings
to the tape with the help of her translation assistants, Mrs. Ross was
able to recover the texts of the tales.)

Tata Manga, regardless of the size of his audience, entered fully
into the spirit of each tale he told, dramatizing the dialogues, varying
his tone and his speed, utilizing the full range of Lonkundo locutions,
and employing every opportunity for the increasing of suspense. His
lively sense of humor was evidenced in his handling of Tales 19 and
73, and his ability to extract the maximum degree of drama from a
tale already twice told was demonstrated in Tale 69. In every instance,
his performance—and it *was* a dramatic performance—was keenly
relished by his listeners. But his narrative technique went deeper than
the mime and the dialogue displayed; at no point was the underlying
lesson lost: whether the dramatis personae consisted of people or
nonpeople, the cultural values presented were clearly Nkundo, and
those values were imperishably impressed upon his listeners by the
outwardly apparent narrative techniques he employed. Tata Itofi's
narrative techniques are difficult to assess from a single sample, a
cumulative tale (Tale 87). His initial choice of this one as a tale to
tell was sound, since such a tale involves the repetition dear to Nkundo
listeners. His mastery of both content and style was borne out by his
unflawed handling of the cumulative songs; his flexibility and his
awareness of his audience were shown by his sharing of their merri-
ment and his alteration of pacing to make room for their laughter
and still not lose the narrative thread. His subtle switch from the
ludicrous series of bargains to the poignancy of the conclusion and
the listeners' response to that shift demonstrated both his artistry
and the strong influence that a skillful narrator can have on the
thoughts and the emotions of his listeners. The storytelling techniques
displayed by Ikwa Isilombe underwent a most interesting change

during the course of his exposure to Mrs. Ross: in the first three narratives he told (Tales 52, 55, and 58), the delivery, though competent, was conditioned largely by the few coins he had been promised for their telling. Tales 55 and 58, patently moralistic recountings, seemed to prompt in him no particular fire or commitment: they were "proper" choices for a missionary hearer; Tale 52 was sufficiently removed from personal application so that—aside from its tumbling-over-itself conclusion—it could be presented with relatively little exertion. But somewhere during the telling of Tale 67, Ikwa Isilombe sensed the challenge and the opportunity afforded a genuine storyteller. Piqued by his own devaluation of his prior performances, he concluded that tale and then, after announcing that he was going to retell that tale with more detail and with some songs, he shouted, "*Bokolo-ki! Bokolo-ki!*" as a signal that now the *real* storytelling was going to begin; he had caught the spirit of a genuine storyteller. In Tale 68 he exercised all the dramatic devices that had been dormant in his earlier tellings—mime, mimicry, prompting of choral response, changes in pacing, rising and falling inflections, attention to details, inclusion of "echoes" in his reuse of the small antelope and the large antelope in the transformation episodes, and various suspense-building techniques—and earned a reward far greater than coins: the clapping, the laughter, and the vocal approbation of his peers. Physically limited by her being seated in a low, overly large chair, Bofaya Efalaiso confined her dramatization of Tale 32 to vocal intonation, eschewing bodily motions entirely. As a consequence, her performance lacked the drama inherent in the tale itself. That the tale possessed the quality it evidences in print can be attributed to her unflagging persistence in the face of odds that would have overwhelmed a less absorbed storyteller: her advanced age and her unclear diction, the crowded room, and the unpatterned, disruptive noises from many different sources. The vocal efforts she made to capture and retain the listeners' interest suggest that under more favorable circumstances she would be capable of a memorable performance. Bolumbu Elakankoi, too, though entirely engrossed in her storytelling, was frustrated in the display of her talents as a storyteller by the intrusive sounds and motions present during her telling of Tales 48 and 56. Both tales have tremendous potential for display of narrative techniques, potential apparent in the texts of the tales as recorded by the narrator, but no efforts at embellishment apart from vocal ones were utilized by Bolumbu in her telling of either tale. That she was concerned to maintain the story line in both tales despite the constant commotion around her suggests that under more encouraging conditions she would have achieved more fully the dramatic potential of the tales.

Four of the five narrators used in Boende were elderly, and the fifth storyteller, Bolumbu, was merely visiting Boende; the likelihood of a later field collector's using these particular narrators may thus be limited. But with the continued growth of the city, the steady stream of visitors, and the presence there of both a good secondary school and a hospital—magnets for those living in the surrounding area—the richness of Boende as a collecting site cannot be overlooked. The interest engendered by Mrs. Ross's collecting, however brief her stay, was widespread; the acceptance accorded strangers in Boende, added to the interest already evidenced there in the collecting of verbal art, offers considerable hope for one either well versed in Lonkundo or accompanied by an Nkundo adept at locating and winning the confidence and cooperation of the competent narrators in that city.

BÓLÈNGÈ

Situated about nine kilometers southwest of Mbandaka, Bólèngè is an old and densely populated village. It extends along the Zaïre (formerly the Congo) River for well over a kilometer and serves as the trading center for the immediate area. The secondary school there was one of the earliest to be established in the entire country, and the Bólèngè hospital throughout most of the past seventy years has been well staffed with trained technicians.

Mrs. Ross's informants in Bólèngè were selected at her request by her long-term friend and translation assistant Bokunge Jacques, so she had no need to seek tale-tellers through other possible channels: the secondary school and the hospital. Bokunge Jacques, though well acquainted with a number of competent storytellers in the village, decided that Mrs. Ross would benefit most by working with just two narrators, Bokunge Jacques himself and one of Bokunge Jacques' distant relatives, Bongonda Michele. Quite unexpectedly, Bongonda's wife, Amba Engombe Telesa, also volunteered to narrate, and her offer was readily accepted.

Bokunge Jacques had correctly assessed his own narrative potential. An examination of the considerable range of tales told by this competent narrator suggests that he was determined to share with Mrs. Ross the widest possible spectrum of Nkundo verbal art.

Of his fifteen narratives and three additional accounts, included in the notes, two are *pourquoi* tales (Tales 7 and 9), three—two using animal dramatis personae and the other a man and a dog—deal with the obligations of extra-familial friendships (Tales 22, 29, and 47), one (Tale 39) is an animal trickster tale, one considers the values of mercy and gratitude (Tale 43), one reflects the Nkundo concerns for ownership and the matter of impossible restitution (Tale 84), one (Tale 42) exemplifies a method by which the Nkundo vent their resentment against the abuse of authority, two (Tales 88 and 94) are dilemma tales, with the latter including also a *pourquoi* element, two (Tales 62 and 66) deal with Nkundo awe of the supernatural in quite different samples of ogre tales, and the remaining five present accounts of tribal history and tribal customs: Tales 3 and 4 are origins tales, and the rest, furnished within the notes (note 26 for Tale 2, note 8 for Tale 54, and note 9 for Tales 84 and 85), deal, respectively, with tribal beginnings, arrangements within a polygynous household, and the reasoning behind tribal markings. All of these tales, of course, contain additional elements of Nkundo life and culture and provide a rich study of the Nkundo themselves, whether thinly disguised as nonpeople or openly as human beings; the bulk of Bokunge Jacques' tales employed nonpeople dramatis personae—reptiles, birds, animals, trees, and supernatural beings. In curious contrast, the tales told by Bongonda Michele and by his wife, Amba, employed solely people as the characters. All but two (Tales 74 and 82) of Bongonda's narratives included supernatural elements—life tokens, miraculous births, transformations, forest spirits, a witch-bird, a talking skull, ogres, and other awe-inspiring evidences. Tale 2 offers a considerable portion of the Nkundo oral epic; Tale 65 reflects the consequences of tabu-breaking; Tales 72, 74, 75, and 76 combine the basic Nkundo concerns of nuclear-family loyalty and of sharing; Tale 82 examines certain areas of polygynous marriage and deals with the danger of false accusation of theft. Amba's two narratives grapple with delicate family issues: Tale 57 probes the relationships among in-laws, and Tale 86 examines nuclear-family adjustments in the light of individual ownership (the latter includes an instance of seemingly impossible restitution). Both of Amba's tales included supernatural elements.

Bokunge Jacques, sixty-five years old at the time of the tale-telling, had just retired from an active life as a general repairman, an occupation at which he had been singularly successful. Both his work success and his extensive education (eleven years of formal schooling) had brought him considerable social status. His particular combination of personality traits—even-temperedness, willingness to work,

ease with people, and knowledgeability—made him an ideal liaison
between Mrs. Ross and possible narrators in the heavily populated
village. His relatively extensive education also enabled him to transcribe the tales (told in Old Lonkundo) into a form of Lonkundo
more readily understood by Mrs. Ross; his thorough familiarity with
the details of the Nkundo hunting and fishing culture—details that
had lain outside her own areas of experience—proved invaluable to
Mrs. Ross in her work with the tales. His unflagging zeal during the
entire project and his willingness to share with her some intimate
insights into Nkundo oral history indicate his own conviction of the
importance of collecting and preserving Nkundo oral narrative.
Bongonda Michele, elderly and crippled with arthritis, had apparently
had little or no formal schooling; his education had come through
the oral tradition, the customary means for preparing Nkundo for
living within their own culture. Details concerning this informant's
personal life and former occupation were not furnished. Bongonda's
wife, Amba, nearing fifty, was considerably younger than her husband; a late addition to his family, she had been acquired to care for
him in his old age. No information concerning her previous circumstances was provided, although she had probably had two years of
elementary schooling, sufficient to enable her to read a little and to
handle money, the latter a skill necessary in the trading of garden
produce in which Nkundo village women engage.

After each morning of taping tales told by Bongonda and his
wife, Bokunge Jacques and Mrs. Ross returned to the church-owned
missionary house where the tapes were replayed and translated into
modern Lonkundo (these translations were later checked by other
multilingual Nkundo). Each time after this exacting task had been
completed, Bokunge Jacques was eager to provide a tale or two of his
own. Apart from Mrs. Ross, there was no continuous audience for
these tellings, but various people—some black and some white, all
Lonkundo-speaking—stopped by to make comments in the course of
their business in the household. The only extraneous sounds, those
from the road passing directly in front of the house, were provided
by an occasional car or truck and by children or adults passing from
one part of the village to another. Bongonda Michele's tale-telling
was done on the front porch of his house, where Amba had arranged
chairs for Bongonda, Bokunge, and Mrs. Ross; others who came to
listen and to participate either brought their own stools, sat on the
ground, or stood near enough to hear easily and to make whatever
contributions seemed appropriate. Since Bongonda lived at a distance
from the highway, no traffic noises intruded upon the storytelling.

Occasionally the crowing of a rooster or the barking of a dog could be heard, sounds disturbing neither to the narrator nor to the listeners. The few women, children, and old men not occupied elsewhere came quickly to hear the tales, since any diversion catches the interest of Nkundo villagers; none of these dared to correct or dispute with the narrator, but all participated in the choruses not only with singing but with clapping and other rhythmic movements. After Mrs. Ross had gone to their home several times, Amba asked if she might tell a tale, the first time in Mrs. Ross's field collecting in which a woman had volunteered as a narrator. At the end of the two different occasions on which Amba told a tale, Bongonda demanded at least half of the small amount paid for her participation in the telling, a portion not relinquished in either instance in Mrs. Ross's presence.

Unfortunately, after transcription and retranslation, the tales recorded during these sessions were erased to make room for other recordings, so we cannot demonstrate the skill with which Bokunge Jacques invited the listeners into the situation presented by a tale. With reference to one tale (Tale 29) for instances of his use of miming, Mrs. Ross clearly recalls his lively performance in the display of gifts, the stacking of firewood, the repeated holding up of the crocodile's single remaining egg, and the pursuit by the baby crocodile. His verbal play, despite his limited audience, is amply demonstrated in that same tale in the use of dialogue, the cracking of the crocodile eggs, the counting of the "fifty" young, and the protesting cries of the newborn crocodile. The element of suspense (still citing Tale 29), initiated by the visit to Crocodile's underwater home, increases as Tortoise is permitted to stay in the "treasury," and mounts as he discovers and destroys one by one most of his friend's "children," "counts" them to prove his trustworthiness, is returned safely to the river bank despite the accusation of the baby crocodile, and then is pursued by the outraged father. This detailed commentary on a single tale told by Bokunge Jacques is an accurate indication of the degree to which this narrator involved himself vocally and bodily in all his tale-telling for Mrs. Ross. Bongonda Michele, too, was totally caught up in his own storytelling. Though unable to move about freely because of his arthritis, he still identified himself with the husband (Tale 72), with Jibanza (Tale 2), with the child (Tale 65)—to cite but three dramatic instances—making loud and appropriate noises to suggest both sound and action attending the various narrative situations. His sense of drama increased with each auditing of his own tales on tape, influencing the power of his telling of subsequent tales. Amba's superb skill as a storyteller is evidenced in her subtle handling of the delicate and age-old problems of in-law and nuclear-family relationships. Her use of miming and her excellent command both of the songs and of the narrative line were marked in the telling of Tale 86. Her intonations and her further use of drama—for example, marking on her own body the successive levels reached by the water rising to submerge the guilty girl—and of song (both in Tale 57) greatly increased the impact of that tale on her hearers. (Additional details on Amba's narrative techniques are furnished in the notes for her two narratives.) Her audience responded as fully to Amba Telesa's tale-telling as to that of her husband.

Bólèngè, rich in oral tradition and in narrators preserving verbal art, has barely been tapped in the present study; opportunities for further field work there exceed those of most sites with which Mrs. Ross is familiar. Bólèngè's convenient location (accessible, as it is, either by air or by water), its ample hotel and restaurant facilities, and the feeling of hospitality present there make it an inviting situation for one comfortable with the Lonkundo language and eager to explore further the wide range of Nkundo oral narratives.

BONGA-ITELI

Mrs. Ross herself did not have an opportunity to visit Bonga-Iteli during her field collecting for the present volume, but Robert Stewart, a Peace Corps teacher who had observed with considerable interest the folktale collecting done in Boende, went to Bonga-Iteli and recorded for Mrs. Ross in a single tale-telling session all the narrative samples furnished here from that village. The portions of the following materials appearing as quotations have been taken verbatim, with Bob's permission, from a letter written early in January of 1974 to Mrs. Ross concerning his Bonga-Iteli visit.

> Bonga [more fully identified as Bonga-Iteli in Bob's permission letter, dated May 22, 1977] is a village of perhaps fourteen families, located between the Salonga and Louila [sic] Rivers, 113 km south of Boende [via winding paths] and in the secteur of Nongo. The people of the area are Yongos and speak a dialect of Lonkundo called Yongo. Houses are generally larger than in the Boende area with high ndele roofs of four sides rather than the conventional two. Behind each house is a kitchen, as large as many normal sized houses in Boende; all of the kitchens stand in a neat row and the open space between the houses and kitchens serves as a general community gathering area. There's a strong sense of community

in the village. Fetishing is not a popular pastime. Hunting is, at least more so than in the Boende area.

The single source for informants was Robert Stewart, who at the time of the tale-collecting had spent two years as a Peace Corps teacher in the secondary school at Boende. Bob commented,

> Just returned from a great bicycle trip with one of my students to Monkoto-Ifumo [sic] and back—in one week and one day. Most of the time was spent in the student's village, Bonga, about half way between here [Boende] and Monkoto. . . . While in Bonga the village people arranged to have a storytelling time one night which I managed to record for you.

About the informant, Bob wrote,

> The storyteller is Mpanga Iyende; age approximate late 30's or early 40's. He's a nonsubsidized primary school teacher in Bonga, a good hunter, and well respected citizen in the village. He also has quite an aptitude for learning English; he worked on it at his own pace during the four days we were there and really learned quite a lot.

It is interesting to note that Mpanga Iyende told only one tale employing animal dramatis personae, Tale 25, reflecting the wily tortoise's (and the Nkundo's) concern with ownership. Three of the eight tales told involved chiefs and their families (Tales 51, 53, and 54), the largest percentage of such high-ranking figures in the Ross collection to be derived from one location; of these three tales, respectively, one concerns the courtship and abortive marriage of the chief's granddaughter, another deals with the relationship between the chief, his pampered daughter, and the rest of his household, and the third reflects parent-child relationships. Also involving parents and children are two other tales: one (Tale 77) of children who disobeyed and were swallowed by an ogre and the other (Tale 78) of a disobedient daughter whose breaking of an injunction, with its consequences, brought embarrassment to her family and to her community. Tale 61 emphasizes the significance of nuclear-family loyalty; Tale 83 underlines the high cost of marital infidelity. Supernatural elements appear in three of the narratives (Tales 61, 77, and 83). Curiously, in his selection of tales to tell, Mpanga Iyende was more consistently moralistic than were those who told tales directly to Mrs. Ross, a characteristic that surprised us both.

Bob's letter included this comment about the storytelling situation: "It [the storytelling time] turned out to be a series of stories, one after the other, given by one man with vocal accompaniment by the group." Fortunately, the tape recording Bob made of the session was of excellent quality; we have chosen to enter all of the information on performance details, audience participation, and interruptive sounds within the notes for the eight tales told by the narrator. Mpanga Iyende's tales are the most fully documented set of narratives in this respect in the present volume, offering the reader as complete an opportunity as possible to experience the actual storytelling for himself. The dialect used—Yongo—was sufficiently similar to the Lonkundo spoken by Bokunge Jacques to allow that competent translation aide to capture the text, though not the songs, of the tales told by Mpanga Iyende; points at which the material was not clearly understood are indicated in the notes for the tales.

No information was furnished by Bob Stewart concerning Mpanga Iyende's narrative techniques. Such indications as can be derived from our repeated listenings to the taped tellings (each time to our greater delight) have been provided in the notes for his tales. The tales told by this accomplished narrator, under traditional storytelling conditions and with a fully Nkundo audience (aside from Bob Stewart), can fairly be said to represent verbal art as it is currently being presented among Nkundo villagers.

Fortunately, tale-telling is still alive and well in Bonga-Iteli, and Mpanga Iyende is still young enough so that further field collecting might well be done there drawing upon what appears to be an extensive repertory of a splendid storyteller. An ideal combination for this purpose would be an ethnomusicologist, a linguist proficient both in Old Lonkundo and in Yongo, and a folk-narrative collector of whatever discipline might best complement the other two fields of study. Such investigations are imperative if an adequate assessment of African verbal art is to be made.

ILONGO-KINDO

A curious interlude was spent by Mrs. Ross in Ilongo-Kindo, reputed to be an excellent location for folktale collecting. This remote village, approximately sixteen kilometers southeast of Boende, is accessible from Boende only by a very rough road. Mrs. Ross's first impression of the village—as was that of the Boende elders who had taken her there by Volkswagen van—was a negative one: lounging about in the middle of the village toward noonday, jobless and apparently disinterested in working, were a number of strong, healthy young men. (The tribal identity of these young men was not ascertained. If—as is possible—they derived from the nearby Ngonje-Ngombe peoples, their "idleness" could be explained in the light of their tribal traditions. For information on these traditions, see Wolfe, *In the Ngombe Tradition* ... [1961], pp. 14–15.) Little was learned about the village on this brief visit.

Tata Manga and several other Boende elders, on inquiring about possible further recording sites for Mrs. Ross, had been told that there was an excellent narrator in Ilongo-Kindo, Mbilo Esio; since Tata Manga in his early youth had been a pupil of Mbilo Esio and held him in great respect, the Boende elder and his peers agreed to make that particular visit as promptly as possible. Before they had located the narrator they were seeking, Tata Manga and his group encountered the idle young men, all of whom expressed an interest in being recorded on tape; that chance encounter yielded two short narratives, and the subsequent session with Mbilo Esio yielded two slightly longer tales. Although the yield from this visit was much smaller than she had been led to expect, Mrs. Ross recognized the benefit of experiencing a relatively "dry-well" encounter with narrators: her appreciation of collecting sites yielding a substantial return was thereby increased.

From the jumbled comments taped among the young idlers, Mrs. Ross salvaged Tale 36, a spare telling of the race-won-by-deception animal narrative, told by Bakonga Bolingo, and an animal tale dealing with the stability of extra-familial friendships (Tale 21), told by Ifoma Itaitonga. The two narratives furnished by Mbilo Esio included a *pourquoi* tale (Tale 11) and a story expressing each man's right to pursue his own way, regardless of its result (Tale 70).

No information was available about the young men aside from what visual observation had yielded. Mbilo Esio at the time of Mrs. Ross's visit was quite an old man, retired, and living in his home village, where he had previously taught and preached for many years.

The two young men stood among their peers as they told the tales included in this volume. Both of them appeared embarrassed and ill at ease in their roles as voluntary narrators. On the other hand, the storytelling situation for Mbilo Esio was a more normal and inviting one: the audience was mixed, including men, women, and children of various ages, and shelter from the heat was provided by a tree beneath which a number of chairs had been set out, largely for the visitors from Boende. The narrator himself sat on a low stool, as was the custom of his fathers. Early in the tale-telling there was an interruption by a small child; otherwise, the audience was quiet, not even providing choral responses. Now and then, a rooster crowed, but this extraneous sound appeared to disturb neither the storyteller nor his listeners.

The two young men delivered their narratives with a greater degree of animation and variety in pacing than can be indicated in the printed texts. As for Tale 36, both the vocabulary and the speech patterns of the narrator presented such difficulties for Mrs. Ross's translation assistant that the translation of the text was truncated to include only those details of which the aide could be certain. The taped version of the tale is longer and much more enthusiastic, with a lively handling of the dialogue not conveyed in the printed version. Although Ifoma Itaitonga's presentation was less dramatic than that of his associate, concern for the good opinion of his peers prompted him to handle the tale convincingly. The substantial audience provided sufficient incentive for Mbilo Esio to use the only dramatic tool available to him: his voice. (He was too feeble to mime or to gesticulate; either or both of these narration embellishments would have increased the dramatic impact of the tale-telling.) Mbilo Esio used his voice quite effectively, providing, for example, a high pitch for the antelope's speeches and a bass for the leopard's remarks (Tale 11).

From her own experience, Mrs. Ross considers Ilongo-Kindo a relatively unpromising site for further collecting. She suspects that much collecting could be achieved if one were to live near a series of small villages, come to know the inhabitants well, and then, having won their trust, invite them to share their narratives. In small villages, the residents tend to rely quite heavily on oral narratives as a means of education as well as of preserving the value system, and there should thus be at least one reasonably competent narrator in each village willing to record a sampling of tales on tape.

LONGA

Longa, the first storytelling site visited by Mrs. Ross in her field collecting, proved for an entirely understandable reason one of the least fruitful locations for the accumulation of Nkundo oral narratives. Scene of one of the early mission stations established in Africa by the Disciples of Christ, Longa is located on a high bank overlooking the Ruki River not too far beyond the point where the Lomela and the Momboyo rivers join to form the Ruki. Life in the village revolves around events in the church, and Longa itself is the site of many church conferences, largely because of its midpoint location in the Disciples' Zaïrian mission-station pattern. Since the death of Ray Eldred (the Disciples missionary stationed at Longa to whom Vachel Lindsay dedicated his poem "The Congo") early in the second decade of the twentieth century, there have been no Western missionaries assigned to Longa, and that village retains to this day the stamp of the early missionary effort. At the time of Ray Eldred's service there, the Disciples shared the view of many other Western denominations that local tales and oral traditions needed to be replaced by tales and traditions drawn from Christian sources; not long after that time, this view gave way to the one held today, that within African oral culture lie strong foundations for the building of Christian insight, and that these foundations might well be used as a bridge toward the Christian ethic. In many other areas of Zaïre, areas provided with mission teachers, this new view has provided the incentive for preserving in print those oral narratives carrying personal, social, and ethical values, resulting in a considerable body of oral material's being included in readers, language textbooks, and other works designed for use in the local languages, including Lonkundo (one example of such a collection is *Bekolo Bėmỏ Bendemba Ba-Nkundo*, compiled at Monieka). Anthropologists, ethnologists, folklorists, and other scholars of African ways and words have unquestionably been aided through this recording of samples of verbal art by those working with various missions, both Catholic and Protestant. Unfortunately, Longa missed the benefits that could have accrued in a similarly active preservation of its own oral traditions.

Mrs. Ross's source for informants was the Longa elementary-school director, Bȯlinsȯmi Pierre, a long-time friend and colleague. Too busily engaged with his administrative work to assist with the collecting himself, he invited several of the elders of the local church to meet with Mrs. Ross and furnish both narrators and audience for the storytelling. Once these contacts had been established, he returned to his own work.

Ngoi Ekoletonga proved to be the only one of this group willing to tell tales for Mrs. Ross, although he received a considerable amount of advice and vocal support from his audience; Ngoi as their leader relished holding center stage as he told four tales and a short bit of social history. Three of the four tales had animal dramatis personae: Tales 15 and 31 concerned relationships between the dog and the porcupine, and the third furnished Mrs. Ross's only field-collected sample of the deceptive-tug-of-war narrative staple (Tale 37). The fourth story (Tale 49), involving a "wise" man and a "fool," reflected the Nkundo concern about theft. Note 17 for Tales 58 and 59 includes Ngoi's brief description of sharing as it had been observed during earlier days among the Nkundo. All of these contributions made either a social or a moral point: even Tale 37, an out-and-out trickster tale, carried the underlying social message that brains could outweigh brawn.

Ngoi Ekoletonga, nearly seventy years old at the time of the tale-telling, had doubtless had no formal schooling. However, because of the strong mission influence in that village, he had probably learned to read sufficiently well to manage the simple passages from the Bible required for his position as elder of the church. He must surely have had a lifetime of exposure to the Nkundo oral tradition, the primary source of education for those deprived of formal schooling, but his selection of tales reflects an understandable reluctance to share with Mrs. Ross and his peers in the church any tales not appropriate to his church post. Further information about this narrator is not available to us.

The brief Lonkundo-language storytelling session, held in the morning in the living room of the school director's home, was more stormy and more punctuated by interruptions than the printed Ngoi Ekoletonga tales indicate. The tape on which the tales were recorded was among those erased to make room for additional tales, so comments cannot be furnished in the notes to specify these interruptions, but Mrs. Ross recalls vividly the efforts made by Ngoi Ekoletonga's listeners to improve his tale-telling. The fact that he was their leader in no way deterred them from inserting corrections or additions. Ngoi Ekoletonga endured these interruptions reasonably well, but he made no allowance at all for the prompting by small children who listened at the edges of the group; young ones offering remarks were promptly sent out of the room for their lack of proper respect for their elders. A lively debate concerning the authenticity of one of the four tales was in progress in the room even during the telling of the tale. *Bekolo Bemo ...* was mentioned several times during the discussion of what tales ought to be told for Mrs. Ross; apparently, several of the elders were familiar with that collection and, feeling that tales compiled by mission teachers would be acceptable to a missionary-collector, they managed to suggest two from *Bekolo Bemo ...* that Ngoi Ekoletonga could tell (Tales 15 and 49 in the present volume). Interestingly, there were sufficiently marked differences between Ngoi Ekoletonga's versions and those provided in the school reader to suggest that the Longa narrator had acquired his own versions directly from the oral tradition rather than from the text-book and to extend the hope that the Longa oral tradition had not actually been lost, but still existed "underground."

Despite the interruptions by his peers, the narrator entered wholeheartedly into his storytelling, enthusiastically playing the role of each character, whether man or beast. As soon as he had heard the playback of his first tale, he increased the drama of his tale-telling even more, not only for the benefit of Mrs. Ross and of his peers but for his personal delight in hearing his own mimicry and com-municated excitement come out of the tape recorder. (A second tape recorder for the capturing of the comments made during the play-back would have been invaluable for documentation.)

The presence of an elementary school in Longa and the evidence that some oral narratives have persisted despite the initial mission resistance against them are both encouraging factors. We trust that future collectors will study this phenomenon in Longa and stimulate the recovery of the samples of verbal art still available there.

MBANDAKA

Mbandaka, known during the Belgian regime as Coquilhatville, is representative of a number of Zaïrian cities in that its major growth occurred after independence was declared in 1960. Crowded with unemployed, unassimilated people, largely those who had previously been "frozen" in or near their own villages by the Belgian adminis-trators, Mbandaka and its sister cities have struggled without success to deal with the problems accompanying sudden urbanization.

In view of the city's size and condition, Mrs. Ross despaired of finding narrators there until she discovered that Mbambo Jean, an old-time friend from Lotumbe, lived not far from the missionary home where she was staying. Mbambo Jean himself furnished the only tales collected by Mrs. Ross in Mbandaka.

Mbambo Jean provided three narratives for the present volume: an animal tale dealing with extra-familial friendship (Tale 18), an account of a young woman who violated a tabu and subsequently became the wife of an ogre (Tale 63), and—after considerable hesitation and great creative anguish—a tale he himself had con-structed at Mrs. Ross's request (Tale 1), the last narrative told by

Mbambo Jean and the last tale collected by Mrs. Ross for this volume.

Mbambo Jean (now Mbambo Mbalaka Ilake), in his late sixties when he recorded these narratives, was teaching in a primary school and assisting his wife in her bakery shop. The childless couple have always been deeply involved in community life wherever Mbambo Jean's work has taken him—he was head teacher of the elementary school in Lotumbe when Mrs. Ross first met him, in 1950—and they have already established sound roots in Mbandaka, their retirement site. Mbambo Jean, though he has had unusually extensive training (three years of high school education), has an inquiring mind and a thirst for learning, and consequently he is well informed about the concerns and values of his people.

Because Mbambo Jean's home is located on a busy street, he and Mrs. Ross went to a reasonably quiet room, well away from the street, to record his narratives. Still, the recording was marred by street noises throughout the entire telling. For the two narratives (Tales 18 and 63) recorded at his home, the Lonkundo-speaking storyteller had as an audience only Mrs. Ross and the tape recorder, a circumstance that unquestionably limited the provocation to dramatize what he was telling: an interested group of listeners tends to encourage the narrator and to afford participation in the many-dimensioned dramatic and musical production that a fully developed Nkundo folktale can be. The circumstances for the narration of Tale 1 were even more restrictive: the creation story was told in a private cabin on a large hospital boat docked at Mbandaka, and no extraneous sounds or audience response attended the telling. The tale itself was clearly a monumental task both to construct and to deliver; after months of deliberation, the author had carefully written the tale out, and then had difficulty in reading it aloud to his satisfaction—for a short period, it appeared that he was undergoing a truly traumatic experience. But, finally put at his ease, he was able to deliver the created work with the flavor he had intended. It is unlikely that Mbambo Jean would have attempted this undertaking for anyone other than Mrs. Ross.

Mbambo Jean's use of Lonkundo diction was exceptionally limited in all three of the tales he told, perhaps because he had no Nkundo listeners. Despite his small audience, the narrator exercised his dramatic talents in mimicking each of the actors in Tale 18; in his telling of Tale 63, the use of a Lonkundo slang term and of many songs, as well as his splendid sense of humor, enabled him to offer a sound performance. (One special note must be included here concerning Mbambo Jean's humor: from his earliest school years, he has been exposed to—and influenced by—Western missionaries, a fact that may account for his humor's appealing to Western analysts.) With a large, traditional Nkundo audience, he would probably prove to be an excellent narrator.

A researcher planning to do field collecting in Mbandaka would be well advised to seek the counsel and support of G. Hulstaert, for many years of his life a Catholic missionary in or near Mbandaka, and at last notice still living in Mbandaka; Hulstaert has been with good reason considered the most outstanding non-Nkundo authority on Nkundo folklore.

MONIEKA

Located on a curve of the Tshuapa River and high above it, Monieka is a large, spread-out, and most attractive village. Even though it is not a government center, for many years it has been a cultural and medical center for a large surrounding area. Supplementing the offerings of the elementary school are teacher-training courses as well as refresher courses for pastors and teachers of the small villages nearby. Serving not only thousands of Africans but also many European plantation workers is a well-equipped and well-staffed hospital. Monieka's educational and medical advantages continue to draw both new residents and visitors.

Monieka was the site of compilation of two Nkundo tale collections, one in Lonkundo and the other in English. The compilers of *Bekolo Bemo Bendemba Ba-Nkundo* and also the author of *Wembi, the Singer of Songs* had access to a large selection of narrators. Teachers, nurses, pastors, workmen, salespeople, and a steady stream of visitors would be available to share their folk narratives with any one of these four women; all the potential narrators needed was an audience. Unfortunately, no names, sites, or dates related to the telling of the tales are recorded in either book, nor is there any indication of the degree to which the oral versions might have been adapted to suit the purposes of the collectors.

Three veteran missionaries, long-time teachers in the elementary school at Monieka—Mrs. Wilma Jaggard (now Hobgood), Miss Martha Bateman, and Mrs. Lillian Hedges—cooperated in the compilation of *Bekolo Bemo*.... At approximately the same time and also in Monieka, another long-time missionary and teacher, Alice Cobble, was preparing for American publication a group of Nkundo folktales translated from Lonkundo and then freely retold in English. Her book, *Wembi . . .*, included versions of twenty-five tales within a framework of structured tale-telling sessions in a single village by a single storyteller, Wembi; each tale is told ostensibly to meet a declared need or answer a specific question of some member of the village. (An assessment of this volume including a sample passage may be found in Coughlan's *Folklore from Africa to the United States* [1976], p. 76.) In the present study we have included Mrs. Ross's translations of eighteen tales from *Bekolo Bèmò . . .*, all used either as variants of the Ross-collected narratives or within the notes with the exception of the one furnished as Tale 95. Selected from the sixty tales in the Lonkundo volume are eleven animal narratives (our Tales 10, 12, 17, 20, 24, 26, 28, 30, 40, 95, and one included within note 1 for Tale 36), three stories about people (our Tales 50, 59, and 85), one tale about an ogre and his relationships with people (our Tale 64), one about a chimpanzee and a man as friends (our Tale 45), another in which trees call the chimpanzee to judge a palaver (our Tale 89), and one in which an ogre lives among animals (see note 4 for Tales 39 and 40). The wide variety of narrative forms in this selection of tales from *Bekolo Bèmò . . .* can be sensed from the inclusion of two dilemma tales, five trickster tales, and three *pourquoi* tales. (Only eighteen of the narratives in *Bekolo Bèmò . . .* have human dramatis personae; *Wembi . . .* includes only eight such tales.) Many of Mrs. Cobble's retellings are loose variants of the narratives collected by Mrs. Ross, although at no time did the latter collect tales in the Monieka area.

All four of these mission teachers at the time of their writing had spent many years in the Nkundo area of Zaïre, most of the time in Monieka. Lonkundo had become a second language for them; French was also an everyday tongue. The fact that in order to become a nonnative teacher in Belgian-controlled Belgian Congo one must have completed specified courses beyond the acquisition of a university undergraduate education indicates the degree of formal schooling to which all four women had been exposed. The amount of formal schooling experienced by the narrators providing tales for the two volumes was nowhere either suggested or implied.

Bekolo Bèmò . . ., intended for Lonkundo-language classroom use, was displaced as a teaching tool as soon as French had been declared the language of school instruction (approximately two years after the book's publication); it continued in circulation, however, among those able to read Lonkundo and with access to no reading materials other than that volume and the Bible, as long as the paperback copies could survive handling. The didactic intentions of the compilers are reflected both in the moral emphasis of many of the tales and in the types of grammatical usage demonstrated in the text. *Wembi* ..., intended for American children, was sold for a number of years within the church denomination the author had represented in Zaïre; it is no longer listed as being in print.

For one equipped with a good tape recorder and a knowledge of Lonkundo, Monieka should be an excellent site for field collecting. The large proportion of elderly people there suggests access to those whose education has come either largely or entirely from the oral tradition.

TONDO

Situated on Lake Tumba and bordering on the Lonkundo-speaking area is the village of Tondo, housing several hundred people. The local residents speak Lontumba, a tongue easily understood by the Nkundo. Tondo is the center of a British Baptist mission and has both a large hospital staffed by British nurses and an excellent second-ary school. For one or another of these special advantages, people come from various directions—many from a considerable distance away—either to become permanent residents or to pay occasional visits. The visitors include a number of Nkundo whose stock of oral narratives might reasonably be expected to be enriched during the time spent in Tondo and who might in turn contribute tales that would put down roots among the oral repertories of Tondo residents and of Lonkundo- or Lontumba-speaking visitors. It therefore seemed to us an ideal site for the assembling of tales subject to diffusion.

The two most productive sources of narrators in Tondo were the secondary school and the hospital, the former because of its co-operative director and competent narrator Lontomba Samuel and the latter through the guidance of Mary Hitchings, a missionary nurse who took Mrs. Ross through the entire hospital introducing her to all the Nkundo who had come there for medical care. Among these patients, two narrators were tape recorded, Bomponge Joseph and Njoli Bombongo.

Lontomba Samuel told tales on two different tapes, the first one including Tales 13, 14, and 27, all animal tales, and the second including Tales 6, 8, 34, 38, 41, 46, and 81, all except the last two also narratives with solely animal dramatis personae; Tale 46 concerned a hunter rescued from many-headed dogs by a leopard he had spared, and Tale 81 dealt with a barren woman whose beautiful daughter, acquired by magic, was able to identify the "father" she had never seen. Bomponge Joseph recounted Tales 33, 44, and 71, the first about the Nkundo's favorite animal trickster—the dwarf antelope—the second a tale in which a hunter and a chimpanzee helped each other, and the third showing two men with exactly opposite attitudes on the matter of sharing. Njoli Bombongo narrated Tales 23, 60, and 93, ranging from an animal trickster tale through the account of a hunter and an ogre in partnership to a dilemma tale.

The three narrators differed widely in their ages, their formal schooling, their personal situations, and their reasons for recording the tales. Lontomba Samuel, the only one of Mrs. Ross's narrators who had had a university education (in Washington, D.C.), has used folktales in his teaching and regards the oral tradition as a custodian of cultural values. Thirty-six years old at the time he told the tales, Lontomba Samuel has a well-educated wife who encourages his interest in oral narrative, as well as several children who benefit from his tale-telling. Initially asked by Mrs. Ross to translate some samples of verbal art his father had recorded, Sam completed that task and then furnished tales he felt would best convey the two basic functions of oral narratives in the Tondo area: (1) to explain certain phenomena or physical features found in nature; (2) to teach, or to carry a moral application. Bomponge Joseph—away from his home in Besenge, near Kalamba, for treatment at the Tondo hospital— was a male in his late sixties; his formal schooling was apparently quite limited, though no information was provided either about his educational background or about his means of earning a living. Bomponge Joseph had been tempted initially into recording tales by the fee promised (a dollar or so). However, he had a seven-year-old grandson (aiding him during his hospital stay) who accompanied him to the tale-telling, and the narrator's awareness that this descendant needed to grow on "the tales of the ancestors" quickly outweighed the monetary factor; both his selection of the tales to tell and the quality of his storytelling were conditioned by the presence in the audience of this important listener. Njoli Bombongo, a nineteen-year-old secondary-school student in Tondo but whose home was in Kalamba, was under surveillance for diabetes at the hospital; his work with Mrs. Ross in translating various tales collected earlier had persuaded him that he could tell narratives that surpassed the others in quality, and desire for the good opinion of his schoolmates attending the storytelling session prompted him to a sound performance.

Lontomba Samuel's first three tales were related during the daytime, with no audience other than his own tape recorder, in the relative isolation of his room. He acknowledged that according to tradition, if these tales were told in the daylight, the teller would not grow any older, but he felt that since he had already reached the age of thirty-six without harm from such activity, he would be unlikely to be damaged by recording the tales for Mrs. Ross. Despite Sam's care in isolating himself, the usual signs of life in a busy village intruded on the tape, although these noises did not interrupt the tale-telling. The tales Sam included on the second tape were told in the middle of the night, again in his own room, with a considerable reduction of extraneous sounds. Since Sam's first language was Lontumba, one that presented difficulties for Mrs. Ross, he told all eleven of his tales in English. For one accustomed to the grace and diction of the language of the original telling, the narrating of traditional tales in English robs the teller of the opportunity to innovate, to utilize allusions meaningful to local listeners, and to "plug in" episodes that in a normal storytelling situation would enrich and expand the narration. In weighing the literary and other artistic merits of these particular tales, one needs to bear in mind the special difficulties under which this narrator was laboring. Sam is known in the Tondo area as a splendid storyteller, and we trust that his exposure to Mrs. Ross's enthusiasm for the tales will lead him to record and preserve in Lontumba the tales for which he has become noted. Bomponge Joseph, accompanied by his grandson, came to the porch of Mary Hitchings's home in the morning to tell his tales. Since the porch was only twenty meters or less from the main path to the Tondo market, there was considerable background noise: the comments of women on their way to market, various traffic noises, and the sounds of activity within the house and within nearby buildings. Even for Lonkundo-speaking listeners, the aging man's speech was slurred and taxing to follow; the Lontumba-speaking residents who paused to listen before continuing on the path, or who sat on the porch steps to hear, could understand the Lonkundo in which the tales were told, but they apparently felt reluctant to query or contribute in a second language. Njoli Bombongo came to Mary Hitchings's house (the missionary home) toward evening to tell his tales; there he found a ready audience among those of his classmates who customarily did their homework in that hospitable setting. Though the young narrator was dignified and undertook his performance seriously indeed, the tales he chose to tell suggest that he had an abundant well of humor and that he recognized the social value of storytelling within his own culture. Household noises constituted the only extraneous sounds, and these were ignored both by the narrator and by his hearers.

Despite the handicaps of his narrating his tales in English and of his lacking a live audience, Lontomba Samuel evidenced considerable animation in his tale-telling. His use of dialogue—both spoken and shouted—of dramatic pauses, of suspense-building factors, of rising and falling inflections, and of songs, as well as his variations in pacing, revealed Sam's total involvement in the act of storytelling. He clearly visualized the larger audience that would be reached, and he overlooked no opportunity to reach that audience. Bomponge Joseph was totally caught up in the excitement of telling tales he enjoyed to a small though interested audience; the stories told were so lively and so filled with dialogue and with familiar narrative figures that their content and the dramatic way in which they were recounted outweighed the transcription problems posed by the slurred diction. Mrs. Ross feels that if Bomponge Joseph had included a tale or two incorporating songs, the language barrier might have been leaped through the marked Zaïrian love of musical participation. We are both convinced that the evident satisfaction of the storyteller in his performance and in the audience response were in large measure occasioned by the presence of the narrator's grandson. Njoli Bombongo, both encouraged and somewhat inhibited by an audience consisting largely of his peers, did not include any songs in his tale-telling, but he utilized both his voice and numerous gestures to increase the dramatic impact of his narratives. The content alone would have been sufficient to captivate an audience of any age; the manner of delivery, competent and infused with humor, aroused animated response from his audience, a response that would have been even more enthusiastic had he included songs allowing choral participation.

The opportunities for further field collecting in Tondo are limited only by the matter of language: future collectors will need to command both Lonkundo and Lontumba if they hope to extract the maximum possible benefit from work at this site, the gathering place for people of many different backgrounds and storytelling repertories and with sufficient free time to share their tales with those who value verbal art as a reflection of the culture out of which it has grown.

Part I

How the Nkundo World Began

Introduction

Introduction

IN COMMON WITH OTHER peoples around the globe, the Nkundo feel a deep interest in both the natural and the supernatural worlds. How did life begin? Who determined the scattering of quite different tribes or nations throughout the earth? How did fire originate? What accounts for various spiritual and physical traits of people and of other animals? What initiated the curious and puzzling habits observable among the wide range of rain-forest inhabitants? Such questions as these are answered in an unlettered society by the creation of myths, epics, legends, and *pourquoi* tales; these explanatory tales survive the introduction of print and the forces of acculturation because they continue to meet a need satisfied in no other way. To understand the stability of a tribe long investigated but still little understood and appreciated, one must explore the means by which that tribe's culture has been preserved: the folk narrative. The sampling of origins accounts and *pourquoi* tales presented in part 1 suggests the sizable array of viable keys to the culture of the Nkundo.

The creation tale with which part 1 begins evidences the earnest effort made by Nkundo narrators to meet the needs—whether sensed or stated—of a storytelling audience; itself a creation of its teller, Tale 1 draws on a lifetime of Mbambo Jean's exposure to oral tradition and the encroachment of Westernization, yet it bears the stamp of original genius that has kept tale-telling alive.

A portion of the Mongo-Nkundo oral epic follows (Tale 2), an epic still current among the Nkundo and strongly affirmed as the explanation for the origin and scattering of the tribes. Until this tale had been investigated in the light of Boelaert's and de Rop's studies, we had been unaware of the tale's broader cultural significance as part of an epic cycle. (Other portions of the cycle have since been identified, and one of them is included in the present volume as Tale 69.) A brief passage of Nkundo oral history, included in the notes for Tale 2, offers another approach to tribal origins.

Three other origins narratives (Tales 3, 4, and 5) account for the beginning of fire, for the development of animistic belief, and for the incompatibility of good and evil; the long-continued Nkundo practice of enslavement of the Batswa is illuminated by Tale 3 and its notes, and the subtle melting of animism into a form of verbal art often incorporated into the folktale, the proverb, is suggested in a note for Tale 4. The Nkundo personalizing of traits as well as of animals and of purportedly inanimate objects is made vivid in Tale 5, rich in cultural associations and in Lonkundo locutions.

The remaining tales included in part 1 fall under the *pourquoi* classification. Several of these explain the "why" of natural phenomena observed in the Nkundo setting: the bat's nocturnal habits (Tale 6); the low position accorded the snake by other creatures, as well as the serpent's practice of attacking other animals (Tale 7); the hawk's flying into the smoke of the burning bush or grassland (Tale 8); and fowls' looking up as they drink (Tale 13). In the course of these tales and Tales 9 through 12 and 14 through 17, much is communicated of Nkundo life, practices, and values, since the animal principals are viewed as living in houses and in villages, as employing guns and hunting dogs in seeking their prey, as electing officers, as burying their dead in accordance with prevailing tabus, as using doctors and medicines, as seeking brides for whom they surrender bridewealth, as keeping goats, as eating from plates, and as conducting palavers.

Tales 9 and 10 are similar to Tales 11 and 12 in their handling of fear: initially, one creature fears another because of some apparently threatening physical feature—the huge eyes of the owl, the pointed antlers of the antelope—and, having that fear assuaged, the reassured creature preys upon the one formerly feared. In common with Tales 7, 14, and 15 through 17, these narratives account for the pursuit-and-attack patterns observed by the Nkundo in their equatorial-forest setting; they also strengthen the listeners' ability to handle their own feelings concerning fear, physical differences, false friendship, and deep disappointment. The thin disguise afforded by fur, scales, or feathers places the human concern at a sufficient distance from both narrator and audience to allow examination of such anxieties and doubts without embarrassment or irritability. In the absence of zoologists and psychiatrists, the narrator of such tales enables the Nkundo to cope with both their outer and their inner worlds.

Investing the animal actors with Nkundo patterns of cultural behavior, the narrator, with his inheritance of compelling tales, deepens and strengthens the hearers' concepts of their own culture and its system of values: the importance of sharing (Tale 7), the assumption of responsibility in hunting (Tales 9 and 10), the protection of the young (Tales 11 and 12), the respect for tabus (Tales 14 through 17), the custom of bridewealth (Tales 15 through 17), the demands of true extra-familial friendship (Tales 14 through 17), the exercise of patience (Tales 9, 10, and 14), the function of the palaver in settling disputes (Tale 7), the wisdom of discretion in speech and in personal behavior (all nine tales cited), the significance of the parents in the arranging of marriages (Tales 15 through 17), the proper division of the spoils of the hunt (Tales 9 and 10), due regard for individual differences (Tales 14 through 17), and still other aspects of the value system that evidence themselves not only through these nine *pourquoi* tales but in most of the narratives throughout this volume.

The seven narrators furnishing the tales for part 1, all men in their fifties or older, remain close to the Nkundo oral tradition despite their wide disparity in formal schooling, ranging from that of Bongonda Michele (little or none) to that of Lontomba Samuel (university education abroad). As might be anticipated, those who teach or taught school tend to tell instructional tales; on the other hand, Bokunge Jacques tells of tribal traditions, and Bongonda Michele recounts a substantial portion of the Nkundo oral epic. The wide differentiation in the narrators' educational and occupational backgrounds is complemented by the equally broad variety of narrative techniques displayed. Here, each man in his own way opens a window on the Nkundo world.

Narrator: Mbambo Jean
Location: Mbandaka
Date: May 1974

1.   The Creation Story

From the middle of the fire came the Word.[1] The Word went everywhere to see what was there. He named the place he found The-Place-to-Sit.[2] Then he took a rest.

He said, "My name is Sprout-from-the-Seed, for I sprouted from the fire. The one who made the fire is The-One-Who-Knows-the-Place.[3] The earth on which I live is The-Earth-Which-Is-Known. My work is to believe the words. My name will be One-Who-Causes-to-Grow."[4]

The Beginning. One-Who-Causes-to-Grow felt very lonely. He said, "I shall call another so that there will be two of us." So he went to the fire and called another to be with him. This one grew out of the fire. This one came to be with One-Who-Causes-to-Grow.

This one said, "One-Who-Causes-to-Grow, I have come because you called me."

"I called you to be with me because I was very lonely. Help me. Let us multiply."

This second one agreed. They loved one another.

The first one said, "I am the first One-Who-Causes-to-Grow. You are One-Who-Causes-to-Grow, Who-Causes-to-Increase, Who-Guards-or-Cares-For.[5] Your work is one who works and one who causes increase."

The second One-Who-Causes-to-Grow agreed.

"I was born first and I called you to help me. You can keep me from being lonely. I shall call you One-Who-Causes-to-Grow who has come, One-Who-Steers-or-Guides, One-Who-Cares-For."

One-Who-Causes-to-Grow said, "My loneliness is finished. Let us grow a family."

The second One-Who-Causes-to-Grow agreed.

The first, "We can no longer call a family from the fire from which we came. Only two of us can be born that way.[6] It isn't possible to have three that way. We ourselves must join. Let us cause others to be born—the two of us. I can unite with you and we will bring forth others like us."

They united.[7]

Then One-Who-Causes-to-Grow said, "We are two people. We can each care for another. I am the one who guides us.[8] I was born first, but we go together."

After that, two were born as one—both at the same time, as one. One-Who-Causes-to-Grow felt that he should divide them. He pulled them apart, and they were separate,[9] as two people.

One-Who-Causes-to-Grow said, "Now you are two, and each can seek his own way."

So one went to the right of him and chose his place for living. The other went to the left[10] of him and chose his place for living. Two more were born,[11] and one went before One-Who-Causes-to-Grow and one went in back of him.[12]

One-Who-Causes-to-Grow said, "Each of the four I will call 'Spirit.'"[13]

They said, "Let us go to Father and ask for a helper. The loneliness is too great."

They returned to their father. One-Who-Causes-to-Grow went to the second One-Who-Causes-to-Grow. "Each child is asking for a helper. They say that they are too lonely. We are two, but each of them is alone. Let us hunt others to help them—the two of us."

They sprouted two others who came together as one. One-Who-Causes-to-Grow divided them and told them that they were to be helpers of these others. He called each of them "Spirit," as he had called the first ones. They grew and began to fly. One went to the right of One-Who-Causes-to-Grow and one to his left.

Then the first two who had been born came to One-Who-Causes-to-Grow and asked for a place to live with a house. One-Who-Causes-to-Grow agreed. "Each one of you go to the place you have chosen. Then each one can build as he wishes in that place."

Spirit who was on the right of One-Who-Causes-to-Grow was called God.[14] Spirit on the left side was called Satan.[15] One-Who-Causes-to-Grow said that Satan would be known as Difficulties. The other, God, would be known as Sunrise.[16]

Difficulties found a large place where he could settle. "I'll build my place to live here."

Sunrise found his place and began to build there.[17] He built a very large enclosure with much wealth—even gold. He built a strong fence around it with only one opening. This opening he called Place-of-Arriving. If anyone entered he could not leave.

Sunrise built a good road from his father's house to his own gate. There were three places in the enclosure—one for the elders, one for the teacher, and one for himself.[18]

Difficulties also built a large and very beautiful enclosure. He also built a road from his father's house to his own gate. His gate was called Place-of-Arriving. People could enter, but not leave.

"Let's go to Father's house and tell him that we have finished building the villages that we started out to build. The work you sent us to do is finished."

"I am happy that it is finished. Every sprout does as it likes to do."[19]

Sunrise became known as Goodness, and Difficulties was known as Badness.[20]

Their father called them to build him a house. Goodness brought much clay which was good. Badness brought clay which was bad. The two were mixed together in the home for One-Who-Causes-to-Grow.

[Unfinished by the narrator]

Various accounts of the Creation have been recorded by those working among the Nkundo, and a lengthy analysis of such accounts accompanies several origins tales in de Rop's . . . *woordkunst* . . . , chapter 5. For a period of two years, Mrs. Ross had requested of each of her narrators an Nkundo creation story, but no such tale had been told. Mbambo Jean had shared on tape two other stories, but it was not until their last session that he offered a creation story of his own. He had spent most of the preceding night developing the tale that he wanted to tell, the only narrative in the Ross collection drawn directly from the imagination of an individual storyteller. The tale as told in Lonkundo evidenced the responsibility and significance attached by the Nkundo to the function of naming.

We have been unable to attach unconditionally to this tale any of the existing type or motif numbers; elements found in one type and in more than a dozen motifs are, however, present in the tale. Lambrecht's type 5 includes a reference to fire in connection with creation: "Man is the son of the fire's daughter and the toad"; the good comes from the fire and the bad from the toad.

Motifs:

T	A1290.	Creation of man—other motifs.
T	A1280.	First man (woman).
T	A1270.	Primeval human pair.
T	A1275.	Creation of first man's (woman's) mate.
T	A1570.	Origin of regulations within the family.
T	A1350.	Origin of sex functions.

T	A1352.	Origin of sexual intercourse.
T	A1552.3.	Brother-sister marriage of children of first parents.
L	A1273.2.	Multiplication of people from two sets of twins (children of primeval pair).
T	A1277.	Offspring of first parents.
T	A1470.	Beginning of social relationships.
T	A1370.	Origin of mental and moral characteristics.
T	A1330.	Beginnings of trouble for man.

1. Mbambo Jean's beginning his creation story with Word, or *Jói*, reflects the importance of this term in the everyday life of the Nkundo.

2. In village life, the Nkundo has almost no privacy; the teller would thus feel the necessity of including a "place to sit."

3. "The-One-Who-Knows-the-Place" apparently refers to the Creator.

4. At this point, the narrator changes the name of the progenitor from Sprout-from-the-Seed to One-Who-Causes-to-Grow; the latter is retained.

5. This multiple name sums up the basic responsibilities of the woman in the Nkundo culture.

6. Mbambo Jean was aware that only one pair can be a *creation* and that any additional human beings must come from the union of this original pair.

7. The narrator's use of the word "united" is an effective and dignified way of expressing "had sexual intercourse."

8. Apparently Mbambo Jean forgot that this task had already been assigned to the second One-Who-Causes-to-Grow.

9. This refers not to the separation of Siamese twins but to the separation from the mother, from the placenta, and from each other.

10. The word translated "right" is literally "the hand of the husband"; the word translated "left" is literally "the place of the woman."

11. The third and fourth offspring are ignored in the remainder of this narrative. Had the narrator finished his account, these two might well have been provided for in the narration.

12. Mbambo Jean recognizes the fact that the inhabitants of the earth must be scattered, an event described in Tale 2.

13. The word for "spirit" as used in the Lonkundo translation of the New Testament means "The Holy Spirit," creating a dilemma for the older Nkundo, long taught to fear the erratic spirits inhabiting the forest, the river, and various other geographical locations.

14. Mbambo Jean uses the term *Mbombianda* for "God"; the Lonkundo Christian Bible uses *Nzakomba*, apparently considered by Mbambo to be higher and more distant from the plight of humans than was Mbombianda.

An account of the origin of *Mbombianda* as the term used among the Lombole to identify the Supreme Being is furnished in de Rop's ... *woordkunst* ... (p. 87). Translated from the Flemish, it reads as follows:

> *Moma* is the Lombole word for *Mbomba. Mbomba*, in some regions, is used as the name for the Supreme Being. Elsewhere it is *Ianda*. But mostly the fusion of the two occurs: *Mbombianda*.

15. The Lonkundo has no exact equivalent for "Satan." It is curious that "Satan" was identified as "left," or "woman." See the concluding comment in Tale 83 for evidence that the association of "woman" with "Satan" is perpetuated in a folktale in an area at least 300 kilometers away from Mbambo Jean's location.

16. A summary of an Mbóle myth (recorded in 1927 by P. Hulstaert) recounting the creation of the sun and explaining sunrise and sunset is furnished on page 87 of de Rop's ... *woordkunst*.... Translated from the Flemish, this summary reads as follows:

> God had three sons: Sun of God, Moon of God, and Man of God. All three had to execute an order. Because one was lazier than the other, each of them was punished according to the fault committed. The sun had to die every day and to rise the next ...

17. At this point, the narrator reflects the Nkundo pattern; in short, he has created an anthropomorphic god and an anthropomorphic satanic figure.

18. Mbambo Jean, a teacher, reflects here the prestige accorded the elder, the teacher, and the chief in his own community.

19. The narrator did not identify the speakers in this dialogue.

20. "Goodness" and "Badness" are personified in Tale 5, collected in Boende, well over 300 kilometers from Mbambo Jean's present home. Since the latter tale was clearly a part of the oral tradition, Mbambo Jean may well have been familiar with it.

Narrator:	Bongonda Michele
Location:	Bólèngè
Date:	March 1973

2. How the Tribes of the Earth Began

A husband, Ilele,[1] and his wife, Mbombe,[2] went into the forest together. They went to hunt meat. First they built a temporary shelter and then Ilele spread out a net for catching animals. They were hoping to catch porcupines. After a long while, a porcupine came out of his hole and was trapped in the net. Ilele took it to his wife to cook. He sang,

> Mbombe, cook it.
> Cook the meat for me.

Mbombe took the meat and prepared it.

When the food was ready, Ilele said, "Mbombe, Mbombe, wait a bit. Let's ask the owner of the forest[3] if it is all right for a woman to eat this meat. Owner of the Forest, Owner of the Forest, is it all right for Mbombe to eat this meat?"

> Don't eat it; don't eat it,
> Lest your trap line see no meat.

Each day they caught porcupines, and Ilele would sing,

> Mbombe, cook it.
> Cook the meat for me.

Then Mbombe would cook some of it and dry some of it. Each day Ilele ate the meat, and Mbombe had none. After six days, Mbombe became angry. She announced, "I'm going home."

She started, but only went a little way until she decided to hide. When Ilele passed that way, she jumped out at him, "O-ou!" He was frightened[4] and ran. She ran after him.

He called, "Mbombe, come, but don't kill me or even frighten me again."

He went on down the path, and an *itòji* bird fluffed his feathers, *fu-u-u-u*.[5] Ilele jumped again, and Mbombe was there, "O-ou!"

Ilele shouted, "Don't kill me; don't kill me!"

She frightened him many times on that path. Finally they reached home.

Shortly, Mbombe found that she was pregnant. She began to refuse foods, but had a great desire for *nsabu* fruits. These she ate and ate and wanted all the time.

Ilele asked her, "What's the matter with you?"

She sang,

> Hornbill, hornbill, take it!
> The hornbill takes the fruit which I want.

The hornbill dropped one nsabu. Mbombe picked it up, cooked it, and ate it. She wanted more.

Ilele asked her, "What food do you really want to eat? Tell me."

"The hornbill let one fall; I picked it up and ate it."

"Where will I find more?" he asked.

"If a hornbill or a parrot flies over, follow it." After not a long while, a parrot flew over. Ilele followed him and picked up the nsabu that the parrot dropped. He gave these to Mbombe and she was pleased.

The parrot went again to the nsabu tree, and Ilele followed him. Ilele left his baskets on the ground and climbed into the tree. There he found a sentry[6] who was set to watch the fruit. He didn't object to the birds' eating the fruit, but he was trying to keep people from taking the nsabu.

Ilele filled one basket with fruit. Then he climbed higher and filled the second basket.

The sentry called, "You are picking nsabu. Don't you know that it is forbidden?"

Ilele hit him.

The sentry cried out so as to be heard at home, "Nsabusabu,[7] Ilele is picking nsabu and he hit me."

The owner of the tree, Ingele, came with a net and spread it under the tree. He said, "I'll catch him in the net and kill him."

Ilele climbed out of the tree and was caught in the net of Ingele. Ingele sang,

> Ingele has caught him
> Even though he is very tall.

Ilele tore the net to pieces and, taking the two baskets of nsabu, went home to Mbombe. She ate and ate the nsabu until they were all gone. They were what she desired most.

Then Ilele returned to the nsabu tree. As he climbed the tree he said, "What will I do with the boy who is the sentry?" He picked nsabu and carried that basket away from the tree. Then he picked more nsabu and carried those away. The sentry came. "Weren't you in enough trouble before? Why do you come back again?"

Ilele hit the sentry and the sentry called out, "Nsabusabu, Ilele is picking nsabu and has hit me again. The nsabu are finished by now."

This time Ntókulakèndè came and spread a net. Again Ilele was caught, and Ntókulakèndè began to sing a song of rejoicing. About then, Ilele broke the net and began to sing his own song:

> He broke the net.
> [choral response]

Ilele went along the path and got into the net of Bankilinga Belenge. Bankilinga began to sing, but Ilele broke loose and sang his own song:

> He broke the net.
> [choral response]

Ilele was caught in the net of Bolongi and freed himself again. This happened a number of times.[8]

Later, Ilele returned to the nsabu tree and climbed up to pick more fruit. While he was up in the tree a tortoise, Ulu, came along and saw Ilele. He pulled strips from a banana stalk and made a net of those and put it under the tree.

When Ilele climbed out of the tree, he found himself caught in Tortoise's net made of the banana-stalk strips. There were people all around watching. When he wasn't able to break out, he sang,

> The tortoise has caught me.
> [choral response]

Ilele pleaded with the tortoise that he free him from the net. Tortoise refused, and the people nearby killed him [Ilele].[9]

Before Ilele had left home this time, he had said to Mbombe, "I have been caught many times and lived. However, this time I feel that I will die. If you see rain before I return, you will know that I am dead. Also, if you see soldier ants who are scattered and not in line, you will know for sure that I am dead."[10]

Mbombe waited and waited. Finally she said, "He must be dead." It began to rain, a soft gentle rain. Very soon she saw soldier ants coming along and then beginning to scatter. She sang her song of mourning:

> The soldier ants are scattered;
> Ilele is dead.

The time had come for her baby to be born. When the pains came, she didn't want anyone to know that they were labor pains; she sang,

> I don't really cry;
> But I have a terrible toothache.[11]

This was not her first baby. She had had many different kinds of births and as many kinds of babies.[12] The baby was making a real effort to be born, and she sang again:

> A friend gives birth to a child;
> The tooth continues to hurt.

This child was an Nkundo. Mbombe called, "Mother, a girl child has been born. She has a chair and sits on it."

The child answered, "I am Nsongo."[13]

Then Jibanza,[14] Mbombe's boy child who was older, took some chalk and rubbed it on Mbombe's leg as a sign that she was a new mother.

Pao—Jibanza had a spear, a shield, and a pointed hat with feathers.

Another child was coming, and Jibanza said, "The child will kill the mother." However, Mbombe gave birth to a boy baby, Boilenge.[15]

Boilenge asked, "Where is my father?"

Mbombe answered, "You find him and find out what happened."

"I want to know where he lives."

"You find out."

"Father, where did you go?"

Since Jibanza was now a soldier, he went to find where his father had died. He found Bankilinga Belenge, but he denied knowing anything about it.

Then Jibanza asked Bosokonda, but he knew nothing of Ilele.

Next Jibanza found Bolongi, who told him, "I saw your father come hunting nsabu in the territory of the Nsabusabu. They caught him and he died there."

Jibanza went to the village of the Nsabusabu and said, "I am ready for a fight, but I don't want it in the village. Too many innocent people would be killed."

The Nsabusabu asked him, "When a child isn't dry around the navel, should he have such a palaver as this?"

"A child must avenge his father," was the retort.

So they agreed to fight. Each side got his soldiers together and they fought. The people of Nsabusabu called the wasps to help them. When the wasps were finished, they called the hornets.[16]

Jibanza was afraid of losing, but Boilenge came to help him.[17]

Jibanza captured the king of the Nsabusabu. Boilenge said, "Let's kill him."

Nsongo objected. "No, don't kill him."

"Why not?" inquired her brothers.

"I want him for my husband."[18]

So they all celebrated the wedding of Nsongo and the king of the Nsabusabu. Then Jibanza went with his soldiers, the Nsabusabu soldiers, Nsongo and her husband, and Boilenge.

As they were going on their journey, they found a man named Yėndė Yėngili who was playing a *longombi*.[19] They listened while he played. He was an Nsabusabu and had boasted, "If I see Jibanza, I will challenge him."

When Jibanza arrived there, all at once he became a child.[20] He watched Yėndė Yėngili for a while and said, "I want to play your longombi."

"How can you play it when you are only a small child?"

"I know how. Give it to me."

"No! You can't know."

"Give it to me."

Yėndė Yėngili finally gave it to him. Jibanza grabbed it and held it close to his body. "I have it now. It's mine."

Just then, Yėndė Yėngili recognized him. "*Mo!* You are Jibanza."

"Me! I'm not Jibanza. I couldn't be he. Jibanza is a king, and I am a child. I'm not like him, not I." Then Jibanza grabbed Yėndė Yėngili and said, "We will kill him."

Just then, Jibanza became an adult once more. "I am the one who will lead in battle. I will have my soldiers."

The soldiers of Jibanza heard that Bapunungu Bainabolongi had been threatening them, so they decided to hunt for him. Jibanza was sure they could conquer him. They decided to trap him, so they left some tobacco[21] in the path hoping that Bapunungu Bainabolongi would find it.

Bainabolongi came and saw the tobacco but was afraid to touch it. He said, "If you are the tobacco of Jibanza, go quickly."

The tobacco went to another place. Bainabolongi followed it and hid. "Now if Jibanza comes, you keep agitating."

Soon Jibanza came near, and the tobacco began to agitate. Then Bainabolongi left. Jibanza found the tobacco gone. "How will I ever catch him?"

It wasn't long until Jibanza found him and quickly captured him.

Jibanza was conquering everywhere. Then another Jibanza came along, Jibanza Jolombongo.[22] The son of Ilele was Jibanza Bolekunge.

Jolombongo said, "I've come here with my soldiers and you have yours. If I win, all the soldiers will go with me. If you win, they'll all go with you."

Each Jibanza had a younger sister named Nsongo.

Jolombongo won the battle and called to his sister, "Nsongo, bring me my knife, Lombolimbongo; I want to kill him." She brought the knife and Jolombongo hit Bolekunge with it. There was a big flash of fire and when it cleared, Bolekunge wasn't there. He had disappeared.

Jolombongo said, "He is dead."

"But you don't see his grave, do you? How can he be dead?" asked Bolekunge's sister.

Jolombongo gathered his soldiers together and the soldiers of

Bolekunge, his sister and the sister of Bolekunge, and prepared to leave. It was raining, but Nsongo, the sister of Jolombongo, sent the other Nsongo in the rain to get water. She went, crying all the way. After she had filled the gourd with water, Bolekunge came and asked her why she was crying. After she told him he said, "Break the gourd."

"I don't want to break it. They will beat me if I do."

So Bolekunge took the gourd and broke it.

"But you are dead. How can you break a gourd?"

"Did you see my grave? I'm not dead."

She went back to the others and said, "The gourd is broken."

Nsongo, the sister of Jolombongo, was angry. She took up a whip with several strands of buffalo hide and raised her arm to strike the girl to the ground. Her arm was paralyzed in the air. She tried several times, but each time it was the same. She finally called someone to help her. This one tried, but his arm was paralyzed. Then she called another and another, and each time it was the same. Finally they called Jolombongo. He raised his arm with the whip, but Bolekunge grabbed his arm and held it there.

Jolombongo said, "I killed you, didn't I?"

They began to wrestle. Bolekunge wrapped his leg around Jolombongo the way a vine wraps itself around a tree trunk and threw him to the ground. His sister brought him the knife, Lombolimbongo, and he cut off the head of Jolombongo.

Jibanza Bolekunge congratulated himself and proudly stated, "I won." Some of the soldiers sang,

> Jibanza is a very strong man.
> He killed his enemy.

Jibanza gathered all the soldiers together and the two Nsongos, and they all went singing down the path.

They went on until they came to Mbombianda, which is god himself. Jibanza said, "Now I want to have the sun.[23] How can I get it?" Then Mbombianda called a fly and said, "Fly up there and bring back the sun for Jibanza."

They waited and waited and finally the fly returned. "I didn't get it," he told them. So they called a wasp and sent him to get the sun. After a long while he came back and said, "I didn't get it. How can I get it?"

He finally called the hawk and said he'd send him. He said to him, "Come and get this present and take it to Elima, the god of heaven."

Hawk took the package and flew up toward heaven, *baw, baw*. He arrived there and found Elima. Hawk said, "Give me the sun for Jibanza." He waited and waited. Then Elima came and gave him a clock. Hawk took the clock and carried it back to earth. He gave it to Jibanza, and Jibanza shared it with his sister.

Jibanza proudly announced, "I am now a king."

He gathered all his people together and they started out. This was their song:

> We have many things
> Because we went on a journey.

As they went along the way, Jibanza left people at different places so that they could start tribes of their own. His mother had given birth to children of each tribe, and now Jibanza was leaving them in their places. He told each one the name of his tribe.

Then he crossed the ocean[24] and left people on every continent in the world. When he died, another king was chosen in his place.[25]

This was the beginning of all the people of the world and how they became scattered each in his own place.[26]

This tale, which appears at first merely a haphazard grouping of various incidents leading eventually to the scattering of the tribes, is more cohesive and more culturally oriented than it seems. Since the Nkundo are primarily involved in hunting and fishing, it is singularly appropriate that a tale accounting for (1) the origin of the Nkundo and (2) the scattering of the tribes should have its beginning in a hunting scene. Tradition among the Nkundo determines the division of meat or fish; a dispute over the disposition of the porcupine caught by Ilele would catch the interest of any Nkundo listener. The introduction of the itóji injects the supernatural element very early into the tale, a sound first link in the chain of often miraculous events which develops what must be acknowledged as an "origins" story. The cleverness of Mbombe, first in countering her husband's selfishness and then in requiring, during her pregnancy, fruits whose acquisition involves considerable risk, makes her a formidable Earth-mother founder for the tribes later scattered throughout the world by her son Jibanza [identified in most published accounts as *Lianja*. See, among other references, Finnegan's *Oral Literature in Africa* (1970), pp. 109–110 and 370–371; de Rop's ... *woordkunst* ..., p. 53; and his *Lianja: L'Épopée des Móngo* (1964), *passim*]. Nsongo, the child identified as an Nkundo, is as clever as her mother; in fact, the wit in much of this tale seems to lie with the women, suggesting that the position of women in Nkundo culture has not always been as subservient as outsiders might conclude.

The account was furnished in truncated form for a most ironic reason: the reel of tape on which the field recording was being made had relatively little room left on it, and the interpreter Bokunge Jacques kept urging the narrator to hurry in his telling so that the end of the tale could be reached before the tape had been exhausted. Any narrator, no matter how accomplished, would furnish a somewhat flawed performance under such discomfiting pressure.

The songs, an important factor in the tale—though by no means as plentiful as might be expected in an "epic"—proved difficult to record and to translate, for they were sung in Old Lonkundo. Since the tape of this tale was erased after its transcription, there is unfortunately no way of verifying the Lonkundo texts for the songs. Close study of the Nkundo *cante fables*, with emphasis on the fugitive "creation" tales, needs to be undertaken by collectors with full understanding both of Old Lonkundo and of ethnomusicology. It is likely that an unhurried version of the present tale would yield more songs than did this particular performance.

Lambrecht's tale type 3260 (based on a story published by Weeks in 1904 utilizing the name *Libanza* for the hero) bears some similarity to this narrative; both are clearly variants of what some scholars (Bascom, Boelaert, and de Rop, among others) have termed "the Mongo epic," the lengthy and vivid account of the culture hero Lianja. It is tantalizing to consider the many similarities which exist between the present tale and the "Lianja epic," a work that "in its most fully published form" totals 120 pages of print (Finnegan, *Oral Literature* . . . , p. 109; see also Biebuyck's "The Epic as a Genre in Congo Oral Literature," in *African Folklore*, ed. Dorson [1972]). The epic includes "the deeds of Lianja's parents, his mother's pregnancy, and the birth of the hero and his sister Nsongo, Lianja's battles with his father's murderer, his wanderings in search of a place for his people and his settlement of them there . . . and, finally, his ascent into the sky" (Finnegan, *op. cit.*, p. 371). Apart from the name of the protagonist—*Jibanza* as opposed to *Lianja*—the Ross-collected account in its major features is quite similar to the Lianja epic as described above. If Bascom's test of the setting appropriate for the telling of a myth, legend, or myth-legend is applied (Bascom, "The Forms of Folklore," chart p. 6 [1965]) to the present tale, this narrative could qualify, by virtue of being told in the daytime, as a tale expected to be believed by the listeners—as, indeed, it *is* believed by the Nkundo to account for the distribution of the tribes. The present telling appears also to meet the minimum of three key episodes necessary for a complete version of the Lianja epic as stipulated by Boelaert (in his *Lianja, het Nationaal Epos der Móngo*, p. 18): the fight for the forbidden fruit, the birth of the hero Lianja [here, Lianja has already been born and is sufficiently well grown to be present at the birth of his sister and brother] and Nsongo his sister and the ensuing avenging of their father's murder, and the trip to the promised land [here not defined as a promised land, but as the whole world, populated by the tribes developed from Mbombe's various children]. A detailed comparison of the Ross-collected fragments of the Lianja epic with the various versions published in French, Flemish, and English is presently under study by Ross and Walker.

Motifs:

T	C220.	Tabu: eating certain things.
C	T251.+.**.	Pregnant wife demands special food involving great risk to husband.
T	H936.	Tasks assigned because of longings of pregnant woman.
T	E761.7.**.	Life token: miscellaneous—rain and disordered soldier ants as signs of speaker's death.
T	A524.2.**.	Extraordinary weapons and hat of culture hero miraculously appear.
T	D631.1.	Person changes size at will.
T	D55.	Magic change of person's size.
T	A526.7.	Culture hero performs remarkable feats of strength and skill.
T	F62.0.1.**.	Bird flies to upper world to get "sun" (clock) for culture hero.
T	A220.	Sun-god.
T	F17.**.	Visit to land of the sun: emissary sent to acquire "sun" (clock).
T	H1149.	Miscellaneous superhuman tasks.
T	H1264.**.	Quest to upper world for "sun" (clock).
T	R260.	Pursuits.
T	A1620.	Distribution of tribes.
T	A530.	Culture hero establishes law and order.

1. Ilele, or Ilelăngonda (literally, "branch of the forest" [see de Rop's *Lianja* . . . , p. 54]), according to various published versions of the Lianja epic, had initially been named Itonde. The unborn child's practice of leaving his mother Ilankaka's womb during the night to eat the rats she had smoked for her own consumption had roused in the parents of the child such fear that after he had been born, he was abandoned in the forest. There he made his way quite comfortably, aided by a "chenille" bird and various magic articles; eventually he went back to find his parents and was renamed Ilele because of the circumstances of his birth and early youth.

A current oral version of Ilankaka's pregnancy, her insatiable appetite for rats during that period, and the birth and early youth of Itonde has been recorded on tape for Mrs. Ross by Ikolo, of Lotumbe, and is presently under study by us. Mamet's Bolia and French translations of the Nkundo account of Itonde's birth and early years (in *La Langage des Bolia*, pp. 124–129) provide another lively variant of this portion of the Lianja epic [Lambrecht's tale type 3221].

2. *Mbombe* is the name used for Ilele's wife in the versions of the Lianja epic published by E. Boelaert, as well as in the Ross-collected tale. One version (Boelaert's "Nsong'à Lianja," *Congo*, pp. 52–55) identifies Mbombe as the first female created by Mbombianda; other versions place her somewhat later in human history, commonly in the third or fourth generation. The Ross-collected variant makes no attempt to place either Ilele or Mbombe in time.

3. "Owner of the forest" evidences the continuing animistic belief among the Nkundo. The exchange involving the sharing of the meat appears in none of the other versions examined.

4. Ilele, though in most respects both strong and fearless, had a wholesome regard both for the dangers present for one alone in the forest and for his wife's prowess, factors apparently familiar enough to the narrator's audience so that they did not require elaboration here.

Considerable relish was exhibited both by the narrator and by his listeners for this entertaining portion of the tale.

5. Itòji's surprising appearance and the fluffing of his feathers at such an unusual hour seemed bad omens to Ilele, increasing his sense of guilt at having deprived his wife of a share of the meat.

6. The various exchanges between the sentry and Ilele were keenly enjoyed both by the storyteller and by his hearers. Further details of these confrontations are furnished in the French translations (see de Rop's *Lianja* . . . , pp. 74–75).

7. *Nsabu*, like various other Lonkundo words, can be lengthened by doubling the last two syllables of the word; this device is used in constructing the name *Nsabu-sabu*, the identification of the tribe that owned the fruit tree and that must be conquered by the culture hero Jibanza in avenging his father's death.

De Rop's *Lianja* . . . cites *losáú*, permitted to birds but not to men, as the fruits for which Mbombe longed, and the Sausáú as the tribe owning the tree bearing these fruits (p. 74). In Boelaert's "Nsong'â Lianja: L'Épopée nationale des Nkundó," *Aequatoria* (1949), the identity of the fruit was unknown to Mbombe; she had by chance picked up, cooked, and eaten one of the fruits dropped from the beak of a bird who later showed Ilele the way to the forbidden tree.

8. Since the tape recording of this tale was erased to make room for other narratives, there is no way to determine whether the repetition was thus truncated by the narrator or whether one or another of the multilingual translators shortened the account; whatever the cause, there has clearly been a reduction of the repetition savored by listeners and valued by a competent narrator as a means of increasing suspense as well as of emphasizing the prowess of the character in question.

9. The tortoise, sharing with Mboloko, the dwarf antelope, among the Nkundo the palm as trickster-clever one, here proves successful in capturing Ilele, a feature held in common with accounts published in French translation (see de Rop, *Lianja* . . . , p. 27).

10. These symbols of the "external soul" or the "life force" of Ilele—unseasonal rain and a disordered column of soldier ants—are particular to the area of the Nkundo as signs of distress or disaster. *Bafumba*, stinging ants often called "soldier ants," normally travel in a line with soldierlike ants on either side of the line keeping them in the right direction and getting them back into line if they are disturbed; their diet consists largely of meat and insects.

In other variants of the Lianja epic, certain other signs are included, among them the unnatural boiling of the water in Ilele's magic horn, the filling of the horn with blood, the weeping of monkeys before his house, and the trampling of the ground by elephants.

11. Mbombe—as is true with Nkundo women today—did not want the rest of the village to know that she was in labor; thus she sang a song about having a toothache. In this version, contrary to custom, she was not assisted by the old women of the family in the birth.

In the published versions of the Lianja epic, women do assist at the births of Lianja and of his sister; furthermore, Nsongo is born before Lianja, often bringing with her her own stool, or chair. In these versions, Nsongo is fully adult when born, and "belle comme le soleil" (de Rop, *Lianja* . . . , p. 80). In none of the published versions cited by de Rop is the birth of Boilenge recorded, although a male sibling named Entonto, termed *"frère aîné de Lianja"* but at whose birth Lianja is present, appears and serves—as does Boilenge—with Lianja in the combat against the tribe of Ilele's murderer.

12. This appears to be an instance of truncation (perhaps an abbreviation of a long passage recounting the individual births, since each of the children born was of a different tribe); motivation for the truncation may have been the shortage of recording tape, or, on the other hand, purely personal choice on the part of the narrator in terms of the interests of his audience. It would have been useful to have the narrator include at least the circumstances of the birth of Jibanza, since in the published variants that birth is preceded by the child's speaking from the womb, occurs through the mother's tibia, and is accompanied by the warrior-hero's famous spear and knife, his father's stick and bell, a gong and his hunting horn, his necklace, and his arrows.

13. As soon as this child was born, she announced her own name, *Nsongo*, "moon" or "month." (The naming practices of the Nkundo are deserving of a separate study.) Appropriately, Nsongo, an influential character in this heroic tale, is identified as an Nkundo.

Among the Nkundo, one who sits on a chair holds a prestigious position. According to Nkundo tradition, the item most strongly desired from Europeans by the Bantu-speaking peoples was the chair, with the table the second most-wanted item; the bed was a much later entry.

14. *Jibanza* is the name of a national hero of all the tribes of the Nkundo, the Mongo, Ngombe, and Baloki. The weapons and the pointed hat which miraculously appear are believed to be the signs of a divinely appointed leader among these peoples. [Information furnished, on questioning, by Bokunge Jacques.]

15. This narrative suggests that Nsongo and Boilenge were born within a few minutes of one another, fraternal twins; according to de Rop's *Lianja* . . . (p. 79), Nsongo and Lianja were likewise twins. Like Nsongo, Boilenge was precocious; in other variants of the epic, the questions asked by Boilenge here were posed instead by Lianja himself. The narrator may have been confused at this point in the narrative: he has Jibanza, not Boilenge, seek the fallen father.

An additional instance of a newborn child's asking, "Where is my father?" may be found in Uche Okeke's *Tales of Land of Death: Igbo Folk Tales* (1971), pp. 46–48; the son subsequently slew the monster responsible for his father's death, and gave his father's body decent burial.

An indication of Old Testament influence upon the Nkundo became apparent during the telling of this tale: when Boilenge joined the battle, Bokunge Jacques intoned solemnly, "Saul hath slain his thousands, and David his ten thousands."

16. [Explanatory material inserted by the narrator at this point: "These sting and then return to the nest to get another sting. Then they could continue to torment the soldiers of Jibanza."]

In Lambrecht's tale type 3260, the culture hero's birth was preceded by a series of "birth products": three different kinds of flies, bees, mosquitoes, the night fly, an animal, a tortoise, and Nsongo; Libanza, called from the womb by his mother, first "threw out a chair, an iron shield, spears, and then came out." (See Lambrecht's "A Tale Type Index for Central Africa," pp. 224–225, for a summary of the version published by Weeks just after the beginning of the twentieth century.) Through the interesting mutation which occurs in the process of oral transmission, insects in the present version are used by the enemy against Jibanza, their "brother."

17. [Explanatory material inserted by the narrator at this point: "When a new leader comes, the soldiers take new heart. Each time a soldier wounded one on the other side, they all sang a song of praise to him."]

Truncation may have been at work here in the tale, also: under traditional Nkundo storytelling circumstances, songs are sung whenever the dramatic situation calls for them; a full version of the Jibanza story would seem to require inclusion of each of the praise songs, since praise songs are a significant part of Zaïrian oral literature. In the present version, only one praise song is sung, and that one seems far too brief and understated for the circumstance under which it is being sung: Jibanza's beheading of the enemy leader.

De Rop notes in his *Lianja . . .* (p. 20) that the published forms of the Lianja epic have consisted largely of prose, occasionally interrupted by short rhymed verses introduced by the narrator and continued by his collaborators; the songs, he contends, are used largely to ornament the prose text, and use words in archaic form. The present version suggests that songs constitute a larger portion of the contemporary tellings than earlier variants have indicated; further field work may yet yield a form of the Lianja epic in which the poetic passages function as they have in epics recorded in other cultures, as integral to the forward movement of the plot, rather than as embellishments.

18. Nsongo, with Jibanza throughout the combat, has the cunning to claim the king of the enemy as her husband; intermarriage in this instance would presumably effect peace between Jibanza's tribe and the Nsabusabu. The Ross-collected tale is the only known narrative of the Lianja cycle in which this particular marriage is cited.

During intertribal warfare, Nkundo women often went along to cook for the soldiers; usually, abstinence from sexual intercourse was required of the soldiers. Intermarriage between these women and members of conquered tribes vied with enslavement as means of subjugating the conquered tribes and ensuring their support.

19. A guitarlike instrument. The *longombi* (spelled alternatively *longombe*), described in G. Hulstaert's "Note sur les instruments de Musique à l'Équateur," *Congo* (1935), is included in a version of the epic published by Boelaert; according to de Rop, it is one of the stringed instruments most frequently used among the Mongo (see his *Lianja . . .* , p. 59).

20. In the published versions of the Lianja epic, Lianja's transformation to child from adult occurs instead during his struggle to destroy the ogres; having eliminated by fire all but the ogres' witch doctor and his wife, Lianja on the itóji's advice becomes an infant in order to destroy these two remaining ogres. (See notes for Tales 67–69, bearing evidence of other fragments of the Lianja epic collected by Mrs. Ross apart from the present tale.)

21. Tobacco was not introduced into Central African culture until the coming of the Portuguese; inclusion of tobacco in this tale is perhaps a consequence of acculturation. Why the tobacco agitated, the narrator did not explain; animism may account for this response of the tobacco to verbal command.

22. The portion of this narrative involving a second Jibanza with a sister Nsongo seems to have been unrecorded in any published version of the Lianja epic. The supernatural powers exercised here are not, however, foreign to the cycle as published; there are undoubtedly other variants of this set of episodes alive in Nkundo oral tradition and awaiting recording.

23. The requesting of the sun (*jefa*) as a gift was a device both of conferring power and of recognizing time. Until the coming of the Europeans, the Nkundo told time by the sun; most Nkundo can still tell time accurately by this means, though clocks and watches are readily available now. The word "*jefa*" is used both for "sun" and for "clock." In the Ross-collected account, Jibanza considers his kingship confirmed by the gift, a condition necessary before his work of distributing the tribes can be undertaken.

The presence of both Mbombianda ("god himself") and Elima ("the god of heaven"), the former aiding Jibanza in securing the sun (a mark of divine approval) from the latter, is puzzling, and the narrator himself seems confused as to the hierarchy and how it can be handled; in the heretofore-published versions of the Lianja epic, only one god—Mbombianda—is named (de Rop, *Lianja* . . . , p. 60).

De Rop, in his . . . *woordkunst* . . . (p. 95), presents in Flemish [the Lonkundo original appears on p. 94] an account of Lianja's sending the hawk and the fly to "go and get the sun from God." The mission was accomplished, but it was undertaken "in the beginning," when "the world was full of darkness," and *jefa* in this account was actually the sun. De Rop's *Lianja* . . . (pp. 36–37) mentions a variant of the epic in which Lianja himself touches the sun with his hands and seems utterly consumed, but recovers because he manages to retain his magic hand-bell.

24. The origin of white men is accounted for in several variants of the Lianja epic, as well as in de Rop's . . . *woordkunst* . . . (p. 53, with the footnote citing Boelaert's publication of the text in 1954 in a Catholic Mission journal titled *Pax*), all drawn from Nkundo oral tradition, crediting the twin daughter of Lianja, Yendembe, with producing by means of a virgin birth white twins who mated and became the progenitors of the white race. De Rop's *Lianja* . . . (p. 16) declares that this episode is invariably included by a narrator of the epic if there are any whites in the audience.

25. The present narrative omits the details attending the death of Jibanza. In several of the published versions of the Lianja epic, the hero, having completed his double task of avenging his father's death and of establishing civilization, ascends to the sky via a towering palm tree, bearing with him his beloved sister Nsongo, his mother Mbombe, and Entonto. Before he leaves, he commissions the various tribes to continue the work he has begun for them. Since this portion of the epic has wide distribution (see de Rop's *Lianja* . . . , *passim*), the narrator may have omitted the details of the hero's spectacular departure because of the pressures of tape-recording time rather than because of unfamiliarity with this crowning touch of the Nkundo epic.

26. Among the Nkundo oral-history materials confided to Mrs. Ross was Bokunge Jacques' "Tribal Origins," included as Tale 2A.

Narrator: Bokunge Jacques
Location: Bólèngè
Date: March 1973

2A.   *Tribal Origins*

A very long time ago, people thought that we Nkundo wished for the place of Ba-Tetela, which is also called Yankata (that the people come).

We Nkundo are the people of Mbondze, who are our fathers. Mbondze gave birth to Simba, and elder Simba was the father of the people of Bofidzi; Bolemelongi was the father of the people of Ntomba; Eale was the father of the people of Lifumba, which is the territory of Bokatola. Their sister is Mputela, and she gave birth to the people of Ekonda. To this day the people of Ekonda are looked down upon as though they were women.

Our forefathers were on the river at Lofole and some of these stayed there even until today. These are the fisher people called by the foreigners "riverine people."

Narrator: Bokunge Jacques
Location: Bólèngè
Date: March 1973

3.   *The Coming of Fire*

Long ago the Nkundo did not have fire, but ate their meat raw, as animals eat theirs. They got fire from a semipygmy tribe that lived in the forest. These semipygmies are called *Batswa* [literally, "slaves"].

The Batswa knew all the things of the forest, and they discovered fire by rubbing pieces of dry wood together. They found one certain tree, *bokumo*, that would produce fire more quickly than any other when two pieces were rubbed together. At that time, the Nkundo would plant gardens and trade their garden produce for meat from the Batswa. To this day, the Batswa do not like to plant gardens, but are still people of the forest. This is in spite of the fact that they live in villages, often send their children to school, and share in many of the things that come with modern living.

The Batswa became slaves of the Nkundo. This was because they were not as strong as the Nkundo and therefore the Nkundo could govern them. Even now, many Nkundo families still consider certain Batswa as their own slaves. Many Nkundo think of Batswa as animals, rather than people, and do not want them to have the advantages of being people. This means that segregation is a very real problem.

The Nkundo found the Batswa in the forest in hovels and have never been able to admit that people would live that way. Today many Batswa do very well in school, and no doubt in time to come they will be accepted on a level with anyone else. Through the centuries there has been very little intermarriage between the Batswa and other tribes because there have been very strong tabus[1] concerning the eating of food cooked by a Batswa. This has kept men of other tribes entirely away from Batswa women.

It is generally very difficult to break down barriers until there is intermarriage, or at least children from a union of the tribes.

It is singular for an Nkundo to admit Nkundo indebtedness to a Batswa even to one of his own family; in this "tale," he confesses it to a white foreigner. The collector, Mrs. Ross, had by this time established a close relationship with Bokunge (he had just discovered that they were *baninga* ["friends"], ones born on the same day). Before telling this and other "histories," Bokunge admitted that information such as that found in these "histories" was seldom given outside the culture. "I wouldn't tell this to everyone," he would say, "but I thought you ought to know more of how it really was."

A. de Rop's ... *woordkunst* ... includes on page 88 an explanation of the origin of the differences between the Baoto [Nkundo] and the Batswa. The translation from the Flemish is as follows:

Also the origin of man belongs here, especially the origin of Batswa and Baoto. In the beginning of the world the Batswa were blacksmiths and invented fire. But every time a monkey passed by in a tree, they left fire and forge to go after the monkey, so they lost all their knowledge and skill in their desire to hunt for meat. They have like new Esau's forfeited their birth-right for food . . .

The Nkundo followed the Batswa at the smithy.

De Rop furnishes also (pp. 100–103) in . . . *woordkunst* . . . an account titled "Verdeling van Nkundó en Batswá" ("Partitioning Between the Nkundo and the Batswa"), collected from Mbele (Bombwanja), Ntomb'e (Wangata), and Itsifo (Lifumba), explaining the Nkundo's obtaining dominance over the Batswa at the Batswa's express request: the Batswa, preferring hunting in the jungle [sic] to "the jabbering at the meetings on the village square" (p. 101), relinquished to the Nkundo the responsibility for administration of "the inheritance" and preservation of their common traditions. The Nkundo were made responsible for maintaining gardens, and the Batswa for providing meat, with goods to be exchanged for mutual suste-nance. [All translations from de Rop are by van Hylckama.]

A narrative, "Het Vuur" ("The Fire"), furnished in the same volume by de Rop (p. 103) but not credited to local informants, attributes the bringing of fire to the tortoise, who—unlike the animals sent earlier by "the forefather of mankind" to secure from God "the names of things"—succeeded in learning from God the technique of preparing fire from wood of the *bofumbo* tree through the use of a "fire plane" and a "striker," and carried back both the word "fire" and the technique of preparing "the thing with which one prepares food and on which you warm yourself when it is cold."

Interestingly, the animals sent earlier had forgotten the message in climbing over a huge tree trunk which blocked the road between them and God; the tortoise "walked around" the tree trunk, retained the message, and "since that time . . . refuses to climb over fallen tree trunks lest he lose this wit." This practice of the tortoise has been retained in various Nkundo folktales, including a dilemma tale found in the school text *Bekolo Bémó* . . . (translated as Tale 95 in the present volume).

Another tale summarized by de Rop in Chapter V of . . . *woordkunst* . . . , titled "De Mythen" ("Myths"), on page 88, credits the discovery of fire to a fisherman's dog who warmed himself at a bofumbo tree while his master was fishing. The third day, the fisherman followed his dog to the source of warmth, cooked his food on it, found the cooked food good, and named the means "fire."

Lambrecht's tale type 3 tells of the Spirit who created man (*Ngòi*) and then gave him fire and the bow. Again, Lambrecht's tale type 35 refers to the Spirit as giving fire to man. There appears to be no definite tale type for this history of the relationship between Nkundo and Batswa and the gift of fire. We have placed it, therefore, with the Creation, origin, and *pourquoi* tales, though it might be as com-fortable under the heading "memorat" (or "memorate") if such a heading could be created to accommodate the many examples of this form of oral narrative in the African treasury.

Motifs:

T   A1414.7.1.**.   Tree as repository of fire: discovered in *bokumo* tree by
                         despised group.

1. Nkundo boys are taught that certain death will be the result of eating food cooked by a Batswa woman. Tabus of this nature build barriers between peoples that are almost impossible to break down.

Narrator:	Bokunge Jacques
Location:	Bòlèngè
Date:	March 1973

4.   *How the Worship of Many Gods Began*

Long, long ago the grandfathers of our grandfather believed that God was there. They were aware that God had made the world and all that is in it including man. However, they felt that God was far away and did not understand the way in which God wanted man to go. As a result, each person took his own private god, each one choosing a god who would help him in what he did and wanted to do. Some of them took a special bird to be god; others took a certain animal; some even took a ghost or a spirit to be god to them; others took a special kind of medicine as god, until there were almost as many gods as there were men in the world—perhaps more.

Sometimes the gods were good and sometimes they were bad. For instance, two men would go on a path through the forest, the younger brother following the older brother. The older brother went along the path and saw no meat, but the second brother following along behind saw meat.[1] Then the older brother would say, "I went first and saw no meat, but you followed and saw much meat. Therefore your god is good and mine is bad."

In spite of this feeling that one's own god is bad and the other god is good, everyone would cling to his own god. Changing one's god just wasn't done.[2]

In the time of our forefathers, a man and a leopard could be friends and talk together. The man could choose this leopard to be his god. No one else would be aware of this relationship. If a war came along, that man could have the wisdom of the leopard in the fight.

When the man has a son, he will teach him about the leopard and when the man dies, the leopard will be the god of the eldest son. Each of the other sons will need to seek a god for himself.[3] If the man dies with no sons, the god will go to his younger brother.

This family will never kill a leopard, nor will they eat the meat of a leopard.

This tale was told toward noon, with only Mrs. Ross and Bokunge Jacques present. The entire morning had been spent in taping and transcribing, and the last tale transcribed raised the question of the old gods of the Nkundo. Bokunge's response to the question furnishes the text of the "tale."

This fragment, told as a "history" by the narrator, belongs with the "origins" group of tales more nearly than with any other of the four subdivisions according to Aarne-Thompson's *Index*. It is interesting to note the strong parallel here between the Nkundo personal gods and the totems found among various groups of American Indians.

We have not been able to find an adequate type number for this item in any of the indexes used, perhaps because this information is normally not furnished to collectors of verbal art. These beliefs are very much a part of the Bantu-speaking peoples' animistic daily life, and accounts of their origin may well increase as interest in preservation of "endangered" folk history develops among the Nkundo themselves.

Motifs:

T   A113.   Totemistic gods.
T   A490.   Miscellaneous gods of the earth.

1. For "meat" the narrator used the Lonkundo term *nyama*, which may refer either to an animal usable for meat or to meat already prepared or in any stage of preparation. The term *nyama* occurs for "meat" or "animal" in a number of Bantu dialects.

2. The phrase "just wasn't done" appears initially to be an expression drawn from outside the Nkundo culture. However, in the sense in which it was used by the narrator, it indicated the serious, irrevocable allegiance between an Nkundo and his personal god: whether his choice be right or wrong, he was bound to honor it.

3. The circumstances under which one would choose a god for himself would of course vary widely; the choice would in many instances be determined by some sort of "sign" or miraculous happening, a happening not excluded from life in twentieth-century Zaïre.

A hospital nurse at Lotumbe, where Mrs. Ross and her husband spent many years, had at some time had an encounter with a certain small forest animal bearing a light-colored stripe around its middle similar to a belt. This encounter so impressed him that he used the name of that animal for his *losako*, or proverb, when his proverb was solicited. If questioned, he would launch into a lengthy account of that animal. Had this encounter happened to one strongly committed to animism, that animal could well have become his god.

Animism as still a strong force in Zaïrian thinking operates in an interesting fashion in instances where an Nkundo patient dies while under a white doctor's care: fortunately for the doctor, the medical personnel are not held responsible for the death; the patient's family attributes the death to the working of a malevolent god or spirit. Even among families long affiliated with a Christian denomination, such "spirits" continue to be real indeed.

Narrator:	Tata Manga
Location:	Boende
Date:	November 1973

5. *Goodness and Badness*

A man lived with his wife for a long while with no children. They finally had one child and gave him the name of Goodness. The name of that child was Goodness. Then Goodness grew and began to get very much wealth which came to him—wives given to him,[1] much money, and the boy had much success where he lived.

He asked his father, he said, "I am Goodness. Everything I see is good. This is good. This is good. I have wives and they have many children. My wives have children. When I have many children, I have goodness. Everything I have is goodness itself.[2] Where is the badness? There are two people on the earth, Goodness and Badness. Where is Badness?"

Then his father answered, "There is no reason for you to hunt Badness. Goodness is with you and you live well. You do not have a reason for seeking Badness."

He said, "*Nyè*, I need to hunt Badness and find out where he is. This is because people are the two, Goodness and Badness. Here we have Goodness, but where is Badness?"

His parents were quite disturbed with the way he was talking.
He said, "I am going to hunt Badness. I'll take my wives with
me."

He left with two wives, going to hunt Badness.

They went and went and went. His father had prohibited his
going, but he couldn't hear these words. His mother had prohibited
him, but he could not hear her. He said, "I am Goodness, and I
am hunting my friend, Badness."

They went, *tee-tee-tee*, until they reached the bank of a river.
His wives and children sat down to rest. He said, "You sit there;
let me hunt; let me call Badness."

He called, "Badness, Badness, Badness!" There was no answer.
"Where can he be? I'll call again. Badness, Badness, Badness!"

Badness answered, "Yes."[3]

He said, "Come here. Come here and greet me. I am Goodness.
I am waiting for you and am hunting where you live."

"Wait for me." Then Badness came with a canoe.[4] He crossed
the river, *te-te-te*, and brought the canoe to shore near Goodness
and his wives.

He was greeted by Goodness and his wives. "You have come!"

He said, "Yes! I have come. You are Goodness?"

He said, "Yes. And you are Badness?"

"Yes."

He said, "*Bonne!*[5] Let us go to your home."

He said, Badness said, "*Bonne!* My canoe is small, and is not
sufficient for your wives and all of you. I will go, I and your wives;[6]
then I'll return for you."

Then Badness went with his wives and children. They went.

Goodness waited and waited on the bank of the river a little, a
little. All that day passed. Then he began to call, "Badness, Badness,
Badness." But he had no answer.

Again in the morning he called and called. Finally Badness
came. Badness asked, "Are you hunting me?"

He said, "Yes. I am hunting you."

As soon as Badness had greeted him, he hit Goodness on a leg.
Then he hit him in the side. Then he hit him on the other leg. After
that, Badness left and said, "Wait a bit and I will come for you."

"Where are my wives?"

He said, "Just wait a bit. I will come and get you. Wait. I will
come for you."

When he had left him and his friend had gone, Goodness his
leg began to swell until it was very large. His side began to swell
until it was huge.

After that, the other leg swelled until it was also very large. He wanted to go home, but the opportunity was not there to go.

He said, "How is this?" Then he began to go on his way, very slowly, slowly. His home from the river bank was about five kilometers. He went from the river to his home, going, going, going[7] from morning until night because he could not go at all well. He arrived at the home of his father and mother at night. He knocked at the door.[8]

"Open the door! Open the door!"

His father called, "Who is there?"

"I am Goodness. But I am very sick. Ever since I found Badness I have had sickness."

Then the mother opened the door. "Our child has gotten enormous. He has become very bad,[9] not at all like himself. His body is huge and his legs are also. He can't get well at all, *nyé.*"

The father said, "*Nyé.* I don't want him in our home at all. This is because you wouldn't listen when I tried to tell you. I didn't want you to hunt Badness, but you did. Now you have badness yourself."

His mother said, "Take him from me. He is very bad; he can't live here again because he has already hunted badness. Now he is like badness[10] and now he has arrived in a palaver. He is badness itself."[11]

He lived for a little while after that. After three days the boy died. This is the result of seeking after badness.[12]

The story is finished.

It seems unlikely that this story originated with the narrator; it is too closely linked with the Nkundo value system to have been told merely to impress a missionary listener. The narrator's experience in teaching at the elementary level may have caused him to re-evaluate this particular tale and to see the importance of its being included in a collection representative of his culture's values and teachings, among them the need to "hear" (heed) good counsel, a principle reiterated in a number of narratives in this volume.

Although both Arewa and Lambrecht initiate their lists of types with tales about the beginnings of things, neither index offers a classification helpful in the present instance, nor does Klipple's study provide assistance here. Aarne-Thompson's tale type 326 appears to furnish the closest indexed parallel to this tale. "Seeking Poverty," in Herskovitses' *Dahomean Narrative* . . . (pp. 209–211), not yet indexed, provides the best African companion piece to Tale 5 and suggests that this may indeed be a staple in African storytelling. Among Turkish variants of the type,

"The Trouble Bird," Story 220 in the Archive of Turkish Oral Narrative at Texas Tech University, offers a horrendous series of "troubles" to the princess who sought to know what "trouble" was. In none of these samples cited, however—the Aarne-Thompson tale type, the Dahomean "divination" tale, or any of the Turkish variants—does the inquirer pay with his life for his inquiry. The Nkundo oral tradition assigns to this particular tale a "playing for keeps" role that may well cause it to outlive more entertaining narratives.

Motifs:

C	Z139.+.**.	Goodness and badness personified.
C	W167.+.	Willful boy goes out against mother's orders to seek trouble.
T	J450.	Association of the good and the evil.
T	J460.	Unnecessary choices.
T	J652.	Inattention to warnings.
T	J230.	Choice: real and apparent values.
C	C941.+.	Elephantiasis for breaking tabu.

1. Multiple wives have traditionally been considered an economic asset in the Nkundo family, a tradition gradually yielding under the impact of the introduction of a cash economy and the movement of rural populations to the large cities. (See "Africa's Food Producers: The Impact of Change on Rural Women," *Focus* [January-February 1975], pp. 1–7.)

2. There is no better way in Lonkundo of expressing "goodness" in the superlative than by using the reflexive form after it, a characteristic locution among the Nkundo; the same device is used later in the tale to intensify "evil."

3. *O*, the response to any greeting, means "Yes." If the non-Nkundo neglects or forgets to make this response, he will usually hear, "He isn't very polite." If he makes the response, he will excite the comment "He knows Lonkundo."

4. The canoes of the Nkundo are dugouts. The tree for the canoe is carefully selected by the one who is to hew it; the tree is felled; the stages in the preparation of the canoe are carefully planned; then the hewer shapes it and hollows it out of the log. (Since the kind of tree used for canoe-making is always waterlogged, hollowing the log by the use of fire is not feasible.) In most cases, the hewer can live at home and return to the work site each day until the canoe is finished. If it is hewn in a swamp, the canoe can be floated out to the river when the water is at high level; if it is hewn on dry land, the men of the entire village will come to the aid of the hewer. A canoe small enough to be carried will be lifted to their shoulders and thus moved to the river. If the canoe is too large and too heavy to be carried, they will arrange good-sized saplings crosswise of the path as rollers and move the canoe thus. Either of these procedures will be accompanied by the singing of work songs to lighten the labor involved. Often these songs will include comments either on the hewer of the canoe or on its owner. De Rop, in a section of his ... *woordkunst* ... titled "Verantwoording van de Benamingen 'Zang en Lied'"—pp. 16–20—furnishes a detailed discussion of both the melody and the content of Nkundo songs, which had previously not been sufficiently appreciated. Classifying the songs as

genuine oral art, with the text in the Nkundo songs "rhythmic by itself," de Rop comments, "Whether the Bakongo are musical or not, we don't know. But we do know that the Nkundo are" [p. 18].)

5. Use of a dialectal form of the French term *bon* here marks one of the rare instances of intrusion of the language of formal instruction into the narration of tales in the Ross collection.

6. In Lonkundo locution, the speaker invariably names himself first and then the other or others concerned: "I and your wives" and "I and you," for example.

7. This is one of countless occurrences of the Nkundo use of word repetition to emphasize the idea expressed.

8. The Nkundo have a proverb *"Bonto owa mpifo, afōkōsule"* [A man of importance doesn't cough]. A person of ordinary status will cough at a door when he seeks the householder. If the door had been closed for the night, the son would probably call for admittance. Knocking is definite evidence of acculturation.

The fact that they had a door indicates that they were a family of considerable wealth and social station. Wood for a door is an expensive item; the ordinary person would have a door of palm fronds.

9. The Lonkundo narrator used the word *"aofitana,"* meaning "spoiled." This word often refers to a cadaver after the person is dead; however, it may also be used to describe food that is spoiled.

10. Bad associations are to be avoided. The English proverb "Birds of a feather flock together" has an Nkundo corollary: *"Wengi'onto eleng'ekae"* [Every person to his own way].

11. In this tale, the narrator personifies "evil" and appears to indicate that it cannot be a part of "good," whereas the narrator of Tale 1 allows the two to be mingled, as with the clay used in the building of the house for One-Who-Causes-to-Grow.

12. The pointing of a moral at the conclusion of a tale—whether in the form of a bald statement, as occurs here, or in terms of a proverb—illustrates the primary function of storytelling among the Nkundo as a means of teaching and of perpetuating traditional values.

Narrator: Lontomba Samuel
Location: Tondo
Date: July 1973

6. *Why the Bat Comes Out Only at Night* [1]

A long time ago, the bat and the sun were good friends. One day
the son of the sun became very sick; he was very ill. So the sun came
to see the bat because he was his good friend. He asked him if he
could help him to find some good medicine so that he could heal his
child.

Bat agreed. He went into his back yard. He looked for a certain
kind of leaves. He handed them to the sun, who was his friend. The
sun took this medicine and went back to his place away in the sky.
He put this medicine around his son's body, and his son recovered.

The following day, he met the bat. The bat saw him coming from
the horizon blazing with happiness. Bat asked the sun how his son
was. The sun replied that his son had recovered from his illness. So
both of them were happy because the boy had recovered.

Two weeks later, the son of the bat in his turn became very
sick, seriously sick. As he was sick, Bat met the sun, his friend, in
the evening. He asked him if he had a good medicine to advise. The
bat had tried the medicine that he had given to the sun to heal his
son, but the bat's son didn't get well. So the sun replied to him,
"Look! I came back all the way from the horizon. It is evening now,
and I am going down to the west. I can't go back to my place in the
horizon to get the medicine for you. You should wait until tomorrow,
when I can rise back from my house. Then I can bring you the medicine."

Bat said, "Oh, my friend. My son is dying. My son is very sick.
My boy is going to die. Please go back to the east, get the medicine,
and bring it to my child."

But the sun didn't like to listen to his friend, the bat. He carried
on his way down west.

Bat was very sad. He went to his house, and his son was ill and
died. He lost his child. This was a very sad story. Bat started to cry.
He cried all night. Early in the morning he saw the sun rising from
the horizon blazing. He cried and shouted, "You are a bad friend, a
very bad friend. I helped you to heal your child. Now when my child

was ill, I asked you to go back to your house to get medicine to help to heal my son. You didn't like to listen to me. I will never be your friend again. My child is dead, and from now on I will never look at you. We will never be friends again. If you are coming on this road, I will never work in the daylight where you are blazing in the sky. I will be looking for my food and eating only during the night."

The bat turned his head upside down so that he would never see the sun. That is why we see today that the bats always hang upside down with their heads down looking toward the earth because they don't like to look at the sun. They will never look for their food during the daylight because the sun is there. That's why they travel and pick up their food during the night.

The tales collected from Lontomba Samuel have special interest for those studying the Nkundo oral tradition because Tondo, the narrator's home as well as the site for collection of the tales, lies adjacent to the Nkundo area. Presentation of a sampling of tales from Tondo affords the student of folktale diffusion a fine opportunity to examine the process of diffusion in action. (See comments on Tondo on pp. 67–70.) It would be interesting to go back ten or more years from now, both to Tondo and to the Nkundo area, to see whether one or more of the tales told for Mrs. Ross had been absorbed into the oral repertories of the neighboring peoples. Since this tale, as well as several of the others told in Tondo, could be replayed from the tapes (either reel-to-reel or cassette), changes—if any—in the texts could be noted and examined for evidences of accommodations made to one or the other of the two cultures.

The hesitations natural to one telling in a second language (English) a tale long familiar in his native tongue are apparent on the tape of this narrative; such hesitations suggest the likelihood that many, if not most, of the tales dear to listeners in their own language will be lost if and when that language falls out of currency, since the tales are in truth oral literature linked to the language of origin.

The bat assumes various roles in tales told among the Nkundo and their neighbors; in some of these roles, he appears clever—either a trickster or the trickster's aide—whereas in others he seems blind to the dangers that surround him (see, for example, Tale 25 in the present volume). His ambiguity of appearance—part animal, part bird—has prompted numerous tales turning on this point: in a war between the quadrupeds and the birds, on which side does he belong? In many of the latter tales, the bat's nocturnal habits are traced from some ancient dispute concerning his identity. The present tale and one other, found in Badibanga's *L'Éléphant* ... (p. 28), plus one cited in Lambrecht (p. 37) as appearing in volume 104 (p. 818) of *La Voix du Congolais*, are apparently the only tales thus far identified which attribute the bat's antipathy to sunlight to a broken friendship between the bat and the sun.

Interestingly, all three tales were drawn from the area now known as Zaïre, and all three concern either death or burial. Of the three, the present tale is the only one which provides evidence that the bat had fulfilled his obligations with regard to the friendship; it is the only one of the three which also requests something of equal value with the favor previously done for the sun by the bat. The other two tales involve the bat's plea that the sun stay his journey across the sky so that Bat can give his mother proper (daylight) burial; the sun refuses to honor the bat's request, necessitating the bat's interring his mother's body at an hour considered improper for burial. Since great emphasis is placed in this culture upon proper burial, the bat is justly indignant, and has since then refused to have any dealings with the sun.

A fourth tale, cited by Klipple as an example of Motif A2491.1. and found also in Area IV (Congo), omits the initial-friendship theme and turns on the sun's refusal to delay its setting until Bat has finished burying his father; Bat's resentment at this refusal prompts his declaration "'I shall never see you again.'" [See Frobenius, *Atlantis*, XII, 374, "Mudima."]

Although all four tales could certainly be termed *pourquoi* narratives, as well as "animal" tales, they unquestionably mirror the social values to be found today among the Zaïrians. Surely there must be many variants of this tale still awaiting collecting and classification.

The only tale-type entry that we have been able to locate for this particular tale in any of the indexes consulted is listed in Lambrecht: her type 80 (1) details the bat's request to his friend the sun that he "stop for a while" to permit the proper burial of the bat's mother; the sun's refusal led to a moonlight burial, sacrifices to appease the offended ancestors, and continued avoidance of the sun by the bat; her type 80 (2), based on Badibanga's Lulua tale, accurately conveys both the brevity and the poignancy of the French presentation by Badibanga, who had heard the tale in his Lulua tongue and felt no need to embellish it.

Motifs:

T	E100.	Resuscitation by medicines.
T	H1558.	Tests of friendship.
T	A2494.12.**.	Miscellaneous enmities of mammals: enmity between bat and sun.
T	A2491.1.	Why bat flies by night.
T	A2491.1.1.	Why bat sleeps by day.
C	A2491.1.1.+.	Why bat hangs with feet up and head down.

1. [Narrator's explanatory comment: "This story is about a natural phenomenon that we observe here. The story tries to explain this phenomenon. You probably know that the bird (*sic*) that we call in English 'bat' in daylight hangs upside down; that is, it turns its head down. It never looks at the sun during the daylight. At night it goes out picking up its food and eating. It tries to eat fruit in the night. But in daylight it doesn't eat; all bats hang on the trees with their heads upside down. This story is to explain why this happens."]

Narrator: Bokunge Jacques
Location: Bólèngè
Date: March 1973

7. *Why the Snake Is Scorned by Other Animals*

All the animals gathered together to have a meeting of their own. They wanted to have a big feast, and this meeting was to plan it. Everyone was there except the fish, and they couldn't come because they were in the water.

When they met, they organized.[1] They agreed on Elephant as president and Hippopotamus as vice president. With the birds, Eagle as their president and Hawk vice president. They rejoiced. In the place of the snakes, Python as their president and Cobra as their vice president. As each one would divide it, they set up the plan for their feast.[2]

Elephant spoke. He said, "I and my animals eat food, but we don't eat all that is there. We always leave some so that people who come may have some part of the food from me the elephant."

Then Hippopotamus spoke in the same manner.

Eagle spoke. He said, "I eat food and leave some for people. Because my wife when she is sitting on the nest caring for our eggs, I kill meat, and bits of that meat will fall to the ground, and people come in the enclosure perhaps to look at the traps, and they like this."[3]

Then Hawk spoke just as Eagle had spoken. When he ate, bits fell, and the forest rats and squirrels could eat it. A little bit is left people or insects down below to pick up.

Then it arrived at the opportunity of the snakes.[4] When they came to Python and his family, they were dissatisfied. Python didn't have a word to say because Python will make a huge round trap of his body. He will trap a deer, perhaps a wild pig, there. He will swallow it, *a-o-o-o*. He does not give any to people at all, *nyè*. Then their vice president, Cobra, is the same. He can catch a squirrel, perhaps a bird; he will swallow all of it, *a-o-o-o*. He won't leave even a little, *nyè*. And people do not have an opportunity for any of it, *nyè*. No one else has any help from either of them at all, *nyè*.

There is another snake who is small, and his name is Ilekele.

Ilekele is another snake who lives in the nest where a hen lays eggs.
Then he bores a small hole and sucks all of the egg, *nyè.* He will leave
the shell only.[5]

The snakes felt very irked and very angry. Then they called the
king of them all, who is like a person itself, Chimpanzee. Chimpanzee
came to cut that palaver.[6]

He said, "You, Elephant, you win, because when you go into
a person's garden, you eat the corn, but you leave corn. You eat the
plantains; you leave plantain. You eat squash; you leave squash. In
that way you leave the owner of the garden some food. You do not
finish it, *nyè.* You do goodness itself.

"And you, Hippopotamus, you do the same. You eat the rushes;
you leave some. What you leave is for certain fish who eat the food
that is left by you. You do goodness itself.

"And you, Eagle, you do very good things. Because when your
wife is on the nest caring for the eggs, you kill a monkey and take it
to your wife. Your wife eats it, but many pieces of meat are let fall
down. You do not pick it up to take it; you leave it, and people who
come and look will pick it up. Everyone rejoices very much. Often
when someone sees your nest way up, they will not bother you
because of the profit you have for animals every day by day who
pick up meat that makes them live which you have thrown away.

"And you, Hawk, you are like that. Even though you catch the
children of a chicken, you do not finish all of it. You will eat some,
but you will leave for the owner of the chickens some chicken. What
you do is goodness itself.

"But with you, Python, and your younger brother, you lose the
palaver. Because you, Python, kill a wild pig, which is a very large
animal. You squeeze it until it is dead. You put your spit on it until
it is slick and slimy. Then you swallow it whole and you don't leave
even a little, *nyè.* Also people do not rejoice in the way you eat your
food. Again, Python, you will set your trap and kill an antelope, which
is very large—larger than a wild pig—even one with two horns. Then
you spread your spit on it and swallow every bit of it in one swallow,
nyè.

"And you, Cobra, are the same way. You catch an animal.
Then you lick it until it is slick and swallow it. You catch a squirrel;
you lick it and swallow it. You do not leave for people or insects.
They do not have a scrap of the food which is there. Only he has
finished swallowing it.

"Your younger brother, Ilekele, is a tormentor of people in the
same way. He will crawl into a hen's nest belonging to a person.

There may be ten eggs or perhaps eight, or perhaps seven;[7] he will make a hole in each egg and suck and suck and suck out all the goodness from inside the shell, *nyė*. He will leave the shells only. The owner of the chicken will expect the hen to hatch chicks, but your younger brother has already finished the eggs, *nyė*. You lose the palaver."

Also all the snakes felt anger itself, especially toward Chimpanzee and his family. They called all of the snakes together and Python said, "All of you who are my younger brothers, whenever you are near to an animal, strike him. Whenever you see a person near you, strike him. They are all bad because Chimpanzee is like a person and he has given us a real palaver." And snakes have anger for animals, people, and for chimpanzees, also.

And like that a snake will strike a dog when he follows an animal and comes near to him and the dog will be dead. In the same way, if a snake passes an animal, he will strike him and very soon that animal will be dead. Soon if a man himself is on the path and the snake sees him, he will hide and then strike him,[8] and the man will be dead.

"Like that, you snakes, you excel in badness. You snakes, they follow you who excel in behalf of the badness which is yours and which you did from long ago. All snakes have anger for people, for animals, and for birds also.

"All of you snakes, you are very bad. You will never have arms and legs because of the evil you have done in ages past. Another snake, Jibate, has a gun in his teeth and when he sees a bird up in a tree, he will throw his slime;[9] it will hit that bird. Soon the bird will fall. You will lick it and then eat it today."

So to this day snakes are the enemies of animals, birds, chimpanzees, and people.

Do not do evil as the snake; in his evil he is enveloped in slime.

This somewhat rambling and disjointed tale presents through animals' voices certain basic observations about animals' habits doubtless made among the Nkundo themselves. Though the tale seems to apply only to the animal characters involved, listeners and readers alike find in it a basic human lesson on the willingness to share, a trait stressed in Nkundo culture. Since the narrator normally uses this tale as a means of teaching his urban grandchildren something of forest lore as well as of their tribal values, he pursues the details of animal habits somewhat beyond a point that would be of interest to an evening storytelling audience.

Truck noises are especially intrusive on this portion of the tape, in curious contrast to the setting and content of the tale; the noises in no way reduce the narrator's concern with his subject.

Lambrecht's tale type 65 offers evidence of the Creator's initial criticism and condemnation of the snake because of his eating practices. We have been unable to isolate a type that precisely accommodates this tale, perhaps because the tale itself resists classification in its shifting focus.

Motifs:

T	B236.0.1.**.	Animal official chosen as result of an election.
T	B240.**.	Elected officer of animals.
T	B236.1.**.	Election of president and vice president of birds.
T	J400.	Choice of associates.
T	B263.4.	War between birds and reptiles.
T	B274.	Animal as judge.
C	A2433.3.+.**.	Why pythons and other snakes hide themselves and attack other creatures.

1. The need to "organize" suggests acculturation, especially in the titles given to the leaders. Leadership among the Nkundo existed, however, well before the coming of the white man to Central Africa.

2. In this instance, the storyteller uses a narrative hook, "They set up the plan for their feast," purely as a device for introducing his main argument. The feast-planning itself is abandoned in the tale, yielding to a diatribe against snakes and even to a hint of a *pourquoi*.

3. The term "people" is used by Nkundo narrators to identify all animals, not just humans; the reference to looking at the traps reflects the narrators' tendency to attach human practices to life among the animals in the bush.

4. [Narrator's explanatory comment: "They had set the snakes apart because a snake is truly an animal, but the snake has no legs. The snake has no arms. All animals have two legs and two arms. Birds have two legs, and their wings are similar to arms."]

5. There is also a snake that swallows an egg whole rather than sucking it from the shell. This particular snake lifts an egg up and out of a nest without breaking it; then he licks the egg to make it slimy and swallows it, shell and all.

6. At this point, whatever intention the narrator had had of telling a tale has given way to his determination to weigh the snakes' selfishness in the scales of a palaver. The choice of Chimpanzee as judge—seen also in Tales 88–90—invites this emphasis on manlike reasoning and argumentation.

7. Despite his European acculturation, the narrator cannot escape the grip of his tradition: when he tells of the stealing of the eggs, his counting assumes the customary Nkundo pattern, moving from the higher number to the smaller ones, as in this case—"ten eggs or perhaps eight or perhaps seven." (See *Dahomean Narrative* ..., p. 53, for a similar convention among the Dahomeans.)

8. It is doubtful that a snake would hide and wait for a man; generally, a snake

fears man and will not strike unless cornered. This supposedly vengeful behavior attributed to the snake is, rather, a reflection of the Nkundo's fear of such creatures; even harmless snakes are termed poisonous, vipers.

9. The *jibate*, or *libate*, a variegated snake, can throw his slime many feet from the ground well into the branches of a tree.

Narrator:	Lontomba Samuel
Location:	Tondo
Date:	July 1973

8. *Why the Hawk Flies into the Smoke*[1]

Bokulu (Eagle) who lives near water and Nkoiambe (Hawk) who lives on land were good friends. One day Hawk's wife became pregnant, as many ladies do. His wife was fond of eating electric fish. She told her husband, Hawk, "When I am pregnant now I don't want to eat anything but electric fish."

So Hawk went to see Eagle, who lives near water, to help him to kill an electric fish.

Eagle said, "I will try, but it is very hard. Electric fish are very dangerous."

Anyway, two days later Eagle managed to catch an electric fish. It was swimming near the bank of the lake. There was a big fight between Eagle and the electric fish. But Eagle killed the fish and took it to his friend Hawk so that Hawk could take it to his wife.

Not long after that, Hawk received word from Eagle's wife, who in turn had become pregnant. This wife said that while she was pregnant she wanted only one thing. That thing was smoke—smoke from the fire or from anything that is being burnt.[2] So Eagle said, "That's O.K. I'll go to see my friend Hawk, who lives in a land where there is much fire burning and much smoke. I'll ask him to catch some smoke for you."

He told Hawk what he wanted. "That's O.K. I will try. You know it is very difficult to catch smoke."

He went one day to try to get smoke where they were burning some grassland. He tried to get the smoke, but he couldn't catch any. It kept getting in his nose, but still he couldn't catch it. He came back very tired.

He told his friend Eagle that he couldn't catch any quantity of smoke to bring to his wife.

Eagle said, "No. You have to. Go back and try again."

So Hawk went again into an area that was being burnt. He tried and tried and couldn't make it. He came back very discouraged. He reported to his friend.

Eagle said, "If you do like that and you can't get smoke for my wife, you and I will never be friends again."

So Hawk went back and tried again to get smoke but he couldn't. So that is why today whenever we burn an area, we see Hawk in the air trying to get some smoke. He is trying to fulfill his duty to his friend.

That's the end.

Told in an area including grassland, this tale is a likely candidate for diffusion from Tondo into adjoining regions because the practice of slash-and-burn agriculture found among the Nkundo and neighboring tribes could well provide the smoke needed to satisfy Eagle's pregnant wife. The theme of an extra-familial relationship's being broken is entirely compatible with Nkundo oral tradition and culture, as can be seen in many of the samples in the present volume. A similar tale may well have been circulating among the riverine peoples shortly after the beginning of the twentieth century, for Weeks in his *Congo Life and Folklore* (1911) says, "While the fire was burning hawks and fish-eagles circled above the burning bush, not 'to drink in the smoke,' as the natives [*sic*] say, but in search of any hapless rats and snakes cut off from escape by the raging fire" (p. 201). In the *pourquoi* entitled "Why the Dog and the Palm-Rat Hate Each Other" (Weeks, *op. cit.*, pp. 382–383), Dog, Palm-Rat, and Eagle wait while Hawk eats locusts and until he has "drunk in the smoke from the fire" of the burning brush (p. 382); here, the factor of the hawk's flying into the smoke is present, but the entire thrust of the narrative is different from that found in the present tale.

No satisfactory type number for this tale has been identified in any of the available type indexes.

Motifs:

T	H1110.	Tedious tasks.
T	H1558.	Tests of friendship.

T	W27.	Gratitude.
T	H936.	Tasks assigned because of longings of pregnant woman.
C	T251.+.**.	Pregnant wife demands special food involving great risk to husband (husband's friend).
C	A2433.4.+.	Why hawks are so frequently seen flying in smoke of fires.

1. [Narrator's explanatory comment: "This is about one kind of eagle and another kind of hawk. This is not the big eagle, but is one that lives near water all the time. *Bokulu* is the kind of eagle that lives near the water. *Nkoiambe* is the hawk. He doesn't live in the water but is the hawk that catches small chicks and usually lives on land. The story is about the friendship between Bokulu and Nkoiambe."]

2. [Narrator's explanatory comment: "She wanted to swallow smoke."]

Narrator: Bokunge Jacques
Location: Bólèngè
Date: March 1973

9. Why the Eagle's Fear of the Owl Is Finished [1]

On another day, Mpongo (Eagle) and Esukulu (Owl) went together as friends.[2] Eagle was attached to Owl, but he felt much awesome fear for him because of his huge round eyes.

One day they went hunting together.[3] They found a band of monkeys playing together in the trees. Eagle said, "You who are my best friend, go and hide. I'll shake the leaves and frighten the monkeys that they run your way."

Owl agreed to this and hid. Eagle shook his feathers among the leaves, *pao-pao*.[4] The monkeys ran right to where Owl was hiding. As they passed him, he was not able to kill a single one of them, *nyè*.

After the monkeys had passed, some small bush babies[5] went by, and Owl caught and killed one of them. Then he called out, "Eagle, come quickly. I am struggling with their leader."

When Eagle came, he found only a little bush baby. He asked

Owl, "There were a great many monkeys, and you catch only a little bush baby?"

Owl answered, "Who came this way except some small bush babies?"

Eagle said, "All right. I have no palaver. Let's try again. This time, you shake the tree and drive them my way."

So once more they flew along together until they found some more monkeys. Owl flapped his wings in the leaves while Eagle hid. Owl followed the monkeys and they went right to Eagle's hiding place. Eagle killed five of them.

Then came the time of dividing the catch. Eagle said, "Here. You take the bush baby and I'll take the monkeys."

But Owl cried out, "I want some monkey meat."

Eagle asked, "Just how ferocious are you?" He had been friends with Owl all this time because of his fear of his big round eyes.

Owl answered, "My fierceness is for bush babies and birds only."

When Eagle heard this, he no longer feared him. He said, "I'm going to kill you yourself."[6]

When Owl heard this, he departed and always made sure that there was a path between them.[7]

The lesson for all of us is that if a friend appears to be very large, let us not say that we are strong lest we become as the eagle and the owl.

A young antelope does not go about in a herd of wild pigs.[8]

[Notes to Tale 9 follow Tale 10.]

	Source:	Bekolo Bèmò ...
		Zaïrian school reader
		(in Lonkundo)
	Translator:	Mabel Ross
	Date of Translation:	January 1976

10. Why the Eagle's Fear of the Owl Is Finished (Variant)

The eagle and the owl went as friends. The eagle feared the owl and felt awe itself because of the staring of his eyes. They went hunting and found a group of monkeys playing.

The eagle said, "You, friend, go and hide and I will blow the leaves."

The owl agreed. The eagle shook his feathers, and the monkeys ran to the place where the owl was. When they passed the owl, he was not able to kill a single monkey, *nyè*.

After the monkeys had passed, some bush babies came, and the owl captured one of them. Then he called out, he said, "Eagle, come; I have battled and killed."

When the eagle came, he found only a bush baby. He asked the owl, he said, "Very many monkeys, and you capture only a bush baby."

The owl said, "What came here was a bush baby only."

The eagle said, "Never mind; we'll go again. You blow them to me."

They went again and found some monkeys. The owl blew as raindrops falling, and the eagle hid. The owl followed the monkeys, and the eagle caught five.

When they were in the act of dividing, the eagle said, "You take the bush baby and I will take the monkeys."

But the owl said, "I want monkey."

The eagle asked him, he said, "Do you have fierceness?" For he feared the owl because of his eyes.

The owl answered, "My fierceness is for bush babies and birds only."

When he heard him talking like that, the eagle finished fearing him and he told him, he said, "I will kill you yourself."

When the owl heard this, he divided their paths.

The teaching for us is that when a friend clothes himself as a good friend, let us not say that we are strong lest we become as the eagle and the owl.[9]

Tales 9 and 10 are a pair of *pourquoi* tales and depict creatures' fear of some misunderstood physical feature and the subsequent revealing of that feature's harmlessness. The strong similarity between the field-collected tale and the textbook version suggests either that the compilers of the reader captured accurately the content and the flavor of the version then current (early in the 1950's) in the Cuvette or that Bokunge Jacques had encountered the tale in the textbook, had vividly recalled it, and had had his recollection reinforced by either telling the tale himself or hearing it told over a twenty-year period. The instances of Lonkundo locution both strengthen and supplement each other, as do the evidences of the mirroring of Nkundo culture in oral narrative.

Arewa's tale types 1571 (1) and 1571 (2) and Lambrecht's tale type 1571 (3) tell of the animals' fearing the cock because of his red crest; a Yoruba variant of the cock's fatal self-revelation appears in Walker and Walker's *Nigerian Folk Tales* (1961), page 29. In all these instances, the others find that the crest is not dangerous, and thereafter the cock becomes vulnerable to attack. Arewa's tale type 1075, another variant, tells of the porcupine who thought the hare's ears were horns; again, the hare's revelation opens him to attack by stronger animals. Only in the last-named type is any claim made by the feared creature that prompts the fear; on the other hand, in none of the tale types cited does the feared creature himself speak his own death sentence in revealing his vulnerability: in each instance, some other creature discovers or discloses the fact that the dreaded physical feature is indeed not harmful at all. Aside from that point, all four tale types mentioned are useful in classifying the present pair of Ross-provided tales.

Motifs:

T	K1710.	Ogre (large animal) overawed.
T	J1900.	Absurd disregard or ignorance of animal's nature or habits.
T	J613.	Wise fear of the weak for the strong.
T	J811.	Wisdom of concessions to power.

1. "Is finished" is a standard Lonkundo expression for "no longer exists" (the term in Lonkundo is *"aosila,"* also used as a formulaic ending or as a chorus for many Nkundo folktales).

[Narrator's introductory comment: "The eagle, Mpongo, is the big brother of all birds. He has claws like a leopard and can kill a monkey and other small animals. The owl, Esukulu, has huge round eyes and has claws very like the claws of an eagle. He talks at night and very often frightens people, '*Oh-ku-lu-lu-lu.*' His neck is limber, and he can turn his head all the way around to his back."]

Bokunge Jacques during his narrating and translation sessions with Mrs. Ross frequently expressed his gratification that these tales were to be carried abroad. Realizing that listeners and readers in other countries might not be familiar with objects and animals in the Nkundo setting, he furnished ample explanatory material, as did Lontomba Samuel for the same purpose.

2. This sentence employs a common Nkundo narrative opening, "On another day, *A* and *B* went together as friends." The Lonkundo for "on another day" (*"Bòkòl'òmò"*) sounds much more melodious and inviting than does its English transliteration.

3. In this tale, as in a number of others, two or more animals go hunting or fishing together, reflecting the occupational patterns found among the Nkundo themselves. In the present instances, the eagle does not use a dog; he does, however, employ the Nkundo hunting strategy of one hunter's driving the game toward another or others equipped to catch them.

4. *Pao-pao* (the sound of thunder) seems somewhat exaggerated as an ideophone representing the shaking of an eagle's feathers among leaves, but arresting sounds and dramatic action are attendant on any Nkundo storytelling.

5. The bush baby, or tarsier, is of the tree-dwelling lemur family, similar in some respects to the monkey but belonging to a distinct superfamily rather than to the monkey family. Bush babies tend to be smaller than monkeys, and rarely appear in the daytime. They have foxlike muzzles and large eyes, and are well covered—prehensile tail and all—with soft, woolly fur. Their nocturnal habits and their size make them appropriate prey for the owl.

6. A common Lonkundo locution, the reflexive form "yourself" after "you" intensifies the *you* and the threat the statement poses for the owl.

7. That the eagle and the owl would be separated from one another by a "path" furnishes another reflection of Nkundo cultural patterns. "Along the path" provides the scene for everyday encounters and greetings, as well as the means of approach both for enemies and for friends. The eagle and the owl, both air-borne, would be unlikely to need a "path" as a protective boundary, but it would be an entirely acceptable and graphic demarcation for Nkundo listeners to the tale.

8. This proverb is the Nkundo equivalent of "Birds of a feather flock together."

9. The Lonkundo version, titled "Mpongo l'esukulu," is Tale 33 in *Bekolo Bèmò* . . . and is found on pages 48–49.

Narrator: Mbilo Esio, retired
               teacher and preacher
Location: Ilongo-Kindo
Date: November 1973

11.   *Why the Leopard No Longer Fears the Antelope*

The antelope had children. One day the antelope was taking a walk with his children. The children were wandering from side to side. The antelope had very tall antlers and the leopard was awed by them. One day one child of the antelope crossed the path where the leopard lived.[1]

"Big Brother Antelope, why does your child follow me and disturb me? I go to this side and he follows me; I go to the other side and he follows me, *ngonza-ngonza.*"[2]

"You are afraid of me because I have these tall antlers. I am here as nothing."

The leopard wonders, "I thought they were deadly weapons, but instead they are not useful to him."

He grabbed the child and punished him.[3]

The leopard was sitting on a fallen tree and the baby antelope crawled over the tree.[4]

"Why did your child cross my fallen tree?"

"I told you before that my antlers were nothing. You have my permission."[5]

The next day he tried to accuse the antelope of crossing into his area. He jumped on him. "I thought he was strong, but he is nothing."

> The tale is ended,
> Ended!
> The tale is ended,
> Ended!

[Notes for Tale 11 follow Tale 12.]

Source: *Bekolo Bémó* ...
Zaïrian school reader
(in Lonkundo)
Translator: Mabel Ross
Date of Translation: November 1972

12. *Why the Leopard No Longer Fears the Antelope* (Variant)

The leopard and the antelope were friends.

The leopard had no children, *nyé*. The antelope had three children.

The antelope appeared with pride itself in his body because he had tall antlers on his head, and the leopard had fear, fearing itself of him because of these antlers.

One day they went on a journey, the two of them and the children of the antelope also. The antelope went first. Then his children followed near him, and the leopard came last.

The leopard asked the antelope that, "Your antlers have much fierceness.[6] Will they kill someone quickly?"

The antelope answered; he said, "My antlers do not have fierceness, *nyé*. They have grown very tall, but they would not kill anyone."

The leopard was finished with his fear of the antelope, and he began to torment the children of the antelope. He told lies and said to the antelope that, "Your children torment me." The antelope said, "No quarrel."[7] Then the leopard killed one baby and ate it.

They continued going and the leopard said to the antelope again that, "Your children torment me again." The antelope said, "No quarrel." Then the leopard ate another baby again.

They continued going and the leopard to the antelope that, "Your children still torment me." The antelope said, "No quarrel." Then the leopard killed another and ate it.

The children were finished, and the antelope did not know because the antelope was in front. Then the leopard said to the antelope himself that, "Why do you torment me?" And he killed the antelope himself.

If someone fears you, you yourself do not say, "I do not have fierceness," because he will come to kill you.[8]

The narrator and the school-text compilers both illustrate in Tales 11 and 12 the fact that unequals can be friends as long as the stronger is in awe of the weaker. In the present tale and its variant, the leopard stood in awe of the antelope's antlers; as soon as he found that they were not dangerous, he killed the antelope and ate him. A relevant proverb, "Don't give away the secret of your power," is clearly evidenced in the Biblical account of Samson's downfall (Judges 16:17–19), as one of the audience was quick to point out.

Weeks' tale "The Leopard Pays Homage to the Goat" (*Congo Life and Folklore*, pp. 433–435), not included in any of the indexes consulted, provides an extra dimension to the pattern of the tales thus far described: Gazelle tells Leopard, who fears Goat's beard and horns, that Goat is not strong; the next day, Goat's teeth are tested by his being given a kola nut, upon which Gazelle "made a sign with his lips to Leopard" that the goat had no teeth. The leopard killed the goat and has never feared goats since that time.

The same classifications are applicable for this pair of tales as for Tales 9 and 10: Arewa's tale types 1571 (1), 1571 (2), and 1075 and Lambrecht's tale type 1571 (3); see discussion of these tale types in the notes for Tales 9 and 10.

Motifs:

T	K1710.	Ogre (large animal) overawed.
T	J1900.	Absurd disregard or ignorance of animal's nature or habits.
C	A2435.3.17.+.**.	Why leopards eat antelopes.
T	J613.	Wise fear of the weak for the strong.
T	J811.	Wisdom of concessions to power.
C	X1790.+.**.	Leopard fears sharp antlers of antelope.

1. In this version, an act of the antelope's child provokes the leopard's first complaint, whereas in the Variant the leopard initiates his complaints only after his discovery that the antelope's antlers are not to be feared.

2. Ideophone describing the child's way of walking from side to side.

3. [Narrator's explanatory comment: "This was by eating him."]

4. This kind of behavior violates Nkundo etiquette.

5. The father antelope's apparent encouragement of the leopard's eating of his children is not in keeping with Nkundo emphasis on the worth of children, a contradiction not explained by the narrator.

6. In the Variant, the leopard inquires quite early in the tale about the "fierceness" of the antlers, a logical and artistic location for a query essential to narrative development. It would be interesting to know whether this was an alteration of an oral account by the textbook compilers in an effort to "improve" the story for young readers.

7. Another meaning for the Lonkundo term used here by the narrator, "*wakunde*," is "bury it." The leopard chose this interpretation and ate the baby.

8. This "teaching" seems more relevant to the narrative than does the one held in common by Tales 9 and 10.

The Lonkundo version of this tale, titled "Nkòi la Mbuli" ("The Leopard and the Antelope"), appears on page 62 of *Bekolo Bèmö.* . . .

Narrator:	Lontomba Samuel, director of the British Baptist secondary school at Tondo
Location:	Tondo
Date:	July 1973

13. *Why the Bird Looks Up as He Drinks*

There is a tale that tells that one day there was a great drought[1] in the country and the birds couldn't find water anywhere. So everybody was crying, every bird was crying, and children were dying and the chicks were dying. And so one day the king of the birds—that's the eagle—called on all birds. One day he called all of them in a great gathering, and he told them that, "Now, listen. We have a great drought. There is no water anywhere. So what we will do is that all of us, we are going to fly all over the world[2] and try to find where we can find water. And if somebody finds this water, he can come back and he will tell all of us and we can go there and drink this water."

So he spread out all the birds and they went out, set out all over, and by the midnight some birds came back and there was a lot of noise at night, and the king came out and asked what it was. Two birds reported that they had found water somewhere very far, that it was left over in a tree stump. In this tree was a hole, and there was water in it. So the next morning all the birds flew to that area. They started drinking, and drinking, drinking.[3] There were a lot of people that were busy with the water.

Then suddenly a tree branch of rotten wood fell out of the tree and exactly knocked this eagle on his legs and each leg was broken. And all the birds were very sad because the king had broken his legs, so they carried the eagle back to his place and for two weeks nobody could go to drink water because the king was sick.

Then at the end of two weeks he got very well; he was very well healed, and they flew back to the area to carry on with drinking water. But now when they started drinking water the king stopped all of them and told them that, "Look! Last time when we drank water together, we had an accident. Now, we are going to make a rule that every bird who drinks water should drink, *zip-e-zip, zip,* for a while, then look up to the sky to see if there is another piece of wood coming, rotten wood coming. So if he sees it he can tell everybody, warn them that rotten wood is falling off of the tree, and they can get out of that place. So that's my decision."

They started drinking one by one. As he said, drank a little bit and looked up to the sky, drank a little bit and looked up to the sky, to see if there is another piece of wood coming, of rotten wood.

That's why—our forefathers explained—the reason why birds, when they drink water, why they drink a little bit and look toward the sky. This is one of the stories which explains a phenomenon, a natural phenomenon.

The narrator's unprompted use—even in English—of the artistic devices of internal rhyme and of repetition in the second sentence and of onomatopoeia in *zip-e-zip, zip,* as well as the inclusion of the traditional thinking of his own people, suggests that Lontomba Samuel envisioned a responsive audience as present, and gave as full a performance as might have been called forth by listeners actually there in the flesh. Tonal variations, changes in narrative pace, and other vocal indications of his total involvement in the storytelling have been preserved on tape.

The eagle is accepted in many tales as the king of the birds. For another tale in the present collection affording the eagle this position, see Tale 42. The drinking habits not only of wild birds but of domestic fowl kept by Bantu-speaking peoples might quite reasonably have prompted varying folk explanations for birds' habitual behavior. Among the Akan in Ghana a proverb states, "When a fowl drinks water it shows it to Nyame [supreme deity of the Ashanti and other Akan peoples]" (Courlander, *A Treasury of African Folklore* [1975], p. 101). Further field collecting of *pourquoi* tales will surely yield explanations as varied as the cultures out of which they have arisen.

In Aarne-Thompson's tale type 220 The Council of Birds the eagle is accepted as judge and assigns each of the other birds his place and work. We have been unable to isolate a tale type accounting for the eagle's function in determining the drinking habits of birds.

Motifs:

T   B242.1.1.   Eagle king of birds.
T   B238.1.**.   Eagle as king of birds assigns work to all.

1. Lontomba Samuel lives on a lake and in a rain forest, where drought would seem unlikely. Since a number of oral narratives derived from various parts of Africa —particularly West Africa—employ formulaic openings describing "a time of great drought," it is entirely possible that this *pourquoi* has entered the oral-narrative stream of Central Africa through the process of diffusion. On the other hand, the rainy-season—dry-season alternation present in much of Zaïre might be sufficient to account for terming an unusually prolonged dry season a "drought" in a normally well-watered area. In any event, the tale is current in Mbandaka, despite its apparent inappropriateness to its geographical setting.

2. The narrator is well aware of the size of the world. However, he was true to the traditional telling of the tale in his assumption that the search for water could be worldwide.

3. The repetition of a participle for emphasis is common in Lontumba as well as in Lonkundo. The narrator is aware that this is nonEnglish locution, but he feels compelled to use the narrative artistry appropriate to a tale told by his own people.

His use of "a lot of people" in describing the birds "busy with the water" is an instance of the narrow line between people and animals in Zaïrian folk narrative.

Narrator:	Lontomba Samuel, director of the British Baptist secondary school at Tondo
Location:	Tondo
Date:	July 1973

14. *Why the Dog Chases Others*

There were three animals: a bird called Embenga, a dog, and a wild animal which is usually known as Encibili. All three of them were going on a trip, the dog, Encibili, and the pigeon.

They came to a palm[1] tree; and there they found one who was full of palm nuts but they were not ripened yet; they were not ready to eat yet. So the bird, pigeon, he asked his friends to stay there with him, to live there, until this palm nut would be ready to eat, because this bird, pigeon, who looks like a parrot, usually likes to eat these palm nuts.

So his friends said, "That's all right. We'll stay with you until these palm trees, palm nuts, are ready to eat, ready to eat." So they stay on. It took them about two weeks. Then the palm nuts were ready, and the bird ate them. So they carried on on their trip. They were going for a long, long trip.

They ran into a bush area that had been burned out by fire.[2] So Encibili told the bird and he told also the dog that, "We should stay here until this grassland, burned out, starts again getting new grass, so I can eat this grass and till it is finished; we can carry on, continue our trip."

So they stayed there, his friends agreed, and they stayed there, for nearly a month. So new grass came out, and Encibili, this animal, ate grass and they were waiting for him. And he finished, and they carried on their trip.

Then the dog said after one day of walking, said that, "We have been walking for a long time now. I think it is time to rest. And I think that the best thing that you can do for me is that we've got the fire, we've got the wood,[3] and to make a big fire because my nose is always wet. Then I will be there near the fire. You will make a big fire, and I will turn up my nose toward the fire until my nose dries out completely, and so then we can carry on our trip."

So they said, "O.K. We agree." They started the first day. They made a very big fire. The dog kept his nose to the fire the whole day. The nose got a little dry, but it was wet again as soon as he took it out from the fire. So they carried on the second day, the third day, the fourth day, but the nose was still wet. So his friends said, "Oh, we are tired. We don't like to stay here for a long time."

He said, "No! Look! You are my good, my best, friends. I have been doing you favors that you have asked for. You should stay on and make a fire for me."

So the bird said, "No! We shouldn't. We don't like it." The bird flew and ran away.

And Encibili also flew, not flew, but went away in the forest, and ran away.

So from that day on, the dog was very angry at the bird and at this animal. That's why from this event he became very upset and he became the enemy of all the birds and all animals. That's why today, you see, when the dog sees any animal, he chases them, he chases them. If he sees any birds, he goes around them, only to try to catch them and try to hit them because they wouldn't like to come to help him dry his nose.[4]

This tale, told on tape with no live audience, provides a useful instance of the earnest concern of certain well-educated Zaïrians to preserve as much as possible of their oral tradition and to make this tradition available to readers and storytellers abroad. On the tape (available only in English), the narrator places the story in the order of its telling on the tape: "The third tale . . . ," a wording altered here because it does not fit the arrangement of the tales in this volume. In this and in others of Sam's accounts, we have preserved as closely as feasible the narrator's exact words, including his repetitions and rewordings manifesting his effort to arrive at the best possible phrasing. There is evidence present also of the narrator's five-year exposure to American English in such expressions as "going on a trip" and "O.K."

The most satisfactory classification we have found for this tale is Lambrecht's tale type 1038. Although in the tale on which Lambrecht has based this type (drawn from de Bouveignes' *Sur des Levres Congolaises* [n.d.]) the animals accompanying the dog (the buffalo, the parrot, and the cock, engaged in trade together) differ from those in the present tale, each wishes—as in the Ross-collected tale—to have the others wait while he refreshes himself in his own individual fashion. The de Bouveignes tale is not treated as a *pourquoi*, but culminates instead in a moral: the dog observes that "if everyone along the road wanted to satisfy his personal interests rather than the well-being of the group, they would never succeed" (Lambrecht, p. 84). In both tales, the dog's request comes last, and in each tale the inability of his friends to meet his need provides an admirable springboard for the particular kind of conclusion selected by the narrator, further evidence of the flexibility and viability of oral narration among the Zaïrians.

Motifs:

T	B211.1.7.	Speaking dog.
T	B211.3.**.	Speaking bird: pigeon (*Embenga*).
T	B211.2.**.	Speaking beast—wild: ungulate (*encibili*).
T	H1110.	Tedious tasks.
T	H1558.	Tests of friendship.
T	W26.**.	Patience: patient dog.
T	W26.**.	Patience: patient wild ungulate (*encibili*).
T	W26.**.	Patience: patient pigeon (*Embenga*).
T	Q321.	Laziness punished.
T	W196.	Lack of patience.
C	Q380.+.	Impatience punished.
C	A2427.2.+.**.	Why the dog chases birds and other animals.
T	A2452.1.	Why dogs hunt.

1. Of the many species of palm trees present in Zaïre, the oil palm is the one whose harvest is awaited in this tale.

2. In Zaïre, as in a number of other African countries, brush and grassland areas are deliberately burned over for two major purposes: to drive small animals out of hiding so that they can be captured for meat, and to control the amount of nonproductive vegetation. This burning-over normally occurs twice a year, just prior

to the two rainy seasons (the longer one during their spring season and the shorter one during their autumn season).

3. Wood, the most common fuel for cooking and heating, is readily obtainable both in the Nkundo area of Zaïre and in Lontomba Samuel's sector, adjoining the Nkundo area. The wood, left to dry after the men have cleared space for the gardens, is free for anyone who wishes to gather it.

4. A parallel even closer to the present tale than is Lambrecht's tale type 1038 appears in Weeks' *Congo Life and Folklore* (pp. 382–383); unfortunately, this one has not yet been indexed. In Weeks' tale, "Why the Dog and the Palm-Rat Hate Each Other"—recorded early in the twentieth century in what is now Zaïre—Dog, Palm-Rat, Hawk, and Eagle go on a journey together, first having agreed not to "thwart each other in any matter." All wait while Eagle watches for palm-nuts to ripen so he can eat them. All wait while Hawk eats locusts and has "drunk in the smoke from the fire" of the burning brush. All wait some months until the new growth of grass and canes has come on the burned-over area, a feast for Palm-Rat. When Dog wants to dry his nose, they build a fire, but as soon as Dog's nose dries, he wets it again. Hawk and Eagle fly away, vexed; Palm-Rat runs, but is chased, caught, and killed because he would not wait until Dog's nose was dry.

The *pourquoi* element forms the major thrust, as it does in the Ross-collected tale; the dog, still the central character, here prompts his own disappointment, adding an extra dimension to what is clearly a staple in Zaïrian oral narration.

Narrator:	Ngoi Ekoletonga, a village elder
Location:	Longa
Date:	December 7, 1972

15. *Why the Dog Hunts the Porcupine*

Mbwa (Dog) was going away to seek a wife.[1] He had chosen a very lovely creature who lived in another village, and her family had agreed to the marriage.[2] She was a beautiful striped cat from the civet family.[3] Dog was delighted to take her for his wife.

As he went, he happened upon a porcupine. Porcupine saw him and asked where he was going.[4]

"I am going to Boende[5] to get my bride. She is a very beautiful young lady, and I am anxious to see her again."

Porcupine was most interested and wanted to go along. They had always been good friends, and Dog was pleased to have him come with him.[6] So the two of them went along the path, *cwa-cwa-cwa*, going, going,[7] to the village where the family of the prospective bride lived.

When they finally arrived at her home, her family was delighted to see them and gave them a welcome. As is the custom, they prepared a big dinner for them: fish, chicken, goat,[8] manioc, bananas, and many other tasty things.[9] While they were waiting for the food to be prepared and brought to them, Dog explained to his friend Porcupine, "My friend, we will eat a great deal of food here since this is a special time for me and for my bride's family. Let me caution you about one peculiarity of mine. When you finish eating meat of any kind, you must not throw the bones away. To me they are very good food. I can never throw away any part of the meat, *nyé*, and I have a definite tabu[10] about throwing bones away. Please leave them on the table[11] and I will eat them."

The food was brought to the table and it was truly a feast. They began to eat and were enjoying it very much. Very soon, Porcupine forgot all about Dog's tabu and began throwing bones out the door and into the street. Dog couldn't leave them there, but quickly ran out and retrieved them.[12] "You have forgotten all about my request and are throwing good bones away. Please don't do this again, but leave them here on the table as I told you," said Dog.

After not a long time, when Porcupine was busily eating, he began to throw his bones out the door once more. Dog was truly disturbed. He said, "My friend, you have forgotten again. Do not throw the bones away. Can't you understand?" Quickly he rushed out the door, picked up the bones, and returned them to the table.

After another while, Porcupine absentmindedly began throwing bones into the street.[13] Dog was quite angry with him this time and began to pick the bones up. He chided his friend, "Can't you remember a simple thing when I ask you?"

All this time, the bride's family was trying to figure out why Dog kept picking up the discarded bones when there was certainly plenty of food left to be eaten. They didn't understand the problem and began to be quite disturbed by his actions. They began to wonder if they wanted anyone like that in their family. Finally they were sure that he was either strange or very greedy. Then they told Dog that he could go on home. They had decided that he couldn't marry their daughter.[14]

Dog was sick at heart and more than disappointed. He and Porcupine started reluctantly down the path for home. The more he thought about it, the more angry Dog became. Porcupine had certainly ruined his chances to have a lovely wife. He kept complaining about it and brooding on the matter. The outcome was that he killed Porcupine and ate him right there.

From that day to this, the dog and the porcupine have not been friends. Whenever and wherever they meet, the dog will kill and eat the porcupine. Also, from that time on, the dog has refused a wife from another group of animals, but will marry only another dog.

The teaching: If you are going with a friend on a journey, find one who thinks and does as you do.

[Notes to Tale 15 follow Tale 17.]

Narrator:	Tata Manga
Location:	Boende
Date:	November 1973

16. *Why the Dog Hunts the Porcupine* (Variant I)

A dog and a porcupine went to the home of the in-laws of the dog. He had his wife and he and the porcupine went to her home. As soon as they were on the path, the dog said to the porcupine, he said, "When we arrive, my wife will give us food. Don't throw any bones on the floor or outside in the open. Don't throw bones; don't throw bones. I eat them."

The porcupine said, "Oh! Like that!" The porcupine said, "I know what you are saying. There is a certain leaf. When I have that leaf, I do not like to have it thrown into the open because I like that certain leaf frequently."[15]

They arrived at the home of the dog's in-laws. The family prepared food that was excellent. They greeted the dog and his friend.

They brought the food and put it on the table. In his own way the dog sat up to the table and the porcupine sat at the table that they eat food. The in-laws said, "Eat the food. The food is ready."

The porcupine had a bad streak. He ate and threw the bones out the door. The dog saw him and felt some anger. The porcupine tested him.[16] Then they kept on eating, eating, eating, and the porcupine threw his bones out the door. The dog finally went out and got the bones and ate them.

His in-laws were surprised. "Our in-law, we give him good food, so why does he go out and eat the bones that are in the dirt?" They felt sorrow itself. "Our child should not be married to that kind of a man. We'll try again another day."

The dog and the porcupine stayed another day. The in-laws cooked a lot of food once more that they eat.

The dog said to the porcupine, "Why did you throw the bones away? Why did you do it? I told you not to throw them away. Today when we eat, do not throw the bones away."

The porcupine answered, "I won't throw them this time."

Then when they were called to eat, they ate food, and ate food, and ate food. The porcupine ate and threw the bones out the door. The dog saw him, left the food that was on the table, and went out to get the bones.

The in-laws, "Ah! Look at him. He's a very bad person. He just keeps eating the bones that are in the dirt."

The dog said to himself, "What am I going to do? I and the porcupine, we will have a palaver[17] because I am a person who likes bones. Bones are my very food." Again the porcupine threw the bones, and the in-laws didn't understand. "They will not let me take their daughter. What will I do?"

When the time came for them to return home, the dog said, "Give me my wife. We must go."

The in-laws said, "You. We will send her afterwards. You go on home and we will send your wife afterwards."

The dog was angry. "This is because I ate the bones and you didn't like it. I now have a palaver with the porcupine."

The dog and the porcupine returned home, but there was real war between them. They fought, and the dog killed the porcupine.

"You ruined my marriage. I asked you not to throw your bones away, but you insisted on doing it. Then I had to get the bones, since they are my food. Now because of you I do not have a wife—because of you.[18] Now we have a palaver and I kill the porcupine."

Even today if a dog sees a porcupine, he will always kill it. If he sees it, he will follow it, *te-te-te*, until he can kill it. Afterwards he won't leave it at all, *nyè*. This is because the porcupine ruined his chances.

[Notes to Tale 16 follow Tale 17.]

Source:	*Bekolo Bèmò . . .*
	Zaïrian school reader
	(in Lonkundo)
Translator:	Mabel Ross
Date of Translation:	November 1972

17. *Why the Dog Hunts the Porcupine* (Variant II)

The dog saw in a certain village a wife which he wanted.

The family of the woman said to him, "Return with the bridewealth, and you may take the wife."

The dog went home to get the bridewealth. His family supplemented his bridewealth, and the dog went to claim his wife.

As he went, a porcupine saw him. He said, "Elder Brother,[19] why do you yourself carry the bridewealth?"

The dog answered, "I don't have a younger brother to carry it for me."

The porcupine said, "Let me carry it for you." Then the porcupine carried the basket.[20]

As they went like that, the dog said to the porcupine, "Look! I have a medicine[21] that you must not throw away the bone of an animal."

The porcupine agreed, and they arrived at the in-laws'. The in-laws killed two chickens. They cooked them and brought them.

As they ate, the porcupine threw a bone into the street. And the dog went out and picked up the bone. He said, "What about you? Didn't you hear?"

The porcupine said, "I forgot."

When the wife's family saw that the dog picked up the bone like that, they said, "Perhaps our in-law wasn't filled with the food which was first. It is fitting that we kill two goats."[22]

Afterwards they brought goats which were two, and again the porcupine threw a bone away.

The dog said, "How come? Why don't you hear my words?" And he went to pick up the bone.

When the family of the wife saw, they said, "We will not give him our daughter, *nyé*. He smears us with shame.[23] He is a very greedy person for food."

The dog didn't feel at all well when he was lacking a wife, and he and the porcupine went home. When they were on the path, the dog said that, "I do not have a wife because of you." And he killed the porcupine dead.[24]

Forgetters do not heal people.[25]

In one form or another, this tale, collected by Mrs. Ross both at Longa and at Boende, has been in the Nkundo oral tradition for at least a quarter of a century, as evidenced by the version published in *Bekolo Bêmô* . . . ; all three forms are included here as Tales 15, 16, and 17 for purposes of comparison. Whether or not the current narrators first encountered the tale in the schoolbook version was not determined; successive retellings have introduced a significant number of departures from the text form to evidence both the viability of the basic tale and the liberty of the narrators to reshape the features of the narrative to suit both themselves and their audiences.

Only one of the three versions identifies the bride (or wife): Tale 15 presents her as a civet, an identification needed artistically to prepare the audience for the narrator's pointed observation that the dog no longer marries outside his own kind; this is the only version of the three to offer two *pourquoi* elements. The *pourquoi* in Tale 17 is nowhere directly stated; lack of another kind of focus suggests that the tale functioned as a *pourquoi*, though the text compilers elected not to include that touch.

The Longa text offers the fullest description of the meal provided; furnishing of this detailed information was prompted by the narrator's having a substantial audience with a relish for the listing of delicious foods. The Boende narrator, lacking an Nkundo audience, gave scant notice to what was served, stressing instead the serving of *two* meals, with the porcupine's malicious behavior apparent at each meal and the dog's consequent distress occupying center stage in the drama.

The attaching of a "teaching" to Tales 15 and 17 is not uncommon in *pourquoi* tale-telling among the Nkundo; it offers further proof that the primary objective of oral narrative there continues to be instructional, largely either moral or social in emphasis, though the narrative situation may appear to confine itself to animals and their interrelationships. The school-text tale closes with an established Nkundo proverb: *Mbabunga afoiky'anto* (literally, "Forgetters do not heal people"), a conclusion artistically in keeping with the false-friend theme that underlies that version; in the hands of another narrator, the tale would lend itself equally well to an openly stated *pourquoi* form.

Cobble's *Wembi . . .* offers a variant of the basic tale including a lengthy explanation of the rationale for the porcupine's accompanying the dog, material more characteristic of a "literary set-piece" than of an oral version transcribed; otherwise, the Cobble version has approximately the same core content as do the three furnished here.

Aarne-Thompson's tale type 910A offers some parallels for this cluster of narratives; Aarne-Thompson's tale type 893 also offers help in placing the tales. A development of Aarne-Thompson's tale type 1332—perhaps 1332D Thoughtless Behavior of Friend Causes Journey to Become Fruitless—would best serve the classificatory needs of this tale and its variants.

Motifs:

T	B280.	Animal weddings.
C	B282.+.**.	Animal marriage: dog and civet cat.
T	A2435.3.1.**.	Food of dog: bones.
T	J410.	Association of equals and unequals.
C	C680.+.**.	Injunction: do not throw bones away.
T	J652.	Inattention to warnings.
T	Z71.1.	Formulistic number: three.
T	H1558.	Tests of friendship.
T	C921.	Immediate death for breaking tabu.
C	A2494.4.+.	Origin of enmity between dog and porcupine.
C	C680.+.**.	Injunction: do not throw away a certain leaf.
T	U130.**.	The power of habit: dog picks up bones at feast.
T	Q261.	Treachery punished.
T	Q327.	Discourtesy punished.
C	Q272.+.**.	Assumed greed punished.

1. Among the Nkundo, a man very rarely is able to marry someone from his own village, largely because of the restrictions on kinship degree within which marriage is permitted in their culture. This pattern is observed by the dog in his seeking a wife "away."

2. As among the Nkundo, consent of both families is required for marriage.

3. In Nkundo folktales, mating can bring together what seem quite unlikely partners, conceivably to strengthen by example the misfortune attending those not following Nkundo traditions involving marriage. (See, for instance, Tales 34 and 80.)

4. The porcupine's curiosity about the dog's errand mirrors the Nkundo's

own curiosity; among the Nkundo, there are no secrets that are not sooner or later revealed. For a narrative employing this fact as its theme, see Tale 72.

5. In the area in which Mrs. Ross worked, there were several villages and a city named "Boende," but the narrator did not specify which Boende the dog and the porcupine visited; localizing the scene doubtless increased the audience's interest in the action, whereas the choice of a widely distributed name made the tale a likely candidate for diffusion. Curiously, this is the only population center actually given a name in any of the Nkundo folktales examined, either among the Ross-collected narratives or in the volumes in French and in Flemish which present tales reasonably faithfully from Lonkundo.

6. Normally among the Nkundo, one or more relatives or friends accompany the prospective bridegroom. The self-invitation by the porcupine, in addition to its offer of a service, is in good keeping with the Nkundo practice of companionable travel.

The narrator's device here for including the porcupine is in interesting contrast to that used in Tale 16. In Tale 16, no device is stated; from the beginning, an extra-familial-friendship situation is assumed.

7. *Cwa-cwa-cwa* is reinforced in its suggestion of the uninterrupted progress of the two companions by the use of "going, going," a common Lonkundo locution.

8. The inclusion of goat on the menu indicates the warm welcome given the groom-to-be. Goats, a luxury, are killed only for special occasions: a birth, a marriage, a death. Obviously, the in-laws intend that the marriage agreement be carried through. This detail increases the dramatic impact of the reversal in plans as a consequence of the dog's betrayal by the porcupine.

The time involved in food preparation seems not to concern the Nkundo. Though meat and fish are smoked if the supply exceeds the immediate demands, more often animals are killed, cooked, and eaten as the occasion requires.

9. [Narrator's explanatory material: "They both were aware that the really big feast would be prepared at the time of the wedding."]

10. Identification of the throwing away of bones as tabu for the dog places special responsibility upon his friend the porcupine to refrain, out of friendship and loyalty, from throwing away any bones himself.

11. The use of a table has become common among the Nkundo—at least, for the serving of men, male guests, white women, and male children old enough to be under the training of their fathers. The Nkundo women, small boys, and girls of all ages tend to sit on low wooden stools in the kitchen—a separate building, *ku-ku*— to eat their meals. They do not eat until the men and all guests have been provided for.

12. The dog's concern about the breaking of his tabu reflects the Nkundo's own anxiety about tabus and about the dangers attendant upon breaking them. The porcupine's violation of the dog's tabu, especially on such an important occasion, was inexcusably rude, and posed a decided threat to their friendship.

13. The violation of the tabu three times by the porcupine is an interesting reflection of the universality of the use of formulistic numbers; the use of three foolish antelopes in Tale 19, another instance of the occurrence of "three times and out" in the Ross collection, suggests that the importance of this number may be greater

among the Nkundo than has commonly been observed. In the absence of firm data on the significance of "three" in Nkundo culture, we have felt it reasonably safe to assume that this element may have entered the tale either by accident or as a borrowing from a nearby cultural group attaching special significance to this number. Continued field collecting will perhaps yield sufficient additional instances of the formulistic use of "three" to provide ground for a tenable conclusion.

14. A marriage agreement can be broken at any time among the Nkundo; although no mention is made here of the return of the bridewealth, in this case the entire amount would be returned to the groom.

15. Since the porcupine confessed himself to be an observer of a similar tabu, he should have felt doubly obliged to respect the tabu of his friend the dog; this detail, too, strengthens the dramatic impact of the betrayal.

16. In this variant, Porcupine's testing of Dog's tabu is treated by the narrator as deliberate and malicious, rather than a matter of carelessness or forgetfulness; the artistry of the narrator in this instance as well as in the liveliness of the dialogue is noteworthy.

17. The word used here for "palaver" was *"jikambo,"* conveying the sense of "quarrel." *"Jikambo"* is regularly used among the Nkundo for one-to-one or small-group disputes, ones not involving the participation of the village elders and other community elders.

18. The bitterness expressed by the dog at the loss of his wife is an accurate reflection of the despondence and resentment an Nkundo would experience in the face of such a situation. To possess a wife is to have prestige in the community: the wife represents the wealth needed to acquire her, the children she will bear, the income her work will produce, and the creature comforts she can bring to the life of her husband and family. To be deprived of all these blessings through the misdemeanors of a supposed friend is to be attacked at two basic points in the Nkundo value system: (1) marital accord and (2) stability of extra-familial friendships.

19. "Elder Brother" (in Lonkundo, with the literal meaning "older sibling of the same sex," *Botomolo*) is used here as a polite term, a term of respect.

20. As do Nkundo males when they must carry a load, the porcupine would carry the bridewealth on his head. Carrying anything on the head tends to give a better balance to the body and thus makes the load easier to carry.

21. "Medicine" is an acceptable alternative both for "tabu" and for "secret practice." (See note 8 for Tale 60.)

22. The pronounced trait of hospitality found among the Nkundo is clearly reflected in the in-laws' concern that the son-in-law be "filled" with food. Though they had already cooked and served two chickens, they went to the trouble and expense of killing two goats to supplement the meal. They were understandably shocked and dismayed when, after all that sacrifice, their son-in-law still went out to pick up the bones. Such boorish response to open-handed treatment marked him as greedy indeed.

23. The Lonkundo term used here for "smear" is *"bisa."*

24. The use of the word "dead" in "He killed the porcupine dead" indicates that the porcupine was completely and thoroughly dead, finished.

25. The Lonkundo title for Tale 17 is "Mbwa l'Iko" ("The Dog and the Porcupine"); the original text appears on pages 36–37 of *Bekolo Bemo*. . . .

Part II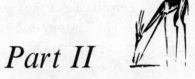

THE NKUNDO IN FUR OR FEATHERS

*Nkundo Cultural Patterns Reflected in Animal Behavior and
Animal Interrelationships*

Introduction

Introduction

DE BOUVEIGNES, in the playful Foreword to his *Sur des Levres Congolaises*, puts into the mouth of Mudimbi, the storyteller of tales from the Kasai area, a comment as helpful in the appreciation of the significance of these Nkundo animal tales as of those told among the neighbors to the south:

> ... "He [Kubuluku, the wily rabbit] has grasped the end that all stories and fables of all time have striven for. Men love to hear them and tell them only to purge themselves of their faults and to enrich themselves with their experiences. Perhaps the usefulness of stories is not always perceived, and that is better. Their lesson is less displeasing when it comes forth after the fact, as with good wine, when one savors it again, after it is swallowed." [translated from page 12]

Trickery and deceit are rife in all the tales in part 2. Is this preoccupation with trickery a peculiarity of the Nkundo themselves? Such a conclusion seems unwarranted in the light of the popularity of trickster narratives in the whole range of African verbal art. Rather, the abundance of such tales in the Nkundo oral repertory seems a likely concomitant to the disadvantageous position in which the Nkundo find themselves among the Mongo tribes occupying the heart of the equatorial rain forest. Largely impoverished, threatened with the loss of their native tongue and the oral literature it carries, seemingly always at the beck and call of some power greater and stronger than they, the Nkundo have sought an outlet for their hopes and anxieties and resentments in the folktale (often, to maintain a thin disguise, in the animal tale), thus venting the concerns that, otherwise aired, might reap the whirlwind. At the same time, the Nkundo can share their feelings and their values with one another and with their children by a technique far more lasting than legislation or "book-learning": told by accomplished narrators, such tales can keep a culture alive long past the time its death might have been predicted. There are values in the Nkundo culture that *must* not be lost; they have worth far beyond the Cuvette, and long past the present generation. The need for viable, stable extra-familial friendships, for example, with their attendant obligations and benefits, is felt in many cultures outside that of the Nkundo; a verbalizing of that need through well-told tales is a decided contribution toward human understanding.

Tales 18 through 30 reflect precisely this grave concern felt by the Nkundo: the central thrust of these thirteen tales lies in the frailty of such relationships despite the earnest intentions of one or another of the parties to the friendship. Too few of the tales beginning "On another day————and————went together as friends" end as all hope they will end—with the friendship still intact. In Tale 21, the dwarf antelope, determined to preserve the friendship she and the leopard profess for one another, deliberately removes the temptation (access to her toothsome children) that would have broken the relationship; this narrative is the only one of the thirteen in which the initial friendship is retained.

Two tales in this section reveal the Nkundo attitude toward ownership and care of property. The obligation to return what has been borrowed is carried beyond reasonable limits in Tale 32: the demanded return of *precisely* the item borrowed, reflected also in several tales in part 3, is deplored by the Nkundo, with this attitude made clear through the dénouements of the various tales. However, a fair and reasonable repayment *is* expected for those items lent in trust (see Tale 31). In a culture holding most goods in common, special value is attached to property clearly one's own—valuables saved, one's drinking gourd—and little sympathy is extended to those who fail to respect such ownership. The two tales sampled here could well serve, in a community storytelling situation, to air a grievance over lost property and secure its replacement with minimal friction.

The Nkundo delight in clever argumentation and the play of

wit in words are clearly revealed in Tale 33. Since most legal cases—those apart from murder—are still decided at the village level through palavers judged by the village elders, skill in argumentation and the ability to "think on one's feet" are highly valued among the Nkundo. (Their interest in dilemma tales, "dry runs" for cases brought up for palaver, is evidenced in part 4 of this volume.)

In Tale 34 two basic Nkundo concerns appear: the genuine demonstration of gratitude for help rendered and the anxiety arising from unstable marital relationships. Reflecting the Nkundo's own conviction that help needed, once recognized, should be offered, the female antelope rescues the leopard. Her fear of the leopard allayed by his marrying her, she conceives his children and then learns the bitter cost of mismatched mating (a point made in several other Ross-collected tales, as well). The whole fabric of Nkundo life is woven, warp and woof, of mutual aid and of mutual trust; in the playing out of the drama in Tale 34, that fabric is torn and then shredded, leaving both listeners and readers to ponder anew their own values.

Overweening pride, in Nkundo tales as well as in those of many other cultural groups, more often than not leads to a fall. In Tale 35, the turtle, usually the winner in the unlikeliest of contests, oversteps himself and pays a heavy price indeed for his cocksure imitation of the ground rat, a sobering reminder to those who would venture beyond proper limits, be they physical, social, or moral.

Tales 36 through 41 pit the weak against the mighty and—as befits the Nkundo's own human need—the "weak" one wins through wit. The highly abbreviated account of a race between an antelope and a tortoise (Tale 36) reflects in its brief course still another basic element in the Nkundo value system: loyalty and unity among members of the extended family. The hoary tale of the small creature who "wins" a pulling contest against two much larger creatures here employs the tortoise, the elephant, and the hippopotamus (Tale 37) in making the point relished by generations of Nkundo: wit wins. Likewise, the hippopotamus learns—too late—that more than a leg can be lost if one's greed exceeds one's means, strong support for the Nkundo stress on sharing and on community interests.

The Nkundo's concern for a reasonable degree of physical security, especially as measured in sufficient meat and fish for himself and his family, is evidenced in Tales 39 and 40 as a factor prompting the use of wit: that both the crocodile and the leopard are "dead dead" and the tortoise alive and prosperous is a fitting outcome of the tortoise's wiliness in those two tales; here is food for thought, as

well as food for the tortoise. The wife of the turtle proves her mettle
in Tale 41: by sheer determination and raw courage (and perhaps a
trace of curiosity characteristic of the Nkundo themselves) she
unmasks the hoax that has kept the larger animals waterless for
weeks—wit, yes, and wisdom, as the narrator points out, may be
found in the unlikeliest of packages.

Tale 42 reflects the Nkundo's regard for justice and the unrest
kindled by abuse of power in high places: beneath the eagle's feathers,
the chief who establishes a law for his people and then freely breaks
that law himself as it suits his convenience is dealt a socially safe
but resentment-venting blow. Rattray in the Preface to his *Akan-
Ashanti Folk-Tales* points up the wide use of folktales, especially
animal tales, as a means of releasing "'repressions' . . . for what
might otherwise become a dangerous complex" (p. xii); Tale 42,
brief though it is, allows the Nkundo to air one such grievance with
impunity.

That part 2 is satisfactorily representative of the animal tales—
and of the cultural values—in the Cuvette can be demonstrated
statistically in terms of the number of narrators contributing (eleven,
including one woman), the full geographical range of ten villages,
towns, or cities from north to south (Mbandaka and Boende to
Ekoto) and from east to west (Ilongo-Kindo to Mbandaka), the
variation in narrators' ages from the teens (Njoli Bombongo) through
the fifties (Tata Manga) to the seventies (Bofaya Efalaiso), the
"stretch" in formal schooling from little or none to university level
(Bofaya Efalaiso to Lontomba Samuel), and in narrative technique
from the seemingly bland (Bakonga Bolingo's Tale 36, which in
print appears sterile but was in fact told with considerable vocal
animation) to the highly dramatic, rich in Lonkundo locutions and
provocative of splendid audience response and participation (Mpanga
Iyende's Tale 25). The sampling of six variants from *Bekolo Bémò . . .*,
drawn from the oral tradition in the Monieka area in the 1940s and
early 1950s, furnishes evidence that some of the current tales have
persisted in one form or another among the Nkundo for at least the
past quarter-century.

In sum, though only one human being speaks in this section (in
Tale 33), part 2 plays out through its animal dramatis personae a
number of significant features in the Nkundo value system. Especially
notable are the emphasis on the maintenance of extra-familial
friendships, the demonstration of family loyalty, the importance of
genuine hospitality, the legitimate use of wit and of trickery to "dress
the balance" in unequal relationships, the observance of a strict code

concerning ownership and borrowing, the propriety of gratitude for help rendered, the concern with marital deceit, recognition of the high risk involved in overweening pride, and care for the wise handling of feelings about those in authority. Through the eyes and actions of "animals," we see the Nkundo themselves.

Narrator: Mbambo Jean
Location: Mbandaka
Date: August 1973

18.   *The Leopard and the Antelopes*

A foolish antelope and a wise antelope had a friend who was a leopard. The leopard said to the foolish antelope, "Friend, come and go with me to the home of my in-laws, the family of my wife."

The leopard said [false start] The antelope said, "I agree."

After they had gone quite a way into the forest, they came to a ghost village where people no longer lived.[1] There they found a large tree with many, many *nsabu*.

The leopard said to the foolish antelope, "Friend, come and let us pick this fruit that we may eat."

They climbed up into the tree and the leopard explained, "Friend, you pick the fruit that is almost white, for that is the good fruit." The foolish antelope agreed to this and picked only the very light-colored fruit, while the leopard picked the purple fruit.[2]

They built a fire and cooked the fruit. The fruit of the leopard were ripe, and he ate well. The fruit of the foolish antelope were not ripe and did not get soft so that he could eat them. He asked, "Why is it that my *nsabu* are not soft and ready to eat?"

He said, "Continue to cook them some more. The water isn't hot enough."

The foolish antelope continued to cook his fruit until finally they were burned. The antelope was hungry that night and had nothing to eat.

The next morning they continued in the forest, the foolish antelope first and the leopard following him. The leopard saw a long piece of wood there that was shaped similar to a knife. He picked it up and put it in his shoulder bag.[3] They kept going until they reached the bank of a river which they needed to cross. They got into a canoe.[4]

When they reached the middle of the river, the leopard said to the antelope, "Antelope," he said, "come let us throw our knives into the river. Then when we have crossed the river, we will find them on the other bank."[5]

The leopard took the piece of wood out of his satchel and threw it into the river.[6] The foolish antelope took his knife and threw it into the river. They kept going and going until they reached the other bank. They disembarked from the canoe. The leopard took his knife from his shoulder bag. He said, "See, my knife had already crossed the river and is here waiting for me."

The foolish antelope hunted for his knife but couldn't see it anywhere. He said, "Friend, do you see that I can't find my knife?"

The leopard answered, "You didn't cross the river properly, or it would be here. Let us go now, and one knife will have to serve the two of us. It doesn't matter."

They continued on their way, but before they had gone far the leopard said to the antelope, "Friend, when we reach the family of my wife and before we eat the food that they will bring us, you will come back here to get drinking water."[7]

They went until they reached the leopard's in-laws'. The in-laws greeted them and very soon brought food. Before they had eaten the food the leopard said to the foolish antelope, "Before we eat this, go and get drinking water where we landed on the bank of the river."

The foolish antelope took a gourd and went to the beach for water. As soon as he had gone and left the leopard behind, the leopard ate all of his own food and all of the food on the plate of the foolish antelope. He left only fish bones[8] for the foolish antelope.

The foolish antelope returned with the water, and went to eat his food. However, he found only his plate with the fish bones. The antelope asked the leopard, he said, "Friend, why did your in-laws give me only a plate and some fish bones?"

The leopard said, "Friend, I want to tell you truly. Don't speak unkindly of my in-laws. If they hear that you are talking that way, they will call me an in-law[9] and a thief. My wife will refuse me."

So the foolish antelope stopped complaining and ate the fish bones that were on his plate.

Soon evening came. The leopard said to the foolish antelope, he said, "Often there is a fight in the night. We do not have a way for leaving quickly. It might be well if we made paths from here to the main path. Then if a fight comes in the night, we will be able to leave quickly." The leopard said, he said, "I'll make a path for you and you make one for me."[10]

They both took knives[11] and went to the back of the house to clear paths to the main path. The foolish antelope made a path for the leopard that reached from the house to the main path. The leopard started his path for the antelope, but stopped working so that the path ended in a big tree.

They went to bed. The leopard went to bed with his wife, and the foolish antelope went to his own bed. After the leopard was in bed with his wife, the leopard couldn't sleep at all. Everyone knows that the leopard prefers meat that hasn't been cooked and is bloody. He knew that the goat pen[12] of his in-laws was near the house. The leopard didn't have the patience to wait for daylight. He left his wife in the house. He went to the goat pen. He chased the largest goat that was there out into the open and ran after him. As soon as the family heard that someone was after a goat and perhaps had caught a goat, they ran out with knives, spears and bows and arrows that they might fight with whoever was after their goat. As soon as they ran out ready to fight, the foolish antelope heard them and knew that they were ready for battle. He didn't know the reason for it, but he said, "I'll wait here on the path that the leopard made for me." The antelope ran out.

The leopard caught the goat and took it to the big path that the foolish antelope had made. The leopard ran into the large path which the antelope had made. He ran into the forest. The antelope ran into the path that the leopard had made and into the tree. There was no path and it was still dark and he couldn't see where to go. He did not have a path.

When the family returned from following the thief, they found the foolish antelope in the path that the leopard had made. They quickly killed him,[13] while the leopard went on back to his home.

Soon the leopard wanted to go to find another wife in another village. He had not done well with the first wife.[14] He went to visit the wise antelope and said, "Friend, I need an antelope of wisdom to go to the home of my wife's family."

The wise antelope agreed. "Let us go!"

The leopard and the wise antelope started off together on the path that the leopard and the foolish antelope had traveled. Soon they came to the deserted village with the *nsabu* tree.

The leopard said to the wise antelope, "You choose and pick the pale fruit and I will pick the dark ones. The light ones are the good fruit, and the dark ones are those that are not ready to eat."

They climbed the tree and began to pick fruit. The wise antelope picked the purple fruit. The leopard picked the purple fruit. They climbed out of the tree and went into the house, where they built a fire and cooked the fruit. The fruit of the wise antelope were good and the fruit of the leopard were good. They both ate.

The leopard asked the wise antelope, "Are your *nsabu* soft and ready to eat?"

The wise antelope answered, "Yes, they are very good."

The leopard kept pursuing the subject. "Your friend didn't find them good at all."

They went on their way until they reached the small clearing in the forest. Again the leopard found a piece of wood shaped like a knife and put it in his shoulder bag. The leopard went first and the antelope followed. The wise antelope found a piece of wood shaped like a knife and put it in his shoulder bag. They went on their way and reached the river bank. They got into a canoe. When they were in the middle of the river, the leopard said, "Friend, let us throw our knives in the river; then we will find that the knives have reached the shore when we arrive there."

The wise antelope said, "You throw yours first." The leopard took the piece of wood out of his bag and threw it in the river. Then the wise antelope took his piece of wood out of his bag and threw it in the river. They went.

They landed on the beach. The leopard took his knife out of his shoulder bag. "See! Here is my knife. It has come to me out of the river."

The wise antelope took his knife out of his shoulder bag. He said, "Friend, here is my knife, also!"

The leopard thought about this. "The friend who is with me is not like the friend who went with me first. Let's go on! When we reach the home of my in-laws and before we eat, you will need to return here to get drinking water."

The leopard started on down the path; the antelope followed. The wise antelope called, "Wait a bit. I have some stomach cramps and must go to the toilet." He returned to the river and put some water in his shoulder bag. He caught up with the leopard and said, "Friend! Let's go!"

They went and went and reached the home of the leopard's wife. She soon brought food to them. The leopard said to the wise antelope, "Before we eat this food, go and get some water. Then we can eat."

The wise antelope answered, "Here is water. Let us drink it."

The wise antelope and the leopard sat, ate their food, and drank water.

The sun had set. Before the sun set the leopard said, "Let us make paths that reach the main road. Then if there is a fight in the night, we will not be in it. We can leave quickly and go home."

They went out with their knives, and the leopard said, "I'll make a path for you to the large path and you make a path for me to the large path." The wise antelope agreed. The wise antelope made a path for the leopard that ran into a big tree. The leopard started a path for the wise antelope, but stopped it at a big tree. They met.

The leopard asked, "Friend, you have finished the path?"

The wise antelope answered, "Yes. I have made a path that reaches all the way to the main road. You have finished a path for me?"

The leopard answered, "Yes. I have cleared a path that goes all the way to the big path. Now if there is a fight, we can leave quickly and go home."

They started back to the house, with the leopard going first. Before they had gone far, the wise antelope called out, "Friend, wait a bit. I have cramps in my stomach. I must go to the toilet."

Antelope followed the path that the leopard had made for him and cut it out until it reached the big path. He came back to where the leopard was waiting, and they returned to the house together.

Soon night came. The wise antelope went to his bed, and the leopard and his wife to theirs.[15] As usual, the leopard wanted raw meat with blood. He knew that the goats of his in-laws were in a pen near by. He went out in the dark[16] and found a very large goat and chased it out of the pen. When the family heard that someone was stealing a goat, they all came out with spears, knives, and bows and arrows that they might catch and kill the thief and rescue their goat.

The wise antelope heard all the noise. He quickly went down the path and went home. The leopard ran down the path that the wise antelope had made for him, but soon came to the tree in the path. The family found him there with the goat and killed him.

Think of the leopard and his deceits: the way he deceived the foolish antelope until that one was dead. But he didn't succeed with the wise antelope because that one was too wise to be deceived and the wise antelope had more wisdom than the leopard.

When you go with a friend, watch him. Some friends are deceitful and want to hurt their friends.

[Notes to Tale 18 follow Tale 20.]

Narrator: Tata Manga
Location: Boende
Date: November 1973

19.   The Leopard and the Antelopes
(Variant I)[17]

Leopard and Dwarf Antelope went together as friends. And Leopard said to Dwarf Antelope, he said, "Let's go together on a trip tomorrow." They went on a journey, the two of them.

As they went on their journey, *té*, they came to a certain place and Leopard said, he said, "Friend, I feel sick. Get a certain medicine for me. I'll take it and drink it and I will live."

Dwarf Antelope said, "No quarrel." While he was gone, Leopard ate all their lunch.

As they went along the path, Leopard said, "Just in case I get sick again, put some of that medicine in your sack. Then if I need it you can give it to me and I'll be well. Let's go on."

Soon they reached the river bank. Both of them had knives. Leopard had already hunted a stick that was shaped like his knife so that you could hardly tell the difference.

When they got in the middle of the river, Leopard said, "Let's throw our knives in the river." Leopard threw the stick into the river and Dwarf Antelope threw his knife in the river also. Both fell to the bottom.

When they reached the bank, Leopard said, "Ah! Here is my knife."

Remove![18] Dark Brown Antelope went first and Dwarf Antelope went afterwards. Leopard went with Dwarf Antelope and all the animals who are short of wisdom. Dwarf Antelope has wisdom like Leopard, and don't forget that he did not kill him. The animals are as many as five that go before Dwarf Antelope.[19]

Leopard threw the stick and Dark Brown Antelope threw his knife. Then they went. Leopard said, "Here is my knife."

Dark Brown Antelope said, "Mine is gone."

Leopard said, "No matter. Let's go."

They went, *té-é-é*, until they reached the home of Leopard's in-laws. When they arrived at his in-laws', he said, "Now we will work paths before we reach my in-laws'. You make one for me and I'll work one for you."

Leopard made a path for Dark Brown Antelope, but he ran it into a tree and stopped there, a *bokungu* tree. However, Dark Brown Antelope cut a path, *tëë-tëë-tëë*,[20] for Leopard that reached the big road.

Then Leopard said, "You have finished a path for me?"

Dark Brown Antelope said, "Yes."

Leopard said, "I have finished one for you. Let's go."

They arrived at the in-laws'. The in-laws greeted them. "You have come. You have come."[21]

They sat in the home of Leopard's in-laws. His law was that at night Leopard wanted to get a goat, even though it was the home of his in-laws. Then that night after everyone was asleep, even Leopard, Dark Brown Antelope shook him. "Wake up! Wake up! Let's get a goat."[22]

He[23] said, "Because while we have been here, they haven't fed us well. Let's get a goat and then go home."

He said, "Eh!" because Dark Brown Antelope had learned that a person who does not eat will not live.

They went out and grabbed a goat. The goat yelled, "Baa-a!"

Then the family rushed out and followed them. They ran fast, *wu-u-u*. Leopard ran down the path that Dark Brown Antelope had made and ran on farther. Dark Brown Antelope ran down the path that Leopard had made, and found the tree in the path. The in-laws grabbed Dark Brown Antelope and killed him. Leopard said, "Even though I brought him, it is just as well that you killed him."[24]

After a while he returned with Marsh Antelope. They went on their way. After a while they came to a clearing. He said in this way, he said to him, "Marsh Antelope," he said, "this medicine you will give me if I get sick and I will live."

While Marsh Antelope was gone, Leopard ate all the lunch they had brought.

Leopard he said to Marsh Antelope in this manner, he said, "Let's throw our knives in the river and pick them up on the shore."

Leopard threw in a stick and it sank. Then Marsh Antelope threw his knife and it sank. When they reached the bank, Leopard produced his knife.

"See. My knife is here."

"I can't find mine."

"Never mind. We only need one."

When they came near to the home of his in-laws, Leopard said, "When we get to my in-laws', we will capture a goat and we will have sufficient." Leopard said, "It is well that we make paths, *tè*. You make one for me and I'll make one for you." Marsh Antelope made a good path for Leopard to the main road. Leopard made a path that ended in a tree.

They ate much food, *tè-è-è*. Then the sun set and night came, and Leopard had a great desire to capture a goat. Leopard said, "I have a real desire for a goat. Let's grab one."

They got the goat, but the goat screamed, "Oh! Leopard! Leopard!"

The family rushed out. Leopard ran down the path that Marsh Antelope had made. Marsh Antelope ran down the path that Leopard had made. He was at the tree, was caught and killed by the family.

After some time, Leopard went to see Large Antelope. "Large Antelope, let's go together to the home of my in-laws. There's lots of good food there. We can go tomorrow."

Large Antelope said, "I hear you. I'll be ready."

He went the way with Large Antelope, in the way of Dark Brown Antelope and Marsh Antelope. He told Large Antelope when they reached the middle of the river as before. Leopard wanted them to throw their knives in the river and retrieve them on the bank. Leopard threw the wooden knife as before and had his knife for the rest of the journey.

When they neared the house, Leopard wanted to build paths to the main road. Large Antelope cut a good path, but Leopard made his stop at the big tree.

As before, Leopard wanted a goat, so they went out in the night. They grabbed the goat. Large Antelope ran down the path into the tree and was killed by the family. Leopard was free.

After a while, Leopard found it was the opportunity of Dwarf Antelope.[25] He called Dwarf Antelope. "Dwarf Antelope, the village of my in-laws is a very good place. The fellowship is good and the food is excellent. Let's go there together tomorrow."

Dwarf Antelope asked, "It's a good place, is it?"

He said, "Yes. Very good."

Dwarf Antelope said, "Your wife lives there?"

He said, "Yes. It's the home of my in-laws."

Dwarf Antelope said, "Very good. I'll be ready."

They went and went, *ti-ti-ti*, until they came to the clearing. Then Leopard said, "I am very sick. If I had a certain medicine, I would live."

Dwarf Antelope said, "I have some in my bag."

They went on to the river. When they were in the middle, Leopard said, "Let's throw our knives in the river and retrieve them on the bank."

Dwarf Antelope said, "Eh!"

Leopard threw a stick in and it sank. Dwarf Antelope also threw a stick and it sank. When they reached the shore, Leopard said, "Ah! Here is my knife."

Dwarf Antelope said, "Here is mine." Leopard was surprised.

Then they reached the place where Leopard wanted to build the small paths. Leopard cut a path for Dwarf Antelope and Dwarf Antelope cut a path for Leopard. Leopard cut the path into a tree and stopped. Dwarf Antelope cut his path into a tree and stopped. Dwarf Antelope with his wisdom said, "Let's go on." As they went, Dwarf Antelope returned and checked the path that Leopard had made.[26] He said, "Ah!" He cut it around the tree to the main path.

Then that night Leopard said, "Dwarf Antelope, before we go out to catch a goat, it would be well if we took some of the medicine that you brought. Then we will be stronger for getting the goat."

Dwarf Antelope said, "Eh!"

So they took the medicine. Leopard mixed his with water, but added pepper to it. Dwarf Antelope mixed his with water only. Each was fixing for the other. Then Dwarf Antelope traded them about. They slept, *té-té-é-é*, then woke up.

Dwarf Antelope said, "Let's be sure and take the medicine."

"Yes."

Leopard took what he thought was the good medicine that Dwarf Antelope had prepared, not knowing that Dwarf Antelope had reversed them. The pepper was hot, and he was hurt.

He said, "What happened? This has pepper."

Dwarf Antelope said, "It's the one that you fixed. What's wrong?"

Leopard said, "O.K.! No matter."

Leopard was having difficulty with his eyes because of the pepper. He kept bumping into things and wasn't sure where he was going. They finally got a large goat. The family rushed out to catch them. Because Leopard couldn't see well, he was going all directions.[27]

Dwarf Antelope said, "The goat is dead. You take it. Then you will have it."

Leopard said, "That is good." He finally bumped into the tree on the path that Dwarf Antelope had made. The family caught Leopard and killed him. They succeeded.

Dwarf Antelope returned. "You have killed Leopard?"

"He has been killing our goats.[28] He was very bad."

Dwarf Antelope said, "Now that you have killed him, let me have a piece of leopard meat." Dwarf Antelope went home with it.

He found the children of Leopard. He said, "Your father is coming. He sent this meat to you and will come along after a while."

Then, because their father had sent it, the young leopards ate the meat of their father with relish.[29] They waited and waited, *tè-tè-tè*, but their father didn't come. Finally they went to the witch doctor. "Why hasn't our father come home? Has something happened to him?"

He said, "Your father is dead. The meat that you ate was the flesh of your father."[30]

The children were shocked. "Dwarf Antelope gave us the flesh of our father. We ate the flesh of our father. We haven't seen Dwarf Antelope for a long while."

To this day, the leopard and the antelope do not go together nor see each other. If the dwarf antelope sees the leopard on the path, he hides.[31]

Bôkô bosila mongo.[32] That one is really finished.

[Notes to Tale 19 follow Tale 20.]

Source:	Bekolo Bèmô . . .
	Zaïrian school reader
	(in Lonkundo)
Translator:	Mabel Ross
Date of Translation:	March 1976

20. *The Leopard and the Antelopes* (Variant II)

The leopard had a wife, and that wife went home. The leopard said to the antelope that, "Come entreat with me in the home of my wife." The antelope said, "No word." And they went.

As they went, they arrived at the river. The leopard said to the antelope that, "Come let us throw our knives into the river." The antelope agreed. But the leopard planned his very arms only, and his knife stuck in the ground in exchange for a stick which was behind him. The antelope threw his knife into the river. The leopard drew his knife out of the ground, but the antelope did not see his knife at all, *nyé*.

They went and they arrived at the home of his wife. They greeted them with happiness! The wife of the leopard cooked very much food. They brought food to the leopard. The leopard said, "I am dead with pain in my stomach. Antelope, go extract for me the medicine in the path which is the path at home."

The antelope ran to get the medicine. The leopard ate all of the food, and he left for the antelope only a little. The antelope came with the medicine, and he gave the leopard that medicine. The leopard said, "Now the pain is finished." The antelope ate the little bit of food which the leopard had left him.

The sun was arriving evening, and the leopard that, "Antelope, come; we will make paths that we capture goats. You make a path for me, and I make one for you, so that we go forth to our very homes."

They went to make paths in that manner. But the leopard went in the path of the antelope another place, and he finished it in the trunk of a bokungu tree. Then they threw a net over goats and they ran, he and the antelope. The people followed afterwards. The leopard went to his home. But the antelope went to be disclosed in the trunk of the bokungu tree, and the people captured him, and they killed him completely. That antelope was a foolish antelope.

The leopard went to call another antelope who had wisdom. He said, "Come; go to my wife's home." The antelope of wisdom agreed. And they went.

As they went, they arrived at the river, and the leopard said, "Come; throw our knives into the river." The antelope of wisdom agreed; he said, "No palaver."

The leopard pretended to throw his knife in the place of the river, but he stuck it in the ground behind him. The antelope pretended to throw his in the place of the river, but he stuck it in the ground behind him, also. The leopard extracted his knife, and the antelope extracted his also. The leopard said, "This is a very bad journey!" The antelope that, "For what reason?" The leopard that, "No matter." And they went.

The antelope took along the medicine in the path. They arrived at the home of the wife, and they welcomed them very well. The wife of the leopard cooked food. And she brought the food. The leopard said, "I am dead with a pain in my stomach. Antelope, extract for me medicine."

The antelope said, "The medicine is here."

The leopard was surprised in his heart. He said, "No word; give me the medicine." Then they ate the food, the two of them.

The sun was arriving evening; the leopard said, "Antelope, come; we will make paths that we capture goats. You make my path and I go to make yours until they reach our very homes."

They went to make paths. The leopard made the antelope's path, but he terminated it at the trunk of the bokungu tree. The antelope of wisdom made the leopard's path, and he terminated it at the trunk of the bokungu tree also. Then he took the place of the leopard to see the path which he had made for him, but he saw that that path terminated at the trunk of the bokungu tree. He himself arranged his path well. He caused it to reach to his very home. The leopard did not regard his at all, *nyê*. When they followed the goats in the night, the antelope ran with his goat in his good path and he went out home there. But when the leopard ran with his goat, he was turned aside in the trunk of the bokungu tree, and the owners of the goat killed him completely.[33]

The false-friendship theme, the trickster-outtricked element, and numerous details of Nkundo customs and beliefs make this cluster, Tales 18, 19, and 20, especially representative of Nkundo oral tradition. Though the core of the narrative is present in all three versions, the storytelling techniques, the dramatic devices, the dramatis personae, and the handling of dialogue vary widely enough among the three to make a sound comparative study not only possible but rewarding.

As in all traditional tale-telling, a narrator occasionally misspeaks himself—appears confused in his character identification, omits a significant incident and then repairs the omission with greater or less artistry, or otherwise revises his narrative in the course of the storytelling. This particular cluster of tales affords several clear examples of these narrative "slips," and we feel their inclusion can bring readers closer to the actual storytelling situation if the "slips" are entered in the transcriptions precisely where they occurred. Such inclusions differ from the "explanatory material," furnished for Mrs. Ross's use and therefore not a part of the tale-telling performance; they belong not in the notes, but right in the living form that is the tale itself, in an effort to share the humanness, earnestness, and eager commitment of the narrators.

Also, certain observations about the Zaïrian school reader *Bekolo Bêmô* . . . have been reserved for comment with this tale cluster; although detailed discussion of the form and teaching techniques employed in the Lonkundo reader seems unwarranted, we consider it necessary to note that the tales in *Bekolo Bemo ...* were arranged by the compilers so as to demonstrate certain forms of grammar. This arrangement is most apparent in our Tale 20, initially selected by the teacher-compilers to make clear a grammatical form called the "Subsequent Imperative," created by combining the imperative form of one Lonkundo word with the subjunctive form of another Lonkundo verb having "*yo*" as a prefix. Two examples follow:

> *Yaka yombonde:* "Come entreat with me."
> *Kenda yonkooza:* "Go extract."

In addition, in this tale much use is made of the subjunctive in general:

> *Yaka tusake:* "Come let us throw ..."
> *Yaka tokale:* "Come let us make paths."

Note also the constructions "that we capture goats," "that we go forth ..."; "said to the antelope that, 'Come entreat ...'" and "said to the antelope that, 'Come let us throw ...'"; and the omission of the verb in "The sun was arriving evening, and the leopard that, 'Antelope, come; we will make paths....'" All the above forms are found in formal Lonkundo grammar as well as in both conversation and storytelling; those readers interested in linguistics will relish the detective work invited by a close reading of *all* the transliterated tales in the present volume.

Both Arewa and Lambrecht index variants of one or more of these tales; Lambrecht's samples, drawn from Central Africa, offer understandably closer parallels than do those of Arewa, derived from the Northern East African cattle area. Arewa's tale types 550 (4) and 550 (5) involve a lion and a hare; the hare is victorious, and the deceptive lion is killed. Arewa's tale type 1191 also has several elements that parallel those in the present cluster; again, the dramatis personae (the hyena and the cat) place this tale outside the geographical boundaries of the Cuvette, though an adept storyteller among the Nkundo might easily substitute a dull-witted antelope for the cat and the dwarf antelope for the hare and a leopard for the hyena and offer his listeners a tale quite in keeping with Nkundo oral tradition.

Lambrecht's tale types 550 (6), 550 (7), 550 (8), and 550 (9) involve a leopard's taking a companion or successive companions to visit his parents-in-law; the companions vary from a goat and a gazelle to various antelopes, with the mongoose as the clever companion in one instance. In a tale from the Kasai, south of the Nkundo area, the leopard makes only one trip, and the only trick is the accusation of the antelope as the killer of the goat; from all indications, the leopard does not die for his crime. In each of these cases, smeared blood identifies the guilty party. The details of knife-throwing, of sending the dupe after medicine or some other substance, and of warning the dupe not to complain about the inadequacy of the in-laws' food are found in one or more of the indexed variants. The tale type most closely related to the present cluster appears to be Lambrecht's 550 (8).

Motifs:

T J400.   Choice of associates.
C C680.+.**   Injunction: pick only certain (unripe) fruit.

T	J1241.**.	Leopard directs dull-witted antelope to pick only light-colored (unripe) fruit while he himself picks ripe fruit.
T	K343.3.	Companion sent away so that rascal may steal common food supply.
T	J2173.	Short-sighted fool loses his food.
T	K1141.	Dupe persuaded to throw away his knife.
T	K2155.**.	Evidence of crime left so that dupe is blamed (dead-end path leaves dupe subject to capture after theft of goat and escape by leopard).
T	K661.	Escape from suspicion of crime.
L	Q382.	Punishment (loss of food, death) for helping.
T	K2150.	Innocent made to appear guilty.
T	K427.	Clever animal betrays thief.
T	J670.**.	Forethought in defences against others: dwarf antelope prepares wooden knife, medicine, and escape path to prevent foul play by leopard.
T	J620.	Forethought in prevention of others' plans.
T	H506.	Test of resourcefulness.
T	J1510.	The cheater cheated.
T	L315.	Small animal overcomes large.
T	K1600.	Deceiver falls into own trap.
T	Q260.	Deceptions punished.
T	J1117.	Animal as trickster.
C	K499.8.+.	Greedy trickster takes companion on visit, keeps him from meal.
T	Q212.	Theft punished.
T	J2300.	Gullible fools.
T	G61.**.	Relative's (father's) flesh eaten unwittingly.

1. Before the arrival of the white man, the Nkundo would live in an area for several years; then they would remove everything that they possessed to another place. Here they would clear the forest, build new houses, and plant gardens. Meanwhile, the old gardens could return to their previous forested condition and thus be renewed. Such deserted villages were often used as shelters by travelers.

2. In order to be edible, *nsabu* must either be heated through in the fire or placed in boiling water. That the foolish antelope did not know when the fruit was ripe was a detail needed by the narrator in order to emphasize the antelope's obtuseness, just as the tree-climbing ability of the antelope and the fire-building art of the leopard were needed to complete the demonstration of this obtuseness, to make clear the antelope's function as a dupe. When questioned about any such "unanimallike" action, this particular narrator would look at Mrs. Ross in surprise and say, "But, Mama, you know this is only a story."

3. On a journey, an Nkundo man will use a bag thrown over his shoulder and hanging to his side. In this bag he carries the things he needs for the journey: a sleeping mat woven of reeds and folded into a ball-like bundle, perhaps a small cooking pot, his knife or machete, and various other accoutrements.

4. In the Cuvette, most families living along a river or near a small stream have at least one canoe. A traveler afoot approaching a waterway too difficult to wade across will almost always find a canoe available. The owner of the canoe expects some remuneration for its use, but if the passengers are willing to do their own paddling, the use of the canoe is usually inexpensive.

5. The ritual of throwing the knives (or machetes) into the river reflects the Nkundo propitiation of the river god or spirit. Since knives are not easy to acquire, people have learned to substitute a sham knife, discovering that the imitation is as efficacious for this purpose as a genuine one.

6. The wooden knife sinks as readily as the genuine knife, so the dupe is not aware of the deceit of the leopard. The instantaneous sinking of a wooden knife, a matter of surprise to listeners unfamiliar with tropical woods, would be expected by an Nkundo; in the rain-forest area, almost any piece of wood will sink until it has been dried for many months.

7. In this instance, as at any other feast, each guest brings his own drinking water, not only because carrying sufficient water for a crowd is burdensome for the host but also because few families would have adequate containers for water for guests. In Tale 95, the civet cat states that he must have drinking water from his own special drinking place: a spring of good water near the river may have afforded the leopard the excuse he sought for sending the dupe on an errand that would leave the leopard free to eat the dupe's food.

8. The leopard's in-laws served the guests fish, even though they had goats and might have served goat meat. This suggests both that the leopard was not visiting there for the first time and that the in-laws, uncertain of the leopard's time of arrival, served the food that was at hand and ready.

9. Obviously the leopard wished not to offend his in-laws and thus draw upon himself the unfavorable use of the term "in-law." The word "*bokilo*," or "in-law," is often used affectionately, but it can also be spat out in a very biting fashion, unwelcome to the listener.

10. Neither the leopard nor the antelope would need a path through the bush; Nkundo needs are the ones under consideration here. Except for the narrative value of having two different paths, one should have been sufficient for both: a narrow, rough path hacked out through the forest. The large tree—perhaps a *bokungu* (one of the largest trees in the Nkundo forested area), an African mahogany tree, or a redwood tree, or *bosio*—would have undergrowth so tightly packed around it that passage would be completely shut off.

11. The narrator did not account for the antelope's having a knife with which to cut the path; the dramatic situation required a knife, and at this point realism yielded to the forward movement of the plot.

12. Many Nkundo families keep goats but eat them only for special occasions. Allowed to run free through the day, wreaking destruction to gardens and other property, at night the goats are penned in an enclosure consisting of a fence of saplings pounded into the ground and then woven with vines.

Among the Nkundo, goats have an interesting social significance: An Nkundo man is completely separated from his mother-in-law when he marries her daughter; however, if he presents her with a goat, they can continue to be friends as before.

13. The antelope had to pay with his life for the theft of the goat even though there was no evidence against him, a reflection of the Nkundo abhorrence of theft.

14. Why the leopard "had not done well with the first wife" was not explained by the narrator. Among the Nkundo, two factors may have accounted for an unsatisfactory marriage: the husband (leopard) may have rejected his wife because she had produced no young, or the family may have rejected him because of his not paying the required bridewealth.

15. The second bride is referred to as his "wife," and the leopard sleeps with her, as he had with the first one. This is an accepted practice among the Nkundo, who feel that no one wants to pay for something that he has not looked over and tried out.

16. In the first encounter, the leopard "didn't have the patience to wait for daylight" to seek a goat, while in the second he went out "in the dark." Evidently in the first instance the narrator was thinking of human habits and in the second of the nocturnal habits of the leopard.

17. This variant is in many ways more interesting than the preceding account, perhaps because the narrator had a large audience of Nkundo elders who thoroughly relished the tale and thus motivated Tata Manga to make the telling as dramatic as possible. That it was an informal gathering, with a most responsive audience arguing and adding details, was evident in the many relistenings to the tape in the process of transliterating the tale.

The narrator's use of a characteristic Nkundo formulaic beginning "went together as friends" confirms the continuing importance of stable extra-familial friendships in the Nkundo value system. Countless tales (using animals as the safest vent) tell of untrustworthy friends, of friendships that develop into bitter enmities, of deceptions the more galling because they have been perpetrated by ones assumed to be friends. On the other hand, the continued presence of tales of deep and abiding relationships, of risks taken—even unto death—for the sake of friendship, indicates that the Nkundo are preserving among themselves and stressing to their children the importance of friendships in Nkundo culture.

18. At this point, the narrator recognizes that he has erred in beginning with Dwarf Antelope. As with the preceding narrator and his "false start" early in the tale, Tata Manga feels free to set matters straight.

19. By the narrator's own statement, five companions preceded Dwarf Antelope (*mboloko*). The narrator employs only three of the five: Dark Brown Antelope (*bofala*), Marsh Antelope (*bongunju*), and Large Antelope (*bomende*). To assume that the use of three foolish antelopes indicates a formulistic-number tradition, especially in the light of the narrator's statement that there were five, seems risky to us. Instead, we suspect that truncation is at work here, rather than the observance of the formulistic number *three*; truncation certainly is employed in the account of the episode involving Large Antelope.

Another instance of the narrator's sense of freedom in tale-telling is his handling of the medicine: the leopard urges the antelope to put some of the medicine in his sack (shoulder bag), but the medicine is subsequently ignored in the course of further trickery.

20. The cutting of a path in the dense undergrowth requires exactly the kind

of persistence suggested by this ideophonic expression, *tëë-tëë-tëë*. The antelope's loyalty requires that he complete the path for his friend; the leopard's betrayal of his friend is presaged by his running the path for the antelope directly into a tree.

21. The repetition of the greeting, traditional among the Nkundo, is found here among animals; the politeness practices, the living quarters, and the code of "death for theft" are envisioned as present in the animal world.

22. Though the antelope himself would not hunger for a goat at that hour, his respect for his leopard friend's appetite prompts him to awaken Leopard. The risk attached to theft, even from Leopard's own in-laws, is willingly undertaken for the sake of friendship.

23. The narrator identifies the speakers in this dialogue by vocal mimicry, lost to the reader; the first speaker is Leopard and the following speaker is Dark Brown Antelope.

24. Leopard carries his betrayal of his antelope friend even beyond the antelope's unwarranted death in his verbal approval of the punishment meted out by his in-laws, a bitter mockery of friendship.

25. The tricky leopard at last errs in his selection of a dupe; he has met more than his match in Dwarf Antelope. The dwarf antelope, very common in the Equatorial Province forests, is normally considered both clever and wise, as is evidenced in a number of the tales in this collection. From the start—note his questioning of Leopard before he agrees to undertake the journey to Leopard's in-laws'—Dwarf Antelope is on his guard against this supposed friend, and Leopard's stratagems are foiled at every turn. The narrator's audience, well aware of Dwarf Antelope's wiliness, expressed much satisfaction and delight at each coup of the clever companion, especially at Dwarf Antelope's switching the medicines, at his leaving the dead goat with Leopard, and at his tricking the young leopards into eating their own father's flesh.

26. The narrator of this variant does not offer the excuse that Dwarf Antelope gave for finishing his path. It is possible that Tata Manga was embarrassed to say that the antelope made the excuse of going to the toilet; after all, a white woman missionary was very much a part of his audience. On the other hand, it is entirely possible that Mbambo Jean, skilled storyteller that he is, had added the "toilet" excuse as his own personal flourish to the telling of a folktale that needed additional flavor in its sterile, relatively audienceless setting.

27. The leopard, outwitted in his earlier attempts to trick the dwarf antelope, relies at last on the medicine that his companion had been prudent enough to bring. The backfiring of this ruse, together with his being found with the dead goat on the dead-end path cut for him, brings the leopard's false friendships to a fitting conclusion: his revelation as the thief and deceiver.

28. In this variant, involving four visits to the same set of in-laws, the in-laws at last realize that their own son-in-law has all along been guilty of the thefts. Since theft carries certain punishment quite outside the area of extended-family loyalties, the leopard's in-laws do not hesitate to kill him for his evil deeds, just as they have earlier killed the luckless antelopes suspected of the thefts. Though these deaths occur in an animal tale, they accurately reflect the Nkundo value system; deprived

in this instance of embarrassing human identification, they nonetheless drive home the lesson: theft is costly for the thief.

29. In this tale, Dwarf Antelope delivers the final and ironic twist; in his feeding of Leopard's flesh to Leopard's children, he has amply rewarded his deceitful friend.

This is the only version of the three which indicates that Leopard already has a family; the wife he is seeking appears to be a second one, suggesting both a polygynistic social tradition as the original source of this version and the likelihood that this version was present in the oral tradition even before the school-text variant had been collected and printed.

30. The witch doctor, with his special skills and abilities, is able to tell Leopard's children what has happened to their father, including their consumption of part of their father's flesh.

Both in Nkundo tradition and in many other African cultures, notably in those of West Africa, a witch doctor does not need to be informed of any of the facts or circumstances; he already knows or can detect without overt clues (by means of sand-cutting, the manipulation of palm nuts, or the tossing of a chain, for example) the problems besetting those who consult him. Not discussed in this tale but widely practiced are various means of divination used by witch doctors in arriving at their conclusions (see Bascom's *Ifa Divination* [1969], *passim*, for a splendid study of such techniques).

31. The *pourquoi* element introduced here suggests that in the hands of a different narrator this tale could function as a lengthy explanation of the origin of an observed animal enmity; as the tale continues in the oral tradition, it might conceivably shift sufficiently in its focus to move into the "origins" group. Presently, however, this single passage is the only indication that the tale might be in a state of flux.

32. The Lonkundo has been retained along with its transliteration because it communicates even across the barrier of language the sense of narrator-audience satisfaction with the completion of the action and the rightness of its resolution.

33. The Lonkundo original, titled "Nkói la mboloko ife; e'olole la ea wanya" ("The Leopard and the Two Antelopes; The Foolish One and the Wise One"), is Story 45, found on pages 66–68 of *Bekolo Bémó*. . . .

Narrator: Ifoma Itaitongo
Location: Ilongo-Kindo
Date: November 1973

21.   Strategy among Friends

The dwarf antelope and the leopard went together as friends.[1] One day the antelope had no food in his[2] house. He had only fish, but was out of cassava.

He said to his children, "What will we eat? Go to the house of the leopard and ask him if you can borrow some cassava.[3] While you are there, be sure and listen carefully to anything the leopard has to say."

So the children of the antelope went off down the path until they came to the house of the leopard. They called, "Friend Leopard, we are the children of the antelope. We have come to ask if we can borrow some cassava."

"You are really the antelope's children?"

"Yes."

"Where do you live?"

"We live just down the path and near the big tree."

"That isn't far away. Is that really where you live?"

"Yes. That's the place."

Then he gave them some cassava and they went home. Their father met them at the door. "What did the leopard have to say?"

"He seemed surprised that we were your children and asked us where we lived."

"Did you tell him?"

"Yes, we pointed out the place[4] and he seemed satisfied with that. Then he gave us this cassava."

"We had better move. The leopard does not give something for nothing. He will come at night."

That day, the antelope gathered his family and his possessions together and moved to another place.[5] He feared that the leopard might come when he wasn't home and eat his children.[6]

The leopard came that night and did not find them.

The tale is ended.[7]

Tale 21 combines the teachings suggested in two Nkundo proverbs: "Do not show caterpillars leaves" and "Your supposed friend will deceive and kill you." Aware of these two truths, the narrator points the way to a wise handling of human tyranny as well as of animals' superior strength and power. For narratives that present less amicable relationships developed between the leopard and the dwarf antelope, see Tales 19 and 33.

Lambrecht's tale type 462 provides adequate classification for the present tale. Although several of the details differ, the basic thrust of both tales is the protection of the young from a leopard. In Lambrecht's tale, collected in the Congo area, the buzzard concludes by declaring her friendship with the leopard terminated, though the young buzzards have been saved by the parent's precaution; the clever antelope in the Ross-collected tale appears to have preserved both the children and the friendship.

Motifs:

T	J1117.	Animal as trickster.
T	H1558.	Tests of friendship.
T	J643.	Care against future tyranny.
T	K427.**.	Clever animal betrays would-be thief.
T	L390.**.	Triumph of the weak—miscellaneous: small animals protect themselves against larger ones.
T	J1176.	Decisions based on experimental tests.
T	K500.	Escape from death or danger by deception.
T	K515.	Escape by hiding.
T	B393.	Animals grateful for shelter.
T	Q91.**.	Reward for cleverness: safety.

1. That a trusting, loyal, extra-familial relationship, usually between two males, is highly valued among the Nkundo is amply demonstrated by the large proportion of tales in the oral tradition reflecting the concern for the stability of such friendships. In the present tale, the fact that the weaker creature is the wily dwarf antelope, *mboloko*, renders this a "safer" friendship than it might at first appear to be.

2. There is no gender in Lonkundo for pronouns, and the narrator did not specify at any point the sex of the parent. For convenience's sake, all creatures of unspecified sex have been assumed to be male.

3. Sharing is one of the basic assumptions in a sound friendship. The leopard would therefore not suspect a ruse if he were asked by his friend's children for food.

4. Among the Nkundo, pointing out a direction is accomplished by one's extending his lower lip toward the path or place in question, leaving both hands free for carrying loads or for performing other tasks.

5. The clever antelope, quite content to be the leopard's friend, is unwilling to trust him too far. He therefore removes the temptation in order to maintain the friendship.

6. The fact that they go "together as friends" does not render the antelope or his children immune from attack and consumption by the leopard; in such a conflict of values, food usually surpasses friendship.

7. The Lonkundo formulaic ending used here is "*Bokolo-ki*."

Narrator: Bokunge Jacques
Location: Bólèngè
Date: February 1973

22.   *The Tortoise Visits the Hawk*

On another day, the tortoise (Ulu) and the hawk (Nkombe) went together as friends. The home of Hawk was high up in a tree. There he had a nest with his wife and children.

Tortoise had a wife and children in his home on the ground. Even though they lived far apart, Tortoise and Hawk were still good friends. One day Hawk went to visit Tortoise and his wife and children. Tortoise wanted to give Hawk a special gift, so he gave him some *baumba*. Hawk was very pleased, and carried the gift up into the tree to his nest[1] and showed his wife and children.

Hawk's wife and children were delighted, and they said, "Tortoise does not have wings. How can he come up here to our home to see us?"[2] Then they laughed and laughed, knowing how impossible this would be.

Then Tortoise, who was an animal with wisdom itself, called his wife and children to him and said, "Bring me many leaves." When they had done this, he said, "Sew the leaves together with heavy cord. Then wrap me up in it to make a package. When Hawk comes again, tell him the package is another gift which he is to carry to his nest in the tree." Tortoise's wife and children did as Tortoise had told them.

When Hawk came again, Tortoise's wife said to him, "Tortoise is in the forest. See the package which he left for you. He says for you to carry it to your home in the tree." All this while, Tortoise was inside the package, listening.

Hawk was pleased. He talked a while with Tortoise's wife and children. Then he took the package and flew with it up into the tree. When he reached his nest, his wife and children were surprised to see the big package. He told them, "I went to the home of Tortoise and found his wife and children there. They told me that Tortoise had gone into the forest but had left this gift for me. She told me to bring it here to you, and here it is."

They all gathered around while he unwrapped the package. All they could say was "*Mo!* Oh! Oh!" They were so surprised they could hardly talk when they saw Tortoise. Finally they asked, "Now you are here? How will you ever get back to earth again? You do not have wings."

The package in which Tortoise had come was ruined beyond repair. He took up too much space in the nest, and Hawk did not want the problem of caring for him. So they pushed Tortoise out of the nest and he fell—plop—to the ground. Fortunately, his heavy shell protected him, and he wasn't seriously hurt.

Do not have a friendship such as the one between the tortoise and the hawk.

When you have succeeded, do not do evil. If you exceed in lying to friends, know that you will continue to do so each time. Do not lie to a friend in something, but teach him a better way.

[Notes to Tale 22 follow Tale 24.]

Narrator:	Njoli Bombongo
Location:	Tondo, but narrator's home was in Kalamba
Date:	June 1973

23. *The Tortoise Visits the Hawk* (Variant I)

The tale of the tortoise and the hawk is like this:

Tortoise[3] was friends, he and Hawk. Then afterwards many times Hawk came to the home of Tortoise to eat food. When he went there to eat food at the home of Tortoise, he saw that Tortoise had no wings to carry him to the nest of Hawk. He went there many times.

"My home is far and you cannot get there at all, *nyé.*"

Tortoise saw this and he said, "Ah! Your nest is how far? How can I get to your nest there in the home of Hawk? Hawk's nest is far above and I live down below with only legs. How will I get there?''

Every time Hawk was in Tortoise's home, Tortoise considered this and thought about it. He said, "I will arrive in the home of Hawk into his nest."

One day Tortoise told his children that, "Children, cut some large leaves. When you have cut the large leaves, when Hawk comes tell him, 'See! Here is a package which Mama prepared in the forest. Pick it up and carry it with you.'"

Hawk arrived at Tortoise's and he said, "*Mo!* We will have a great celebration here at our house. I am going to seek palm wine here for the great celebration up above in the nest." Afterwards, when Tortoise had finished preparing, Hawk did not know. He left the package. When he had finished wrapping the package, the children of Tortoise told Hawk to take the package. When Hawk came to their house, the children said, "Father[4] isn't here. See the package he left. The package is here from Tortoise for Hawk."

When he left the package for Hawk, Hawk carried it to his home. Hawk arrived up above at his nest. He unwrapped it and saw Tortoise. He laughed and laughed.

Tortoise said, "I have arrived in the nest of Hawk. My legs wouldn't bring me, but I have gotten here today. See that I am here. You said that I couldn't come to your celebration in your nest. I have already come. Here I am and I have seen your nest. You said that I couldn't come without wings."

Hawk felt chagrin. Tortoise was up in the tree with the birds. The story is finished. We teach this way.

If you succeed you will not do evil. You will not tell your friend lies or you know you will tell more each time. You do not cheat a friend in anything, but teach the good way.

It is finished. Do this way and you profit. The story is finished with distinction.

[Notes to Tale 23 follow Tale 24.]

Source: *Bekolo Bémò*
Zaïrian school reader
(in Lonkundo)
Translator: Mabel Ross
Date of Translation: January 1976

24.   *The Tortoise Visits the Hawk* (Variant II)

The hawk and the tortoise went as friends. The hawk accepted the treasures of the tortoise.

He said, "Tortoise, you will not come to my house. I live in a tree which is tallness itself. You do not know the top. You can't climb there." He mounted up with all the treasures.

The tortoise said to his children like this: "You get leaves. You wrap me in those leaves. You wait at the tree stump which is under the nest of the hawk. Call the parrots. Let the parrots carry me above."

The children wrapped the tortoise in leaves. They left him on the tree stump.

The children called the parrots that, "Parrots, carry this gift to the hawk. Say to the hawk that, 'The gift which is from the tortoise is here.'"

The parrots mounted up above with the gift. They put the gift there in the nest of the hawk.

The hawk unwrapped the gift and saw the tortoise. He said, "*Mo!*"

The tortoise asked him, "I can't reach your nest? I don't know the top?"

The hawk paid the tortoise the treasures which were fitting. Afterwards, he threw the tortoise down, *pao*.

The tortoise did not feel pain, since his back is very hard.[5]

The two field-collected versions (Tales 22 and 23) of this trickster-tricked tale, though both told in Lonkundo by Nkundo, are distinctly different in flavor and provide a good opportunity for comparison of narrative style. The core of both tales is held in common: The tortoise manages by trickery to visit the hawk's nest.

(An Nkundo proverb is singularly apt here: "Where there is a friend [relative], he is never too far away to be visited.") Each version, however, has its own distinctive style, and the stylistic differences appear in ideal balance with the basic similarities in content.

Beneath the individual touches of the tales, both hold essentially the same major elements (including an obvious relish of the function of the tortoise as the ultimate trickster and of the trickster-tricked motif) and the same theme, that of friendship (actually, *false* friendship), a reflection of the Nkundo emphasis on the rewards, obligations, and risks of an extra-familial friendship. Although the emphasis of the second narrator seems to rest on Tortoise's determination to achieve the "impossible," the "impossible task" is directly related to the theme: the returning of a friend's visit, with the acceptance of the gifts traditionally offered by the host on such an occasion. Both tales record a clearly one-sided friendship, and both endings are consistent with the texts.

The use of "plop" instead of a traditional Lonkundo onomatopoetic expression and the inclusion of the lengthy "teaching" may seem to be flaws, but such touches are the prerogative of the narrator.

In the version presented in the Lonkundo school text (Tale 24), the hawk returns the *baumba* which he has received from the tortoise before he pushes the tortoise out of the nest. This and other features—for instance, the differences in the order in which the details of the narrative are presented—provide evidence that Bokunge Jacques' version was not merely a memorization of the text printed in 1957. It is interesting to note, also, that this particular tale can be documented as present in the Nkundo oral tradition over a period of at least two decades. In Badibanga's version from the Kasai area of Zaïre, not cited by Lambrecht, the tortoise —failing to exact from the sparrow-hawk the promised gifts-in-return—causes the nest to fall, killing the little sparrow-hawks (*L'Éléphant* . . . , p. 15). In Badibanga's version (drawn from his Lulua tribal oral tradition), the tortoise has his children fasten him to the breast of a hen; when the sparrow-hawk chooses that slow-moving hen as his prey and carries it to his nest, he finds the hen's "passenger," the tortoise, who thus has the opportunity of soliciting his return gift in the sparrow-hawk's own home. The Lulua tribe is located near enough to the Nkundo area so that this version, adapted to the Nkundo environment, might well become a part of that neighboring oral tradition, an instance of diffusion worth looking for; by a reverse process, one or another of the Nkundo versions might one day find itself at home in the Kasai.

Lambrecht's tale type 1080 fits both of the Ross-collected tales: the turtle visits the hawk's nest by tricking the hawk into carrying him there in a bundle of dry grass. Lambrecht's tale type 1082, based on de Bouveignes' "La Grenouille et le Milan" (*Sur des Levres Congolaises*, pp. 182–189), combines two elements: (1) a frog's determination to collect on a loan he had made to the hawk, and (2) the frog's arriving at the hawk's nest through deception and leaving *"Comme je suis venue au sommet"* (he feigned death from a bush fire he himself had set, at the suggestion of his old aunt, and the hawk threw him into his game bag); concealing himself that night in the game bag, the frog was returned to the ground by the unsuspecting hawk.

Motifs:

A	A2493.12.2.**.	Friendship between tortoise and hawk.
C	H1220.1.+.**.	Quest undertaken to pay debt (repay visit).
T	J1020.**.	Strength in unity: tortoise and family work together to convey tortoise to hawk's nest.
T	J1117.	Animal as trickster: clever tortoise has family wrap him as "gift" to ensure his transportation to hawk's nest.
T	J2349.**.	Nature of gullibility—miscellaneous: hawk carries "gift" to nest and finds trickster tortoise concealed in it.
T	K310.	Means of entering house or treasury (nest).
T	K1810.	Deception by disguise.
T	J570.	Wisdom of deliberation.
T	J1040.	Decisiveness of conduct.
T	J180.	Possession of wisdom.
T	K1892.1.1.**.	Trickster hides in leaf package in order to be carried.
T	H1558.	Tests of friendship.
T	B469.9.	Helpful parrot(s).
T	B469.9.**.	Helpful parrot(s): carry "gift" to hawk's nest.

1. The impossibility of the hawk's carrying such a heavy load as iron or copper bars (*baumba*) to his nest is a reminder of the Nkundo tendency to attribute to nonhumans the behavioral patterns and feelings and value system of the Nkundo themselves.

2. A gift or a visit requires a return courtesy in Nkundo communities, so it is not surprising that the hawks' first question after receiving the present would concern Tortoise's visit to their own home. Relieved that the tortoise had no wings, they laughed; they were thinking, as people would be expected to do, but their reasoning was birdlike: no wings, no visit to the nest. In Variant I, the hawk assumes at once the role of a trickster, since each time he visits the tortoise he reminds himself *and* the tortoise that Tortoise "cannot get there at all, *nyè*." But Tortoise's thinking is not tortoiselike; it is peoplelike: he outtricks the trickster. In the Bokunge Jacques version, only one visit of the hawk to the tortoise is mentioned, but since they were identified as "good friends" it can be assumed that this visit had not been the only one paid. The hawk in this version is not given as clearcut a role as initial trickster as he is in Variant I, evidence that the narrators have exercised their freedom to tell the basic tale as they please.

3. "*Maulu*," used by this narrator for "Tortoise," is an alternative Lonkundo form for "*Ulu*."

4. "*Fafa*," employed here by the narrator for "Father" or "Daddy," is used both in Lonkundo and in Lontumba, the primary language spoken in Tondo. The Lingala word for "father" is "*tata*" (chosen in Tale 34 for "Papa" by Sam, a native of the Tondo area); "Tata" is also used as an honorific for older men, as may be seen in the names of two of Mrs. Ross's narrators, Tata Manga and Tata Itofi.

5. The Lonkundo textbook version, titled "Nkombe la ulu," appears on pages 44–45 of *Bekolo Bèmò*. . . .

Narrator: Mpanga Iyende
Location: Bonga-Iteli
Date: December 1973

25.   *The Tortoise and His Flute*[1]

Once Ulu (Tortoise) and Lolema (Bat) went into the garden of Tortoise's in-laws. It was a very large garden, and the two of them were going to work there.[2] Bat was Tortoise's friend at that time. They arrived in the very early morning. They sharpened their knives and hoes and worked and worked. But Bat worked and worked and worked especially hard. However, Tortoise soon went into the shade and stayed there resting but not working, *O mpampa*.[3]

Bat said, "*Mo!* The two of us have come to work in the garden. It's the garden of your wife's family. I am working, so why don't you work also?"

"You are right. My work is in the house. Let's return to the house in the village and I will work."

They returned to the village and went into the house. They built up the fire in the house. The house burned easily and quickly.[4] Bat went up and perched on the rafters. Tortoise found a broken pot that was full of water. He crawled into it and hid there.

The flames became bigger and bigger. Bat began to fly about, calling Tortoise and hunting him. It was not long until the roof fell in, and he was under it and was killed.[5]

As soon as things had cooled down, Tortoise came out of hiding. He found four bones that had been a part of Bat. He cleaned the marrow out by blowing, *fwe-fwe-fwe*, and then found that they made excellent flutes. "*Hwa!*" He was very pleased. "This is my very own flute. I'll go everywhere with it."[6]

So he started out visiting with his flute.

> Here I have the bone of Bat.
> Only Tortoise can blow on it,
> I, myself, the tortoise.
> *Hwa-hwa-hwa!*[7]

Then Botomba (Forest Rat) heard him. "That is very nice. I want to blow on the bone also."

"Very good. Wait a minute."

Tortoise went off a way. He had made some glue which he put in the bone.

"Here is the bone. Blow on it."

Well, Forest Rat could not make any noise with it. He said, "Friend, what have you done?"

Tortoise said, "Wait a minute." And he put it in his pocket and took out a different one.[8]

> *Narrator:* When me and Bat went
> *Chorus[9]:* Yes?
> *Narrator and*
> *Chorus:* We went into the fire.
> Bat was burned in the fire.
> Yes, me and Bat went,
> And Bat was burned in the fire,
> The way he was flying around,
> Charred in the fire, charred in the fire.[10]

Nsombe (Wild Pig) came along and heard the song. "Friend, give it me for a little bit."

Tortoise said, "Chief,"[11] and gave him the bone with the glue in it.

He took it and tried to play.

> *Narrator:* When me and Bat went
> *Chorus:* Yes?
> *Narrator and*
> *Chorus:* We went into the fire.
> Bat was burned in the fire.
> Yes, me and Bat went,
> And Bat was burned in the fire,
> The way he was flying around,
> Charred in the fire, charred in the fire.

He returned it and took care of it and made a trade.[12]

Wild Pig said, "Friend, it doesn't play well for me. Tortoise, why do you do this to me?"

> *Narrator:* When me and Bat went
> *Chorus:* Yes?
> *Narrator and*
> *Chorus:* We went into the fire.
> Bat was burned in the fire.
> Yes, me and Bat went,
> And Bat was burned in the fire,

                The way he was flying around,
                Charred in the fire, charred in the fire.

"*Mo!* The one you gave me, it just won't sing."
"Chief, return it. I want to ask you."

Narrator:	When me and Bat went
Chorus:	Yes?
Narrator and	
Chorus:	We went into the fire.
	Bat was burned in the fire.
	Yes, me and Bat went,
	And Bat was burned in the fire.
	The way he was flying around,
	Charred in the fire, charred in the fire.

He arrived at the water.[13] Nkòndè (Crocodile) heard the flute.
He came and he said, "*Mo!* Tortoise! What do you have that makes
such a noise?"
"Wait a minute." Then he said, "Take it."

Narrator:	When me and Bat went
Chorus:	Yes?
Narrator and	
Chorus:	We went into the fire.
	Bat was burned in the fire.
	Yes, me and Bat went,
	And Bat was burned in the fire,
	The way he was flying around,
	Charred in the fire, charred in the fire.

Crocodile said, "You haven't really blown it. Let me try."
But Tortoise played again.

Narrator:	When me and Bat went
Chorus:	Yes?
Narrator and	
Chorus:	We went into the fire.
	Bat was burned in the fire.
	Yes, me and Bat went,
	And Bat was burned in the fire,
	The way he was flying around,
	Charred in the fire, charred in the fire.

Crocodile said, "But what makes the noise? I want to try it."

He[14] handed Crocodile the flute that wouldn't blow. Crocodile tried, but the flute wouldn't blow.

Then Tortoise blew his flute.

Narrator:	When me and Bat went
Chorus:	Yes?
Narrator and	
Chorus:	We went into the fire.
	Bat was burned in the fire.
	Yes, me and Bat went—[15]

Bu-bu! He went with the good flute.

Tortoise cried and he cried and he cried and he cried and he cried. "What am I going to do? It was the very bone of Bat, and he has stolen it. I ask you, how can I get it back? He was up here, and now he's down there! He went, and what am I going to do, me with the crocodile?"[16]

Eeke (Egret) heard Tortoise crying and said, "*Mo!* I know where to find Crocodile. If you go get *nkaka* fish for me, I'll help you find the crocodile."

Tortoise agreed. Then Tortoise went to hunt the fish, two baskets full.

Narrator:	Eeke the bird, the fish are placed.
	Eeke, the bird.
Chorus:	The fish are placed.
Narrator:	Eeke the bird, the fish are placed.
Chorus:	Eeke the bird, the fish are placed.

The bird heard and came and ate until all the fish in the baskets were finished. Then he took the tortoise to see the crocodile. The crocodile was on a big rock asleep in the sun.

Narrator:	When me and Bat went
Chorus:	Yes?
Narrator and	
Chorus:	We went into the fire.
	Bat was burned in the fire.
	Yes, me and Bat went,
	And Bat was burned in the fire,
	The way he was flying around,
	Charred in the fire, charred in the fire.

The tortoise arrived there with great joy. But when he saw the crocodile, he found that the bone was crosswise in his mouth and his teeth were closed over it.

The tortoise cried and cried.

The bird came again. "Try a spear. Get me more fish and I'll find him again when you are ready."

Tortoise came with three baskets of fish and sang,

> *Narrator:* Eeke the bird, the fish are placed.
> Eeke, the bird.
> *Chorus:* The fish are placed.
> *Narrator:* Eeke the bird, the fish are placed.
> *Chorus:* Eeke the bird, the fish are placed.

Egret heard and came and ate all the fish that were in the three baskets. They went, *te-ee-ee*, and Crocodile was on a big rock asleep in the sun, and there it was in his mouth.

> *Narrator:* We tie him up; he is sunning himself.
> *Chorus:* He is sunning himself.
> *Narrator:* Go! Capture! He is sunning himself.
> Thus we catch each other; he is sunning himself.
> *Chorus:* He is sunning himself.

"*A-samba-samba-samba.*[17] But it is enough." He took the spear. *U-u-u!* He put the spear in him and then he took the flute from the mouth and then he rejoiced.

The people came, wanting the meat. They rejoiced. Tortoise said, "I don't want the meat. I have my flute. I don't need anything else."

He took the flute and went home singing.

> *Narrator:* When me and Bat went
> *Chorus:* Yes?
> *Narrator and*
> *Chorus:* We went into the fire.
> Bat was burned in the fire.
> Yes, me and Bat went,
> And Bat was burned in the fire,
> The way he was flying around,
> Charred in the fire, charred in the fire.

Well, if you know someone who calls, "Thief, thief!" it is like the tortoise and the crocodile who is dead.[18]

> *Narrator:* The sun is set.
> *Chorus:* The action is complete.

[Notes to Tale 25 follow Tale 26.]

Source: *Bekolo Bèmö* ...
Zaïrian school reader
(in Lonkundo)
Translator: Mabel Ross
Date of Translation: January 1976

26. *The Tortoise and His Flute* (Variant)

The tortoise, the bat, and the rat went hunting and killed many animals. They smoked some of the meat and cooked some.

The tortoise said, "Before you eat the food let us go a little way to bathe in water." They all agreed to do in that manner, and they went to bathe in water.

When they arrived at the swamp, the tortoise said, "Let us submerge in the water that we see thus who can stay under water the longest."

The rat submerged in the water, but he could not continue a long time and he came to the surface. The bat submerged, but he also could not continue under water. But the tortoise went under and surfaced in another place where they could not see him, and he came ashore on the bank and went home. He went and ate all the food, eating, and completely finished it. Then he submerged again in the place where he had surfaced and surfaced again where the bat and the rat were. "You see my ability to stay under?"

They answered, "Oh, yes. We see. You have great ability for that." Then they returned home.

When they arrived home, they saw that the food wasn't there. They blamed each other, blaming a great deal. Afterwards the tortoise said, "It is well that we burn[19] in some houses which are in a deserted village where no people live. He who is scorched with the fire, it is he who ate the food."

The bat said, "I have no complaint. Let us go there."

They went into a house and closed the openings very well. The tortoise said, "It is fitting that you go out, and let you burn me in the house."

The bat and the rat went out and they burned the tortoise in the house. After a long time of burning the house, the tortoise came out of a hole at the back of the house. After the burning of the house was finished, the tortoise came out in the ashes and said, "Bat, see. I am here! I am not burned at all."

They burned the rat in another house, but the rat went into a cave which was in the ground, and the house burned. Afterwards the rat came out, but he was not scorched at all.

The bat entered into another house and they burned it. But the bat was hung on a cross beam of the house, and was ensnared, ensnared, ensnared. Because he did not have the wisdom, he was burned in the fire.

The tortoise and the rat said, "He who ate the food was the bat."

The tortoise took a bone of the bat and made an ivory[20] whistle. All the animals came for the exhibition of the whistle.

The rat said, "You whistle on the whistle that I hear it." The tortoise whistled. The rat appropriated it from the tortoise and ran with it that he carry it. The tortoise cast a magic spell[21] behind him, and the rat cried with pain and said, "Brother, lift the magic spell. Take the whistle, your whistle." Then the tortoise took his whistle and lifted his magic spell.

All the animals came in that manner that they hear the whistle because that famous whistle is of the king of the animals. But the tortoise with his wisdom cast the magic spell that his whistle be not taken from him.

But when the crocodile came he took the whistle, taking itself, and took it into the river. The tortoise tried to spear him with the magic spell, but the magic spell went into the water, *pao!* The tortoise cried day and day for his whistle.

After not a short while he saw a bird, an egret, who passed above and he said to him, "Egret, it is fitting that I and you go as friends. The reason is that the crocodile took my whistle. If you see the crocodile, call me, and if I see *nkaka* fish,[22] let me call you that you come and eat it."

The tortoise went a very long way and he saw some food for the egret. He called the egret with a song. He sang,

> Egret bird, egret bird, *nkaka* fish is here!
> Egret bird, egret bird, *nkaka* fish is here!

The egret came and he ate that *nkaka* fish.

Another day, the egret saw the crocodile, and he called the tortoise with his song:

> A bit of nose—
> we see the disturbance of the water.
> We see a reflection of light;
> we see the disturbance of the water.
> A bit of nose—
> we see the disturbance of the water.
> We see a reflection of light;
> we see the disturbance of the water.

The tortoise came, but he did not cast his magic spell upon the crocodile, and the crocodile went into the water.

The tortoise cried with much crying. Then he went and he saw some *nkaka* fish, and called the egret with his song again.

> Egret bird, *nkaka* fish is here!
> Egret bird, *nkaka* fish is here!

The egret came and ate that food of *nkaka* fish.

After not a short while, the egret saw the crocodile again and called the tortoise with his song again:

> A bit of nose—
> we see the disturbance of the water.
> We see a reflection of light;
> we see the disturbance of the water.
> A bit of nose—
> we see the disturbance of the water.
> We see a reflection of light;
> we see the disturbance of the water.

The tortoise came with speed. He found the crocodile; he was sunning on a fallen tree which was on the river bank. He enticed him with much wisdom, carefully, carefully, and he defeated him with his magic spell. The crocodile was soon dead, and he and the egret cut him up. They divided the meat of the crocodile.[23] Then the tortoise retrieved his whistle.[24]

Mpanga Iyende, surrounded by a responsive audience ranging in years from infancy to old age, thoroughly relished the telling of Tale 25. The account of the wily tortoise was enhanced by much animated dialogue and by the ample use of songs involving enthusiastic choric support with frequent harmony and what appeared to be two-part-round singing, evidenced especially in the first and fourth lines of the second song. (At one point, a child who did not know all the words or the tune sang with the chorus in a monotone, beginning and ending at precisely the right moments.) We have been unable to transcribe all of the local dialect of the Lonkundo songs, so we have presented none of it here; the content, we feel, has been sufficiently represented in English translation.

The focus in the present Ross-collected tale is not clear: the narrative begins with attention directed to the friendship between the tortoise and the bat, apparently a close friendship indeed, or Bat, a male, would not have been willing to do a female's kind of work in the garden of Tortoise's in-laws. Bat maintains his care and concern for Tortoise until his own life is lost in the collapse of the roof. Tortoise's concern for the friendship appears superficial, at best; instead of mourning his friend's death, he utilizes the bones—which, according to Nkundo custom, should have been given proper burial—to make flutes employed solely to satisfy his own ego, first by the making of music and then by the duping of those who wished to duplicate the tortoise's tuneful sounds. There is no indication that the flutes are being played to memorialize Bat; in fact, the song sung by Tortoise places the blame for the bat's death on his "flying around," a criticism maintained throughout the frequent repetitions of the song. Two basic values in the Nkundo value system appear to be in conflict here: the concern for stability in extra-familial friendships and the strong sense of individual ownership of an item of property. In this instance, Tortoise's pride in possession of the flute which he alone could play, reiterated in Tortoise's concluding statement, has obliterated whatever concern he might have expressed about the death of his friend. Judging from the care Mpanga Iyende took in making the tale unforgettable—the miming, the animation in dialogue, the dramatic impact of the songs, the use of the traditional hesitation word *"Nkanko"* ("then") and of the customary formulaic ending (*"Ili!" "Yo!"*), and the driving home of the lesson with a "teaching" that reinforces the Nkundo prohibition against theft—we must assume that the storyteller had not arrived at this combination by accident but by intent, and that the pairing serves a social and cultural function outside the ken of Western readers and listeners.

The wavering of the narrative line in the field-collected Tale 25 may reflect an ambivalence in the minds of the Nkundo themselves, occasioned to some degree by the proliferation of material goods in a culture quite limited economically, between the traditional value system and the inroads of other value systems necessitating a choice between real and apparent goods.

A variant of a portion of the Ross-collected tale is offered in Cobble's *Wembi* . . . (pp. 51–53). In Cobble's version, "The Bat and the Turtle," the bat becomes angry with the turtle because the latter is so happy. He suggests that each burn the other in a hut made of leaves. The turtle makes his escape by digging underground, but the bat is burned in the fire. There is no flute-making or flute-playing episode or any other narrative development beyond the contest's conclusion.

Lambrecht's tale type 579, the closest indexed parallel we have found—there are several *unindexed* parallels not cited here—includes a hawk and a turtle who undergo an ordeal by fire. The hawk is killed, but the turtle has the rats make him an escape tunnel. The turtle makes a flute of the hawk's leg bone and sings his victory song.

Motifs:

T	B449.3.	Helpful bat.
T	K515.4.**.	Tortoise's escape from fire by hiding in water jar.
T	Q2.	Kind and unkind.
C	F988.3.+.**.	Tortoise makes flutes from friend bat's hollowed bones.
T	K1700.	Deception through bluffing.
T	B211.3.	Speaking bird.
T	B463.2.**.	Helpful heron (egret): aids tortoise in recovering flute taken by crocodile.
C	C980.+.**.	Tabu broken without penalty: tortoise violates friendship pact with bat without punishment.
C	C980.+.**.	Crocodile killed for breaking tabu concerning theft.
T	H221.	Ordeal by fire.
T	K2090.	Other hypocritical acts.
T	D1389.2.**.	Charm (hex) enables tortoise to retain possession of flute.
T	J1117.	Animal as trickster.
T	Q212.	Theft punished.

1. [Narrator's introductory phrase: "Now then."] The narrator used this or a similar verbal bridge between the discussion following one story and the beginning of the next tale, to terminate the discussion and to get total audience attention for the narrative to come.

The word "*nkanko*," translated in all the Ross-collected tales as "then," is perhaps the most popular "phatic communication" signal in Lonkundo. The familiarity of this speech signal provides one more tie between oral literature and life in the Cuvette.

2. Normally, males among the Nkundo do no gardening work beyond the clearing of the trees and brush from the garden plot prior to its cultivation. Since this particular garden plot belonged to Tortoise's in-laws, he may have made some pre-marriage commitment to provide manual labor as part of the bridewealth, a common practice among other sub-Sahara tribes though not customary among the Nkundo. This detail may have been borrowed from some neighboring oral tradition in order to show Bat's complete dedication to the friendship pact in his willingness to share Tortoise's "women's work."

3. An ideophone expressing "Nothing" or "Not at all," "*O mpampa*" is common both in conversation and in tale-telling.

4. The low fire kept burning in a house, constantly ready for revival, tends to dry out the house quickly and render it highly flammable. A house fire in a village prompts the formation of a bucket brigade by the villagers as a means of preserving

the neighboring huts. Afterwards, the neighbors share cooking equipment with the stricken family.

5. Bat, accustomed to life outdoors, apparently died trying to help his friend Tortoise escape from the burning house. Tortoise, already stung by Bat's criticism of his indolence, showed no concern for Bat's safety, a development Nkundo listeners would be expecting in a tale coupling a known trickster with any other character; such relationships almost invariably fall into the classification "false friendships."

6. Tortoise's delight in the flute reflects both the Nkundo's innate response to rhythm and the pride of ownership. The unwillingness to share is not condemned in this tale: to all appearances, Tortoise *does* "share," but his trickery makes a mockery of the sharing. That the flute is considered rightfully Tortoise's property is pointed up by the proverb cautioning against theft.

7. In this song, very little musical range is used; a third is the largest interval included. Lines 1, 2, and 3 descend in pitch gradually from the top to the bottom of the third; the fourth line, sung on the bottom note in a monotone, duplicates the sound of the flute. The term "flute" fails to suggest the "horn" sound represented by "*hwa-hwa-hwa!*" at the pitch used by the narrator.

8. Considerable animation informed the dialogue here, and both narrator and audience relished Tortoise's exchanging the flutes; the storyteller's mirth was evidenced in his voice, and the audience's in giggles and chuckles.

9. The "chorus" includes all those who want to participate. The men's voices—somewhat shrill in this area—seem more pronounced; also, the men tended to sit nearer the tape recorder because of their greater social prestige, adding volume because of their nearness. People of all ages and both sexes shared in the singing, however.

10. This song presented real problems in translation, not only for Mrs. Ross but also for her principal translation assistant, Bokunge Jacques. Complicating the matter was the presence of spontaneous harmony among singers in the audience—not a rigid, "perfect-pitch" form of harmony, but clearly an enthusiastic accompanying line (usually roughly a third either above or below the melody line, as the individual himself chose), showing both familiarity with the tale and its songs and a warm sense of participation in the act of storytelling. At no time did the narrator appear other than pleased with this assistance from his engrossed listeners.

We have checked various printed sources for evidence that the "two-part round" effect we discerned and/or vocal harmony occur in other music recorded in the Cuvette. Thus far, we have found no reference to the use of rounds in the choric tale, nor have we been able to confirm the occurrence in any other tales of a harmony line for the *sung portion*. Trilles, in his two-part discussion in *Anthropos* of "Les Légendes des Béna Kanioka et le Folk-lore Bantou" (1909, 1910), shows several instances of harmony (Vol. 4, p. 954, and Vol. 5, p. 172, for example), but in each case these were furnished by the Ngome harp, a 7-stringed instrument used to accompany singing among the group Trilles studied—Bantu-speaking people, but not the Nkundo.

More attention appears to have been given in journals to sacred music versus indigenous music than to painstaking examination of the forms of music used in *cante fables* among the Nkundo. For a spirited discussion of the merits of indigenous music found in the "Congo" area, see Hulstaert's "Musique indigène et musique sacrée" (*Aequatoria*, 12 [1949], 86–88).

11. The Lonkundo word "*bokulaka*," translated as "king," "ruler," or "chief," an honorific normally reserved for far more important persons than Wild Pig, was here employed to increase the humor and teasing in the telling. An amused stir among the audience confirmed the storyteller's deft touch, doubtless a personal and original one.

12. Mime was apparently used by the narrator here to convey the unstated action: Tortoise put the glue-stopped bone in his pocket and, pretending he was providing a substitute, pulled out the same voiceless flute. That this was indeed the "trade" made is evidenced by Wild Pig's complaint that "it doesn't play well" and his assumption that some such trickery had been afoot: "Tortoise, why do you do this to me?"

Various "people" details throughout the narrative—the work in the in-laws' garden, the ordeal-by-burning episode, Tortoise's pocket, Tortoise's furnishing the *nkaka* fish in baskets, and the use of a spear to kill the crocodile—are reflections of the Nkundo's or neighboring tribes' own practices played out by animal characters to allow the emotional distance necessary for the audience's accepting the "teaching."

13. The two or three words for which we have supplied "Nkóndè (Crocodile)" we have been unable to extract from the tape. Clearly, the new actor on the scene is the crocodile: he is mentioned by name just after the next singing of the song, and no other point has been provided for his introduction. What, if anything, is said by the narrator here to set the scene or define the character or alert the audience cannot, of course, be fabricated; we have not furnished what we cannot support.

14. The narrator's comfortable use of "he" with no particular concern for the clarity of the reference is puzzling and perhaps irritating to a Western reader attempting to follow the narrative line. But it presents no problem in a natural storytelling situation where "narration" includes nods, gestures, pointing with the lower lip, shoulder shrugs—miming of all kinds—as well as rising and falling inflections, exclamations of surprise, disgust, or amusement, laughter, vocal tone suggesting a sneer or mockery or approval or pity, and physical interaction with one or more of the listeners to dramatize an encounter; the *words* of the story and of incorporated songs are insufficient to carry the story as it is being conveyed through all the means of "verbal art" in its broadest sense.

15. The song was interrupted at this point by "*Bu-bu!*" representing the rushing sound as the crocodile emerged from the water to snatch the flute.

16. The narrator movingly communicated the distress and helplessness of Tortoise in the face of this apparently insurmountable problem posed by Crocodile: Mpanga Iyende's voice played upon the sympathies of the listeners (even of non-Nkundo listeners) until they were firmly established as defenders of Tortoise's right to that flute: whatever indiscretions he had committed up to that point, Tortoise was now the "man" in trouble, and the listeners' efforts were bent toward helping the narrator extricate him. Participation in the singing became feverish; all the listeners called to summon Egret; all ate the two baskets of fish; all grieved with Tortoise to discover that Crocodile had fallen asleep with his teeth closed over the flute (contrary to his usual practice of sleeping with his jaws wide open); all rejoiced

when Tortoise recovered his flute. That Tortoise left the meat for "the people" met with universal approval.

17. An ideophone, delivered in a stuttering fashion, suggesting "It lacks"; it indicates the enormity of the job and the insufficiency of the weapon.

18. Tortoise's carefree conclusion and the directing of the proverb toward the crocodile's theft of the flute rather than the tortoise's misdeeds raise additional questions about the narrative unity of this tale; the trickster element appears to have reduced the impact of the close-friendship beginning and distorted the traditional Nkundo emphasis on extra-familial ties, a subtle mutation that demonstrates the narrator's freedom to use apparently conflicting values in a highly effective and artistic fashion.

19. The tortoise proposes an ordeal which will fix the guilt for the theft on one, and only one, of the three. Testing by burning occurs more frequently in Nkundo tales with animal dramatis personae than in narratives involving thefts among people; in the latter tales, the preferred method among the Nkundo is the "water test" (see, for example, Tales 57 and 78). Tests by poison are found occasionally in tales in the Cuvette, but are more frequently utilized as ordeals outside this area. Burning as a "game" proposed by a trickster occurs frequently also in narratives involving no test of guilt at all.

20. The narrator actually identified the instrument as an *ivory* ("*bompate*," meaning "elephant tusk" or "ivory") whistle, and we have kept that term.

21. "*Ndangi ekae e'ekila*" ("*ekila*" in Lonkundo may be interpreted as "tabu," "spell," or "hex"). This is the only instance in Nkundo narrative where we have encountered either the word or the concept of "spell." As far as we can determine, none of the volumes translating Nkundo texts—by de Rop, Hulstaert and de Rop, or de Bouveignes—presents any character, whether human or nonhuman, as capable of "hexing" others. This may have been a borrowing from some other oral tradition either on the part of an especially innovative Nkundo narrator or on the part of one of the three compilers of the school text. Certainly, "hexing" as a technique for controlling the actions of others functions in various African cultures (and elsewhere) to this day, and enters into the practice of witch doctors with telling effect; magic medicines (for increasing success in hunting or fishing, for increasing or ensuring fertility, for resuscitation) abound.

Various other forms of magic do appear in the Ross-collected tales, with the nearest approach to a magic spell found in Tale 2; there, those who would strike Jibanza's sister find their arms strangely paralyzed. Additional evidences of magic include the healing of an almost-severed tree trunk, transformation of an egg into a child, change in form from person to fish and vice versa, magic changes in size from man to infant and the reverse, and the use of certain leaves in a potion aiding a hunting dog.

22. "*Nkaka*," the same kind of fish requested in the field-collected tale, could not be rendered into English by the translator.

23. The tortoise's taking half of the crocodile meat makes good cultural sense in this instance, since neither alone could have consumed the meat; the omission of "the people" from this version also serves artistically in that the dramatis personae continue to the end to consist only of animals other than people. In many "animal"

tales, a division of meat occurs, though in the natural world outside the narrative the disposing of the meat would not be formalized. Still, we feel there is in this version a loss of narrative effectiveness with the recovery of the whistle not the *sole* and verbalized gain of the tortoise; this diversion from the major thrust of the tortoise's action is nonetheless not surprising in a tale told to protein-short listeners.

24. The original Lonkundo version, titled "Ulu la Lolema la Mpo" ("The Tortoise, the Bat, and the Rat"), appears on pages 82–85 of *Bekolo Bémô*. . . .

Narrator:	Lontomba Samuel, director of the British Baptist secondary school at Tondo
Location:	Tondo
Date:	July 1973

27. *The Crocodile Returns the Monkey's Hospitality*

A black monkey called in this area Ngila was living in good friendship with Crocodile.

One day, Monkey—the monkey—invited—cooked a very good dinner, this monkey cooked a very good dinner, very good meal, large meal, and he invited all his friends; he invited them.[1] Then he made all the chairs and tables,[2] and he asked that everybody come to this meal should sit on a chair so that he could eat the good meat. And, as you know, a feast, a big feast like that, attracts a lot of people.

So Crocodile came, too, and he wanted to sit on the table. But the law was that he should sit on a chair. But you know that Crocodile has a very long tail, and he can hardly sit on a chair. So this black monkey, Ngila,[3] who was the host, insisted, "Everybody sits on a chair." They tried to make Crocodile sit on a chair. He couldn't, because his tail was l-o-n-g,[4] and they couldn't make it to fit properly in the chair, on a chair. So it was very hard, and Ngila the monkey wouldn't change his mind.

He said, "Well, I'm sorry, my friend, because everybody has to sit on a chair like that, but if you can't, then I can't allow you to be in my feast." So Ngila decided that his friend should go out, go back.

And the crocodile went back home in the lake sadly because he couldn't participate in this feast. That was too bad.

So a month later or so, Crocodile made a big feast, too. He cooked a good meal and invited all his friends. Then in this he insisted that everybody who comes to eat this food has to wash his hands; every, every, everybody has to have very clean hands, white hands. But this monkey, Ngila, who had cooked the previous meal, he has black hands. His hands can never be white. He just looks like other monkeys, like most of the monkeys, but his hands are naturally black. Well, anyway, everybody who was in the feast was washing his hands, and before he got in the dining hall,[5] he had to show his hands to the host, so. But one after another, one after another— Then came Ngila, the monkey. He showed his friend his hands, but his friend said, "I'm sorry. Your hands are not clean enough. Get the soap[6] and wash them again."

Monkey Ngila went and tried to wash his hands; he washed and he washed. He went again to his friend, his hands showed him, but the hands were not improved; they were still black.

So the friend said, "Well, I'm sorry. It's the time to start eating now, and I can't just waste my time here waiting for you cleaning your hands. You just go home."

So Ngila went home and he couldn't participate in this feast.

That's why today you see Ngila would never trespass where the crocodile is.[7] They are enemies.

Anyway, in the teaching, the moral application, it is not very difficult: What you do to your friend one day, he can do it to you, too. So that we want to show to all the people that we shouldn't do bad things to our friends or laugh at somebody because he has some infirmities because you don't know; one day, something could happen to you, too.

[Notes to Tale 27 follow Tale 28.]

Source: Bekolo Bèmò . . .
                 Zaïrian school reader
                 (in Lonkundo)
Translator: Mabel Ross
Date of Translation: January 1976

28.   *The Crocodile Returns the Monkey's Hospitality* (Variant)

The *ngila* monkey and the tortoise went as friends.

The tortoise said, "Ngila, come let us go to my house; let us eat food."

The tortoise cooked a very large feast. He passed the food to the *ngila* monkey. He said, "Before you eat the food you go and wash your hands first."

The *ngila* monkey washed his hands, washing, washing. They did not wash clean.

The tortoise said, "You will not eat food because your hands excel in dirt." In his manner he went. He ate no food at the tortoise's house, *nyè*.

Another time, the *ngila* monkey said, "Tortoise, it is well that we go to my house."

Then they went to the house of the *ngila* monkey, and the *ngila* monkey cooked much food. He found a reclining stool made from the forked branch of a tree and brought it near to the tortoise. He said, "Friend, you lean against this stool."

The tortoise answered, "No matter. I will lean there." Then he leaned, but he fell into the palm sauce because the tortoise is not tall.

Everybody laughed at the tortoise for this reason; therefore then the *ngila* monkey had imitated the badness which the tortoise had done first.

What is to be avoided? Not like the tortoise?
The last badness is worse than the first.[8]

Although Lontomba Samuel had no audience other than the tape recorder and was recording Tale 27 in English, not his native tongue, his tale was recounted with a considerable amount of animation; the narrator's use of dramatic pauses, rising and falling inflections, and variations in pacing reveals his total involvement in the act of storytelling. We feel the exact transcription of Sam's narration has captured enough of his excitement to allow readers to sense his appreciation of the tale and its reflection of Nkundo culture and values.

Sam's narrative and the related Tale 28 from *Bekolo Bèmö* . . . have been handled together here; despite readily apparent differences in the order of the visits and in the second principal (Crocodile vs. the tortoise)—differences evidenced also in the indexed variants cited below—they are basically the same tale, an amusing and widely distributed sub-Sahara African form of the Aarne-Thompson tale type 60.

Klipple summarizes as variants of the type several that are similar to the present pair of tales in that the guest on one of the visits is required to wash his hands or feet "white and clean," an impossible task whether he be baboon, ape, or black monkey. The Klipple-cited narratives that involve the burning of grass or brush so that the guest's paws might be repeatedly dirtied are, of course, less close to the Ross-collected tale than are those in which the paws of the guest are by nature black; both of the latter tales are derived from the Congo area. In none of the Klipple variants is any of the principals a crocodile, nor is a creature physically unable to sit required to sit in order to eat.

Three of the four versions of Arewa's tale type 1001 (a renumbering of Aarne-Thompson's tale type 60) require the turtle or tortoise to sit to eat; the only one in which the turtle's attempt to sit causes him to fall into the food is 1001 (1). The other member in 1001 (1) and 1001 (2), the macaque, is required to wash his hands before eating, but each time dirties them on ashes strewn by the turtle. The crocodile does not appear in any of Arewa's versions.

Lambrecht's tale type 1001 (5), drawn from de Bouveignes' *Sur des Levres Congolaises*, most nearly fits the Ross-collected tale in several respects: it involves both a crocodile and a black-pawed monkey; both entertainments are feasts or celebrations, with many witnesses of the guest's discomfiture; the crocodile is required to sit on a chair in order to eat or drink; and the "inappropriate entertainment repaid" results in enmity between the two principals. The other three variants summarized by Lambrecht (from the Badibanga and Stappers volumes cited elsewhere) involve both hand-washing and impossible seating, but the toad replaces the crocodile in the dramatis personae and the guest's embarrassment is witnessed only by the host or by the host and the host's wife.

Various forms of the field-collected tale appear in folktale collections from many parts of sub-Sahara Africa and have been especially plentiful in volumes published for children; among the latter, one elaborately retold but highly entertaining version from Rhodesia utilizes the tortoise rather than the crocodile, and presents the tortoise as being served food and beer in long-necked jars—on the return visit, the tortoise's guests have been prompted to rebuke the black monkey for putting his "dirty" hands into the common bowl (see Elliot's *Where the Leopard Passes* [1949], pp. 87–94).

Motifs:

T	H1558.	Tests of friendship.
C	C680.+.**.	Injunction : everyone, including crocodile, must sit on a chair to eat.
T	J10.	Wisdom (knowledge) acquired from experience.
T	J1565.	Inappropriate entertainment repaid.
C	C680.+.**.	Injunction: everyone, including the black monkey, must wash his hands clean and white before eating.
T	H1024.	Tasks contrary to the nature of animals.
L	A2494.5.37.	Enmity between monkey and crocodile.

1. As among the Nkundo, here a fine dinner—a feast—is an occasion for a community-wide gathering. Exclusion from such a gathering is cause for embarrassment and resentment.

2. Acculturation and anthropomorphization are both apparent in the mention of the monkey's making chairs and tables for an animal feast.

3. We have retained both "*Ngila*" and "Monkey" wherever the narrator used them.

4. In a normal Nkundo storytelling session, this tale would have provided an ideal vehicle for gesturings, bodily posturings, and vocal dramatizations, all relished by the audience. Some suggestion of the last-named feature is afforded by Sam's drawing out of the word "long."

5. "Dining hall" may well be a linguistic survival from the narrator's university experience in the United States.

6. The Nkundo are accustomed to keeping their bodies clean and oiled (the latter for beauty as well as for comfort's sake). Soap is a popular item among the Nkundo (see also Tale 78 for another narrative making this point), and its use here to "clean" the black monkey's paws is a direct reflection of Nkundo culture.

7. Here, the narrator introduces a *pourquoi* element that may or may not have been present in the oral version from which the compilers provided the schoolbook form. Since the narrators of the tales included in *Bekolo Bèmò* . . . were not identified by the compilers, it is not possible to determine whether or not this element suggested a drift from the "inhospitality repaid" folktale toward a *pourquoi* tale.

8. The Lonkundo original, titled "Ngila l'Ulu," is found on page 53 of *Bekolo Bèmo.* . . .

Narrator: Bokunge Jacques
Location: Bòlèngè
Date: February 1973

29. *The Tortoise Betrays the Crocodile's Hospitality*

On another day the tortoise, Ulu, and the crocodile, Nkòndè, went together as friends.[1] Crocodile went to the home of Tortoise and they exchanged gifts; then Crocodile returned to his home in the water. He called his wife and children and showed them the gifts given to him by Tortoise.

Some days later Crocodile went again to visit Tortoise. Tortoise said, "Crocodile, I am going to visit you in your home."[2]

Crocodile agreed, and they went together to the home of Crocodile in the water.[3]

Tortoise said to Crocodile, "Crocodile, we have been close friends for a long while. Could I sleep in that room that is reserved for your family and closest friends?"[4]

Crocodile agreed, and led Tortoise to that room and left him there. Tortoise found that Crocodile had left fifty eggs in that room ready to hatch. When Tortoise saw the fifty eggs, he called out to Crocodile, "Bring me some good firewood. In the evening when I go to bed, I will build a fire."[5]

So Crocodile brought the firewood, and Tortoise stacked it in the room where he was. When evening came, he built a fire. Then he cooked one of the eggs in the fire and ate it. During the night he cooked the eggs one at a time and ate them. However, each time he cooked an egg it would burst open, *ba-u*. Crocodile kept hearing this noise, and finally he went to the door of the room and called, "Tortoise, I keep hearing a cracking noise, *ba-u*, *ba-u*. Where is it coming from?"

Tortoise went to the door and answered, "The firewood you brought keeps cracking in the fire, and the noise is from that."

By morning, Tortoise had eaten forty-nine of the eggs and each egg had cracked open, *ba-u*, *ba-u*. He called to Crocodile, "Crocodile, return me to my home this morning. But before I go, I want to show you that all of your eggs are here." He took the remaining egg and held it up to a hole in the door and began to count, "One." He put that egg down and picked it up again, saying "Two." He put it down and picked it up again: "Three." He did this, using the same egg each time, until he had counted all fifty eggs. This was so that Crocodile could know that his eggs were all there and safe.[6]

Then Tortoise got on Crocodile's back so that Crocodile could take him to the bank of the river.

In the meantime the one crocodile egg that was left hatched, and soon the baby crocodile began to call, "Daddy, dump him in the river; he ate all the eggs."[7]

Crocodile called back, "No! No! We counted the eggs."

But the young one continued to call, "But Daddy, he ate the eggs."

Crocodile did not believe him, and left Tortoise on the river bank. However, when he returned home, he realized that what his child had said was true,[8] and Tortoise had eaten all the eggs but one. He was very angry, and rushed to the bank of the river. By then, Tortoise had disappeared in the forest. To this day the crocodile is still hunting for the tortoise.[9]

Don't be like the tortoise who ate the children of his friend the crocodile.

[Notes for Tale 29 follow Tale 30.]

Source: Bekelo Bémó . . .
                     Zaïrian school reader
                     (in Lonkundo)
Translator: Mabel Ross
Date of Translation: January 1976

30.   *The Tortoise Betrays the Crocodile's Hospitality* (Variant)

The tortoise and the crocodile went as friends. One time the tortoise called the crocodile and gave him very many gifts. The crocodile carried them home.

After a while the crocodile sent a messenger to call the tortoise for dinner. The tortoise came and he said, "Friend, go and fight the leopard, the very leopard; bring him to me." Then the crocodile went and fought the leopard and brought it. After that the tortoise said, "Friend, spread a bed for me in your forbidden room." And the crocodile spread a bed for him in that room. And in that room were the eggs which the wife of the crocodile had laid there.

After a while the tortoise said to the crocodile, "Friend, I will return home tomorrow, and I want you to leave me today. And in the morning you take me in your canoe[10] to my home."

The crocodile gave the tortoise very many gifts. Then they slept. In the night the tortoise ate all the eggs. When he cooked an egg in the fire,[11] it cracked, "*tao, tao*"[12] and the crocodile asked, "Friend, what was that?" The tortoise answered, "That was the leopard which you fought; it exploded."[13] The tortoise ate all the eggs. He left only one egg.[14]

At the end of the night before he went he said, "Crocodile, see that all of your eggs are here. Let me count now, that you do not come to blame me afterwards." Then he raised up that one egg, raising it many times in his counting until fifty raisings. The crocodile thought that all the eggs were there because they were in that room. And he said to his child,[15] "You count the eggs after my going when the sun is well up." Then he and the tortoise got into the canoe and went.

Before they had gone far, the child went to see, but he found one egg only. Then he called out, "Daddy, Daddy, bring back the tortoise who has finished the eggs." The tortoise said, "He said to you, 'Paddle very hard because the waves are very many in the river!' Paddle! The child fears that you will die."

Then the crocodile continued to paddle the tortoise and left him on the river bank near his home.

But when he returned home, his child said to him, "Father, I called you that you return with the tortoise; he finished the eggs. Now why didn't you return with him?" The crocodile paddled again that he catch the tortoise, but he found that the tortoise had finished going.[16]

In Tales 29 and 30 the Nkundo deal again with the theme of friendship betrayed; as is true in Tales 39 and 40, both the tortoise and the crocodile are characters, and as in Tales 39 and 40 the smaller creature is victorious over the larger. But the present narratives—one current in the Cuvette and the other printed in Lonkundo from the oral tradition roughly a quarter of a century earlier—suggest a closer initial friendship and a deeper degree of betrayal than do the others: in these, the crocodile trusts the tortoise sufficiently to house him in the family treasure room, and the tortoise in turn deals the most telling of blows in a child-valued culture—he eats the generous host's children. Evidence that even this grim situation can be vented by laughter is afforded in the Variant by the trickster incidents involving the egg-counting and the misquoted message. Still, the warning carried in both versions is clear to Nkundo listeners and readers: seek only trustworthy friends, and treat them honestly and honorably.

In none of the many African variants cited by Klipple for the likeliest type classification, Aarne-Thompson's tale type 37, do the tortoise and the crocodile appear together; the crocodile enters only one variant (from the Ewe), and the false friend [nurse] therein is a hare. Children in egg form are not consumed in any of the variants. None of Arewa's variants of Aarne-Thompson's tale type 37 (re-numbered 855) involves either crocodiles or eggs. The parallel in Lambrecht's tale type 855 (9), though it deals with a female dog and a female leopard rather than a male tortoise and a male crocodile, does begin with an apparently genuine friendship and end with the friendship broken, though no *pourquoi* statement is included; in the Lambrecht-cited tale, published in 1958 in *Kongo Overzee*, the outraged mother dog returns the leopard's unkindness by eating the leopard's cubs before the friendship is terminated. There appears to be no satisfactory classificatory number in any of the present indexes that serves the needs of the Ross-collected tale and its textbook variant; this particular combination of features seems entirely confined to Nkundo oral tradition. Further study of the friendship—false-friendship tales current elsewhere in Central Africa may eventually yield enough additional samples to warrant assigning this tale a type number.

Further evidence of earlier currency of this tale among the Nkundo is afforded by a somewhat adulterated English-language retelling of the basic narrative in

Cobble's *Wembi* . . . , based on tales circulating orally in the Cuvette two or three
decades prior to the date of publication in the United States.

Motifs:

T	H1558.	Tests of friendship.
T	K310.	Means of entering house or treasury.
T	K346.	Thief trusted to guard goods (crocodile's eggs).
T	K359.**.	Tortoise thief gains access to crocodile's eggs on basis of close friendship tie.
T	B535.**.	Animal guardian: tortoise allowed to sleep in same room with crocodile's eggs.
C	C229.+.**.	Tabu: eating eggs of hospitable crocodile.
C	K411.1.+.**	Tortoise claims sound of crackling fire as alibi for cracking sound of cooked crocodile eggs.
C	W154.+.**.	Ungrateful tortoise eats eggs of crocodile host.
T	J670.**.	Forethought in defences against others: tortoise holds up single remaining crocodile egg fifty times for counting by crocodile.
C	B491.3.+.**.	Helpful crocodile: provides transportation for deceitful tortoise.
T	J1144.**.	Eaters (eater) of stolen food (crocodile's eggs) detected.
T	K435.	Child's song incriminates (cries incriminate) thief.
T	J652.	Inattention to warnings.
C	K571.+.**.	Tortoise escapes capture and punishment by misquoting child's shouted warning.
T	R260.	Pursuits.
C	A2494.6.2.+.**.	Enmity between tortoise and crocodile.

1. [Narrator's explanatory comment: "Tortoise lived on the ground and
Crocodile lived in the water."]

2. For Tortoise to omit a return visit would have been unthinkable.

3. [Narrator's explanatory comment: "In every home there is a room where
no one goes but the family."] Many Nkundo homes have such a special room for
storage of their dress-up clothing as well as for concealment of a lockable metal
box for papers and other valuables.

4. Tortoise's request to sleep in that special room might reasonably have been
interpreted by Crocodile as a test of the stability of their friendship. There is no
indication given by the narrator that any abuse of that friendship is initially con-
templated by either of the principals.

5. Tortoise's planning to build a fire in Crocodile's underwater home—though
it might have been instantly suspected by a Western reader as an indication of
mischief afoot—would arouse no suspicion on the part of Nkundo listeners: the
dramatis personae consists of animals, but the cultural milieu is pure Nkundo, and
the Nkundo themselves appreciate the warmth of a fire at night. In this instance,
a delicious opportunity knocked, and Tortoise promptly opened the door.

6. This device is commonly used in trickster tales collected both in widely separated African cultures and in non-African sources; often, a deceptive "nurse-maid" repeatedly presents one of the remaining young to demonstrate to the mother the health and safety of the children. Bokunge Jacques' relish of this particular detail was clearly evidenced in the telling.

7. Fully as common in verbal art is the "truth will out" theme, with the informer sometimes a bird or a dog, sometimes a bone or the skull of the victim, sometimes a small child, sometimes even a child still in the womb. As Torrend remarked in his *Specimens of Bantu Folk-Lore* ... (p. 27, fn. 7), "the revealer is a little being which might have been thought to have no notion of right or wrong." Further instances of this theme may be found throughout the present volume.

8. Various Nkundo tales and proverbs stress the wisdom of listening to un-expected sources—including young children—and heeding what is said. See, for example, Tales 65 and 72.

9. This conclusion for the tale offers a hint of a *pourquoi* element which affords room for interesting speculation. Those accustomed to encountering folktales only in written and rather "literary" form might persuade themselves that this tag serves to tie off the tale in a neat and tidy fashion. A "precious" ending is not, fortunately, a characteristic of the tales Mrs. Ross encountered in her field collecting; two likelier alternatives present themselves in this instance. The primary purpose of the concluding line may be strictly functional: it definitely establishes a "so *that's* why the crocodile pursues the tortoise" opportunity for Nkundo listeners to answer one or another of the puzzling questions about phenomena observed in nature. True, the major thrust of the narrative is directed against the rupture of friendship, a central concern in the present Nkundo value system. But if over succeeding genera-tions that concern should lose its force, the tale still has within it the wherewithal for a *pourquoi* that need not be tied to the value system; whatever the value system, the natural sense of wonder persists. In this tale one *may*, then, be observing the earliest stage of a folktale in a state of flux, a narrative worth pursuing by later collectors to determine its altered function as the Nkundo gradually become absorbed linguistically and culturally into a larger group.

On the other hand, attaching a *pourquoi* "signal" to a tale centered on another theme may be something added for lagniappe, as an extra flourish which particularly pleases this narrator himself, at that moment the center of attention and the arbiter of what is to be included in his distinctive version of that particular tale. The im-provisation encouraged among Nkundo narrators is readily apparent throughout the narratives in the present collection, a tantalizing sampling of the combinations and permutations of what is unquestionably a wealth of traditional verbal art still present in the Cuvette.

For another Nkundo instance of this added-*pourquoi* flourish, see de Rop's "De Luipaard, de Dwergantiloop en de Bosrat" (... *woordkunst* ... , pp. 254–259); for a non-Nkundo example, see the Gã folktale "The Pineapple Child" in Whiteley's *A Selection of African Prose. 1. Traditional Oral Texts* [1964] (pp. 164–165).

10. The inclusion of the canoe as a means of transportation where the crocodile's back would have sufficed is a direct reflection of Nkundo material culture; the

crocodile's position as a property-holder is readily perceived by the listeners. (A canoe is utilized also in Cobble's English-language retelling in *Wembi. . . .*)

11. Here, a detail present in the current oral version is lacking in the schoolbook form; the assumption is that the guest's room would afford the comfort of a fire. Limitation of space and of complexity may have caused the compilers of the text to abbreviate the oral form they had heard; on the other hand, Bokunge Jacques himself may have elected to include the fire-building touch because of the dramatic possibilities with a live audience, a touch that points up Tortoise's determination to press his unexpected opportunity for a feast. The fire-building episode is included in Cobble's retelling of the earlier oral version; whether this detail is to be attributed to the reteller or to her source is unclear.

12. The onomatopoetic expression representing the sound of the exploding egg differs from the one used by Bokunge Jacques partly because the narrators themselves were free to choose the sounds they considered most representative and partly because of the way in which the respective listeners *heard* those sounds. Ideophonic and onomatopoetic expressions pose interesting and challenging problems for transcribers and translators. (Note: The calcareous shells of crocodilian eggs are considerably thicker than those of domesticated hens.)

13. The explanation afforded here, while less "logical" or "defensible" than the one furnished in Bokunge Jacques' version, still reveals the narrator's effort to tie together the various elements in his tale. In Cobble's retelling, the sound is attributed to the "light wood" brought by the crocodile for the fire in the tortoise's room.

14. The apparent contradiction between "The tortoise ate all the eggs" and "He left only one" is an accurate mirroring of an Nkundo speech pattern used both in conversation and in storytelling. Mrs. Ross has many times heard such statements paired, with no indication from either speaker or listener that anything is irregular about the combination. Actually, the device serves the narrator well: he can indicate the thoroughness with which the tortoise completed what he had started, and he can mime and otherwise prompt response and suspense by emphasizing that the wily tortoise had "hedged" against the probable unpleasant consequence of his act

Bokunge Jacques, perhaps aware that the usual Nkundo speech pattern would seem illogical to Western readers, adapted his own handling of the number to fit the Western practice of precise enumeration.

15. This "child" is apparently of an earlier hatching, since he finds the remaining egg when he goes, following his father's instructions, to count the eggs.

This "family" touch and the bit of humor in the tortoise's deliberately misquoting the child's message to his father may well have been present in the oral tale on which the text was based; in *Wembi. . .* (p. 30), Cobble states "The Crocodile was very hard of hearing. He asked the Tortoise what his child was saying. The Tortoise replied, 'Your child is saying to paddle hard for a storm is coming up. Paddle for your life!'" Such touches are keenly relished by Nkundo listeners.

16. The Lonkundo textbook original of this tale, titled "Ulu la Nkonde," appears on pages 94–95 of *Bekolo Bémò. . . .*

Narrator: Ngoi Ekoletonga, village elder
Location: Longa
Date: December 7, 1972

31. *The Porcupine Borrows from the Dog*

Iko (Porcupine) found that he needed some money,[1] so he went to Mbwa (Dog) and borrowed from him. After some time he found that he didn't have the means of repaying the debt. As a result he began to hide from Dog. He found good hiding places in holes made in the roots of large trees in the forest. He would come out only occasionally; most of the time he stayed hidden in the hole in the tree.

In due time, Dog wanted his money and began to hunt Porcupine. He went to a man for help. He told Man that, "Porcupine has a debt with me. I can never catch him in order to collect. Perhaps you could help."

Man was pleased. He answered that, "I would be glad to help you. I am hungry for porcupine meat. Let's go together that we hunt him."[2]

"That's fine with me," said Dog. "I can seek him out with my nose. Also, I know his way and the kinds of places where he hides. You, yourself, will need to catch him."

Man made a net of strong vines.[3] It was similar to the kind he used for fishing, only it was smaller. Dog started out ahead with his nose to the ground, seeking the hiding place of Porcupine. Man followed close behind. When they found the hole where Porcupine was hiding, Man spread out the net on the ground around the hole. He fastened it all around the edges with heavy sticks and stones that Porcupine couldn't get away from it. They waited in the nearby bushes to see what would happen. When Porcupine came out of his hiding place, he found that he was securely caught in the net.

Both Man and Dog were satisfied, and Man had a good meal.

If you make a debt with someone, he will hunt you and keep hunting you until he finds you.

Debt kills love and friendship.[4]

The Nkundo often says that if he borrows from a friend, that person is no longer his friend because debts do not mix with friendships; on many occasions, Mrs. Ross has heard an Nkundo say, "If I lend you money, I will not see you again. If you see me coming, you will go another way in order to avoid me. I prefer to keep you as my friend." As is suggested in Tale 86, indebtedness constitutes a kind of slavery too burdensome to bear.

The present tale reflects the Nkundo cultural stricture against lending and borrowing, with the "teaching" made more acceptable by the drama's being played out by animals. Neither animal would, in the natural world, have any need for "money." The element of revenge is apparent in the Ross-collected tale: the dog is satisfied with the outcome of the action, even though he has not recovered his money.

In Lambrecht's tale type 1082, the hawk refuses to repay the loan made by the frog. The frog is aided by his old aunt in recovering the money: through deception, the frog succeeds in being carried to the hawk's nest and obtaining his money; by hiding in the hawk's gamebag he manages to return safely to the ground. In Arewa's tale type 762, the chicken's inability to find and return the razor borrowed from the hawk accounts for the hawk's practice of preying on "chicken's children"; this tale type does not involve the borrowing of *money*, a distinctive feature of the Ross-collected tale and of Lambrecht's tale type 1082.

In an unindexed tale found in Weeks' *Congo Life and Folklore* (pp. 371–373), "How the Fowl Evaded His Debt," the leopard lent money to the fowl, who on being solicited for repayment had his slaves dupe the leopard into having his head cut off in order that it "be combed and cleaned"; in this version, the creditor loses not only his loan but his life. In the same volume (pp. 419–421), in "How the Frog Collected His Debt from the Hawk," the hawk borrowed one thousand brass rods (the equivalent of money) from the frog and failed for six months to repay his creditor on the assumption that the frog, having "neither feathers nor wings," would be unable to collect on the debt; the frog, concealing himself on market day in the satchel of saucepans bought by the hawk, had himself carried to the hawk's nest, where he demanded and received the payment due, and—subsequently concealing himself once more in the satchel—was carried safely to market, where he told the astounded hawk, "Well, I came by the road by which I travelled" (p. 421).

Though each of the indexed and unindexed tales cited above resembles the field-collected tale in the matter of an animal's refusal to repay a loan and the creditor's effort to collect on the loan, none seems sufficiently close to the present tale to afford assistance in assigning a tale-type number to it.

Motifs:

T	A2241.	Animal characteristics: borrowing and not returning.
C	C549.+.**.	Tabu: borrowing and failing to return someone else's property.
T	K231.	Debtor refuses to pay his debt.
T	K232.	Refusal to return borrowed goods.
T	K515.	Escape by hiding.
T	R311.1.**.	Hole in root of tree as refuge.
T	J670.**.	Forethought in defences against others: porcupine hides from his creditor, the dog.

T B560.**. Animals advise men: dog leads man to concealed porcupine.
T J1020.**. Strength in unity: dog and man cooperate to capture and kill
porcupine.
C Q270.+. Cheating punished.
C Q380.+. Breaking tabu punished.
T Q411.13.**. Death as punishment for failure to return borrowed goods.

1. The narrator could not explain why the porcupine would need money; he was willing to accept the suggestion that it might have been needed to purchase food. He was much more interested in the problem of borrowing and not repaying than he was in the occasion prompting the loan.

2. Among the Nkundo, hunting is more often than not a cooperative venture, partly because the forest is dangerous for an unaccompanied hunter and partly because group hunting methods are more productive than are those of a single hunter. Here, each one will gain something suitable and more accessible through united effort than through solitary labor.

3. The narrator explained, on questioning, that the vine used was *ngóji*, flexible and durable as well as readily available in the rain forest.

4. The narrator also furnished a second proverb, one that, with other connotations, he had used several times before: "Join two incompatibles—the relationship is uncertain."

Narrator:	Bofaya Efalaiso, an elderly woman
Location:	Boende, but narrator came previously from Ekoto
Date:	October 1973

32. *The Wise and Foolish Antelopes*

Once there were two small brown antelopes who were good friends. One was a very wise antelope and the other was a very foolish one with no wisdom at all. The foolish antelope had a gourd[1] of his own. One day when he was going to his garden, the wise antelope asked if he could borrow the gourd so that he could go to the river and get water. While he was there, the water rushed up and grabbed the gourd and carried it on down the river.

He went back home calling, "Friend, friend. Your gourd was taken by the current and carried down river."[2]

"Oh, no! I want my gourd. Go and get my gourd."

"I can't get your gourd. It is gone. However, I will bring you one that is as good as yours."

"No, no! I don't want another gourd. I want my very own gourd."

After a while, the wise antelope knew that he had better hunt the very gourd that had been lost. He got a canoe and started down river. He went and went.

All along the way, people called greetings to him. "Are you there? Where are you going?"[3]

"I'm hunting my friend's gourd."

"Go well."

He went and went.

"Where are you going?"

"I'm hunting my friend's gourd."

"Go well."

He went and went. After a while, he passed a hut where a very old man lived. The old man called, "Come, come! Come here! Where are you going?"

"My friend had a gourd. I took it to get water, and the river carried it away. I don't know where it is, but I am trying to find it. I need it, need it, need it. I'm hunting, hunting, hunting."

"If you will stay here and help me, I'll tell you how to find it. Wait! Wait! Wait! I'll help you find the right way of the two."[4]

So the wise antelope cleaned the old man's garden, he cleaned his house, he picked the bugs out of his hair,[5] washed his clothes and washed him.[6] He slept there, and slept there, and slept there. Then the old man told him, "Go down this road. You will come to a fork in the road and will see that one is a wide road and one is narrow. You are to go down the narrow path."

So the wise antelope left the old man and started down the path. Soon he came to the division of the two roads. He went down the narrow path and soon met some people.

"Where are you going?"

"I'm hunting my gourd. It belongs to my friend. I took it to the river to get water and the river carried it away."

"Sit a bit."[7]

So he sat down, and soon they brought the gourd to him. The

wise antelope went home and returned the gourd to the foolish antelope.

"How did you find it? I didn't think you could."

Soon the wise antelope found that the foolish antelope had taken a certain food called eggplant[8] from his garden. "I want the eggplant which you took."

"But I ate it. I'll get you some other."

"No, no! I must have that one. I returned your gourd. You must return my eggplant."[9]

Finally the foolish antelope started off in a canoe. He went on down the river, but refused to greet anyone or talk with anyone. He landed near the old man and started down the road. Since he had not asked for help, when he came to the division of the road he chose the wide road.

As he went along this road he met some people. "Where are you going?"

"I ate some eggplant from my friend's garden and he wants it. I am hunting it."

"You want your eggplant?"

"Yes. That's right."

They didn't like his looks or his story, so they killed him.[10]

Inclusion in this narrative of such expressions as "the water rushed up and grabbed the gourd," "the very gourd that had been lost," and "Go well" preserves the flavor of Lonkundo diction. The extensive employment of dialogue without identification of the speaker provides excellent internal evidence of the narrator's effective use of mime and gesture throughout the telling of the tale, in effect a mini-drama.

In Bofaya's tale, as in a number of others in the Nkundo oral tradition, the sacredness of ownership is stressed. A number of "ownership" tales employ a human cast of characters (see, for example, Tale 86). Fully as often, such tales employ animal characters endowed with human traits and imbued with the Nkundo value system to vent safely strong feelings concerning ownership. In both tales mentioned, as well as in Tales 84 and 85, the narrators' theme appears to be one of sound judgment in claims of individual ownership.

Lambrecht's tale type 3590 (3) provides the most satisfactory classification for this tale. Lambrecht's sample narrative tells of a poor boy who loses in the river the calabash of a rich boy. After helping an old lady, he is able to find the lost calabash. When the rich boy eats the food of the poor one and is sent to replace the food eaten, he encounters the old lady, refuses to help her, and, as a consequence of her unoffered advice about the right path, is killed.

Motifs:

T	N350.	Accidental loss of property.
C	C680.+.**.	Injunction: borrower must return to owner the exact object borrowed and lost.
C	C549.+.**.	Tabu: losing anyone else's property.
C	H1220.1.+.	Quest undertaken to pay debt.
T	H1219.**.	Quest: recovery of borrowed and lost gourd.
T	H1132.	Task: recovering lost objects.
T	B443.2.	Helpful antelope.
T	N825.2.	Old man helper.
T	Q40.	Kindness rewarded.
T	J151.	Wisdom from old person.
C	C680.+.**.	Injunction: do not take the wide path; take the narrow path.
T	J1511.	A rule must work both ways.
T	H1219.**.	Quest: recovery of eaten eggplant.
T	Q338.	Immoderate request punished.
T	Q2.	Kind and unkind.

1. A common sight in the Cuvette is a spread-out vine with gourds, planted and nourished by the women in their gardens. Gourds are commonly used for carrying water from the river or swamp to the house, as well as for transporting drinking water while traveling.

2. The narrator cried out this message loudly and with great anxiety.

3. Among the Nkundo, to omit response to a greeting is to commit a breach of etiquette. Normally, "Stay well" would follow "Go well."

4. Age is greatly respected, even venerated. It is not at all unusual that the antelope stopped and cared for the old man, even to the extent of tending his garden (apparently there were no women in the family to do this kind of work). The old man made a bargain with the antelope and had no question but that he could fulfill his part of that bargain; an exchange of service for service is as old as oral tradition.

The Wise Old Man is a widely recognized archetype (see *Collected Works of C. G. Jung*, IX, i, pp. 207–254); for other instances of The Wise Old Man, or Wise Old Counselor (often a woman instead of a man), see Tales 84 and 85.

5. It is considered a kindness to pick bugs (usually lice) out of someone else's hair; not uncommonly, pupils remain after school to provide this kind of service for the teacher. This courteous practice is by no means limited to Zaïre, or, for that matter, to Africa.

6. In Tale 84, the first woman stopped along the way to bathe and clean an elderly person. In the present tale, the wise antelope renders the same service. In each instance, the one who stopped to render aid succeeded in the task ahead.

7. They had to fulfill all the host's obligations of courtesy before they could bring the gourd to the antelope. No mention is made of bringing food and drink, but very probably that was part of the courtesy extended.

8. Among the nonnative vegetables now grown by the Nkundo is the *nsolo*, or eggplant (occasionally called egg-fruit); its value as a food is suggested by the

frequency with which its ownership is a matter of dispute in the tales of the Ross collection.

9. How either antelope thought that the already eaten and digested eggplant could be found and returned is not a matter of concern to the narrator. In this instance, as well as in the demand for the return of a specific scarring needle (in Tales 84 and 85), the motivation appears to be spite, or vengeance, as suggested on page 56 of Bremond's "'The Impossible Restitution' as a Specifically African Theme" (*Conch* [September 1970], pp. 54–58).

For a penetrating discussion of this theme and a comparison of Aarne-Thompson's tale type 480 with five African samples, Bremond's aforementioned article is unparalleled. We suspect, however, that a broader sampling of African tales is needed than the author has furnished in support of his comment that "since the objects involved are simply ordinary examples of a type, without any magical power or particular characteristics, a properly-understood social egoism would be completely satisfied by the substitution of an object functionally equivalent to the lost one [.]"

10. By Western standards, the ending is abrupt. Quite obviously, the Nkundo narrator felt that the action of the hosts was both reasonable and well justified, and that the audience would find the conclusion acceptable.

Narrator:	Bomponge Joseph
Location:	Tondo, but narrator's home was in Besenge, near Kalamba
Date:	June 1973

33. *Quick Wit Saves the Antelope from the Leopard*

A certain man went into the forest to cut some palm leaves. He cut leaves and cut leaves, and stacked them one upon another until he had a large package of them.

While he was cutting palm leaves, a dwarf antelope came running with much speed through the forest and hid in the midst of the cut palm leaves. The antelope ran into the midst of the palm leaves.[1] As soon as the antelope was out of sight, a leopard came into the place.

The leopard asked the man, "Have you seen my antelope?"

The man didn't give him a direct answer, but told him a parable. He said and he said that, "Antelope has ears; Leopard has eyes. This stacked bunch of palm leaves is not large enough for both of them."

The antelope heard what the man had said and stuck his head out of the palm leaves. "The way that man talks makes good sense.[2] Antelope has ears; Leopard has eyes. The stack of palm leaves is not large enough for both of them."

The antelope saw his chance and ran, running, *pao*,[3] into the forest.

As soon as the leopard realized what had happened, he ran after the antelope. Even though he followed him and followed him, the leopard never did catch up with the antelope.

The narrator used in his title for this tale—"The Parable of the Antelope and the Leopard"—the Lonkundo word translated "parable." This narrative is not really a parable as the word is used in English; it involves more nearly a play on words. The antelope readily understands the application of the man's words and takes prompt advantage of the fact that the leopard is slow in comprehending their meaning. The leopard's slow-wittedness gives the antelope sufficient time to make his escape; still, the leopard cannot accuse the man of failing to assist him in his pursuit of the antelope. By his veiled remark, the man has saved both the antelope and himself.

Arewa's tale types 2086 (1) and 2086 (2), in both of which the hare escapes from the lion by being thrown from a tree (or lowered from a tree) in a bundle of straw, accommodate a portion of this tale, though both are lengthier and more complex in incidents than is the present narrative. The word-play element involved in the Ross-collected tale has not been identified in a pursuit-and-escape pattern in any of the indexes consulted.

An unindexed variant of this tale furnishes one episode in an Nkundo narrative supplied both in Lonkundo and in Flemish by A. de Rop (. . . *woordkunst* . . . , pp. 254–258; the episode is found in Flemish on p. 257) titled "The Leopard, the Dwarf Antelope, and the Forest Rat." In the de Rop variant, attributed to P. Bokanga, the fleeing dwarf antelope encounters a man cutting *nkosa* stems and piling them into a basket. The dwarf antelope, crawling into the basket with his feet protruding to resemble *nkosa* stems, heeds the man's answer to the leopard's question ("The dwarf antelope has ears; the leopard has eyes; my bundle of *nkosa* has gotten so thick!") and, leaping out of the basket, escapes from the leopard. De Rop's version deserves more extended analysis than we can furnish here: it involves at least six distinctly different motifs in the Thompson *Index* alone, as well as incorporating a *pourquoi* element as a tag ending. Most of the motifs present in this tale have been collected in the field either as separate narrative foci or within more fully developed narratives with quite different emphases. The question naturally arises as to whether a narrator's acquaintance with the Bokanga/de Rop version provided the impetus for at least this one of the Ross-collected tales or whether, on the other hand, the form provided in ... *woordkunst* ... is, instead, the creation of Bokanga from a wealth of oral bits here joined to prolong suspense and sustain audience interest.

Motifs:

T	J830.	Adaptability to overpowering force.
T	K515.	Escape by hiding.
T	K521.**.	Escape by disguise: antelope escapes leopard by hiding in pile of cut palm leaves.
A	K1800.1.**.	Hiding so only the bulk (mass) of the body shows.
T	J80.**.	Wisdom taught by play on words.
T	J1250.	Clever verbal retorts—general.
T	J1050.	Attention to warnings.
T	J670.**.	Forethought in defences against others: dwarf antelope profits from man's hint and leaves inadequate refuge before detection by pursuing leopard.
T	W200.**.	Cleverness: dwarf antelope pursued by leopard discerns warning by man and leaves inadequate concealment.
T	L390.	Triumph of the weak—miscellaneous.
T	B390.**.	Antelope grateful for man's assistance in escape.
T	J570.	Wisdom of deliberation.

1. The *mpete* leaves in which the antelope hid come from a certain type of palm that grows well back in the rain forest, often in a swamp. The fronds are longer and wider than most palm fronds and are used for thatching roofs both in the villages and in some urban areas.

2. The narrator said, literally, "The way that man talks is like a man talking," equally well expressed in "The way that man talks makes good sense."

3. The construction "ran, running" is a traditional Lonkundo locution. The addition of *pao* here was a dramatic touch keenly relished by the narrator; actually, "*pao*" is too heavy a sound to suggest an antelope's running.

Narrator: Lontomba Samuel
Location: Tondo
Date: July 1973

34.   The Marriage of the Antelope and the Leopard[1]

Nkulupa (Antelope) was one day working in the forest.[2] Suddenly she happened to work near a big and large deep hole that has been dug by man, the hunters. In the bottom of this hole, Leopard was there. He had fallen in this big hole.[3] He couldn't get out. When Leopard saw Antelope, he asked her if she could help him to get out. Antelope disagreed because she knew that if Leopard got out of the hole, he might decide to eat her.[4] But Leopard said, "Please, go cut a big string—big rope—and try to help to pull me out. And since you are a female antelope, I will not eat you, but I will marry you."

So Antelope at the end agreed. She went and cut a big long rope[5] and threw it where Leopard had fallen, and she pulled him out of the hole. Leopard was very thankful to Antelope, and he told her that they were to be married together. They were married.

Before not too long a time, Antelope became pregnant, and the children in the womb grew and grew. As the time of delivery was nearing, these small babies in Antelope, children, started singing. They were singing inside of their mother's womb, and the song was like this:

> Our father Leopard has very bad eyes.
> His eyes are meagre.
> His eyes look like he was very hungry.

When Leopard heard this, he told his wife Antelope that, "I love you so much, but I *hate* your children. I *hate* the children that are in your womb."

So the next day the children started again to sing:

> Our father Leopard[6]

So the leopard got a good excuse. He said, "Well, I loved you, but the children in your womb don't like me, so I am going to kill you."

So Leopard went on and killed Antelope and ate her.

Here, Leopard had tried to find an excuse to eat this animal, his wife.

When you are a bad person and you have a bad feeling against someone, whether you pretend to love him, you will always try to get something that can put you in conflict. Love between Leopard and Antelope was not a real love. They were married because Leopard pretended to love Antelope. But when his need to kill Antelope and to eat her grew worse, Leopard ate Antelope.

As is true with others of the tales told by Lontomba Samuel, this narrative is intended to teach something to the listeners. Since Sam had only the tape recorder as an audience, we are unable to determine whether or not the song summarized here is customarily provided by the narrator and a chorus rather than by the narrator alone, as Sam was impelled to provide it; we judge, however, that in the light of his handling of the song for Tale 81 (see note 10 for that tale) the song in the present tale would not be presented antiphonally. It *was sung*, and considerable animation was present in the telling; apparently the narrator envisioned the wider audience that the tale was meant to reach. The challenge of telling the tale in English, not his native tongue, doubtless caused some loss of flavor in the telling: the reduced use of dialogue is a case in point.

Again, an animal cast of characters plays out a central Nkundo concern, this time the aura of distrust that surrounds the relationships between husband and wife in Nkundo culture. Among the Nkundo, the blood tie is far stronger than the marriage bond; in the present tale, even the consanguineal tie is insufficiently strong to overcome the leopard's appetite for antelope meat. Quite apart from its concern with trust in one's marriage partner, the tale points up the Nkundo's strong feeling against ingratitude.

In none of the indexes consulted have we found a tale-type number even remotely suitable for this tale. Klipple's 48 African versions of Aarne-Thompson's tale type 155 and Arewa's and Lambrecht's samples for tale type 2751 (based on Aarne-Thompson's tale type 155) in most instances involve the use of an arbitrator rather than an assistant in revenge; none of them includes a marriage between rescuer and rescued. Klipple's second Kweli variant ("Leopard und Antilope") includes an antelope which frees a leopard and is killed by the leopard but eaten by the snake that had confined the leopard; there is neither judge nor marriage in the tale. Of Klipple's versions of Aarne-Thompson's tale type 155, eleven appear also among the variants cited by Arewa for his tale type 2751; none of the Klipple versions appears in Lambrecht's index. (Lambrecht's index does include versions drawn from Stappers, de Bouveignes, and Badibanga, sources significant for the present study but either not yet published or not available to Klipple.)

Motifs:

T	K735.	Capture in pitfall.
C	M246.+.**.	Leopard promises he will do antelope no harm if antelope will help him out of pitfall.
T	B443.2.**.	Helpful antelope: pulls leopard out of pit trap.
C	M268.+.**.	Antelope rescues leopard from pitfall on promise of marriage.
T	B364.1.	Animal grateful for rescue from trap (pitfall).
C	J2199.+.**.	Antelope helps leopard out of pit, is shortly thereafter eaten on flimsy pretext.
C	U120.+.**.	Antelope rescues leopard from pitfall, is shortly thereafter eaten on flimsy pretext.
T	T100.	Marriage.
T	B280.**.	Animal weddings (leopard and antelope).
C	B282.+.**.	Animal marriage: leopard and antelope.
C	T230.+.**.	Faithful wife, unfaithful husband (antelope and leopard).
T	K2010.**.	Hypocrite husband (leopard) pretends love but attacks wife (antelope).
T	W154.2.1.**.	Rescued animal later threatens rescuer, and eats her and their unborn children.
C	M340.5.+.**.	Children in womb warn of danger from father (leopard).
C	T299.+.**.	Husband (leopard) kills and eats wife (antelope) because unborn children speaking from womb distrust him.
T	S11.	Cruel father (leopard).
C	S62.+.**.	Father (leopard) slays wife (antelope) because unborn children distrust him.
T	S302.**.	Unborn children murdered by father (leopard).
T	Q2.	Kind and unkind.
L	Q382.	Punishment for helping.
L	H1292.12.	What is food for leopard.
L	A2435.3.9.	Food of leopard.

1. [Narrator's explanatory introduction: "The next story is about two animals. These are the leopard and the antelope. This antelope is a special kind called *Nkulupa*."]

2. [Narrator's explanatory comment: "It was a female Nkulupa."]

3. A pit trap, apparently not furnished with sharpened stakes at the bottom to impale the prey.

4. [Narrator's explanatory comment: "The leopard is an animal that eats the other animals."]

5. The "rope" used was *ngòji*, the term used here by the narrator. All of Mrs. Ross's translation assistants had trouble arriving at what they considered a satisfactory English equivalent of "*ngòji*."

6. Leopard interrupts the unborn children's song here.

Narrator:	Lontomba Samuel
Location:	Tondo
Date:	July 1973

35. *The Contest between the Turtle and the Ground Rat*[1]

One day this rat which we call *Montomba* (Ground Rat) found a big field. He cut the big trees. It was a really large field.[2]

Ground Rat cut down the trees, and the time came when the field was ready to be burned. He called all his friends—men, animals, and everybody in his home town. He told them, "You will see how I burn my field. There is magic in burning my field. Come and see."

Many people came. They were anxious to see this new method of burning a field.

Ground Rat took a torch of fire and started burning in one end of the field. He went around the whole field with the fire. He burned all the edges while keeping himself in the middle. The fire surrounded him. Everybody was wondering where he would be getting out.

The fire became very high—flaming all over. The people began to shout, "Ground Rat is going to die! Ground Rat is going to die! The fire has surrounded him, and the flames are near him."

Ground Rat had a hole. As the fire was nearing him, he got in his hole, and the fire cooked the place where he had been standing.

Everybody shouted, "Oh! Ground Rat is dead! Ground Rat is dead! He is burned up."

When they were shouting around, they heard a voice in the forest, "My friends! Let's go! I am here."

Everybody was very surprised. They said, "*Ho!* He is standing there. He is not in the fire."

But Ground Rat, when the fire was near him, had to go into the tunnel that he had dug and come out the other opening.

His friend Ulu (Turtle) was there, too. He was very surprised. He looked at him and said, "Gee![3] This is very serious. This is very amazing. I am going to cut my field, and I will do the same thing."

So Turtle cut down his big field. He waited until it had dried. When he was ready to set the blaze, he called two friends. "Let's go to see me. I will burn my field in the miraculous way."

People gathered around as the turtle was getting ready to set the whole field ablaze. He surrounded himself with fire. The fire started to smoke. A big flame was approaching him with smoke and a big wind. Turtle was surrounded by the fire. Turtle began to get hot. He began to wonder about the way he was going to pass.

He asked himself, "How did Ground Rat get out of here?"[4]

The fire came nearer and nearer. Turtle didn't know where to go. At the end, the people saw Turtle was burned. He was completely burned, and died because he didn't know. He didn't have a tunnel; he didn't have holes to run away in. He did that to try to imitate what Ground Rat had done, but he didn't understand why Ground Rat could do so. He died.[5]

The moral application is that we shouldn't do things because our friends have done them. We don't know what is behind them or what power they have.

That's the end.

This tale falls among the group of narratives told in Tondo which Lontomba Samuel himself classified as "tales that teach or have a moral application." As a teacher himself, Sam would be likely to have a substantial number of such tales in his own repertory; quite apart from their usefulness to children and young people, these tales have a continuing appeal to adult Nkundo and other Bantu-speaking peoples: at the expense of vain or foolish animal characters, adult listeners can be reminded of truths that have application at all ages and to all conditions of life. Lontomba Samuel overlooked no opportunity to heighten excitement and suspense: his use of dialogue, both spoken and shouted, enlivened the telling of this patently moralistic tale.

Unlike the trickster tales in this volume, the present tale does not pit a trickster against a dupe; instead, the conceit of Turtle leads him into a fatal imitation. Tales of fatal imitation occur in most of the collections of Zaïrian tales examined. De Bouveignes' volumes include a substantial sampling (more useful for content than for genuine oral-narrative style), among which our personal favorite is found in *En écoutant conter les noirs*—a witty tale in which the cock, having claimed that he could do anything a duck could do, found swimming a trick he could not master and paid for his vanity with his life. Stappers in *Textes Luba* . . . and Mamet in *La Langage des Bolia* offer further samples of this Zaïrian staple of oral art.

Lambrecht's tale type 1462A offers the closest parallel to the present tale in that one character (the mongoose) is able to escape from the fire with his life, whereas the partridge, lacking a burrow, is burned to death. The tale cited by Lambrecht, however, carries the narrative beyond the death of the imitator: the mongoose, in serving the young partridges the cooked flesh of their father, incurs their wrath and, tempted into an imitation of their "headless" state, has his head cut off so that he, too, can dance to the music of their flutes.

Motifs:

T   J2413.   Fatal imitation by an animal.
T   J512.   Animal should not try to change his nature.
T   J2300.   Gullible fools.

1. [Narrator's introduction to tale: "This story is about two animals, a turtle and a kind of ground rat. This rat is a rat that digs a hole in the ground, and then digs a tunnel and comes out in another opening."]

2. [Narrator's explanatory material: "As they do in this area, they wait until all the leaves and the trees that have been cut down get dry. Then people will go and set fire so that this field can be burnt."]

3. An expression probably adopted during his study in the United States. In his own language, Sam would use "*Mo!*" or "*Ho!*"

4. Turtle's anxiety is vividly suggested here in the narrator's voice and animation.

5. Again, the perplexity and distress of Turtle and the finality of his experiment are conveyed by the narrator's tone and inflections.

Narrator:	Bakonga Bolingo
Location:	Ilongo-Kindo
Date:	November 1973

36.   *The Race*

The tortoise and the antelope challenged each other to have a race. They planned their course and arranged to meet at a certain spot the next morning. The tortoise arranged to have other members of his family along the course of the race so that the antelope would see them along the way. The course was long and difficult, and the antelope became so tired that he couldn't quite make it. As a result, the tortoise who was waiting nearby was able to cross the line and win the race.

He who is swift does not win; he wins who has patience and wisdom.[1]

Both the speech patterns and the vocabulary of Bakonga Bolingo presented decided difficulties for Mrs. Ross and her translation assistant Tata Itofi. Our repeated listenings to the taped tale have confirmed our suspicion that this translation was a considerably truncated version of the tale actually told, and that it fails to convey the animation, the dialogue, and the pacing with which the storyteller initially delivered it. (Its brevity alone is insufficient to mark it as an inadequate translation: Botsang Mosienyane has told Barbara K. Walker that the Setswana-language version of the same tale currently told in Botswana is as spare as the present narrative.) Someone thoroughly familiar with the dialect spoken at Ilongo-Kindo, the site of this tale-telling, might well be able so to extract the narrative from the tape that it would do greater justice both to the tale and to its narrator.

It had seemed to us unlikely that a tale—even a fable—so telescoped, so shorn of the repetition and onomatopoeia and other stylistic features found in the bulk of the Zaïrian tales in the Ross collection, would have lasted in the oral tradition in its present form. The challenge must normally have greater dramatic impact, the course of the race must be more fully described, the plotting of the wily tortoise with his family members must receive more attention, and the outcome of this "uneven" race must be handled by an accomplished storyteller with more finesse than the present translation suggests. Our function here, however, was not to rewrite, or retell, but to transliterate and then explicate, so we have left the tale in the form in which Lonkundo-speaking translators were able to deliver it from its dialectal original. Presence of even this skeletal version confirms our supposition that the race-won-by-deception narrative is still present among the Nkundo, though the dramatis personae may differ from one version to another; see note 1 for a form of the tale current among the Nkundo in the Cuvette at the time of the compilation of the Lonkundo school reader *Bekolo Bèmò.* . . .

Aarne-Thompson's tale type 1074 provides the basic classification for this tale. Arewa's tale type 1157 (2), pitting the hawk against the turtle, and his 1157 (5), pitting a man against a tortoise, are also helpful, with 1157 (2) the better choice because the race thus classified is run purely as a contest, with no reward or stake, and the conclusion is drawn that the turtle through her wisdom was able to win the race. Of Lambrecht's variants for the basic type, the most useful for the present narrative is tale type 1157 (8), in which the antelope and the turtle race solely as a contest, the turtle's relatives are used, and the conclusion drawn is that of the two characteristics—intelligence and strength—the former is the more important.

Klipple cites more than twenty African variants of Aarne-Thompson's tale type 1074 in which the tortoise, pitted against an antelope or an antelopelike animal in a race, wins by stationing his or her relatives en route to deceive the competitor; additional variants cited utilize companions rather than relatives, furnish a protagonist other than the tortoise, or employ stratagems of somewhat different kinds to allow wit to overcome speed. In all, 39 versions of the basic type are supplied by Klipple.

Mamet's "L'antilope et la tortue (fable)," included on pages 80–81 of his *Le Langage des Bolia* and cited by Lambrecht for her tale type 1157 (8), deserves close examination here in terms of what it reveals of the translator's handling in French of an African-language tale. Although the Lia are also Zaïrians, their language—Bolia—is unlike Lonkundo, so we cannot determine how true the French translation is to the original diction. But the lengths of the two versions are approximately equal, and the French is direct and unelaborate; the preliminary "A certain day" is common in Zaïrian storytelling; the inclusion of traditional greetings is a widely found feature; the liveliness and mime of an oral telling are indicated by the dialogue, the questions and exclamations, and the frequent use of dashes, suggesting the response of a storyteller to the interest and enthusiasm of his listeners. We suspect that an equally lively version of "The Race" is within the repertory of more than one Nkundo narrator, and indeed might be present in Bakonga Bolingo's own telling of "The Race," furnished here in rather sterile and wooden translation because of language gaps. The Bolia translation's closing statement, "*L'intelligence et la force, ce qui compte: l'intelligence*," or a close local form of it characterizes most examples of this fable that we have found, whether sketchily or more elaborately told.

An interesting turn on the "tired antelope" conclusion is apparent in Brazil. The children's magazine *Sesinho* (December 1959, pp. 10–12) carried a retelling of the antelope's race against the tortoise in which the antelope feigned a fainting spell soon after the start of the race; the tortoise's relatives came out of hiding to see what was the matter, and the tortoise's deception was thus revealed. The moral following the Brazilian version suggested that deceit could not be forever hidden. Whether this new twist in a narrative already well explored was actually found in the Brazilian oral tradition or whether it was, in fact, an invention by the reteller (unidentified) is open to debate; in either case, the basic tale was being used through print in order to *teach*, an updating in medium but not in function of oral narrative.

Motifs:

T	J1117.	Animal as trickster.
T	K11.1.	Race won by deception: relative helpers.
T	B491.5.	Helpful turtle(s) (tortoise[s]).
T	H970.	Help in performing tasks.
T	K1840.	Deception by substitution.
T	K1000.	Deception into self-injury.
L	K96.	Awe-incurring contest won by deception.

1. The tale in *Bekolo Bèmó* . . . (pp. 42–43) titled by the compilers "Likokolo la Likolo" ("The Butterfly and the Snail") affords an interesting contrast to the spare telling of the present tale. It follows as Tale 36A.

Source: Bekolo Bèmò . . .
             Zaïrian school reader
             (in Lonkundo)
Translator: Mabel Ross
Date: April 1977

36A. *The Butterfly and the Snail*

The butterfly and the snail contended about the way of traveling in the mornings. The butterfly tormented the snail, tormenting.

He said, "You, Snail, you do not have legs, you do not have wings for flying quickly as I do. How does your journey succeed?" He teased the snail, teasing. "I go out in the morning early. I will arrive at a place; you will not have yet awakened from sleep."

The snail answered that, "Let us contend. We will contend from one place. We shall stop here. If you go to a place upstream, I will go to a place downstream. We will sleep in places that are there. The forests are equal. Let us go in the morning to measure the trip for our mornings. He who arrives here first is the winner."

The butterfly crossed the forest and slept in the village where he had promised. In the morning when the sun rose, he departed. He flew, flying, that he arrive where they had argued before the snail.

But the snail had finished arriving first. He did not know that the snail did not go a long way, *nyè*. The snail had hidden in the forest. He went slowly, slowly, all night and arrived first.

The butterfly was surprised and said, "Click-click! You, no legs, you, no feet, you arrive slyly."

None of the variants that we have encountered offers a parallel to the *Bekolo Bèmò* . . . narrative; in this tale, no helpers other than the snail's own wit and persistence aid him in winning the race.

The term "measure" used by the snail is not intended to suggest "scout" or "measure off" as a preliminary to the race; it applies to the snail's own method of forward motion, and might be interpreted either as "make" or "compare."

The Lonkundo sound "*Liko-liko!*" here translated "Click-click!" is an ideophone suggesting both disbelief and disapproval; it resembles the sound of a gun trigger or the cracking of one's knuckles.

Narrator: Ngoi Ekoletonga,
              a village elder
Location: Longa
Date: December 7, 1972

37. The Tortoise Tricks an Elephant and a Hippopotamus[1]

On another day Ulu (Tortoise) went to Ngubu (Hippopotamus) and said, "In one minute's time I can beat you in a pulling contest even though you are large and I am small." Hippopotamus agreed to the contest, to be held at any time Tortoise wished it.

Then Tortoise went to Njòku (Elephant) and said, "In one minute I can beat you in a pulling contest even though you are large and I am small." Elephant agreed to the contest, to be held at any time Tortoise wished it.

Not too long after that, Hippopotamus saw Tortoise near the river bank. He called to him,[2] "I am ready for our competition. Come. Let us have a pulling contest, the two of us together. Let me show you how strong I am."

"Very well. I will go and find some rope[3] and we will contend together."[4]

In not a long time, Elephant saw Tortoise on the path and called to him, "I am ready for our competition. Come. Let us have a pulling contest, the two of us together. Let me show you how strong I am."

"Very well. I will go and find some rope. I will return very soon and tie it to your leg. Then I will show you that you aren't so strong."

So Tortoise went for the rope. He tied one end of it to the leg of Elephant. "I will go into the forest,"[5] he said. "When I am ready, I will call out to you. It will take me only a minute to pull you along the path."

Then Tortoise took the other end of the rope and tied it around the leg of Hippopotamus. Then he said to him, "I will go into the forest. I am ready to show you that I can pull you out of the river quickly. When I call, you begin to pull."

Tortoise went into the bushes so that he could watch the contest.[6] Then he called loudly, "I am ready to pull." Hippopotamus pulled and pulled. Elephant pulled and pulled. After not a short time and much pulling, they saw that neither was winning. Each one thought that Tortoise was very strong indeed, and each conceded the contest to Tortoise.

Peace doesn't last long with three people.[7]

It is not surprising that this widely distributed tale should appear among those collected by Mrs. Ross. The wiliness of the small, slow tortoise that allows him to trick two much larger animals into conceding the victory to him echoes the Nkundo's own need to use his wits in competing with those other Bantu-speaking tribes and with those white men from the west and north who can determine for him what language he must speak, what medium of exchange he must employ, and what faith he must profess in order to deal with others in a confusing and complex time. Whether or not he succeeds in his own personal struggle for preferment, the Nkundo can "win" with the tortoise in this time-tested yet timely tale.

Aarne-Thompson's tale type 291 provides the basic classification for the tug-of-war narrative; it is the only one we have found applicable to this tale. Arewa equates his tale type 1134 with Aarne-Thompson's 291; in Arewa's single sample, drawn from the Yao tribe, the hare challenges the elephant and the hippopotamus to a tug of war, with each loser to pay a wager, and the hare collects both wagers since each of the larger animals thinks he has lost the contest. Lambrecht equates her tale type 1550 with Aarne-Thompson's 291, and she furnishes two samples for the type, one presumably from the Luba (based on de Bouveignes' *Ce que Content les Noirs* [1934], a volume we were unable to examine) and the other from the Lulua (drawn from Badibanga's *L'Éléphant . . .*, pp. 65–66). The former sample presents the antelope as pitting his two creditors—the elephant and the crocodile—against one another on their assumption that each is pulling the bull the antelope has promised him as payment for his debt; the antelope leaves before the two creditors detect the deception. The second sample, in some ways closer than the first to the Ross-collected tale, presents the mongoose—the trickster in the Luluabourg area—as arranging the tug of war to prove he is stronger than either the elephant or the hippopotamus; in the struggle, both larger creatures die, and the mongoose offers their flesh as a feast for the men who have come to help him build his house. The Badibanga version differs from the present tale in that in the former the dupes die as a result of the pulling; in the Ross-collected tale, the tortoise is seeking ego satisfaction rather than the death of the duped contestants, an accurate reflection of the Nkundo's hope in his own social and economic struggle.

Various unindexed versions of the tug-of-war tale are of interest for comparison's sake; for examples, see Jablow's *Yes and No . . .* (pp. 95–98), Cobble's *Wembi . . .* (pp. 104–107), and Walker and Walker's *Nigerian Folk Tales* (pp. 59–60). Of special interest—especially as evidence that in one form or another the tug-of-war tale has been told among the Nkundo for at least half a century—see Weeks' *Congo*

Life and Folklore ("How the Sparrow Set the Elephant and the Crocodile to Pull Against Each Other"—pp. 39–42).

The dramatis personae may vary somewhat from one tale in its cultural setting to another, but in each instance wit overcomes weight, a reassuring outcome that fills a continuing need among the peoples we have studied. The Ross-collected tale seems well suited to its purpose.

Motifs:

T	J1117.	Animal as trickster.
T	K22.	Deceptive tug-of-war.
T	H1562.**.	Test of strength: pulling, with elephant and hippopotamus pulling against one another, each assuming he is pulling against the tortoise.
T	W200.**.	Cleverness: tortoise pits elephant and hippopotamus against one another in pulling contest and by deception "outpulls" both.
L	K96.	Awe-incurring contest won by deception.

1. [Narrator's introductory comment: "Ngubu is a very large and powerful animal who lives in the river. Njòku is a very large and powerful animal who lives in the forest. Ulu is a small animal who must be clever in order to make up for his lack of strength and lack of size. He very much likes to prove his prowess over the larger animals and often will seek various feats of competition with them."]

2. The expression "He called to him" is ambiguous in the text. Did the hippopotamus call, or did the tortoise call? It is at points like these that mime and vocal mimicry come into use as tools of the master storyteller's trade. The narrator's voice and posture made it clear that the hippopotamus said, "I am ready for our competition." Again, the same tools are used to clarify the ambiguous comment when it appears later in the confrontation with the elephant. In this tale, as in many others in the Ross collection, the narrator omits the name of the speaker because he conveys the speaker's identity by some livelier, more dramatic means. His is both oral art and dramatic literature, made real by body language that is difficult to communicate in print but that stamps the tale indelibly in the minds of his hearers-participators.

3. *Ngòji*, the strong vine used here, has been translated as "rope" rather than "cord" or "string" (all three are valid translations) because of the pull that will be exerted on it. The term "tie-tie" is used in a number of uncited variants we have encountered in the course of our reading.

4. The Lonkundo term "*swela*" ("contend together") can also be rendered "contend in a fight (Tale 51) and "settle this by fighting" (Tale 65).

5. Here the narrator appears to have mistaken the direction in which Tortoise needed to carry the other end of the rope in order to make the contest feasible. "Toward the river" or "to the water" would have been more logical. No protest was made by the listeners, who accepted this slip in sense in the interest of moving on with the tale.

6. Tortoise reflects here the curiosity natural to the Nkundo themselves. With Tortoise, the listeners watch gleefully the progress of the contest, confident of the

outcome. If Mboloko, the dwarf antelope, had been chosen by the narrator as the perpetrator of this hoax—as could easily have happened, since the tortoise and the dwarf antelope are equally popular in the role of "winner by wit"—he, too, would have watched the contest from the bush.

7. The proverb is a most appropriate one in terms of Nkundo society, a reflection in animal hides of the relationships among people. The elephant and the hippopotamus, both very large and of approximately the same strength, get along very well by letting each other alone. But when a third party—no matter how small— comes between them or aligns himself with one of them against the other, there is sure to be trouble. A recognition of the tendency to "take sides" prompts the members of an Nkundo hunting party to build their own separate shelters and to care for their own meat, thus gaining the protection of the group but maintaining sufficient independence of one another to avoid interpersonal friction.

Narrator:	Lontomba Samuel
Location:	Tondo
Date:	July 1973

38.   *The Cock Tricks the Hippopotamus*[1]

One day a cock decided to go and sell a lot of things. He gathered corn, manioc, rice, flour, and all kinds of grains that he could pick up in his yard. He took all those things and put them in a canoe. He took also his wives, chickens, and chicks, and put all of them inside. It was a big load, all those things. He was going to cross the lake to sell them and get a lot of money.

As they were paddling across the lake, they saw a hippopotamus floating in the lake. So when the cock saw the hippopotamus, he jumped out of the bottom of the canoe and went to fish on the top of some of his goods. He pulled one leg up under him so that he was standing on one leg and the other leg was hidden inside his wing. The hippopotamus when he saw the cock yelled at him, "Where are you going with all this wealth? You have many things, many grains in this canoe. How did you manage to get all these things?"

The cock answered, "Oh, it's easy! You see I am standing here with only one leg. What I did was that I cut one of my legs and I sold it to people in our town. And out of this leg I made a lot of money so that I was able to buy all of these things."

The hippopotamus was surprised and shocked. "Is that so?"

The cock said, "Yes. I sold this leg."

"That is an interesting story."

"If you want to become as rich as I am and get a lot of things like this, you should cut your leg off and go and sell it."

"That is wonderful. The cock has a small leg and has much wealth. I have a big leg and should make more money."

So he went to his home town. He asked his brothers and sisters and parents to cut off his leg so he could sell it. But his friends said, "Don't do it. Don't do it. You will die if you do."

"No, no! I have seen the cock with one leg, and he has a lot of things. I am going to cut mine. Mine is larger and heavier. I will sell it and make much money."

They tried to discourage him from doing this, but he didn't like to listen to them. So they agreed and started cutting his leg. As they cut his leg, he felt a lot of pain. He died and didn't make any money.[2]

Tales of small creatures' outwitting or tricking larger, stronger ones are common in Nkundo storytelling, as well as in African oral narrative as a whole. In this instance, the cock appears motivated purely by malice in inflicting injury on one who had given him no offense. The dialogue in the tale was delivered in highly animated fashion, and by a curious coincidence a cock was crowing throughout the telling.

Arewa's tale type 479 is based on a *pourquoi* tale in which a hen tells a hawk that if he cuts off his leg—as the hen pretends to have done—he will have money to buy meat; the hawk follows the hen's advice and, finding he can no longer walk, begins in revenge to hunt hens and chickens. Lambrecht's tale type 1401 C, in which a chicken convinces a wading bird that by cutting off his leg he will have a successful fishing party—advice costing the wading bird his life—offers in the first portion of the tale a reasonably similar situation to that in the Ross-collected tale, but concludes, as does the Arewa sample, as a *pourquoi* tale, a feature not found in Tale 38. All three tales involve a hen (or cock) as the trickster, with the dupe also a fowl; the identity of the dupe and the absence of a *pourquoi* conclusion in the present tale suggest that neither Arewa's nor Lambrecht's classification will serve the Ross narrative.

Motifs:

T	J1117.	Animal as trickster.
T	J2413.4.1.	Fowl makes another animal believe that he has had his leg cut off.
T	J2413.4.	Animal dupe cuts off limb.
T	J652.	Inattention to warnings.
T	K1000.	Deception into self-injury.
T	Q272.	Avarice punished.
T	J230.	Choice: real and apparent values.
T	J2400.	Foolish imitation.
T	J2401.	Fatal imitation.
T	J2413.	Foolish imitation by an animal.
T	K890.	Dupe tricked into killing himself.

1. [Explanatory material: "This next story is a trading story."]

A "trading story" could be expected among an Nkundo narrator's repertory since for generations a number of Nkundo have earned their livings by carrying goods to the nearest market and selling them; the river system in the Cuvette affords convenient transportation for trade goods, and with the increasing movement toward urban centers the need for such goods has grown. Mrs. Ross had asked for a "trading story" with the hope of securing one involving successive better or worse bargains; the narrator, misunderstanding her request, furnished the present tale.

2. [Explanatory material: "He wanted to become rich but he didn't understand how. Some people want to become rich and they do not know how. They need to work harder to become rich. By trying to become rich in one day, we are losing our lives."]

This paragraph does not resemble the customary Nkundo "teaching" following a folktale; it is instead a personal expression of conviction for the narrator, himself a teacher and a hard worker.

Narrator: Bokunge Jacques
Location: Bóléngé
Date: February 1973

39. *The Tortoise Tricks the Leopard and the Crocodile*

On another day, back when the tortoise was a friend of both the leopard and the crocodile, Ulu (Tortoise) went to his friend Nkòi (Leopard) and said to him, "Leopard, kill some meat and give it to me and I will give you a man."

Then Tortoise went to his friend Nkóndè (Crocodile) and said, "Crocodile, catch fish for me and I will give you a man."

Leopard killed much meat and gave it to Tortoise. Crocodile caught many fish and gave them to Tortoise. One day Leopard said to Tortoise, "Tortoise, I have given you much of my meat. Now, when will you bring Man to me?"

Tortoise answered, "Very soon I will bring Man. When you see a creature with large scales on his skin, you will know that this is Man. Seize him, for he is yours."

Very soon after that, Crocodile saw Tortoise and asked him, "I have given you much fish. When will you bring Man to me?"

Tortoise answered, "When you see a creature that has spots all over him, you can be sure this is Man. If he says 'fu-fu-tu' when he speaks, this will indeed be Man. Seize him, for he is yours."

Then Tortoise went back a little way under a tree and watched. Leopard came and Crocodile came. Crocodile saw someone coming who had many spots. He heard him say "fu-fu-tu" and he knew this was Man. Leopard saw the one with the large scales and he knew this was Man. Each seized the other, as Tortoise had told them to do. They fought and fought until neither could fight any more. Both had many serious cuts and injuries. Crocodile went back into the river to nurse his wounds, and died there. Leopard went with his wounds into the forest, and died there. The troubles of each of them were finished completely, *nyé*.

Tortoise could return to his home in peace.

When we secretly plot to pit one person against another, we are like the tortoise with the crocodile and the leopard.[1]

[Notes to Tale 39 follow Tale 40.]

Source: Bekolo Bemo . . .
               Zaïrian school reader
               (in Lonkundo)
Translator: Mabel Ross
Date of Translation: January 1976

40. *The Tortoise Tricks the Leopard and the Crocodile* (Variant)

The tortoise asked the crocodile that he provide fish. He left a promise with the crocodile that he would have a man.

Then the tortoise went to the leopard and asked him that he provide meat. He said to the leopard, "As you give me meat, I will give you a man."

The crocodile caught many fish. He gave fish to the tortoise every day. The leopard spread nets for meat[2] and gave it to the tortoise. The tortoise was very satisfied.[3]

The crocodile became tired of giving fish to the tortoise. He asked him for his man.

The tortoise said to him, "Tomorrow you will find me with another animal who has spots everywhere on his body. You will know that he is your man by the very spots which are there. You catch him."

The leopard was tired of spreading nets to catch meat for the tortoise. He asked him for his man.

The tortoise told him that, "Tomorrow you will find me with a man covered with scales on his body; he is your man. Catch him."

The next day, the crocodile went to the home of the tortoise. He found that he was in the forest. Then the leopard came to hunt his man at the home of the tortoise. He knew that the crocodile who had the scales was his man. And the crocodile knew that the leopard who had the spots was his man.

They fought all day. The leopard said, "You are my man; it is you."

The crocodile said, "No, no, you are my man; it is you."

The two of them left with severe wounds. The crocodile went into the water with the wounds which were the leopard and died there. The leopard went into the forest with the wounds which were the crocodile and died there. But the tortoise lived and did not lack for meat.[4]

Various creatures appear as tricksters in the abundant treasury of wit-vs.-weight, brain-vs.-brawn tales to be found in African oral literature. Among the Nkundo, the tortoise and the dwarf antelope are equally popular among narrators for this choice role; with the Yoruba of Nigeria, the tortoise takes the palm as trickster; in Sierra Leone, as in Ghana and several other West African countries, Spider outtricks the rest (see, for example, Verna Aardema Vugteveen's retelling of "How Spider Sold a Big 'Dog,'" in Walker's *Laughing Together: Giggles and Grins* . . . [1977], p. 63); other small but clever animal tricksters in Africa include the hare and the mongoose (see especially "Le lion, la mangouste et le léopard" in Badibanga's *L'Éléphant* . . . , p. 73, for a variant of these two tales). Whatever animal form the trickster may wear, his play of wit is thoroughly relished, and his continued role in verbal art appears assured.

In Tales 39 and 40, Tortoise—small and slow, but clever—outwits both the crocodile and the leopard. Ostensibly, he seeks food; quite as important as the food, however, is the satisfaction of having duped those larger and stronger than he, the primary source of satisfaction also to Nkundo listeners, themselves considered of small significance in their own country.

Lambrecht's tale type 1553 (1), based on the tale from Badibanga's *L'Éléphant* . . . mentioned above, serves most adequately as the classification for the present pair of tales despite the type's use of the mongoose rather than the tortoise, the promise of a watchdog rather than a man, and the acceptance of payment other than food prior to the receipt of the promised reward. The deceptive bargain in all three instances constitutes the entire tale; in each instance, both dupes are larger and less clever than the trickster; in each case, the dupes are summoned to appear simultaneously to claim their reward; each dupe assumes the other is the promised dog (or man); each dupe leaps on the other to capture the purchased creature; the trickster in each instance escapes unharmed. No tale type *precisely* fits the Ross-furnished tales because no other indexed tale that we have found includes the promise of a man to an animal as food, a feature that adds both humor and dimension to the present tales.

Motifs:

T	J1117.	Animal as trickster.
T	Q91.**.	Reward for cleverness: tortoise gains food from both leopard and crocodile.
T	K1020.	Deception into disastrous attempt to procure food.
T	K2030.	Double dealers.
L	K978.1.2.**.	Leopard and crocodile both sent for the "man."
T	K810.	Fatal deception into trickster's power.
T	K234.	Trickster summons all (both) creditors at once, precipitates fight, and escapes payment.
T	J1750.**.	One animal mistaken for another: leopard and crocodile attack one another, each told by tortoise that the other is his "man."
T	B266.	Animals fight.
T	N338.	Death as result of mistaken identity: wrong person killed.

C   K441.+.**.   Tortoise promises "man" to crocodile and to leopard; both
                        come simultaneously for him.

T   J670.**.   Forethought in defences against others: tortoise abandons scene
                        at moment when crocodile and leopard come to claim the
                        "man" promised to each.

T   K1840.   Deception by substitution.

T   K1000.**.   Deception into self-injury (death).

1. Bokunge Jacques' reference in his "teaching" to the relationships among the characters in the tale (a device used also in Tales 10, 22, 25, 29, and 43, among others) serves to point up another dimension of the proverb as a form of verbal art: it can serve as a kind of oral "shorthand" among those familiar with the tale, to call to memory the tale giving rise to the proverb without the speaker's needing to tell the story.

Postma in her *Tales from the Basotho* (p. 43) uses a proverb in this fashion to suggest a folktale in the common treasury. In the tale "Roaqo, the Woman Who Ate People" (pp. 42–49), the hero, Masilo, is puzzled by the silence and inactivity in a village consisting of many huts. To make vivid Masilo's surprise at the absence of hens and chickens on the ash heaps, the narrator says, "He had never seen an ash heap where the hens and the chicks were not searching for the needle of the hawk, as the old story tells." (The tale to which the proverblike allusion is made appears as "Hen, Hawk, and the Needle" in Postma's *Tales from the Basotho* [pp. 37–41].)

2. In the natural world, the leopard would not "spread nets" in order to catch his prey. This anthropomorphic touch reinforces the assumption that the animals in Nkundo tales are actually disguised Nkundo, playing out their conflicts and concerns with animal dramatis personae.

The "meat" the leopard would be most likely to secure for the tortoise would be drawn from the rodent and the cat families.

3. Among the Nkundo, one must really be *stuffed* to be "satisfied." One of Mrs. Ross's informants expressed the men's eating until their stomachs feel heavy as eating "until they feel pregnant." An Nkundo proverb states, "A man with a heavy stomach is a happy man."

4. The Lonkundo original of this tale, titled "Nkonde l'Ulu la Nkòi," appears on pages 93–94 of *Bekolo Bèmò*. . . .

Another Nkundo tale included in *Bekolo Bèmò* . . . ("Ulu la Eloko la Ngubu" —pp. 85–86) deserves reproduction here because, although it is not close enough to Tale 39 to be labeled "Variant II," it contains much of the dramatic conflict furnished in the present pair of tales, with the added elements of inclusion of an ogre as one of the dupes and of further trickery on the part of the tortoise following the dupes' detection of his deception. The tale follows as Tale 40A.

Source: Bekolo Běmò . . .
             Zaïrian school reader
             (in Lonkundo)
Translator: Mabel Ross
Date: April 1977

40A.   The Tortoise, the Ogre, and the Hippopotamus

The tortoise went to the ogre and said to him, "Give me your man;[1] let me pay that which is required of me."

The ogre said, "Take the man who is sitting in my yard." And the tortoise took the man which the ogre showed him, and carried him to his home.

Then he went again to the hippopotamus and said to him, "Give me a man; let me pay the price." The hippopotamus gave him a man, and he went home with the man which was of the hippopotamus.

The tortoise went to the ogre. He said, "Come on Sunday.[2] If you find a man sitting, he is your man; take him captive." And he went to the hippopotamus. He said, "Come Sunday. If you find a man sitting,[3] he is your man; capture him."

The ogre came on that day, he and the hippopotamus. And the tortoise saw the ogre and he saw the hippopotamus. The ogre came with anger that he capture the hippopotamus, and the hippopotamus came with anger that he capture the ogre, and the two struggled with a very hard battle. The tortoise left. He went to all of the tortoises in his tribe.

The ogre and the hippopotamus stopped their fight. The ogre asked the hippopotamus. He said, "You are not my man which the tortoise purchased?"

And the hippopotamus answered. He said, "I do not suppose that you are my man. It was the tortoise who spurred us on."

Then the two went to hunt the tortoise, and they saw the tribe of tortoises. They said, "The tortoise who took our men out of the way, he must give us our men."

But all of the tortoises said, "You command the tortoise who spoke to you."

But they regarded all the tortoises, and did not know that one who took their men, nyè. And the debt was finished in that manner.

In this literal translation from the Lonkundo, there are a number of puzzling elements, chief among them the presence of an ogre in an animal tale. Too, there appears to be an anticipated trading of "men," none of whom is clearly identified. What payment was made—what price—for the "men" the tortoise received is not indicated, nor do the compilers of the school reader tell what the tortoise did with the "men" he solicited and received. This much is certain: that the tortoise assumed the role of a trickster from the very beginning, playing off one dupe against the other, and that he maintained that role consistently throughout the tale, even to the point of "losing" himself among his relatives and thus making his identity undiscoverable. Despite its puzzling aspects, this trickster tale has a genuinely Nkundo flavor even in the Lonkundo-translated-into-English form, and it whets one's appetite for the translation of the rest of the tales in this ephemeral volume. Knowing that such a tale was alive in the oral tradition as recently as a quarter of a century ago, one might well go "fishing" with it and other puzzling tales in search of the forms those tales have assumed with the passage of time.

Motifs:

T	J1117.	Animal as trickster.
T	G501.**.	Gullible ogre.
T	Q91.**.	Reward for cleverness: tortoise gains "man" from both ogre and hippopotamus.
C	K441.+.**.	Tortoise promises "man" to ogre and to hippopotamus; both come simultaneously for him.
T	K1840.	Deception by substitution.
T	G520.	Ogre deceived into self-injury.
T	K1000.**.	Deception into self-injury: hippopotamus, by tortoise.
T	K234.	Trickster summons all (both) creditors at once, precipitates fight, and escapes payment.
T	K231.	Debtor refuses to pay his debt.

1. Neither the meaning of "man" nor the full nature of the bargain is clear here. Apparently, the tortoise promised the ogre a "man" in return. Whether he also paid something for the "man" he took from the ogre's yard is not indicated; the "pay" may have referred to a future repayment rather than to an immediate compensation.

2. This is one of two instances in the Ross-furnished tales in which a specific day of the week is mentioned. Since the book *Bekolo Bemo . . .* was compiled by missionary-teachers, one might not be too surprised to find an awareness of Sunday communicated to prospective Christians; ironically, it was a *Sunday* that was selected by the tortoise for the perpetration of his mean trick. We are at a loss to explain this feature of the tale. It may possibly represent an Nkundo in-group joke of which the compilers themselves were unaware.

3. Here, as is true earlier also in the tale, "sitting" is not to be taken literally; rather, it is to be understood as "located" or "settled" or "present at that place." (See note 8 for Tales 43, 44, and 45.)

Narrator: Lontomba Samuel
Location: Tondo
Date: July 1973

41. The Wife of the Turtle and Her Brave Act

One day all the animals decided to go hunting in the forest. They went and made a hunting camp. It was close to a well where people can get water. After hunting for several days they got thirsty, so they sent a man[1] first to that well to try to get water out of it. In that well there was a snail that has fallen in it, and he was afraid that whenever they come to get the water, they might pick up him and break him.

So they send first—the first animal they sent was the animal that we call Mboloko (Dwarf Antelope).[2] He went there, and as he went there was a need to pick up water out of the well. He heard the snail singing, but he didn't know it was a snail. He just heard a song from the water, like this:

> In this well, nobody can pick up water,
> Kongo.[3]
> Especially those people who are slaves.
> Kongo.
> In this well, nobody can pick up water,
> Kongo.
> Especially those people who are slaves.
> Kongo.
> In this well, nobody can pick up water,
> Kongo.
> Especially those people who are slaves.
> Kongo.
> In this well, nobody can pick up water,
> Kongo.
> Especially those people who are slaves.
> Kongo.

So when this small antelope heard this song, he turned back and ran away. Dwarf Antelope ran away and he said that, "I heard a very mysterious song from under the water, and it is terribly dangerous. I cannot go there."

So the animals laughed at him and decided to send the leopard, who is strong and who can't be afraid of anything.

So Leopard went in his turn to try to pick up water. But as he was nearing the well he heard again the song:

> Leopard, you shouldn't approach here.
> *Kongo.*
> This is prohibited.
> *Kongo.*
> It's dangerous for you to come down here.
> *Kongo.*
> Slaves should not drink water out of this.
> *Kongo.*
> Leopard, you shouldn't approach here.
> *Kongo.*
> This is prohibited.
> *Kongo.*
> It's dangerous for you to come down here.
> *Kongo.*
> Slaves should not drink water out of this.
> *Kongo.*

So he was very afraid and worried and he ran back. So he told the people like that—he told—he went back to his friends in the hunting camp and he told his friends about this mysterious song from under water.

So after Leopard, they sent Elephant. He went and he found the same thing.[4]

As the time was going on, it became very difficult in that area because they couldn't get water. And they stayed there for nearly two weeks without water. All the wild animals who were very strong and very fierce were there, but they were all afraid.

At the end, Nkulu (Wife of the Turtle) decided to go to get the water. She said, "Let me go, and I'll go there and get that water."

So all the people just burst with laughter. They said, "Ho! Could you go there? The brave animals—brave men like Leopard and Lion and Elephant—have been there and didn't get this water. You would not be capable of doing this."

But Wife of the Turtle went and went, and as she was nearing the well she also heard this song coming out of the water:

> Wife of the Turtle, don't approach this well.
> *Kongo.*
> No slave should drink this water.

Kongo.
If you drink water out of this,
Kongo,
We will be in trouble with you.
Kongo.
Wife of the Turtle, don't approach this well.
Kongo.
No slave should drink this water.
Kongo.
If you drink water out of this,
Kongo,
We will be in trouble with you.
Kongo.

But Wife of the Turtle didn't like to listen to this, and she said, "I will drop into the water and go to the bottom to see which kind of animal is singing that."

And she went down into the water, and the snail sang and he sang harder and louder, but Wife of the Turtle decided to drop in, and she dived—dove—and she found at the end near the bottom there was a snail. So she picked it up, went back to the water surface, and brought the snail to the hunting camp, and everybody was very surprised and praised this woman turtle.

Really, this story shows us that Turtle, who doesn't even walk very fast, who can not be considered as strong, who in this story was just a woman turtle—a female turtle—she was brave, and she saved the lives of all the animals in this fishing camp. So we should not look down upon the people we think are weak, because they can be brave—even more brave than we would think.

In most of the Ross-collected animal tales, the hero or victor is assumed to be male, though in Lonkundo the lack of gender for the third-person-singular pronoun causes some blurring of sex lines. The present tale stresses the sex ("just a woman turtle—a female turtle") as well as the obvious physical limitations of a turtle of either sex in a task requiring courage, affording a curious and interesting extra dimension in Nkundo tale-telling.

The narrator, recording the tale without a visible audience, gave a richly dramatic performance for his unseen listeners, including a representation of the chorus normally participating in the telling of a *cante fable*. His self-imposed requirement that for the convenience of Mrs. Ross he tell the tale in English, despite the difficulties it presented for him, produced a clear instance of the earnestness with which he and other narrators responded to Mrs. Ross's request for "tales told by the fathers."

Of the indexed tales, Lambrecht's sample for her tale type 2235 affords the closest parallel to the present narrative: a portion of the sample tells of a rabbit which, faced with detection of his dishonest dealings with the chief, frightened away each animal sent to represent his creditor by hiding and calling to him in a voice vastly magnified by a horn; each time, he greeted the investigator, stepped out of sight on a feigned errand, and shouted a threat from an imaginary pursuer of that particular animal, requesting "Father" to "Hand me your gun!" and thus causing the agent to flee.

Closer parallels to the present tale—ones consisting solely of the kind of conflict forming the whole of Tale 41—are more abundant than the indexes would suggest. In an unindexed tale in Weeks' *Congo Life and Folklore* ("Why the Chameleon Cut Off His Own Head"—pp. 445–446), a chameleon frightens various large animals from the frog's house, of which she has taken possession. Finally the sparrow discovers the perpetrator of the hoax and dupes the chameleon into cutting off her own head in order to dance as well as the sparrows. Herskovitses' *Dahomean Narrative* . . . (in "How Pig Came to Live with Man"—pp. 212–214) furnishes another instance —this time featuring Pig as the hero—in which a small creature, a frog, frightens away a succession of larger animals sent to a stream to fetch water for making clay; Pig, undeterred by "The Thing" speaking from the water, consults a diviner and on his advice spears the speaker, finds it is only a frog, and brings water back to his co-workers. From that time, Pig has always been "in the house with man" (p. 214). Torrend's "I Am Tembwe" (. . . *Bantu Folk-Lore* . . . , pp. 62–64) includes a male tortoise which, disregarding its own safety, secured the fire being withheld by the sleight of a hornet that had intimidated larger animals by its song threatening death and disembowelment to anyone who entered the hut appropriated by the hornet. In footnote 4 (p. 64), Torrend indicates that the story was "current on the Zambesi" at the time the book was published [1921]. Torrend adds this interesting comment: "It is an allegory explaining how the natives [sic] used, occasionally, to get rid of foreigners, when these without ceremony took possession of their springs or their fields." Torrend does not offer any source for this observation; it would be illuminating to pursue this question among the Nkundo to see whether they, too, view the present tale as allegorical.

Motifs:

T	J1117.	Animal as trickster.
C	K335.+.**.	Snail threatens and frightens away animals wishing to drink at well in which he is hiding.
C	K2320.+.**.	Snail shouts threats from well to frighten other animals from well.
T	K1700.	Deception through bluffing.
T	K2320.	Deception by frightening.
T	K1887.	Illusory sounds.

T W32.**.   Bravery: prompts wife of turtle to investigate threatening song
                        in the well.
C L290.+.**.   Modest wife of turtle, mocked by larger animals for her pre-
                        sumption, succeeds in detecting source of frightening sounds
                        from well (snail) and makes water from well available to
                        other animals.
T B491.5.**.   Helpful turtle (tortoise): wife of turtle—confronts terrorizing
                        snail possessing well and wins water for comrades.
T B390.**.   Animals grateful for wife of turtle's detecting cause of terrifying
                        sounds in well and thus making water available to them.

1. "Man" is not intended literally here: instead, "someone" or "some creature"
expresses the narrator's intention; "brave men" and "all the people" occur later in
the tale, though the characters are identified as wild animals. These slips over the
thin line between man and other animals make clearly evident the primary function
of animal tales among the Nkundo: to present human situations at a sufficient
emotional distance to allow them to be considered objectively.

2. [Narrator's explanatory comment: "He is supposed to be more clever than
the others."]

3. "*Kongo*," normally the chorus's response, was furnished by the narrator
himself at a different pitch from the verse proper, to suggest the antiphonal character
of the song in a traditional storytelling situation. The word "*kongo*" is used here
for its sound, rather than for its sense—as Bascom suggests, it serves "to make the
song sweet" (see his *Ifa Divination*, p. 255, n. 7).

4. Truncation is evident here; this time, the narrator himself shortens the tale,
eliminating the snail's song sung to the elephant and the elephant's report to his
thirsty friends as well as the entire episode of the lion at the well, mentioned later
when Wife of the Turtle offers to fetch water for the animals. Truncation at this
point appears artistically valid in that it reserves the major emphasis for the "brave
act" pointing to the social conclusion drawn by the tale-teller.

Narrator: Bokunge Jacques
Location: Bòlèngè
Date: February 1973

42.   *The Eagle Violates His Own Law*[1]

On another day the eagle, who is the king of all the riverine birds, called them all together. He said, "We are all aware that the people[2] come to this river to drink.[3] Therefore I feel that it should be kept clean, so I am making a law that no bird of any sort is to drop droppings in the river."

Everyone agreed to this, and the birds went their various ways.

Not many days later the eagle flew out over the river, alighted on a tree branch, and dropped his droppings into the river.

A great outcry began. All the birds cried and shouted, "This is badness itself."

We do not like laws such as the eagle passes.

This brief tale may well serve to vent the feelings of the narrator and his audience concerning the oppression to which they themselves have been subjected by the whims and autocratic decisions of their rulers, whether tribal chiefs, European masters, or court judges. As is indicated in Rattray's *Akan-Ashanti Folk-Tales* (pp. x–xi), this opportunity for release of pent-up resentment is an important social service afforded by oral narrative; the use of animals—or birds—as principals allows the participants in the storytelling situation to air their own grievances with impunity.

The researcher has been unable to find in any of the indexes a type number appropriate for the present tale. In Aarne-Thompson's tale type 220, "the eagle as judge assigns each his place and work," whereas in the present tale he gives them only one directive. Klipple's variant of Aarne-Thompson's tale type 221, The Election of the Bird-King, drawn from Nigeria (in Dayrell's *Folk Stories from Southern Nigeria* [1910]), comments, "the fishing eagle sits quietly in the tree, and his terrible beak and cruel claws make him master," but no overt abuse of his authority is suggested.

Motifs:

T   J1511.   A rule must work both ways.
C   P522.+.**.   King (eagle) makes law that no bird may excrete into river.

1. [Explanatory material inserted by narrator at this point: "The birds who fish for a living will sit on the branch of a tree that hangs over the river. They will excrete a dropping and wait for a fish to grab it and then they will catch the fish."]

2. "People" here includes all living creatures. The eagle's concern appears to be both ecological and magnanimous, but proves instead to be monopolistic and abusive; such abuses have been observed among human leaders by the Nkundo and have likewise been resented.

3. Rivers are used for all purposes by the Nkundo. In a single trip to the river, one can bathe, relieve himself, wash his clothes, and carry water back to his hut for drinking and cooking. The concern of the birds with the purity of the water may reflect an increasing awareness among the Nkundo of the relationship between pollution and disease; stories illustrating the contrast between statement and action as seen in autocratic and peremptory leaders were being told in Lonkundo long before the present emphasis on ecology.

Part III

PEOPLE

*Problems and Solutions
as Seen by the Nkundo*

Introduction

Introduction

EVEN MORE FUNCTIONAL than animal tales in communicating the values, customs, and basic concerns of any given group of people are the narratives in which people themselves furnish the dramatis personae. Contrary to our expectations in the light of the widespread assumption that African tales tend to be primarily those with animal actors and with simple, spare narrative style, we found among the Ross-collected items slightly more "people" tales than "nonpeople" tales—forty-two, as opposed to thirty-eight—reckoned on the basis of dramatis personae alone, in addition to ten in which a person serves as one of the major characters. Moreover, these narratives proved for the most part to be well-developed examples of verbal art, complex in structure and yet consistent in story line, and evidencing the controlled interplay of characters marked in good literature whether written or oral.

In this portion of the volume are found forty-four primarily "people" tales, including thirty-nine Ross-collected narratives and five variants translated from *Bekolo Bémó*.... Within this group of forty-four narratives falling under the Aarne-Thompson classification "Ordinary Folk-Tales" can be found a mirroring of seven basic elements in the Nkundo value system: (1) integrity in filial, fraternal, and parental obligations; (2) the twin concerns of ownership and of sharing; (3) stability in marital relationships; (4) the showing of kindness and the response of gratitude; (5) respect for individuality; (6) respect for established customs of courtship and of marital-partner choice; and (7) recognition and appropriate awe of the supernatural. As is true in Nkundo life itself, two or more of these values may either overlap or appear in conflict with one another within a single narrative; too, Nkundo values not included among the seven listed here but still strongly held by the Nkundo may well be present in one or more of the tales. The measure of a narrator's skill is indicated in the degree to which he can leave with the listener a valid key to acceptable moral and social behavior, a guide to the making of a responsible choice, within the framework of his own culture. Although one narrator consistently maintained, when questioned by Mrs. Ross on some point or another, "But, Mama, this is a *story*," the truth lies deeper than that demurral: the "story" is the working out of Nkundo real-life situations in an effort to find solid ground in the shifting sands of inner and outer conflicts. *Are* there ogres? *Is* there cannibalism? *Do* friends betray one another, family members waver in their loyalty to one another, marital partners falter in their bonds? These and other concerns are not found among the Nkundo alone, but the Nkundo through oral narrative persist in bringing them to light time and time again for re-examination and re-evaluation, as is demonstrated by the samples in part 3.

For convenience in analysis, we have arrived at the following groupings of the forty-four tales. Nine tales appear to stress consanguineal obligations: Tales 53, 54, 55, 57, 74, 75, 76, 77, and 78. Eight narratives seem to emphasize matters of sharing and/or of ownership: Tales 49, 50, 58, 59, 60, 84, 85, and 86. Stability in marital relationships receives primary emphasis in six narratives: Tales 72, 73, 79, 81, 82, and 83. Seven tales stress the reciprocal traits of kindness and gratitude: Tales 43, 44, 45, 46, 47, 48, and 80. The Nkundo respect for individuality is indicated in three narratives: Tales 56, 70, and 71. Two tales impress upon listeners the worth of traditional courtship and mate-selection customs: Tales 51 and 52. Recognition and/or appropriate awe of the supernatural can be seen as assuming the commanding role in nine narratives: Tales 61, 62, 63, 64, 65, 66, 67, 68, and 69.

Immediately, each classification will prompt a question or a battery of questions. Of primary concern—and, unfortunately, unanswerable—is this query: Do the Nkundo narrators and their audiences see in these tales the values and concerns that Western analysts consider "obvious"? Countless additional investigations, by field collectors of every conceivable discipline and equipped with tape recorders to preserve the preliminary discussions, the comments and amendments made by the audience during the telling, the playback of the tale and the responses of the teller and the listeners to the second hearing of the tale, and subsequent observation of possible changes in social behavior traceable to the "teaching" in the tale, might still fail to answer that compelling question. In token of the complexity of the preceding query, consider this question: If "awe of the supernatural" is the central concern of Tale 66, why is the story titled "The Man Who Described an Ogre and Still Lived" [our title]? Doesn't this suggest that the Nkundo *aren't* really awed by the supernatural? We maintain that the very fact of the ogre's inclusion in a tale—whether or not he is "bested" by the protagonist —evidences a continuing anxiety among the Nkundo for the main- tenance of a safe relationship between man and supernatural forces. That Imana succeeds in outwitting the ogre and thus escaping with his life lends a measure of reassurance, perhaps, but it still does not blink the issue that the supernatural must be reckoned with. A narrator desiring to underline the importance of awe of the super- natural is free to choose his "weapon": he can use fear, laughter, victory (with an uneasy sense that this is a victory that will have to be won over and over again), or whatever other tool best serves his own temperament and the mood of his listeners. But he must make the choice himself, and he must so structure the tale that that choice proves the right one for driving home the lesson. From the treasury of tales that he has garnered since early childhood, he will tend to select what best served his own needs; thus are tales preserved from generation to generation.

From the present sampling, it is obvious that each reader could reclassify the tales in the light of the lessons he himself derives. That a multiplicity of arrangements is possible accounts for the con- tinuing appeal and effectiveness of these "people" tales: each listener or reader brings his own concerns to the "hearing" of a given tale, and takes away from that "hearing" something applicable—either a positive finding or a negative one, conceivably even one that the narrator had not envisioned—to that concern. Since each of the tales tends to have more than one factor or value within it, the same tale can answer different needs for different observers. To cite but one example from part 3, Tale 56 affords insights into several major areas besides the one we have considered as stressed, respect for individuality: consanguineal obligations (the daughter's duty to respect her father's wishes, and the father's responsibility to safeguard his daughter), ownership (the father owns his daughter by right of paternity, but the husband owns his wife by payment of the required bridewealth), marital stability (the importance of honoring agreed terms, but the threat to the husband's traditional dominant role in the family posed by the condition that he share his wife's misfortunes), courtship (the abduction of the bride—a violation of the traditional pattern—in balance with the father's unreasonable attitude with regard to his daughter's marrying at all—also a violation of the traditional pattern), marriage conditions (the acceptable practice of the surrender of bridewealth, made unacceptable by the father's vengeful bridewealth terms) ... and a host of other ponderables.

Each tale in part 3, with the possible exception of Tale 55, can stretch to include a variety of Nkundo personal or social needs; the range of tales reveals the complexity of what the uninformed too often term a "primitive" culture. We invite you to explore this world of the Nkundo through the eyes of its own people.

Narrator: Bokunge Jacques
Location: Bòlëngè
Date: February 1973

43. *The Hunter and the Chimpanzee Help One Another*

On another day the men of a certain village decided to go into the forest to hunt meat. Since many were going, they took a net along to stretch out over a large area of the forest.[1]

The net was spread and many animals were trapped. This included a chimpanzee, which was surprising.[2]

All at once a loud cry was heard. "Lomboto, Lomboto! Hurry and help. There is trouble in the net, and all the animals are coming in your direction."

Eza, the chimpanzee, heard the name and hurried, *tee-tee-tee*, in that direction. "Lomboto," he said, "make me live. I'll be able to help you sometime."

When Lomboto heard his plea, he released him from the net. Chimpanzee ran off into the forest.

Lomboto dropped the net on the other animals. Each hunter had meat to take home. Each divided his meat according to the customs of the fathers.

Chimpanzee did not forget the name "Lomboto" and carried it in his heart.[3]

On another day the wife of Lomboto needed some palm fruit[4] so that she could cook the foods that her family liked. She called Lomboto. "Please go into the forest and get some palm fruit for our dinner."

Lomboto took his climbing belt. With this and his machete he set off into the forest.

When he found a palm tree on which the fruit was ripe, he began to climb, climbing, climbing, up to the fruit. Any palm fronds that were hanging in his path he cut as he went and let them fall to the ground. He reached the fruit and saw that it was good. He stepped out of his climbing belt and cut the bunch of fruit. As the fruit fell, it caught the climbing belt, and both fruit and climbing belt fell to the ground.

Lomboto looked all about, hoping to find a way to get out of the tree. When he could see no possible way he began to call, "Someone come and help me. I am Lomboto and I am in real difficulty. I climbed into a palm tree and can't get down. Unless someone comes, I will die here in the tree. I am Lomboto."

Even though Lomboto's voice would carry through the forest for many miles, it was still doubtful that anyone would hear him.

However, Chimpanzee had not forgotten the name "Lomboto." When he heard it, he went quickly to find out what the difficulty was. When he found Lomboto up in the tree, he called, "Lomboto, Lomboto."

Lomboto answered, "Yes."

"I recognized your name. I am the chimpanzee which you helped when I was caught in the net for catching animals. What is it that you wish?"

"Chimpanzee, I am seeking just any way of getting out of this palm tree. My climbing belt has fallen to the ground and I myself am calling anyone who can help me get down. You have come. Can you bring my climbing belt up into the palm tree to me? Then I can climb down."

Chimpanzee put the climbing belt around his waist and climbed the palm tree just as a man would. He knew that when he reached Lomboto they couldn't both use it for climbing down. He handed the climbing belt to Lomboto; then he himself jumped out of the tree, *poom*.[5]

Lomboto came down out of the palm tree using his climbing belt. He thanked Chimpanzee with many words of thanks.[6] He well knew that he could easily have died in the palm tree before anyone would have found him there.[7]

We help each other even as the chimpanzee and Lomboto helped each other.

[Notes for Tale 43 follow Tale 45.]

Narrator: Bomponge Joseph
Location: Tondo, but narrator's home
               was in Besenge, near Kalamba
Date: June 1973

44. *The Hunter and the Chimpanzee Help One Another* (Variant I)

This is the story of Eza and Lomboto.

Eza (Chimpanzee) lived in the forest. He went into a village where Lomboto lived. Some of the people wanted to kill him, but Lomboto said, "No, he must be allowed to live."

While Chimpanzee sat[8] there, Lomboto gave him, gave him, gave him food and then more and more food. Chimpanzee ate and ate and ate. Finally Chimpanzee went home to where his family lived.

Then one day Lomboto went into the forest. When he went into the forest, *te-te-te*, he came to a family of chimpanzees. They said, "There is nothing to do but kill him."

When they were about to kill him but before they did, Chimpanzee came and said, "No, you must not kill him. He took care of me and gave me food when I needed it. I rejoiced and rejoiced with him. Let him return home in safety."

This is the end of the story of Chimpanzee and Lomboto.

You are to live as Lomboto let live and as Chimpanzee protected Lomboto from death in the forest.

[Notes for Tale 44 follow Tale 45.]

Source: Bekolo Bèmò . . .
               Zaïrian school reader
               (in Lonkundo)
Translator: Mabel Ross
Date of Translation: March 1977

45. *The Hunter and the Chimpanzee Help One Another* (Variant II)

Father of Boele[9] had a wife. One time the wife desired *mbeele*, fruit of the *boele* tree, with much desire.

She sent her husband, she said, "Seek *mbeele* for me; do this truly."

And her husband picked a great many *mbeele*, but his wife was not satisfied, *nyè*.[10]

The husband went into the forest very far. He found some *boele* trees that were very large. He cut a vine for a climbing belt, and tied it to the tree; then he climbed.

When he arrived, he cut many branches of the *boele* tree, but one branch carried his climbing belt away. It fell below, and Father of Boele was helpless up above. How long a time!

He saw in the distance an ape was coming. The ape found him. He asked him, he said, "Father of Boele, what are you doing here?"

Father of Boele said, "I came to pick *mbeele* fruit for my wife. I climbed with a climbing belt, but when a branch fell, it caught the climbing belt. The climbing belt fell down, and I am helpless here."

The ape felt mercy, and he pulled a branch of another tree and he said, "Father of Boele, come and pass."

Father of Boele perched on the back of the ape and he jumped to the other tree;[11] then he went down and he went home.

A long time after that, a man saw the ape. He called the people, "Come, bring nets; then let us restrain the ape."

All the people brought their nets, and Father of Boele took up his net that they restrain the ape.

The ape heard that there was one in the place whom they called Father of Boele. Then he heard the name Father of Boele. He went to that place. He fell[12] into the net of Father of Boele. Then the ape said, "Father of Boele, release me."

Father of Boele remembered the mercy which was of the ape, and he released his net; then the ape went, going.

The ape lived because he had felt mercy for the man.[13]

Although the narrators of the two field-collected versions, Tales 43 and 44, lived many kilometers from one another and differed considerably in background, they both used the same name for the man and the same creature rescued and rescuer in turn. Of the two storytellers, Bokunge Jacques furnished the more detailed and animated version, employing a dramatic occasion for the initial encounter, an artistic handling of dialogue, incorporation of various cultural factors, many traditional locutions, and a deft plot line. Though the methods of mutual assistance varied widely in the two versions, the conclusion with a proverb or near-proverb, in both instances one utilizing the names of the leading characters, suggests that one form or another of the tale is a staple in Nkundo repertories. The fact that Lontumba-speaking listeners added details to Bomponge Joseph's variant indicates that the narrative is known outside the Lonkundo-speaking area, as well.

There are several interesting differences between the version translated from *Bekolo Bèmò* ... (Tale 45) and the two field-collected narratives: in the school reader, the order of the rescues has been reversed; the nature of the rescue is a physical, bodily one; the animal is identified as an ape (from its size and strength, probably a gorilla rather than a chimpanzee—a change artistically essential to permit the man's being "perched" on the rescuer's back); the name of the man is altered, and the "ape" is unnamed; the motivation for the man's tree-climbing differs (in Tale 43, the palm fruit is needed for the family; in Tale 45, the *mbeele* are to satisfy the wife's own longing—perhaps a pregnancy-prompted craving, though this is not stated in the text; under normal circumstances, an Nkundo would not thus pamper his wife). The similarities are equally arresting: the use of traditional Lonkundo diction is present in all three; in all three, the animal speaks as a man and is understood by the man; all three employ a man and a primate as the principal characters; recollection of the man's name (in Tales 43 and 45) by the animal provides the key to the identification of the imperiled animal; the climbing belt is used in two of the three tales; in all three, the theme "Live and let live" takes precedence over the need for food.

The tale of a lone animal grateful for a human's act of kindness and in turn helpful to his benefactor appears to be widely distributed. Aarne-Thompson lists two tale types—156 and 156A—based on a considerable number of samples (apparently including the one cited by Klipple under tale type 156 and drawn from Somalia [formerly Somaliland]); Arewa lists six tale types in addition to a renumbering of Aarne-Thompson's type 156A—2421, 2486, 2498, 2527 (1), 2540, and 2578—all based on single samples drawn from the northern east-African cattle area he was investigating; Lambrecht offers three tale types—2410, 2426, and 2427 —each based on a single sample derived from the collections of tales from Central Africa available to her. Tale 45 in the present volume has no parallel in any of the

samples cited; it is possible that one of the eleven "African" samples on which
Aarne-Thompson's tale type 75 was based involves a man, rather than an animal,
as the "weak" (helpless) one initially rescued. Of all the tale types listed above,
Arewa's 2578 most nearly approaches the circumstances in the fuller of the two Ross-
collected tales (Tale 43) and therefore warrants its being identified as the most
appropriate classification presently available. In Arewa's tale type 2578 (drawn from
the Iraqw in 1929 or earlier), a boy secretly released an elephant from a trap set
by the boy's father; in the absence of confession, the father took the son to hunt
honey in a baobab tree, removed all the steps that would have permitted the boy's
descent, and abandoned him; the rescued elephant later came and freed the boy
from the tree. [The boy's subsequent murder of his father is an added element in the
Iraqw tale; otherwise, the tree-trap rescue patterns in Arewa 2578 and in Ross's
Tale 43 are satisfactorily similar.] No suitable type number has been identified in
any of the indexes to accommodate Tale 45.

Motifs:

T	B364.1.	Animal grateful for rescue from trap.
T	B370.	Animal grateful to captor for release.
T	B360.**.	Chimpanzee grateful for rescue from peril of death.
T	B441.1.1.**.	Helpful chimpanzee.
T	Q40.	Kindness rewarded.
T	B547.	Animal rescues man from dangerous place.
T	B391.**.	Animal grateful for food and shelter.
T	B547.**.	Animal rescues man from dangerous situation.
T	B542.**.	Helpful ape: rescues man by carrying him.
C	B322.+.**.	Man allows helpful ape to escape from net.

1. [Narrator's explanatory material: "With this they hoped to catch many
animals. Some of the hunters would frighten animals in the direction of the net and
these animals would be caught in its meshes."]

Many varieties of small animals, such as civets, antelopes, and rodents, are
caught in this way; often a wild pig is captured thus.

2. [Narrator's explanatory material: "A chimpanzee is too much like a man
to be caught in such a situation."]

3. [Narrator's explanatory material: "An animal will almost always remember
a kindness."]

4. These small golden-brown fruit, made up largely of oil and fibers, grow in
a large cluster well up in the fronds of the tree; their seed is nutlike and hard. The
women cook the fruit, pound it to get rid of the fibers, and use the delicious sauce
with meat, fish, greens, and other foods. They can also heat the fruit and extract
the pure oil for use in frying plantains, banana cakes, and other foods that would
otherwise lack sufficient flavor. The oil both from the fruit and from the nut is used
commercially, as well.

5. *Poom*, an ideophone representing the graceful, hurt-free descent of a chimpanzee, reflects the Nkundo understanding that a chimpanzee can roll himself into
a ball and fall a long way without injury other than jarring on impact.

6. For "with many words of thanks," the narrator used *"Eoto, eoto"* (literally, "Relative, relative"). In Lonkundo there is no exact equivalent for the expression "Thank you"; the nearest approach among the Nkundo on such occasions is "relative," since there it is normally relatives who render aid prompting thankfulness.

7. [Narrator's explanatory material: "The Nkundo people continue to follow the custom of helping people in distress even to this very day."]

Under certain circumstances, the Nkundo recognize the securing of food as less important than the showing of mercy, a factor in the value system perpetuated both through numerous proverbs and through oral tales.

8. The term "sat," meaning "settled," is used also among the Luba; see Burton's "A Luba Folk-Tale," *Bantu Studies* (1935), page 69.

9. This name is an honorific used as a substitute for the man's given name (see Tale 93 for another instance of such nomenclature); here, the Lonkundo equivalent is *"Is'e'oele."* This naming practice reflects the dignity accorded to parenthood by the Nkundo.

10. Omission of a mention of pregnancy as inducing the wife's strong desire for more and more *mbeele* is less likely to have occurred as a result of the compilers' "sheltering" the young children reading the book than as a consequence of their recognition that the readers would understand the wife's condition without being prompted, since there is little privacy about *any* matters in an Nkundo village.

11. Exactly what happens here is not clear: (1) the ape provides a "perch" from which the man can jump to another tree; or, (2) the ape, with the man perched on his back, jumps to the other tree. In either case, it constitutes a rescue method for which we have found no parallel elsewhere in published sources.

12. The method planned for netting the ape is not clear. If the ape (gorilla) were large enough to support a man, he could scarcely be shaken out of the tree, yet apparently the hunters expect him to fall, as indeed he does, choosing Father of Boele's net as his trap.

13. The original Lonkundo title, "Is'e'oele la Ngondo," is translated thus: "Father of Boele and the Ape" (the Lonkundo version appears on pages 55–56 of *Bekolo Bėmȯ . . .*).

Narrator: Lontomba Samuel
Location: Tondo
Date: July 1973

46. *The Leopard Rewards the Hunter's Kindness*[1]

One day a man who was a hunter went into the forest and put there a lot of traps to get animals. One day when he went into the forest to look at his traps, he found that Nkòi (Leopard) had been caught in one of them. When Leopard saw this hunter coming with bow and arrows, he begged him. He asked him to feel sorry for him and let him go away. He could just cut the wire and let him go. Leopard told the man, "You should help me because one day I might help you out, too."

The man thought for a while and decided that he would agree. So he cut the rope,[2] and Leopard ran away.

One day this man, who was a single hunter, wanted to go to the next town to look for a lady that he could marry. He had seen a girl in this next town and he wanted to go there to get married. As he was walking through the forest between those two towns, he saw a dog coming out of the bush[3] to keep him company. The man said, "Hello. I was alone on my road. Now you join me. We can go together."

So they went together until they arrived at the town. The man met his fiancée, or the lady he wanted to marry. They arranged things. They stayed overnight. In the morning the marriage was concluded; the dowry[4] was paid to his wife's family. They collected their luggage and belongings, and pretty soon they were on the way back to his village. The dog was with them.

They walked and walked until they came to the junction where the dog had to turn to return to the place where he had come out from the bush. The dog said to the man, "I was your companion. I helped you to go and get this wife. Now you have to divide the things that we got there into two equal parts."

The man said, "O.K."[5]

The money, the food, and all kinds of stuff[6] that they had gotten, they divided into two. So the man said, "That's enough now. Good-bye."

But the dog said, "No, you can't do that. You still have one thing that you haven't divided."

"Which thing?"

"This lady. You are to split this lady in two. Then you can have part and I can have part."

The man said, "No. I can't do that."

As they were talking, suddenly another dog but with two heads came out of the forest and said, "What's the trouble?"

So the dog reported and the man also reported. The dog with the two heads backed his friend, the dog. "Yeah! You have to divide this wife into two."

The man disagreed. As they were talking, another dog appeared from the forest. This one had three heads. He also agreed with his friends. It went on and on, and finally the last dog which came had ten heads. They were all making trouble and they all said, "You have to divide this wife in two."

So the man was very sad. He was surrounded by these monstrous animals. He decided to go and look for leaves[7] so that he could divide his wife in pieces.

The dog stayed on the road with the wife. The man went into the forest. As he walked there, he saw that Leopard was there, the leopard that he had saved from the trap. He told him about his problem.

The leopard said, "Don't worry. Get some big, big leaves and wrap me around and take me into the middle of these dogs."

So the man cut down a lot of leaves and made a big pile. He wrapped the leopard completely and carried him on his back into the middle and said to the dog, "These are the leaves. You yourself open them."

As they opened the leaves, the leopard came out and killed and devoured the dogs.

Leopard said, "You have saved me from your trap. I am saving you from this trouble. Now take your wife and go home."

Leopard went, and the man went home with his wife.

Moral application: We should help our friends when they are in trouble, whether they are mighty or weak. We should help because one day they might save us, too.

Tales reflecting the trait of gratitude are plentiful among the Nkundo. This high regard for mutual consideration is echoed also in many Nkundo proverbs, sound mirrors of the value system.

Arewa lists a number of tale types which involve the return of kindnesses of one form or another: 2421, 2512, 2540; Lambrecht's tale types 2410 and 2426 also offer accounts of kindness or mercy rewarded. As the treasury of African tales continues to be made more available, a large section will need to be reserved for "kindness-rewarded" narratives in a type index devoted to African tales; certainly the variants found for the Ross-collected tales alone in French and in Flemish would support that contention. (Cobble's *Wembi . . .* furnishes a variant in English: an antelope which had rescued a spider was in turn protected by the spider, who spun webs over the antelope's tracks to deceive the hunter into thinking the tracks were old ones. This and others of Cobble's tales warrant examination for content, though few clues to Nkundo narrative style can be found there.)

Motifs:

T	B364.1.	Animal grateful for rescue from trap.
T	B375.7.	Leopard released: grateful.
T	W27.	Gratitude.
C	B435.+.**.	Companionable wild dog.
T	G351.1.	Dog as ogre.
C	G261.+.**.	Dog-devil demands half of the bride in return for his accompanying the hunter to get her.
C	G361.+.**.	Ten wild dogs, the first with one head, the second with two heads, and so on, to the tenth with ten heads.
T	B431.1.	Helpful leopard.
L	B449.6.	Helpful leopard.
C	B549.+.**.	Helpful leopard arranges plan for hunter's escape from monstrous dogs.
T	J1020.**.	Strength in unity: threatened hunter and grateful leopard cooperate to destroy monstrous dogs.
T	J670.**.	Forethought in defences against others: man directs monstrous dogs to open leaf package themselves (package contains leopard, who devours them).
T	G520.**.	Monstrous dogs deceived into self-injury.
T	G512.9.1.**.	Monstrous dogs killed by helpful leopard.
C	B524.+.**.	Helpful leopard kills monstrous dogs for hunter.
T	Q40.	Kindness rewarded.

1. [Narrator's explanatory comment: "The next story is about leopard and man. This is the kind of a grateful story—a grateful animal and a grateful man."]

2. Here the narrator has used "rope" instead of "wire" as the material from which the trap had been made. The Lonkundo term "*ngòji*," used in both instances, presents a problem in translation for many others besides Sam.

3. When the narrator refers to the dog's coming out of the "bush," the term

"forest" should be understood for "bush." The narrator himself lives in a tropical forest on a lake. The term "jungle" to refer to such forested areas is considered offensive and unless it has appeared in a literal translation (see pp. 307–8), we have scrupulously avoided it.

4. The term "dowry" is not used here in the sense in which it is employed in Western culture: to describe the gifts that go with the bride to her husband; "bride-wealth" is intended here.

5. "O.K." is a reflection of Sam's exposure to American English during his university work in Washington, D.C.; another such reflection of linguistic acculturation can be seen in "Yeah," later in this tale.

6. "All kinds of stuff"—however relaxed the expression may appear—clearly does not refer to the bridewealth, since that was left with the bride's family. Apparently the bride's family had sent some goods with the bride as gifts for the new household, a perfectly acceptable practice among the Nkundo, especially if the bride's family lives in more comfortable circumstances than does the groom's family or if there is a distant family relationship between bride and groom (see Tale 82 for another example of this kind of gift).

7. The leaves would be used for wrapping the two halves of the bride into bundles that could be carried by their respective owners.

Narrator:	Bokunge Jacques
Location:	Bòlèngè
Date:	February 1973

47. *The Broken Friendship between the Man and His Dog*

Many long years ago a certain man named Likata (Hand) had a dog, Mbwa.[1] Hand did not have any *baumba*,[2] nor did he have any brothers who might help him. In fact, he had no family at all.[3] Because of this, he and Dog lived together as a family. Hand cared for Dog and fed him much as he cared for himself. As a result, Dog grew to be large and very beautiful.

One day Hand said to himself, "I do not have a sister; I do not have a brother; I do not have any family who can help me to buy a wife. I will take my sleeping mat and hunting things and go with Dog into the forest and hunt meat."

He took his dog bell, *elofo*, and put it around Dog's neck.[4] Hand and Dog went into the forest together. They were hardly settled in a shelter until Dog picked up the scent of a porcupine. He followed the scent and Hand followed Dog as best he could. Then Dog began to call, "Wu, wu, woof! Hurry up, Master."[5] Hand quickly found Dog with the porcupine. He killed the porcupine and carried it back to their shelter.[6] They shared the spoils of the hunt as friends working together.

Hand and Dog stayed in the forest a long while. Each day they found meat. Each had an abundance to eat, and there was plenty left to dry and sell. One day Hand realized that he had enough *baumba* so that he could buy a wife.

In the days that followed, Dog was left to find food for himself. Hand's wife had taken Dog's place in that home.

As time went on, Dog became very angry and finally refused to hunt meat for Hand. Dog said to him, "Hand, I will not hunt meat for you again. You have treated me very badly."[7] Then Dog went into the forest and did not return ever again.[8]

Do not refuse to give food to a man who feeds you when you are hungry.[9]

After working with tales taped in the village, Bokunge Jacques wanted to tell a tale himself. The tape recorder was set up on the dining-room table in the missionary home, with now and then either a missionary or an Nkundo passing by, listening, and making comments. The subject of hunting dogs could not fail to interest any member of this hunting and fishing culture.

This tale presents a curious problem in "typing": structured as a fable, complete with "moral," it would seem that countless parallels could be found for it. But the skill of the narrator and the value system of the Nkundo have so subtly affected the focus of this tale that the major thrust lies neither with the dog nor with the man, but with the relationship, the partnership, the friendship. Each partner benefits from the other beyond the point where "gratitude" is an appropriate response. The dog—functioning both as family and as extra-familial friend—becomes the agent of his own rejection: he enables his master to secure a wife. Thereafter, he is cast aside, ignored—as a partner—but still expected to serve the interests of his erstwhile comrade. In this acorn of a tale lies a forest of Nkundo culture: importance of family, significance of friendships, centrality of sharing, awe of the supernatural (witness the leaf potion prepared for the dog), recognition of immeasurable indebtedness, the bitter dilemma posed by a choice between wife and comrade—all these are firmly rooted here in the scene and artifacts and customs of the Nkundo.

Helpful dogs appear elsewhere, of course, in tales collected by Mrs. Ross: animals as well as people use hunting dogs, and even quarrel over the share of the booty to be given to the dog; faithful dogs rescue their fleeing masters from ogres; dogs display inordinate patience with their comrades' individual quirks. But *this* dog is more than the usual helpful animal, and we have been unable to find his equal elsewhere.

The second portion of Aarne-Thompson's tale type 211∗∗, in which a dog leaves his stingy master, offers a slender peg for classification of this tale. Help is offered also in Klipple's variants on Aarne-Thompson's tale type 545: the Swahili tale cited, because of the hero's shabby treatment of his erstwhile comrade the gazelle, and the Hausa narrative both stress the strength of the initial comradeship; the outcomes of these comradeships vary for the animal principals in that they are rewarded quite differently, but in both instances the tales are carried beyond the point at which Bokunge Jacques concludes his narrative. We have found no entirely satisfactory tale-type number for this poignant tale.

Motifs:

T	B421.	Helpful dog.
C	C680.+.∗∗.	Injunction: certain parts of prey must be given to hunting dog.
C	D1444.+.∗∗.	Magic leaves cooked with food enable dog to hunt better for his master.
T	B581.∗∗.	Dog enables hunter to catch enough game to pay bridewealth.
T	H1558.	Tests of friendship.
C	C935.+.∗∗.	Hunter's dog abandons him because of violation of injunction about division of prey.
C	B299.1.+.∗∗.	Dog leaves master who fails to set out food.
T	Q2.	Kind and unkind.
T	Q281.	Ingratitude punished.
T	Q280.	Unkindness punished.

1. *Mbwa*, the Lonkundo generic name for "dog," and *Likata*, meaning "hand," furnish the characters' names in this narrative. Since "Hand" seems to symbolize the care and protection initially given to the dog and withdrawn with the man's acquisition of a wife, we have retained it as the man's name; obviously it functions artistically in the telling of the tale, since "heart" is committed readily to the wife once she has been acquired.

With very little effort, one can substitute "extra-familial friend" for "dog" and detect a clear social function in its telling; the single sentence "Hand's wife had taken Dog's place in that home"—provocative of a smirk or a smile, perhaps, among Western readers—is a totally serious observation in an Nkundo setting. This is, indeed, a people-people story, not a people-animal story, despite its outward cast of characters.

2. [Narrator's explanatory material: "or the pieces of copper used by his people for buying a wife."] The narrator is careful to make evident at the very start of the telling that Hand has no resources other than Dog, and that marriage is Hand's objective.

3. It is most unusual for an Nkundo to have no family. Cousins, aunts, uncles, brothers, and sisters are generally abundant, though through some misfortune one or both of the parents may have been lost. The narrator may have structured this situation to illustrate the need for family, since family members would normally assist the man in securing a wife.

4. [Narrator's explanatory material: "With the bell he could know where Dog was at any time."]

The dog bell, *elofo* or *bolefo*, commonly attached to a collar around the dog's neck is made of wood or from the stone of a fruit or from some other resonant substance; the clapper is carved from the *isike* (of the spurge family).

5. The narrator here has apparently slipped into viewing the dog as human and as communicating vocally; Nkundo dogs are as a rule voiceless and must be located by the dog bell. The "slip" may well have been an artistic device to increase audience sympathy for Dog [or "extra-familial friend"] as a partner for the hunter and to make the dénouement more moving.

6. [Narrator's explanatory material: "Certain parts of any animal that Dog helped to catch belonged to him. When Hand cut up the porcupine, he hung the liver, the heart, the stomach, and perhaps some other parts up in a tree. This was an unwritten law that these parts belonged to the hunting dog. Then the owner of the dog would get leaves from a certain tree in the forest. The next morning he would cook the meat belonging to the dog with these leaves. The leaves had a special power and were like a potion which would help the dog to hunt for his master. Hand did all of this each time Dog helped him."]

7. Again, the narrator has Dog communicate vocally with Hand, this time to point out the man's faithlessness to his trust and obligation. Again, the narrator apparently views the message of the broken relationship as taking priority over what Westerners might term "logic"; to Nkundo listeners, slipping comfortably back and forth across the thin line which separates humans from other animals, this narrative device would come as no surprise.

8. Dog's lot alone in the woods is not pursued by the narrator, since the major point has already been driven home. Like other Nkundo narrators encountered by Mrs. Ross, Bokunge Jacques stopped when the story was finished, leaving the listeners to debate whatever points they chose; discussion centered in this instance not on the dog's future but on the relationship broken by faithlessness, mirrored in human-human bonds as well as in human-animal associations (see, for example, Tale 80).

9. The ambiguity of the "teaching" allows the listeners to review the narrative themselves in the light of Dog's potential faithfulness despite his master's neglect, encouraging a subsequent renewal of the bond between master and dog as comrades. Nkundo concern with interpersonal relationships is nourished by what goes on *after* the story is finished, and is conditioned by the degree of verbal art exercised by the narrator.

Narrator: Bolumbu Elakankoi,
               a woman
Location: Boende, but narrator's
               home was in Wema
Date: October 1973

48.   *The Ungrateful Friend*

A certain man who lives with us on the earth has the name Mbunga[1] of the Village. He went into the forest to hunt meat. When he got into the forest he went and went, *ti-ti-ti*. He met a man along the way.

He asked him, "Where are you going?"[2]

"Why do you ask me where I'm going? I live in the village and you live here in the forest. I come to hunt animals. How can we be friends, since we do not live together?"

He said, "I want you for a friend, the two of us."[3]

"I don't know you. You live in the forest and I live in the village. Why should we go together?"

"I am hunting a friend. Let us go together."

Then they went off together. They went and went, *ti-ti-ti*, until they reached a certain place. They stopped and sat for a bit.

The second one asked, "What's your name?"

"My name is Mbunga of the Village."

"Oh! You are Mbunga of the Village. I am Mbunga itself. I am Mbunga of the Forest."

"Oh! You see. We are two people with one name."

Then they sat together for a while, the two of them.

"You are Mbunga of the Village. I am Mbunga of the Forest. Are you sure that you will not reject me?"

"No, no! I can never reject you. I and you are people with the same name."

They slept that night, and Mbunga of the Village dreamed that his mother was dead and that Mbunga of the Forest brought her to life.[4] Then each went home. He found that his mother was dead. He ran to the home of Mbunga of the Forest. "My mother is dead. What will I do?"[5]

Mbunga of the Forest said, "What? That is difficult." He found some medicine and gave it to Mbunga of the Village. Mbunga of the Village took the medicine and went home a little, a little, to his mother. He put the medicine up her nose and she came alive and got up.[6]

Soon Mbunga of the Village returned to the home of Mbunga of the Forest. Mbunga of the Forest said, "Why have you come? What is your problem?"

"I took the medicine that you gave me and put it in my mother's nose and she lived."

"Oh! That is good."

He stayed that night and dreamed that his father was dead. He went home, *ti-ti-ti*, and found that his father was dead. He ran back to the home of Mbunga of the Forest. "My father is dead."

Mbunga of the Forest asked, "You still do not reject the way we talked at first?"

"No, no! I'll never reject that, *nyé*."

Mbunga of the Forest gave him some more of the medicine, and he hurried home. He found his father dead. He took the medicine and put it in his nose. His father then lived.

He returned to the home of Mbunga of the Forest and found that Mbunga of the Forest was dead and the insects were eating the body. He cried and wailed and wailed and wailed until he was tired. He said, "Friend, Friend, Friend. He is so fat."[7]

He went to get a knife, and while he was wailing, he cut a piece of flesh from his friend. He wrapped it in leaves and put it in the fire and cooked it quickly. He put the flesh and plantains on his plate ready to eat. While he was eating, his friend began to breathe and woke up. He had only been asleep.

"Go ahead and eat me. We'll talk afterwards."

"No, no! This is not you. This is another kind of food."[8]

"You mean this is not from my body? Don't you see this hole you took from my body? You seem to have rejected the way we talked together. Remember when your mother died, I gave you a fetish which gave her life. Then your father died, and I gave you a fetish for him. Now you find me dead and instead of helping me, you eat me."

"No, no! I can't eat it." He wailed again.

"You had better eat it. If you don't, I'll kill you right away."

So Mbunga of the Village ate the flesh of his friend.

Then Mbunga of the Forest called all the Mbungas. "One day I met Mbunga of the Village." Then he told the story of their friendship so that they could decide what to do with him and decide which one should die.[9]

"I saw someone come from the village. I asked him that we go

together. I asked him his name and he said, 'Mbunga of the Village.'
I told him I am Mbunga of the Forest. Which one of us will not be
loyal to the other first? The Mbunga of the Village had said, 'Not I.
How can I ever be unfaithful to you?' He dreamed that his mother
was dead. He had the same dream about his father. Each time I
gave him a fetish that revived them. Then he came and found me
dead. He cut my stomach and took the meat. Now you tell me
what I am going to do with him. Whichever is wrong will kill the
other, and you will eat the meat.[10] If I lose the case, leave him
alone. He will be all right."[11]

Mbunga of the Village lost, and they killed him.

Among the Nkundo, extra-familial friendships are highly valued, matters of
deep and continuing concern. Such friendships carry both benefits and obligations;
responsibility in maintaining such friendships is exhibited by the degree to which
each party to the friendship shows his gratitude for the benefits and fulfills his proper
obligations. Twin to the desire for fidelity in extra-familial friendships is the strong
tie that exists between men (or women) of the same age group (especially in the Wema
area), exceeded only by the bond that unites those bearing the same name.

Since a culture's strongest desires and fears evidence themselves in oral narratives
and other forms of verbal art, it is not surprising to find among the Nkundo many
tales—some involving animals and others involving people—concerning friendships
and false friendships. The present tale, told by a woman totally engrossed in her tale-
telling, is especially poignant because it demonstrates the disintegration of the
friendship between two men bearing the same name, Mbunga, a friendship in which
the Mbunga who had received the greatest benefits from the friendship committed
the most heinous indignity: assuming that his loyal friend had died, he cut and cooked
a portion of his benefactor's flesh, weeping all the while because the friend had died.
On awaking, the abused friend sought and received a judgment against his erstwhile
friend, a judgment handed down by all those others named Mbunga, most certain
of all to exact a just retribution. Such a tale is likely to endure in the oral tradition
as a horrifying example of the violation of one of the dearest institutions in the tribal
culture. The ingratitude shown by the false friend compounded the injury, a combination neither forgiven nor forgotten by the listeners.

None of the indexes furnished a tale-type number that meets the needs of the
present tale. It is to be hoped that subsequent indexes will provide a classification
for such tales as this and the published but unindexed "people" narratives described
below.

Jablow's *Yes and No* ... (pp. 115–117) in a Vai dilemma tale presents in quite
a different light the situation of a friendship based on similar names: Kamo in the
West, desiring to visit his friend Kamo in the East, consulted a diviner who "cut

sand" and then warned him not to go out at night during his visit; one night at his friend's home, his friend's life was imperiled by a snake, and Kamo of the West rushed out and saved him but was blinded by the snake's blood. Kamo in the East, after consulting a diviner who also "cut sand" and then advised him to kill his own son and apply his blood to the friend's face, killed the child and restored his friend's sight. Which, then, was the greater friend?

Still another dimension is afforded such friendships by de Rop's . . . *woordkunst* . . in a narrative titled "The Two Bembándo" (pp. 198–203). The friendship of these two was so close that when it came time for them to marry, the one insisted that they both marry the same woman. After a surprised protest, the other agreed, and they found a desirable bride, Bolúmbú, in a village where neither Bembándo had any relatives at all. Since both the bride's family and the grooms' families were enthusiastic about the planned marriage, the initial instalment of the bridewealth was paid. Shortly before they went to claim the bride, one of the Bembándo died and was buried; his death was deeply mourned by his friend. As the other Bembándo passed the cemetery en route to the bride's village, his dead comrade called, "Wait for me, so we can go together." Shaking with fear, the live Bembándo waited, and then he and his dead friend went to fetch the bride; they completed the wedding arrangements (with the bride's family's full knowledge that the one Bembándo was indeed dead), celebrated the wedding feast, and left for home with their bride and with many gifts from the bride's family. As they approached the cemetery, the dead Bembándo insisted on his share of the goods, and the fearful comrade promptly divided with him until the matter of sharing the bride arose. When the living Bembándo offered to surrender his portion of the material goods in exchange for his dead friend's half of the bride, the two men quarreled bitterly, and the quarrel was suddenly resolved by the dead one's disappearing with the bride. The living Bembándo came home crying, "and everybody was very much amazed about all this." The moral drawn is as follows: "Although you have concluded a pact of friendship with somebody, don't marry *one* woman if you don't want to share the fate of the two Bembándo" (p. 203). [Summary based on translation by Dr. Tinco E. A. van Hylckama]

See also Whiteley's tale "The Four Uouas," in his *A Selection of African Prose* . . . (pp. 51–55), in which four sisters, all taking the same husband, demonstrate the unlike characters of namesakes.

Motifs:

T	J400.**.	Choice of associates (namesake).
T	H1558.**.	Tests of friendship (of namesake).
T	K2010.**.	Hypocrite namesake pretends friendship but attacks.
T	Q2.	Kind and unkind.
C	K1860.+.**.	Namesake feigns death so that supposed friend will reveal his false claim of friendship.
C	H1556.1.+.**.	Man feigns death to test namesake's stated loyalty.
C	K2090.+.**.	False friend feigns grief at death of namesake, cuts flesh from namesake's body for food while he weeps.

T	E1.**.	Resuscitation to prove infidelity of man's namesake.
C	J1214.+.**.	Man refuses to accept declaration of friendship following false friend's eating some of his flesh during namesake's feigned death.
T	Q281.	Ingratitude punished.
T	Q215.**.	Cannibalism of namesake punished.

1. *"Mbunga"* is the first-person-singular form of the Lonkundo verb *"bunga,"* meaning "to be ungrateful." Other meanings of the verb include the following: "to be delinquent, incorrect, irregular, oblivious; to blunder, err, fail, forget, go amiss, go wrong, lapse" and almost a dozen more (see entry for *"bunga"* in Ruskins' *Dictionary of the Lomongo Language* [n.d.]). Pierre Sangana, one of Mrs. Ross's translation assistants, considered even "ungrateful" as inadequate for this purpose— no English translation, he felt, fully expressed the multiplicity of meanings of *"bunga."*

2. As is true in many Nkundo tales, the narrator does not name the speaker here; from the context, it becomes apparent that the speaker is Mbunga of the Forest, initiator of the friendship even before he knows the similarity in their names.

3. This simple statement expresses the hunger for friendship felt among the Nkundo. In his trust, Mbunga of the Forest renders himself vulnerable to the shifty Mbunga of the Village. Throughout the tale, Mbunga persists in his intention of establishing a sound friendship, though from time to time his anxiety concerning his new-found friend's fidelity prompts him to ask, "Are you sure that you will not reject me?" If, as is suggested by the instructions given prior to the palaver, "all the Mbungas" find cannibalism an acceptable practice, this knowledge might well have increased Mbunga of the Forest's concern about the stability of this new friendship. From the start, it is a one-sided relationship.

It is interesting to note that the faithful one comes from the "forest," or the bush, whereas the faithless one derives from the village. Whether or not these names suggest an unrest concerning the increasing urbanization (and consequent depersonalization) in the Cuvette would be a provocative point to pursue.

4. This is the only Ross-collected tale in which dreams are mentioned, a curious omission in a culture where much importance is attached to dreams, especially to those believed to be prompted by the spirits of deceased members of the family. That the dreams in this instance and in the following one prove to be true would tend to strengthen among the listeners the significance of dreams.

5. The narrator does not indicate that Mbunga of the Village's report of his dream about his mother's death included her being cured by Mbunga of the Forest, but whether or not he had been given this information, Mbunga of the Forest has a friendship obligation: to attempt to resuscitate the mother. Though he has not been described as gifted in medicine, for the purpose of the narrative he is able to furnish a medication that meets the need of his friend's dead mother.

6. In the Cuvette, medicine is often inserted up the nose, though it may also be given as an enema or simply inserted into the anus.

7. The sorry circumstance of Mbunga of the Forest's death does not blind Mbunga of the Village to the fact that here is good meat at hand, meat to satisfy his hunger. The Nkundo are almost a century away from cannibalism, but cannibal-

istic acts persist in the tales. The statement "He is so fat" (a quality making meat taste more delicious) follows so promptly upon the heels of "Friend, Friend, Friend" that few Nkundo listeners would be surprised at the cannibalistic act which follows the noisy grieving. The fact that the body is insect-infested does not deter him: the opportunistic Mbunga of the Village, already heavily indebted to the man presumably dead before him, snatches this last benefit for himself, condemning himself in the eyes of the audience not only by the act itself but by the ingratitude lying behind it.

8. Here, Mbunga of the Village proves himself not only a hypocrite but a coward. In a culture where both truth and courage have long been valued, the anti-hero has delivered upon himself the final blow.

9. Despite the evidence clearly at hand, the case is subjected to palaver, with both Mbungas to be bound by the judges' decision.

10. Mbunga of the Forest proposes not only the death but the eating of the one adjudged guilty, a suggestion that cannibalistic acts themselves were not condemned by "all the Mbungas," but that the eating of one's friends was tabu. We assume that this tale is a survival from earlier times among the Nkundo; all other cannibalistic behavior is reserved in the Ross-collected tales to ogres and to monstrous dogs.

11. Here, Mbunga of the Forest displays mercy for the one who has abused him. As has been shown in earlier tales in this volume, mercy is a trait valued among the Nkundo.

Narrator:	Ngoi Ekoletonga, a village elder
Location:	Longa
Date:	December 7, 1972

49. *The Wise Man Outwitted by the Fool*

Bolole (Fool) and Bont'owa Wanya (Wise Man)[1] went together to hunt meat. As soon as they reached the hunting place, each one built his own small shelter.[2] Then they each built traps for the animals.[3]

The very first day, Fool found meat in one of his traps. But Wise Man found nothing. Fool took his meat to his hut. He cleaned it and smoked it over his fire. Then he stored it carefully near his hut.[4]

The next day, Fool went to check his traps again. While he was gone, Wise Man took Fool's meat from its hiding place and hid it near his own hut.

When Fool returned, he found that his meat was gone. He sought out Wise Man and asked, "Where is my meat? I had a basket of it yesterday, but today it is gone."

Wise Man answered that, "You are nothing but a fool. You don't have any meat and never did have. You have forgotten what you had. Go your way and stop accusing me."

The second day, Fool found meat in his traps. He cleaned it, smoked it, and stored it carefully. When he was gone to hunt again, Wise Man took it and put it away for himself. When Fool complained, he reminded him that, "You are just a fool. You don't know what you have."

This happened day and day.[5] Fool began to make a plan. He went out along the path until he met a man. He killed him, cut up the meat, smoked it, and stored it as he had his other meat.[6]

In not a long while, the family of the man came into the forest hunting him. "Where is the man who came into the forest?" they asked Fool.

Fool said, "No word."

Knowing that Fool was not a wise man, they weren't willing to trust him. They looked for Fool's meat, but found that he had none at all.

Then they asked Wise Man about their relative. "Have you seen the man who came into the forest a few days ago?"

Wise Man answered, "I have not seen him and I have heard no news of him."

However, they decided to search the meat of Wise Man. *Mo!* There they found the flesh of the very man they were seeking.

The result was that Fool went home with no meat and no problems. However, Wise Man found himself with a real palaver, judged by the elders of the village. All evidence was against him, and he had no chance of being vindicated.

Often a fool has more wisdom than people think he has.

[Notes to Tale 49 follow Tale 50.]

Source:	*Bekolo Bèmò . . .*
	Zaïrian school reader
	(in Lonkundo)
Translator:	Mabel Ross
Date of Translation:	March 1976

50. *The Wise Man Outwitted by the Fool* *(Variant)*

Fool and Real Person[7] went for a period to hunt. They built temporary huts. Then they went to hunt meat. Fool killed a wild pig. Real Person killed a dark brown antelope. Then they went into their huts.

Fool hid his wild pig behind his house. Real Person came to uncover that wild pig; he brought it to his house. Then he asked Fool, "What did you kill?" Fool said that, "I killed a wild pig." Real Person said, "I killed a wild pig also."

Real Person said, "Let us cut up that meat now." Then Fool went to uncover the wild pig; he found nothing at all, *nyè*. He felt much sorrow in his heart. Real Person cut up the wild pig and smoked it very well.

Real Person did Fool in this manner many doings. Then Fool understood, and he knew that Real Person had done deceitfully to him.

They went hunting again. But Real Person had no meat that day at all, *nyè*. Fool encountered with a woman, the wife of a certain chief. He killed that woman, and he hung her in a basket. Then he said to Real Person that, "It is well that we go home today." Real Person agreed. But when they stood up that they go, Real Person took that basket by force from Fool. He supposed that it was a basket of meat.

When they arrived home, they asked Fool that, "Where is your meat?" Fool that,[8] "I do not have meat." Then the people asked them that, "Did you see a woman there in the forest? They hunt, hunt, hunt for her but they do not see her, *nyè*."

Fool answered; he said, "Real Person killed that woman whom you seek."

Real Person denied it; he said, "Not I." But when they unpacked his basket, they saw the woman. Then they acquitted Fool from the palaver. Real Person paid the owner of the wife with very many things.[9]

The trickster-tricked pattern offered in the present pair of tales is found more often in the Ross collection as being played out by animal actors than by humans (see, for example, Tales 18–20 and 22–24). Evidently the narrator of Tale 49 was the oldest in the circle of elders involved in the narration; even when members of his audience made suggestions or additions, he tended to ignore them.

Klipple's first variant for Aarne-Thompson's tale type 9 (The Unjust Partner), based on the Congolese tale "How the Crow Cheated the Dove and Got into Difficulty through It" (in Weeks' *Jungle Life and Jungle Stories* [1923], pp. 401 ff.), is the only sample that fits these two stories; Klipple's variant utilizes animals rather than people as characters, but the situation is strikingly similar to that found in the Ross-provided narratives. (A summary of the sample cited by Klipple for her variant appears below.) None of the samples furnished in either Arewa's or Lambrecht's index appears to afford help in classifying these tales.

In Weeks' "How the Crow Cheated the Dove and Got into Difficulty through It" (available to us in his *Congo Life and Folklore*, pp. 401–402), the crow (represented as the clever one) and the dove (represented as the dupe) go hunting together, taking with them their guns, charms, dogs, and chief huntsman. Every animal the dove kills is claimed by the crow until the dove accidentally shoots and kills the chief huntsman; the crow claims that prey also until he sees it is the huntsman, when he promptly disclaims it. The case is brought up for palaver, and the judges determine that the crow, because he has claimed all the earlier prey, must bury the huntsman's body properly and pay all the expenses of the funeral.

In "Bokombi oa Lokombo" ("The Builder of Traps"), found on pages 11 and 12 of *Bekolo Bèmò* . . . , a delightful twist is given to the "meat in the basket" element found in the Ross-provided narratives: a hunter who violates a tabu finds mushrooms growing in the path and picks them in lieu of the meat his traps had failed to catch (he had been told not to complain if his traps failed to catch meat); the mushrooms become portions of a missing goat, and the arbitrators of the palaver decide that the hunter must pay the owner of the goat a suitable amount of money. The miscreant is understandably and disagreeably surprised at the character of the meat in his basket, but by violating an aspect of the Nkundo value system (the respect for tabus) he has richly earned his punishment.

Motifs:

T	H509.**.	Tests of cleverness or ability: miscellaneous—unwitting contest between two men to see which has better sense.
C	C549.+.	Tabu: touching anyone else's property.
T	J514.**.	Deceitful friend steals fool's meat, and his greed, detected, causes him to lose the palaver.

T	J1500.**.	Clever practical retort (responsive act).
T	J670.**.	Forethought in defences against others: "fool" kills man (woman) and hides meat in basket to be stolen and claimed by false friend, ensuring thief's detection.
C	J1110.+.**.	Clever fool hides human flesh in meat basket rifled by false friend and thus incriminates thief.
T	J1510.	The cheater cheated.
T	K2155.	Evidence of crime left so that dupe is blamed.
C	L390.+.	Clever "fool" outwits his deceitful "wise" hunting partner.
T	K661.	Escape from suspicion of crime.
T	K1600.	Deceiver falls into own trap.
C	Q380.+.	Breaking tabu punished.
T	Q212.	Theft punished.
T	L430.	Arrogance repaid.
T	L140.	The unpromising surpasses the promising.

1. In this case, the "praise name" "*Bont'owa Wanya*" proves to have been unwisely conferred.

2. [Narrator's explanatory comment: "This not only gave him shelter from rain, but also protected him at night from wild animals."]

3. [Narrator's explanatory comment: "This was composed of a long fence made of poles and leaves with traps here and there the length of the fence. A small animal would hunt a way through the fence. The only opening he could find opened directly into a trap. Later the hunter could follow along the fence and check each trap for his prey."]

Such fence-traps are commonly used by the Nkundo, especially by men going out singly rather than as members of a large hunting party; large hunting parties normally resort to huge nets, which are worked cooperatively (see Tale 44 for a group hunting venture of this sort).

4. The meat was stored outside the hut both to keep it fresher and to leave room inside the small shelter for the preparation of meat caught on subsequent days.

5. "Day and day" is the Lonkundo equivalent of the English "Day after day" or "For many days." Neither the "wise man" nor the audience would expect the fool to know what was going on, at least for a while. After all, he was a fool.

Attitudes toward maniacs and lunatics vary widely from culture to culture. Among the bulk of the cultures that we have investigated concerning this point, the overall tendency of the group seems to be to fear and confine the maniac but to protect—and even, on occasion, revere—the imbecile or lunatic. We cite but one source of the many consulted: Westermarck (*Ritual and Belief in Morocco* [1926], Vol. I, pp. 47–49) notes that in Morocco mental derangement is always "attributed to supernatural influences." Harmless lunatics "are venerated as saints, whose reason is in heaven while the body is on earth" (p. 48). If—as appears among the Nkundo folktales we have examined—he who abuses or takes unfair advantage of a fool invariably loses, one might have reason to suspect that among the Nkundo, as well as in many other cultures, the fool is not considered fair game for the would-be cheat.

6. Certain acts of honor are a part of the Nkundo value system. Anyone can

pick cassava leaves if the plants are growing along the path; whatever is found or abandoned on the path itself is by agreement the property of the finder. (Several trickster tales in de Bouveignes' volumes play on this point.) If two men go out to hunt together, however, it is accepted that neither will bother the meat of the other. The so-called "wise man" apparently felt that he need not abide by the rules when he was dealing with a fool. Fool, who was less a "fool" than he appeared, relied on his knowledge of the character of his "friend" in his plan: he could trust Wise Man to steal the meat and thus clear Fool of the crime.

7. The translation into English of the name "onto Mongo" is not easy. It can be transliterated "The Man Himself," "The True Man," or "Real Person." Since among the Nkundo a fool is frequently regarded as other than a whole (or real) person, we have chosen "Real Person" here to point up the major difference between the two that would be remarked by the Nkundo themselves.

8. The omission of "said" in a dialogue is frequent among the Nkundo, both in conversation and in narration.

9. The Lonkundo original, titled "Bolole l'onto-Mongo" ("The Fool and the Man-Himself"), appears on pages 9–10 in *Bekolo Bémò.*...

Narrator:	Mpanga Iyende
Location:	Bonga-Iteli
Date:	December 1973

51. *The Chief's Granddaughter and Her Suitors*[1]

Another man had a daughter[2] and then she had a daughter. Then the child there found it hard because man and man bothered the chief. Then many came to ask for her. Then Iko (Porcupine) came and stood. "Tell the child that I am here."

Then the man went to the child[3] of the chief. While he was in the house, another man was there who was the guard. The porcupine said, "I want the child of the chief."[4]

"You want her?" He showed disgust.[5]

Then the porcupine went; he returned. She refused him. *Té-è-è.*

Then, *te-e-e*, Mboloko (Dwarf Antelope) came. He was wearing

an undershirt, a shirt, and trousers.[6] He came to get the hand of the
wife of the chief.[7] Then Dwarf Antelope came. He asked the guard
for information. "Is the child of the chief there?"

"*E-e-e*, it's like that."[8]

"I'm waiting till you tell her I have come."

Dwarf Antelope returned. After he returned, then Nkòi (Leopard) came.

Leopard came, looking handsome. He came to see what was
going on there. He said, "The porcupine and the dwarf antelope
came to take the child of the chief.[9] Now I've also come. Do you
hear me?"

He said, "See that I am the leopard. Tell her that I have come
to take the child of the chief."

"Wait and I'll ask her."

For the wife he sang his song.[10]

He returned; he left with shame itself because the child of the
chief had refused him. Some laughed at him. "You did bad, and
then she refused you."

Then at that time Njòku (Elephant) came. He went through the
forest carelessly knocking down trees along the path, and picking
leaves from the trees.[11]

Then he reached Pierre.[12] He arrived.

"You hear: what person?"

He said, "I am Elephant."

"*E-e*. What do you want?"

"*E-e*. I came to ask to take the child of the chief. Do you hear
me? Go and ask her."

"I'll ask her."[13]

Elephant left with all shame.

Then another who is like the leopard but is smaller[14]—he wanted
to come to Pierre himself, only Pierre. He came creeping along the
path with his beautiful coat. He arrived and asked the place of the
chief. He slept. In the morning[15] he said, "I have come. Where is
the child of the chief?"

Then he arrived and the guard grabbed him at the door of the
house.

He asked him to ask for the child of the chief. Then,[16]

She said, "Bring him in. I want to see him."

Lion came and she saw him. She said, "*N-n-n*. My husband,
what do you have? I will have him."

Then the chief had a feast and gifts.[17] Then Lion took his wife
and they went. Those who went went with difficulty.

As they went, someone said, "You have the child of the chief.

You may not pass here until you contend in a fight. If you win, you may go with your wife. If I win, you leave your wife."

Then, "How? Porcupine?"

"Until we fight, the child of the chief may not pass."

They took the things for the fight. "If we must fight before we pass, I don't refuse."[18]

A long time, a long time, they met and came and came and fought.[19]

They fought, and Lion won. He went with his wife.[20]

Then they arrived, they at the place of Nsombe (Wild Pig).[21] He said, "You may not pass here until we fight. If you win, you may take your wife. If I win, the wife stays here."

He said, "Come on." They fought.[22] They fought and fought. He won. Lion went with his wife.

Then another person said, "*Mu!* You pass. You want to pass here with your wife. You can't pass until you fight with me. If you win, she goes with you, and if I win, she will stay here."

Then they fought.[23]

Then they fought and fought.[24] The trees fell. They struggled, *nyè*. The leaves flew . . . They rolled over in all the paths. They fought, and Lion won.

Then Ulu (Tortoise) came from there seeking an opportunity. He said, "You and I,[25] both of us, asked for the child of the chief. Now I and you we will try. If you come up from the dirt, you take the wife, but if I come up from the dirt I take the wife."

Then, "I don't refuse. Come."

They fought.[26]

They fought and fought and fought and fought and fought. They stopped. He said, "You haven't won, and I want to take the wife and then I want to go."[27]

"When you came from the trip with your wife, you yourself . . ."

"I want to go."

"Until you overthrow me, you cannot go with your wife."

"I have no word. We'll fight." Then they fought again at that place.[28]

They fought and fought and fought, and Tortoise won.[29] Tortoise said, "Your wife stays here as my wife, but you may go on. You go on, but leave your wife here."

The wife said, "*Mo!* I think that since I didn't choose Tortoise, if I can't go with my husband I'm going home."

Then the wife returned to the place of her father. Lion went, and Tortoise remained in his home.

When you hear a rumor, friend, leave it. I am there.

Lion had a good wife at home. Tortoise ruined his chances with the child of the child.[30] Do you hear?

Narrator: I am parched![31]
Chorus: The action is completed!

Although to a Western reader Tale 51 may have rather humorous overtones, there is no laughter at all from the Nkundo audience during its telling. Clearly, the narrative is a serious one, intended to teach rather than to entertain: the matters of courtship and marriage, with the interference possible in human marital arrangement, are too close to the core of Nkundo life to serve as subjects for humor. The prompt choral participation suggests that the listeners were already familiar with the tale and relished the opportunity to participate in its telling. Much animation was displayed in the narrating, and the tale-teller's skillful use of inflection and of changes in pace increased the story's dramatic impact.

The account of a woman—not always a chief's "child"—courted by a number of "men" (all animals) is a staple among the folktales of various African cultures. Tests for suitors are universal, although it is more usual to have the suitor prove himself worthy before he can claim his bride than it is to require the suitor to defend his right to the bride after he has won her.

Even though the "child" was well guarded, she was given the privilege of choosing her own husband, an opportunity not in keeping with Nkundo practice. The marriage of people and nonpeople—animals, supernatural creatures, objects— is not uncommon in the Nkundo oral tradition, but in none of the Ross-collected narratives with the possible exception of Tale 80 are there offspring of such a union; the children of this latter union—if, indeed, they *are* the children of the fish-woman and her husband and not those of the husband by the slave-wives given to him— disappear with the wives following the husband's breaking of the tabu. Since propagation is highly valued by the Nkundo, perhaps "unnatural" marriages are included, each with an unfortunate outcome, to inculcate adherence to the Nkundo cultural patterns regarding courtship, bridewealth, and marriage.

The curious mixture of Nkundolike and non-Nkundolike elements in this tale prompts the question of its origin. Is it perhaps a "stray" from another cultural group, not yet fully accommodated to the Nkundo value system? Is it, on the other hand, a relic from an earlier Nkundo oral tradition, reflecting a value system that has since given way to the present one? In either instance, it offers interesting possibilities for the study of folktale alteration and diffusion.

Apart from Arewa's tale type 201, which includes combat for the retention of a bride, there appears to be no satisfactory classificatory aid for this tale.

Motifs:

C	M90.+.**.	Father (grandfather) decrees that daughter will be allowed to choose her own husband from among all animal suitors.
C	M90.+.**.	Chief decrees that granddaughter will be allowed to choose her own husband from among all animal suitors.
T	T131.0.1.	Princess has unrestricted choice of husband.
T	B620.**.	Series of animal suitors for human bride.
T	T110.	Unusual marriage.
T	H310.**.	Suitor tests: initial choice left entirely to bride-to-be.
T	H326.1.2.**.	Suitor test (post-marriage): skill in wrestling.
T	H331.4.1.	(Animal) suitors contest with groom in wrestling to determine owner of human bride.
T	H1562.9.**.	Test of strength: wrestling with lion groom for possession of human bride.
T	B263.8.**.	Wrestling contest between lion (bridegroom) and other animals (rejected suitors of human bride).
T	B266.	Animals fight.
T	H335.0.1.**.	Bride helps suitor perform his tasks by singing praise song.
T	L315.	Small animal overcomes large.
C	L315.+.**.	Tortoise wins suitor contest in wrestling match, overcoming lion bridegroom after larger animals have failed.
T	L430.**.	Arrogance repaid: tortoise, victorious in wrestling contest with lion bridegroom, is rejected as husband by human bride.

1. The narrator makes a false start, "Another woman did ...," then exclaims "*A!*" After a very brief pause, he starts again, with full confidence, to tell the tale he has undertaken. The entire tale is delivered at a very fast pace.

2. Here someone from the audience grumbles about the narrator's shift in beginnings, opening his protest with "*Mo!*" This was the only real complaint about the narrator's performance voiced throughout the entire eight-tale session.

3. "Child" here and elsewhere in the tale is to be understood as the granddaughter of the chief.

4. A child in the audience is heard singing and talking at this point.

5. Here the narrator *announces* the song to be sung by furnishing the first two words of the song. Although this story was clearly a *cante fable*, the speed with which the songs were sung, combined with the unfamiliarity of the dialect, made the words exceedingly difficult to decipher. After a number of efforts to reproduce the songs— there were slight variations from one singing to another—we have had to accept the fact that we cannot do them justice in translation. At each point where the song is sung in the narrative, we have indicated the number of lines sung, and special changes in content, and comments on the chorus's function, leaving the opportunity of a literal translation to some later specialist in ethnomusicology who can also unlock the dialect of Lonkundo used by the narrator.

This first song has five lines of text—as do all but one of the other courtship songs sung in this tale—each followed by the same one-line chorus. The content of the song presents Porcupine's candidacy for the hand of the chief's granddaughter and the eligibility of both for such a match. The nonsense sound *"ya"* was used at the ends of the fourth and fifth text lines "to make the song sweet" (see Bascom's *Ifa Divination*, p. 255, n. 7, for this use of nonsense sounds in songs).

6. Dwarf Antelope's wearing of human clothing is at once evidence of acculturation and an engaging instance of "one-up-manship" on the part of a creature noted for his quick wit. (See Tales 18–20 and 33, narratives capitalizing on this trait of the dwarf antelope.)

7. The narrator immediately corrects this error, saying "child of the chief" after a barely perceptible pause. No embarrassment is apparent in association with this slip of the tongue.

8. Dwarf Antelope's song is sung here; it is identical to the first song with two exceptions: "Mboloko" replaces "Iko" in the fourth line, and there is a substitution of *"i"* for *"ke,"* underscoring the special quality of this clever fellow. There is a brief hesitation following the end of the song before the narrator picks up the story line.

9. The rapid spread of gossip characteristic in an Nkundo village is here extended to the entire forest community, with one "man's" business becoming everybody's affair.

10. A voice can be heard at the back of the audience, saying, "It isn't there," meaning, "Leopard isn't going to win her."

The leopard's song is sung here, using "Nkòi" as the first word in the fourth text line. There is no hesitation this time between the end of the song and the continuation of the narrative.

11. [*Translator's* comment: "as a man eats peanuts when he is going to seek a wife because of the joy in his heart." The translator gestured to show the elephant's carefree behavior, and laughed with pleasure at the episode.]

12. Use of a French name in addressing a guard is most certainly an original touch on the part of the narrator.

13. Elephant's courting song is sung here, but his name is omitted in the fourth text line.

14. This is Simba (lion), as is made evident in the song sung for him by the narrator. Lions, found east and southeast of the Cuvette, are not native to the Nkundo area, a fact that may account for the narrator's rather hazy and misleading description of the final suitor.

15. Lion timed his arrival strategically. As a Zaïrian proverb states, "No monkey eats during the night" [i.e., "Ask favors in the daytime"]. Also, a suitor up and about early in the day is likely to prove an industrious and prosperous husband.

16. A *four*-line song, complete with chorus lines, is sung for Lion; "Simba" is included in line 4. In his song, Lion is more tactful in his announcement of his intention than the other suitors have been.

17. Apparently, no bridewealth was asked of Lion or his family. On the contrary, the groom gained not only the princess but a substantial dowry as well. This

reversal of the customary Nkundo gift presentation suggests that this narrative may have been imported from a culture with quite different marriage customs and that not all of the necessary narrative accommodations have yet been made to fit the story to its new cultural milieu.

18. Male prowess is valued among the Nkundo, especially where it relates to hunting and to self-defense. The "prize" in this instance was an especially valuable piece of property, a wife. (Since prowess in battle figures in many other tribal cultures besides that of the Nkundo, this feature does not mark the tale as unquestionably Nkundo in origin.)

19. Although a translation of the song sung by the lion's bride proved too difficult to manage, we were able through repeated listenings to determine in the Lonkundo dialect the "two-part-round" effect we had noted in Mpanga Iyende's *cante fables* before. The words and the overlapping pattern of lines are furnished here following a description of the plan for the singing.

The narrator himself sings the four-word line three times all the way through, without intermission. When the narrator begins *"'kul'ine"* the second time, the chorus begins singing the same four-word line, singing it three times through, also without intermission.

Narrator:	*Simba bome'kul'ine.*
	Simba bome'kul'ine.
Chorus:	*Simba bom*
Narrator:	*Simba bome'kul'ine.*
Chorus:	*e'kul'ine. Simba*
	bome'kul'ine. Simba
	bome'kul'ine.

The line sung appears to be an elision of these words: *Simba bome akula ine*; the sense of the words is "Simba my husband overthrows him," sung by the bride to encourage her husband in the struggle. There is no attempt made by the narrator to imitate a female voice.

20. The storyteller makes a false start after this word, but he recovers himself and proceeds, unflustered, with the narrative.

21. Wild Pig did not sue for the hand of the chief's granddaughter during the course of the tale, though he may have been one of the many "men" who had "bothered the chief." From this point on, the animals who fight with the lion do not tally with the ones who came courting. Why this shift in dramatis personae occurred was not explained. We suspect that the rush of combatants reflects the Nkundo's own interest in being involved in whatever action is going on, and that the fact there *is* plenty of action makes the identity of the actors rather unimportant to the listeners. Logic seems not to be the determining factor here.

22. The same song pattern described in note 19 is repeated here.

23. Again the song is repeated, as above.

24. Throughout this description of the fight, great excitement is exhibited on the part of both narrator and audience; such enthusiasm is shown in the reporting that several words were lost to translation (ellipsis dots indicate the gaps).

25. Here the narrator reverses the customary order in the naming of persons, an order mended in the following sentence.

26. Again the song is sung by narrator and chorus as described in note 19. The choral participation becomes positively frenzied.

27. Again the narrator makes a false start ("You from . . ."), but quickly replaces those words with the ones intended. As the next passage is related, he places great emphasis on repetition, increasing his volume and really squabbling in the process of handling the dialogue.

28. Again, the bride's encouraging song is sung by narrator and chorus.

29. There was considerable response from the audience when the winner was announced.

30. This is precisely what the narrator said.

31. Here the narrator substitutes for his usual "*Ili!*" the word "*Nyiti!*", similar enough in sound—and delivered with a rising inflection—to signal the end of the tale, but clear enough to command a well-earned drink.

Narrator:	Ikwa Isilombe
Location:	Boende
Date:	November 1973

52. *The Girl Who Chose Her Own Husband*

That child was very beautiful, and all the animals wanted that woman. The father came.

Mam'olilo, Mam'olilo of my mother,[1]
　　Ko kongole.[2]
I have found a husband for you.
　　Ko kongole.
Isio, the animal,[3] is that husband.
　　Ko kongole.
Give him the chair[4] that he may go home.
　　Ko kongole.

She refused, and the porcupine came.

Mam'olilo, Mam'olilo of my mother,
　　Ko kongole.

I have found a husband for you.
> *Ko kongole.*

The porcupine is that husband.
> *Ko kongole.*

Give him the chair that he may go home.
> *Ko kongole.*

She refused, and the dwarf antelope came.

Mam'olilo, Mam'olilo of my mother,
> *Ko kongole.*

I have found a husband for you.
> *Ko kongole.*

The dwarf antelope is that husband.
> *Ko kongole.*

Give him the chair that he may go home.
> *Ko kongole.*

She refused him, and the large antelope came.

Mam'olilo, Mam'olilo of my mother,
> *Ko kongole.*

I have found a husband for you.
> *Ko kongole.*

The large antelope is that husband.
> *Ko kongole.*

Give him the chair that he may go home.
> *Ko kongole.*

She refused him, and the wild pig came.

Mam'olilo, Mam'olilo of my mother,
> *Ko kongole.*

I have found a husband for you.
> *Ko kongole.*

The wild pig is that husband.
> *Ko kongole.*

Give him the chair that he may go home.
> *Ko kongole.*

She refused him, and the large brown antelope came.

Mam'olilo, Mam'olilo of my mother,
> *Ko kongole.*

I have found a husband for you.
> *Ko kongole.*

The large brown antelope is that husband.
Ko kongole.
Give him the chair that he may go home.
Ko kongole.

She refused him, and the speckled fowl came.

Mam'olilo, Mam'olilo of my mother,
Ko kongole.
I have found a husband for you.
Ko kongole.
The speckled fowl is that husband.
Ko kongole.
Give him the chair that he may go home.
Ko kongole.

She refused him, and the leopard came.

Mam'olilo, Mam'olilo of my mother,
Ko kongole.
I have found a husband for you.
Ko kongole.
The leopard is that husband.
Ko kongole.
Give him the chair that he may go home.
Ko kongole.

She refused him, and the large bluish bird[5] came.

Mam'olilo, Mam'olilo of my mother,
Ko kongole.
I have found a husband for you.
Ko kongole.
The large bluish bird is that husband.
Ko kongole.
Give him the chair that he may go home.
Ko kongole.

She refused him, and the wild goose came.

Mam'olilo, Mam'olilo of my mother,
Ko kongole.
I have found a husband for you.
Ko kongole.
The wild goose is that husband.
Ko kongole.

Give him the chair that he may go home.
Ko kongole.

She refused him, and the elephant came.

Mam'olilo, Mam'olilo of my mother,
Ko kongole.
I have found a husband for you.
Ko kongole.
The elephant is that husband.
Ko kongole.
Give him the chair that he may go home.
Ko kongole.

She refused him, and the chicken came.

Mam'olilo, Mam'olilo of my mother,
Ko kongole.
I have found a husband for you.
Ko kongole.
The chicken is that husband.
Ko kongole.
Give him the chair that he may sit down.[6]
Ko kongole.

The people are all excited. She had refused them all and is taking the chicken. The women prepare food for the feast. They bring chairs and tables and spoons and forks. They were eating at the tables. During the feast it began to rain. The worms came out in the rain. When the chicken saw the worms, he ran after them. The chicken had shamed the princess because even though she had refused all the others, now her husband was running after worms.

Because the differences between this *cante fable* and the preceding one (Tale 51) outweigh their similarities, we felt that one could not be considered a variant of the other. In print, the two belie their strongest common feature: the extensive use of song to carry the narrative forward. Fortunately, Mrs. Ross was able with the help of Pierre Sangana to capture both the wording of the songs for the present tale and the way in which the songs were tied to the brief spoken portions. The telling was direct, and the audience thoroughly relished the repetition involved in the singing. Again, as in Tale 51, the content of the tale was not provocative of laughter; regardless of the identity of the suitors, each of the candidates was taken seriously, and the earnestness and hopefulness of the father in presenting each candidate communicated itself in the narrator's voice. Artistically, this sober handling provides a telling contrast with the outcome of the tale: The choice made after a series of solemn considerations proves to have been an unwise one, and once more the listeners are reminded by inference that the tribal way, the traditional way, of marital choice is sound. A tale that to Western listeners may appear to make little sense serves to reinforce the cultural values of the society out of which it grew, with the moral made even more effective because the narrator leaves the hearers to derive it themselves.

None of the indexes consulted furnishes a tale-type number appropriate for this *cante fable*. There is need for a type number, however, since this tale does not stand alone in the vast range of African narratives if one is to judge from the published but unindexed variants available. We cite but two such variants here.

Okeke's *Tales of Land of Death* presents in "Onalu" (pp. 66–68) an Igbo *cante fable* of a beautiful girl courted by a number of animals; the elephant, the leopard, the goat, the snake, and "a great many others" were turned back by Onalu's mother, who was waiting for one special suitor, a "spotted being" who had long ago given a gift in earnest of his suit. On his arrival—a tardy arrival, for the sake of the narrative —the spotted bush rat was awarded the bride. The narrative concludes, "Ogini's good fortune was a great source of pride to the lowly" (p. 68). It is entirely possible that Tale 52 originated outside the Cuvette as an effort to make the same point but that in the new cultural environment that point has been eroded.

Dayrell's "The King Who Married the Cock's Daughter" (in his *Folk Stories from Southern Nigeria* . . . [1910], pp. 42–45) includes an element strikingly similar to that providing the crux of the present tale. A king still not satisfied with his 250 wives, learning that Cock had an exceptionally beautiful daughter, sought her as his bride. Cock cautioned the king that "if he married his daughter he must not forget that she had the natural instincts of a hen, and that he should not blame Adia unen [his daughter] if she picked up corn whenever she saw it" (pp. 42–43). The king married her nonetheless and so favored her that the wife previously favored deliberately exposed Cock's daughter's weakness for corn in public and thus shamed the king, who returned Adia unen to her father. Later informed by his third wife of the jealous one's deliberate provocation of this disgrace, he rejected the jealous wife and a year or so afterwards died of a broken heart. The concluding statement of this tale points up the narrative's purpose: "[T]hey passed a law that for the future no one should marry any bird or animal" (p. 45). In effect, the Nkundo tale makes a similar point: that a marriage should include partners appropriate to one another and to the Nkundo cultural pattern.

Motifs:

T	T131.0.1.	Princess has unrestricted choice of husband.
C	W165.+.**.	Woman refuses all suitors except chicken.
T	B620.**.	Series of animal suitors for human bride.
T	H310.**.	Suitor tests: initial choice left entirely to bride.
T	T100.	Marriage.

T   B620.1.   Daughter promised to animal suitor (chicken).
T   B602.**.   Marriage to chicken.
T   T110.   Unusual marriage (human bride to chicken).
T   U130.**.   The power of habit: chicken chases worms at own wedding
                     feast.

1. "Of my mother" is equivalent to "of my kin" or "dear to me." No special meaning is attached to the "child's" name.

2. "*Ko kongole*," sung by the chorus throughout the tale, is used purely for its musical sound, "to make the song sweet" (see note 3 for Tale 41), as has been true in several other songs found in the present collection (for example, "*Kongo*" [Tale 41] and "*ya*" [Tale 51]).

Though no attempt was made by the narrator to imitate the female voice, the first three text lines appear to be sung by the father and the fourth text line by the prospective bride.

3. None of Mrs. Ross's translation assistants was able to identify "Isio" apart from his being an "animal."

4. "Give him the chair," signifying the completion of the "child's" evaluation of the prospective bridegroom, has no connection with Nkundo practice that we have been able to discern. The chair as a form of property has long been highly valued by the Nkundo, and serves as a symbol of authority (see note 13 for Tale 2 on this matter).

5. The large bluish bird, a clumsy, ugly bird very common in the Nkundo area, makes a noise like "*lokula-kôkô*," an observation that has given it the Lonkundo name "*lokulakôkô*." Its cry is said to be a warning of the approach of enemies.

6. With the exception of the changing names of the candidates, "that he may sit down," the mark of the "child's" approval of the suitor, is the only variation in the song sung throughout the *cante fable*.

The procession of suitors having been completed, the narrator proceeds quickly and economically to the dénouement: the excitement attending the nuptial feast, and the embarrassment visited upon the whole community (though only "the princess" is named) when the chicken, obeying his instincts, runs after worms. The tumbling-over-itself of the concluding portion is suggested by the intermixture of verb tenses and by the rapidity with which the events are summarized. The contrast between the orderliness of the courtship procedure and the mad scramble accompanying the unsuitable marriage serves to underscore the moral the narrator expects the listeners to draw from the tale. The narrative technique is admirably designed for its didactic purpose.

Narrator:	Mpanga Iyende
Location:	Bonga-Iteli
Date:	December 1973

53.   *The Chief's Daughter and the Hawk*

A certain chief had a daughter who couldn't do any work, *nyė*. Her work was eating and bathing.

He got up and was going on a long journey, he and his wife. They went from their village. The one he left,[1] he said, "Mama, now I am going on a trip. This girl must not do any work at all, *nyė*. Her work is only to eat and to bathe." Then he left, *te-e-e*. He stayed there months.[2]

The mother went into the forest to work in her garden. While she was there, she felt very, very tired. "*Mo!* I am weakened and tired from working in the garden. Go get me some water that I may live."

She said, "You know that Father said I couldn't work like that."

She said, "Go bring some water."[3]

She took off an iron necklace, iron bracelets, and iron anklets.[4] She took a *yuka*[5] and she took a jug, and she went to the swamp.

While she was at the swamp getting water, Nkombe (Hawk) grabbed her in his claws and carried her high into a tree and put her in his nest. While she was there, every bird came and left droppings on her body until she was covered with the droppings. Then they scratched her with their claws.[6]

Her father hadn't come yet. Then people came, and then more came.[7]

"Father is near. He is coming." Then she heard the noise of a barge.[8] They passed. Then some more came with a motor.[9]

Then they[10] said, "Your father went and arrived there[11] yesterday. When he came back from his trip, he brought many, many slaves and things of all kinds. He gave up to the child of elegance all the things that he brought in her behalf."

Then she understood.[12]

Then one said, "Who is there?"

She said, "I, the child." Then she saw the big boat, a very long boat.

He[13] said, "Every slave is to go up in the tree until he reaches the nest."

One slave climbed and climbed and climbed, but he didn't get there. They cut his throat. *A-i-i!*[14]

Another slave came and climbed and climbed, *ti-i-i,*[15] but he didn't get there. They cut his throat.

They all climbed and tried and tried, *O nyĕ.*

Another slave tried and tried and tried and tried and tried. He arrived where the child was. He took her and he came down with her. Then they went home.

All the wealth which he had brought, his riches, she heard about. They washed her in water. Then she felt of all the things which he had brought from the journey.[16]

Then when a person loses his freedom, he cannot free himself; he must merit his freedom.[17]

When the mother did badness to the child of her child, she did not only to the child but to other people.

> *Narrator:* The sun has set!
> *Audience:* The action is completed.[18]
> *Narrator:* The sun has set!
> *Audience:* The action is completed!

The frank and open handling here, with a human cast of characters, of the delicate relationships existing within a presumably polygynous household indicates the skill of this particular narrator. As is true among the Nkundo, any favoritism shown carries its price; the father's decided favoring of his daughter is covertly condemned by the narrator, not so much by words as by the humiliating period the favored one is forced to spend in the hawk's nest. Curiously, this exposure of the privileged one is cathartic to the Nkundo listeners, who through this tale can vent with impunity their feelings of frustration and resentment concerning their own low position in the Zaïrian economic structure.

Many insights into life among the Nkundo are afforded by the tale: the use of injunctions, the pleasures of eating and of bathing, the assignment of responsibility for the care of a child or children to another during the parents' absence, the onerous character of the woman's work, the obedience to the elders required of a younger person, the elaborate forms of adornment, the means of securing water, the closeness of the people to their environment and to its other tenants, the continuing presence of slavery, the high value set on the life of a child—*any* child—and the wonder felt at the acquisition of wealth. Also amply demonstrated are such linguistic features as the use of words for emphasis and as interjections ("*nyĕ*" and "*O nyĕ*" and "*Mo!*"), the employment of ideophones and of onomatopoeia ("*te-e-e*," "*ti-i-i*," and "*A-i-i!*"), and the omission of words where the meaning without them will be understood by Nkundo listeners. Certain indications of narrative technique are present, as well, in the formulaic beginning and ending, the omission of identification of the speakers in a dialogue—conveyed instead by mime or by intonation—the use of repetition ("climbed and climbed and climbed" and "tried and tried and tried and tried and tried"), the inclusion of one or more proverbs or "teachings" to drive home the point of the tale, and the freedom of the narrator to improvise and to manipulate his audience (see note 18).

The only indexed tale affording any parallel at all to this one is that for Lambrecht's tale type 855 (8); in Lambrecht's sample, a bird carries a child away, but no other elements of the two tales are similar. We cannot at present assign a type number to this narrative.

Motifs:

C	C680.+.**.	Injunction: do not permit beautiful daughter to do any work except eating and bathing.
C	B299.1.+.**.	Hawk abducts chief's daughter.
C	C927.+.**.	Girl carried away by hawk when forced to work (injunction violated).
T	B552.**.	Girl carried by hawk: abducted and imprisoned in hawk's nest.
C	M2.+.**.	Chief executes every slave incapable of rescuing his daughter from hawk's nest.
C	P175.+.**.	Slaves killed for failure to rescue chief's daughter from hawk's nest.
T	R153.**.	Parent (father) effects rescue of child by use of slaves.

1. The relationship of the daughter to "the one he left" is unclear. Any woman older than the girl in an Nkundo village may be addressed as "Mama." It is possible, on one hand, that she and the girl's mother are co-wives and that her violation of the injunction against the girl's working is a consequence of the commonly observed rivalry among co-wives, venting itself upon the absent wife's daughter. On the other hand, the concluding "teaching" suggests that the "Mama" was the chief's own mother. In either event, "Mama" was considered responsible not only for the girl's unfortunate experience but also for the deaths of the slaves unable to rescue the girl from the hawk's nest.

2. A child is heard talking at this point on the tape.

3. The quarrelsome tone of voice used by the narrator in this exchange is an effective dramatic device. Protest as she will, the girl is well aware that—whatever the father's injunction before he left—she is compelled to obey the order of "Mama" as her elder.

4. The ornaments worn by the girl are marks of her father's indulgence normally reserved for the favorite wife, not for a daughter. In most cases, such adornments are hammered on and are thus not easily removed; apparently room has been left

for her growth, allowing her to take them off without cutting them. Had she been wearing her anklets, bracelets, and necklace, the chief's daughter would not as readily have been carried away by the hawk; her removal of these possessions is necessary to the development of the narrative.

5. The *yuka*, or basket, is used for carrying the heavy water jug.

6. At this point in the story, a listener asks, "Did the chief come?" and the narrator answers, "No. The chief had gone, *ti-i-i*, on a journey. Listen!"

Following this exchange, the narrator sings a song of six text lines, each one followed by a choral response, "*Yele, yele, ye!*" from the audience. A line-by-line translation proved impossible to secure; the content of the song is reproachful, detailing the girl's abhorrent situation but containing no reference to the family members.

7. Here the narrator sings, with choral response from the audience, almost the same song described in note 6.

8. The barge, or *ebei*, is intended for the transporting of supplies and trade goods, and is not powered by a motor but by poles or by paddles, depending on the depth of the water and the character of the soil beneath the water; the use of a barge suggests the immense wealth that later proves to belong to the chief's daughter.

The daughter could "hear" the barge because those propelling it were singing a work song to make their difficult work seem lighter. In order to maintain the rhythm of the paddling or poling, someone in the barge would normally beat out the rhythm on the side or edge of the barge. For a useful discussion of the place of "rowers' songs" in Nkundo verbal art, see de Rop's . . . *woodkunst* . . . , pages 16–20.

9. The narrator sings a seven-line song, with each line followed by choral response; this time, several family references are made in the girl's bitter complaint about her miserable fate in the hawk's nest.

10. The speakers are not identified, but they bring the message the chief's daughter had almost lost hope of hearing.

11. "There" is the home of the chief and his family.

12. Here the narrator sings a seven-line song, again with each line followed by the same choral response; this fourth song is not a repetition of the third one, though it includes several of the lines of that song, emphasizing the girl's complaint about her abandonment by her parents.

13. "He" is the chief, father of the girl in the hawk's nest.

14. The narrator delivers a strangled cry, represented here by "*A-i-i!*"

15. On this ideophone, the narrator has the vocal support of the children in the audience.

16. At this point there is a decided change in the narrator's tone: a moralizing sort of delivery emphasizes the seriousness of the "teaching." The narrator's apparent assumption that the "mother" was the guilty one would be vociferously disputed by an Nkundo audience; the "mother" was exacting from the favored daughter a service younger ones in that culture are expected to furnish for their elders. Dispute is a concomitant to tale-telling among the Nkundo, and provides a most effective method of reinforcing values because the conclusions drawn are those of the listeners, prompted by an ingenious narrator's creating the occasion for discussion and resolution of a delicate problem.

17. None of Mrs. Ross's translators was able to solve the ambiguity of this particular observation. It has been translated literally here, but doubtless some key element peculiar to the dialect has been missed in the translation: the relevance of "he must merit his freedom" to the girl's situation escapes us.

18. The narrator, dissatisfied with the volume of this choral response, repeats "*Ili!*" and receives a much more enthusiastic "*Yo!*"

Narrator:	Mpanga Iyende
Location:	Bonga-Iteli
Date:	December 1973

54. *The Chief Who Did Not Love His Children*

Then a chief was in a village[1] ... A large chief had many wives and many children also. Well, then, he didn't like to see small children inside, *nyè.* Each child when he passed, he would strike their ears and shout at them in anger and tell them to go home.[2]

One day real trouble came to the chief, for he was very, very sick,[3] a very, very hard sickness. When they saw that he was in trouble, "In this way, sickness has arrived, and it will be very hard unless the children bring water and bathe your body. If it isn't like that, you will never get well again."

They called a young girl child to go to the swamp for water. Then, when she arrived there, she saw the elegantly plumed *nkoku*[4] birds that were there. She didn't get the water.

After a long time, she didn't return, somebody said, "Somebody should follow her. We don't know the problem she found there. The water hasn't come."

Then another one followed her. She called out,[5] "Friend, friend, come with the water. The chief is in great need of it."

She said, "Friend, when I arrived here to get the water, I found like this:

Come. Shh! The insect hunters crowd and scratch.
Yes, crowds and crowds alight; the insects have come.[6]

Then someone said, "Friend hasn't yet come, but now follow her, now "

Come. Shh! The insect hunters crowd and scratch.
Yes, crowds and crowds alight; the insects have come.

Another girl came from there. "Botamba, Botamba, come! Come here! The chief is in bad condition."
They said, "Another friend has come. A friend has come here."

Come. Shh! The insect hunters crowd and scratch.
Yes, crowds and crowds alight; the insects have come.

Then another one came to the beach there. She said, "*Mo!* And the thing is getting difficult. Bring the water."
The others said, "When we came to get water,

Come. Shh! The insect hunters crowd and scratch.
Yes, crowds and crowds alight; the insects have come.

Then another one came. She said, "The thing is getting difficult. Bring the water. Why are you staying there? Bring the water! It isn't coming back. Hurry. The chief needs water. Hurry! Come!"[7]
"Another one has come. Friend, come and see."

Come. Shh! The insect hunters crowd and scratch.
Yes, crowds and crowds alight; the insects have come.

Then a follower went to get the children. While all that was going on, the chief died.

He was a chief, and children are children. If they had had a chance in his house—but he had blunted the children's understanding before they went to get the water.
According to the rules of our world, we find that some talk like this, but not the way the chief talked in his manner of doing.

Every person who does evil will find evil afterwards. Every person who does good will afterwards find good.

> *Narrator:* The sun has set!
> *Chorus:* The action is finished![8]

Reflected in Tale 54 is the deep and genuine concern felt by the Nkundo for their own children and for the children in their extended-family community. The position of children in a polygynous household is dramatically exposed here: despite their numbers, each child is still individual, childlike in her curiosity, and prone to share with her peers her interest in and excitement about the features of her own environment. Drawn more closely together by their abuse by their father, the chief, these children could be expected to forget their unfeeling father's need for water in the pleasure felt in observing the *nkoku* birds' behavior.

Here, as in several other tales in the Ross collection, two cultural values are in strong conflict: (1) the requirement of filial obedience and (2) the immense importance attached to children. The narrator himself resolves that conflict in a conclusion acceptable to his hearers: if the children had been treated well, they would have met their father's need—have shown filial obedience—but the chief through his prior behavior had "blunted their understanding," and their neglect of him in his extremity was thus both understandable and excusable. A subtle preparation for this conclusion becomes apparent upon close examination of the text; in not a single instance does a child call the dying man "Father"—the term consistently used is "the chief." The man who had in no way other than by procreation proved a "father" to his children richly deserved to be ignored as a "father" in his hour of need. The narrator suggests in "In this way, sickness has arrived" that the chief's cruel behavior toward his children had in fact produced his "very hard sickness," and that it could be cured only by the showing of mercy by those who had received no mercy at his hands, a suggestion confirmed by the proverb closing the tale.

We have found no tale-type number suitable for classifying this poignant narrative.

Motifs:

T	S11.	Cruel father.
C	M2.+.**.	Chief punishes his own children whenever they approach him or enter his house.
T	W137.**.	Curiosity: prompts children to watch feeding birds instead of fetching water for bathing dying father.
T	Q285.**.	Cruelty punished: father cruel to his children dies when they fail to bring water to bathe and heal him.
C	Q411.+.	Death as punishment for (outcome of) cruelty.
T	Q280.	Unkindness punished.

1. An intrusive sound by a small child in the audience interrupted the narration, and Mpanga Iyende began anew.

2. Presumably, he sent the children to their respective mothers' huts.

3. A yawn from someone in the audience is clearly audible on the tape at this point. The narrator, sensitive to audience reaction, moved very quickly thereafter to dialogue, and maintained a pattern of animated dialogue and song throughout the rest of the tale itself, returning to a more sober pace only during the "teaching" at the end.

4. Plural in Lonkundo for "guinea fowl."

5. Here the narrator shouts as the friend would shout, but he does not imitate a girl's voice.

6. Bokunge Jacques had as much difficulty in unlocking the songs in this tale as he experienced in translating those in the other tales told by Mpanga Iyende. He caught, however, the *sense* of the song in the following free translation: "I see the *nkoku* scratch and peck." A fuller translation of the recorded song was provided by Pierre Sangana.

7. A decidedly scolding tone is used by the narrator here.

8. As is true with others of Mpanga Iyende's tales, the formulaic ending "*Ili!*" "*Yo!*" concludes this narrative.

An item of cultural interest furnished by Bokunge Jacques seems appropriate as an adjunct to these notes. In response to Mrs. Ross's questioning, her primary translation assistant and long-time friend furnished information concerning the arrangements found within a polygynous household; his comments follow:

Narrator:	Bokunge Jacques
Location:	Bólèngè
Date:	March 1973

The Relation of a Man with His Wives

A man of any importance has as many as forty wives. He builds for himself a good-sized house. Then he builds a smaller house for each wife as she is added to his harem [sic]. The first wife is always "one" with her husband and has precedence over all the others—a sort of queen in the compound.

Each wife prepares food and brings some to him each day. She would be most distressed if he didn't partake of what she had brought. The matter of which one with whom he is to sleep each night is prescribed by an unwritten law. He builds the houses in a line stretching on either side of his house. The wife in the first house comes to his house for three consecutive nights; the one in the second house then comes for three nights. Thus they pass this on down the line until each wife has had a turn. Then they start over.

When a woman is pregnant, she is excused from her turn until her child is born and has reached about two years of age. This gives the child time enough to be strong and able to eat solid food, and the mother can wean it. They take no chances on a mother's being pregnant again until her child no longer needs her milk.

Narrator: Ikwa Isilombe, formerly
a teacher living near Wema
but now in Boende
Location: Boende
Date: October 1973

55.   *The Good Son and the Bad Son*

A chief had very many wives and children also. He had a first-born son and a second-born son. The first-born was a very wicked child. He wouldn't listen to his father, *nyė*, nor do as he said, *nyė*. And also the child who came after him thought much of his father, everything which his father said, perhaps work, perhaps of him. The first child if the father gave him a task did not listen at all, *nyė*. The second child would listen and would finish all, all,[1] for his father with much tightness and heat. He brought good fish and prepared the fire. When the older son had fish, he didn't give his father, or anything of any sort did he give him, nor did he think of the father.

When the father died, a great many of his children came. They blessed the second son with many blessings because he had cared for their father with such care.

With all of them the first son had hopes everywhere, but we do not know how much a father leaves a child. Yet he blesses according to the life that a son had lived, and this father blessed in that way. The one son was more fit to have the blessing.[2]

Ikwa Isilombe initially told this decidedly moralistic tale largely to hear his own voice on tape. Once he had experienced this satisfaction, he went on to tell a quite different and more fully developed narrative (see Tale 58). The tape of Tale 55 provides evidence that the narrator wanted to continue moralizing but that Tata Itofi, another narrator, deliberately cut him off.

Despite the didactic content of the present tale, the story was delivered with considerable concern; obviously, the matters of filial obedience and loyalty and of the consanguineal tie were of deep import to the teller, as, indeed, they are in the Nkundo value system as a whole. That filial obedience has continued to be a cultural imperative among the Nkundo and other Bantu-speaking peoples is stated without equivocation in Dodge's "Missions and Anthropology . . . " (1944): "Filial respect, especially to the father, is expected. . . . [T]he younger are always expected to honor and obey their elders" (p. 77).

We suspect that, had the occasion been a traditional evening storytelling session, the tale would have taken the dilemma-tale form in which substantially this same narrative is found, credited to Elímá Jean, in Hulstaert and de Rop's *Rechtspraak-fabels . . .* (Tale 33—"Een man en zijn twee kinderen"—pp. 114–117). One footnote and the "solution" for the dilemma-tale version (both on p. 115) afford an interesting additional dimension to Ikwa Isilombe's narrative. Translated from the Flemish, they read as follows:

> [1]*Alotake nkói:* as a token of their authority, elders and other notable people carry a band, cut from a leopard skin, over the shoulder. The band runs over front and back and is held together at the hip on the other side.
>
> After the father's death, the leopard skin, the sign of authority, goes to his eldest son. [In the dilemma tale, the leopard skin had been left to the second son. B.K.W.]

Solution

In this dispute between the older and younger brothers, the following is true: the authority comes by order of God and by order of the father and the mother. During the time that the father was still living, the older brother didn't treat him right. The father refused him his blessing and refused to give him his authority. He gave that to the younger brother. No sooner is the father dead than the older brother claims the authority. Doesn't he realize that the father has refused to give him this authority? The older brother loses the lawsuit. He may be the oldest, but the father has put him in the second place.

[Translated by Dr. Tinco E. A. van Hylckama]

It is obvious from the heat generated in the "solution" for the jurisprudence tale that the apparently flat and prosaic form in which Tale 55 appears on the page gives little indication of its vitality and probable service in the Nkundo oral tradition: it is meant to be *argued*, not preached; the taped original carries sufficient evidence of the sparks of controversy to support our assumption that the narrator was familiar with the tale in its function as a practice for palavers rather than as a folktale with a beginning, middle, and end, a minidrama.

Unable to find in any of the indexes a suitable tale-type number for this tale, we have created one based on the Aarne-Thompson tale type 949 (The Faithful Servitor); until a permanent number has been assigned, we have amended the type number as follows: 949** The Faithful Son.

Motifs:

C	P236.+.**.	Undutiful children: first-born son refuses to provide for his father's needs.
C	S21.+.**.	Cruel son: first-born son refuses to provide for his father's needs.
T	L13.**.	Younger son helps father.

T   Q2.   Kind and unkind.
T   Q86.   Reward for industry.
C   Q111.+.**.   Father's property as reward for younger son's faithful service.
C   Q68.+.**.   Obedient son rewarded by inheritance of father's property.
T   Q325.   Disobedience punished.
T   Q595.**.   Forfeiture of wealth as punishment for unwillingness to provide
                       for father's needs.
C   L430.+.**.   Arrogant lack of consideration for parent repaid.

1. "All, all" is the literal translation of the Lonkundo for "all of everything."

2. Denial of the father's blessing is a far more serious loss among the Nkundo than is the loss of material inheritance since the Nkundo regard for and relationship with departed ancestors is both deep and aweful. The influence of the dead continues to be felt throughout the following generations; by failing to receive his father's blessing, the older son has visited trouble and anxiety upon his children and his children's children. (For another instance of a father's refusal to bless his children, see Tale 74.)

Narrator:	Bolumbu Elakankoi, a woman
Location:	Boende, but narrator's home was in Wema
Date:	October 1973

56. *The Unusual Bridal Agreement and the Determined Husband*

A certain man who was the head of the village had one child, a daughter. Nearby were a man and wife who had had no children for a long while, but finally had a son. The son was called Ntut'afeka.[1] His parents wanted him to take a wife, but he said, "No, I'm still not a man."

However, he saw the chief's daughter and wanted her. Her parents didn't want her to get married; they wanted to keep her at home. His parents tried to tell him that he couldn't take the chief's daughter, but he was sure that she was the one to be his wife.

He realized that he would have difficulty getting her, so he went by night to her home.

He asked, "Where does the girl sleep?" Then he took her and went home with her.

When the chief found that she was gone, he sent police[2] out to hunt for her. After three days they saw her when she had gone to the spring to get water.

The police came back. "Don't cry any more. We have seen your daughter. She is married."

"But she has no husband."

"We found her near the garden of her husband."

The chief was really angry and sent his commissioner after her, but he couldn't bring her home. Then he sent his *capita*, but he didn't succeed, either. He finally gathered his soldiers together and prepared for war.

When Only Once realized that war was coming, he went to the chief and bowed down to the ground before him. "You are the great chief, and I bow before you."

"Why did you take my daughter from my house?"

Only Once said, "I took her to be my wife. What is the bride-wealth for your daughter? Then I can finish our palaver."

The chief was ready for the question and still had no desire to give up his daughter. "I want four water buckets,[3] and four cars of the white man's money; I want four trucks full of iron anklets and iron bars."

Only Once brought the four water buckets, the four cars of white man's money, and four trucks of iron anklets and iron bars. Then he asked, "Now what else must I do?"

The chief said, "When my child bruises herself, you must have a bruise in the same place. If she has a fever, you must have a fever; if she cuts her leg, you must cut yours. Whatever she suffers, you must suffer the same."[4]

After two Saturdays had passed, the young wife had a fever. In three days she was dead. The young husband went to order the box for burying. "Make two boxes both alike. My wife is dead and I need them."

When they were finished, he took them home. Everyone came and was surprised. "Why are there two boxes? Only one person is dead. We don't understand this at all. Why two boxes?"

The husband put his wife in one box and got into the other one himself. His parents asked, "Why are you in the box?"

"Don't forget that my name is Only Once."

The carpenter put the lids on the boxes and hammered the nails into them to secure them.

The parents of Only Once cried, "We don't understand this. Our son isn't dead and yet he is to be buried." They cried and cried.

The men went out and dug the hole for the boxes. They dug and dug. They put the box with the wife in first, and then the box with her husband. The hole wasn't big enough for both boxes. His father called out, "The room in the ground isn't big enough. Take the box out with the boy."

They heard Only Once knock on his box.

"Take out the nails."

"What?"

"Take out the nails."

They took them out, and Only Once got out of the box. "The chance is finished. I am Only Once. Put the dirt in the hole."

The chief came to him. "What do you mean by not staying in the hole? You agreed to suffer whatever my daughter had happen to her."

"All right. Now you may shoot me with a gun."

The chief was angry and called all of his soldiers together. "He took my daughter from my house and carried her home to be his wife. He killed her. He agreed that he would suffer whatever happened to her."

Only Once answered, "I won't talk with the soldiers or the chief. I do not have two mouths[5] in this; I have only one mouth and will talk only once."

The chief said, "Very well. You can tell the judge who settles palavers your story."

When the judge came, Only Once began his story.[6] "I really liked the chief's daughter, but he wouldn't let her go. I went at night and took her home. Her father found her, and I asked her price. He told me four water buckets, four cars full of the white man's money, and four trucks full of iron bars and iron anklets. You understand."

"I understand."

"Afterwards I returned to him and asked what else was in this price. He answered that any sickness my wife had, I was to have also. If she had a fever, I was to have a fever. If she cut her arm, I was to cut mine. If she hurt her leg, I was to hurt mine in the same way. So when she died, I had two boxes made. They dug and dug. They put her in the grave and then they put me in. They found that the hole wasn't big enough. So they took my box out and filled the hole over the box of the girl. Then I refused the second time. The chief came with his soldiers and their guns and wanted to know why I hadn't been buried also. I am still Only Once."

The judge gave him the palaver, and the chief took his soldiers and went home.

The significance of naming among Bantu-speaking peoples becomes apparent in Tale 56: without his bearing the name "Only Once" and behaving consistently in keeping with that name, the protagonist would indeed have suffered the burial alive that the vengeful chief had intended for him. (Helpful comments on naming practices among Bantu-speaking peoples may be found in Dodge's "Missions and Anthropology . . . ," pp. 87–88.) Whether Only Once received his name from his parents because of his being born late in their lives or whether he himself adopted the name—a practice not uncommon among the Nkundo—both he and the others in the community identified the man with the name and with his concording patterns of behavior.

It is curious that a woman would tell a tale in which the bride's family appeared to be "bested" by the groom. Clearly, Bolumbu considered the decision of the palaver as well justified; she had no quarrel with the fashion in which the unusual bridewealth condition had been met. (Although a number of the Ross-collected tales involved the giving or receiving of bridewealth, this is the only narrative she encountered in which a verbal commitment to share misfortunes was included.)

Lambrecht's tale type 2175, based on a single tale published by de Bouveignes in *Sur des Levres Congolaises* . . . (pp. 72–77) and titled "Celui que ne se répète jamais," fits the present tale in its central point: the fact that the bridegroom's name saves him from an untimely death. In de Bouveignes' tale, presumably collected among the Luba, the young man obtains his wife honorably, by familial agreement, and he and his wife have many happy years together, produce several children, and are prosperous; the woman's family feels that the son-in-law has met his commitments admirably, and there is thus no need for a palaver to determine the justice of the husband's refusal to be buried a second time with his wife. In the present tale, the wife is obtained covertly; the excessive material bridewealth and the accompanying "sufferings" are determined ex post facto; the bride dies shortly after the marriage; the young man alerts his parents to the means for rescuing him from untimely burial ("Don't forget that my name is Only Once"); the bride's vengeful father refers the dispute for palaver. These two tales provide an excellent instance of the wide range of variation possible when the same central theme falls into the imaginations of two different narrators. The Luba version presents the protagonist as protected by the "tabou" indicated in his name in every act he undertakes; the perfect consistency of the protagonist in the matter of nonrepetition—of words and of acts (greatly detailed in the French translation)—renders a palaver unnecessary. The Nkundo narrator sees the protagonist as an opportunist, bent on having his own way, and enabled to effect his own rescue by convincing the judge at the palaver that he had indeed met his commitments, resting his case on the telling point "I am still Only Once." The tone of the Luba tale is somewhat moralizing, and the tale reads better, we suspect, than it would tell: the details in de Bouveignes' version are numerous, but might well be dropped by one who wished to retain the tale for later telling since they are embellishments not central to the action; it seems, in effect, to be a literary retelling rather than a direct translation of a tale actually taken from a living narrator. In the Nkundo version, on the other hand, suspense is rife and opportunities for gestures and for miming are ample; those factors were fully utilized by the narrator, wholly caught up in her storytelling. It would be interesting to capture an oral variant of de Bouveignes' tale to see how much of the elegance of narrative structure and dialogue is present in Luba oral transmission, a crucial test for the reliability of any translation or retelling.

There is a possibility that in the hands of a different narrator or under circumstances more nearly approaching a traditional evening tale-telling session, the present story could be offered in the form of a dilemma tale; the telling here is relatively spare, and the conclusion is certainly open to lively debate.

Motifs:

T	J1280.	Repartee with ruler (judge, etc.).
C	M2.+.**.	Chief decrees that daughter's bridegroom must suffer everything that daughter suffers, including burial.
T	Q456.**.	Burial alive as punishment: condition made a part of bridal agreement by father of abducted girl.
T	M254.	Promise to be buried with wife if she dies first.
T	C762.**.	Tabu: doing things more than once.
T	Q91.**.	Reward for cleverness: death order evaded.
C	J1113.+.**.	Clever bridegroom avoids burial alive by application of his own name, "Only Once."
C	J1530.+.**.	One absurdity rebukes another: young man buried alive as part of bridewealth agreement escapes death when grave cannot accommodate two coffins, cites his name, "Only Once," in refusal to be reburied.

1. This name can be translated in any one of several ways: "No Return Afterwards," "Never Twice," or "Only Once." We have selected "Only Once" as the most appropriate appellation for the protagonist in this tale. The translation Lambrecht furnishes (see p. 184 of her "A Tale Type Index . . . ") for a similar Luba name, "He who never does the same thing twice," seemed to us more cumbersome and no more helpful than "Only Once."

2. In this area during the period of Belgian rule, the names for military and government officials were expressed in French. The chief's commissioner was his

personal officer, and his *capita* was the head of all his workmen. These references, including the police reference, are not a part of early Nkundo culture, but—as often happens—they have been incorporated, along with other new things, into the old tales.

3. Although "four water buckets" seems a peculiarly small request to make in the light of the chief's much heavier financial demands, water buckets are greatly desired by the Nkundo because these containers are much easier to carry than the traditional water gourds or the jugs supported by baskets (see note 5 for Tale 53); they are in a sense prestige items.

4. The demands concerning bridewealth made by the chief were not only excessive, but truly vengeful; in addition to fulfilling what appeared to be impossible financial tasks, the young man was required to be subordinate to his wife in that he must accept her physical limitations. The financial requirements, though extreme, would arouse no more than wonder among the listeners; the personal requirements would be offensive to both males and females in the audience, long accustomed to the male's dominant role in the household. From this point onward, the audience's sympathy would lie with Only Once, despite his having secured his bride initially in a surreptitious manner.

5. Among the Nkundo, "I do not have two mouths" has two possible meanings: (1) I am telling the truth; (2) I will tell my story only once. The latter meaning, intended here, was readily accepted both by the chief and by the judge.

6. The narrator's artistry is evidenced by her choosing to have Only Once recount the whole series of events rather than to summarize the situation. Besides the audience-pleasing factor involved in repetition, the relating of the conditions concerning the bridewealth and his faithfulness in meeting those conditions predisposed both the judge and the audience in his favor. It is precisely this kind of handling that makes Tale 56 readily adaptable to the dilemma-tale form.

(In Torrend's . . . *Bantu Folk-Lore* . . . , pp. 20–22, a dog named "Be-Thankful," when mistreated by his new owners, returns home, singing, "As I am Be-Thankful, I go, I go back," furnishing evidence that the matter of identification of animals with their names is as strong among Bantu-speaking peoples as is the identification of humans with their names.)

Narrator: Amba Engombe Telesa
Location: Bòlèngè
Date: March 1973

57. *Goodness between In-Laws*

A woman had four daughters. The oldest one, Nsòmi, was married. She still had three daughters at home.

One day she planted many squash in her back yard. Once after they had grown to be large, she was going into the forest. She called the three together and said, "Don't eat the squash! Don't eat the squash! If you eat it, you will die."[1]

The three girls heard her and understood her. After she had gone, the girl who was married, Nsòmi, came to visit her. She saw those big lovely squash and said, "I'm going to pick some squash."

Her sisters were shocked. "No, no! Mother said that we mustn't pick them or we would die."

"If I pick them and cook them, why shouldn't I eat them?"

So she picked and cooked some squash. Then she ate all she wanted, but her sisters refused to touch it. "Mother said for us not to eat it, and we are afraid to."

So they sat and talked until their mother came back from the forest. She looked and saw that one squash was missing. "Who picked the squash?"

They all denied picking it.

"Then who ate it?"

Again they denied it entirely.

"Let's go to the river and find some *mbondo* fruit and make some *samba* from it."[2]

They all went to the river with her and prepared the *samba* potion. They all ate it.

Then the second daughter went into the river while the others sang,

> I didn't eat my mother's squash,
> The squash of Monjeka,
> So I won't die from it.

She came out of the river with no problems.

Then the third daughter went into the river and the sisters sang again,

> I didn't eat my mother's squash,
> The squash of Monjeka,
> So I won't die from it.

This sister came out of the river.
Then the youngest girl went in, with the same song:

> I didn't eat my mother's squash,
> The squash of Monjeka,
> So I won't die from it.

This youngest daughter came out of the river.
Nsòmi, the married one, went in and they sang. Soon the water came to her thigh and they kept singing. Then it came to her waist and they sang. It came to her neck and they sang. Then she went under the water and was gone.
Nsòmi's husband, Ilele, heard that his wife had gone home. She had picked and eaten her mother's squash and her mother had killed her.[3]
He was angry. He took his knife, his spear, and his shield and went to the home of his wife's mother. "I want my wife. She came here yesterday. I heard that she had died. I want my wife."
He took Monjeka, the mother, and tied her up tight and then tied her to one of the timbers that held up the roof.
The three sisters began to cry,

> Ilele has tied up our mother Monjeka.
> Ilele.

The second sister said, "Take me for your wife in the place of my sister. Then untie my mother." Then they all sang,

> Ilele has tied up our mother Monjeka.
> Ilele.

"No, no! I want my own wife."
Then the next sister offered herself. They sang,

> Ilele has tied up our mother Monjeka.[4]

"No, no! I want my own wife."
The youngest daughter stood before him. "Take me for your wife, but untie Mother."

> Ilele has tied up our mother Monjeka.
> Ilele.

"No, no! I want my own wife."

The elders of the family[5] came together and said, "Choose the one you want for your wife. Forget the one who is dead. Then go your way."

"No, no! I won't change wives. These are all different, and I want my own. These may be pretty girls, but they aren't the same."

They talked and talked, but it was still the same. Even the sisters begged him again, but he only wanted his own wife.

Then from away back in the forest they heard singing:

Ilele has tied up our mother Monjeka.
Ilele.[6]

"Listen, everyone. It's the voice of Nsómi and it is like a star." From that time on, her name was Bókóci.[7]

Everyone was quiet. The voice kept singing and coming closer and closer.

Then she was there, *pu.* "Bókóci has come. Bókóci has come."[8]

She stood in front of her husband. Everyone was very quiet.

Then Ilele began to untie the mother. He untied and untied until she was free.[9]

He said, "My wife has come, and I can accept it. I rejoice and I will go home."

The mother said, "You can't go without eating."

So she prepared duck,[10] chicken, and many other good things, and they had a feast.[11] Then he took his wife home safely.

There is goodness between in-laws when the child is in the middle.

Tale 57, related briefly but with telling effect by a superb narrator, offers several departures from other Ross-collected tales: the use of a "truth potion" in combination with an ordeal by water; a direct, people-centered handling of the delicate matter of relationships between in-laws; evidence of the function of the sororate among the Nkundo; refusal of acceptance of a palaver verdict; and demonstration of the trait of forgiveness, a trait not reflected in the tales told by other narrators. (The trait of *mercy* appears in other tales; see Tales 43–46 and 93, for example.) Given this wide range of unusual elements, each having some weight in Nkundo culture and in the continuing value system, Amba threads her way through the narrative without hesitation, and succeeds in handling a thorny human problem without recourse to animal actors or to encounters with ogres, devices used by narrators of other tales in this volume to deal with relationships between in-laws.

Certain elements found in other Ross-collected tales are also included here: violation of an injunction, use of songs at dramatic points, drowning of the guilty one, use of a palaver to settle a dispute, insistence on recovering the exact object lost, repetition, the Nkundo tendency to gossip, violation of a tabu or injunction without more than temporary punishment, and the listing of foods served at a feast. Clearly, Amba is aware of the main stream of Nkundo oral narrative, and pleases her listeners by including elements familiar to them. She *does* exercise her prerogative as a narrator, however, by combining these familiar elements with others to present a tale distinctly her own.

We have been unable to find in any of the indexes consulted any tale type comprehensive enough to warrant attaching an established type number to this tale.

Motifs:

C	C680.+.**.	Injunction: certain food must not be eaten without permission of owner.
T	H210.	Test of guilt or innocence.
T	H223.**.	Ordeal by "truth potion."
T	H225.**.	Ordeal by water.
T	Q325.	Disobedience punished.
C	Q380.+.**.	Punishment for violating injunction concerning eating of forbidden food (squash).
T	F930.**.	Extraordinary rising of water in swamp or river to indicate guilt of one being tested.
T	F420.**.	Water spirits: river spirit can cause water to rise to drown one guilty of theft and lying.
T	J1144.	Eater of stolen food detected.
C	Q428.+.**.	Death by drowning for stealing mother's property.
C	Q467.+.**.	Drowning as punishment for violating injunction concerning eating of forbidden food (squash).
C	W188.+.**.	Son-in-law insists on return of drowned wife, refuses any substitute.
T	W167.	Stubbornness.
C	Q469.+.**.	Punishment of woman by son-in-law: being tied to house post until his lost wife is restored.
T	D22.**.	Transformation: common woman to "starlike" woman.
C	W10.+.**.	Mother-in-law shows forgiveness to son-in-law who had kept her tied to post.

1. Children in the Nkundo culture—especially girls, since they share the gardening work with their mothers—would understand that the squash were not poisonous, but that they were forbidden by the mother's injunction. Traditional respect for parental authority would lend strength to the effectiveness of the mother's threat.

2. "*Samba*" is a kind of "truth potion," one of a number used in Central African cultures to determine the identity of a malefactor. Sometimes the potion

is put into the eyes of the suspects; only the guilty one is afflicted with pain and torment from the "serum." More often, it is swallowed, producing vomiting, severe pain, and death. Here it occurs in combination with a "water test," a coupling we have not found elsewhere.

3. Gossip travels quickly in an Nkundo village. The details of this particular event would be recounted in full, even though there is no evidence in the tale that the ordeal was witnessed by anyone other than the members of the immediate family.

That the mother had "killed" Nsómi reflects the growth of a bit of gossip in its travel. Actually, Nsómi had perished as a consequence of her own violation of an injunction, but the notion of a "murder" had more appeal for gossips than did the idea of just retribution.

4. The narrator omitted here the repetition of the name "Ilele."

5. Since Nkundo villages normally consist of the members of a single extended family, it is to be assumed here that the "elders" were those in the entire village and that this was a full-scale palaver, with its decision one to be final. Ilele's refusal to accept the verdict points up both his stubborn intention to recover his own property and the touchiness of the issue of in-laws in Nkundo culture. Like Only Once (see Tale 56), Ilele was a firm and determined man and held strongly to his own rights. Nkundo respect for individuality here comes into conflict with Nkundo regard for obedience to the judgment of the elders and to the function of the palaver; when two or more cultural values come into conflict, the tale as a mirror of the culture is certain to appear distorted.

6. The supernatural character of the revived Nsómi is first suggested by her singing the song she could not possibly have heard, about an event she was not there to witness. Here, the use of the same song serves to effect narrative unity as well as to prepare the listeners for Nsómi's changed character and name.

7. The Lonkundo word meaning "star." The interpreter explained that "a small bright light" seen in the forest became brighter as the voice drew nearer, and became Nsómi.

In the presence of such a wonder, both quiet and awe would halt the usual babble of Nkundo voices, and the quiet observed by the family would increase suspense and awe among the listeners to the tale, evidence of Amba's superior narrative technique (see Tale 86 for another example of this narrator's skill).

8. The speaker of this line was not identified by the narrator. The line assumes the double function of a self-introduction and of a greeting; the reader is left to determine whether the wife names herself—another supernatural touch—or whether the observers greet her in her new character.

9. The fact that Monjeka had remained tied throughout the lengthy palaver and its subsequent events, to be released only by the one who had so confined her, offers evidence that the elders recognized some degree of justice in Ilele's complaint. It also indicates that the initial relationship between Ilele and his mother-in-law had not been a friendly one, certainly not one eased by the gift of a goat (see note 12 for Tales 18–20).

10. This is the only Ross-collected tale in which duck is included in the list of foods served.

11. That Monjeka would not only insist that her stubborn son-in-law receive the traditional Nkundo hospitality but would also serve such a feast indicates a kind of forgiveness not suggested elsewhere in the Ross collection. Monjeka's act sets the scene for the "goodness between in-laws" proverb with which Amba concludes the tale.

Narrator: Ikwa Isilombe
Location: Boende
Date: November 1973

58. *The Rightful Owner*

A father and son went into the forest to hunt meat.[1] They gathered cassava[2] and other food as well as their hunting equipment[3] to take with them. When they got into the forest, they set traps, traps for ensnaring animals. The father set traps on the ground where they could catch antelopes, wild pigs,[4] and other animals. The son went up into the trees and set traps for monkeys, birds, and animals that went in the trees. Then they built a shelter for themselves and for the meat that they caught.

When night came the father said, "Son, go and check the traps we have set to see if we have any animals in them."[5] He sent his son since the father was getting old and not able to do as much as formerly. The son found a very large wild pig in one of the traps his father had set.[6] He killed it,[7] put it across his shoulder, and took it back to where his father was and showed him the wild pig.

He said, "Father, I found this wild pig in one of the traps in the tree where I had set them. I found it, a very large wild pig."

The father said, "Is that true?"

"Yes. That's where I found it."

"Very good."

The son called, "Let's cut it up and care for the wild pig there."[8]

The father said, "But for a wild pig like this I need a special knife which I left at home. Go home and ask your mother to give you the knife which I call *Iteneinoso*. Because I have not heard of such a thing before, get this knife and bring it to me."[9]

The son went rapidly on the path, *kao-kao-kao-kao*, until he reached home. He found his mother there.

"You have come," she greeted him.

"Yes, I have come."

"You have come."

"Yes, I have come."

"What's your problem? Why have you come?"

"Mother, we were in the forest and I went out to check the traps. I found a wild pig in one of the traps that I had set in the tree. Father said that we couldn't properly cut it up until he had the right knife for the task. He had left the knife here and sent me to get it from you. It is the knife which he calls *Iteneinoso*. I have come to get it."

His mother just couldn't understand.[10] Anyway, she sent a knife with him hoping that it would be right for the job. "This is your father's knife. Take it to him. Go."

The boy ran through the forest, *tee-tee-ee*. He arrived.

His father asked him, "What did your mother have to say?"

He said, "She wasn't at all sure about what you wanted, even though I told her about the wild pig. She didn't know which knife was named *Iteneinoso*, so she sent this one to you."

Father said, "No, it isn't that one. Go back home and get another knife. She must know which knife I want."

The boy ran home, *tee-tee-ee*, until he reached his mother. "Mother, this knife that you gave me is not the one that Father wants. He wants the one he calls *Iteneinoso*. Give me the one he asked for."

The mother looked around for another knife and gave it to her son.

"Ah!" And he ran off into the forest to take it quickly to his father.

His father met him. "How did you do?"

He said, "Father, Mother gave me this knife to bring to you. She couldn't find any other."

Father said, "No. Not that one. We can't cut up the wild pig with that knife. Go back to your mother; give her this knife and tell her to send my own knife called *Iteneinoso*."

Quickly the boy ran back through the forest, *ti-i-i*. He found his mother and gave her the knife. "Mother, this isn't the knife that Father wants. He wants the one called *Iteneinoso*."

The mother sat and looked at him. "My son! What am I to do?
Tell me. Who killed the wild pig?"

"I did, Mother, with my knife."

"How did you kill the wild pig?"

"We fixed traps; Father set those on the ground, and I set
those in the trees. When I checked the traps, this wild pig was in
a trap in a tree. I killed it, and Father sent me for his special knife."[11]

The mother laughed. "You say that the wild pig is yours because
you found it in a trap in a tree. Pigs do not go up into trees. I have
never before heard of such a thing. They always travel on the ground.
Are you sure that this isn't your father's wild pig and not yours?"

The boy went back, tee-te-ee-ee, to his father.

"Well, what did your mother have to say this time?"

"She told me to come back and admit that I was lying to you.
The wild pig is really yours."

The father said, "No quarrel. Now let's go and cut it up."[12]

So they went out and cut up the wild pig.

Even though a young person has much wisdom of his own, he
should not forget that his parents have even more.[13]

[Notes for Tale 58 follow Tale 59.]

Source:	Bekolo Bêmö . . .
	Zaïrian school reader
	(in Lonkundo)
Translator:	Mabel Ross
Date of Translation:	November 1972

59. *The Rightful Owner* (Variant)

A father and son went to trap animals. When they arrived they
were busy with setting traps.

In the morning they went to see, and they untangled a forest
rat.[14]

The son baked the rat and some plantain. He unwrapped the meat and divided it. He took the part that was suitable for the father and placed it for himself, and took that suitable for himself and placed it for the father.[15]

The father saw this division and he said in his heart that he wouldn't eat it. He said, "My son, the rat is not fully cooked. Bake it again."

The son baked it again. He divided it as he had done at first, and the father wouldn't eat it. He said once more, "It isn't done."[16]

Then the plantain was cooked. The father said, "It is well that you take the plantain home."

The son took the plantain home. His mother asked him, "How was everything when you went into the forest?"

The son said, "We arrived and Father killed a rat. After I cooked it, I took the part that was suitable for Father and placed it for me. That suitable for me I placed for Father. And Father said that the rat wasn't done. Even though it had baked a very long while, he continued to say that it wasn't done."

The mother said, "You, one in need of wisdom! Go! Take that which is with you and give it to your father. That which is with your father, you take."

The son returned and he did as his mother had told him. The father tried it and he said, "The rat is cooked very well."

The father was well filled, and the son did not lack for meat.[17]

Tales 58 and 59 are two of many tales in the Nkundo oral tradition in which the proper division of meat and other foods is stressed; such tales are told repeatedly to reinforce this important truth not only for children but for adults. Nkundo children are early taught that Father and the village elders must have the first share of any meat or fish trapped. The son in the first tale was certainly aware of this tradition, and the father was determined not to permit him to ignore it. The second tale emphasizes the additional point that prescribed parts of the animal or fish caught belong properly to the elders. Another narrative in this volume (Tale 74) presents basically the same lessons, but the resolution is necessarily altered by the fact that the meat in the latter tale has already been eaten without its being properly shared, whereas in the present pair of tales the faulty division is not irreparable.

Another narrative from the school reader *Bekolo Bemo* . . . (pp. 78–80), titled "Is'ea Ntoanya la Lisoko" ("The Father of Ntoanya and the Antelope"), concerns an adult hunter who snared a large antelope and skinned it. The antelope, somehow surviving the skinning, ran from the hunter as soon as the *ngòji* confining him had been cut. The hunter warned his fleeing prey that a skinned antelope would be rejected by his kind; in turn, the antelope warned the hunter that he, too, would be rejected by his family because he had not brought home the antelope's meat. Both predictions proved accurate: the antelope, not allowed to associate with other animals because of his unnatural condition, was forced to live alone in the forest; the hunter, unacceptable to his family because they assumed he had failed to share the antelope's meat in the prescribed fashion, was not allowed to "light a fire" either with his own family or with his in-laws. A poignant tale, this one mirrors the stress that continues to be placed on the importance of sharing, ranking it above maternal protection and extended-family ties.

No tale type that we have found provides adequate classification for this pair of narratives. Aarne-Thompson's tale type 9 (The Unjust Partner), from its title a likely candidate for this purpose, emphasizes trickery and cheating of an entirely different kind; Lambrecht's tale type 553 (her renumbering of Aarne-Thompson's tale type 9) and Klipple's variants of Aarne-Thompson's tale type 9 are inadequate classifications for the same reason: the focus is not on a tradition of sharing as a social responsibility—as among the Nkundo—but, rather, fair division on a business basis. A new tale-type number is needed for narratives of the present sort.

Motifs:

T	N827.	Child as helper.
T	K735.	Capture in pitfall.
T	K254.**.	Goods misappropriated: son claims as his the pig caught in the father's trap.
T	W157.	Dishonesty.
T	J230.	Choice: real and apparent values.
T	F838.**.	Special knife named "*Iteneinoso*" ("I-Never-Heard-of-Such-a-Thing-Before") needed for cutting up father's game unjustly claimed by son.
T	J1020.**.	Strength in unity: mother and father cooperate in teaching son importance of truth.
T	Z71.1.	Formulistic number: three.
T	J514.**.	Son claims father's prey as his and is rebuked.
T	J10.**.	Wisdom (knowledge) acquired from experience: son learns to claim only game he himself has caught.
C	C680.+.**.	Injunction: certain formula for division of spoils of hunting and fishing must be observed.
T	K254.**.	Goods misappropriated: son keeps father's portion of food, gives father share proper for son.
C	P690.+.	Custom of hunter sharing meat.
T	J514.**.	Son claims father's portion for himself and is rebuked.
T	P632.2.	Cuts of meat distributed according to rank.
T	J10.**.	Wisdom (knowledge) acquired from experience: son learns to respect traditional division of spoils of hunt.

1. Traditionally, the training of the sons among the Nkundo has been the responsibility of the father, with the classroom in this hunting economy the rain forest of Zaïre and with much to be taught by experience, rather than in words. This boy's first hunting experience yielded a valuable moral and cultural lesson as well as the more obvious ones related to hunting, trapping, and meat preparation.

2. Cassava, the staple of the Nkundo diet, is pure starch, an adequate source of sustenance until meat can be procured to supplement it. Various dishes prepared from cassava can be readily carried in the shoulder bag or in a basket on the head, freeing the hands for clearing a path through the thick underbrush to the hunting site.

3. The hunting equipment normally includes bows and arrows, spears, knives, nets, and snares of various sizes, as well as a machete for clearing a path and for digging pitfalls.

4. Wild pigs are fairly common in the forests of the Cuvette. They are fighters, and a hunter must be careful in handling them. Their meat is excellent, more like beef than like pork in texture and in flavor.

5. By sunset, whatever daytime foragers lived in the area would have left their daytime haunts and retired to rest. If any of these animals had been caught, they needed to be killed and their meat prepared, usually by smoking, so that it would not be spoiled or lost to nocturnal animals in search of food. Twilight furnished sufficient light for checking the traps, and at that hour the son would not be likely to alarm the nocturnal animals he and his father hoped to trap during the nighttime hours. The father's age provided a fine excuse for his offering the son the excitement and responsibility of checking the traps.

6. Probably a pit trap, dug deep in the soft earth by the father's machete and then camouflaged with small branches and leaves.

7. A knife would be used for dispatching the pig. Boys in the Nkundo culture are very early taught by their fathers the many uses of knives.

8. Although this was his first hunt, the son recognized the need for immediate preparation of the meat of "his" pig.

9. The wisdom of the father in not shaming his son—or, indeed, losing his own dignity in an unseemly quarrel—but, instead, enabling the boy by his father's ruse to learn the proper respect for ownership, could well be emulated in any culture. The fact that the father was the hunter who had trapped the pig had to be established. The father, instead of accusing his son of lying, sent him for the special knife whose name (meaning "I never heard of such a thing before") should have given the boy the clue necessary for solving the problem. There was much appreciative laughter among the audience at the father's comment that he needed a special knife to cut up "a wild pig like this."

10. The boy hid nothing in his account to his mother, but—perhaps for the narrator's purpose of increasing the dramatic impact—neither he nor his mother drew the connection between the boy's act and the name of the knife.

11. On his third return home, the son furnished, at his mother's request, all the details of "his" catch, providing the mother with the necessary clue.

The mother probably sat on the same sort of low wooden stool used by women during the eating of meals.

12. Once the true ownership of the pig had been established, the meat could be prepared.

13. This "teaching" extends the focus of the tale to reflect the stress placed on filial obedience and on willingness to accept counsel that constitute other important features of the Nkundo value system.

14. The rat caught was a *botomba*, approximately the size of a large rabbit.

15. All foods served in an Nkundo family are divided in definitely prescribed ways, and certain parts properly belong to the father; the less choice portions go to other members of the family.

16. The Lonkundo way of saying that the food is not done is "It hasn't come." Nkundo are called to a meal with the same kind of expression: "The food has come."

17. The Lonkundo original for this tale, titled "Ise l'Ona" ("Father and Son"), appears on pages 8–9 of *Bekolo Bėmò*....

A brief note on Nkundo social history provided by Ngoi Ekoletonga, a village elder, is illuminating in the context of the present tales.

Narrator: Ngoi Ekoletonga
Location: Longa
Date: December 7, 1972

Sharing

Long ago when a child caught his first fish or trapped his first animal or bird, he himself didn't eat it. He gave it to his elders: father, uncles, older brother. Everything from his garden—fruit or anything else—must first be shared with the elders. Even the first house that he built was not for himself but for his elders. The Nkundo no longer follow this custom.

Narrator: Njoli Bombongo
Location: Tondo, but narrator's
             home was in Kalamba
Date: June 1973

60.   *The Hunter and the Ogre as Partners*

A man had always lived in a village, he and his family. Ogre lived in the forest, he and his family. One day the man said that, "I go to set traps in the forest." When the sun rose, he said to his wife, "Make me some cakes. I am going to set traps[1] in the forest that I find much meat there that we can live."

As soon as he reached the forest, he began to set traps for catching animals. After he had prepared three traps, he met an ogre. There in the forest it was a very wilderness. He met Ogre and Ogre greeted him. The man greeted Ogre.

The man asked, "Who are you?"

Ogre answered, "I am Ogre, the owner of this forest."

The man said, "Where do you live?"

Ogre said, "I live in all of the forest." Ogre returned to the man, "Who are you?"

He said, "I am greater than all things with strength."

When Ogre heard this, he was filled with awe. Ogre asked, "You really exceed all men in power and strength?"

"Eh! I exceed all men in strength. What do you do?" The man said also, "I have come to set traps in the forest which is a wilderness."

Ogre said, he said, "Can we set traps together here in the forest, I and you? Now I and you will set traps in the forest, the two of us."[2]

The man agreed; he said, "We will go together as friends, I and you.[3] We will dig many holes as traps and kill many animals."

Ogre agreed, "We will be busy setting traps, I and that man." That day they set 436 traps.

Ogre said to the man that, "If we kill any male animals, you will take the males. If we catch any female animals, I will take any female animals that we trap."

That man agreed; he said, "Eh! I will take male animals and you, Ogre, take the female animals."[4] They set traps like that.

The sun rose. When they looked at the first trap, they saw that they had six male wild pigs, seven male small antelopes, eight male larger antelopes, and one male elephant. They had not trapped any female animals, *nyė*.[5]

Ogre looked it over and said, "You have finished doing the traps. You were to take all the male animals. The males you release and take with you."

The man took all the animals to his village and divided them among all the family, and they ate. Then the man returned to the forest to meet Ogre. While he and Ogre set traps, the sun set. Ogre sat with hunger; he had no food.

When the sun rose next morning, they went to look in their traps. Once again they found males: male monkeys, male porcupines, and many other male animals. They did not have any females at all, *nyė*.

Ogre said, he said, "Take them all that are males, because we agreed that you take the male animals and I take the female animals."

Once more the man took all the meat into his village and divided it among his family, and they ate.

His wife said, "My husband does what? He goes into the forest as though he were the owner of it. I will follow him and take him food to help him while he hunts."[6]

As soon as she had prepared the food, she went; she followed her husband until she came to the wilderness. She went, *k-a-o*, as she went on the path cut by the hunters. She fell into one of the pits that Ogre and her husband had made. There was no one to help her out.

At sunset Ogre and the man went out to see what animals they had caught in their traps. They found the wife of the man in one of the pits.

Ogre began to dance and said,

> I have meat.
> I have meat.
> I have meat.
> I have meat.
> I have meat.

The man looked at him with surprise. "Don't you know that that is my wife?"

Ogre answered, "Eh! We have finished. But we have already agreed that any animals we find in the traps that are females are my meat. You have already had much meat. Now I have meat.[7]

> I have meat.
> I have meat.
> I have meat.
> Ogre of the forest,
> I have meat.
> Ogre of the forest,
> I have meat.
> Owner of the forest,
> I have meat.

Ogre rejoiced very much.

The man said, he said, "That is my wife. Why do you keep rejoicing that you have meat?" Then he looked at his wife and asked, "How did you get here?"

She answered, "I was following you, my husband. I fell in the pit that you had dug and the Ogre had dug."

The man was very angry.[8] Ogre called his family to come and get the meat. That man called all the family from the village who had shared in eating the meat that he had given them. They came.

Ogre told his family, he said, "We divided all the female animals that we take them and that we kill them. She is a woman in the pit."

Then some people came who had much wisdom, more than anyone else. This was wisdom that they had gotten as a gift from God.[9] They said, "Here is the family of the man who was hunting in the forest. All of his family are here, many people, and all of Ogre's family are here, many ogres." They began to listen to the palaver and think about it.

One man said, "This is our wife.[10] It isn't at all fitting they take her, *nyė*."

Ogre said, "No, it isn't that way at all. We have an agreement that any female animals that we catch belong to us, the ogres, and male animals are yours, the people of the village. You have eaten a great many animals, and we have had none. A woman is our meat for us to eat."[11]

The people of the village did not rejoice with this at all, *nyė*.

There was one man there who had more wisdom.[12] He said, "Your meat which is female is in the pit. Tell one of your ogres to go into the pit to help pull her out."[13]

One of the ogres went into the pit. "Our very own meat. No one should take our meat. Let us take it and eat it. This is our own meat."

The man of wisdom agreed. "Now there are two animals in the

pit; one is a male, and one is a female. We will take the male, and you take the female."

But Ogre said, "No, no! Not that way. You are not to take one of us just because he is in the pit."

The man of wisdom answered, "But he is in the pit and he is a male. That means that he is ours. If you take the woman and kill her, then we will take the male. If you must kill the woman, we must kill the male."

They pulled them both out of the pit. Ogre said, "You take the woman, and we will take the male which is ours."

The story stops like this.

A man shares the hunt with the family; he will fail in the forest without a family. We have already seen that when that man shared food with the family, the family helped him in the forest where he found the ogre.

The story is ended.

Since Tale 60 is the first of the "people" narratives to introduce the *eloko*, the Nkundo ogre (or "bogeyman," as he is termed in Flemish: *boeman*), substantial note ought to be taken of this recurring folk type.

Mrs. Ross found it very difficult—though most of her narrators wanted to tell an ogre tale—to extract from any Nkundo a coherent description of an ogre. In part, this reluctance may be accounted for by the tabu apparently associated with the describing of an ogre (see Tale 66). To an even greater extent, it may be explained by the circumstance that of those who encounter an ogre, few live to tell the tale (see Tale 79 for an account of a victim whose unhappy end demonstrates two truths in the Nkundo culture: 1. one must beware of an ogre; 2. one must hear [heed] "the mouth of the husband"). All are agreed, however, that an ogre has a decided preference for human flesh and that he can on occasion be overcome—usually by superior wit.

De Rop, in his ... *woordkunst* ..., titles chapter XIV "Boemenfabels." Here (in van Hylckama's translation of pages 240–241) is de Rop's commentary on the Nkundo ogre and on the tale cycle that has grown up around him:

> The eloko is a very mysterious being. He is a kind of jungle [*sic*] man with a repulsive appearance. He is dressed in the bark of trees or in leaves. The description of the bogeyman is not exactly fit for dinner talk, because one would soon lose all appetite.
>
> The bogeys have human names, speak a human language, and live in villages in the heart of the jungle [*sic*]. They have their own hunting grounds and fishponds. They have wives and children. There are bogey villages with

only women. The man who happens to get there is accepted as husband and well taken care of, but he is watched over, so he cannot walk away.

The bogey has no place in the religious conceptions of the Nkundo. The Supreme Being, the nature spirits, and the dead are worshiped. But there is none of that as far as the bogeys are concerned.

Although fantastic things happen in bogey stories, they have nothing in common with heroic legends. Even though the bogey tales are widespread, there is no unity in the whole cycle. In the animal fairy tales we have mostly the Tortoise and the Dwarf-Antelope. In the bogey tales, even that unity is not apparent. They are all loosely knit pieces in which fantastic imagination runs rampant. Sometimes they are creepy ghostly tales about a singing finger, a leg that cuts palm nuts, a jaw-bone that chews, skulls that empty a fishpond, and so on.

The bogey plays the people dirty pranks [;] on the other hand he's at times fooled by humans, often with stupid tricks. Sometimes a bogey likes a person and helps him while hunting or fishing. But then he [the person] has to obey rigorously the bogey laws and adhere to bogey customs. Whoever fails to do so, loses in the end. Sometimes he makes sure people find game, keeping himself invisible. One hears him call: "There's an antelope for you." Don't be curious then and try to see the giver, because that will cost you dearly.

Most of the time, though, the bogey is hostile to humans. He's out for food prepared by humans; but his favorite diet is human meat.

For people like the Nkundo, who live in the heart of the jungle [sic], when behind every tree there are hidden dangers and surprises, which can unexpectedly jump out at you—the big moral lesson of these bogey stories is: "Watch out in the forest."

It is a reckless deed to enter the jungle [sic] alone. Especially girls and women have to be careful in the jungle [sic] if there is not a man with them.

Carelessness, stubbornness, thanklessness, in a word, every sin has its punishments in the bogey stories. It is as if, for every misdeed or imprudence, a bogey stands prepared to administer a well-earned penalty.

As de Rop indicates in his delineation of the *eloko* and of his place in the Nkundo oral tradition, there does seem to be a motley mass of tales about this interestingly inconsistent ogre. There had been no particular pattern in the tales Mrs. Ross had collected, but we had assumed that a lengthier collection would reveal some framework into which the field tales could be fitted, an assumption that thus far has proved groundless. P. Boelaert's volume *Eloko, de boeman der Nkundó* (n.d.) and a pamphlet titled "Bekolo bya biloko" (n.d.)—the former in Flemish and the latter in Lonkundo—are the two studies on which de Rop based his observations. An equally awesome monster, the forest Imp, appeared in 1911 in Weeks' *Congo Life and Folklore* in several tales, suggesting the longevity of the monster as a Zaïrian folk type at least during the twentieth century.

Mrs. Ross's first exposure to an ogre tale in Zaïre came in her translation of "The Woman and the Ogre" (Tale 64 in the present volume) from *Bekolo Bémó*. . . . Excited by this tantalizing sample, she "fished" among the Nkundo, using that tale as bait, and found the fishing good indeed. Included in the Ross/Walker study are all of the ogre tales she caught, as well as the school-text tale and references to variants from the French and from the Flemish wherever those collections included what seemed to be the same basic tales Mrs. Ross had found still current in the 1970s. It is to be hoped that with access to versions from all three languages, some non-missionary, non-literary-artist investigator will pursue the elusive *eloko* on his native ground and discover a unity in the tales which has thus far not been discerned. The ogre tales have been entered wherever in the present volume their central thrust has appeared to lie within one or another of the elements of the Nkundo value system.

Aarne-Thompson's tale type 9 does not quite fit this tale because the original partnership in "The Hunter and the Ogre as Partners" involved no tricky intentions —at least, none that were indicated by the narrator. The present tale comes closer to Aarne-Thompson's tale type 1030. Lambrecht's tale type 2040 has some similarity to the present narrative: a lion claims to own the bush where the hunter sets his traps, and demands all the entrails of the catch. A wife is caught in a trap, and the lion demands her entrails. A mouse saves her by tricking the lion into the trap. An unindexed tale in Weeks' *Congo Life and Folklore* (pp. 422–424), however, offers the closest parallel found: a man and a forest Imp agree to share what falls into a pit; the man will take the males and the Imp the females. Only males are caught until the man's wife falls into the pit, is claimed by the Imp and his summoned Imp friends, and is rescued by the woman's son by precisely the same ruse employed by the wise elder in the present tale.

Motifs:

T	G570.	Ogre overawed.
T	G580.**.	Ogre goes into partnership with hero.
C	T258.+.	The curious wife.
T	K735.	Capture in pitfall.
T	Q341.	Curiosity punished.
T	J151.	Wisdom from old person.
T	J1170.	Clever judicial decisions.
T	G501.	Stupid ogre.
T	K171.0.1.	Giant (ogre) cheated in division of spoils of the chase.
T	G560.	Ogre deceived into releasing prisoner.

1. Pit traps are used in several other tales (see especially Tales 58 and 65). The smaller traps, made with reeds and twigs, are used for very small animals and for birds. A trap large enough to catch an elephant—or a woman—would be dug in the soft, moist earth with a machete and then camouflaged by a network of thin saplings overlaid with leaves and with scraps of fallen matter normally found on the forest floor. It is fortunate in this instance that the hunters had not embedded into the floor of the pit a set of sharpened stakes on which to impale the trapped animal.

2. Ogre was gullible from the outset; he believed the man's intention that they

work together as partners, an intention that might well have been honored had not the hunter's wife's curiosity complicated the matter.

3. The "go together as friends" relationship is usually found in non-ogre tales. Often an Nkundo tale that begins with two unlike characters' "going together as friends" concludes with the breaking of that friendship. This traditional pattern in oral narrative, together with the highly unusual combination, introduces an element of suspense readily appreciated by the Nkundo listeners.

4. There is no suggestion in the tale that this had not been conceived as a fair partnership. As de Rop's comments indicate, an ogre has been known to befriend a hunter, and the hunter would normally be in sufficient awe of the ogre to keep the terms of the agreement.

5. It seems unlikely that so many traps would catch only male animals; this situation is required, however, as a suspense-building element, and underscores Ogre's appreciation of the female meat that he finally trapped. (In Weeks' tale, the man laughs and says, "Did you not know that only male animals go about in search of food?") In each instance, the ogre himself had specified the basis on which the spoils were to be divided, a basis scrupulously observed by both until the catching of the man's wife threatened the agreement.

Narrators delight in listing for their hunting-culture listeners the many kinds of animals caught in a hunt.

6. The hunter's wife might well wonder at the amount of meat her husband was bringing home. The setting of 436 traps by the hunter and the ogre in partnership far exceeds the means of a single hunter.

7. Ogre had an entirely just claim, since the agreement had specified "male" and "female" and had excluded no species as "uncountable."

8. Curiosity on the part of Nkundo women, especially as related to hunting matters, is an open invitation to disaster. Unless a woman is invited to accompany her husband on a hunting expedition—to cook for him and to preserve the meat from the hunt—she is not expected to intrude upon this male enterprise.

The Nkundo school text *Bekolo Bėmȯ* . . . offers an interesting variant (in Tale 15, not included in the present volume) of this tale: A young sister becomes curious about the consistent success of her hunter-brother in bringing home game. Following him secretly one day to his hunting shelter, she discovers that his special "medicine" for hunting consists in removing his head and laying it on the bed before he goes out to hunt. When he returns, he feels around until he finds his head, puts it back in place on his neck, and proceeds to prepare the meat he has caught. When the younger sister reports this fact to her older sister and discovers that the sister wants to see this miracle for herself, she cautions her elder to leave the head right where the hunter has put it. The older sister, disregarding this counsel, snatches the head and runs home with it. Before she is able to return it to its place—at the pleading of the younger sister—the brother has returned from a successful hunt and is distraught at his inability to find and replace his head. Its return restores his confidence, and the meat is prepared as usual. But the near-disastrous consequence of the girls' interference with a man's work comes through very clearly to an Nkundo audience. (A parallel among Samoan legends accounts for the origin of the coconut.)

9. The narrator does not identify the people with "much wisdom." (The expression "wisdom that they had gotten as a gift from God" may have been added by the narrator as a concession to the missionary listener-collector; if so, this is an indication of acculturation as well as of courtesy.) The inference is that they were elders of the hunter's family and village.

10. The villagers refer to the woman as "our wife." They would not use this term unless there were an actual extended-family relationship. The exogamous principles upon which marriages are contracted among the Nkundo and the observance of the sororate compound the puzzle of marital relationships for those accustomed to other combinations and permutations of family matching.

11. As is true among the Nkundo themselves, the ogres are represented as honoring the practice of sharing among kinfolk the meat or fish caught. Other reflections of Nkundo culture in the customs attributed to the ogres (the presence of ogre elders and witch doctors in the ogres' social structure) may be found elsewhere in this collection, including Tales 67 and 68. The "whistling-in-the-dark" attitude suggested in the very titling of these latter two tales indicates the powerful hold on Nkundo imagination which the ogre maintains to this day. The ogre, filling—as he does—the important post of giant-dragon-formidable adversary, can scarcely be dispensed with in a viable oral tradition.

12. The one wise man may well have had help from the other elders in "cutting the palaver" (settling the dispute). The hunter's winning the palaver through trickery is by no means the only instance in Nkundo tale-telling of such a device, though this instance is more graphic than the one included in Tale 93.

13. If both the woman and the ogre could be "pulled out" of the pit, the gullibility of the ogres is emphasized by the elder's ruse in sending an ogre into the pit to "help pull her out," a fact that would prepare Nkundo listeners for the dénouement as well as reinforce their respect for the elder's wisdom.

In Weeks' tale, the son urges his father, "Let him take this one," whereupon the Imp, jumping into the pit to claim his prey, becomes a "male animal" and to save his own life has to give up the woman. The earlier narrative provides an instance of an equally strong motif in Nkundo oral tradition supporting the innate wisdom of a young child as informer or counselor.

Narrator: Mpanga Iyende
Location: Bonga-Iteli
Date: December 1973

61. *The Brother and Sister Who Escaped from the Ogres*[1]

A woman had brothers. One was a girl and six of the children were boys. They were grown, and one day she went into the forest that she hunt caterpillars for her brothers to eat.[2] She went and went, *ki-i-i*, and she didn't know the path. Suddenly she was in the place of the ogres.

A very large ogre saw her and said, "I have a wife."

She said, "I have a husband."[3]

Then, *te-e-e*, the people of her village hunted and hunted and hunted, but they did not see her. They hunted and hunted, *nyë*.

Her oldest brother said, "*Mu!* We haven't seen our sister. She must be lost in the swamp. I'm going to follow her."

He went and followed and followed and followed and followed, and arrived where she was.

She saw it was her brother.[4] She took him behind her house, and saw it was certainly her oldest brother. "*Mu!* What are you doing here? This is the house of the ogre. You can't live if you stay here."

He said, "If I can't live, there's no reason. Nevertheless, I have come that I take you home."

"My husband and the other ogres have gone into the forest to hunt food. They eat only meat, but they prefer human flesh. Now that you are here, let's sit a little bit. But when you come after dark, my husband will be sleeping on the side of the bed nearest the fire, and I'll sleep away from the fire. Take your spear, and some spears have a pointed end. Put it in the fire. Come to my husband and he will yell out, 'I've been speared!'[5] He'll hear, and in the end he will call out, 'I've been speared.' Do you understand?"

"I understand."

"Before the sun is fully set and it becomes very dark, you hide in the forest near the house. Do you hear?"

"I hear."

Then Ogre returned from the forest and came into the house. The ogre noticed the smell. "*Sweo-sweo-sweo.*"

The woman began to cry. She rolled in the dirt and cried and cried. "As long as we've lived together as people, you still do not like my odor. Perhaps I ought to leave if you feel that way." She kept crying and rolling in the dirt.[6]

A chief of the birds came and came into the house of the ogre and he was singing.[7]

.   .   .

Then the ogre said, "What are you doing here? Go!" He hit at the bird with a stick and he left.

All the ogres came and brought their meat, and the wife cooked and cooked and cooked, *ki-i-i.* They ate, and they went to bed when the sun went down.

As soon as it was quiet, the brother came out and took up his spear with the sharp point that he get the ogre. Then he came over by the bed. He took the dull end and put it where his sister was. He put the sharp end into the ogre.[8] Then Ogre took his l-o-n-g thumbnail, which was one meter,[9] and reached out from the bed and cut the throat of the brother and killed him.[10]

"*A-i!* You didn't tell me your brother was here, and now he is dead." The ogre cried and cried. "He was a part of the family. I didn't know where he was."[11]

Then, *te-e-e,* in the morning all the ogres came to greet the meat.[12] The wife had no way to cry in the open, so she cried in secret so he wouldn't see her. Then, *ti-i-i,* they ate. And so they went again.

After two days the second brother came. "Your older brother was just here and he was killed, and now you come. For what reason?"

"Wherever you are, it must be finished. I won't return, *nyé.*"

She cooked for him and gave him food and manioc bread.[13]

"Now, before we sleep, get a spear that's dull on one end and sharp on the other and put it in the fire. You know that my husband is very fierce, and he will call out, 'What's the matter? What's the matter?' But take the dull end of the spear and put it against me and I'll call out. Then you put the point of the spear into the ogre. Do you hear?"

"I hear."

They came in from hunting, and, "Sniff, sniff, sniff. *Sweo-sweo-sweo!*"

Then the woman began to cry and cry and roll in the dirt.

"As long as we've lived together as people, you still don't know my odor. Maybe I should go home." Then she stopped rolling.

Then, *te-e-e*, the little bird arrived.[14]

Ogre was angry, and he[15] left.

After the sun had set, they went to bed, and the brother came. He tried and he heated the spear. He poked his sister with the dull end. She sat up, complaining, " . . ."[16] Then he thrust the hot, pointed end into Ogre, but missed.[17] Ogre reached out with his meter-long thumbnail and cut his throat. Then, *te-e-e*, he had succeeded with two of the brothers.

He killed another.

He killed another.

He killed another.[18]

The last brother, who was a very child, said that he would go to rescue his sister. "I can go."

When he arrived, the sister saw him and she cried and cried, and said, "All the others are dead. If you are killed, what will I do? I'll be all alone."

The child brother said to her, "I won't eat your food.[19] I'm not hungry. I've had food."

Before he started on his journey, he had collected fierce insects of many kinds, *bajwa balolonga*. After he arrived there, he made a house of leaves and put them in it. All of the things were very fierce.

Then, then,[20] *te-e-e*, the sun went down, and the young boy hid with all his things. He came, *ti-i-i*, in the quiet of the night. He cooked the sharp end of his spear, *tso-tso*, in the fire until it was very hot. He put the dull end of the spear near his sister and the pointed end near the ogre. Then he woke his sister with the dull end and she sat up, complaining, " . . ."[21] He thrust the hot, sharp end in the place of the ogre, and it pinned him to the ground. Ogre reached out and his thumbnail went into the ground, *nyė*. He was dead.

After the ogre was dead, then he collected his insects. "In the morning the ogres will come to greet me. When you see them coming, tell them that the brother of your husband came yesterday. They will come and I will release the fierce and poisonous insects to kill them."

"Eh."

Then, *te-e-e*, the ogres came, calling, "The brother of the ogre is here. Let's go and see him. He seems to be fierce." Then, "Ogres, the husband has fallen."

He said, "..."[22]

He had finished killing all of the ogres, *nyé*.[23]

After he finished killing the ogres, he took his sister, he took the *baumba*, he took all the things that were there; he took and took.[24] Then, *ti-ti-ti-ti*, they left it[25] near the edge of the swamp.

A small child who was bathing in the swamp saw them. She ran to their mother, shouting, "Mama, come and see. The brother and sister have already finished coming there."

"The children are not finished at all?"

"No, no. Not at all."

"There is no palaver—except for God."

"They have returned in that manner."

Then they came to see all the things—*toma-touma, baumba-baumba*—little, little, little, and then they went into the house and had a great feast.

But if you go into a village of other people, you ask about the work that is there, and then you ask about the talking about the brother and sister and they'll tell you about the brother and sister who killed all the ogres.[26]

Included in Tale 61 are several features about ogres that conflict both with those of the ogres in other Ross-collected tales and with established Nkundo practices normally attributed by narrators to ogres. Here, Mpanga Iyende has the ogres go to bed at sunset; in Tales 67 through 69, emphasis is placed on moonlit nighttime as the ogres' time to work. Here, also, the ogre weeps before his wife; on the other hand, the wife does not weep before the ogre about the deaths of her brothers (though she counterfeits mourning to impress upon the ogre her grief that he does not yet know her odor), but cries instead in secret, a pattern observed elsewhere in the tales. Here, the ogres eat in the morning as well as at night; the Nkundo normally have one daily meal, in the evening. These and other curious departures in the narration aroused no comment or contradiction from the audience, which respected the narrator's prerogative to affix his individual stamp to the tale.

Various disruptive sounds are present on the tape recording of the tale, but none of the extraneous noises appeared to disturb either the narrator or his listeners. At one point or another, the following sounds can be heard: coughing, the voice of a small child, an older child's singing in the background, someone shouting in the distance (Nkundo often shout to one another from one end of the village to the other), and the laughter of a child in the crowd—perhaps at a private joke, since the passage being narrated was not considered amusing by the rest of the listeners. Also, there is the sound of a chicken, roosting on a branch and apparently disturbed by the tale-telling.

Sounds and actions relevant to the narrative itself have been indicated in the footnotes for the tale. Both the audience and the storyteller participated actively in the drama played out in the tale. As has often been observed, a quiet African audience is a rarity; this particular audience was totally and vocally involved in the telling of the tale.

We have been unable to locate in any of the indexes a type including enough elements of the present tale to warrant attaching that type number to it. Lambrecht's tale type 3981 and Arewa's tale type 3979 each contain some of the elements, but the combination resulting in each instance seems insufficiently close to the Ross-collected narrative. It is hoped that as more and more of the Nkundo ogre tales become available—Boelaert and de Rop have in various studies paved the way for such investigations—enough samples can be mustered to encourage the establishment of a type number that will include this and similar tales.

Motifs:

T	T111.	Marriage of mortal and supernatural being.
T	T135.1.**.	Formulistic exchange of marriage vows between supernatural being and human: "I have a wife." "I have a husband."
T	G81.	Unwitting marriage to cannibal.
T	G84.**.	*Sweo-sweo-sweo* [Lonkundo equivalent of "Fee-fi-fo-fum"].
T	B211.3.	Speaking bird.
C	B569.+.**.	Bird's song warns ogre of impending danger from human wife.
T	J652.	Inattention to warnings.
T	H1385.6.	Quest for lost sister.
T	G530.**.	Ogre's human wife aids hero (her brother).
C	C680.+.**.	Injunction: strike ogre's wife with blunt end of spear and ogre with heated pointed end of spear.
C	F529.+.**.	Ogre with thumbnail one meter long.
T	G88.**.	Cannibal has long thumbnail.
T	G551.1.	Rescue of sister from ogre by brother.
C	G512.8.+.**.	Young man spears ogre; ogre killed.
T	G512.1.**.	Ogre killed with spear.
T	L310.	Weak overcomes strong in conflict.
T	G519.**.	Ogres killed through other tricks: fierce insects.

1. The formulaic opening is lacking on the tape.

2. An Nkundo woman seldom goes far into the forest alone because of the dangers and difficulties to be encountered there. After the girl's disappearance, the villagers would have called repeatedly, hoping she could follow their voices to safety. Apparently she had left enough signs so that if necessary she could be sought and rescued.

3. This exchange was used throughout the Ross-collected tales when a marriage occurred between an Nkundo and a supernatural creature, whether the latter happened to be malevolent or benign. See, for example, Tales 62 through 64, 80, and 83.

4. At this point, there was a high-pitched gasp by the narrator, representing the dismay the girl felt when she saw her brother in that dangerous place.

This was the first tale in the Ross collection in which the narrator had increased the dramatic impact of the story by assuming a higher voice to represent a female character, a pitch maintained with a high degree of consistency throughout the girl's speeches.

5. Omitted by the narrator here was the girl's instruction concerning use of the spear's dull end to prompt her outcry, an omission mended in her directions to the second brother.

The girl's instructions here were given very rapidly, as if the ogre's arrival were imminent, a factor heightening the drama and suspense.

6. The actions of the girl were precipitated by the ogre's exclamation "*Sweo-sweo-sweo*," the Lonkundo equivalent of "Fee-fi-fo-fum," an expression of the detection of the odor of human flesh. In an effort to divert the ogre's attention from her brother to herself, she exhibited the signs of true mourning among the Nkundo.

7. The bird was not identified, nor could enough of the text of the bird's song be translated to warrant its inclusion in the tale, since it was sung in a dialect unfamiliar to the translators; omission of the song from the text has been indicated by ellipsis dots.

Certain observations can be made about the song's form and content: (1) it was "lined out" by the narrator for the audience and was apparently new to them, though they quickly caught the pattern and thereafter furnished the chorus, each line of which began with the word "*Jili*," the name of an Nkundo children's riddling game; (2) there are five lines of text, each followed by the chorused "*Jili mama*," with a concluding eleventh line consisting only of "*Jili*"; (3) the bird's song warns the ogre to beware of his wife, since she is concealing something, and thus avoid destruction.

8. Here the narrator made first a noise representing the sister's response and then a deeper sound for the ogre's response to the pricking of the spear.

9. With great relish, the narrator demonstrated the length of the ogre's thumbnail.

Tales from neighboring culture areas include ogres with excessively long, strong fingernails used in various ways, extending even to their use in cutting down trees. See, for example, Postma's *Tales from the Basotho* (1974), pages 136–141.

10. The narrator paused here, to allow greater dramatic effect for the ogre's display of regret which followed the killing of his in-law. The ogre had had no indication of the young man's identity; he would not—according to the Nkundo value system—have deliberately killed his wife's brother.

11. Here the narrator provided a thoroughly convincing demonstration of the ogre's grief, a grief which in no way reduced his willingness to feast on the flesh of his wife's brother.

12. The term used here—*sésa nyama*—is a direct reflection of Nkundo practice: to "bless ['greet'] the meat" includes cutting it up, dividing it.

13. In Nkundo storytelling, whether the characters in the tale are wild animals, ogres, or people, the foods served are those found in the Nkundo diet, with the notable exception of human flesh relished by the ogres. Presumably, the girl would have sustained herself on these foods during her stay with the ogre.

14. At this point the narrator "lined out" a slightly enlarged version of the bird's warning song: a new line and the chorus "*Jili mama*" are added after the chorus of the original third text line; a new line and the chorus also follow the chorus of the original fifth line; as before, the song concludes with "*Jili.*" The material added in this song serves to re-emphasize the ogre's threatened position.

15. "He" is the bird.

16. A shouting outside the audience obscured the words on the tape expressing the sister's complaint here.

17. It is curious that neither of the first two brothers had succeeded in reaching a vital spot in the ogre with the point of the spear. In all likelihood, the narrator intended to prolong the story to increase suspense and to reserve the crown of success for the youngest brother, a narrative staple worldwide.

18. Although repetition is relished, the narrator here chose to omit the details of the three ensuing rescue efforts and to concentrate instead on the youngest brother's attempt to recover the girl.

19. Even within the account of the youngest brother's visit, the narrator eliminated the details by now thoroughly familiar, moving directly to the hero's preparation for his battle with the ogres; these and earlier evidences of truncation were readily accepted by the listeners. The chanted ideophone *bajwa balolonga* used by the storyteller suggests the poisons carried by the insects; the chant employed a diminished-third interval.

20. "Then," "*nkanko*" in Lonkundo, is the favorite hesitation word among the Nkundo both in conversation and in tale-telling.

21. Ironically, a child's shouting not far from the storytelling site distorted the content of the girl's complaint; the translators were unable to decipher the words.

22. Unaccountably, there was a blank space on the tape at this point. When the sound resumed, the narrator was crying out in a low, rough voice—imitative of the ogres—the Lonkundo equivalent of "They follow us! Things which are fierce!"

23. The audience as a whole chorused the "*nyé.*"

24. In Lonkundo there is a patterned chant used to describe the gathering up of such goods: "*Baumba, baumba,* / *Toma, touma,* / *Isisi, isisi, isisi.* / *L'isis'isisi.* / *L'isis'isisi.*" Roughly translated, it means "Copper bars, copper bars, / Things, all the things, / Gradually, little by little /", with a satisfying, elided repetition of the third line peculiarly pleasing in the Lonkundo original.

25. "It" here indicated "the treasure"—everything brought home.

26. This is the only tale in the Ross collection that offers an ending purporting to authenticate the narrative. Artistically, use of the formulaic ending would have been anticlimactic.

Narrator: Bokunge Jacques
Location: Bólêngé
Date: February 1973

62.   The Woman and the Ogre

On another day several young women went out into the swampy
parts of the forest to hunt fish.[1] One of the women wandered on
ahead seeking a better place to fish. She never seemed to be quite
satisfied, and kept wandering on in hopes of a better place. All at
once she realized that she was a long way from her friends. She
turned back, feeling that it was time she joined them again. Soon
she was completely lost, and found that she was going here and there
in the forest and becoming more lost all the time.

As evening was coming on, she met an ogre in the path. This
is a fearful thing, and she was very frightened. In any event, here
was the young woman, Lifoku,[2] lost in the forest and face to face
with Ogre himself.[3] She was alone and had been frightened before
she met Ogre. Meeting Ogre made her all the more frightened, but
there was no way in which she could avoid him. He looked her over
and decided that he could use her for preparing his meat.

Therefore he said to her, "I have a wife."

She answered, "I have a husband."[4]

That night, Lifoku's family began to call her. They would call
and call and then listen to hear if she answered.[5] The next day,
they began to search all through the forest. For many days they
searched and called, but it was all to no avail. When everyone else
had given up the search, Lifoku's two brothers continued to seek
her in the forest. One of these brothers had four ferocious dogs
that he took along on the search. The dogs were named by their
special talents. One was called Ntenafelefele because when he
attacked a person, he would cut the person in half just above the
waistline. Another was Elengolakwete because he would jump for
the throat of the person and almost cut the head off. The third was
Lofongankobuna because he wanted to prolong the fight as long
as possible, as though he wished to entertain an audience. The last
of these dogs was Ecikakabetsampunungu. He was the one who
severed the head from the body and left it some distance from the
body. Even with such excellent help, the brothers searched a long
while with no success.

In due time, the brother with the dogs found her deep in the forest. Then he saw Ogre and also the meat drying over the fire. The meat was obviously human flesh.

Lifoku ran to him and fell into his arms. She was crying and so was her brother. When Lifoku was able to speak, she began to express her fear for her brother. "You must know that he is very bad. He will surely kill you."

"No, no. He will not be able to harm me. My four dogs will protect me. They are my protectors. I have no fear."

Ogre greeted Lifoku's brother, calling him Ekilo (Brother-in-Law), and gave him a welcome. He had Lifoku prepare a suitable meal for him and expressed the desire that he stay for a while with them.

When night came, Ogre took Brother-in-Law into the house. "You may sleep in this room. I hope that you will be comfortable."

In the night, when all was quiet, Ogre went to the room where Brother-in-Law was sleeping, planning to kill him for a future meal. However, the four dogs wouldn't so much as let him enter the room.

One morning shortly after that, Ogre said to Brother-in-Law, "I want to go into the forest. Let us go together and pick the fruit that grows on the rubber vine."[6]

Brother-in-Law was pleased with the prospect of finding this fruit and was soon ready to go with Ogre. He left his dogs in the care of Lifoku, since he knew that Ogre wouldn't be comfortable if they went along. "Shut the dogs up in the house. Ogre and I will go alone into the forest. If I need the help of the dogs, I will call them and they will tell you that I have called."

The two of them walked through the forest searching for the special fruit. When they found it, Ogre said, "You climb up and get the fruit." So Brother-in-Law climbed well up into the tree where the fruit was growing.

Then Ogre began to cut the tree with his axe, *seko-seko-seko.*[7] As he cut he sang a song:

> Cutting, cutting, the tree is going to fall.
> Cutting, cutting, the tree is going to fall, cutting.
> In the forest between the villages is fruit.
> In the forest between the villages man can eat.

Even though Ogre kept cutting at the tree with his axe, strangely enough it did not cut.

The brother in the tree knew that he needed help, and decided to call his dogs. He began calling them by name: "Ntenafelefele,

Elengolakwete, Lofongankobuna, Ecikakabetsampunungu." They heard his voice and began to tell Lifoku that she must turn them loose.

As soon as the dogs were released, they quickly picked up the scent of their master and were soon following his trail, *ngòi-ngòi-ngòi*,[8] until they reached the tree where Brother-in-Law was. Then Brother-in-Law commanded them, "Fight him. Fight him hard." The dogs jumped on Ogre and killed him until he was completely dead, *nyè*.

Brother-in-Law came down out of the tree and with his dogs returned to the home of Ogre. He and his sister wrapped all the meat except the human flesh into packages. These were tied on the backs of the dogs, and Lifoku carried what was left. When they arrived at their village, there was much rejoicing. With all the meat that they brought, a great feast was prepared, and all the people came to honor Lifoku's safe return home.

Do not kill a dog; a dog is a true helper.

[Notes to Tale 62 follow Tale 64.]

Narrator:	Mbambo Jean
Location:	Mbandaka
Date:	August 1973

63.   *The Woman and the Ogre* (Variant I)

A certain man had two sons and a daughter. The daughter was named Mpucu Tòlòkò. She had palavers with people everywhere. She was always fighting and arguing. She could never hear the teachings of her father or mother.

That particular year, there was a great dry season.[9] However, Ogre owned the nearby swamp, and no one dared to hunt fish there. He made it a forbidden place, and everyone was afraid to go there.

On either side of this swamp there was a village. One day the
people across the swamp from Mpucu's village had a big celebration
where there would be feasting, drinking, and many games.[10] Some
of the young people of Mpucu's village decided to go to the celebration. Before they reached the swamp, the oldest girl among them
said, "There is a special tabu here in this swamp. While we are
crossing it, no one should spit."

When they reached the swamp, they found dead fish[11] everywhere, and as a result the odor was very bad.

Mpucu cried out, "*Mongoyeka!*[12] The odor here is terrible. Why
can't I spit to relieve myself of it?"[13]

In spite of the warning she had been given, she spat into the
swamp. The girls with her were very sorry that she had.

They all went on to the village where the celebration was. They
played and played until they had tried everything. Then they started
for home. When they reached the swamp where they had crossed
before, they found that the water had risen until it was very high.[14]
They began to sing a special song before they crossed:

> I did not spit.
> It was Mpucu Tòlòkò who spat.
> Mpucu Tòlòkò caused the strife.
> Mpucu Tòlòkò did.

They kept singing while the first girl crossed. She arrived safely
on the other side. Then the second girl went into the swamp while
the song kept on:

> I did not spit.
> It was Mpucu Tòlòkò who spat.
> Mpucu Tòlòkò caused the strife.
> Mpucu Tòlòkò did.

She arrived safely on the other side. The third girl went into
the swamp, singing as she went,

> I did not spit.
> It was Mpucu Tòlòkò who spat.
> Mpucu Tòlòkò caused the strife.
> Mpucu Tòlòkò did.

As soon as she was safely on the other side, it was Mpucu's
turn to cross. She said, "My friends sang as they crossed. I'll sing
the same song as I cross and I'll be safe also."

> I did not spit.
> It was Mpucu Tòlòkò who spat.
> Mpucu Tòlòkò caused the strife.
> Mpucu Tòlòkò did.

Her friends had crossed safely and were waiting for her on the other side. However, Mpucu found the swamp to be much deeper than they had. The water came to her ankles and she sang,

> I did not spit.
> It was Mpucu Tòlòkò who spat.
> Mpucu Tòlòkò caused the strife.
> Mpucu Tòlòkò did.

It came to her knees and she sang the same story:

> I did not spit.
> It was Mpucu Tòlòkò who spat.
> Mpucu Tòlòkò caused the strife.
> Mpucu Tòlòkò did.

It came to her thighs as she sang,

> I did not spit.
> It was Mpucu Tòlòkò who spat.
> Mpucu Tòlòkò caused the strife.
> Mpucu Tòlòkò did.

The water came up to her waist and she kept singing,

> I did not spit.
> It was Mpucu Tòlòkò who spat.
> Mpucu Tòlòkò caused the strife.
> Mpucu Tòlòkò did.

It came to her neck and the song continued:

> I did not spit.
> It was Mpucu Tòlòkò who spat.
> Mpucu Tòlòkò caused the strife.
> Mpucu Tòlòkò did.

Then the water covered her completely, and they could no longer hear her or see her.

Her friends saw that she was gone in the swamp and they went home to tell her parents. "Mpucu went with us. Now she is drowned in the swamp."

Everyone wept for her. They went to hunt her body in the swamp, but never found it.

When Mpucu found herself under water in the swamp, she went into one of the fish traps belonging to Ogre. When he came and found her there, he was pleased and danced for joy. He was a bachelor and he shouted, "I now have a wife."

He sang again, "I have a wife."

Mpucu answered, "I have a husband."

"I have a wife."

"I have a husband."

Ogre brought a canoe for her and took her to the village of the ogres. Ogre gave her kitchen equipment and the things needed for the house.[15] When she went inside, she found that he had great wealth.

Soon, Mpucu's older brother, Empompo, decided that he would go to find the reason for Mpucu's death. He knew that her friends had safely crossed the swamp and that the water wasn't very deep. First, he went to get help from Itòji.[16]

Itòji told Empompo, "Your sister refused to listen to the teachings of others. Her friends told her that it was tabu to spit in the swamp. Now she is with Ogre as his wife."

Empompo asked, "How can I help my sister and take her home?"

Itòji answered, "Go and get three hundred dogs, some wasps and hornets, and some driver ants.[17] When you come near to the village of the ogres, you will find a man. He is a chief. Ask him where Ogre who kills strangers lives. He will tell you where you will find your sister."

Empompo went to get all the things that he needed to take with him—three hundred dogs, wasps, hornets, and driver ants. The dogs could follow him, but the insects he put in the bag that he carried on his shoulder.[18] He then got a canoe, put everything into it, and crossed to the other side of the swamp. When he came near to the village of the ogres, he met a man on the path.

He asked, "Father, where is the home of Ogre who kills strangers?"

The chief answered, "Listen. You have little chance of reaching the home of Ogre. He doesn't like strangers to come, and kills them when they arrive. However, you may arrive there and find your sister. Do not go openly as a man, but go in hiding. Then, if your sister offers you food, eat it. If Ogre offers you food, do not eat it."[19]

At that time, Ogre was in the forest hunting meat. In this way

Empompo reached the house and found his sister. When Mpucu saw her brother, she felt sad. She said, "Ogre does not like strangers to come. He will kill you when he sees you here."

Empompo said, "Hide me under the bed. Then when Ogre comes, if you give me food, I'll eat. If Ogre gives me food, I'll refuse it. You understand."

Mpucu answered, "I hear you."

Ogre was nearly home by then, and Mpucu hid Empompo under the bed. Soon Ogre arrived with the meat of people and the meat of the forest. He gave the meat to Mpucu and she cooked and cooked until it was all prepared. Then they were ready to eat dinner.

After Ogre had eaten, he said, "We have finished eating. Now, even though we have no guests, you sing a song. Sing."

Mpucu sang,

> I ate food with my father and mother.
> My hand goes to my mouth;
> Then it goes under the bed.
> I put the food under the bed; I put the food
> under the bed.

Mpucu put food under the bed as she sang.
Ogre said, "Sing again."
She sang,

> I ate food with my father and mother.
> My hand goes to my mouth;
> Then it goes under the bed.
> I put the food under the bed; I put the food
> under the bed.

Mpucu put the food under the bed as she sang.
Ogre said, "Sing again."
She sang,

> I ate food with my father and mother.
> My hand goes to my mouth;
> Then it goes under the bed.
> I put the food under the bed; I put the food
> under the bed.

As she sang, Ogre held food under the bed. When Empompo saw the hand with food, he was afraid to refuse it, and he ate it. Ogre found Empompo there under the bed. Empompo was frightened. Ogre said, "Here I find food right in my own house."

He took a huge cane that an ogre uses for killing animals, and killed Mpucu's brother. Mpucu saw that her brother was dead. She refused to weep when Ogre could see her, so she decided to go to bed. She told Ogre, "I feel sick. I feel sick."

Ogre thought it best that she sleep until she felt better.

Ogre cut up Empompo and divided the meat with his friends, and they all ate well.

The months passed, and Mpucu stayed in bed and wasn't able to work in the house. After three months she got up and began to work again.

Mpucu's younger brother was wondering about his brother and sister, since no news of them had come. He said, "My brother has gone to hunt Mpucu and even now is there. I do not know why my sister died or where my brother is. I am going to talk with Itòji."

He went and told Itòji his story. Itòji told him the same as he had told Empompo. He said, "Your brother is already dead because he wasn't courageous. But you are man. You take three hundred dogs, some hornets, some wasps, and some driver ants. Take them in a canoe and you will arrive there as did your brother."

Botekoli Mpulu'ofombo put the insects in his shoulder bag and took the dogs with him. He crossed the swamp in a canoe. As he neared the village of the ogres he met a chief on the path. He asked him, "Where does Ogre who kills strangers live?"

The chief told him as he had told his brother. "Hide under the bed when you arrive there. If your sister gives you food, eat it. But if Ogre gives you food, refuse it. At night, Ogre and his wife will talk together in the room. Before Ogre's wife tells him that her brother has come, they will eat dinner."

Soon Botekoli arrived at the house of his sister. When Mpucu saw him, she felt much sorrow. She cried, "My older brother is dead; now my younger brother has come, and Ogre will kill him also."

Botekoli said, "Even though our brother is dead, each person is of a different kind. I have come that we might talk it over."

Mpucu warned, "You had better hide under the bed now. Very soon Ogre will return from hunting. If I give you food, eat it. But if Ogre gives you food, refuse it."

Then Botekoli hid under the bed. Ogre came with the meat of man and the meat of the forest. He cut it up and Mpucu cooked and cooked. Then they came to the time of eating.

Ogre said to her, "Sing."

Mpucu sang the same song as before:

> I ate food with my father and mother.
> My hand goes to my mouth;
> Then it goes under the bed.
> I put the food under the bed; I put the food
>   under the bed.

As she sang, Mpucu put food under the bed, and her brother ate it. Ogre passed food under the bed, and Botekoli refused to eat it. "I can't eat that food." So Ogre ate it himself.

Soon it was time to go to bed. Mpucu explained to Ogre that this was her brother and his brother-in-law and that he should treat him as family. Ogre listened to her and said, "No. I wouldn't harm my own family. I would like to greet him. 'Brother-in-Law! You are here!'"

Botekoli answered, "Yes! Proverb!"

Ogre answered, "The relative of a person is in the family even though he is an in-law."

Botekoli explained that he had come to visit his sister. Ogre said, "Come and I'll show you the room where you are to sleep." Botekoli went to the bedroom that Ogre showed him. He took his dogs, his wasps, his hornets, and his driver ants with him there. He closed the door and braced it with a strong wooden rod.

After Botekoli was asleep, Ogre came out of his bed very quietly, leaving his wife asleep. He went to the room where his brother-in-law slept. He carefully tried to open the door but could only open it a crack. However, the insects who were on guard rushed out and began to sting him.

Ogre cried out, "My brother-in-law has wasps. Why?" He called to Botekoli, "Stop your insects from tormenting me. Stop them. Stop them."

The insects left when Botekoli called them. "Why are you here in the night like this?" he asked.

Ogre said, "I am hunting a pipe for smoking." Ogre went back to bed, and soon it was morning.

Ogre said, "Brother-in-Law, I want to hunt honey.[20] Wouldn't you like to go with me?"

Botekoli answered, "I'd like that. Let's go."

Ogre went into the village and told the ogres, "My brother-in-law has come, and we are going to hunt honey. You follow, and when he is in the tree, we'll cut it down and have a feast."

Botekoli said to Mpucu, "We are going into the forest to hunt honey. If I need help, I'll call the dogs and you can turn them loose."

So Ogre and Botekoli went into the forest to search for honey. Ogre spotted the tree with the honey up in the branches. He said, "There is the honey. Climb into the tree and get it."

So Botekoli climbed into the tree where the honey was. He had a torch with fire which he used to get the bees away. As soon as he was there, all of the ogres came to the tree. "We must kill him. He has come to take our wife. We must kill him."

They began to cut the tree with their axes, *kao-kao*. The tree was very large, but after a while it was about to fall. Botekoli reached into the honey nest and took out handfuls of honey. He threw a great amount of it down to the ogres. They grabbed it and began to eat it with relish. In the meantime, they forgot all about Botekoli.

While they were eating the honey, Botekoli began to shout, "*Bangongoloko! Etenafefele!* Come!" He was calling his dogs and all of his insects. Mpucu heard the dogs complaining and knew that they were being called. She let them out of the room where he had left them. The dogs and insects went to the place where Botekoli was in the tree. They attacked the ogres and quickly killed them. The witch doctor of the ogres wasn't there and therefore wasn't killed. He alone was left to return home.[21]

When all the ogres were dead, Botekoli took his honey and climbed out of the tree. He went back to the village and found his sister. He said, "The ogres tried to cut the tree down and kill me, but now they are all dead. Let us get our things together and go home."

They gathered the things which Ogre had taken from the people he had killed. They took those things with them and returned home. When they arrived, they prepared a great feast. They beat the drums, calling all the people to come and celebrate with them.

If a child says that she will not heed the teachings of the people who tell her what she should do, she gets herself into difficulty. Now, Mpucu Tòlòkò did as she pleased, and her brother died because of her obstinacy, all this because she refused to hear the teachings of her friends, and as a result she felt great shame.

[Notes to Tale 63 follow Tale 64.]

Source: Bekolo Bèmò ...
Zaïrian school reader
(in Lonkundo)
Translator: Mabel Ross
Date of Translation: November 1972

64. *The Woman and the Ogre* (Variant II)

Some women went after *bieya*. There were seven women.

When they reached the place of searching for the bieya, they divided paths, each woman on her own path.[22] When a certain woman went on her path, she found an ogre standing. The ogre said to her, "I have a wife." Then he said to her, the woman, "You say that, 'I have a husband!'" And she felt much fear, and she said, "I have a husband." Then they went to the home of the ogre.

The food of the ogre is the very flesh of people. And the woman found the very many heads of people which were in his garbage pit, which was a hollow in the bokungu tree. And she felt fear itself and awe.

In the family of that woman she had seven brothers, six older and one child.

The first went to hunt his sister in the forest, and he found her in the yard of the ogre. When the sister saw him, she felt much sorrow and cried with tears. And she said, "Why did you come here? The ogre took me as wife, and his food is the flesh of people." Then she showed him the heads of people in the hollow of the bokungu tree.

Soon the ogre came with a basket of the flesh of people. Then the woman hid her brother under the bed. The ogre put down the basket with the flesh of people and he said, "I smell a terrible odor. I smell a terrible odor!"[23] Then he walked everywhere hunting the place the person was hiding. Then his wife told him that, "The one who comes is your brother-in-law, my brother." And he greeted the brother, "In-law, you are here? You are here?" And the brother of the wife answered him, and he came out from under the bed and he sat down. Then the sister gave him food and he ate.

At night, he slept in the room which the ogre showed him. But throughout the night the ogre came with a big stick and quickly killed him. He cut off his head and carried the head to throw it in his garbage pit; then he brought the meat itself to his wife. In the morning the wife knew that it was the very flesh of her brother, and she cried with the very cries of sorrow.

Five more of her brothers came in the same way, and the ogre killed all of them, *nyé*. The only one who was left was the youngest child. He went to the witch doctor. The witch doctor said to him, "Get some wasps and bees and some fierce animals; then go seek your sister. The sister is not yet dead, but your brothers have finished dying." The child took all of the fierce things, and he went.

When he went, he found his sister. When the sister saw him, she cried. She said, "We have all come to an end here, I and my brothers." But the brother felt no fear, and he did not want to be hidden at all, *nyé*. He sat with his fierce dogs which he had brought, and his bees and wasps. Then the ogre came and greeted him. "In-law. You are here? You are here?"

He answered, "I am here."

In the evening, the ogre showed him the room for sleeping. The child took his fierce dogs and all the fierce things and he put them in the doorway.

Throughout the night, that ogre came with cunning itself, that he kill that child. But the fierce insects challenged him, and he cried out with crying itself and screaming. The dogs growled with much fierceness. The ogre said, "In-law, call your dogs!"

The boy asked him, "In-law, what do you come here to do?"

The ogre said, "I have come that I might light a fire." And the child called the dogs and slept.

In the morning the ogre asked the child that, "In-law, do you like to hunt honey?"

The child answered, "Yes, I like to hunt honey."

The ogre said, "Come, let us go that I get honey; let us hunt honey."

The child left his dogs and fierce insects in the house. He told his sister that if she heard the dogs running about and crying, she was to open the door for them that they go. Then he went, he and the ogre.

When they went, they arrived at the honey tree; the child climbed that he have honey. But the ogre called all of the ogres; he said, "Come, and we will have good meat." Then all the ogres came and they chopped that tree. Then they sang their song,

> Cutting the tree, *kao-kao*!
> The branch of the tree bends, *kao-kao*!
> The devils of the forest, *kao-kao*,
> Cutting the tree, *kao-kao*!
>
> Cutting the tree, *kao-kao*!
> The branch of the tree bends, *kao-kao*!
> The devils of the forest, *kao-kao*,
> Cutting the tree, *kao-kao*!
>
> Cutting the tree, *kao-kao*!
> The branch of the tree bends, *kao-kao*!
> The devils of the forest, *kao-kao*,
> Cutting the tree, *kao-kao*!
>
> Cutting the tree, *kao-kao*!
> The branch of the tree bends, *kao-kao*!
> The devils of the forest, *kao-kao*,
> Cutting the tree, *kao-kao*!

The tree was very nearly ready to fall, but the child slapped the tree a blow with his hand, and the cut of the tree was whole again.

The ogres said, "This child has witchcraft. The tree had very nearly fallen, and he slapped a blow with his hand and the tree is healed of its cuts."

The witch doctor of the ogres was there and he said, "I am going for a bit of a drink; then I'll return." Thus he went on a journey. And some ogres who remained sang the song again:

> Cutting the tree, *kao-kao*!
> The branch of the tree bends, *kao-kao*!
> The devils of the forest, *kao-kao*,
> Cutting the tree, *kao-kao*!

The tree sought that it fall again, but the child slapped the tree with his hand again, and the wound was healed once more. Then he called his dogs, the one who was named Botenaifefele and another who was called Ifumbwatelele.[24] When the child's sister heard the dogs pacing and crying in the room, she opened the door for them and they went out, they and the fierce insects; and they all ran, running itself, out of breath.

When they arrived, they bit the ogres with severe bites, and the fierce insects stung them, and they killed all of the ogres with death itself. The witch doctor of the ogres lived because he had gone before the dogs and the insects had come.

The child came down and went to get his sister, and he and his sister went home.[25]

Tales 62, 63, and 64, all dealing with the marriage of an unwilling woman to an ogre and her subsequent rescue by one of her brothers, reflect much of Nkundo nuclear family loyalty, of friction and distrust between in-laws, and of Nkundo customs as well as of the awe of the supernatural that constitutes an important factor in the value system. Among the many features held in common, each of the narratives begins with a communal activity; each one presents the marriage formula adopted for the bond between a human woman and a supernatural being; each includes a tree refuge for the hero; each includes two or more brothers who seek the lost woman; each involves the use of dogs in the killing of the ogres; each includes at least some sung portions; and each ends with the safe return of the successful brother and his long-sought sister.

But it is the differences among the tales that give them special interest for the student of narrative techniques. In Tale 63, presented as a *cante fable* though there was no audience (apart from Mrs. Ross) to sing the choral response, the narrator *said* the first line of each song and *sang* the remaining lines, a pattern not observed elsewhere in the Ross-collected tales. That same tale—63—has additional dimension in its inclusion of tabu violation and a subsequent submersion of the tabu violator. In Tale 62, the narrator provides a considerable amount of explanatory material, quoted in the notes, that indicates the tale-teller's concern for the listener's full understanding of the setting, characters, and events in the story, material that would not be supplied for an all-Nkundo audience but that places the tale solidly within the framework of the culture for a non-Nkundo reader. Another notable difference between Tale 62 and the other two in the cluster is that in the first narrative neither of the woman's brothers loses his life in the process of rescuing his sister. The proverb concluding Tale 62 marks still another interesting departure of that tale from its variants: the emphasis placed upon the value of the dogs in the rescue mission; the dogs, acknowledged early in the tale as sufficient protection for their owner, render the second brother's efforts unnecessary, and serve a peoplelike function in their carrying of the parcels of meat, a use of dogs by people that appears nowhere else in the Ross collection. No mention is made in Tale 62 either of the itòji or of the ogre witch doctor, curious omissions in an ogre tale; these omissions serve to strengthen the significance of the dogs in the tale, since one can safely assume that with those four dogs on the scene, a consultation with the itòji was unnecessary and not even a witch doctor could have escaped death at the action's conclusion. It is interesting to note that fierce insects were required in both of the variants, in addition to the dogs, in order to overcome the ogres, and that in both instances the witch doctor managed to avoid the death meted out to the rest of the ogres.

The disparities between Tale 63 and Tale 64 outweigh their many similarities, evidence that even if Mbambo Jean had been familiar with the school-reader version, he felt free to develop a narrative memorably different from the published form. Because of the narrator's own fine, subtle wit, there are decidedly humorous overtones in Tale 63 that are absent in the other two versions, among them the humor of exaggeration (300 dogs carried in a canoe), the humor in the conversational exchanges with the second brother—including the ogre's alibi for his nighttime visit to his in-law's room—and the humor of situation (ogres' being distracted from human flesh by handfuls of honey thrown down by the hero). It is unfortunate that Mbambo Jean had no Nkundo audience for this tale, since the audience's reaction would have provided the soundest possible clue as to whether or not what Western analysts perceive as "humorous overtones" are actually humorous to the Nkundo. As is evident in several other tales in the present collection (for example, Tales 51 and 52), situations that would prompt laughter from Western readers do not always provoke laughter from members of the culture giving rise to the tale, nor do situations prompting laughter from an Nkundo audience (see Tale 87) appear humorous to many Western readers. A final mark of Mbambo Jean's artistry in Tale 63 is his coming full circle in his narration by tying the "teaching" to the tabu-breaking that had led to the series of episodes with the ogres; his is the only people-related "teaching" offered in this set of three "people" tales, narratives that deserve closer examination than space in the present volume allows.

Aarne-Thompson's tale type 312C provides the basic classification for this set of tales. No satisfactory variants for the basic type were located in Klipple's, Arewa's, or Lambrecht's indexes.

Motifs:

T	G400.**.	Person wanders into ogre's power.
T	F400.	Spirits and demons (general).
T	T135.1.**.	Formulistic exchange of marriage vows between supernatural being and human: "I have a wife." "I have a husband."
T	G81.**.	Knowing but awed and unwilling marriage to cannibal ogre.
C	F402.1.4.+.**.	Ogre takes human wife.
T	T111.	Marriage of mortal and supernatural being (ogre).
T	H1220.	Quests voluntarily undertaken.
T	H1385.6.	Quest for lost sister.
T	B421.	Helpful dog (dogs).
T	B521.**.	Animals (dogs) aware of fatal danger from ogres.
T	R251.**.	Flight (errand) on a tree, which ogre tries (ogres try) to cut down.
T	G275.2.	Witch (ogre) overcome by helpful dogs of hero.
T	G552.	Rescue from ogre (ogres) by helpful animals (dogs).
T	B524.1.	Animals overcome man's adversary by force.
T	B540.	Animal rescuer or retriever.
T	G512.9.1.	Ogre killed by helpful dogs.

T	G500.	Ogre(s) defeated.
T	R156.	Brother rescues sister.
T	C40.**.	Tabu: offending spirits of swamp (by spitting).
T	J652.	Inattention to warnings.
C	W167.+.**.	Girl persists in spitting in tabu area.
C	F949.+.**.	Stream (swamp) floods when profaned by woman's spitting.
C	F253.1.+.**.	Swamp spirit can cause water to rise if swamp is profaned.
T	F420.**.	Water-spirits: swamp spirits.
T	H220.**.	Ordeal by water: water will rise to drown guilty one.
C	M90.+.**.	Trial by ordeal: each girl to enter river (swamp). Innocent will not be drowned.
T	H225.**.	Ordeal by water.
C	C925.+.**.	Trial by water ordeal for breaking tabu.
C	Q380.+.	Breaking tabu punished.
T	C920.**.	Apparent death for breaking tabu.
T	F940.	Extraordinary underground (underwater) disappearance.
C	Q467.+.**.	Apparent drowning as punishment for breaking tabu.
C	H1229.+.**.	Brothers set out one after another to seek lost sister.
C	D1711.+.**.	Small-bird (itòji) witch doctor.
C	D1726.+.**.	Itòji bird magician: aids hero in defeat of ogres.
C	B569.+.**.	Bird (itòji) instructs hero in method of defeating ogres and of rescuing his sister.
T	C0.	Tabu: contact with supernatural.
C	C219.+.**.	Tabu: eating food offered by ogre's hand.
T	C240.**.	Tabu: eating food of (from) certain person.
T	C220.	Tabu: eating certain things.
C	P690.+.	Custom of hunter (ogre) sharing meat.
T	G532.**.	Hero hidden and ogre deceived by his wife.
C	B579.+.**.	Helpful bees and wasps guard door for hero in ogre's house.
T	B481.3.**.	Helpful bees: frighten ogre from sleeping hero, sting ogres to death.
T	B481.4.**.	Helpful wasps: frighten ogre from sleeping hero, sting ogres to death.
C	G317.+.**.	Ogre entices hero away from protective dogs and insects by ruse of honey hunt.
T	G582.1.**.	Ogre bribed with food: escape from pursuing ogres by throwing down handfuls of honey as distraction.
T	G530.**.	Ogre's human wife aids hero (her brother).
T	G512.**.	Ogre (ogres) killed by wasps, bees, and other fierce insects.
T	F405.**.	Means of combatting spirits: bees and wasps and dogs used in overcoming ogres.
T	B524.1.1.	Dogs kill attacking cannibals (ogres).
T	G551.1.	Rescue of sister from ogre by brother.
T	F531.6.12.**.	Disappearance or death of ogres.
T	G81.	Unwitting marriage to cannibal.

T	G84.**.	*Sweo-sweo-sweo* [Lonkundo equivalent of "Fee-fi-fo-fum"].
C	G11.15.+.**.	Ogre with human wife kills and eats all but youngest of her brothers in their attempts to rescue her.
T	D1711.	Magician (witch doctor).
T	P253.	Younger (youngest) brother aids in escape of captive sister.
T	P253.**.	Younger (youngest) brother rescues sister captured by ogre.
C	F810.+.**.	Tree healed by blow of hero's hand when almost felled by ogres.
T	D1602.2.2.**.	Tree magically healed by blow of hero's hand when cut by ogres.

1. [Narrator's explanatory comment: "They carried sievelike dippers as well as the baskets which they strapped about their shoulders and carried on their backs. When they found a water-filled hole in the swamp, they would stop to see if there were any fish there. They would scoop the water up with their sieves and then put the fish in their baskets. Often when there were several women, they would separate a bit so that only one or two at the most would be working at one water hole. This would mean that they would probably catch more fish, and at the end of the day, the ones who had the most could share with those who didn't have so many."]

2. "*Lifoku*," the Lonkundo equivalent of "young woman," is used here as a proper name.

3. [Narrator's explanatory comment: "She could recognize him because of two things that seem to be common to ogres. He had hair that was very long, hanging to his waist, and he carried a heavy stick which he used for killing meat."]

4. [Narrator's explanatory comment: "For this is the way an ogre takes a woman to be his wife."]

5. [Narrator's explanatory comment: "If she could hear them, she could follow the voices home."]

6. [Narrator's explanatory comment: "Now, this is a thick vine that winds itself around the forest trees. Its sap is very like the sap of the rubber tree, but it has fruit that is sweetness itself, and pleasing. One needs to be careful when eating it, however. In the mouth it is pleasant, but if it gets onto one's lips, it hardens like a coat of rubber."]

7. An ideophone suggesting "continuously."

8. An ideophone indicating "like that" or "in that way."

9. [Narrator's explanatory comment: "This meant that fishing was good."]

10. The "big celebration" is termed by the Nkundo an *nteke*. At a proper *nteke*, everyone will be drunk before the event is over. Such celebrations, held after the birth of a child or after a period of mourning, have the flavor of carnivals, and attract many visitors from other villages; in this particular instance, since there were several young people going together, their parents permitted them to go. The "games" include both those involving chance and those involving skill.

11. When the water recedes from the swamps as the dry season begins, fish are often left aground. Usually the local people gather these fish before they begin to deteriorate. However, since the ogre guarded this particular swamp so well, no one dared to harvest the fish and they were left there to rot, causing the offensive odor.

12. A vigorously expressed slang expression common among the Nkundo; there is no exact English equivalent for it.

13. The Nkundo often spit as an expression of disgust; in fact, spitting is almost an art among them. Whether Mpucu wished to spit for this reason or whether she really felt relief from the odor would be thus effected is not indicated.

14. The girls, immediately assuming that the river had risen as a consequence of Mpucu's violation of the tabu against spitting, made no effort to protect her from the consequences of her act; they were primarily concerned with their own safe crossing of this spirit-induced barrier.

15. The ogre here is represented as living in Nkundolike circumstances. In such marriages as this one, the human wife would be able to find food to her own liking in the forest, and prepare it according to her own custom, without recourse to the human flesh that pleased her husband.

16. [Narrator's explanatory comment: "Itóji is a small bird who is consulted and has the same powers as a witch doctor."]

17. Only a storyteller could summon such a formidable collection of "weapons." Dogs in Zaïre are generally feared because more often than not they are left to hunt their own food and are therefore prone to attack. The combination of flying insects (wasps and hornets) with crawling insects (driver ants), all of them with fierce stings or bites, posed a decided threat to the ogre; ogres usually are represented as fearful of insects. Although no mention is made of a protective medicine provided by the witch doctor for Empompo, it is assumed that he has been thus safeguarded. The narrator did not indicate the means used by Empompo to accumulate either three hundred dogs or the array of insects; a "willing suspension of disbelief" on the part of the audience is expected.

18. Most Nkundo men going on a journey into the forest take with them an *ikoma*, a tightly woven mesh bag either carried on the shoulder or fastened to the belt.

19. Since eating together is a sign of accepted friendship and hospitality, the brother was warned not to accept food from Ogre until after he had been properly received into the household. The successful second brother not only heeded this warning, but took care to show the courtesy of asking Ogre for his proverb, an act certain to win his favor.

20. Honey is a great delicacy, highly desired both by the Nkundo and by ogres. The narrator's choice of this item as the object of a joint hunt was indeed strategic.

When honey is found in the forest, it is carried home in a package, a *boteta*, made of leaves. In the *boteta* with the honey are the honeycomb, a motley assortment of bees, bits of leaves and bark, and whatever other scraps happened to be on or near the honey when it was found.

21. All the ogres were killed except the witch doctor; this significant personage survives in all other tales in the present volume except for Tales 67, 68, and 69, when he and his wife, the only survivors in the ogre community, become the objects of the hero's determined search in his effort to eradicate the ogres.

Mrs. Ross, interested in this apparent immunity of ogre witch doctors, questioned Mbambo Jean about the matter. After he had offered the explanation he usually furnished in response to unanswerable questions—"Remember, Mama, that this is a story"—he admitted that a witch doctor should not be killed.

Among the Nkundo, the profession of the witch doctor is an honored one. Passing from father to son the knowledge of the various medicines based on forest materials, the witch doctor—whether human or ogre—lives in the village but is careful to keep his secrets hidden. Whatever is the source of his abilities to foresee events, know mystically of things that have happened but of which no information has been furnished to him, and produce magic that seems to be effective, the existence of these abilities is readily conceded by the Nkundo, as well as by many other peoples. (See Bascom's *Ifa Divination, passim,* for an extensive treatment of these and other powers of the babalawo, or diviner, practicing within the cult of Ifa.)

22. Very often, Nkundo women go together into the forest to work—to fish in the swampy areas, to hunt caterpillars, to seek *bieya* and other choice vegetables not grown in their gardens. If some places are better than others for securing the food sought, the older women will have the preferred places. However, when the women come together again at the predetermined meeting point, they tend to share the product of the hunt with those who have been less successful in their search, whether or not all the women are members of the same family.

Bieya, closely resembling asparagus both in appearance and in flavor, grows in damp, cleared areas of the forest; it is spearlike, with each spear tightly wrapped by thin leaves. The gatherer cuts it, peels off the overlapping leaves, and prepares it in much the same manner as asparagus is made ready for eating.

23. Why this ogre considered human odor "terrible" when he—in common with other ogres—finds "the flesh of people" highly desirable meat is puzzling. The "fee-fi-fo-fum" motif is present in several of the Ross-collected tales, but this is the only one in which the ogre actually describes the odor as "terrible." The human wife's assumption that her ogre husband found human odor offensive is present in Tale 61; in that tale, the assumption underlies a ruse employed as an effective narrative device.

Torrend in his ... *Bantu Folk-Lore* ... includes a tale titled "To be Marked!" (pp. 75–80) in which a cannibalistic son exclaims, "There is a smell of something human.... There is something that smells.... I want to eat it." Apparently in this instance, the odor is not unpleasing, but merely tantalizing.

That the heads of people are not eaten by ogres is another detail verbalized only in the present narrative. Nowhere in the Ross-provided tales is any reference made to the disposition of human bones following the eating of the flesh by ogres with the exception of Tale 76, in which the disappointed ogres find the burned skeleton of Older Sister's baby and eat it; apparently the bones are consumed along with the meat. Any portions rejected by the ogres would be quickly devoured by forest animals and insects or, if inedible, would decompose and become part of the soil.

24. These names mean, respectively, "The-One-Who-Cuts-Sharp" and "The-One-Who-Is-Very-Fierce."

25. The Lonkundo original of this tale, titled "Bomoto l'Eloko" ("The Woman and the Ogre"), appears on pages 25–28 of *Bekolo Bemo.* ...

Narrator: Bongonda Michele
Location: Bòlèngè
Date: March 1973

65.   *The Slave Becomes the Master*

Bolumbu married and had a child. Before their child had many years, her husband said, "Bolumbu, go with the child to your parents that they see her. Then come home."[1]

Then Bolumbu began her journey with her child. On her way she had to pass through a small forest between two villages. There was a tabu in this forest place. No child must eat the fruit growing there, not the *lomunga*, not the *lòmbòlè*.[2] Yet these the child wanted. The child began to sing to her mother,

> Mother, *lòmbòlè*; Mother, *lomunga*.
> Mother, *lòmbòlè*; Mother, *lomunga*.

After a time, the mother picked some fruit and gave it to the child.

Then the owner of the forest, Bolili Likumbe,[3] came, *pu-u-u*. She asked the mother, "Did you give *lòmbòlè* and *lomunga* to your child?"

Bolumbu answered, "Yes." Truly she had.

Bolili said, "All right. We will settle this by fighting."

They struggled and struggled. Bolumbu was killed. Bolili dressed herself in Bolumbu's clothing. She put Bolumbu's basket on her shoulders. She tied the child to her hip. She possessed Bolumbu's spirit. When she had finished, she looked as Bolumbu had looked when she left her village.

They went along the path toward the home of Bolumbu's family, *ikao-ikao-ikao*. They reached a village. When the people saw them, they were delighted. They said, "Oh-h. Bolumbu has come. Bolumbu and her child are here. Eh-h-h." Some of the family took the child. The child said,

> Mother is not this one.
> Spy it out carefully.[4]
> That is Bolili from the bend in the path.
> Spy it out carefully.

> She wrestled with Mother.
> Spy it out carefully.

The people all came to see what was there. Bolili took the child. She wanted to go on. She said, "This child keeps talking and talking." Then they went and went, *te-e-e*.

They came to another group of people. These people, too, were pleased to see the child. "Oh-h! Bolumbu has come. She has her child."

They took the child. Quickly the child said, "She is not my mother. She has taken the spirit of my mother."

> Mother is not this one.
> Spy it out carefully.
> That is Bolili from the bend in the path.
> Spy it out carefully.
> She wrestled with Mother.
> Spy it out carefully.

The child sang the song, singing, singing.[5]

The people said, "*Mo!* This child says that this isn't her mother. It is only the spirit of her mother. What'll we do?"

Bolili said, "A child is talking. She talks, talking. Truly I am her mother."

Then they went until they reached the village of Bolumbu's mother. The child's grandmother took the child. She cried for joy. Then she looked at Bolili. "Bolumbu has changed; truly she hasn't changed like that."

Then the child began her song:

> Mother is not this one.
> Spy it out carefully.
> That is Bolili from the bend in the path.
> Spy it out carefully.
> She wrestled with Mother.
> Spy it out carefully.

The grandmother asked, "What do you mean?"

The child said, "That is not my mother."

Night came, and the grandmother prepared food for everyone. They all ate.

When morning came the people said, "Let us go to our gardens in the forest. Our corn is planted there. Unless we care for it, the birds will eat it."

Then they went to the forest. They found many birds. It was
fitting that a slave protect the corn from them.

Bolili said, "Take this child. Let her protect the corn."[6]

The people said, "The spirit of Bolumbu will come in a bird,
Nkanga.[7] He is the bird of our own village." The bird sang,

> The witch doctor is angry.
> *Yoyo-yo-yo.*
> I feel shame because of the slave.
> *Yoyo-yo-yo.*
> The witch doctor is angry.
> *Yoyo-yo-yo.*
> I feel shame because of the slave.
> *Yoyo-yo-yo.*
> The witch doctor is angry.
> *Yoyo-yo-yo.*
> I feel shame because of the slave.
> *Yoyo-yo-yo.*[8]

The people of the village wondered, wondering. They said,
"This is very difficult. He says that the slave will become the master.
Why does he speak that way?"

Then they knew that the child was wise. She had tried, trying,
to tell them the truth concerning her mother.

The grandmother asked the child, "Why do you say these things?
Why does the bird say that the master will be the slave and the slave
will be the master? Tell us all things."

"As we went along the path, I and my mother, I wanted the
fruit that was growing in the small forest, *lómbólé* and *lomunga.*
Mother got the fruit and I ate it. Then Bolili came. She struggled
with Mother. When she killed Mother, she took all of Mother's
clothes and things. She said that I was her child."

Night came. The grandmother dug a hole that was not only
deep, but wide across, digging, digging. Then she took small limbs
the size of a man's thumb and laid them across the hole. In the
middle she put a much larger limb, the size of a man's thigh. This
would make it strong.

That night she took Bolili there and said, "I have made this
bed for you and the child. Truly you will sleep well here."

So Bolili and the child went to sleep on the tree limbs. How
could they know that the pit was there?[9]

In the night the grandmother came quietly, quietly. She picked
up the child. Then she grasped the large limb that was in the center

of the bed. She jerked it, jerking. The bed and Bolili dropped into the pit, *bwó*.

Bolili called, "I have no palaver with you. No matter. If I die here, your child and I together."

The grandmother answered, "Not my child. My child is here with me."

Then, throwing, throwing, she threw the dirt back into the pit. In not a little while the hole was gone. The ground was level as before:

> The slave is dead.
> The imposter is dead.
> The slave is dead.
> The imposter is dead.

He who stops the rain for a friend, he himself will be drenched.

Tale 65 provides the only instance among the Ross-collected narratives in which there is physical combat between a spirit and a person. The Nkundo belief in animism and the accompanying awe of the supernatural are clearly apparent in the presence and the remarkable powers of the "owner of the forest." As in Tale 80, the spirit materializes as a "person" able to make and enforce demands prompted by the violation of a tabu; in Tale 80, the demands are temporarily satisfied by the violator's relinquishing of adornments, whereas in the present tale the requirement is a physical one, a wrestling match, that has permanent consequences both for Bolumbu and for Bolili. It is interesting to note that this particular spirit was assumed to be dispatched by her being buried alive ("The imposter is dead"). No other Ross-provided tale suggests that a *spirit* can be destroyed, although the death of ogres and of monstrous dogs is included in tales involving those supernatural creatures, and the "supernatural" paramour in Tale 83 perishes at the hand of the offended husband's friend. The permanence of a "spirit" is a difficult matter to determine; the narrator here does not deal at length with that problem because the central action of the tale has been completed by Bolili's burial. The fluctuations in the handling of supernatural elements suggest one or another of two possibilities: (1) the Nkundo belief in animism may be in the process of losing its force; (2) tales reflecting a strong belief in animism may be going "underground."

Klipple's variant of Aarne-Thompson's tale type 780 (The Singing Bones), "The Story of Kiali and Her Husband Kumba," involves the disguise of a porcupine as a child's mother. When the porcupine takes the child to the grandmother, the child sings that the porcupine ate Kiali in the road. Finally the grandmother goes, finds Kiali in a hole in the road, and brings her home and strengthens her; then the porcupine is thrown into the fireplace. The rest of the elements in this variant are not relevant to the present tale. Portions of the two samples given for Klipple's tale type 781* are closely related to the present tale: in "How Can I Silence Katubi?" (Torrend's . . . *Bantu Folk-Lore* . . . , pp. 9–12), the wife eats a large fig denied her by her husband; he kills her with his assegai and goes with his son and the baby, Katubi, to his wife's parents' home. The son sings of his mother's murder, and the grandmother seats the murderer on a mat over a pit; when he falls into the pit, he is scalded to death. In the other variant, also from Torrend's . . . *Bantu Folk-Lore* . . . (pp. 14–17), "Father, Wait for Me," a pregnant wife unjustly accused of eating fruit shaken from a tree by her husband is killed by him; leaving her body exposed for the vultures, he proceeds to his in-laws', followed by the unborn child dragging its umbilical cord and singing of the murder. Killed and buried repeatedly by the father, the unborn child reappears, still revealing the murder. On learning the truth, his wife's family kill the murderer and expose his body for beasts of prey.

Motifs:

T	C40.	Tabu: offending spirits of water, mountain, etc.
C	C621.+.**.	Tabu: picking certain kinds of fruits.
T	C225.**.	Tabu: eating of certain fruit by children.
C	P233.+.**.	Indulgent mother gives child fruits (tabu) because child demands them.
T	J1144.**.	Eaters of stolen (tabu) fruit detected.
T	F441.**.	Forest spirits.
T	F400.	Spirits and demons (general).
C	W167.+.**.	Child persists in asking for tabu fruits.
T	F402.1.2.**.	Forest spirit blocks path of woman who has violated tabu.
T	F402.1.4.**.	Demon assumes human form in order to deceive.
C	F402.1.4.+.**.	Spirit in human form takes human child.
T	F402.1.4.**.	Forest spirit inhabits body of slain woman and appropriates child in order to deceive woman's family.
T	G440.	Ogre (spirit) abducts person.
C	F253.1.+.**.	Forest spirit can inhabit the body of a woman overcome and killed by wrestling.
C	D537.+.**.	Forest spirit transformed to woman by overcoming woman (killed by wrestling) and taking on cloth and appearance and spirit of slain woman.
T	D42.2.**.	Transformation: forest spirit assumes shape of woman overcome by wrestling for violating tabu.
A	K1988.1.**.	Imposter: forest spirit wears a murdered mother's clothes and is taken for the mother.
T	N827.	Child as helper.
T	K435.	Child's song incriminates thief (and murderer).
C	B569.+.**.	Bird identifies murderer and imposter in song.
C	B569.+.**.	Bird tells girl's grandmother of girl's mother's murder and impersonation by forest spirit.
C	N275.+.	Bird's song reveals woman's duplicity.

T	B131.2.	Bird reveals treachery.
C	E231.+.**.	In bird's song, murdered woman whose body is inhabited by malevolent forest spirit supports child's report to grandmother of the murder.
T	E230.**.	Return of spirit of murdered woman in form of bird to ensure punishment for murder.
T	R153.**.	Parent (grandparent) rescues child.
C	Q411.+.	Death as punishment for cruelty.
T	Q456.	Burial alive as punishment.

1. The Nkundo, members of a patrilineal society, feel that a child—especially the firstborn—should be taken as soon as possible to visit its maternal grandparents. Such a visit cannot be made without the husband's consent. The visit of this child had apparently been delayed; she must have been at least three or four years old at the time the visit described in the tale was undertaken.

2. Both the *lómbólé* and the *lomunga* fruits are common in many forest areas in the Cuvette. Why a tabu was attached in this particular forest to their being eaten by children was not indicated.

3. "*Bolili*" is a stick for making fire by friction, and "*likumbe*" is derived from the verb "to bend." The latter portion of the spirit's name is used here to indicate her habitation: she comes from "the bend in the path."

4. In the antiphonal singing employed in the telling of this tale, the chorus line "Spy it out carefully" included a word, "*kési*," that had no function aside from completing the rhythm; it is a nonsense sound that enhances the sound of the song without furnishing information. In a report titled "First Research on the Structure of Five Lonkundo Poems," published by Boelaert (in *Reports of the Meetings of the CBKO* ([1952], pp. 348–365), the author concludes that the "dynamic accent" is the most important factor in the structure of Lonkundo poetry. The use of "*kési*" in the present song appears to provide exactly that kind of dynamic accent illustrated in the poems, giving what Boelaert terms "life and color to the oral art."

5. Since this tale was erased from the tape after translation, we cannot determine exactly how many times the child sang the song.

6. Bolili's offer of the child as a guard for the corn indicates that she regarded the child as a slave; no conscientious Nkundo mother would leave her own very young child alone in a forest garden. This offer should have alerted the villagers—as, indeed, it alerted the listeners in the audience—to the truth of the child's song, a truth eventually recognized by the grandmother. The Nkundo proverb "Only lay hold of a child and you will see its mother" proves true here of grandmothers, as well.

7. The term "*Nkanga*," normally used to identify a witch doctor (see note 5 for Tale 75), is here applied to a bird, "the bird of our own village"; this is the only Ross-collected tale in which Nkanga appears as a bird. The witch doctor, as seen by the Nkundo, is physician, counselor, magician, soothsayer; it is as soothsayer that Nkanga serves in the present tale. In this instance, Nkanga also houses the spirit of the slain Bolumbu.

8. Unfortunately, the song text is incomplete; the portion providing evidence that "the slave will become the master" was not preserved in the translation. The chorus line "*Yoyo-yo-yo*" suggests the imperative need for prompt action: "*yoyo*" in Lonkundo means, among other things, "quickly," "hastily," or "hurriedly"; the repetition of "*yo*" would intensify the "*yoyo*."

9. Among the Nkundo, to make for a guest a bed with fresh branches is to offer a gesture of real courtesy. For this reason, Bolili would not suspect that the bed camouflaged a pitfall. Bolili's response when she found herself trapped echoes her vengeful attitude toward Bolumbu from the start; it also reflects the narrator's artistry in coming full circle on his characterization of the "owner of the forest." Both the listeners and subsequent readers of the tale are led to accept Bolili's burial alive as a fate well deserved.

The term "*bwȯ*," used here for emphasis, means "right away" or "all together"; it is well chosen to indicate the force and completeness with which Bolili fell into the pit.

Narrator:	Bokunge Jacques
Location:	Bȯlėngė
Date:	March 1973

66. *The Man Who Described an Ogre and Still Lived*

On another day a man called Imana[1] went into the forest to hunt palm fruit. He found a palm tree that had ripe fruit on it. He adjusted his climbing belt and went up where the fruit was growing.

While he was there, an ogre came to the foot of the palm tree and called out, "Are you cutting me some palm fruit?"

Imana answered, "I, Imana, am cutting for myself."

Ogre called again, "Imana, those palm fruit are *esombe*,[2] aren't they?"

"Indeed, they are *esombe*," said Imana.

"Drop some of that palm fruit down to me."

So Imana threw some of the palm fruit down to Ogre. After Ogre had eaten some of the palm fruit, he knew that it was *esombe* and excellent fruit. So he called to Imana again, "I want some of that palm fruit. Cut a bunch for me."

Imana looked all around the foot of the tree to find a place where there were thorns and sharp-edged grasses that were long and all tangled together. Then he cut the bunch of fruit and let it fall right into this tightly packed undergrowth, *kee-ee-ee.*

While Ogre was busy trying to get the fruit out of the thorns and undergrowth, Imana climbed out of the tree and left as quickly as he could.

Ogre called out to him, "Imana, Imana, do you see me?"

Imana answered, "I see you."

"How is it that you see me? What do I look like?" asked Ogre.

"I saw you come," said Imana. "You are very, very tall and thin. You have long arms that reach almost to the ground, and on your head is a cranial lump that looks like a bundle of *nkongo*[3] leaves."

Ogre was shocked. "Imana, you do see me. *Mongo!*[4] Now you will go and tell your family how I look. What am I going to do with you, Imana?"

Not really believing, he called out once more, "Imana, do you see me?"[5]

Imana answered again, "I saw you coming. You are very tall and thin and you have long arms that almost reach the ground. On your head is a crown that looks like a bundle of *nkongo* leaves."

Ogre said, "Imana really does see me. *Ngoya!*[6] Now he will tell his family at home how I look."

Ogre felt great anger, but Imana was too far down the path for him to be able to catch him.

So Imana hurried home and told all the people of his village just how an ogre looks.

The Nkundo's awe of ogres and other supernatural creatures is matched only by their eager interest in tales reflecting humans' encounters with these awesome beings. As in several other tales in the Ross collection (see, for example, Tales 60, 62–64, and 67–69), the protagonist through wit combined with care and courage is often able to overcome his formidable adversary the ogre. Although such encounters normally leave little room for humor, Tale 66 and Tale 60 offer evidence that in the hands of an accomplished raconteur at least one form of humor—the humor of discomfiture—can enrich the telling of tales with deeply serious content.

Relief from tension is also afforded by the use of such expressions as "*Mongo!*" and "*Ngoya!*"; these terms enliven the telling and echo the Nkundo's speech patterns in much the same way as the leopard's expletives in Tale 93 bring that tale home to its hearers.

The most useful classification for this narrative appears to be Aarne-Thompson's tale type 336, which presents Death as devouring a girl who questions him about various parts of his anatomy; apparently her action violates a "description" tabu. In the present tale, his cleverness in tossing the fruit into an almost inaccessible spot allows the hero to avoid the death normally meted out for this violation.

Motifs:

T	C0.	Tabu: contact with supernatural.
T	G582.1.**.	Ogre bribed with food: escape from pursuing ogre by throwing down desirable fruit from tree into tangled underbrush.
C	K90.+.**.	Awe-incurring contest (conflict) won by deceit (feigned service for adversary).
T	C820.	Tabu: finding certain secret.
T	C310.	Tabu: looking at certain person or thing.
T	G570.	Ogre overawed.
T	C20.**.	Tabu: describing ogre.
T	C420.	Tabu: uttering secrets.
T	C420.**.	Tabu: describing appearance of ogre.
T	C423.2.	Tabu: speaking of extraordinary sight.
T	G630.	Characteristics of ogres.
T	F401.**.	Appearance of ogre described (tabu).

1. "*Imana*" literally means "go away," or even the stronger "get out," a name well chosen for this protagonist in view of the tale's narrative development.

2. The *esombe* are a small but very juicy and delectable fruit.

3. Of the many leaves in the forest available for packaging, the *nkongo* leaf is the most desirable; it is especially well adapted for wrapping food that is to be steamed or baked in the coals. In the larger population centers, where it is inconvenient for women to get into the forest to cut *nkongo*, bundles of these leaves are sold in the markets.

4. "*Mongo!*" is a common slang expression among the Nkundo. Translation of this mild expletive is difficult; the closest English equivalent is probably "Really!"

5. [Narrator's explanatory comment: "He asked this last question because if a person saw him, he must kill that person, and Imana was already too far down the path for him to catch."] An Igbo proverb (see Okeke's *Tales of Land of Death*, p. 112) doubtless available in some form also among the Nkundo has relevance here: "One does not tire who runs for one's life"; it is in this fashion that Imana was running.

6. "*Ngoya!*" is a much stronger expletive than "*Mongo!*" The word literally means "mother," and in a culture where consanguineal ties are stronger than marriage bonds, invocation of this name expresses a sense of helplessness, of inadequacy in the face of a desperate situation, of total loss, of grief too deep for tears.

Chatelain states in his "African Folk-Life" (p. 25) that "all the affection an African child is capable of is concentrated on its mother, and . . . the insult which most deeply wounds even the adult African is a disrespectful mention of his or her mother." In the light of the significance of the mother, the ogre's expletive has maximum force for the Nkundo listeners.

Narrator: Ikwa Isilombe
Location: Boende
Date: November 1973

67. *The Last of the Ogres*

A father and son lived in the same village. They had heard the reputation of an ogre who lived in a nearby forest. This particular ogre was an elder, and his name was Lomat'ȯnėnė.[1]

Then the father said to his son, "Today either Lomat'ȯnėnė will die or I will die. One of us must."

Then he got out his spear and his knife and sharpened them and sharpened them.

"My son! Let's go into the forest and find the place where Lomat'ȯnėnė passes."

Then they both took their spears and their knives and went into the forest. The son went first so that he could watch for the tracks of Lomat'ȯnėnė. The father was following after him.

Then the son found the tracks of a wild pig. He said to his father, he said, "Father, come and look. These tracks are very large. They must be those of Lomat'ȯnėnė."

The father said, "Ah! Not at all, not Lomat'ȯnėnė. These are the tracks of a wild pig.[2] They aren't the tracks of Lomat'ȯnėnė."

So they went on, the son first and his father following.

They went and saw antelope tracks. "Father, here are some more tracks. Come and look at them."

The father said, "No, no! Not those! Not the tracks of Lomat'ȯnėnė. Those are the tracks of an antelope, not those of Lomat'ȯnėnė."

They went on and the son called again, "Father, here are the tracks of Lomat'ȯnėnė."

The father came and looked. "No, no! These are the tracks of a large brown antelope, not the tracks of Lomat'ȯnėnė at all."

They went on through the forest and kept seeing tracks of many different animals, including leopard and elephant tracks. Each time the son would call his father and ask if these were the tracks of Lomat'ȯnėnė. Each time the father would tell him who had made the tracks.[3]

Then they came upon some very large tracks. These were truly those of Lomat'ȯnėnė and led directly to his house.

The father said, "Ah! This is goodness itself. Dig a deep hole. Bury me in it except for my chin and face."

The son dug and dug[4] until it was deep enough. Then he buried his father up to his chin. Then, *te-e-e-e*, the ogres came along the path, passing, passing one by one, with Lomat'ȯnėnė as the last one. He stumbled over the chin, *ko*,[5] and went back to see what it was. "This is perhaps a mother and child, perhaps a persecutor, or perhaps a trial for Lomat'ȯnėnė."

The ogres gathered around and saw it was a man. "That one is known to us, known to us."[6] Then they saw who it was, and killed the father.

But the son, after he had buried his father, had climbed up in a very tall tree near where his father was buried. He saw that they had killed his father. He began to cry, and his tears fell as great drops on a leaf near Lomat'ȯnėnė.

Lomat'ȯnėnė saw them. "These are either great drops of rain or they are the tears of a person. There must be someone up above."

Then they said, "Come down."

"No! I won't."

"Come down."

"I won't come down."

One of the ogres started up the tree. He climbed and climbed. When he came close to the boy, the boy cut the branch, *kata-kata-kata*, and the ogre fell to the ground, *ka*.[7]

Another ogre climbed the tree. Again, the boy cut the branch, *kata-kata-kata*, and the ogre fell to the ground dead, *ka*. He was dead.

Another ogre started up, but Lomat'ȯnėnė stopped him. "No! There are enough of us dead already.[8] Let's go home." So they all went home.

When the boy came there with his father and he was well up

in the tree, his home was there. He had not yet gone so far or so high. He stayed there a while. The boy finally came down out of the tree. "Ah, many ogres are dead, Father,[9] but Lomat'ȯnėnė is still alive. Why am I still alive? It must be to kill the rest of the ogres, including Lomat'ȯnėnė."

He went to a witch doctor.[10] "Where are the ogres, and how can I kill them?"

"All the ogres are there in a huge hollow tree in the forest. Go there and set a trap in the door of the hollow. When night comes, climb the tree and set a fire above the hollow of the ogres."[11]

Then the boy made a trap and set it in the very door of the hollow. He climbed up in the tree, and when night came he started a fire above the hollow.

The ogres realized that there was a lot of light and said, "The moon is full."[12] They started to pass out, and sparks fell on them. The witch doctor and his wife were there. They said, "No. This isn't the moon. This is some other big palaver. We had better see what it is." The witch doctor and his wife slipped out.

They were all afraid. They said, "It is fitting that Lomat'ȯnėnė pass first." So Lomat'ȯnėnė went first and was caught in the trap. The others were afraid to go out after that. All the other ogres were killed in the fire.[13]

That left only the witch doctor and his wife.[14] The boy said, "They are all dead except for the witch doctor and his wife. Now what do I do?"

He hunted and hunted, te-te-te-te, for the witch doctor and his wife, te-te-te. He hunted and didn't have. He was getting discouraged when he finally thought of an answer. He turned himself into a tiny baby. The wife of the witch doctor found him and picked him up.

The witch doctor said, "Don't take that baby."[15]

Soon they arrived where there were many trees with *etofi* fruit.

The wife said, "When the child is a bit bigger, he can climb up and get the fruit." She really liked *bitofi*.

The boy heard her. "Mother, let me try now." She was a bit surprised, but put him onto the trunk of the tree. He began to climb slowly, and finally reached where the fruit was. He began throwing down fruit and throwing down fruit. Then he found a very large one. "This is a special one and it is for Father." Then he himself crawled inside of the *etofi*. The father opened his mouth wide, and the fruit dropped into his mouth and on into his stomach.

The witch doctor called, "Child, come on down. Let's go."

He heard the song, "I am in the stomach of Father."[16]

"Oh!"

"I am in the stomach of Father."

He beats on his stomach, *kao-kao-kao*. The child sings, "I am in the stomach of Father."

The father is very angry. It was his wife's fault for taking the child. He took a huge stick and killed her with it.

That boy inside had a *lokengo*, *lokengo*,[17] and began to cut, *ka-ka-ka-ka*, his way out. Soon the witch doctor was dead also. This is the reason why ogres are finished on the earth.

[Notes to Tale 67 follow Tale 69.]

Narrator:	Ikwa Isilombe
Location:	Boende
Date:	November 1973

68. *The Last of the Ogres* (Variant I)

Then a father lived in a village, he and his son. He heard the reputation of the ogres. The ogres lived in the forest, the people we fear. This ogre was named Lomat'ònènè, an elder, a very elder.

Then he said, "Today I and Lomat'ònènè, we die. When we meet, we die." Then he took his spear and his sword and sharpened them and sharpened them and sharpened them, *a-o, a-o, a-o, a-o*. Then he took that sword and sharpened it and put it down.

He said, "My son."

"Yes."

He said, "Let us go into the forest to find the place where it is rumored that Lomat'ònènè passes."

Then they took his spear, his sword, and his shield and went to the forest, the father following and the son first. The son passed into the forest. The son called the father.

Narrator:	Father, come see the path,
Audience:	*Yaya-ya-ya-ya.*
Narrator:	The path where pass *bingende'ngende*.[18]
Audience:	*Yaya-ya-ya-ya.*
Narrator:	Father, come see the path,
Audience:	*Yaya-ya-ya-ya.*
Narrator:	The path where pass *bingende'ngende*.
Audience:	*Yaya-ya-ya-ya.*
Narrator:	Father, come see the path,
Audience:	*Yaya-ya-ya-ya.*
Narrator:	The path where pass *bingende'ngende*.
Audience:	*Yaya-ya-ya-ya.*

The father came and passed by. "Oh! Not this one. This is the path of the small antelope. We need the path where Lomat'ȯnėnė passes, not the path of the small antelope."[19]

Then the son called again, and it was the path of the wild pig.

Narrator:	Father, come see the path,
Audience:	*Yaya-ya-ya-ya.*
Narrator:	The path where pass *bingende'ngende*.
Audience:	*Yaya-ya-ya-ya.*
Narrator:	Father, come see the path,
Audience:	*Yaya-ya-ya-ya.*
Narrator:	The path where pass *bingende'ngende*.
Audience:	*Yaya-ya-ya-ya.*

"This is the path of the wild pig, not of Lomat'ȯnėnė. Continue a while." They went on, *te-te-te*.

Narrator:	Father, come see the path,
Audience:	*Yaya-ya-ya-ya.*
Narrator:	The path where pass *bingende'ngende*.
Audience:	*Yaya-ya-ya-ya.*
Narrator:	Father, come see the path,
Audience:	*Yaya-ya-ya-ya.*
Narrator:	The path where pass *bingende'ngende*.
Audience:	*Yaya-ya-ya-ya.*

Then he said, "Ah. This is the path of the large antelope,[20] not Lomat'ȯnėnė. Continue to go." They went, *kao-kao*. They found more tracks.

Narrator:	Father, come see the path,
Audience:	*Yaya-ya-ya-ya.*

> Narrator :   The path where pass *bingende'ngende*.
> Audience :   *Yaya-ya-ya-ya*.
> Narrator :   Father, come see the path,
> Audience :   *Yaya-ya-ya-ya*.
> Narrator :   The path where pass *bingende'ngende*.
> Audience :   *Yaya-ya-ya-ya*.

Then he said, "These are elephant[21] tracks only."

Then they went; they went, the son first and the father afterwards. Now they were in many paths of the ogres. They saw the paths where the ogres went to hunt roofing leaves.[22]

> Narrator :   Father, come see the path,
> Audience :   *Yaya-ya-ya-ya*.
> Narrator :   The path where pass *bingende'ngende*.
> Audience :   *Yaya-ya-ya-ya*.
> Narrator :   Father, come see the path,
> Audience :   *Yaya-ya-ya-ya*.
> Narrator :   The path where pass *bingende'ngende*.
> Audience :   *Yaya-ya-ya-ya*.
> Narrator :   Father, come see the path,
> Audience :   *Yaya-ya-ya-ya*.
> Narrator :   The path where pass *bingende'ngende*.
> Audience :   *Yaya-ya-ya-ya*.

He said, "Ah![23] We've found it. We can work. These resemble them very well. We can take him. You bury me until only my head shows, my chin only. And when he passes, we can kill him."

Then the son dug a hole and dug and dug and buried his father. The son climbed into a tree, a very tall tree, so he could see when the ogres were coming, *te-e-e-e*.[24] The ogres came at that time from down the path. They passed; they passed; they passed; they passed. Then Lomat'ònènè passed afterwards. He stumbled over the chin that was in the hole. *Boom!* He dropped his leaves. "Is this a chin or a stump?"

> Audience :   It is a man's chin.
> Narrator :   Is this a man's chin or a stump?
> Audience :   The chin of a man, the chin of a man, the
>   chin of a man.

He said, "Ah!" They scrutinized the head. They killed the father, *kao*.

When the son saw that his father was dead, then he cried silently, and one tear fell on a leaf near Lomat'ȯnėnė, *tȯ.*

He said, "Is this a small raindrop or the tear of a man?"[25]

The ogres sang,

> *Narrator and Audience:* The tear of a man, the tear of a man.

They lifted their eyes and saw the son in the tree. He said, "What is that up above?"

"The son of the man."

He said, "Come down."

He said, "I won't come down."

"Come down."

"I won't come down."

One of the ogres got a vine[26] and began to climb the tree, *katakata-kata.* The boy cut the branch where the ogre was, *ka.* He was dead.

Another ogre began to climb the tree, *kata-kata-kata.* He cut the branch again, *ka,* and he was dead. *Te-te-te.*[27]

Lomat'ȯnėnė said, "Everyone will be finished. Let's go home. We'll leave the boy here." Then they went.

The boy came down. He said, "Ah! All of them are not dead. There are still enough. Can I kill them? No!"

He went to see the witch doctor. The witch doctor said to him, "They are not far. They live nearby. Where you find a large hollow tree, that is their home. Do you understand? Follow them there. Get a trap and put it in the opening of the hollow. And near the opening build a fire, that they be burned when they leave."

Then that boy went to set a trap and to build a fire in the opening of the hollow tree. When the ogres saw the light of the fire from a distance, they said,

> *Narrator:* The moon is showing.
> *Audience:* We go hunting.
> *Narrator:* The moon is showing.
> *Audience:* We go hunting.
> *Narrator:* The moon is showing.
> *Audience:* Let's go!
> *Narrator:* *Boko-ki!*
> *Audience:* *Ki!*

Then another witch doctor of the ogres was there, a little witch doctor.[28] He called his wife and said, "Not at all. This is not the

moon. It is a fire. This is something else. We are going to perish.
Let's flee." He and his wife left in his own secret hole.

The fire became hot. They cried out to Lomat'ȯnȯnė, "The fire
is hot. It is well if Lomat'ȯnȯnė passes first. He is our chief." Then
Lomat'ȯnȯnė passed and was caught in the trap. *Gboom!*[29] He
was so large that the entrance was blocked.

> *Narrator :*   Press forward.
> *Audience:*   Lomata is tied with cords.[30]
> *Narrator :*   Press forward.
> *Audience:*   Lomata is tied up with cords.
> *Narrator :*   Press forward.
> *Audience:*   Lomata is tied up with cords.

Then all the ogres were dead in the fire.

That boy went to the witch doctor again. He said, "You tell
me that of the ogres one remained. Perhaps he is dead."

He said, "No! The witch doctor remains, he and his wife. If
he continues to live, he will return to continue to reproduce the
ogre village. Try to kill him and his wife."

Then the boy said, "Ah! He and his wife remain like that. And
I am to kill both of them." Then the boy asked himself how to kill
the witch doctor and his wife.

The witch doctor said, "You must seek the path of the witch
doctor. The witch doctor will follow his own path. He likes that.
Then he will not begin to go elsewhere."

The boy said, "I am to seek the path of the witch doctor. I'll
fall into a trap. I will become an antelope."

He went into a deep trap belonging to the ogre and became a
small antelope.

The witch doctor saw the small antelope. He said, "This is not
an animal. It is not for us. Let's go."

The wife said, "We will leave this meat? It is for us."

"Ah! *Te-e-e-e.* It was like dead. We can't take that. It is not
an animal."

The boy said, "They did not take me. I will become a dead
antelope along the path."

They went on their way. On the way they found a large antelope
dead. The wife wanted it, but the witch doctor said, "No! We are
not going to take a dead animal. That is not an antelope. This is
that man who is hunting us."

"You always give up. This is two animals that we haven't taken.
Why did we come here?"

The witch doctor said, "What have I done that this boy tracks me?"

On another day some women decided to have a cape made from the special skin of a beaver. They wanted this for all of their age group.[31] It was a beautiful skin. They said to the witch doctor's wife, "From now on, we want this skin for all of our age group. We want this skin for a cape. If your husband does not provide you with it, divorce him."

The witch doctor came and wanted to trap the beaver and sell to the women. The boy heard this and knew it was his opportunity. The boy became a dead beaver. The wife of the witch doctor said, "I am fortunate. Here is a dead beaver. I'll take it for the skin."

The witch doctor said, "No! This is not a beaver."

The woman was angry. "You always give up any animals you find, even this beaver. I'm going to divorce you because you will not take the beaver for the skin."

The witch doctor said, "All these animals we are finding are the people who are hunting us."

They continued on their way.

The boy decided to take another form and went to the ashes of the ogre's village and became a baby. They found him crying there. "Maa! Maa!" The wife was delighted. She wanted to keep him.

Then the witch doctor said, "No! Not that one."

"But it is the child of Lomat'ȯnėnė. We should care for him."

"Return him where you found him."

"But it is the very child of Lomat'ȯnėnė."[32]

"Let us go."

They went and went and went. They found a tree with a rubber vine growing up it. It had much fruit on it.

The wife said, "They are to eat. How can I get them? What will I do? My husband cannot climb trees."[33]

The husband said, "We can't get them. They are too far up. Let's go!"

The wife said, "You always leave everything. You left the small antelope; you left the large antelope; you left the beaver. Now you want to leave the *bitofi* fruit."

The child said, "Mother, before we go, let me try to get them. Let me cling to the tree that I try to climb it to get them."

She put him on the tree trunk and he climbed to the fruit, *kaba-kaba-kaba*.[34]

"Father, I see a big fruit there for you."

The mother said, "No! That is too dangerous for you. Don't get it."

The father said, "Yes, get it. It is for me."

He crawled inside the *bitofi* fruit. Then it fell into his father's hands and in one movement into the father's mouth and to his stomach.

Then the mother said, "Child, come on. Let's go."

"I am in the stomach of Father."

"Ah! Let's go."

"I am in the stomach of Father."

"Let's go!"

"I am in the stomach of Father."

The witch doctor said to his wife, he said, "You got us into this palaver. You said this was the child of Lomat'ónènè. I am a witch doctor. I will kill you. You may no longer live." He killed her.

Then the child who was inside of the stomach had a razor.[35] He began to cut the witch doctor. He cut the ogre, *ka*. He was dead.

This is why the ogres are finished on our earth. The boy had succeeded in finishing them, even though his father had erred.

[Notes to Tale 68 follow Tale 69.]

Narrator: Tata Manga
Location: Boende
Date: November 1973

69. *The Last of the Ogres* (Variant II)

Likinda and his mother and father went into the forest. Likinda was a blacksmith. His father hunted meat, and his mother hunted fish. When they arrived at their place, they cleared, and cleared, and cleared; then they built a shelter. The mother of Likinda, the father of Likinda, and Likinda himself worked at it.

In the morning the father went to hunt meat. Then the mother went to hunt fish. Likinda stayed behind and forged metal, *kè-kè-kè-kè*. He forged near the side of the shelter. He said,

He who works spears,
  Some spears and spears.
I, Likinda, make spears,
  Some spears and spears.
Father hunts with spears,
  Some spears and spears.
Mother goes with spears,
  Some spears and spears.
He can't hunt meat or hunt fish without spears,
  Some spears and spears.

Then an ogre appeared. Perhaps he raised up; perhaps he was hiding near the blacksmith's shed. Then Likinda saw the ogre and split him lengthwise with his spear and he was dead. When his mother and father came that evening, he told them what had happened.

His father said, "Very good. You did well."

Another morning the father went to hunt meat and the mother went to hunt fish. Likinda was left alone in the shelter. He worked away at his forge. An ogre with two heads came.

He who works spears,
  Some spears and spears.
I, Likinda, make spears,
  Some spears and spears.
Father hunts with spears,
  Some spears and spears.
Mother goes with spears,
  Some spears and spears.
He can't hunt meat or hunt fish without spears,
  Some spears and spears.

Then the two-headed ogre came near. The ogre came up to Likinda and looked over the forge. Likinda took a knife that he had made and cut off his heads. The ogre was dead. This happened day after day, like that, like that, like that. Likinda killed the ogres.

His mother began to be worried. One day his mother said, "I'll stay tomorrow."

Likinda said, "O, nyë. My mother must not stay here alone. The ogre[36] is very bad. He is very large and very strong."

The mother said, "Nyë! I will stay here."

Likinda finally left her and went to hunt fish. The father went to hunt meat. The mother worked the forge; she worked as a blacksmith.

Soon an ogre was listening to her song.

> He who works spears,
>   Some spears and spears,
> I, his blacksmith, make spears,
>   Some spears and spears.
> My husband hunts with spears,
>   Some spears and spears.
> Likinda hunts fish with spears,
>   Some spears and spears.

Then when the ogre came up to her, she did not know how to cut his head off in the way that Likinda had, so he cut hers off, and she was dead. The ogre and his friends ate her and went on their way.

Then the father, the husband, came and Likinda came and could not find the mother. Then they knew that the ogres had eaten her.

Likinda said, "Father, let us go and hunt where the ogres pass."

So they went down the path, the father first and Likinda following. After they had gone a way, the father saw some tracks, like an elephant's, passing by. "An animal with age," the father said. "Likinda, here are elephant tracks. They are often cantankerous. Come and look."

Likinda said, "No, those are not the tracks we seek. Those are a different kind of animal."

The father said, "These are like the tracks of the ogre. These are like the tracks of the ogre."

Likinda said, "Not like that. Let's go on." They went.

Like that, all the animals went and went and they found their tracks, until they found the path of the very ogres.[37]

The father said, "Perhaps these are the tracks which are greater, which are greater, which are greater."

Then Likinda said, "Ah! Those are their path. The ogres have gone to hunt leaves for roofing. They have gone to find strips of bamboo to make it stronger."[38]

Then the father of Likinda said, "It is well that you dig a hole here and bury me that my head only is above. This is in the manner of our fierceness."[39]

When they had thought about it, Likinda said, "If I bury you, do not forget that you can't kill a person."

The father said, "It is well that you bury me. And when I call you, you can come."

"No word. I'll hide nearby."

The father got into the hole with only a part of his head above ground, and Likinda climbed up into the tree above him. The ogres came and passed and passed and passed over the father, many of them without touching him, until the oldest, Lomat'ȯnėnė. He hit the head and yelled, "This is like the top of the head of a man. It only shows above the chin." They all returned and looked and found Likinda's father there. They rejoiced. They killed him, cut the meat and cut the meat, and ate it.

Likinda was feeling great sorrow, and his tears fell on a leaf near Lomat'ȯnėnė, *tò*.

Lomat'ȯnėnė said, "Either these are drops of rain or they are the tears of a man." They all looked up and saw Likinda.

One of them climbed up into the tree. When he was near to Likinda, Likinda cut the branch, *ka*, where the ogre was, and the ogre fell to the ground.

They said, "You have killed one, but you can't kill two."[40]

Another ogre climbed and climbed and climbed and climbed. As soon as he was near to Likinda, Likinda cut the branch, *ka*, and he fell to the ground dead.

"You killed two, but you can't kill three."

Another ogre climbed and climbed and climbed. As soon as he was near to Likinda, Likinda cut the branch, *ka*, and he fell to the ground.

"You have killed three, but you can't kill four."

This kept happening like that, like that, until he had killed many of them. Then they said, "We had better stop this and not let him kill more of us." They left Likinda. They went on the path.

Likinda came out of the tree and followed their tracks. He stopped to consult a witch doctor. "The ogres came and killed my mother and then my father. What shall I do? I am all that is left."

The witch doctor said, he said, "The ogres live in a hollow tree. Go there and set a trap in the door of the hollow. Then climb up into the tree above the hollow. Then at night light a fire. The tree will be set afire and the ogres will be burned."

Likinda said, "That's good."

So he went. He worked and worked and worked to set a trap in the door of the hollow. Then he climbed up into the tree above the hollow and started a fire there.

When the ogres saw a fire there, they said,

> The moon comes into view.
> We work in it. Let us go forth.
> The moon comes into view.

> We work in it. Let us go forth.
> The moon comes into view.
> We work in it. Let us go forth.
> The moon comes into view.
> We work in it. Let us go forth.[41]

The witch doctor of the ogres saw it and said, "No. That isn't the moon. That is fire." He and his wife, because of his power as a witch doctor, struck the side of the tree and left.

All of the ogres were frightened. "The fire will kill us. Let's go. Lomat'ȯnėnė, you go first." Lomat'ȯnėnė went out and was caught in the trap. Then they sang their song,

> The trap killed Lomata with the cord.
> The trap killed Lomata with the cord.
>   Push, but
> The trap killed Lomata with the cord.
> The trap killed Lomata with the cord.

All of them were burned to cinders, burning, burning, burning, until they were finished, *nyė*. Then only the witch doctor and his wife remained.

Likinda sought wisdom. "They are all dead. The witch doctor only remains. What can I do?"

He went to the edge of the swamp and became a very little baby. He lay there and cried, "Maa! Maa! Maa!"

Then the witch doctor and his wife passed by to get water and saw the baby there. The woman said, "Eh! This must be the baby of Lomat'ȯnėnė. He left it on the edge of the swamp. His father is dead. It is well that we take him."

The husband said, "No! This is not the baby of Lomat'ȯnėnė. This is another baby. You are not to take it."

She said, "Go away! This is the child of Lomat'ȯnėnė, and we should care for him until he is grown."

He said, "You take him up and he is the child of someone else. This is not the child of Lomata, *nyė*."

The wife insisted and she succeeded. They went. He said, "You take the baby when it might be the baby of someone else. You don't know." They went.

As they went they came to a tree that had fruit called *bitofi*. Then the wife wanted some of the fruit very much.

She said, "As soon as this boy grows up a bit, he can climb the tree and get the fruit for me."

Then the baby said, "Mama, I'll climb for you." The mother put him on the trunk. The witch doctor said, "He says he can climb."

The husband said, "Look at him. He is little, and how can he climb?"

The witch doctor said, "Wait a bit. He will grow."

They put him onto the trunk of the tree. He began to climb slowly, slowly and carefully. When they would quit watching him, he would climb fast. Then when they looked again, he would go very slowly. Then he arrived where the fruit was.

He called, "Mama, I have reached the fruit."

She said, "Very good. Throw some to us."

He picked one *etofi* and threw it to his mother. He picked one and threw it to his father. He picked another and threw it to his mother, then to his father again, *ti-ti-ti*. He found a very large *etofi*. He crawled into the middle of it and called, "I have found a very large *etofi* and I want Father to swallow it."

The father said, "Very good. Throw it down."

He said, "Open your mouth wide." Then the *etofi* came down and went into the witch doctor's mouth and he swallowed it.

He said, "That was good. Come on and we'll go on."

He said, "I'm inside of Father."

"What?"

He said, "I'm inside of Father."

"You! How did you get inside of me?" He hit his stomach a hard blow with a pole, *poom*, hoping to bring the fruit up.

The boy sang, "I'm inside of Father."

He said, "If you are really there, cut me."

Likinda cut him and he screamed, "Stop that! Stop that!" He was very angry and turned on his wife. "This is your fault. You insisted on bringing him with us. Now we have a real palaver." He grabbed his knife and killed his wife. Then he began to beat his stomach, *poom*. "I hope you are dead."

Likinda said, "I'm inside of Father. I'm not yet dead."

He said, "Oh! You aren't yet dead?"

"No."

The witch doctor hit again, *poom*. "You hear? Now you are dead."

He said, "No! Not at all! I'm not dead."

Poom! "You aren't dead yet?"

"No."

"Cut me again or I won't believe it." Then he screamed because the boy cut him. "Stop that! Stop!"

The boy began to cut his way out, *ka*, and the witch doctor was dead. He was the last of the ogres. He had succeeded and there are no more to this day.

He went to his home.[42]

In the narrating of Tales 67, 68, and 69, we have an interesting instance of competition among narrators, of "one-up-manship," that was not encountered elsewhere in Mrs. Ross's field collecting. For two reasons, the cluster of tales is arranged in its present order, though all three tales were told on the same day at the same place: (1) that is the order in which they were actually told; (2) the third tale has dimensions that require special comment in the light of its relationship to the purported "oral epic" of the Mongo/Nkundo.

As soon as Ikwa Isilombe had completed the taped telling of Tale 67, told without the inclusion of songs, he was aware that he was dissatisfied with it, and he undertook to retell the story, this time prompting and receiving considerable audience response by the songs included. A close comparison of Tales 67 and 68 reveals that Ikwa Isilombe's alterations in the latter included refinements beyond the addition of songs: the provision of details at points where he had truncated the first time, the interesting device of utilizing a pseudonym for the ogres (indicating the genuine fear and awe of the ogres that was felt by the protagonist), the decidedly increased drama in the dialogues and in the incident involving the destruction of the ogre community, the series of transformations undergone by the hero in his effort to gain access to the witch doctor and his wife (prompting a succession of family arguments), and the verisimilitude attempted in the large fruit's dropping first into the witch doctor's hands and then being placed by the witch doctor himself into his mouth. Examination of the two versions reveals the freedom given the Nkundo narrator to innovate, to add his own personal stamp to a tale, to alter the diction, to shorten or lengthen, to reach for a greater degree of competence in his own rendering of a narrative with no sense of restraint from the listeners. These are clearly not rote-memory productions but individualized, flavorful dramas, each with its own strengths and each quite evidently a folktale development of what might well be told elsewhere with the inclusion of the blacksmith Likinda in a fashion that would relate it directly to the Lianja epic.

The facts that Ikwa Isilombe felt free to "top" his own first tale and that he told the second version with such relish suggest the ease he felt both with his material and with his audience, as well as the challenge he sensed in the knowledge that all the tales Mrs. Ross collected would be reaching a far wider audience than he could normally encounter in his tale-telling: he felt the social and artistic responsibilities incumbent upon a carrier of verbal art reflecting his own cultural milieu.

After Ikwa Isilombe and most of the other elders had left the tale-telling site, Tata Manga declared his own intention of producing a still better version of the basic narrative, and he told Tale 69, a variant that bears a marked relationship to the series of Lianja episodes earlier described (see notes for Tale 2). The encounter between Likinda (or Lianja) and the ogres in which the destruction of "all the ogres" is accomplished occurs, says de Rop (in *Lianja, L'Épopée des Móngo*, pp. 84–86), on the hero's march to the "promised land"; for this chronological detail and the account of the conflict, de Rop draws on "N60, 11–63, 25," a reference identified in the introduction to this illuminating study of the epic. On page 26 of the same study, de Rop attaches the name "Likíndá" to the hero who by the intervention of "la Divinité" transformed himself into an infant in order to kill the ogre Inka-nkanga; for this detail, de Rop cites one of Boelaert's studies of the epic, *Lianja— Verhalen II* (1958). This same Likíndá, said in the "Ekofo version" (presented in Boelaert's longest form of the epic, *Lianja—Verhalen I* [1957]) to be the son of Lianja, "is charged with subjecting the enemy tribes" following his father's death; "the grandson, Lianja, the blacksmith, continues the wars" (de Rop, *Lianja ...*, p. 87). As is obvious from this brief sampling of the bits and pieces studied and put together by scholars in an effort to arrive at some notion of the content and form of this "living epic," an English-language study of the various narrative threads would be a challenging and satisfying project. Those interested in pursuing the epic through its various extant versions (published in French and in Flemish) will do well to begin with the de Rop volume cited above.

Tata Manga's narrative includes a number of the elements furnished on pages 84–86 in de Rop's *Lianja ...* : the hero's determination to destroy the ogres, his consulting a "small bird" about the best means of accomplishing this task, the hollow-tree home of the ogres, the use of fire and of a trap in the extermination, the ogres' mistaking of the fire for moonlight, the killing of "le grand Lomata," the hero's transformation into a baby in order to deceive and kill the ogre witch doctor and his wife, the tossing-of-fruits episode, and the hero's cutting his way out of the witch doctor's belly after the witch doctor has slain his own wife. In short, all the basic elements of the de Rop-cited version are present in Tale 69, giving rise to our speculation that Tata Manga's tale either was derived from a fuller form of the epic or is one of the floating tales from which the epic has been compiled by the scholars whose works we have consulted. The occurrences of "Likinda" and "blacksmith" are not peculiar to Tata Manga's version, though they seem to have slipped out of place chronologically in terms of other versions of this confrontation of the hero with the last of the ogres. Likinda's being accompanied by his parents, the appearance of a two-headed ogre, and the mother's service at the forge have not been met in any of the published versions at our disposal, nor have the burial-to-the-chin and the cutting-of-the-branches details been located outside the tales in the present volume. Given the freedom allowed the Nkundo narrator, it is not surprising that somewhat different details appear in the various versions.

Although other portions of the Lianja epic have been listed in Lambrecht's index, no sample suitable for classification of the present cluster of tales has been entered either in Lambrecht's study or in any other of the indexes examined.

Motifs:

C	H1229.1.+.**.	Quest for certain ogre with objective of killing him.
T	J1800.**.	One thing mistaken for another—miscellaneous: one animal's tracks mistaken for another's.
A	K1800.1.**.	Hiding (being buried) so that only the chin shows.
T	R311.	Tree refuge.
C	G80.+.**.	Cannibal ogres at foot of tree detect hero's presence by a tear shed at their killing of his father.
T	R235.**.	Fugitive cuts branch of tree so that pursuer (ogre) falls to his death.
C	H1229.1.+.**.	Quest for ogre community with objective of killing all of the ogres.
C	D1726.+.**.	Itòji bird magician: aids hero in defeat of ogres.
C	F408.+.**.	Cannibalistic ogres live in hollow tree.
T	J1800.**.	One thing mistaken for another—miscellaneous: fire mistaken for moonlight by ogres.
T	F405.**.	Hero catches ogre leader in doorway trap and thus blocks escapes of other ogres from burning tree home.
T	F405.**.	Hero burns tree home of ogres and destroys all ogres except wily witch doctor and wife.
T	G512.3.	Ogre (ogres) burned to death.
T	G512.	Ogre(s) killed.
T	G500.	Ogre(s) defeated.
T	F531.6.12.**.	Disappearance or death of ogres.
C	H1229.1.+.**.	Quest for ogre witch doctor and wife with objective of killing them.
T	D55.	Magic change of person's size.
C	C680.+.**.	Injunction: do not pick up infant suspected of being hero transformed.
T	T585.	Precocious infant.
C	F628.1.0.1.+.**.	Extraordinary infant kills ogre by concealing himself in fruit he throws down to ogre to be swallowed.
T	F910.**.	Ogre swallows hero concealed in fruit thrown down from tree.
T	F911.	Person (animal) swallowed without killing.
T	F915.**.	Victim (trickster) speaks from swallower's body.
T	G520.	Ogre deceived (tricked) into self-injury.
T	F912.2.**.	Victim (trickster) kills swallower from within by cutting.
T	G510.**.	Last of ogres (witch doctor and wife) killed by hero.
T	C430.	Name tabu.
T	C433.	Tabu: uttering name of malevolent creature (Euminides).
T	C433.2.	Dangerous animals not to be named.
T	D114.1.1.**.	Transformation: boy to small antelope (*mbuji*).
C	C680.+.**.	Injunction: do not pick up animal suspected of being hero transformed.

T	D114.1.1.**.	Transformation: boy to large dead antelope (*lisoko*).
T	D117.**.	Transformation: boy to dead beaver.
T	P447.	Blacksmith.
C	P690.+.**.	Custom of hunter (ogre) sharing meat.
T	Q91.**.	Reward for cleverness: blacksmith, disguised as infant, conceals himself in large fruit swallowed by ogre witch doctor and thus destroys him.
T	A527.3.1.**.	Culture hero can transform self.

1. "*Lomata*," meaning "the bite of a person or a dog," and "*bònènè*," meaning "large," have here been combined by elision to form a cognomen that—in terms of ogre values—would be classified as a praise name. The form in which the name of this ogre appears in several of the Lianja-epic studies is shorter: "Lomata."

Tales 67 and 68 are the only ones in the Ross collection in which someone sets out without immediate provocation to destroy a certain ogre; we suspect that the narrator himself created this arresting beginning in order to heighten suspense as well as to prepare the audience for the death of a man insistent on meddling with a supernatural being who had apparently done him no harm.

2. Although no information is given by Ikwa Isilombe, in either of his tales in this cluster, about the occupation of the father or of the son, it is unlikely that a son in the rain-forest area would be entirely unable to identify animal tracks. Since his faulty interpretations did not prompt laughter among the listeners, we suspect that here the narrator, himself an elder, is allowing the audience to observe that a father's discernment is greater than a son's; respect for the judgment of an elder would normally be confirmed in Nkundo oral art. This series of exchanges in Tales 67 and 68 concerning the tracks serves to increase the dramatic impact of the son's eventual success in obliterating the ogres, a task at which his father had failed. An Nkundo proverb is singularly appropriate under such circumstances: "Unless the father cuts the big trees, the son could not cut the growth," a tribute to "the fathers" reflected also in the custom of the successful hunter's tracing his ancestry in the account of his hunt.

3. Truncation is evident here: the narrator wished to move directly to the human/ogre conflict. It is noteworthy that the narrator used a singsong tone in the naming of the various animals. An extraneous sound is also heard at this point on the tape—the crowing of a rooster.

4. The narrator makes mouthy, gulping noises here to represent the sound of the son's digging of a hole in the swampy earth.

5. This ideophone, suggesting a surprised stumbling, is expressed on the tape with considerable force.

6. Presented in singsong fashion, this line is the closest attempt at singing that the narrator makes in Tale 67.

7. This staccato sound denotes the breaking of something brittle.

8. Since only two ogres have been killed by the hero, this statement appears to be an indication either of truncation or of the ogre elder's softness of heart. The narrator mended this weakness in his next telling by inserting "*te-te-te*," suggesting a continuation of the climbing and the cutting limited only by the listeners' imagination.

9. Although the father is dead, the son assumes—in keeping with Nkundo beliefs—that his father's spirit is nearby, counseling him and prompting him to action. For helpful information on the functions and behavior of family spirits, or *"bekáli,"* see de Rop's *Lianja* . . . , page 63.

10. Despite the absence of the mention of the itòji as the "witch doctor" consulted at this point, Nkundo listeners are expected to understand that the itòji is the only one who can help in humans' dealings with ogres.

11. The insistent crowing of a rooster here in no way distracted either the narrator or his audience from the tale-telling.

12. The audience laughed loudly at this evidence of the ogres' stupidity.

13. Heavy banging noises were made here to represent the catastrophic character of the fire; Mrs. Ross was unable to determine how the sounds were produced except that they were not vocalized.

14. The ogres' witch doctor escapes entirely in all the Ross-collected narratives except those in the present cluster, and a determined effort has to be made by the hero in each of these three tales in order to kill him. The consensus in Nkundo oral tradition favors the invulnerability of the witch doctor, whether he meets humans' or ogres' needs, and this consensus would be mirrored in the folktales.

15. Despite the witch doctor's injunction, his wife does take the baby (a reflection of the Nkundo emphasis on the importance of child-bearing and child-rearing), and the baby proves their undoing (a reflection of the stress placed by the Nkundo on the wife's obedience to her husband). Again, the narrator has chosen to include two conflicting values in the same tale, but here—as is true also in the other two tales in this cluster—the tale-teller himself through the narrative line underscores the Nkundo's firm stand on a delicate situation: the wife's disobedience, her stubborn insistence on her own way, the social inappropriateness of her failure to heed her husband's directions, costs both her life and the life of her husband.

16. In saying *"Fafa,"* the term used here for "Father," the narrator draws out the first syllable as the word is voiced, in singsong, half-mocking and half-exultant fashion.

17. The sharpness of the *"lokengo,"* or razor, is emphasized by the repetition of the noun; the narrator intends no doubt about the effectiveness of the weapon used against the ogre witch doctor.

18. The plural, *"bingende'ngende,"* of the Lonkundo "safety" word for "ogre" —*"ngende"*—accentuates the strength of the tabu against naming either a malevolent creature or a dangerous animal. The customary Lonkundo word for "ogre" is *"eloko,"* and its plural is *"biloko"*; safety and custom both dictate the use of a pseudonym, and the narrator employs the "safe" name to communicate the fear felt by the son that the ogre, hearing his name, might make their mission impossible. This suspense-building touch is a highly effective one since it allows the audience itself to draw the conclusion that the men are afraid, though determined to complete the task they have set for themselves.

This exchange between narrator and audience is one of the two "songs" in the narrative that were actually *sung*; the other passages that appear in the text as "songs" (with the exception of the one in which the ogres mourn the loss of their leader just prior to the burning of the hollow tree) are chanted rather than sung, though they are handled antiphonally.

Once the ogres have been located and the hero's campaign against them has begun, the term *"bingende'ngende"* yields to *"biloko"*; the former has already satisfied its tension-producing function.

19. The "small antelope" in this instance is *"mbuji,"* even smaller than *mboloko,* the dwarf antelope noted in Nkundo tales as very clever.

20. Identified by the narrator as *"lisoko,"* this antelope functions later in the tale as one of the hero's states of transformation.

21. Here the narrator uses a secret name to replace *"njòku,"* the usual term for "elephant," lest the elephant hear his own name and disturb them.

22. The leaves specified by the narrator were *mpete* leaves (see notes for Tale 33). [Narrator's explanatory comment: "These paths criss-crossed and were many."]

23. This sound was considerably drawn out by the tale-teller.

24. The storyteller makes a false start here, "And the son ... ," but quickly abandons it for the appropriate phrasing.

25. If a small drop of water falls from a tree when someone is going through the forest and it isn't raining, such a drop is often described as "the tear of a man," a reflection here of Lonkundo locution.

26. The vine was apparently entwined around the tree, affording a means of the ogres' reaching the branches. Curiously, this cluster of tales contains the only instances Mrs. Ross encountered in which ogres were said to climb trees; in all other Ross-collected tales involving tree-climbing by men associated with ogres, the humans are directed to climb to oblige the ogres (or choose to ascend in order to escape from an ogre or ogres). The hollow tree in which the ogres in this set of narratives live is also a departure from the pattern usually suggested in Nkundo ogre tales; normally, ogres are represented as living very much in the style of the Nkundo themselves.

27. This ideophone, suggesting continuous action, means that one after another of the ogres climbed and was killed. (Review note 8, above, for the corrective function of this ideophone in the tale.)

28. One of Mrs. Ross's translation assistants, Pierre Sangana, explained that the narrator had used the phrase "another witch doctor" because one—the itòji— had already appeared in the tale. The aide also confirmed that the witch doctor was "little" only when his size was compared with that of the other ogres; he was still a formidable figure. His relatively small size served the narrative function of allowing him to leave unnoticed "in his own secret hole."

29. The consonant combinations "gb" and "ngb" are often used by the Nkundo as plosives.

30. Since the ogres cannot move Lomat'ònènè out of the passageway, they assume that he has been bound by a "cord," in this instance the kind used to trap wild pigs.

31. Fraternal and sororal societies are formed among the Nkundo not so much in terms of common interests as in terms of age; such age-sets are less common in the area where the Rosses served than they are in contiguous regions. An example

of such an age-set would be one consisting of menopausal women; there *was* a menopausal age-set in Lotumbe. The members of such groups do tend to be somewhat clannish and to establish rather firm lines concerning both dress and practices.

32. Totally caught up in his tale-telling, the narrator cried as the wife would have cried as he spoke this line.

33. The reason for the ogre witch doctor's inability to climb trees was not explained by the narrator; this lack in the witch doctor provided a narrative gain for the storyteller: it allowed him to send the child up the tree to fetch the fruit, ultimately achieving the hero's purpose of destroying the remaining ogres.

34. An ideophone expressing the process of climbing.

35. On questioning, the narrator provided the French equivalent for this word, since the Lonkundo form was new to Mrs. Ross.

36. The narrator appears to be referring to "the ogre" as a class here; obviously, there are many ogres present in that part of the forest, since Likinda (a name meaning "only child") had already killed one daily for many days in succession.

37. Here is an instance of truncation in the interest of getting on with the action. Since the basic tale had already been told twice at that same tale-telling session, the storyteller could effect this economy without loss of narrative sense.

38. In the preceding sentence, the narrator had used the term "*ndele*"; here he employs "*lokala*," quite a different kind of roofing material from the leaves used for thatching. "*Lokala*" is a mat made of strips of bamboo that serves to keep the thatching in position on the roof; such mats can also be used as floor coverings and as fences for capturing fish.

39. The narrator here provides the key to the puzzle of the father's requesting that the son bury him so that only his head will show (in Tales 67 and 68, he requires that only his chin be visible): this deliberate exposure to danger is a mark of their "fierceness" and presumably a mark of bravery. Arewa's tale types 670 and 1622 present animals' being buried so that only their teeth show, but in neither instance does the burial demonstrate bravery. This element of the tale was readily accepted by the audience in each of the Ross-collected narratives, so apparently it is either reasonably common in Nkundo tales or has some social significance that outweighs its apparent impracticality as a means of capturing ogres. Such puzzles indicate the need for much additional field collecting with an emphasis on the ethnological context in which such arresting details as this one function as narrative devices.

40. "You have killed one, but you can't kill two" suggests a cumulative pattern within an "ordinary" tale; this chant and the subsequent variations of it were delivered with great relish by the storyteller and received with delight by the audience.

41. The ogres' time of hunting is indicated in this cluster of tales as occurring at night; in various other Ross tales including ogres, the ogre comes home at night bringing "human meat and forest meat" for his wife to cook. In each instance, the narrator appears to have suited the ogres' work schedule to the needs of the narrative, his prerogative as a tale-teller dealing in encounters of humans with the supernatural.

42. This closing sentence, occupying the position normally taken by a proverb or a "teaching" or a formulaic ending if the narrator wishes to use one or more of these characteristic closings, seems anticlimactic. Actually, it represents the tale-

teller's own situation at that moment: the story was finished, dinner was ready, and he himself was ready to go to his home. In common with the other competent narrators encountered by Mrs. Ross, he had enjoyed both his own dramatic presentation and the audience's enthusiastic response to the tale-telling, but he had a sound sense of the right time to stop.

Narrator:	Mbilo Esio, retired teacher and preacher
Location:	Ilongo-Kindo
Date:	November 1973

70. *Each Man Has His Own Way*

Two friends, Ekambakamba and Iyèndèyèlèmò, were alike in all things. They built houses alike and furnished them alike. They were equal in everything that concerned them.

One day Iyèndèyèlèmò needed some palm oil, and he decided to make the long trip to where he could get some. He gathered forty gourds together and started on his journey. It was a long trip, going, going, across swamps and rivers, and it was not a few days before he reached the grove of really good palm trees.

When he saw the trees, he was delighted. "Now I can make some good palm oil."

He climbed into a palm tree and began to cut the fruit. Very soon an elder of the ogres came to see who was cutting palm fruit.

He shouted, "Who do you think you are? You can't cut palm fruit here. This grove belongs to us."

Iyèndèyèlèmò took out his bow and shot an arrow at the ogre. He just missed the ogre, who ran to get help. Iyèndèyèlèmò went on cutting bunches of palm fruit and letting them fall to the ground.

After a while, ogres and ogres came to stop him from cutting the fruit. Iyèndèyèlèmò began to shoot arrows among them. They soon said, "We cannot stop him," and they went, going, going.

Iyèndèyèlèmò kept on cutting fruit and cutting fruit. Then he made oil and made oil[1] until his forty gourds were filled. Then he made the long trip home. When he arrived, he kept twenty gourds of oil for his own use and gave twenty to Ekambakamba.

After not a little while, Ekambakamba ran out of oil. He said, "The oil is finished. I will go to the palm grove and get some more."

"No, no! You mustn't do that. If you go there you will have real difficulties. Let me give you a gourd of oil. Then you will have twenty-one and I will have nineteen."[2]

Ekambakamba was unwilling to do this and was determined to go, *nyĕ.* Finally Iyĕndĕyĕlĕmȯ told him, "If you must go, hear my words. Be very careful of the ogres. They will try to stop you. Always keep your bow and arrows with you."

So Ekambakamba gathered forty gourds and started on the journey. As soon as he reached the grove, he climbed a tree and began to cut the fruit. Soon the elder of the ogres came to see who was cutting the fruit. Ekambakamba shot an arrow at him, and he ran to get help. The ogres came pretending that they wanted peace. They brought plantains and sugar cane as gifts[3] and wished to discuss the palaver.

Cautiously, cautiously, Ekambakamba climbed out of the tree. He sat with the ogres, and they discussed many things together. Finally they asked that they see his bow and arrows. "They must surely be a special kind." He gave them the bow and arrows to pass around and see. As soon as the bow and arrows were out of his reach, the ogres grabbed Ekambakamba and killed him.

Friends may be equal, yet one exceeds the other.

Tale 70 is the only tale in the Ross field collection in which ogres prove to be tricksters. In all of the other Nkundo narratives we have encountered—in whatever language they might have been presented—ogres have been represented as more stupid than the human beings they met. (Among the Ross-collected tales, for example, see Tales 60, 66, and 67–69.)

The narrator's purpose in telling the tale, however—if one may judge from the concluding proverb—was not to deal with ogres versus human beings but to stress the uniqueness of character to be found among men as individuals. The Nkundo emphasis on individuality is borne out in proverbs, used both in conversation (as a preamble to a greeting, as a caution or reprimand to children, in the course of palavers of all kinds) and as a conclusion in storytelling. Two proverbs frequently used among the Nkundo but not employed here by the narrator underscore the importance of keeping to one's own way:

Wèngi'onto eleng'ekae. (Every person to his own way.)

Bòn'oa lisoko ntakèndaka nd'otonga wa nsombo. (A young antelope does not go about in a herd of wild pigs.)

We have been unable to locate in any of the indexes consulted a type number providing suitable classification for this tale.

Motifs:

C	W167.+.**.	Willful man goes out against friend's advice to seek palm oil in ogre-infested forest.
C	C680.+.**.	Injunction: keep your bow and arrows with you (to avoid capture by ogres).
C	J2199.+.**.	Man allows himself to be enticed to palaver with ogres and is then killed by them.
T	K815.	Victim lured by kind words approaches trickster(s) and is killed.
T	K1700.	Deception through bluffing.
C	K1715.+.**.	Ogres pretend to examine man's bow and arrows; when they have them, they kill him.
T	K810.**.	Fatal deception into trickster ogres' power.
T	J2137.	Death through lack of foresight.

1. There are a great many varieties of palm fruit, but choice fruit makes the best oil. See note 8 for Tale 87 for a description of the making of palm oil.

2. This is translated precisely as the narrator told it; the lack of logic disturbed neither the narrator nor the audience, eager to get on with the tale.

3. In other tales in the Ross field collection, ogres are shown as having a taste for honey; this is the only indication that ogres have plantains and sugar cane at their disposal, and it doubtless reflects the Nkundo diet as attributed to ogres (as, indeed, it is to animals, also, in Nkundo tales).

Narrator: Bomponge Joseph
Location: Tondo, but narrator's
               home was in Besenge,
               near Kalamba
Date: June 1973

71.   *The Provident Man and His Prodigal Companion*

Two men went into the forest to hunt and to fish. They went to work together both for fish and for meat. One of them was named Bembilibefino and the other was called Becwofefola.[1] First they hunted meat and killed many animals. However, Bembilibefino cooked and ate all of the meat that he had killed. In the meantime, Becwofefola carefully dried most of his meat so that he could take it to his family.

Then they began to catch fish. Again, Bembilibefino prepared his fish and ate and ate all that he had and enjoyed it with much relish. Again, Becwofefola dried his over the fire to take home, and ate very little of it himself.

One day the rains came, and they could no longer hunt meat in the forest or fish in the river.

One of them said, "We might as well go home. There certainly is nothing that we can do here."

The other agreed, and they began to pack up. Bembilibefino said to Becwofefola, "Give me a bit of meat and a bit of fish. As you can see, I don't have any to take home with me."

"No, no. I have a very large family at home. We came here to get food for our families. You haven't saved any. But I have carefully saved so that I can take enough home for my family."

Therefore Bembilibefino went home with nothing to show for his trip and his work.

This brief didactic tale encapsulates the Nkundo's concern for sharing with family members the fish and game that he has caught. At the same time, Tale 71 suggests the individual differences that are respected in Nkundo culture. Though

Becwofefola is well aware of Bembilifefino's lack of foresight in eating all the food acquired through hunting and fishing, he is prudent enough to pursue his own way, leaving his companion to discover the high cost of selfishness and greed: immediate family and community disapproval, as well as future hunger for himself and his family.

We have been able to find in the indexes no suitable type number for this narrative. Aarne-Thompson's tale type 280A (The Ant and the Lazy Cricket), the nearest possible parallel, will not do because neither man in the tale is lazy; both are industrious, but one is more prudent, conservative, and self-denying than the other. Klipple, the only indexer furnishing African variants for Aarne-Thompson's type 280A (under the earlier type number, 249), provided no variants helpful in this instance.

Motifs:

C	J711.2.+.**.	Wise man cooks only what he needs, has plenty to take home for sharing; fool eats all he catches, has none to take home for sharing.
T	U130.**.	The power of habit: wise man cooks only what he needs, has plenty; fool cooks all, runs out.
T	J710.	Forethought in provision for food.

1. The names of the two characters in this tale present less of a problem in pronunciation than in translation. Despite repeated efforts, Mrs. Ross and various translation assistants were unable to secure sufficiently adequate English equivalents for the names to allow use of the English forms in the tale. "Bembilibefino" means roughly "day-by-day food hunter" and "Becwofefola" contains a reference to "continually going"; since neither translation is firm enough to warrant its use here as a proper name, we have retained the names provided by the narrator.

Narrator: Bongonda Michele
Location: Bòlèngè
Date: March 1973

72. *The Husband, the Wife, and the Sharing of Meat*[1]

Waji (Wife), along with Bome (Husband), went into the forest. They went there to set traps for catching animals. The first trap that they set caught a wild pig. Wife cooked it and served it to them.

Just before Wife was ready to eat, Husband said, "Wait a minute. Let's ask the owner of the forest. 'Owner of the Forest, Wife has this meat. What about it?'"[2]

"She musn't eat it, lest you are bewitched at the hunt and find nothing."

Husband said to her that, "You mustn't eat it."

So Wife carried her meat to the swamp and put it down into the water. She caught not a few good fish with it.

She came back. "When you begrudged me the wild pig, I got my own food in the swamp."

Husband didn't like this at all, *nyè*. After she did this several times,[3] he cut her head off and buried it in the ground.

He left and kept rejoicing, "Wife is dead and I will no longer have problems with her. She won't bother me again."

He went back to their shelter in the forest and gathered all her things together. About then, Wife's head[4] began to sing,

> The fool, Botamba, ate the wild pig.
> He refused to share with me.
> Then he cut off my head.

Husband answered, "No matter." He dug up the head and with his knife he cut it into pieces, *kwa-kwa-kwa*.[5] Then he dug another hole and buried it again. He said that, "I want to leave here. I'm going home." He went and went and went. When he was almost home, he heard the head again.

> The fool, Botamba, ate the wild pig.
> He refused to share with me.
> Then he cut off my head.

Husband said that, "Are you following me?" He returned to where the head was buried. After he dug it up, he chopped and chopped until it was in small bits. Then he buried it again. When this was finished, he finally arrived home.

Then the head began to sing again.

> The fool, Botamba, ate the wild pig.
> He refused to share with me.
> Then he cut off my head.

The people heard the song. "You have come. What is it that comes after you? Who is talking?"

Husband asked that, "Where?"

"Can't you hear it in the forest?"

Then her song began again.

> The fool, Botamba, ate the wild pig.
> He refused to share with me.
> Then he cut off my head.

As the people looked down the path, they saw the head coming, rolling along from side to side.[6] Then it arrived.

The people called, "Husband, come here. This is the head of your wife. Did you kill her?"

He had nothing to say.

They asked the head that, "What about this palaver?"[7]

She said, "We went into the forest. Botamba killed a wild pig and refused to give me any. I went to the swamp and caught some fish with the meat and didn't give him any. Then he cut off my head."

The evidence was all there, and Botamba had nothing to say.

When Cain killed Abel, Cain found that the thing was not finished.

or

Nothing is hidden which is not found.

[Notes to Tale 72 follow Tale 73.]

Narrator: Tata Manga
Location: Boende
Date: November 1973

73.   *The Husband, the Wife, and the Sharing of Meat* (Variant)

A woman and her husband went into the forest to hunt meat. When they arrived there, they made a place for sleeping and then a room where they could work. When they were there, the husband went to hunt meat, to hunt, to hunt. He put the meat. When he brought the meat, the wife cooked that meat.

At the time of eating it was passed to the husband that he eat. As the wife was ready to eat, he said, "Don't eat it! Don't eat it just now. I will ask the owner of the forest if you can eat it." He asked, he said, "Owner of the Forest! Owner of the Forest! My wife eats this food?" Then he himself said,[8]

> She eats. I will not spring the trap
> to succeed.
> She eats. I will not spring the trap
> to succeed.
> She eats. I will not spring the trap
> to succeed.

Then he said, "You hear. You hear. You hear. Don't eat." So he ate and ate until it was finished. She had nothing to eat.

In the morning he went out again to hunt food. He went to hunt meat. He came back in the evening with meat. His wife prepared and cooked it even though she had had nothing to eat all day. They got ready to eat.

The man said, "Wait! Don't eat. Don't eat. I'll ask the owner of the forest. Owner of the Forest! Owner of the Forest! Shall my wife eat this meat?"

Then,

> She eats. I will not spring the trap
> to succeed.
> She eats. I will not spring the trap
> to succeed.

The husband said, "You hear that. You hear. You are not to eat it. Don't eat. I only am to eat it."

So the wife went hungry again.

Day after day it was like that. The wife had no food to eat. The wife said, "I and my husband have come into the forest. Day after day he eats and I do not eat. I am very hungry. Now I am nearly dead from hunger.[9] What will I do? Why is my husband doing such badness?"

On another morning the husband went into the forest to hunt meat. The wife got her things together for catching fish in the nearby swamp. She cast her lines, and cast them, and cast them in another place. There she found many, many fish and filled her basket with them.

Before her husband returned and could eat fish, she ate and ate until she was satisfied. She left some for later, since her stomach was full.

Her husband returned from the forest, but this time he had no meat, *nyè.* He had gone in vain. *O mpampa.*

The wife said, "You have no meat. You have no meat at all, *nyè.*"

He asked his wife, he said, "No, no meat at all. What kind of food have you had?"

She said, "I've had fish from the nearby swamp."

The husband said, "Ah! I'll have fish tonight."

Then the wife brought the fish for them to eat.[10] Just as her husband was ready to eat, but before the husband ate, she said, "Wait! Wait! Wait! Don't eat. I must ask the owner of the swamp if you may eat." The wife then asked, "Owner of the Swamp! Owner of the Swamp! My husband may eat this fish because he has none?"

The owner of the swamp said,

> He eats. Let the swamp not create.
> He eats. Let the swamp not create.
> He eats. Let the swamp not create.

Then she said, "Do you hear that? Don't eat! Don't eat! Don't eat!"[11]

Her husband sat. The wife ate, *ti-ti-ti,* until the food was all finished in the pot in which the wife cooked the fish. They slept at night. The husband was very hungry. He had had no food.

Then he said, "What am I going to do?"

He found some palm sauce and a bit of fish in the pot. He ate

and ate and ate all he could get. Then his hunger exceeded his good
sense and he tried to lick the pot.

Soon the pot fell over his head, covering his eyes. His wife
heard her husband pounding, *pomp, pomp*, because of the pot.

The wife said, "What are you hunting?"

The husband, "This pot has grabbed me about the head. It
doesn't have loosening power."[12]

The wife said, "Eh! I certainly wish you'd be quiet. If you keep
pounding around, you'll break the pot."

She went back to bed, and her husband kept trying to remove
the pot.

I want that the husband treated his wife badly first. Then the
badness that came to him was greater than that he had done to her
and he had the punishment with the pot on his head.[13]

Although the basic Nkundo concerns for satisfactory marital relationships
and for the importance of sharing are present in both Tale 72 and 73, the plot developments are vastly different. The first narrator details a series of sobering—even
grisly—events and concludes with the expected capital punishment of the guilty
husband; the second narrator approaches the same subject from a humorous stance,
thoroughly relishes the hoaxes and ridiculous incidents, and shares with his listeners
his pleasure at the outcome of the husband's greed. Despite the entertaining tone
of the second narrative, its central thrust is a matter of serious concern both to the
tale-teller and to the members of his community; he elects to make the lesson more
palatable and more memorable by exercising his splendid sense of the comedy of
human interrelationships. Each tale-teller has managed his narrative line skillfully,
and each tale in its own way succeeds in convincing the listeners of the cultural im-
peratives prompting the telling of the tale. This pair of narratives illustrates the
freedom of the Nkundo narrator to develop a significant theme or themes in the
fashion most suitable to his own style and temperament and most applicable to the
needs and mood of his audience.

Lambrecht's tale type 3070 provides the closest classification we have found for
Tale 72; in Lambrecht's sample, "Histoire de Bakanga et de sa femme," drawn from
Mamet's *Le Langage des Bolia* (pp. 93–96), a wife denied meat by her husband nets
fish and refuses to share them with her mate, who kills her and returns to the village.
His wife, transformed into a bird, sings that Bakanga is a thief and reveals his evil
deeds. The wife's liver, given by the husband to the child to cook, says to the child,
"You cook me, your mother—me, who have given you the breast." The murderer
is thereupon confined to his hut, which is set afire.

Klipple in her Ekoi variant for Thompson's motif number J2131.5.2. furnishes the best classification we have found for Tale 73. The sample cited by Klipple, titled "Why Wives Sometimes Leave Their Husbands," is drawn from Talbot's *In the Shadow of the Bush* (1912), page 114, and concerns a husband who, refusing his wife portions of the three animals he has caught, eats the fish caught and cooked by his wife. When he enters his head into the pot to reach the last of the food, his head becomes stuck there.

The refusal of a husband to share meat with his wife or wives occurs also in Lambrecht's tale types 3705 and 3740; in 3705 the hunter counterfeits the "voice from the forest," and in 3740 the thief (who has secured his meat by a magical charm) is allowed by the abused wife to be caught and killed by his pursuers. In Lambrecht's tale type 3650, a stepmother who has neglected her co-wife's orphaned son samples the food he has prepared for himself from leftovers and gets her head caught in the pot; no one is able to remove the pot except the stepson, who says she has deserved this result of stealing his scraps when she had failed to share fish with him.

Several features in Mamet's variant, "Histoire de Bakanga . . . ," deserve special notice: the frequent and functional use of song, the fine sense of economy shown in the saving of the slain wife's flesh for food, the inability of the hunter to catch the bird that tells of the murder, and the murderer's comment just before his death by burning ("You have the power to kill me because I have killed your child"). In translating into French this tale from the Lake Léopold II area, Mamet has retained some of the marks of Nkundo culture (the characteristic kinds of traps, the temporary hut, the typical foods, the woman's reed fish traps) and a touch of Lonkundo diction: "*il met en route, marche, marche.*" There are doubtless other versions of this tale current in the rain-forest area of Zaïre.

Motifs:

C	W151.+.**.	Greedy husband refuses to share meat with wife.
T	C220.	Tabu: eating certain things.
T	C221.1.1.5.**.	Tabu: eating wild pig.
T	J643.	Care against future tyranny.
T	J710.	Forethought in provision for food.
T	H506.	Test of resourcefulness.
T	J830.	Adaptability to overpowering force.
T	C221.1.3.	Tabu: eating fish.
T	J1511.	A rule must work both ways.
T	Q421.**.	Punishment: beheading for offensive manner in self-provision.
C	Q421.+.**.	Beheading as punishment for failure to share fish with husband.
T	S62.	Cruel husband.
C	S62.+.	Husband slays wife for failure to share her fish after his having denied her a share of his meat.
T	E50.	Resuscitation by magic.
C	E225.+.**.	Ghost of murdered wife—as skull—pursues murderer to home of her parents to reveal murder.

T	D1615.7.	Singing head (skull).
T	D1610.5.	Speaking head (skull).
T	E632.1.	Speaking (singing) bones (skull) of murdered person reveal (reveals) murder.
C	D1318.+.**.	Singing skull incriminates murderer.
T	E230.**.	Return from dead in form of skull to ensure punishment for murder.
T	R261.1.	Pursuit by rolling head.
C	N271.+.**.	Singing skull incriminates murderer.
T	N270.	Crime inevitably comes to light.
C	E231.+.**.	Man at in-laws' accused of murder by rolling, talking skull of murdered wife.
T	Q211.3.	Uxoricide punished.
T	C220.**.	Tabu: eating porcupines.
C	J1112.+.**.	Clever wife: wife uses husband's own ruse and consults swamp spirit to deprive husband of a share of her fish.
T	J1510.	The cheater cheated.
T	J2131.5.2.**.	Greedy husband licks out pot, gets it stuck on head.
C	Q272.+.	Greed punished.
C	X0.+.	Greedy husband gets head stuck in pot.

1. This tale was titled by the narrator "A Parable of Cain and Abel." [Narrator's introductory comment: "If you kill someone, you figure your problems with that one are finished. You think you can hide it in the forest and no one, not even God, will know about it."]

2. Only the sense of the song is provided here; Mrs. Ross and her translators were unable to capture the pattern of the original in English.

The "owner of the forest" provides sound reason for the prohibition, one that the wife in a hunting culture would accept as logical. Interestingly, the wife is allowed to *keep* her share of the meat, although she is not permitted to *eat* it.

3. The narrator himself truncates the narrative here. "This" includes both the wife's fishing and her apparent bragging about her skill in providing for herself.

4. The murdered wife's spirit is henceforth embodied in her skull, which continues to testify to the murder despite the husband's efforts to destroy it.

The husband's real name, furnished in the song, means "tree"; the narrator's reason for the choice of this name is not indicated. Could the name serve as a symbol for "provider"—as is suggested by the proverb concluding Tale 80—and thus demonstrate the irony of this man's refusal to provide for his wife? Names are not light matters among the Bantu-speaking peoples, as several of the tales in this volume reveal.

5. "*Kwa*," an onomatopoetic representation of the ringing sound apparently heard when one is cutting up a skull, is generally used with a verb meaning "to fall with metallic ring or crash."

6. A rolling, talking skull is mentioned also in footnote 2, page 53, in Torrend's . . . *Bantu Folk-Lore* . . . for "Open, Open, Little Bird." In this footnote to the tale furnished in full, still another version of a murdered-wife tale is summarized; in

this version, the wife's head comes rolling several nights to the door of the husband's hut, causing the husband to make expiation for his crime, after which both the head and the community leave him in peace.

7. This is the only Ross-collected tale in which a talking skull serves as a witness in a palaver. Quite apart from the fact that the skull itself was evidence of the crime, the source of the grisly account would lend credence to the witness's testimony in a culture profoundly awed by the supernatural.

8. The narrator here suggests that only the husband "heard" the response to his query and then furnished the "owner of the forest's" answer for his wife. This humorous twist, introduced early in the tale, prepares the listeners for the appropriateness of the comical and embarrassing consequence of the guilty husband's maneuvers.

Again, the "answer," as interpreted by the husband, is well chosen for a hunting culture: the wife would not want to interfere with the success of the hunt.

9. The wife had probably managed to secure various edible roots, such as manioc (cassava), but hunger is only temporarily satisfied by such foods; meat in e form is the food that for the Nkundo truly satisfies hunger.

10. In this version, the wife appears to have been less immediately resourceful in dealing with her hunger for meat than was the wife in Tale 72; on the other hand, her husband had eaten all of the meat he had caught, so she had no highly desirable bait at hand for fishing. Too, she seems less inclined than was the other wife to provoke her husband's anger and resentment; she shares with him the fish she has caught, in keeping with the Nkundo emphasis on the importance of sharing. Her compliance makes her ultimate "victory" more acceptable to an Nkundo audience.

11 At this point, the narrator was laughing heartily, appreciating the wife's imitation of her husband's ruse.

12. Again, the narrator laughs, this time at the ridiculousness of the husband's action.

13. This is the only Ross-collected tale in which the storyteller voiced his intention in the narration. Actually, Tata Manga is combining the "teaching" involved in the tale with a description of the technique used for conveying that "teaching" to the listeners. This kind of analysis appears to be quite uncommon among Nkundo narrators, most of whom tell a tale or tales without an expressed awareness of the communication techniques involved in the tale-telling.

Narrator: Bongonda Michele
Location: Bólèngé
Date: March 1973

74. The Importance of Sharing

On another day Balèngè, Wanga, and Bokune went into the forest to hunt copal.[1] They all had good baskets and sounding sticks. Bokune could learn many things from the older ones.

As they went, going, going, down the path, Balèngè and Wanga killed a snake, an *ndóta*.[2] They said, "Let's not take it home to Father. We wouldn't get much of it. We'd have to give the best part to him."

So Balèngè and Wanga cooked it and ate it. They refused a part to Bokune.

Bokune that, "Why won't you share your meat with me?"

"Did you work for it?"

"No matter."

Then they went on into the forest to the swamp. After they finished filling their baskets with copal, *tò*, they went home. Balèngè that, "When we get home, we won't tell anyone that we killed a snake."

Wanga that, "It was very good meat, and they won't like it if they know we had it."

When they reached a village, everyone greeted them. "All of you, Balèngè, Wanga, Bokune, you have all come."

"Yes. We have come."

Bokune began to sing,

> We saw a really good snake.
> They didn't hear me.
> We killed the snake.
> They refused me.
> They didn't hear me.

They all continued going on the path. They came to where there were other people. "Balèngè, Wanga, Bokune, you have all come."

"Yes. We have come."

Then Bokune began again:

> We saw a really good snake.
> They didn't hear me.
> We killed the snake.
> They refused me.
> They didn't hear me.

Balėngė and Wanga said, "Stop! It is bad when you talk about the *ndòta*."

They went and went and went, *te-e-e*, until they came to the house of their father. They sat to talk with him a little.[3] He that, "Balėngė and Wanga, you had a good journey with Bokune?"

Bokune began again:

> We saw a really good snake.
> They didn't hear me.
> We killed the snake.
> They refused me.
> They didn't hear me.

Their father that, "What about this song of Bokune's?"

"It doesn't mean anything."

But Bokune said, "They killed a snake, an *ndòta*, the kind you like best, Father. They cut it up and cooked it, but they gave none to me."

"You are very bad children—badness itself. You killed a good snake, the kind we like best. You ate it. You did not bring it home to us."

Their father cursed them. He refused to give them his blessing.[4] Truly he felt that they were bad.

Any child that eats in secret and does not share is not worthy of the family.

The emphasis on sharing as one of the key factors in the Nkundo value system constitutes the major thrust of Tale 74. Present also, however, are the delicate matter of sibling interrelationships and the basic requirement of filial obedience. Bongonda Michele's audience was a most appropriate one for this particular combination of values, since the children could be reminded about the cost of sibling disputes and of the failure to defer to the father's dominant position in the family, while the parents could benefit from the reminder that firmness in such matters must be exercised if the value system were to be maintained.

No tale type that we have found has proved satisfactory for the classification of this narrative. In the light of the significance of a prescribed division of the spoils of hunting and fishing in many of the Bantu-speaking tribes, a type number is needed for tales reflecting this emphasis.

Motifs:

C   P690.+.   Custom of hunter sharing meat.
C   C680.+.**.   Injunction: certain formula for division of spoils of hunting and fishing must be observed.
T   C220.   Tabu: eating certain things.
C   Q272.+.**.   Failure to share punished.
C   Q272.+.   Greed punished.
C   Q270.+.   Cheating punished.
C   Q380.+.   Breaking tabu punished.
C   Q595.3.+.**.   Forfeiture of father's blessing as punishment for failure to share.

1. For many years in the Cuvette, forest peoples needing ready cash sought copal, a resin found in swamps and used commercially in making varnish, plastics, paints, and other products. The copal, usually gathered by women and young people, was carried home on the back in a large reed basket with shoulder straps. The sounding sticks, spearlike, with metal unbarbed tips, were poked down here and there into the swampy ground to locate the lumps of "ripened" or hardened copal in the ground; these lumps were seldom large (weighing rarely more than a few ounces), but they possessed decided value in the market and were well worth the labor of digging out and carrying home.

This tale's inclusion of a hunt for copal, a substance that for a number of years has had lessened market value because of the development of synthetics but has gradually recovered some of its value, suggests that the tale has survived the effects of acculturation and still affords a lesson or lessons worth communicating to Nkundo audiences.

2. The *ndóta* snake, not identified either by the narrator or by Mrs. Ross's translation aides, was obviously a delicacy—as, indeed, is *any* source of meat, however small. In keeping with every other catch, it would traditionally be shared with the elders in the family, especially the males.

In this instance, the girls probably wrapped it in leaves and baked it in an open fire.

3. The children would sit either on the ground at their father's feet or—if the household were affluent enough—on low stools. Few households own sufficient chairs to seat the whole family.

4. The fact that the father cursed them and refused his blessing indicated the degree of his anger and the severity of his reprimand. It did not mean that the girls were never to return, or that the father-daughter relationship had been permanently destroyed, but that they would be well advised to stay in their mother's hut and out of their father's sight for a long while.

Narrator: Bongonda Michele
Location: Bòlèngè
Date: March 1973

75. *The High Cost of Selfishness*

On a certain day, some women went into the forest to hunt fish.[1] Two of the women, Botomolo (Older Sister) and Bokune (Younger Sister), took their brother Mpèmpè with them.[2] They left their things in the shelter and snared many fish. Each woman cooked some of her fish and then dried some of it to take home with her. For no reason, Older Sister refused to share her fish with Mpèmpè; he shared the fish of Younger Sister. She did in this manner for many days. After some time, Mpèmpè said, "You! Why won't you give me any food? I don't understand."

Older Sister answered, "Go to Younger Sister. She will give you food."

"But you brought me on this journey?"

On that night, they heard a very large bird. He was near their shelter. He perched and began to sing,

> You take me for Mpèmpè.
> Do not hesitate to learn.
> You ask me for Mpèmpè's mother.
> Do not hesitate to learn.
> You are a knife. I am a knife.
> Do not hesitate to learn.
> You are a shield. I am a shield.
> Do not hesitate to learn.

The bird flapped his wings, *pwu-pwu*,[3] over the shelter as he left.

The next morning Older Sister and Younger Sister went to hunt fish. They returned to the shelter before sunset. They dried some fish and cooked some fish. Younger Sister shared hers with Mpèmpè, and Older Sister ate her own. That evening, *pwu-pwu*, they heard the flapping of the wings of the huge bird:

> You take me for Mpèmpè.
> Do not hesitate to learn.
> You ask me for Mpèmpè's mother.
> Do not hesitate to learn.

> You are a knife. I am a knife.
> Do not hesitate to learn.
> You are a shield. I am a shield.
> Do not hesitate to learn.

Again he flapped his wings in the manner of the night which was finished. He did this seven doings, *ngòkò, ngòkò, ngòkò*.[4]

On another day, Mpèmpè said, "Our food is finished. I will go home and bring some food here."

That night after Mpèmpè had finished going, the bird came again, *pwu-pwu*.

> You take me for Mpèmpè.
> Do not hesitate to learn.
> You ask me for Mpèmpè's mother.
> Do not hesitate to learn.
> You are a knife. I am a knife.
> Do not hesitate to learn.
> You are a shield. I am a shield.
> Do not hesitate to learn.

He flew near the entrance of the shelter and again sang the song. It was quietness itself in the shelter; he went inside. Then he took the eyes of all the people who were there, plucking, plucking. He put the eyes in a small pouch which he carried on his back.

Because of this, when morning came, no one could see the path in front of the shelter. When Mpèmpè came with the food, he found that no person had eyes. "What a palaver! What'll we do?"

He returned home that he talk with the relatives. "There in the shelter a big bird came and he took the eyes of Older Sister and Younger Sister," he said.

"Let's all go and discuss this with the witch doctor."[5] They went.

The witch doctor listened to their news. Then he said to Mpèmpè, "Look! That bird lives in the forest. You go there. You can live in his home in the way of his workman. While you are there, you can learn all of the manner in which he lives and how he cares for his affairs."[6]

Then Mpèmpè did as the witch doctor had said. He went to the home of the big bird and lived there as his workman. While he was there, he was watching the bird that he learn all about him.

On another day the big bird said to Mpèmpè, "I am going to hunt food. You take care of the house while I am gone."

The opportunity had arrived for which Mpėmpė had been waiting. After not a long time, he began to look for the pouch. Quickly he found it and he went on his way. The bird was surprised when he did not find Mpėmpė and the pouch with the eyes.

Mpėmpė returned to the shelter and he gave Younger Sister her eyes. But he refused to give the eyes to Older Sister. "You don't do the right things. You do not hear what is right."

Older Sister begged and she promised until after not a short time Mpėmpė returned her eyes to her.[7] Then he taught her, "You did badness. I do not like that way. If you do, things much worse will happen to all of us. I do not feel happiness in the way you act." Then the three of them went home, *bwó*.[8]

After some days had passed, those three went again to the shelter because all the fish they had gotten had been eaten. While they were going in the path to the shelter, they found a very large mushroom[9] growing. They picked it and carried it with them. That evening Older Sister cooked the mushroom, but she refused to give some of it to Mpėmpė.

In the morning itself, when the first cock crowed, the small cuckoo bird fluffed his wings, *ku-ku-ku*.[10] They heard,

> You picked my mushroom.
> Be crippled.
> You picked my mushroom.
> Be crippled.

Mpėmpė began to collect all their belongings. "Hurry, everybody! The owner of the mushroom is coming. He feels that we have taken his very own child. Come on. Let us go quickly."

> You picked my mushroom.
> Be crippled.
> You picked my mushroom.
> Be crippled.

An ogre followed them, and they were having difficulty that he not arrive near them. He was close.

> You picked my mushroom.
> Be crippled.
> You picked my mushroom.
> Be crippled.

He was near; they felt him. They came to a bokungu tree and Mpėmpė called out, "Lower your limb. We need help." The tree let a large branch fall, and Younger Sister and Mpėmpė climbed on it. Then he tried to keep Older Sister from climbing the tree.

"Leave the tree for me to climb. The ogre will kill me dead dead."

The limb of the bokungu went to sleep and fell to the ground. In time, Older Sister climbed, and the limb of the tree returned above.

The ogre arrived and studied what was there. He had desire for food. "*Na-a-a!* I'll be able to live now. I have very much good meat."

He went home quickly to call the other ogres. "I have found a tree that has many monkeys, *bwė.* Come! Let's go kill them." They took their axes and went to the place of the bokungu tree. One ogre began to cut the tree, *kao-kao.* They all sang,

> We cut the tree, cutting, cutting,
> The earth nourishes us, cutting, cutting.
> We find the fruit between the villages, cutting, cutting.

After he had cut a gash in the tree, the tree began to complain, "Stop! Stop!" And the gash was healed. Then another ogre began to cut the tree, *kao-kao.*

> We cut the tree, cutting, cutting.
> The earth nourishes us, cutting, cutting.
> We find the fruit between the villages, cutting, cutting.

All this time, the ogres were singing their cutting song. At each time that the tree was nearly falling, the gash in the tree was healed. Each ogre cut the tree, and each time it healed itself.

> We cut the tree, cutting, cutting.
> The earth nourishes us, cutting, cutting.
> We find the fruit between the villages, cutting, cutting.

After a time, every ogre had cut, cutting, and all their axes were dull. "What'll we do now?" asked one.

"We'll have to go home and get other axes." Then they left to get sharp axes.

Then Older Sister and Younger Sister and their brother quickly climbed out of the tree and they went on the path. After not a long time, they came to the home of the bird who knows the way of the ogres. Itóji agreed to help them. He said, "Go that you talk with the chief of the ogres. Lokilo lives in a village not too far on the path."

They went on the path toward that village. When they were near to that village, they heard, "*Kao-kao!*" It was the ogres running to where they were. Quickly they were face to face, *ta-ka-ba!*[11]

"Who are you? Aren't you the ones who were up in the tree that we tried to cut down?"

"No! No! Not us! We have been to the blacksmith's to make some spears."[12]

"Truly not you?"

"No! No! Not us!"

"Not you at all?"

"No! No! Not us!" Then, to prove that they were carefree and had no burdens, they all began to dance and to sing,

> I have never seen goodness
> From the time of my birth.

After those three had danced and sung, the ogres said to them, "Go your way. We can see that you aren't those people."

After they had gone not far, they met other ogres, *ta-ka-ba!* "Who are they? They are the people who were in the tree that we tried to cut down."

"No! No! Not us! We have come from the blacksmith's where we made spears."

"But truly you are like them. Truly it isn't you?"

"No! No! Not us!"

"But they were like you."

"No! No! Not us!"

> I have never seen goodness
> From the time of my birth.

After a while, the ogres agreed and told them, "Go. You aren't the people which we seek."

Again they started in the path. Then, *ta-ka-ba!*, other ogres were there.

"Look! Here are the people who were above in the tree which we tried to cut down."

"No! No! Not like that. We have been in the place of the black-smith's that we make some spears."

"But truly we feel that you are those people."

"No! No! Not us!"

"But you are like them."

Again they began to dance and sing:

> I have never seen goodness
> From the time of my birth.

Then these ogres also told them, "Go as you wish. You are not those people."

At that time, they had finished reaching the village. In this village was a house that belonged to some of their family. They ran to that house and they blocked the door and the windows. But the ogres came and they tied the door and the windows from the outside. In this manner no way of escape was there.[13] The ogres rejoiced. "Now we have our meat. We will live well."

The captives paid a small boy to go and tell their relatives of their difficulties.[14] The family was surprised. "What'll we do?"

Then they called a forest rat; they called an aardvark; they called an anteater. They said to them, "Our family is trapped in a house by ogres and can't go. Go and dig them out that they come home." Then these three went to the house where the captives were, and they began digging, digging, under the wall of the house.

While they were digging, the people in the house continued singing that the ogres would know that they were there. And they didn't wish that the ogres hear the animals digging.

When the tunnel was sufficient, they all crawled through it and were free to go home. Then, before they left, they set a trap in the tunnel[15] and left it there. As they went, they sang,

> I have never seen goodness
> From the time of my birth.

After not a long time, the ogres found that even though they had closed the house with force itself, those people were gone. "They have gone. What can we do now?"

The eldest of the ogres, Lomata, began to crawl into the house through the tunnel. His neck was caught in the trap and he was killed dead. The ogres began to wail,

> Lomata, our eldest,
> Has his neck caught in a cord.

They felt sorrow itself. "Here we are. These people who were to be our feast have dug out and are at home. Lomata is dead. What can we do?" The ogres went home with no food and with sorrow.

Mpèmpè and Older Sister and Younger Sister arrived home without another palaver.

Do not return evil for evil; return good for evil.

[Notes to Tale 75 follow Tale 76.]

Narrator: Bongonda Michele
Location: Bòlèngè
Date: March 1973

76. *Compensation for Evil*

Two girls who had the same mother and the same father went to hunt fish. Bokune (Younger Sister) said that, "I'm going to get some salt."

Botomolo (Older Sister) said that, "No, don't go. I'll get enough for both of us."

Older Sister got salt, but Younger Sister also got salt and hid it.

They needed a dipper in order to dip the water out of the hole in the swamp.[16] They remembered that they didn't have one. Younger Sister said that, "I'll go and get mine."

But Older Sister said that, "No, no. Don't bother. I'll bring two."

Younger Sister said that, "I have no complaint." But she got one and hid it nearby.

Then Older Sister said that, "When we finish working here, we'll want to rub ourselves with oil."

"I'll get mine," said Younger Sister.

"No, no. I'll get enough for both of us."

"No matter." But Younger Sister got her own oil and hid it nearby.

When they reached the river bank, many people came, and with them came their brother, Nkana. They all went out in canoes and caught not a few fish and returned to the beach.

Younger Sister cooked hers and Older Sister cooked hers. When they were ready to eat, Nkana said that, "Older Sister, give me salt."

"No. I don't want to. I don't have much, and if I share with you, it will soon be gone."

"Why don't you make some more?"

"How can I do that now?"

"No matter."

Then Younger Sister got her salt and salted the fish.

"I'm glad I didn't share with you. Look. You have your own."

Then they all needed to wash and rub their bodies with oil. Nkana asked Older Sister that, "Give me some oil that I rub it on my body."

Older Sister answered that, "If I give you some, it will be finished very quickly."

"What if it is? How am I to rub my body? But I have no complaint."

Younger Sister got the oil that she had hidden, and they rubbed it on their bodies.

Older Sister said that, "I brought some for you, but I'm glad I didn't give it to you."

Then they decided to go into the forest to hunt fish in a ditch in the swamp. They each needed a dipper for this.[17] Nkana asked that, "Older Sister, give me a dipper."

"No. If I give you one, both of mine will be finished in one day."

"No word. Keep yours. I'll get another one."

Younger Sister got hers and started to dip water with it.[18]

"I'm glad I didn't let you use mine. I didn't know you brought yours."

Not a little while later, Younger Sister and Older Sister each had a baby, both born at about the same time.[19] Older Sister said that, "I want both babies to sleep with me."

"Why do you want this?"

Older Sister answered that, "You are just a child and don't really know how to care for them. I'll sleep with both of them."

She lay down to sleep that night. Her own baby was against her, and Younger Sister's child was on the outside next to the fire. She kept turning and turning in her sleep and was crowding Younger Sister's baby closer to the fire.

But Younger Sister didn't sleep. She had her eyes there. She saw Older Sister push her child nearer the fire little by little. She called, "Now you are really sleeping. Are you caring for the babies?"

"Yes. I'm caring for them."

Older Sister went to sleep again, but she kept turning and pushing the baby toward the fire. Younger Sister watched and then carefully picked up her baby and cared for it herself.

Older Sister didn't know Younger Sister's baby was gone and kept pushing the baby. Then the baby let out a cry and was in the fire. Older Sister called that, "Your baby, Younger Sister. It's in the fire."

Younger Sister answered that, "It's not my child. My baby is here in bed with me. I have already taken it."

Older Sister said that, "What do you mean? Now you have caused my baby to be in the fire."

"No, not I. It was you who pushed it into the fire. You can blame only yourself, with much blaming."

Older Sister thought that, "My child is dead. I must seek revenge." She went into the forest to call some ogres to help her. She thought that, "I myself can't seem to get ahead of her, but I can find help from the ogres."

Nkana and Younger Sister began to plan. "What will we do? Shall we go home, or shall we seek help?" They decided to talk it over with the bird who is like a witch doctor, Itòji. They found him and told him their problem. "Our sister has gone to the ogres. What shall we do about it?"

Itòji said that, "Now, you do like this. You, Nkana, you make a big basket. Then put your sister and her baby in it. You carry it down the path. When you meet ogres, say to them that, 'I am Kotoyakoto. I am from Elanga and I'm going to Buyaeyeka.' When they hear that you are Kotoyakoto, they won't bother you at all but will let you pass. Do you hear?"

"Yes, I hear."

Nkana got the materials for making the basket. Then he put Younger Sister and her baby inside, just as Itòji had told him to do. Then he started down the path. Younger Sister and her baby could not be seen. They went and went and, *sa-ka-fa*,[20] there were the ogres.

They said that, "Who are you?"

Nkana answered that, "I am Kotoyakoto. I am from Elanga and I'm going to Buyaeyeka."

They were surprised. "Ah-h-h. You are Kotoyakoto. That is something. Then dance for us."

Nkana's dance was a dance and a song of joy:

> You don't see me,
> Koto,[21]
> But I look myself over.
> Koto.
> I'm like a beautiful bird,
> Koto,
> A bird from the river.
> Koto.

The ogres said that, "Go ahead. You may pass."

So Nkana went on ahead with his basket. Soon he saw some more ogres coming down the path.

They said that, "Stand where you are. Who are you?"

"I am Kotoyakoto. I am coming from Elanga and am going to Buyaeyeka."

"You are Kotoyakoto himself? Then dance for us."

So Nkana began to sing and dance.

> You don't see me,
> Koto,
> But I look myself over.
> Koto.
> I'm like a beautiful bird,
> Koto,
> A bird from the river.
> Koto.

"Our chief is on a journey," said the ogres.

"Yes, indeed."

"Go your way."

Once more Nkana picked up his basket and went his way. Soon he met some more ogres, and the same ceremony took place and he passed them by.[22] Then he saw some more ogres, but this time Older Sister was with them. She called out that, "There they are; there they are! Those are the ones I told you about. Kill them!"

"No. We are afraid to do anything until we know more about them."

"Look in the basket," she said.

"No. We might have a real palaver if we did. Who are you?" they asked.

Nkana answered that, "I am Kotoyakoto. I am coming from Elanga and am going to Buyaeyeka." Then he sang his song:

> You don't see me,
> Koto,
> But I look myself over.
> Koto.
> I'm like a beautiful bird,
> Koto,
> A bird from the river.
> Koto.

Older Sister said that, "No, that isn't true at all. Look in his basket. You will find people inside."

"That just isn't possible. How could they be there? His is of Kotoyakoto, our chief. How would we dare to look there?"

Older Sister kept telling them that, "Open the basket."

But they refused. They felt that they couldn't without having a real problem. They said that, "Go on your way."

So Nkana picked up the basket and went on down the path.

Older Sister and the ogres went on their way until they came to the place where she and her brother and sister had been sleeping. They found the burned skeleton of Older Sister's baby[23] and ate it.

Then they asked Older Sister that, "Where are the people that you promised us would be here?"

"They are the ones that I pointed out to you on the path."

"No, no. That just can't be."

So since she couldn't give them the food she had promised, they killed her and ate her.

Admittedly, several of the elements in this pair of Bongonda Michele narratives mark Tales 75 and 76 as quite different from one another—for example, the allegiance of the human actors to one another against the ogres in Tale 75 as opposed to the alliance of Older Sister with the ogres against her siblings in Tale 76, the selfishness of Older Sister in Tale 75 as opposed to the outright evil and malice of Older Sister in Tale 76, and the use of animals in effecting an escape from the ogres in Tale 75 as opposed to the use of a basket and a deceptive song in effecting an escape from the ogres and from Older Sister in Tale 76. Despite these and other marked differences, however, the two tales appear to us to belong together because of their common emphasis on certain aspects of the Nkundo value system. The stress on the importance of sharing—whether of fish or of needful supplies—is strong in both tales. Central also is the significance of family loyalty, including the imperative for mutual consideration and protection. Awe of the supernatural and the need for resourcefulness in countering supernatural powers are evidenced in both tales. The trait of mercy, valued by the Nkundo, is emphasized by its presence in Tale 75 and by its absence in Tale 76. Above all, these tales share the Nkundo understanding that violation of cultural values is not without cost—that the price paid for straying from the path set by "the fathers" is one that few are ready or able to pay. No listener to these tales could fail to be reminded of that basic truth.

No tale type that we have found is sufficiently comprehensive to meet the classificatory needs of either or both of these narratives. Help is afforded on certain portions of one or the other of the two Ross-collected stories by two citations, one from Lambrecht and the other from Klipple. In Lambrecht's tale type 3587, based on a tale collected in Stanleyville (now Kisangani) in the area east of the Cuvette, a younger brother accompanying his sister and other girls to fish proved very helpful to them in their work; all the girls shared their fish with him except his sister, "who was still angry." Beyond this point, there is no development in the Lambrecht-cited tale; both of the Ross-collected tales incorporate supernatural elements that increase

their complexity and deepen the listeners' sense of the potential cost of selfishness
and of evil.

In the tale "Alas! Father! at the Temple" (from Torrend's ... *Bantu Folk-
Lore* ..., pp. 32–37), cited by Klipple as an Area IV (Congo) variant of Aarne-
Thompson's tale type 1119, the head wife asks the child of a co-wife to sleep with
her and her child, intending to kill the co-wife's child with a heated knife; the child
changes places with the head wife's child, and the head wife kills her own child
instead. Tale 76 of the Ross collection has the younger sister remove her baby, thus
exposing the older sister's baby to the fate intended for the younger one's child;
this plot development prompts the older sister to seek the aid of the ogres in obtaining
revenge and results eventually in her own death, even as the head wife dies when
her criminal act is revealed to the father by the living child.

Motifs:

C	C680.+.**.	Injunction: certain formula for division of spoils of hunting and fishing must be observed.
C	P690.+.	Custom of hunter sharing meat (fish).
T	Q2.	Kind and unkind.
C	P251.5.+.**.	Elder sister abuses young brother.
C	L31.+.**.	Young brother scorned by selfish older sister but aided by younger sister saves all three from a witch-bird and from ogres.
T	G211.4.5.**.	Witch in form of large eye-plucking bird.
T	B872.**.	Giant bird with witch-doctor powers plucks human eyes and keeps them in pouch.
C	G353.+.**.	Monstrous bird plucks out eyes of sleeping girls.
C	S165.+.**.	Bird plucks out eyes of two girls.
T	F405.**.	Hero learns magic tricks of giant witch-bird and recovers his sisters' stolen eyes.
T	G270.**.	Witch-bird escaped by hero after hero's recovery of pouch of eyes plucked from his sisters.
T	D2161.3.1.1.**.	Eyes plucked out are magically replaced through hero's following directions of witch doctor.
T	G462.**.	Hero as servant in witch-bird's house to learn his ways and to recover pouch of stolen eyes.
C	W10.+.**.	When hero recovers stolen eyes, he returns them to selfish sister who has abused him.
C	D270.+.**.	Transformation: ogre's "child" to huge mushroom.
T	R260.	Pursuits.
T	R311.	Tree refuge.
T	F979.4.**.	Tree bends down to allow hero and sisters to escape from ogres.
T	F811.**.	In response to request, tree bends down to provide escape route for hero and sisters.
T	D950.**.	Magic tree—bends to rescue fleeing hero and sisters.

T	R251.	Flight on a tree, which ogre tries (ogres try) to cut down.
C	F810.+.**.	Tree heals itself when almost severed by ogres.
T	D1602.2.2.**.	Tree of refuge magically heals itself when cut by ogres.
T	D950.**.	Magic tree—heals itself when cut.
T	R243.**.	Fugitives aided by helpful bird (*itóji*).
T	B469.**.	Helpful birds—miscellaneous: *itóji*, helpful in countering powers of ogres.
T	P447.	Blacksmith.
T	G501.	Stupid ogre(s).
T	J1020.**.	Strength in unity: brother and sisters by singing and dancing cooperate to deceive pursuing ogres.
T	G555.**.	Boy and sisters captured by ogres dance and sing to demonstrate that they are not the victims sought, and are released.
T	N827.	Child as helper.
T	K640.	Escape by help of confederate.
T	B524.2.**.	Animals overcome man's (brother and sisters') adversary (adversaries) by strategy.
T	R243.	Fugitives aided by helpful animal(s).
T	B540.	Animal rescuer or retriever.
C	B437.1.+.**.	Helpful forest rat.
T	B544.**.	Forest rat helps dig escape tunnel for hero and sisters.
T	B449.**.	Helpful wild beasts—miscellaneous: (*Tubulidentata*) aardvark.
T	B544.**.	Aardvark helps dig escape tunnel for hero and sisters.
T	B449.**.	Helpful wild beasts—miscellaneous: anteater.
T	B544.**.	Anteater helps dig escape tunnel for hero and sisters.
T	R211.3.	Escape through underground passage.
T	G510.	Ogre killed, maimed, or captured.
T	P253.**.	Younger brother aids in escape of captive sister(s).
T	R156.	Brother rescues sister(s).
T	P690.**.	Customs—miscellaneous: sharing among family members.
T	J10.	Wisdom (knowledge) acquired from experience.
T	S70.**.	Cruel sister.
T	P252.1.1.**.	Elder sister abuses younger sister, attempts murder of sister's child.
T	J670.**.	Forethought in defences against others: mother removes her child from side nearest fire and thus prevents evil sister's effort to roll child into fire.
T	S322.3.**.	Evil sister rolls own child into fire, mistaking child for that of her sister.
T	S302.	Children (child) murdered.
T	N338.	Death as result of mistaken identity: wrong person killed.
T	K1600.	Deceiver falls into own trap.
T	K929.	Murder by strategy—miscellaneous.
T	N812.**.	Ogres, on promise of human meat, aid evil sister in seeking revenge against younger sister.

C	L31.+.**.	Young brother scorned by evil older sister but aided by younger sister saves younger sister from ogres whose aid is enlisted by older sister.
T	P253.2.1.	Brother faithful to persecuted sister.
C	R336.+.**.	Refuge in basket.
T	G555.	Escape from pursuing ogres by singing deceptive song.
T	G570.**.	Escape from pursuing ogres by concealment in basket supposed to belong to ogre chief.
T	Q261.	Treachery punished.
C	Q411.+.	Death as punishment for (outcome of) cruelty.
T	Q415.0.1.	Punishment: being eaten by demon (ogres).

1. [Narrator's explanatory comment: "It was the dry season, when the water in the swamps was low and the fish would be easy to catch."]

Again, the relationship of family members has given the characters their names; in this instance, since "*Nkana*" ("Sibling of the Opposite Sex") was not used by the narrator, it is to be assumed that the women had more than one brother.

2. [Narrator's explanatory comment: "He was their own brother, because he had the same mother and father as they had."]

3. Onomatopoetic representation of the flapping of large wings.

4. In Lonkundo, participial forms of verbs often function thus; "*ngôkô*" is Lonkundo for "doing," here indicated as an act, "a doing." The sense of "*ngôkô*" when it is repeated is "like that, like that, like that."

5. "*Nkanga*," the Lonkundo term for a witch doctor who deals with many kinds of medicines and many forms of witchcraft, was used by the narrator as the proper name of the expert consulted. His advice would of course be followed.

6. There is a suggestion here of a "sorcerer's apprentice" situation, but the narrator does not allow himself to be drawn into a digression that will divert listeners from the central thrust of the narrative.

7. Here, the trait of mercy is shown in a person-to-person situation. (See Tales 43–46 and 93 for instances of person-to-animal and animal-to-person mercy.) At no time in this tale is there evidence, however, that Mpémpé has *forgiven* Older Sister for her unkind behavior. (For a poignant instance of people-to-people mercy, see "Le mari et ses deux femmes," in de Bouveignes' *Entendu dans la Brousse*, pp. 156–160.)

8. "*Bwô*," suggesting "right away," emphasizes the sense of urgency felt by the three after their narrow escape from the witch-bird.

9. In Nkundo folktales, a mushroom tends to be suspect, not only in the Ross field-collected tales but in other narratives as well. In a tale found in de Rop's . . . *woordkunst* . . . (pp. 96–99) involving a marriage between a hunter and an other-worldly woman, mushrooms grow out of the mouths of the dead in the wife's village. See also page 261 of the present volume for a summary of a tale from *Bekolo Bêmô* . . . illustrating the questionable character of mushrooms.

Mushrooms function in other forms of verbal art, as well as in folktales. An attractive illustration is furnished by an Igbo riddle (from Okeke's *Tales of Land of Death*, p. 109):

"What is the chicken of the poor?" "Mushroom."

10. An onomatopoetic sound representing the flapping of small wings.

11. "*Ta-ka-ba*" is an ideophone used here to create the feeling that the ogres were not there and then, suddenly, there they were. The narrator *shouted* this expression each time, as one might say "Boo!" or "Bang-bang!" to startle the listener.

12. The stupidity of the ogres is apparent here; no mention is made of the possession of spears by the human characters, yet the ogres did not question the absence of evidence of a visit to the blacksmith's "to make some spears."

13. The narrator explained, in answer to Mrs. Ross's question, that the ogres had wrapped *ngòji* vines around and around the house, covering the door and the windows and tying them securely. Such vines are considered impossible to break.

14. No explanation was given by the narrator as to how a "small boy" might have been found as a messenger in what apparently was an ogre village. The audience's "willing suspension of disbelief" is confirmed by the unquestioning acceptance of this device for securing aid, as well as of the use of the forest rat, the aardvark, and the anteater—all strong diggers—to dig a tunnel under the house.

15. Again, a trap strong enough to kill the eldest of the ogres is at hand for the captives' use; the Nkundo would use a trap, and a trap is therefore furnished. The narrator's persuasive powers and storytelling skill carry him comfortably through the introduction of this unlikely but indispensable insurance against pursuit of the three by the ogres.

16. [Narrator's explanatory comment: "Then they could pick up the fish that were there."]

17. Nkundo men do not normally use dippers in fishing, nor would a full-grown male fish with a group of women in the swamp. Nkana is obviously too young to go fishing with the men or by himself in a man's fashion, by spearing, netting, or trapping fish. For the sake of the narrative, he is kept here with his sisters, and subsequently serves as the protector of Younger Sister against the malevolence of Older Sister.

Dippers are made of solidly woven reeds; sieves are of reeds woven more loosely. The Nkundo listeners, as well as Nkana, would readily accept Older Sister's reluctance to share her dipper, since by double use it would be worn out after a few hours and would then be of service to neither of them.

18. Nkana appears to have been overlooked by the narrator at this point, but this "oversight" is dramatically sound: the listeners' attention is focused on the development of the animosity of Older Sister toward Younger Sister and the effort of the former to destroy the latter's infant.

19. No indication has been given that either girl is married, nor is any clue given as to the paternity of the two infants. (The matter of the elapsing of time is neatly covered by "Not a little while later.") Since premarital pregnancies among the Nkundo are socially acceptable, this situation would not disturb the members of the audience, intent on the interrelationships of the siblings. The introduction of infants onto the scene sharpens even more the discord between the sisters, since a child is of inestimable worth to any Nkundo woman; each mother would yearn to

care for her own child. Still, Younger Sister would be expected to yield to her elder in the demand that both babies sleep beside Older Sister.

20. Here, Bongonda Michele uses a different ideophone, "*sa-ka-fa*," to express the suddenness of the ogres' appearance; "*sa-ka-fa*" and "*ta-ka-ba*" (in Tale 75) both reflect this narrator's delight in sounds. In the present tale, the storyteller uses this ideophone just once; since he values more highly for narrative purposes the hoax perpetrated on the ogres by Nkana's pretending to be Kotoyakoto, their chief, he saves his dramatic emphasis for the encounters in which this deception is practiced.

21. "*Koto*," the root word for the ogre chief's name, is used by the narrator as the chorus for Nkana's song identifying himself as the chief.

22. This truncation on the part of the tale-teller reserves the primary dramatic impact for the confrontation of the false chief with Older Sister.

23. The crowning sign of Older Sister's inhumanity is provided by her failure to give the body of her murdered child proper burial. Given this indication, those in the audience who had had any sympathy whatsoever for Older Sister would abandon her cause and confirm the proverb with which the narrator concludes his tale. Just as no woman would sell her cooking pot (her dearest material possession), no woman worthy of the name would reject her own family.

Narrator: Mpanga Iyende
Location: Bonga-Iteli
Date: December 1973

77. *The Children and the Two Paths*[1]

A certain woman was going to hunt fish. When she went to hunt fish, when she had gone, *ti-i-i*, a way, she arrived at a division in the path. There in the path, the path was two. One was a very good path, pleasing; the other path was bad. She went on the bad path.

She said to her children, three children, "When I go for fish, if the child cries, when you are on the path pass on the bad path. Do not pass on the good path. You understand."

The children said, "*Bonne*."[2]

"Now I am going." The mother went to hunt fish.

After she had gone for fish, *ti-ti-ti-ti-ti*, the child became fretful, became fretful. She cried. The first child said, "*Mu!* Illness is there. The child is sick."

She said, "We do not know about that. Mother said that we were to follow her."[3]

When they were on the path, the child who was the second arrived at that path. She said, "*Mu!* This path isn't good. Mother said we should go on the bad path. How can we pass on the bad path?"

The first said, "Let us pass on the good path."

"But Mother said for us to go on the bad path."

"It would be very difficult. Here is the good path. Let's go on it."

"Let's go."[4]

Then they went, looking up, looking up.[5]

Suddenly they arrived in the village of the ogres. They found the first ogre.

He asked, "Where are you going?"

They said, "We are going to follow Mother. She went to hunt fish and the youngest cried. We didn't know."

"What of us? You may pass, but first let me tell you the problem. Be careful when you arrive at another ogre. That other ogre, his name is Bokulaka."[6]

Then, "We don't know. We follow Mother. Mother went." Then they went.

Then they arrived at the house of the third,[7] then they arrived at the house of the fourth, then they arrived at the house of the fifth, then they arrived at the house of the sixth, then they arrived at the house of the seventh, then they arrived at the house of the eighth.[8] After they arrived at the house of the eighth ogre, of the ninth, the chief at the tenth.[9] They said, [10]

.   .   .

"Come close a bit. I can't hear you, the things you say. Where are you going?"[11]

.   .   .

"Come here."

Then when they came nearer, he swallowed them.

The mother left her fishing. When she arrived, nobody was in the house. She hunted them. "My children! Where are they?"

"They followed you as you said."[12]

She said, "My children don't always follow the path of wisdom, *nyè.*"

She met someone on the path and was told, "I saw your children going toward the village of the ogres."
She arrived at the first house of the ogres' village.[13]

⋅   ⋅   ⋅

Then she passed. She arrived at the house of the second ogre.[14]

⋅   ⋅   ⋅

Then she passed. She arrived at the third, the fourth, the fifth, the sixth—she arrived.[15]
Then, before she went there she had her small knife, her sack of salt, and she went with her enema bag.[16]
She went and arrived in behalf of[17] the seventh house, the eighth house, the ninth house.[18]

⋅   ⋅   ⋅

She arrived at the ogre at the end, who was their chief.[19]

⋅   ⋅   ⋅

"Come nearer. I can't hear you talk. I can't hear you."[20]

⋅   ⋅   ⋅

"Come still closer. Come a little nearer."
She came nearer.[21]

⋅   ⋅   ⋅

As she spoke that way, he swallowed her. When he swallowed her there, she found many people who were also living there. She saw her children.[22]
"What is the thing you have done? I told you that if you went on the path, follow me. The good path do not follow. Why did you go that way? You do not have wisdom. I said, 'Go on the bad path,' but suddenly you went on the good path."
She had her knife there and she began to bore a hole in the skin[23] of the ogre now. She was succeeding.
Ogre said, "I feel the knife in the place of the food where I swallowed the person; it is not quiet."[24]
The wife said, "*N-n-n?* Perhaps it's because the woman there has fat."[25]
Then the mother cut the skin; she cut, she cut, she bored some more.
He said, "My wife, the thing with me is that I do not feel well. Give me some hot water to drink."

His wife gave him some hot water to drink. *Ti-i-i*, then. That woman cut and continued to cut at the skin.

He said, "Wife, the sickness has become very bad."

Then the mother cut all the first skin itself. The ogre was dead. He fell. Then all the people were set free. They came out of his stomach and thanked the woman for their freedom. Then they went home.

And to you, little children, when your mother tells you don't do in that way, do not cross over as did the two children.[26]

And get water.[27]
It is finished.[28]

During the telling of Tale 77—the last of Mpanga Iyende's tales, recorded in a traditional outdoor evening storytelling session—there were two audience sounds quite apart from those described in the footnotes: a repeated, racking coughing by people of various ages, especially of one small child (characteristic of the pulmonary illnesses afflicting residents of this swampy area with its chilly nights), and the giggling of little children. At one point, a mother in the audience diverted her fretful child by playing a finger- or toe-game with him, and snatches of words of the accompanying rhyme can be heard on the tape. Various audience responses reflected the emotional impact of the story on the listeners: laughs, giggles, groans, one sound equivalent to Western-type booing, and vocal support for ideophones and instances of onomatopoeia.

Lambrecht's tale type 3952 (6) offers some coverage for the present tale in that a mother (the ogre's wife) goes to seek her child, is swallowed by the ogre who had deceived and swallowed the child, finds inside the ogre not only the child she had been seeking but also earlier children taken from her by the ogre (as well as other people he had swallowed), and uses sharp razors to cut an opening in the ogre permitting the escape of all his victims. Arewa's tale type 3952B includes two disobedient children who are eaten by a devil as a consequence of their disobedience; they are later rescued by the obedient third child. Neither of these tale types includes the combination of disobedience by children and rescue from an ogre by the mother, nor does any other tale type in the indexes consulted.

Motifs:

C	C680.+.**.	Injunction: do not take the good path; take the bad path.
T	C614.**.	Forbidden road (path).
T	J652.	Inattention to warnings.
T	Q325.	Disobedience punished.

C	G361.+.**.	Ten ogres, each one higher in rank than the one before.
C	G11.15.+.**.	Lesser ogres reserve choice human victims for cannibal chief's consumption.
T	K815.**.	Victims lured by kind words (question) approach trickster (ogre) and are swallowed.
C	H1229.+.**.	Mother goes on quest for lost children.
T	R153.**.	Parent (mother) rescues three lost children.
T	G551.	Rescue from ogre by relative.
T	G512.1.	Ogre killed with knife (sword).
T	F912.2.	Victim kills swallower from within by cutting.
T	F913.	Victims rescued from swallower's belly.

1. There is no formulaic opening aside from "A certain woman" present on the field tape for this tale. Since on several occasions Mpanga Iyende had used some sort of preliminary expression and since Bob Stewart (taping the tales) had on other occasions interrupted a formulaic ending in order to conserve tape, it is possible that such an economy measure deprived this present version of a traditional opening.

2. Though the tale was being told in a dialect of Lonkundo (Yongo), the narrator puts into the children's reply a local pronunciation of the French word "*bon.*" In a few other instances in Mpanga Iyende's narration, French terms and a proper name were included, in each case given a local pronunciation but recognizably French in origin; this is a surprisingly small degree of linguistic acculturation in view of the fact that French is the language of instruction in Zaïre.

3. A baby is often left in the care of a sister. (Nkundo girls express no desire for a doll, since more often than not there is a baby to care for.) Food for the baby depends entirely upon the mother until the child is weaned at the age of two. Presumably, in order to quiet the child's crying, one or the other of the sisters would have put the baby to her breast, a pacifying technique used by both males and females of the family in the absence of the mother; when that method failed to prove adequate, the sisters would recognize the need for taking the baby to the mother.

4. In Nkundo tales as in many others, the counsel of old people and of younger brothers and sisters normally proves sound; lack of attention to this counsel almost invariably leads to disaster. On the other hand, the younger sister would be expected in the Nkundo culture to defer to her elders' judgment. The need for a decision concerning the paths, initiated by the mother and unwisely resolved here, prepared the listeners for the dramatic events which followed. That the folktale mirrors the culture is a thesis which must be examined in the light of conflicts within the value system under study.

5. At this point, the narrator said "They arrived" and then, considering this a false start, paused to reword the beginning of the next sentence. With a single exception in Mpanga Iyende's narrations, such false starts met with no reproach from the listeners, and appeared in no way to affect his own confidence and enthusiasm in tale-telling.

6. The first nine ogres appeared to be saving this tender meat for the chief of

their village, a courtesy the Nkundo would recognize as proper in terms of the traditional concept of "division of the spoils."

7. The narrator omitted mention of the second ogre, an oversight later mended in the sequence of the mother's visits.

8. The narrator himself shortened the tale in this fashion, perhaps because it was the last one and he sensed a growing restlessness in the audience; on an earlier occasion, however (Tale 61), he had similarly shortened the tale, so this device may be characteristic of his narrative technique in handling a tale which according to the demands of the occasion might or might not include the repetitions dear to Nkundo listeners.

9. The narrator clenched both fists when he named the "tenth," a reflection of the Nkundo counting-by-fives practice in which *five* is represented by one clenched fist and *ten* by two clenched fists.

10. The narrator furnished the children's petition to the tenth ogre in the form of a three-line chant for which we have been unable to secure an adequate translation. (The omission of this and of similarly untranslatable passages has been indicated by three centered ellipsis dots.) The chant made no attempt to achieve a musical effect, but rose and fell in spoken pitch, and the words in this instance had end-rhyme (*—kanga, —yanga,* and*—nunga*); this tale contained the only occurrences of end-rhyming to be found in the Ross-collected tales.

Although there was neither a chorus nor a clearly antiphonal arrangement, some of the children in the audience joined their voices with the narrator's toward the end of each chanted line. Apparently at least some of the listeners had heard this tale before and relished hearing it again.

The narrator, in presenting the ogre's speech immediately following the children's chant, deepened his voice appreciably, to suggest the enormous size and awe-inspiring strength of the chief of the ogres. The raisings and lowerings of pitch were not consistently maintained throughout the tale, but they served to suggest the opposed forces and to increase the drama and suspense.

11. The children's three-line chant was sung here, with a consequent gap in the translated text.

The ogre chief's deep voice, imitated by the narrator, following directly upon the chant's completion, accentuated the horror of the ogre's swallowing of the children.

12. The speaker of this line was not identified by the narrator, but identification is unnecessary. In an Nkundo village—as is true in most other African tribal settings —children are highly valued, and the mother's distress would be quickly apparent to her neighbors, who would doubtless have observed the children's departure and would aid in their recovery. In the village, any child is everybody's child in matters of nurture and protection.

13. The narrator sang once here the mother's song, presented to the ogre but directed to the children she felt were nearby; it carried the message that the child's unwillingness to be a "proper child" led to such misfortunes. There was no chorus, though some effort was made toward antiphonal singing; the song consisted of three near-rhymed lines (*—koka, —bona, —'afya*), with two extra metric feet in the third line. This song has not been furnished in the text.

14. Again, the narrator sang the mother's song, with some vocal support from the audience.

15. The truncation here was the storyteller's, an evident effort to reduce the repetition yet sustain the suspense. At such points, any good narrator "reads" his audience and is free to stretch or shrink the telling to suit that particular group of listeners. It is conceivable that, had the tale been narrated earlier in the sequence of eight stories, more repetition would have been included.

16. Here the narrator inserted some significant information formerly omitted; a Western reader might expect the mother's preparations to be described at the time they were made—at home, before she set out to find her children. The narrator may have overlooked the "tools" until this time; on the other hand, he may have decided to keep the listeners' attention on the search, not diverting them by information not actually required until this particular point in the tale.

Nor did the narrator need to tell his Nkundo audience why the mother took what she took: the listeners would recognize the enema bag as a first-aid item (much of the medication in this area is administered rectally); the salt would provide a medium of exchange in case payment was required to redeem the children from their captor. No Nkundo woman would set out on a rescue mission without a knife—or a small machete—concealed, with the other items, in her *ifuta*.

17. This phrase, in its Lonkundo equivalent (*nd'elok'ea*), is a favorite in all speech activities of the Nkundo. Its significance here is unclear except as it reflects the close ties between conversational and narrative diction.

18. The narrator again sang the mother's song, with some of the audience supporting him.

19. Once again the narrator and some of the listeners sang the mother's song.

20. Here the narrator mimicked the deep, gruff voice of the ogre chief, following the chief's command with another audience-aided singing of the mother's song.

21. For the last time, the narrator and various listeners sang the mother's song.

22. Raising his pitch to mimic a woman's voice, the narrator presented the mother's next passage—directed to her children—in an excited, scolding tone that might have been heard in any village scene where children needed correction. The setting for the scolding—inside the ogre's stomach—in no way reduced the pertinence of the rebuke. The audience appeared entirely in agreement with this "first things first" handling of narrative order.

23. As is true with members of various other African groups, the Nkundo has a rather sketchy anatomical terminology (at least, with respect to Western medical vocabulary). Just as he might fail to distinguish between "artery" and "vein," here the Nkundo narrator overlooks the distinction between "flesh" and "skin." Clearly, "flesh" was meant here, but the word for "skin" was used.

24. Here the narrator used a querulous tone, complaining very much in the fashion of a pain-troubled Nkundo male.

25. The women giggled with delight and appreciation following this comment.

26. The "teaching" offered here is a departure from the pattern found in most of Mpanga Iyende's eight tales, though it is a common and readily accepted Nkundo way of concluding a tale. (Compare this ending with the one for Tale 61 for another innovative "tie-off" by the same narrator.)

27. This is the second instance during the evening session in which the narrator asked for water at the point where he would normally have used some such "sign-off" as "The sun has set," delivered with a rising inflection, with the choral response "The action is finished," delivered with a falling inflection.

28. The audience, recognizing that not only the tale but the tale-telling session had been concluded, chorused "*Aosila*," delivered with a falling inflection.

Narrator:	Mpanga Iyende
Location:	Bonga-Iteli
Date:	December 1973

78.   *The Girl Who Ate Her Mother's Eggplant*[1]

A woman had planted a special vegetable in her garden in back of her house. It is called *nsolo* (eggplant). She wanted to make a trip into the forest with her husband. Before they left, she said to their children, "We are leaving, and the eggplant is about ready to eat. However, no one at all must pick it or eat it while we are gone—not even one piece."

Then she went with her husband and left the children at home, then, *tee-tee-tee*.

In not a long while after they left, the youngest child, a girl, said, "I feel hunger. I am going to pick and eat some of Mother's eggplants."

One of the others that, "No! Don't do that. Mother said not to touch them."

"That is of no concern. I feel hunger."

She went to the garden and picked them. She cooked them and ate them with manioc and oil, *tee-ee*.

After a month the parents returned from their journey. As soon as they reached the house, the mother put her basket down and went[2] out back to look at her garden. She quickly saw that some eggplants were gone.

She ran back into the house. "Who has eaten?"

"Your last child."[3]

The mother didn't like this. "Let's go to the river and find out. Each person and person[4] can go into the river, and the one who ate it won't forget."

So they all went together to the river. As soon as they arrived at the beach, the first child went into the water. As she went in, she sang,

> *Narrator:* I did not eat Mother's eggplant.
> *Chorus:* *Nyė.*
> *Narrator:* Stop the difficulty with Mama.
> *Chorus:* *Nyė.*
> *Narrator:* The water comes up like that.
> *Chorus:* *Ba-nyė.*[5]
> *Narrator:* . . .[6]
> *Chorus:* *Ba-nyė.*
> *Narrator:* I need
> *Chorus:* Soap.[7]
> *Narrator:* I need
> *Chorus:* Soap.

The second child[8] went into the water, singing,

> *Narrator:* I did not eat Mother's eggplant.
> *Chorus:* *Nyė.*
> *Narrator:* Stop the difficulty with Mama.
> *Chorus:* *Nyė.*
> *Narrator:* The water comes up like that.
> *Chorus:* *Ba-nyė.*
> *Narrator:* . . .
> *Chorus:* *Ba-nyė.*
> *Narrator:* I need
> *Chorus:* Soap.
> *Narrator:* I need
> *Chorus:* Soap.

She was raised up, but she didn't fall.[9]

The third went into the water, singing,

> *Narrator:* I did not eat Mother's eggplant.
> *Chorus:* *Nyė.*
> *Narrator:* Stop the difficulty with Mama.
> *Chorus:* *Nyė.*
> *Narrator:* The water comes up like that.
> *Chorus:* *Ba-nyė.*

Narrator:	...
Chorus:	*Ba-nyė.*
Narrator:	I need
Chorus:	Soap.
Narrator:	I need
Chorus:	Soap.

The fourth went into the water, singing,

Narrator:	I did not eat Mother's eggplant.
Chorus:	*Nyė.*
Narrator:	Stop the difficulty with Mama.
Chorus:	*Nyė.*
Narrator:	The water comes up like that.
Chorus:	*Ba-nyė.*
Narrator:	...
Chorus:	*Ba-nyė.*
Narrator:	I need
Chorus:	Soap.
Narrator:	I need
Chorus:	Soap.

The one who was last went into the water:

Narrator:	I did not eat Mother's eggplant.
Chorus:	*Nyė.*
Narrator:	Stop the difficulty with Mama.
Chorus:	*Nyė.*
Narrator:	The water comes up like that.
Chorus:	*Ba-nyė.*
Narrator:	...
Chorus:	*Ba-nyė.*
Narrator:	I need
Chorus:	Soap.
Narrator:	I need
Chorus:	Soap.

The water came up to her stomach.

Narrator:	I did not eat Mother's eggplant.
Chorus:	*Nyė.*
Narrator:	Stop the difficulty with Mama.
Chorus:	*Nyė.*
Narrator:	The water comes up like that.
Chorus:	*Ba-nyė.*

> Narrator: . . .
> Chorus: Ba-nyė.
> Narrator: I need
> Chorus: Soap.
> Narrator: I need
> Chorus: Soap.

The water reached her arms.

> Narrator: I did not eat Mother's eggplant.
> Chorus: Nyė.
> Narrator: Stop the difficulty with Mama.
> Chorus: Nyė.
> Narrator: The water comes up like that.
> Chorus: Ba-nyė.
> Narrator: . . .
> Chorus: Ba-nyė.
> Narrator: I need
> Chorus: Soap.
> Narrator: I need
> Chorus: Soap.

She was submerged.

After a while, the family decided that she was drowned and wouldn't come out of the river, *tee-ee*. They decided to leave her, and they went home.

A fisherman who lived nearby put his traps into the river to catch some fish. One morning he went out to check the traps. The first one had no weight when he lifted, *O mpampa*—also the second, *O mpampa*, and the third, *O mpampa*. The fourth trap, then, was very heavy. He pulled on it, calling out, "Why is this so heavy?"

He heard his words come back: "Why is this so heavy?"

Then he called, "Who is there?"

The voice again: "Who is there?"

He began to pull the trap and found the young girl there.[10] He said, "I have found a little daughter[11] for my wife. We will take her as our own."

He arrived home and took the girl into his household as his very own.

Some people came into his village and saw the girl. "What child is this? Isn't this the girl that the mother rejected because she ate the mother's eggplant?"[12]

Some others came and also recognized her. "This is surely the girl whose mother sold[13] her because she ate the eggplant from her mother's garden."

They went to the mother of the girl. "The girl that you rejected because she ate your eggplant we have seen in a fishing village. She has been accepted there as part of the family."[14]

Her mother and many of the family gathered money together[15] and went to the fishing village. They gave the money to the fisherman and took the girl home.

When you hear someone say, "Stop! Stop!" that is sure to be something bad.[16] Don't do whatever it is. When the girl disobeyed the orders of her parents, she went into the water.[17]

> *Narrator and Chorus:*   The sun has set!
>   The action is finished!

Several facets of the Nkundo value system appear in Tale 78: the requirement of filial obedience, the horror of theft, the necessity of speaking the truth, a strong respect for tabus and for injunctions, the importance of children (especially to a childless couple), the force of community opinion, and the continuing responsibility of the family for each of its members. There are evidences also of Nkundo practices and characteristics, including the use of a "water test" to determine guilt or innocence, the severity of punishment for theft, the tendency toward gossip, and the custom of pooling resources to secure funds sufficient to pay bridewealth or to redeem one temporarily lost to the village community. In this particular tale, the violator of the injunction seems not to have suffered as a consequence of her disobedience. We suspect that an Nkundo audience would understand and inwardly apply the punishment omitted by the narrator, since the tale is intended—as are the others—to reinforce the Nkundo value system.

Aarne-Thompson's tale type 785 offers some assistance in classifying this tale in that there is a denial of the eating of a certain food (the lamb's heart) by Peter's companion, just as in the present tale there is a denial of the daughter's having eaten the proscribed food; no other elements of Tale 78 are similar to those cited for the type, however. In Lambrecht's sample for her tale type 3172 are found several elements similar to portions of the Ross-collected narrative; a "water test" in the river determines the girl guilty of swallowing the chief's spoon; the river submerges and drowns the guilty girl; she is later netted (though transformed into a fish) and brought ashore and prepared for cooking; she is subsequently restored—retransformed into a girl—to her family. On the other hand, the differences between the two tales outweigh their similarities, so we cannot accept that type number as sufficiently precise for the Ross-collected narrative. We have been unable to find in any of the indexes a type number that is adequately suited to Tale 78.

Two unindexed variants offer helpful insights concerning the present tale. On the matter of one's being able to live under water for a period of time and then be restored none the worse for the underwater stay, Weeks' *Congo Life and Folklore* (in "The Water-Fairies Save a Child," pp. 406–409) presents a boy who disobeyed his father and allowed his birds to escape; the father killed the boy and threw his body into the river, where the water-fairies revived him, reared him, made him wealthy, and eventually restored him to his father, with whom he was reconciled. (Here again, the disobedient child seems not to have suffered permanently for his disobedience.) A variant furnished by de Rop in his ... *woordkunst* ... (pp. 149–151) deals with parents who have warned their nine children not to eat either the mother's eggplant or the father's squash; the eldest child picks both vegetables and eats them. During the "water test" that follows, a song is sung:

> I did not eat my mother's eggplant.
> > Jump back!
> I did not eat my father's squash.
> > Jump back!
> The river's water takes me along.
> > Jump back!
> It takes me along; it burns in my heart.
> > Jump back!
> It takes me along; it goes to my head.
> > Jump back!
> Little calabash,
> > Jump back!

Since translation of the songs from a dialectal form of Old Lonkundo presented serious problems for Mrs. Ross and her aides, the translation of this particular song, of which one variant or another may well be used in the present tale, is most helpful to us.

[Translation prepared by Dr. Tinco E. A. van Hylckama]

Motifs:

C	C680.+.**.	Injunction: certain food must not be eaten without permission of owner.
T	J652.	Inattention to warnings.
T	H210.	Test of guilt or innocence.
C	M90.+.**.	Trial by ordeal: each daughter to take "truth serum" and then to enter the river; the innocent will not be drowned.
T	H220.**.	Ordeal by water: water will rise to drown the guilty one.
C	F253.1.+.**.	River spirit can cause water to rise to drown one guilty of theft and lying.
C	Q467.+.**.	Drowning as punishment for violation of injunction.
T	F940.	Extraordinary underground (underwater) disappearance.
T	Q212.	Theft punished.
C	R150.+.	Fisherman as rescuer.

1. The narrator terminated the discussion of his preceding tale and called the attention of the audience to the beginning of this one by the following firm directive: "You sit down. I want to go [begin]."

2. There is pronounced coughing in the audience at this point.

3. The speaker here is not identified; presumably it is not the youngest daughter.

4. Meaning "one by one."

5. The "*Ba-*" is added here to fill out the line in terms of rhythm.

6. The sounds in this line are blurred by the superimposition of another set of voices over the narrator's.

7. No Nkundo will overlook an opportunity to bathe. The daughter, having been cleared of suspicion, takes this opportunity to wash herself. (Weeks pointed out in his *Congo Life and Folklore*, p. 86, that soap-worts can be used for bathing, since they lather well.)

"*Sabon*," the word used by the chorus for "soap," is a truncated version of "*saboni*," the Lonkundo adaptation of the French word "*sabon*"; the demands of the rhythm here caused the dropping of the "*i*." The excited response by the audience in the last line of the chorus prompted the narrator to insert "*Nkanko*" ("then," the hesitation word he uses throughout his tale-telling), effectively quelling the outburst.

8. The narrator effects economy here by omitting detailed comments on the results of the first four daughters' "water tests," going almost immediately into the next singing of the song.

9. A babbling from the audience is apparent at this point on the tape.

10. There is no explanation either in this tale or in any of the other Ross-collected narratives involving water ordeals as to how the "drowned" culprit manages to survive under water. Neither the narrator nor the audience appears to find the survival either miraculous or strange.

11. Here the narrator uses the Lonkundo term "*walèkèlè*" ("mother-and-child"), very much a part of Nkundo imagery, to convey the warm acceptance the girl received at his hands, not as a slave, but as a child born by some miracle into his family.

12. A gossipy tone is employed here, seemingly hypercritical, but effective dramatically.

13. The narrator uses "sold" ("*tekya*") rather than "rejected" ("*tona*") here, perhaps indicating a placing of pressure on the family to recover the girl.

14. To lose a village girl—even as a consequence of an ordeal—and then to have her accepted elsewhere reflects on the entire community, which regards every child of the family as its own. Considerable social pressure would be brought to bear on the natural family to redeem her.

15. Since women are an economic asset, the family could scarcely expect to demand and receive the girl without payment. Such payment would exceed the financial resources of the immediate family, and supplementary funds would be forthcoming from the extended family.

16. Nothing is said about punishment meted out to the girl afterwards for the embarrassment she had brought upon the family and upon the village, but the tone

of the "teaching" suggests strong criticism of the girl's disobedience and a warning to others who might be tempted to pursue the same course.

17. A voice in the background saying "*yu*" covers the narrator's final word, "*Yo!*" On this occasion, the formulaic ending was a joint recital by narrator and chorus, with the usual rising inflection on "*Ili!*" and falling inflection on "*Yo!*"

Narrator:	Tata Manga
Location:	Boende
Date:	November 1973

79. The Woman Who Did Not Hear Her Husband Speak

A certain woman and her husband went into the forest to hunt food. They came to a good place for finding both meat and fish.[1] They built a shelter there.

When they finished the shelter, the husband said to his wife, "When I am going into the forest to hunt meat, if you hear someone calling do not answer. You remain very quiet and do not talk; no matter what you see, do not talk."[2]

The wife said, "Eh! I won't talk."

The husband went to find meat. While he was gone hunting food very far into the forest, his wife heard someone calling from the edge of the forest. The voice said,

Ngao, ngao, ngao, ngao.	[Onomatopoetic sounds][3] The menacer has finished coming. Bring!
Ngao, ngao, ngao, ngao.	[Onomatopoetic sounds] The menacer has finished coming. Bring!

The woman said, "For you. Come!"

It was an ogre, and he had heard her and sang again,

Ngao, ngao, ngao, ngao.	[Onomatopoetic sounds] The menacer has finished coming. Bring!
Ngao, ngao, ngao, ngao.	[Onomatopoetic sounds] The menacer has finished coming. Bring!

The woman called, "Come here!"
"I am coming."
"You have come a long way?"
"Yes! Give me food."
"I have some meat. Would you like that?"
The ogre didn't want that. She offered him several kinds of food, including meat and fish, but he didn't want them.

What he wanted was some of her meat, meat of the woman. He finally cut off a piece of her thigh. When he had eaten it, he went on his way.

The next morning her husband asked her, he said, "You haven't heard anyone calling nearby us?"

"No. I have heard no one.[4] If I go, I won't forget."

"Do not forget. Do not forget."

She remained quiet, and he went on to the forest to hunt meat. The ogre came again and called her.

Ngao, ngao, ngao, ngao.	[Onomatopoetic sounds] The menacer has finished coming. Bring!
Ngao, ngao, ngao, ngao.	[Onomatopoetic sounds] The menacer has finished coming.

"Woman, see me. I'm coming. I'm coming. I'm coming."

He went to the woman. He asked for food. She brought food and he did not want it. She brought meat and he did not want it. She brought fish and he did not want it.

He said, "Give me your flesh." He ate the meat which was of his kind. The ogre left.

Her husband returned and saw that she was not strong and that she seemed to have no joy in living. He asked, "Why don't you have joy in living? What has happened?"

"I'm just very cold in my body. It is nothing."

"All right. Bring me some food that I might eat."

She brought the food and her husband ate heartily.[5] She seemed to have no appetite and ate very little because the wife felt a desire for sickness.

The next morning before he left for the forest, he reminded her, "Remember. If anyone calls or comes, you are not to answer. You are to remain quiet."

He left. Afterwards the ogre came again. He sang his song.

Ngao, ngao, ngao, ngao.   [Onomatopoetic sounds]
The menacer has finished
    coming.
Bring! Bring!

"Do you see me?"

He found her there and she offered him food, *nyė*, meat, *nyė*, and fish, *nyė*. "I want only the meat from your body." He ate meat from her body.

Each day he returned and cut off a piece of the woman and cut her and cut her and cut her.[6] This happened until she was sick and nearly dead.

The husband came and found her in bed and very sick. "What's the matter? Did you answer some evil person who came and called? When we came here, you were strong and well. Now you are weak and sick. What have you done?"

She said, "No. I have done nothing."

The husband said, "I am sure that you must have responded to someone who came."

She finally showed him her body that had had the flesh cut off until there was little left. He had eaten and eaten and eaten.

"I think you must have answered when an ogre came. Now I am going home. If you can come, that is good. However, you refused to listen to me even though I am your husband. If you die, you will know why, because you refused to listen to the word of your husband."[7]

He collected all of their things together and said, "I'm ready. Let's go."

His wife was not able to get up, so he left her there, and in not a long time she was dead.[8] This was because she refused to listen to the mouth of her husband.

She was taught.[9]

The concern for the wife's obedience to her husband is strongly felt among the Nkundo, and the fire with which Tale 79 was told vividly conveys that concern. By inflection, by intonation, by variation of pacing in the narration, and by the frequent rather eerie repetition of the onomatopoetic sound of bell-ringing, the storyteller aroused in his listeners a criticism of the woman's disregard for her husband's "mouth" that found the audience in full accord with the concluding statement, "She was taught."

In Arewa's tale type 3784, the wife is punished for disobedience twice by her husband's tying her to the side of a leopard. Each time, the leopard tries to rub her loose; after the second time, she obeys her husband. In the present tale, the husband does not actually punish his wife; he leaves her to live or die with the punishment she has invited upon herself by her response to the ogre. Apart from the fact that in Arewa's tale type (based on a tale from the Chaga tribe) the wife disobeys and is painfully punished, there is no similarity between it and the Ross-collected tale; the Arewa sample is, however, the closest indexed parallel we have found.

An entertaining but unindexed tale involving a wife's intention (unfulfilled) of disobeying her husband's injunction is furnished by Rattray in "Why It Is the Elders Say We Should Not Repeat Sleeping-Mat Confidences" (*Akan-Ashanti Folk-Tales*, pp. 128–133). Before his wife has completed her stated intention of revealing the trick used by Kwaku Anansi to win her hand, Kwaku Anansi pours water on his sleeping wife's sleeping mat and then threatens to reveal her "shame"; in short, the "punishment" inhibits the disobedience.

Many tales found, both indexed and unindexed, include a wife's disobedience of her husband's injunction (often one concerning the treatment of a child, of a favored bird or animal, or of another wife), but none that we have discovered has incorporated even a suggestion of the artistic combination of elements present in this tale.

Motifs:

C	C680.+.**.	Injunction: do not answer if anyone calls.
T	C20.**.	Answering ogre.
C	C499.+.**.	Tabu: answering ogres.
T	H479.**.	Wife tests—miscellaneous motifs: wife to remain silent if anyone calls.
T	T254.	The disobedient wife.
T	W31.	Obedience.
T	H1557.	Tests of obedience.
T	J652.	Inattention to warnings.
T	G11.2.	Cannibal giant (ogre).
T	G400.	Person falls into ogre's power.
C	G11.15.+.**.	Cannibal ogre refuses other foods, eats instead portions of living flesh from hunter's wife's body.
T	C423.2.	Tabu: speaking of extraordinary sight.
T	Q415.0.1.**.	Punishment: being eaten bit by bit by ogre for violation of injunction.

C   F446.1.+.**.   Forest ogre forces woman to supply pieces of her own living
                        flesh for his food.
T   C921.**.   Lingering death for violating injunction.
T   C940.**.   Weakness by being eaten bit by bit by ogre for violating
                        injunction.
C   Q451.11.+.**.   Woman forced to serve bits of her own flesh to ogre, flesh
                        eaten before her eyes.
C   Q429.+.**.   Death caused by ogre for disobedience of husband's order.

1. Normally in the Nkundo area, when the season is good for fishing, it is relatively poor for hunting, and vice versa. The best hunting season occurs when the waters of the rivers and swamps are high, reducing the amount of exposed ground and forcing the animals toward the small dry area where they can be more readily caught. On the contrary, the best season for fishing occurs when the waters are low, forcing the fish into the pockets of water remaining and into the main streams of the rivers where the women can more easily dip them with their baskets or catch them in their nets. In the present tale, the wife would be expected to do the fishing and her husband the hunting.

The fact that the man had to go "very far into the forest" to find game suggests that they located their shelter in a relatively open area near a fishing site so that the woman's work could be done near the shelter for her own safety. Had the woman busied herself sufficiently with her fishing, as the agreement between them had doubtless been arranged, she would have been less likely to have fallen prey to the ogre.

A hunter's being accompanied by his wife occurs in several tales in the Ross collection (see, for example, Tales 72 and 73). More often, a hunter goes with one or more other men, carrying food prepared by their wives, and spends a number of days hunting and preparing meat to take home (see Tales 44 and 71). Each man builds his own shelter, since the meat each man catches will be stored separately. Ownership of the meat is strictly honored (see Tales 49 and 50 for instances of dishonesty in this respect).

There is no mention of the present couple's children. Occasionally if there is only one child, the child will accompany the parents to the hunting site (see, for example, Tale 84) and thus be under the mother's care, usually slung at her back in a fold of her outer garment, or *ifuta*. The woman's disregard of "the mouth of her husband" and the absence of children suggest that the marriage was relatively new.

2. The concern of Nkundo men and women for ogres and for various spirits inhabiting swamps, springs, waterfalls, forests, and other awesome spots should have made such a warning unnecessary.

3. "*Ngao, ngao, ngao, ngao,*" representing the insistent ringing of a bell, is a series of sounds produced by the narrator's beginning with his mouth wide open and then rolling his mouth into a small circle. Only the sense of the song is given.

4. There is a strong tabu against describing a supernatural sight, a tabu that would have restrained the woman from answering honestly. Her sense of guilt in disregarding her husband's command would also make denial the discreet policy. (Exceptions occur in Tales 66 and 84.)

5. In addition to catching fish, the woman accompanying her husband into the forest is expected to furnish the services normally required of a wife in that culture, including providing meals prepared from what supplies had been carried from home supplemented by the various edible roots and fruits available in the forest. Apparently the ogre's cannibalization of her flesh had not yet rendered her incapable of these services.

6. There is no formulistic number peculiar to the ogre's visits.

7. A wife, a valuable piece of property, is expected among the Nkundo to obey her husband. This disobedient one had lost her value as property; her condition would make her useless either for work or for childbearing. The husband's leaving her behind would not shock Nkundo listeners, who know where the wife fits in the value system.

8. The husband's failure to give her body proper burial marks the final stamp of disapproval of the wife's disobedience.

9. A common formulistic ending for an Nkundo folktale—"*Aosila*," meaning "It is finished"—yields here to "*Aolako*," meaning "She was taught," a firm driving home of the point made doubly effective by its echo of the customary ending allowing the members of the audience to conclude that "it" (the matter of the wife's disobedience) was indeed finished.

Though this particular wife had no way of changing her behavior as a result of being "taught," each wife among the Nkundo listeners would be expected to learn the lesson carried in the tale: it is essential for a wife to obey her husband.

Narrator:	Bongonda Michele
Location:	Bòlèngè
Date:	March 1973

80. *The Fish-Woman and the Broken Tabus*

On another day three young women went from a village to hunt fish. As they went along the path, they had to pass through a small swampy forest. This particular forest had a tabu against spitting.[1]

One of the women was called Bafalafasa Biaji (Tattletale).[2] Tattletale, even though she knew about the tabu, spat in the forest. Her friends chided her. "Why do you spit here in this forest?" She shrugged her shoulders. "It really makes no difference."

They went just a bit farther and met the owner of the forest.[3]

> It is mine; it is mine.
> Take off your sash.[4]

He sang this song many times.[5]

When Tattletale heard his song, she removed the sash that was wrapped about her waist and gave it to him.

The women went a little way farther, and the owner sang again:

> It is mine; it is mine.
> Take off your bells.[6]

Tattletale took off the bells she had around her waist and gave them to one of her friends, and she passed them to the owner.

They went a little farther, and the owner began to sing again:

> It is mine; it is mine.
> Take off your beads.[7]

So Tattletale took off her beads, and the man took these also. By then, Tattletale was feeling very sad and was crying.[8]

However, the young women went on to the swamp to fish. As soon as their baskets were full of fish, they said, "Let's go home."

They started off down the path for home. When they came to the forest where Tattletale had broken the tabu and had all the palavers, they found a very large river there, *bi-i-i!*[9]

They said, "Where did this river come from? Now how do we get home?" As they thought about it, they began to accuse Tattletale for causing the river to be there. They were sure that the owner of the forest had put it there.[10]

Then one of the young women began to walk out into the river. As she went, they sang,

> Kill Mputu Toloke.[11]
> See the one who cried.[12]

They sang this all the time the friend was crossing the river. As soon as she was across, the next woman went into the water, and they began the same song and sang until she had reached the other side:

> Kill Mputu Toloke.
> See the one who cried.

Then Tattletale went into the water to her knees, and they sang,

> Kill Mputu Toloke.
> See the one who cried.

The water came up to her waist, and they sang,

> Kill Mputu Toloke.
> See the one who cried.

It came to her shoulders, and they sang,

> Kill Mputu Toloke.
> See the one who cried.

Then she was completely covered with water, *ba-ba*.

"She is already drowned. There is no use waiting. Let's go home."[13]

In that same village early one morning, a man took his fish traps and went to the river to catch fish. Later, when he checked his traps, he found that among other fish he had a *lokombe*. He returned to his temporary shelter; he ate some of the fish, but the *lokombe* he put up on the drying shelf for food for another day.

The next day, he went out into the river to check his traps. When he returned to the shelter, he found that someone had brought him some delicious food—fish, greens, and cassava—all cooked and ready to eat.

He asked, "Who could have prepared all of this good food for me? Someone from home must have brought it while I was out in my canoe." Without asking any more questions, he ate it and enjoyed it.

The next day, he left to check his traps. When he returned, he found the same kind of meal waiting for him. He no longer asked questions. He just ate it.

The next morning he said, "I won't leave again until I find out who is bringing this food." So he hid where he could watch.

Very soon the fish, *lokombe*, turned into a woman, for this was Tattletale. She put a cloth around her waist[14] and began to prepare food.

He came out of hiding and said, "I have a wife."

She answered, "I have a husband."

"You are the one who has been preparing all the food for me?"

"Yes," she answered.

"That is wonderful. I now truly have a wife."

She said to him, "I will help you to have a better life. However, you must never tell anyone where I came from. Your mouth must never speak of this.[15] Do not drink liquor. Liquor ruins people.[16] If you do drink, you will have some very real problems." They sang,[17]

Narrator:	Where do we succeed?
Audience:	In our mouths.
Narrator:	Where do we fail?
Audience:	In our mouths.

Narrator:	Where do we succeed?
Audience:	In our mouths.
Narrator:	Where do we fail?
Audience:	In our mouths.

After not a long while, Lokombe went to visit her father and mother. They gave her two slaves to take home with her; both of them were young women.[18] She took them with her and gave them to her husband. "These are wives for you." The wives began to build a house for their husband—building, building. As time went by, the wives worked for him and gave him children. As a result, he became a very rich and influential man.

Every day, he began going to the long house in the center of the town where the elders of the village met.[19] One day when he was there, one of his friends asked him, "You come here all the time, but you don't drink liquor with us. Why don't you drink?"

"My wife doesn't approve of my drinking liquor."

"Your wife doesn't want you to? How can you accept that?[20] Come on and drink just a bit."

So he took a cup of the liquor and drank it. Then he drank another cup of it. Then he went home.

Lokombe smelled his breath. "Have you been drinking?"

He answered, "No, no!"

She warned him, "Remember to be careful."

Another day, he went to the center of the village. All of his friends were drinking, and he joined them. He drank until he began to sing. He sang all the way home.

When he arrived home, Lokombe asked, "Have you been drinking?"

He said, "Who do you think you are? You forget that you were a fish and I saved you. How dare you accuse me?"[21]

His children heard this and began to sing,

> Mother, she a *lokombe* fish.
> Mother, she a *lokombe* fish.[22]

Then they all went to bed and to sleep.[23]

When he awoke the next morning, his house was gone, his wives were gone, his children were gone. He was just the way he had been before Lokombe had come to him and as she had warned him.

Right after that, he went into the forest and he heard the voice of his wife:

> Narrator: Where do we succeed?
> Audience: In our mouths.
> Narrator: Where do we fail?
> Audience: In our mouths.

That tree that gives life to the cattle,[24] do not cut it down.

The fact that Bongonda's audience on this occasion consisted largely of women and preschool children may account for his telling Tale 80; it is told from a woman's point of view—though the narrator was an old man—and carries several warnings that women would find familiar and would want their children to hear. The emphasis placed on dress and adornment, the likelihood of women's wanting to "even the score" with a gossip, the concern with the risk involved in drinking liquor, the inclination of the children to support their father's side rather than their mother's (see Tale 87), and the fish-woman's concluding, in effect, with "I told you so" are all common factors in Nkundo female culture. And the proverb which drives home the point of the story is one that the women, overworked and underrated in the male-dominated social structure, would readily appreciate.

Unfortunately, this is one of the tales erased after translation, to make room for new materials, so we are unable to convey fully the degree of audience participation. Mrs. Ross noted that the audience not only sang but clapped during the antiphonal singing, and that Bongonda and his listeners actually marked on their own bodies, as they sang, the various points the water reached on Tattletale. In the telling of this tale, the narrator mimed at every possible point, especially during the dialogues, providing one of the most dramatic tellings encountered during the course of Mrs. Ross's own field work. (The tale-telling at Bonga, since it was done in a traditional evening storytelling session, was unquestionably the most productive performance encountered during the collecting period, but Bob Stewart rather than Mrs. Ross witnessed the drama on that occasion; the flavor of the tale-telling has fortunately been well preserved on tape.)

Lambrecht's tale type 3172 serves three elements of the present tale: the water test, or ordeal, to prove guilt or innocence, transformation of the drowned girl into a fish, and her retransformation into a girl; for the most part, Lambrecht's sample affords insufficient help in classifying the Ross-collected tale. Some of the latter portion of the present tale can be found in Lambrecht's tale type 3752, based on de Bouveignes' Congolese collection *Entendu dans la Brousse* ("Ingratitude, soeur de sottise . . . ," pp. 168–171): the supernatural wife with a horn in her neck provides great wealth for her husband; if he makes fun of her horn, he will lose her and all the wealth she brought. He breaks the tabu and loses everything; the breaking of the tabu is prompted not by his drinking, however, but in his petulance at her not having prepared the bread he had directed her to have ready for him.

Klipple furnishes several variants of the fish-woman tale type under Thompson's motif number C31.2. (Tabu: mentioning origin of supernatural wife), a device used to expand the coverage of African tales carrying no adequate type numbers in the Aarne-Thompson index. Of the variants provided, none includes the original tabu-breaking resulting in the girl's transformation from girl to fish, and only one includes the husband's breaking of the tabu while intoxicated; in one variant, the tabu is never broken. In two of the variants, eating of the kind of fish from which the fish-woman originated is thereafter prohibited to the family and all its descendants. None of the variants offers a fish-woman who has herself broken a tabu and who brings her husband additional wives and other forms of wealth subsequently lost by his breaking a tabu, with both tabus united by the splendid narrative device of the significance of the mouth. In short, none of Klipple's variants adequately meets the classificatory needs of the present tale.

Cobble's *Wembi* . . . provides a short variant of this tale: a man, finding in the river a wife who brings him wealth, promises never to reveal its source; when he shouts at her concerning her origin, she disappears with all of his goods. In "The Hunter and the Deer," a Yoruba tale (Walker and Walker, *Nigerian Folk Tales*, pp. 11–16), the hunter loses both his deer-wife and his senior wife when the latter serves him enough palm wine to loosen his tongue and reveal his supernatural wife's origin and the means of her returning to her former state.

In none of the variants examined, either indexed or unindexed, have we found a tale as rich in themes, motifs, plot development, and narrative artistry as the Ross-collected narrative. We cannot at present assign it a tale-type number.

Motifs:

T	C40.	Tabu: offending spirits of water, mountain, etc.
T	J652.	Inattention to warnings.
C	D1318.17.+.∗∗.	Rising river drowns violator of tabu against spitting.
C	Q380.+.	Breaking tabu punished.
T	D915.	Magic river.
C	Q467.+.∗∗.	Drowning as punishment for breaking tabu against spitting.
T	C923.∗∗.	Drowning as punishment for breaking tabu against spitting.
T	D179.∗∗.	Transformation: woman to fish, following water ordeal for breaking of tabu.
T	D510.	Transformation by breaking tabu.
T	D370.	Transformation: fish to man (woman).
C	N819.2.+.∗∗.	Mysterious housewife: girl transformed from fish.
T	B654.	Marriage to fish in human form.
C	T111.+.∗∗.	Marriage of mortal man and girl transformed from girl to fish to girl.
T	T135.1.∗∗.	Formulistic exchange of marriage vows between supernatural being and human: "I have a wife." "I have a husband."

T	C420.2.	Tabu: not to speak about a certain happening.
T	C441.	Tabu: mentioning original form of transformed person.
T	C35.1.**.	Tabu: mentioning origin of fish-wife.
C	C421.+.	Tabu: revealing secret of supernatural husband (wife).
C	C680.+.**.	Injunction: do not drink alcoholic beverages.
T	J10.**.	Acquisition of wisdom: gossipy woman learns that trouble comes from the mouth and goes in at the mouth.
C	C429.+.	Tabu: revealing source of wealth.
T	F600.	Persons with extraordinary powers.
C	P170.+.**.	Fish-woman gives husband slaves as wives.
C	N455.+.**.	Children learn secret of mother's origin from drunken father.
L	C31.10.	Tabu: making fun of supernatural wife.
T	C31.4.2.	Tabu: scolding supernatural wife.
T	C932.	Loss of wife (husband) for breaking tabu.
T	C920.1.**.	Disappearance of wives and children for breaking tabu.
C	C930.+.**.	Both supernatural wife and accompanying riches disappear because of husband's breaking tabu.
T	C930.	Loss of fortune for breaking tabu.
C	D469.+.	Transformation: village (town) to bush.
C	Q595.3.+.**.	Forfeiture of wealth as punishment for breaking tabu.

1. The narrator does not explain why spitting in the forest was tabu, nor does he state why Tattletale felt free to break the tabu. Such tabus often grow out of events which themselves are not always retained in the folk tradition; possibly someone who had spat there had thereafter had some notable misfortune. The reason behind the tabu might well have been long forgotten, but the tabu itself was real indeed. Tattletale, initially flippant in her attitude toward the tabu—perhaps because she was not alone in the forest, but with friends—soon discovered its seriousness and promptly met every demand of the owner of the forest.

2. [Narrator's explanatory material: "That name was given to her because she was a gossip and liked to pass all sorts of stories about people to others."] We have furnished "Tattletale" at all points where the nickname "Bafalafasa" was used by the narrator.

3. "The owner of the forest" reflects the Nkundo's animistic belief. In this tale, the "owner" appears to have had many rights and much power. At one point the "owner" is termed "the man." Spirits, as is true of ogres, are believed by the Nkundo to have the ability to make themselves visible at will; in this instance, the spirit is male, whereas in Tale 65 the spirit is female. To offend such a spirit is to tread on dangerous ground.

Curiously, Tattletale's breaking of the tabu seems at first to have brought her good fortune: a husband and children. But when her husband in turn breaks a tabu, she disappears completely. In a number of tales in the Ross collection (as well as in various tales found in the collections translated from Lonkundo, from French, and from Flemish), though the matter of broken tabus frequently appears, most of those who violate the tabus do not suffer as much as might have been anticipated. (Tale

79 offers a notable exception.) The motif of the broken tabu persists in Nkundo oral literature, but it seems to have lost its force as a deterrent in the culture mirrored by the tales.

4. A young woman of the Nkundo tribe hangs about her clothes and her body many bulky and decorative items; she has no desire to look thin or wasp-waisted. The wide sash, or *nkamba*, probably of a bright color, was tied around her lower hips and buttocks.

5. Unfortunately, with the erasure of the tape, we have no way of determining exactly how many times the song was sung. Judging from the Nkundo tales which have been preserved from Mrs. Ross's field collecting, the song was sung at least three times; the succeeding songs were also undoubtedly repeatedly sung, since both narrator and audience relish repetition and participation.

6. The bells were worn on a cord around her waist.

7. The beads were under her *ifuta*, or wraparound overskirt, and hung at hip level.

8. Although when she had been deprived of these adornments, Tattletale was still far from naked, she obviously felt that much of her striking appearance had been lost.

9. *Bi-i-i*, an ideophone, is used by the narrator here to heighten the drama; later, when he describes Tattletale's being covered with water, he emphasizes that fact by *ba-ba*, suggesting the gurgling of the drowning girl.

10. The two friends of Tattletale, certain of the cause for the presence of the river where there had been a swamp, had no choice but to wade across. Obviously, the river was not as deep as it was wide, or the guiltless friends would have been unable to cross it safely. As is true in all such "water tests" or "truth tests" or "ordeals" we have encountered in the Nkundo tales, a "magic river" is deep only for the one guilty of the theft or other misdeed being investigated. See Torrend's . . . *Bantu Folk-Lore* . . . (pp. 56–57) for another form of water ordeal: the suspects' being required to cross a river on a cord stretched from bank to bank; the guilty one will be unable to complete the crossing and will thus drown.

11. "Mputu Toloke" was apparently the real name of the tabu-breaker, though her nickname, "Tattletale," was used during the early part of the tale—with the important exception of the "water-test" song—and on occasion during the latter part of the narrative.

It is interesting to note that in another tale, collected by Mrs. Ross from Mbambo Jean [now Mbalaka Ileke Mbambo] in Mbandaka five months later, a girl named "Mpucu Tòlókò" who "had palavers with people everywhere. She was always fighting and arguing . . ." also breaks the spitting tabu, is drowned while crossing the profaned water, and is later caught in a fish trap by an ogre (see Tale 63). It is entirely possible that at least the first part of this tale has fairly wide distribution among the Nkundo, and that either the narrator or Mrs. Ross misheard the names, so much alike that they could easily have been altered in the process of diffusion alone. The song is used in both instances to fix the guilt for tabu violation on the responsible person. The subsequent developments in the two narratives are vastly different; the greater artistic unity appears to lie with the present narrative.

12. The second line of the song singles out for the owner of the forest the one who had been guilty of violating the tabu.

13. Evidently the young women had expected Tattletale to be drowned, since they left almost as soon as she was submerged in the water. To those with a Western orientation, it may seem odd that no effort would be made to rescue someone who was obviously drowning; among the Nkundo, the victim of such a "water test" would already have placed himself beyond the ranks of those deserving aid. His fate had been decided by supernatural forces, and no Nkundo would tamper with such powers. Violation of tabus overrides marital bonds, consanguineal ties, and the community's protection of its own members.

14. Lokombe, or Tattletale, covered her nakedness immediately upon her transformation into human form, even though she was unaware that she was being watched. "Cloth" refers to body covering, of whatever fabric or cut. Where she obtained the "cloth" in a fisherman's shelter was not explained; the narrator here relies on the audience's "willing suspension of disbelief."

15. As long as her husband was willing to keep her secret, Lokombe was ready to help him. The expression of this second tabu increases the degree of suspense in the narrative.

16. The narrator's emphasis on the dangers of liquor was not a deliberate effort on his part to please or impress the missionary-turned-collector; he had evidently seen among his own people some of the tragic results of drinking to excess the only alcoholic beverages that most Nkundo can afford: palm wine and corn liquor. A part of their culture for many generations, these two beverages are more damaging than the imported liquors for those who imbibe regularly. The husband's "real problems" could stem from his becoming so inebriated that he would reveal the secrets of his wife's origin and the source of his own affluence.

17. The antiphonal singing suggests that this tale was a familiar one to the listeners. As for the statement "They sang," it seems unlikely that the "they" refers to the husband, since this was her initial caution to him about matters of the mouth. There is no outright statement that the fisherman promised to honor the tabu she described; his honoring it would normally be assumed.

It is interesting that a woman bearing the nickname "Tattletale" should caution her husband about the danger inherent in the mouth. Actually, her own mouth—in spitting—was the cause of her drowning; she may well have learned from this experience to be more cautious about everything pertaining to the mouth. Quite apart from its obvious logic, this caution strengthens the narrative unity of the tale and increases the poignancy of the song heard at the end, after the husband had lost everything by his failure to heed his wife's warning.

18. Even though Tattletale had drowned and this young woman came with a different name, her parents knew her and readily accepted her. (The place in Nkundo oral literature of those returned from the dead is deserving of a separate study.) The slaves given to her were apparently a sort of dowry. There is no indication that the parents asked the fisherman for the bridewealth customary among them. Lokombe had promised her husband wealth and she was keeping her promise; among the Nkundo, as among other tribes in Zaïre, wealth can be measured in terms of the number of wives a man has.

There are a number of occasions on which "slaves" are mentioned in the Ross collection (see, for example, Tales 3, 53, and 82). Slaves were at one time very much a part of the Nkundo cultural pattern, and constituted an important form of property. The Batswa are still termed "slaves" by many Nkundo; not all slaves are Batswa, however, nor are all Batswa slaves. The origin of the two slave women given to Lokombe for her husband was not specified by the narrator; obviously, they were young and healthy, or they would not have been taken as wives.

19. The fisherman as a man of affluence would have become a man of influence. For this reason, he could meet with the elders of the village in the special shelter provided for that purpose, a rectangular structure with a roof and roof supports but no walls. Here the business of the village and the palavers between individuals are discussed. Most of the time, the men argue and exchange stories.

20. Understandably, the other men ridiculed the fisherman for allowing his wife to dictate to him what he could and could not do. In the Nkundo culture, the husband is considered the dominant figure in the household, and a challenge to that dominance is resented.

21. The story appears to be truncated at this point, perhaps in the interest of providing a speedy conclusion with increased impact because of its brevity. There must have been at least a bitter quarrel, and probably a sound beating, before the children dared to interfere.

22. The children's song provides an excellent instance of the practice in Lonkundo of omitting a form of the verb "to be" in a sentence.

It is doubtful that the children had heard of the origin of their mother before this time. Children are taught to respect and obey their parents, and such a piece of information would have eroded the mother's influence on her children.

The narrator's text of the husband's statement to his wife does not identify her as other than a "fish"; omission of the term *"lokombe"* may have been merely an oversight, since the word would provide a useful and artistic "bridge" to the children's chant. In the mother's name, "Lokombe," and with the clue word "fish" provided by the father, the children might reasonably be expected to guess that she had been a *lokombe*, even without the father's furnishing the actual identification.

23. Curiously, the penalty for the breaking of the tabu is not exacted immediately; in this tale, "they all went to bed and to sleep" after the husband's revelation of his wife's origin. It was not until the next morning that the fisherman discovered the enormity of his loss: all that remained to him was the taunting-poignant song of his wife, heard in the forest.

24. The term "cattle" here is not to be taken literally; it summarizes the children and all other wealth derived from the "tree" that was Lokombe. The Nkundo do not keep cattle because of the prevalence of tsetse flies, though they own goats, chickens, and dogs.

Narrator: Lontomba Samuel
Location: Tondo
Date: July 1973

81. *The Child Who Knew Her Father's Name*

There was in a town a man by the name of Boleliko.[1] He had four wives. Three of his wives were fertile. They bore him many children. But the last one had no children. Her name was Wangekomba.[2] This lady was very sad because her friends[3] used to tease her and tell her that the will[4] of their husband was for them, but not for her because she had no child. She was sad, and she cried day and night.

One day her husband, Boleliko, wanted to go on a trip. He set to go on a trip—long trip. Before leaving, he called on all his wives, and he told them that he was going away, but upon his return he would like to find that every one of them has a child and this child should be a boy, a son. So he left each of them with this rule, that when he comes back, he has to find that each wife has a child, a boy, and furthermore, this boy, when he comes, the boy has to know the name of the father, Boleliko. If upon his arrival he finds a wife who has a child, who has a boy, but the boy doesn't know the father's name, it's not his child. The child will not be considered as his, and he will be killed[5] at once. So the husband left and went on his journey.

While he was there, the other three—all of them were pregnant —three.[6] But Wangekomba, the last one, wasn't, so her friends started again to tease her and to give her a bad time, that "You will be killed; you will be divorced when our husband comes back because you don't bear any child."

So Wangekomba, who was sterile, decided to go away, to go far in other towns to try to find a witch doctor[7] that could help her to have children. She walked along on the road. She came to the first village. She asked if there was a witch doctor that would help her to become pregnant, or to bear children. They replied in the first village that there was no witch doctor.

She went to the next one. She didn't find any. She went to the next one; it was the same way. She became very sad.

When she went to go to the next town, during the daylight as she was walking through this forest, she was very tired and very

hungry. On the side of the road she saw a small bird that we call the
hilohonge.[8] And this lady decided that she was very hungry and she
wanted to kill this bird to eat it. But as she approached her arm, her
hand, to take up this bird to squeeze it, this bird stopped her from
doing it.

And the bird told her, "I know that you want to find a witch
doctor that can help you."[9]

And the bird started singing this song:[10]

> Don't hold me. Don't kill me. Listen.
> I know that you are looking for a witch doctor.
> Don't kill me.
> Take this egg to your house.
> Make a fire and put the egg near the fire so
>   it can be warm.
> Go out and close the door and stay out until you
>   hear this egg bursting three times. When you
>   have heard it bursting the first, the second,
>   and the third time, open the door and you
>   will have a child.[11]

The lady went back through the towns. Each time, the people
asked her if she had found a witch doctor and she said, no, she hadn't.
She pretended to be very sad.

When she reached her village, she went into her house, made a
fire, and did everything as the small bird had told her. She sat outside
her door. After a while she heard the egg bursting—one, two, three
times. She went inside and there was a beautiful nice-looking girl—
very pretty, the most beautiful girl in the town.[12] She didn't tell
anybody. She was still concerned because her husband had wanted
a boy and this was a girl.

Some weeks went by, and one day they heard that the husband
had come. He did not want to enter his house until he had seen all
the wives with their children. The first three wives went happily with
their sons to meet their husband. The husband would not hold any
of the children.

He said, "Put them there." The three were sitting in a row before
him. He wanted to test which of the children knew the name of their
father. They called the fourth wife, Wangekomba, who doesn't
have children. She came, and her husband was angry with her. He
shouted, "Tie Wangekomba to the post and kill her because she
doesn't have a child."

Wangekomba said, "Don't kill me! Don't kill me! Please, I have a child in my house."

"Why didn't you bring your child?"

"Because my child is a girl and you wanted a boy."

"Go get her. We want to see her anyway."

She went with some others to her house and there was this lovely and beautiful girl sitting there. She was the most beautiful daughter in the town. Everyone was happy to see this child, and Wangekomba was happy also. They all asked when did she have this child.[13]

She said, "I had it in secret because people would not like that I have a child."

Now it was time to test the children, the three sons and the daughter, to find out which of them knew the father's name.

He asked the son of the first wife, "What is my name?" The son didn't know. The husband said, "Kill the child." They killed[14] the first son.

He asked the second son and it was the same, so they killed him. The third was the same and they killed him.[15]

He asked the daughter, "What is my name?"

She said, "You are my daddy. Your name is Boleliko."[16]

Everybody was happy, and especially the father. He decided to make this daughter the most important child in his family.

This story shows us that we should not tease people who do not have children or do not have the things that we have because one day they might have something more important than anything that we have.[17]

Despite the fact that Lontomba Samuel was alone with his tape recorder in the middle of the night when he recounted Tale 81, the tape picked up all sorts of interesting sounds of life at that late hour: the shouts and cries of children at play, the bursts of song found at almost any hour among any African groups we have known, the jangling of bells—the cause of the bell-ringing was not explained—men talking together in the street, and the voice of a woman calling her child.

The narrator referred to this story as a "fertility tale." Clearly, the importance—the life-and-death necessity—of childbearing was a major factor in the narrative, and the bulk of the action involved Wangekomba's effort to demonstrate her fertility by securing a child. The interplay among the co-wives from beginning to end suggests, however, that an equally strong concern was felt by the narrator for the problems of co-wives in a harem, as well as for the position of an unfavored wife in the community at large; his concern is evidenced in the conclusion, which goes beyond the immediate subject of fertility to the broader area of interpersonal relationships as a whole.

Though Whiteley has stated (in his *A Selection of African Prose. 1. Traditional Texts* [1964], p. 165) that the matter of barrenness is "one of the most widespread themes in West Africa," we have found only one indexed version that is in any respect useful toward the classification of the present tale. Arewa's tale type 3017 is based on an Ngonde story of a sterile and abused co-wife who cooked four *isebe* fruits each of which changed into a girl child. She kept the secret of their origin from her husband and from them until the first three had married chiefs; during a quarrel with the fourth girl, still at home, the mother told her she was a fruit-child. As soon as the child reported the puzzling name to her sisters, all four "flew up as though they were birds" (Arewa, p. 141) and disappeared.

Among the unindexed tales most poignantly recounted is "The Pineapple Child," a Gã folktale (see Whiteley, pp. 164–165); this tale includes other elements besides the transformation of an object (a pineapple) to a little girl, and a monogamous household is involved rather than a polygynous one, but the sampling it affords of narrative skill in dealing with this significant theme makes it worthy of note. Okeke's *Tales of Land of Death* in "Gourd Daughter" provides a moving example of such a tale from the Igbo oral tradition. A tale from Botswana recorded in Setswana and in English for Barbara K. Walker by Botsang Mosienyane on January 9, 1975, tells of a servant boy who imbibed the fertility potion he had been sent to fetch from the witch doctor for the wife of his master, whereupon he himself conceived and bore the child. It is tantalizing to know that such tales are abundant yet have not been included in indexes so that the present tale and others relating to the serious concern with fertility can be classified.

As is true with all other sterility/co-wives' interrelationships tales, either indexed or unindexed, available to us, Arewa's tale type 3017 fits the Ross-collected tale in only a few respects; it is, however, the closest parallel we have been able to find. We strongly suspect that the story was created by the narrator himself through the skillful interweaving of portions of various other tales in an effort to meet a need felt in his own community.

Motifs:

C	M90.+.**.	Husband decrees that each of his four wives must bear a child during his absence and that on his return home, each child who cannot furnish the father's name will be killed.
C	M244.+.**.	Barren woman releases small bird (hummingbird) on bird's promise to help woman secure a child.
C	B569.+.**.	Helpful bird (hummingbird) tells childless woman how to get a child from a certain egg.
T	D1024.	Magic egg.
C	D829.+.**.	Magic egg (producing beautiful girl) acquired from bird.
T	D1024.**.	Magic egg—produces beautiful female child.

A	D431.4.1.**.	Transformation: egg to child.
C	D431.+.**.	Transformation: egg to beautiful girl child.
T	D1347.**.	Magic object produces supposed fecundity.
C	H175.2.+.**.	People are assembled so that children may name their father and thus escape death.
C	P210.+.**.	Husband orders wife killed because she has no children.
C	T299.+.**.	Husband orders wife killed because she has borne no child.
C	S11.6.+.**.	Father kills own sons who cannot furnish his name.
T	H175.2.**.	Child acquired by barren wife is able to provide her father's name and thus escape death.
T	H481.**.	Infant (child) picks out his (her) unknown father.

1. [Narrator's explanatory comment: "He was a polygamist."] Polygyny is still in evidence in Zaïre, particularly in the bush villages; there it has decided economic benefits for the husband.

2. [Narrator's explanatory comment: "which means a wife who doesn't bear children; she was sterile. She couldn't have a baby, so her name was 'Wangekomba.'"]

3. Sam's reference to "her friends" presumably applies to the other wives of Boleliko; these women scarcely behaved as "friends" in their jeering at Wangekomba for her childlessness.

4. "Will" here is to be interpreted as "desire."

5. Since the power of the father in an Nkundo family is absolute and since filial obedience is a value strongly stressed by the Nkundo, the termination of a child's life for the violation of this paternal injunction would increase audience suspense but would not arouse disapproval from the listeners.

6. [Narrator's explanatory comment: "Apparently they became pregnant from the husband before he left."]

7. According to Chatelain ("African Folk-Life" [1897], p. 24), "[t]he greatest affliction that can befall an African is not blindness, or deafness, or even insanity, but childlessness. No consultation fee of a diviner, nor any sacrifice to the spirits, is deemed too expensive if there is hope of thereby securing the desired blessing." This emphasis on childbearing has not yet lost its force among the Nkundo. In the tale, Wangekomba—as would any other woman in such a situation—made every possible effort to satisfy her husband.

De Rop points out in his ... *woordkunst* ... (p. 89) that the Nkundo believe "God is the original giver of the blessing of parenthood: a childless woman will end her complaint about her infertility with a resigned: '*Elaka nk'Omongo*: it is the will of the Owner.' By Owner they mean God." [Italics ours]

8. [Narrator's explanatory comment: "The *honge* is a small bird, and this bird sucks the juice from new flowers. It has a very long mouth."]

The bird to which the narrator refers is in all probability a hummingbird; there are many near the village where he lives.

9. The bird himself proves to have supernatural powers, indicated initially by his discerning her errand and subsequently by his providing her with a magic egg that, properly handled, will produce the child she seeks.

10. The narrator *sings* both the lead voice and the choral portion (the latter in a different "voice") first in his own tongue—Lontumba—and then explains the song in English. The English version does not attempt to transliterate the song or to reproduce the narrator/chorus form of the original.

11. Here there appears to be use of a formulistic number, *three*, combined with an understood though not stated tabu concerning looking at a certain supernatural event. The element of the closed door, with a tabu forbidding its being opened, occurs nowhere else in the Ross-collected tales.

Awe of the supernatural would have led *any* Nkundo to follow scrupulously whatever directions were provided by a supernatural advisor, no matter how puzzling those directions might seem. Failure to observe the directions would constitute the violation of an injunction.

12. The use of the word "girl" and later evidence about her suggest that the child produced from the egg was not an infant but a girl sufficiently well grown not only to "sit" but to possess remarkable beauty and a perception of what was expected of her.

13. The trait of curiosity characteristic of the Nkundo is apparent here. In an extended-family pattern, the presence of such a girl would scarcely have gone unnoticed. Since the producing of the child had been a supernatural event, Wangekomba would not be unwise enough to reveal that event. The nature of Boleliko's threat and the certainty of its being carried out made Wangekomba understandably reluctant to present her beautiful daughter.

14. The brevity with which the killing is handled by the narrator is artistically motivated: the interest of the narrator (and of the audience) lies in what happens to the girl, the product of a sterile wife. The penalty exacted for the child's inability to meet his father's demand points up the strong emphasis on filial obedience, but it also places in sharp relief the care of the sterile wife in preparing her daughter well for meeting this special requirement of the father.

15. Truncation is evident here; a lengthier handling would have distorted the focus of the tale.

16. Both the father-daughter relationship and the naming of the father establish the girl as belonging to Boleliko. How she knew the name is not explained, nor does the narrator indicate the father's surprise at her sudden appearance on the scene. The "willing suspension of disbelief" on the part of the audience is assumed by the narrator.

17. [Narrator's closing comment: "This is the end."] This was the last of the tales told by Lontomba Samuel, and the comment "This is the end" marks the end of the taping session, not the end of Tale 81.

Narrator: Bongonda Michele
Location: Bòlèngè
Date: March 1973

82. The Jealous Wife

A certain man named Kèlèkèkè went to another village to visit. When he arrived there, he found a woman who was soon to deliver a child.

He said to that woman and her husband, "We are distant relatives. Your wife is pregnant and I am interested in the baby that's coming. If it is a boy, I'll bring many gifts and you bring gifts and we'll exchange them. If it is a girl, it is my wife.¹ Now I'll go home."

After a while the woman had her baby. Liangu was a lovely girl baby. The girl grew and grew until one day the parents said, "Let's take her to her husband."

So they gathered all of her things together and went and went, *kao-kao*.² They arrived at a stretch of forest just as a big storm came up. Thunder roared in their ears—*pao*—and they ran for cover. Her father and mother ran into the forest. However, in the other direction were the gardens of a nearby village. Liangu ran that way and hid under the cassava leaves that were there. The owner of the garden, Nsonga, came to her garden and saw the young girl.

She said, "I have a slave. She's in my garden and has been stealing there. I'll take you for my slave."³

Liangu said, "No. I haven't taken anything from your garden. I was on the path with my father and mother when it began to thunder. We were frightened. My parents went one way, but I came here and hid. I am not a thief.

> When Kèlèkèkè came to the home of my parents,
>   *Yafo, yafo,*
> Mother was weak with a pregnancy.
>   *Yafo, yafo.*
> Kèlèkèkè said if she had a boy they would exchange gifts.
>   *Yafo, yafo.*
> If she had a girl, she was to be his wife.
>   *Yafo, yafo.*
> The day arrived and a baby girl was born.
>   *Yafo, yafo.*

Now we are going so that I may be the wife of Kėlėkėkė.
 Yafo, yafo.
You want to make a slave of me. I was only hiding under
 your cassava.
 Yafo, yafo.
I didn't dig any. Look at my hands and see if they are
 dirty.
 Yafo, yafo.
Look at my back and see if I have the strength to carry
 a basket of cassava roots.
 Yafo, yafo.

They went to a nearby village, and Nsonga accused Liangu
again of being a thief. Liangu sang all of her story to them.

When Kėlėkėkė came to the home of my parents,
 Yafo, yafo,
Mother was weak with a pregnancy.
 Yafo, yafo.
Kėlėkėkė said if she had a boy they would exchange gifts.
 Yafo, yafo.
If she had a girl, she was to be his wife.
 Yafo, yafo.
The day arrived and a baby girl was born.
 Yafo, yafo.
Now we are going so that I may be the wife of Kėlėkėkė.
 Yafo, yafo.
You want to make a slave of me. I was only hiding under
 your cassava.
 Yafo, yafo.
I didn't dig any. Look at my hands and see if they are
 dirty.
 Yafo, yafo.
Look at my back and see if I have the strength to carry a
 basket of cassava roots.
 Yafo, yafo.

The people there looked at her hands and at her back. "She
is still a child and not strong enough to dig or to carry cassava.[4]
You had better let her go. Kėlėkėkė will be very angry." The village
people wanted Nsonga to wait for Liangu's parents, but Nsonga
decided to go on down the path.
Nsonga sneered, "Thief, thief."

Liangu said, "Don't call me that. I'm not a thief."

They went on almost to the village of Kėlėkėkė when they met a group of people.

Nsonga called, "Come and help me. Here is a girl I found in my garden. She was stealing cassava."

Someone said, "She's been stealing cassava?"

Then Liangu began to sing her song again telling of why she was there:

> When Kėlėkėkė came to the home of my parents,
>> Yafo, yafo,
>
> Mother was weak with a pregnancy.
>> Yafo, yafo.
>
> Kėlėkėkė said if she had a boy they would exchange gifts.
>> Yafo, yafo.
>
> If she had a girl, she was to be his wife.
>> Yafo, yafo.
>
> The day arrived and a baby girl was born.
>> Yafo, yafo.
>
> Now we are going so that I may be the wife of Kėlėkėkė.
>> Yafo, yafo.
>
> You want to make a slave of me. I was only hiding under
> your cassava.
>> Yafo, yafo.
>
> I didn't dig any. Look at my hands and see if they are
> dirty.
>> Yafo, yafo.
>
> Look at my back and see if I have the strength to carry a
> basket of cassava roots.
>> Yafo, yafo.

They listened to her song; they examined her hands and her back. They said, "Nsonga, you'd better leave this as it is. If Kėlėkėkė finds out about this, he will be very angry."

She answered, "No, no. I won't leave it."

They went and went. Finally they reached the house of Kėlėkėkė. Then Liangu realized that Nsonga was a wife of Kėlėkėkė.

Kėlėkėkė demanded of her, "Where did you get this girl child?"

"She was stealing cassava from my garden."

He was really surprised.

Liangu began her song once more:

> When Kėlėkėkė came to the home of my parents,

Yafo, yafo,
Mother was weak with a pregnancy.
   Yafo, yafo.
Kėlėkėkė said if she had a boy they would exchange gifts.
   Yafo, yafo.
If she had a girl, she was to be his wife.
   Yafo, yafo.
The day arrived and a baby girl was born.
   Yafo, yafo.
Now we are going so that I may be the wife of Kėlėkėkė.
   Yafo, yafo.
You want to make a slave of me. I was only hiding under
   your cassava.
   Yafo, yafo.
I didn't dig any. Look at my hands and see if they are
   dirty.
   Yafo, yafo.
Look at my back and see if I have the strength to carry a
   basket of cassava roots.
   Yafo, yafo.

Again she sang it all the way through:

When Kėlėkėkė came to the home of my parents,
   Yafo, yafo,
Mother was weak with a pregnancy.
   Yafo, yafo.
Kėlėkėkė said if she had a boy they would exchange gifts.
   Yafo, yafo.
If she had a girl, she was to be his wife.
   Yafo, yafo.
The day arrived and a baby girl was born.
   Yafo, yafo.
Now we are going so that I may be the wife of Kėlėkėkė.
   Yafo, yafo.
You want to make a slave of me. I was only hiding under
   your cassava.
   Yafo, yafo.
I didn't dig any. Look at my hands and see if they are
   dirty.
   Yafo, yafo.
Look at my back and see if I have the strength to carry a
   basket of cassava roots.
   Yafo, yafo.

Then he realized that this was the girl who was to be his wife. "What's going on here? What could this child have done?" he demanded again.

Once more Nsonga told her story: "I found her in my garden stealing my cassava. She is a thief."

He turned to Liangu. "Tell me again." Liangu sang her story for him again.

> When Kėlėkėkė came to the home of my parents,
>> Yafo, yafo,
> Mother was weak with a pregnancy.
>> Yafo, yafo.
> Kėlėkėkė said if she had a boy they would exchange gifts.
>> Yafo, yafo.
> If she had a girl, she was to be his wife.
>> Yafo, yafo.
> The day arrived and a baby girl was born.
>> Yafo, yafo.
> Now we are going so that I may be the wife of Kėlėkėkė.
>> Yafo, yafo.
> You want to make a slave of me. I was only hiding under
>>   your cassava.
>> Yafo, yafo.
> I didn't dig any. Look at my hands and see if they are
>>   dirty.
>> Yafo, yafo.
> Look at my back and see if I have the strength to carry a
>>   basket of cassava roots.
>> Yafo, yafo.

"This is truly the child that I bargained for before she was born."

Her mother and father arrived at the house of Kėlėkėkė just then. The mother was crying because of their lost child. The father began to tell his story. "Remember when you visited us a long while ago. My wife was pregnant. You said that if it was a boy, we would exchange gifts; but if it was a girl, she would be your wife. The day you left, my wife had her baby. Now we have come to bring her to her marriage. But on the way there was a big storm; thunder and lightning frightened us. My wife and I ran, but Liangu went into a garden of cassava and hid there. The garden belonged to your wife. She came and accused Liangu of being a thief. But how could Liangu dig cassava or carry it since she is still a child?"

They called Liangu and examined her hands and found no dirt.

They examined her back and could tell that she hadn't carried a heavy basket on it.

Kėlėkėkė was angry. He said, "My wife must die. I should kill her myself. She is bad and ruins all of our reputations and especially that of Liangu. I could kill her, but I prefer to sell her. Then the new owner can tie her hands down with her clothes, stretch out her neck, and cut her throat."

And that is just what happened to Nsonga. Kėlėkėkė sold her. Her new owner tied her hands with her clothes; he stretched her neck and cut her throat.[5]

If you are forbidden something, leave it alone.

This *cante fable*, Tale 82, combines the repetition dear to Nkundo audiences with a strong ethical lesson that has been marked in Nkundo tale-telling throughout at least the first three quarters of the twentieth century, ranging from the tale "The Water-Fairies Save a Child" in Weeks' *Congo Life and Folklore* (1911) through the *Bekolo Bėmȯ* ... tale "The Thief and His Mother" (1957) to various tales in the Ross collection in which death threatens those guilty of theft. In Tale 78, the parents were ready to punish their daughter by drowning if she were proved the thief; in Tale 86, in which a boy "borrowed" his brother's bird, the boy could have lost his life in the dangerous process of retrieving the bird, which the owner considered as stolen. In the present tale, Liangu is faced with slavery if indeed she has stolen Nsonga's cassava. Clearly, theft in all these instances was considered reprehensible, as, indeed, it had been in countless cultures before that of the Nkundo.

The place of honesty in the Nkundo value system is most pointedly shown in the school-text tale "The Thief and His Mother," in which the thief is finally taken out to be killed. The Lonkundo wording, literally translated, reads thus: "they carried him that they kill him, killing completely." The mother follows, weeping. The son asks to speak with her and promptly cuts off her ear. When she reproaches him, he reminds her that had she taught him well in his youth, neither of them would have had this sorrow—his from death and hers from shame. His final admonition to her is "Stop this evil that it be not yet grown!": the evil of which he speaks is theft.

Lambrecht's tale type 1047 offers a tale from a Lingala-speaking area (closely associated with the Lonkundo-speaking area) in which a father teaches his son through experience "not to become a person who lives by theft." There is no tale type described in any of the indexes that combines the major elements of the present narrative.

Motifs:

T	K2127.	False accusation of theft.
T	K2150.	Innocent made to appear guilty.
T	K2110.	Slanders.
T	K2213.	Treacherous wife.
T	T257.2.	Jealousy of rival wives.
T	Q280.	Unkindness punished.
T	Q261.	Treachery punished.
T	Q331.	Pride punished.
T	L430.	Arrogance repaid.
C	Q411.+.	Death as punishment for mistreating girl.

1. Promising an unborn child in marriage is not uncommon among the Nkundo. A man likes to have a young wife in his old age, to care for him and to keep him warm (note, for example, the present narrator, Bongonda Michele, and his relatively young wife Amba). In this tale, the marriage arrangement was between distant kin and was attractive to both parties.

2. *Kao-kao* suggests heavy footsteps: the travelers were loaded with gifts for Kėlėkėkė and were tired from their journey.

3. Nsonga revealed her character as quickly as she discovered Liangu in her garden: she claimed the young girl as a slave. Whether it was customary to claim a thief as a slave, the narrator did not say; the people in the two encounters seemed willing to accept the condition if Nsonga could prove her claim. They were fair: they listened to Liangu and verified her testimony, and they also cautioned Nsonga of the danger of false accusation. Obviously, the accusation of theft was a very serious one.

4. Cassava is transported from the forest garden to the gardener's home in a *yuka*, a basket carried on the back. This basket, held in place by straps around the arms and shoulders, is very heavy, and the women lean forward and walk pigeon-toed so that they can balance it for carrying. Liangu would have had marks on her back if she had been carrying such loads.

5. In a culture where women have a high economic value, Kėlėkėkė's plan of such a morbid death for Nsonga places further emphasis on the seriousness of an accusation of theft in Nkundo communities.

That someone would buy Nsonga for a slave and then kill her suggests that the purchaser shared Kėlėkėkė's (and the community's) horror of theft and took this expensive means of making his horror known.

Narrator: Mpanga Iyende
Location: Bonga-Iteli
Date: December 1973

83. *The Supernatural Paramour*[1] *Tempted and Destroyed*

One morning a woman who had a husband[2] took her knife and went into the forest to hunt reeds that she make a basket. She went a long way, *ti-i-i-i*, where the reeds were growing, *ti-ti-ti-ti*. She cut and cut, *ki-ki-ki-ki*,[3] until she had enough for her basket; then she went on until she was in the forest itself.

She saw a man there who was shining bright[4] and up in a tree. She felt much fear, and as soon as he came down out of the tree, she bowed down before him.

He said, "I have a wife."

She answered, "I have a husband."

"Where do you come from, and what are you doing?"

"I am Bekombe. I have come from my village to cut reeds that I make a basket."

"I hear you. It is well when you come you call me. I will be here up in the tree. When you come again, call me."[5]

Narrator:	Eciko, come down,
Chorus:	you, you, you.
Narrator:	Someone has called you,
Chorus:	you, you, you.
Narrator:	That one Bekombe bia Bòndèkò calls
Chorus:	you, you, you.[6]

"You understand."

"Yes. I hear you clearly."

Bomoto,[7] *te-e-e, te-e-e*, went home and stayed there for a while, *ti-i-i*, and she stayed there for a while, *ti-i-i*.[8] One morning she took her knife. "I am going to cut reeds for a basket." She cooked food, manioc.

Narrator:	Eciko, come down,
Chorus:	you, you, you.

> *Narrator:* Someone has called you,
> *Chorus:*   you, you, you.
> *Narrator:* That one Bekombe bia Bòndèkò calls
> *Chorus:*   you, you, you.
> *Narrator:* Eciko, come down,
> *Chorus:*   you, you, you.

He came down and ate and ate the food, and they talked and talked and talked. She[9] returned.

Te-e-e, another morning she took food and went into the forest to cut reeds. She arrived there.

> *Narrator:* Eciko, come down,
> *Chorus:*   you, you, you.
> *Narrator:* Someone has called you,
> *Chorus:*   you, you, you.
> *Narrator:* That one Bekombe bia Bòndèkò calls
> *Chorus:*   you, you, you.

Then he came and they ate the food, *ti-i-i.* She returned.

Her husband said, "This woman every day says, 'I have to hunt reeds to make a basket.' A basket is something that a woman needs only one at a time.[10] A basket is something that she only needs one of, and she keeps going to get more." So he decided to follow her, *ti-ti-ti-ti-ti,* Bomoto first, him, Bome,[11] afterwards. They arrived there. She put her basket down and called,

> *Narrator:* Eciko, come down,
> *Chorus:*   you, you, you.
> *Narrator:* Someone has called you,
> *Chorus:*   you, you, you.
> *Narrator:* That one Bekombe bia Bòndèkò calls
> *Chorus:*   you, you, you.
> *Narrator:* Someone has seen you,
> *Chorus:*   you, you, you.
> *Narrator:* .   .   .[12]
> *Chorus:*   you, you, you.

"Someone is hiding nearby."
"I don't see anyone. Where is he?"

> *Narrator:* Eciko, come down,
> *Chorus:*   you, you, you.
> *Narrator:* Someone has called you,
> *Chorus:*   you, you, you.

Narrator:	That one Bekombe bia Bȯndėkȯ calls
Chorus:	you, you, you.
Narrator:	Someone has seen you,[13]
Chorus:	you, you, you.
Narrator:	. . .
Chorus:	you, you, you.

"Where is someone? I don't see anyone." She looked place and place.[14]

However, from his hiding place her husband could see this shining person in the tree. He was afraid, and hurried down the path for home.

Then Eciko came down and ate her food. He ate her food. She returned home.

Her husband told a friend of his experience, and what he had seen in the tree. The friend said, "I'm not afraid. I'll follow her and find out about this."[15] The friend said, "I want to see this shining man. I'm going there."

When she arrived there, the wife first and the friend after, Bomoto arrived.[16]

Narrator:	Eciko, come down,
Chorus:	you, you, you.
Narrator:	Someone has called you,
Chorus:	you, you, you.
Narrator:	That one Bekombe bia Bȯndėkȯ calls
Chorus:	you, you, you.
Narrator:	Someone has seen you,
Chorus:	you, you, you.
Narrator:	. . .
Chorus:	you, you, you.

"Somebody's there!"

"Where is he?" She hunted place and place.[17]

The friend saw the man up in the tree and was afraid and ran away.

Another friend said, "Me until I arrive there." One morning he sharpened his knife, *a-o-siy'a-o-siy'a-o-siy'a*, until it was very sharp. This morning he said, "I am going to follow her until I get there." He followed on another path until he got there, and then he hid.[18]

The wife called,

> *Narrator:* Eciko, come down,
> *Chorus:*   you, you, you.
> *Narrator:* Someone has called you,
> *Chorus:*   you, you, you.
> *Narrator:* That one Bekombe bia Bȯndėkȯ calls
> *Chorus:*   you, you, you.
> *Narrator:* Someone has seen you,[19]
> *Chorus:*   you, you, you.
> *Narrator:* .   .   .
> *Chorus:*   you, you, you.

"I can't see anybody. I've looked place and place, and nobody, nobody."

"But somebody's there."

"Oh, *nyė.* I don't see anybody."

> *Narrator:* Eciko, come down,
> *Chorus:*   you, you, you.
> *Narrator:* Someone has called you,
> *Chorus:*   you, you, you.
> *Narrator:* That one Bekombe bia Bȯndėkȯ calls
> *Chorus:*   you, you, you.
> *Narrator:* Someone has seen you,
> *Chorus:*   you, you, you.
> *Narrator:* .   .   .
> *Chorus:*   you, you, you.

"*Bonne.*[20] I don't want difficulty. If you say that no one is there, I'll come down."

> *Narrator:* Eciko, come down,
> *Chorus:*   you, you, you.
> *Narrator:* Someone has called you,
> *Chorus:*   you, you, you.
> *Narrator:* That one Bekombe bia Bȯndėkȯ calls
> *Chorus:*   you, you, you.
> *Narrator:* Someone has seen you,
> *Chorus:*   you, you, you.
> *Narrator:* .   .   .
> *Chorus:*   you, you, you.

He came down. When he came down, the friend of her husband shot him with an arrow and then finished killing him with his knife.

The wife ran away.[21]

A woman is like Satan. Even though he saw the man, his desire for the woman made him come down, and he died.

> *Narrator:*   The sun has set.
> *Chorus:*   The action is finished.[22]

Tale 83 is a curious mixture of the supernatural and the age-old problem of the "triangle." Eciko, whose name means "an arbor," "a bower," or "a mating place," had human desires and appetites but was in appearance clearly supernatural.

This is the only narrative treatment of marital infidelity encountered in Mrs. Ross's field collecting; Bob Stewart, who recorded this and the other tales in Bonga for Mrs. Ross, was known not to understand the dialect in which the tale was told. Obviously, the tale was presented to a male-female, adult-child audience, indicating that such narratives can be told freely among the Nkundo. The question as to whether this or a similar tale would have been told to a white woman missionary is pertinent; further collecting to determine the answer will be aided by knowledge of the existence of this tale in the current oral tradition.

We were unable to secure a copy of the West African tale cited in Clarke's Motif-Index . . . as the source for his new motif T230.+. It is possible that that tale, drawn from the German-language collection by Himmelheber (*Aura Poku, Volksdichtung aus Westafrika* [1951]), includes at least some of the same elements as are found here.

Aarne-Thompson's tale type 1380 (The Faithless Wife) would seem on the basis of the caption to fit this story; the wife's faithlessness, however, is the only element common to both tales. This narrative might reasonably be assigned a letter in addition to the Aarne-Thompson number, yielding tale type 1380B.

Motifs:

T	F521.3.4.**.	Person whose body shines like silver.
T	F500.**.	Remarkable persons: man with extraordinary shining appearance.
T	C0.	Tabu: contact with supernatural.
T	T111.	Marriage of mortal with supernatural being.
T	T135.1.**.	Formulistic exchange of marriage vows between supernatural being and human: "I have a wife." "I have a husband."
C	T230.+.**.	Faithful husband, unfaithful wife.
C	H1300.+.**.	Quest for "something": husband seeks cause for wife's frequent visits for reeds for baskets.
C	F401.2.+.**.	Luminous spirits: "shining" man becomes paramour/husband of already-married woman.

T	K1550.1.**.	Husband discovers wife's unfaithfulness.
T	T257.	Jealous wife or husband.
T	C169.**.	Tabu connected with marriage—miscellaneous: taking second (supernatural) husband.
C	F401.2.+.**.	Luminous spirits: "shining" man awes men as well as woman.
T	K1569.5.**.	Husband catches paramour by having friend follow unfaithful wife to tryst.
T	K800.	Killing or maiming by deception.

1. Although no details are given to establish the certainty of an adulterous connection, the appearance created by the secret meetings between Eciko and Bekombe suggests adultery.

2. The narrator's initial identification of Bekombe as "a woman who had a husband" presupposes circumspect behavior in keeping with Nkundo standards. Thus the listeners are prepared to judge her irregular relationship with the supernatural stranger as they would weigh it in a palaver. To add emphasis to his disapproval of this liaison, the narrator withholds any mention of the woman's husband until there have been several trysts in the forest.

It would be interesting to hear a female narrator's version of this tale—if, indeed, a female narrator would undertake to tell such a tale—to see what artistic devices she might use to make the woman's position more socially acceptable in an Nkundo setting.

3. An onomatopoetic expression reproducing the sound made by the knife as the reeds were cut.

4. The Lonkundo term *ngesi-ngesi*, translated here and in everyday usage as "shining bright," is the one used for the Transfiguration in the Lonkundo translation of the New Testament.

5. [Explanatory material inserted by the narrator: "She called his name *Eciko* and her name along with her mother's name, *Bekombe bia Bòndèkò*. Her name was Bekombe and she was born of Bòndèkò. This would identify her before he would come down out of the tree."]

As in Tale 87, a song is sung both to summon and to reassure an unusual creature. The same device is used in various *cante fables* in Botswana, notably one in which a servant boy sent to fetch a fertility potion for his master's wife drinks the potion, in due time is delivered of a child, hides the child in a tree, and announces his coming to feed it by a similar identifying song; this song, imitated by the master's wife, enables her to recover the child intended to be hers. [Tale told by Botsang Mosienyane on tape for Barbara K. Walker]

6. At this point, Bekombe's song is presented, in a fashion encountered only rarely among the Ross-collected tales: it has the character of a two-part round in that both the narrator and the chorus are singing at the same time, lines of the same length, but the chorus repeats the same words ("you, you, you") while the narrator varies the words sung; neither the narrator nor the chorus sings alone at any point. In the song, there is no interval greater than a fourth in either part sung.

7. Here the narrator calls her *Woman*, using "*Bomoto*," the Lonkundo equivalent of the word, as a proper name. The tone in which the word is spoken suggests

the disapprobation felt by the narrator, who has already given her name—Bekombe —but chooses here not to accord her that dignity.

8. The repetition here serves to increase suspense as well as to suggest the woman's impatience to be in the forest instead of at home.

9. There is no distinction in Lonkundo between "he" and "she"; the sense here appears to demand "she," since the following paragraph has her starting out from home.

10. The narrator here is deliberately strengthening the case against the woman. Actually, a woman *may* have more than one basket. Though she carries her basket on her back and can thus carry only one at a time, she will probably have another basket full of cassava roots soaking in the swamp. Bekombe's need for so *many* baskets might well make her husband suspicious, however. The fretful tone in which the narrator expresses the husband's perplexity about his wife's basket-making buttresses the audience's sympathy for the husband.

11. *"Bome,"* or "husband," used here as the proper name for the man, takes on extra force in its contrast with *"Bomoto"*; the replacement of the Lonkundo term *"Waji,"* "Wife," by "Woman" underscores the broken relationship between them: he is still functioning as the husband, but she has abandoned her station as a wife.

12. The sense of this line has been lost; the narrator is distracted by an audience sound, and briefly loses his involvement in the song.

13. There is a marked hesitation before the narrator sings this line, and the chorus waits until the narrator begins his line to sing "you, you, you" as an "overlay."

14. A characteristic Lonkundo locution—*wiji la wiji*, literally "place and place" —suggesting "everywhere," in a frenzied type of search.

15. Here the narrator has made a false start—"Then she started out ... " —and he pauses momentarily to rephrase.

16. This narrator has a tendency toward repetition that seems careless but is deftly planned to maintain suspense and to focus the audience's attention on the dramatic action to follow.

17. Great excitement is shown by the narrator in this dialogue, increasing tension in the listeners.

18. [Narrator's explanatory material: "He was on a path that was near, but parallel to the path that she was on."]

19. Again, the narrator hesitates before beginning this line, and again the chorus waits for him.

20. The dialectal form of the French word *"bon"* appears here; the expression "Good" accentuates the irony: the narrator has Bekombe unwittingly entice Eciko out of the tree to meet his death at the hands of the husband's well-armed friend. (The courage of the friend is underlined by his persisting in his intention despite the fear he must have felt—as, indeed, had both the husband and the first friend, as evidenced by their hasty retreats from the scene on viewing the "shining" man— in the light of the long-term influence of animism in the Cuvette.)

Bekombe's eagerness had blinded her to the dangers of their illicit encounters. Though she has looked "place and place," she has protected her paramour's life no more carefully than she has protected her husband's interests.

21. The wife knows that there will be no place for her now in her community, and she is more willing to face the uncertain dangers of the ogre-inhabited bush than the certain outcome of the palaver.

22. The Lonkundo words used in the concluding exchange are "*Ili!*" and "*Yo!*" with a rising inflection on the "*-li!*" and a falling inflection on the "*Yo!*" Both terms are shouted, serving to vent the feeling that has accumulated during the telling of this emotion-charged tale.

Narrator:	Bokunge Jacques
Location:	Bòléngè
Date:	March 1973

84. *The Co-Wife Who Demanded Her Scarring Instrument*

On another day, Waji (Wife), Bome (Husband), and Bòna (Child)[1] went into the forest to hunt. In not a long while, they built a temporary shelter where they could eat and sleep and dry their meat. Then Husband built a fence trap, building, building, that he catch many animals.

The next morning, Husband went out to check his traps. *Mo!* He had caught not a few animals. He took them back to the shelter, and Wife cooked some of the meat for them to eat. What she did not cook, she put on the shelf to dry.[2] Each day, they ate some of the meat and dried some that they save it.

One morning, Husband left to check the traps, as was his work, and Wife stayed at their shelter to care for the meat. After Husband had been gone not a long while, an ogre came to the shelter. He said to Wife, "Eat all the meat that you have, *o-bio!*[3] Eat even all the meat that is drying on the shelf, *o-bio!*" After she had eaten it all, eating, eating, the ogre went away into the forest.[4]

Husband came back from his traps and said, "Bring food that I eat."

Wife felt much fear of Husband. She told him that, "I do not know where the food is." Husband felt anger, and he beat her, beating itself. After that, she said, "An ogre came and ate all the meat."[5]

The next morning, Husband hid with his iron-tipped arrows.[6] After not a long while, he saw the ogre coming. He aimed and shot an arrow. The ogre fell dead, dead dead. Then Husband, Wife, and Child quickly packed their things and went home with haste itself, *lomo-lomo*.[7]

In not a little while after they arrived home, Bokali (Co-Wife) came to see them.[8] Wife had borrowed Co-Wife's *lótèbu* (scarring instrument)[9] to use during the hunting trip. Wife explained to Co-Wife, explaining, explaining, all of the problems about the ogre[10] and that in their haste she had forgotten the scarring instrument and had left it in the hunting shelter. "I'll get you another one," she said.

But Co-Wife was not satisfied, *nyè*. "No, I don't want another one. I must have my very own scarring instrument."

Wife said that, "It isn't possible to return your own. I will give you a hundred scarring instruments instead."[11]

"No, no!" Co-Wife insisted. "I want my very own scarring instrument."

Wife explained, explaining, "If I go into the forest again, the ogres will surely kill me. I pray that you will agree for me to return two hundred scarring instruments to you."

Co-Wife was not satisfied, *nyè*. "I must have my own scarring instrument, the very scarring instrument that is mine."

Finally Wife went back into the forest to hunt Co-Wife's scarring instrument. As she went, she found a very old lady in the path. Ekoto (Old Lady)[12] said that, "Help me to bathe myself and then rub me with oil before you go to get the scarring instrument. If you do this, you will have no difficult problems at all, *nyè*."

So Wife bathed Old Lady and rubbed her with oil. Then Old Lady said that, "Go. The name of the ogre which you killed is Nkok'iyou.[13] When you find many people together who are crying, you go into that *botumba*[14] and you cry with them. When they ask you why you are crying, say that, 'He was one of my very own fathers.' Then you will see the scarring instrument. Take it and put it in the folds of your cloth and go home very fast, *lomo-lomo*."

Wife left Old Lady and went on her way. Soon she came to a house with not a few people who were all crying. She entered and began to cry with them. They asked that, "What are you doing here?" She answered that, "He was one of my very own fathers."

Then she saw the scarring instrument. She took it and put it in the folds of her cloth. Soon she slipped out and went home by night, quickly, quickly. When Co-Wife saw her very own scarring instrument, she was satisfied.

After not many days had passed, Co-Wife borrowed Wife's needle[15] that she sew a cloth. While she had the needle, her child swallowed the needle into its stomach. When Wife heard about this, she went to Co-Wife and said, "I have some sewing to do. Give me my needle."

Co-Wife answered that, "My child has swallowed your needle. It is fitting that I give you two hundred needles instead."[16]

Wife said that, "Do not forget: I wanted to return two hundred scarring instruments to you when I forgot yours and left it in the shelter. But you refused. You said that, 'I want my very own scarring instrument.' Now I will not be satisfied until you give me my very own needle."

So finally they killed Co-Wife's child and found the needle that Wife be satisfied.

Don't oppress a friend by extortion lest you do as Co-Wife and her friend.

[Notes for Tale 84 follow Tale 85.]

Source: Bekolo Bèmò . . .
               Zaïrian school reader
               (in Lonkundo)
Translator: Mabel Ross
Date of Translation: November 1972

85.   The Co-Wife Who Demanded Her Scarring Instrument (Variant)

One day a certain woman went into the forest; she went with her husband and her child.

The husband built a leaf wall for trapping animals. Then he returned to the shelter in the forest. In the morning, he went to check the traps. He had killed many animals. The wife cooked some of the meat, and some they put over the fire to dry. In the evening they ate some meat and stored some.

Another morning, the husband went to check the traps. His wife remained in the shelter. After the husband had gone, an ogre came to the wife. He said, "Eat every bit of the food in one swallow—even the meat that is drying on the shelf." Then he returned into the forest.

Her husband came from the forest and he said, "Bring food."

The wife felt much fear before her husband and said, "I do not know where the meat is." Then her husband beat her very hard. Afterwards, she told her husband, "An ogre ate all the food."

The next morning, the husband hid with iron-tipped arrows. Soon he saw the ogre come and he shot an arrow, and the ogre was dead. He and his wife and child put their things in a bag and they went home fast, *lomo-lomo*.

When they arrived home, the wife had forgotten the scarring instrument of her co-wife. The co-wife said, "You must bring me my very own scarring instrument."

She told her co-wife that she would return one hundred scarring instruments instead. But the co-wife said, "No, no! I want my very own."

And she said, "If I go into the forest, the rest of the ogres will kill me. I entreat you that you agree that I return two hundred scarring instruments."

But the co-wife said, "I want my very own." So she went back into the forest to hunt the scarring instrument of her co-wife.

As she went, she found a very old woman on the path. That old lady said, "You bathe me and rub me with oil; then you go and get the scarring instrument. Then there will be nothing difficult about it."

So she bathed the old woman and rubbed her with oil. Then the old woman said to her, "Go, and the name of the ogre whom you killed is Nkok'iyou. When you find some people who are crying, you go into the gathering place and cry with them. And when they ask you about it, say, 'He is one of our fathers.' And then you will see the scarring instrument. Take it, put it in the fold of your cloth, and go home at night with much haste."

The woman did as the old lady had told her; she saw the scarring instrument; she returned with it at night itself and arrived home safely. Then she gave her co-wife the scarring instrument.

After not many days had passed, the co-wife borrowed her needle in order to sew some cloth. The co-wife's child swallowed the needle right into his stomach.

The woman said to the co-wife, "Give me my needle."

The co-wife said, "My child has swallowed the needle. Let me give you two hundred needles instead."

But the woman said, "I did not return two hundred scarring instruments to you, and I do not like your way. You must give me my very own needle."

So they killed the child of the co-wife and took the woman's needle to her.[17]

The tale of the scarring instrument and the needle had been included some fifteen years earlier in *Bekolo Bėmŏ* ... , a school text. Undoubtedly, Bokunge had read that text at some time or another; unquestionably, he had heard the tale himself from the elders of his village when he was growing up. The version told by Bokunge Jacques, Tale 84, is clearly richer in Lonkundo locutions than is the variant (Tale 85) translated from the school text; the pair of tales affords an excellent opportunity for comparison of content, narrative style, and diction toward a fuller recognition of what can happen to an oral narrative when it is "frozen" into print by recorders whose first language is not that of the narrators.

Despite the fact that in an Nkundo village most things are held in common —if not community-wide, at least within the family—there are certain objects that are individually owned, and possession of these objects is vigorously defended. The "eye-for-an-eye" pattern of retaliation for the violation of such personal property rights is evidenced in several of the tales in the Ross collection (see Tale 32 for an animal tale reflecting this Nkundo practice).

There are variants of the basic tale listed both in Arewa's study and in Lambrecht's, suggesting that the theme is not uncommon in sub-Sahara Africa. Arewa's tale type 3830 furnishes an account of a man who returned to the owner the very cow he had trapped—retrieving it at considerable risk—and then exacted from the cow's owner the bell he had been enticed into swallowing; return of the bell cost the swallower his life. Lambrecht's tale type 3831 tells of a weaver who, tempting the hunter's dog to eat some meat, then claimed the dog had stolen the meat, and—despite many counter offers—killed the dog to recover his meat; subsequently, the weaver's son swallowed a pearl intended for the hunter's daughter, and the hunter claimed the life of the child in order to recover the lost pearl (applying, as he said, the weaver's own rules). But, relenting, he took nothing at all in exchange for the pearl. The latter portion of Lambrecht's tale type 1980 furnishes the closest parallel to the present pair of narratives, however: a co-wife has her axe stolen by a djinn angered by the first wife, and the co-wife demands the return of that very axe. At great hazard to herself, the wife recovers and returns the axe; she retaliates when the co-wife's child swallows one of the wife's cowry shells and is killed to allow recovery of that very cowry shell. (Lambrecht notes that the people of the community approved "for his mother had acted in the same manner previously"; this tale, collected among the Bolia—located not far south of the Nkundo—and published in French by Mamet, indicates that the "eye-for-an-eye" theme does indeed reflect the culture/value system to be found in more than one tribal group in Zaïre.) In neither of the first two types cited above did a child of the original "demander" actually pay with his life in the course of the retaliation; this factor *is* present both in the Ross-offered pair of tales and in Lambrecht's tale type 1980.

Motifs:

T	G512.1.**.	Ogre killed with bow and arrow.
T	C784.**.	Tabu: lending, with return of exact object lent required.
C	H1220.1.+.	Quest undertaken to pay debt.
T	H1289.3.1.	Quest: recovery of scarring needle from ogre-inhabited forest.
T	N825.3.	Old woman helper.
T	H1233.1.1.	Old woman helps on quest.
T	Q40.	Kindness rewarded.
T	Q41.2.**.	Aid in quest provided in return for bathing and oiling skin of old woman.
T	C920.1.**.	Death of child for mother's breaking of tabu: recovery of exact object lent causes death of child.
T	Q338.	Immoderate request punished.
T	J1511.	A rule must work both ways.

1. Here again, a general term furnishes the proper name for each character.

2. The Nkundo, lacking refrigeration in the rural areas, preserve both meat and fish by drying. Every house and temporary shelter has a shelf or rack well above the fire where the meat can be left to be dried and smoked. Foods preserved in this manner are quite palatable.

3. Bokunge did not explain why he included this particular expression except that it emphasized "all" and added flavor to the hearing.

4. No explanation was given by the narrator as to why the ogre made the woman eat the meat instead of eating it himself, nor was any account provided of the child's interaction with either character in the encounter.

5. Wife wisely elected to receive a beating rather than to disclose the fact that an ogre had visited her; one does not generally report contacts with the supernatural (an exception occurs in Tale 66). When she finally confessed that an ogre had come, she still did not reveal *all* of the truth: that she herself had been forced to eat the food. Further punishment would undoubtedly have followed such a revelation, since certain portions of animals are proscribed to women among the Nkundo.

Since the wife is (by fact of purchase as well as by tradition) the property of the husband, nothing prohibits him from treating her as he sees fit. The use of the reflexive "itself" after "beating" indicates the severity with which the wife was beaten.

6. Iron implements, including iron-tipped arrows, were in common use in Central Africa long before the coming of the white man to that continent. The arrows used by the Nkundo vary in design; the barbs make the arrows exceedingly difficult to extract from living flesh. There is no indication that the arrow held any magical power; it was well aimed, and it effected its purpose.

7. *Lomo-lomo*, an ideophone based on the Lonkundo word "*lomo*" ("breathe" or "quick breathing"), is aptly used here to describe the shortness of breath resulting from the family's desperate running.

8. When a man among the Nkundo has more than one wife, he takes turns eating with each one and sharing her sleeping mat; each wife has her own hut and her own kitchen, though the wives normally share the heavy work to be done for the husband. The first wife has somewhat more status than do succeeding wives, but there is considerable jealousy among them, and a good deal of competition for the husband's attention is evident.

"*Bokali*" can mean "spirit," "specter," "ghost," or "co-wife." Because Mrs. Ross encountered this tale in the oral tradition and had the term interpreted as "co-wife," she was able to establish the meaning of this word in the school-text variant. In Lonkundo, as is true with a number of other languages (including Turkish), the third-person-singular pronoun has no gender, so the sex of "*bokali*" could provide no clue. Also, since Nkundo men as well as women sew—most of the tailors are men—the detail concerning the needle would not assist the translator in determining the sex of "*bokali*."

9. Every Nkundo woman owns a *lótèbu* (plural, *ntèbu*), now used for grooming the hair; the sharp end is used for parting the hair, and the razorlike blade on the other end is used for cutting the hair. At one time, this tool was used extensively for making the body markings or tribal scars. Why Wife did not have her own scarring instrument was not explained; the borrowing of a scarring instrument here is of course central to the narrative.

One of the useful and interesting bits of oral history collected by Mrs. Ross after she had won the confidence of Bokunge Jacques serves here to substantiate the origin of tribal markings among the Nkundo, material which belongs logically with tales involving scarring instruments. Since it is part of the Ross field collection, this account follows with a standard headnote, a title, a motif number which seems appropriate, and supplementary notes.

Narrator:	Bokunge Jacques
Location:	Bólèngè
Date:	March 1973

The Origin of Tribal Markings

A very long time ago, our fathers didn't live here in this area but came from a long way away. They moved from one place to another because of one tribal war after another. Then the Arabs came, along with the Portuguese. They came with guns, while the people here had only bows and arrows. The people here also used shields when they fought. These protected them from arrows. But gun-shot would go through the shield and into the person. The Arabs took our fathers by the thousands and sold them in marketplaces just as meat is sold. They were confined with people who could not speak their own language, and this was more difficult.

Long, long before the slave traders came to Africa, many tribes decided to have markings on their faces and bodies. This was so that one tribe could be distinguished from another. You must remember that God put a mark on Cain's forehead so that people would recognize him wherever he went.

Motif:

C   A1687.+.   Origin of tribal marks.

Since Negroid peoples seem to scar easily, forming keloids, the *lòtèbu*, or scarring instrument, could be used for inserting certain medications under the skin to form keloids in whatever pattern was desired. From Bokunge's account, one concludes that marking for tribal identification was well established before the slave traders came. However, during the slave-trading era, more extensive patterns on the body proved protective, because the slave traders, particularly interested in perfect bodies, would often reject a body that had scars on it.

Little or no tribal marking is being done among the Nkundo now. Not only would such decorations—except for facial markings—be covered by modern clothing, but the urgent need for them has passed.

The freedom the narrator felt in innovation in the recounting of this bit of oral history is suggested by the inclusion of a reference to Cain, evidence both of acculturation and of the narrator's awareness of his audience and the importance of fitting the narration to the audience.

10. Wife doubtless omitted—as she had with her husband—the detail that she herself had eaten the meat; such information would speedily have been conveyed to her husband by the co-wife.

11. The offer of a hundred or two hundred *ntèbu* seems to be an exaggeration intended to add flavor to the tale; a woman would have great difficulty in acquiring even fifty scarring instruments. The offer—impossible as it was of fulfillment—serves the narrative function of pointing up the wife's sense of desperation at the

prospect of returning to the ogre-inhabited forest on an even more impossible quest, a sense of desperation readily shared by the audience.

12. *"Ekoto"* is a term of respect used in addressing a very old lady; in this tale, the term furnishes the proper name for the woman herself. Seldom are these elderly people left with no one to care for them. Evidently, Ekoto in this tale had no children or other family members to care for her, and Wife came at precisely the right time. (Tale 32 presents an old man in a similar situation.) Respect for age, a strong element in the Nkundo value system, is repeatedly reflected in the oral narratives both in the Ross collection and in the Nkundo tales available in Flemish and in French.

In the role of the Wise Old Counselor, Old Lady already knows Wife's situation and also that of the ogres. Refusal to follow Old Lady's directions would traditionally have resulted in failure in the quest.

13. This name signifies "grandfathers" or "forefathers."

14. See Tale 80 for other uses of this village gathering place.

15. The borrowing and subsequent loss of a needle in a tale from Lesotho (see Postma's *Tales from the Basotho*, pp. 37–41) accounts for the hawk's relentless pursuit of chickens, as well as for hens' practice of scratching in the ground, searching always for the lost needle.

16. It would be impossible for an Nkundo woman to secure even *fifty* needles. Needles are bought one at a time and are safeguarded. The offer, made to indicate the impossibility of the task, also serves as a narrative device to indicate the extent to which the woman would go to ensure the life of her child. The listeners, well aware of the high value placed in Nkundo culture on the having of children, here faced the conflict of two important elements: the consanguineal tie and the obligation to respect personal ownership. Obviously, the content of Nkundo oral narratives is not lightly considered; such tales cut close to the bone of Nkundo life, and reveal its living tissue.

17. The Lonkundo original of this tale, titled "Bomoto l'okale la Bome l'ona" ("The Woman and Her Co-Wife and Husband and Child"), appears on pages 23–25 of *Bekolo Bèmö.* . . .

Narrator: Amba Engombe Telesa
Location: Bólèngè
Date: March 1973

86.   *The Two Brothers and Their Birds*

A woman had two sons. One day the woman and her sons went into the forest to hunt meat. It had been raining, and they found a large puddle of water there. They found some large branches from a tree and washed them. Then they laid them around the water like spokes of a wheel. Over these branches they spread the raw sap from the rubber tree.

They watched. Soon a flock of birds came to take a bath. When the birds came out of the water, their feathers were caught in the raw rubber. Then the mother and sons collected the birds to sell as food in the market.[1]

The older boy, Botomolo,[2] didn't want to kill all the birds. He said, "I want one of the birds for my own." So they were all killed and marketed except the one bird that he had chosen.

That evening the family gathered to hear Older Brother's bird sing. They said to the bird, "Sing. Let us hear you."

The bird sang his song:

> This is the way he acquired this bird:
> It flew down into the puddle,
> So he has me as his bird;
> It flew down into the puddle.

The news of the bird's song went from village to village and people came. "We want to hear the bird sing."

Older Brother's bird and its song became known far and wide, and Older Brother was pleased. The people paid Older Brother when they heard the bird sing. The bird kept singing the same song, and everyone enjoyed it.

One morning very early Older Brother got up and went into the forest to hunt. His younger brother, Bokune, decided to take the bird out of doors.

His mother said, "No, no!"

His father said, "No, no!"[3]

"I want to take him out to hear him sing. Then I'll bring him back into the house."

As soon as the bird was outside he began to sing,

> This is the way he acquired this bird:
> It flew down into the puddle,
> So he has me as his bird;
> It flew down into the puddle.

As soon as the song was finished it flew onto the roof:

> This is the way he acquired this bird:
> It flew down into the puddle,
> So he has me as his bird;
> It flew down into the puddle.

Then the bird flew over to the top of a banana tree:[4]

> This is the way he acquired this bird:
> It flew down into the puddle,
> So he has me as his bird;
> It flew down into the puddle.

The mother was shocked. "*Mo!*[5] What can we do?"

The bird flew into the very tallest tree. The tree was so tall it had no leaves:[6]

> This is the way he acquired this bird:
> It flew down into the puddle,
> So he has me as his bird;
> It flew down into the puddle.

His father and mother were very angry. "Why did you take him out? Your brother will be very unhappy."

Older Brother came in from the forest that evening. The first thing he did was go to see his bird.

"Where is my bird?"[7]

"Your brother took him out to sing. He flew until he arrived in the very tallest tree."

He tried to call the bird, but to no avail. His parents offered to get him another one, but he must have his own with its own song.

Finally they called the elders of the family to cut the palaver. It was decided that Younger Brother should climb the tree and get the bird.

Younger Brother took the lunch[8] that his mother had prepared for him and put it in a bag over his shoulder. The mother, father, and

Younger Brother went into the forest. Younger Brother fastened his *bolango*[9] around the tree and started to climb. He moved the belt a bit higher as he walked slowly up the tree. His mother and father heard him sing before he was halfway up the tree:[10]

> As the belt makes its way up the tree,
> Jumping, jumping,
> I climb and continue to weep,
> Jumping, jumping.

They watched him climb until he was just over halfway:

> As the belt makes its way up the tree,
> Jumping, jumping,
> I climb and continue to weep,
> Jumping, jumping.

He climbed a bit further and they heard him sing the song again:

> As the belt makes its way up the tree,
> Jumping, jumping,
> I climb and continue to weep,
> Jumping, jumping.

Then as he climbed they could see him only partially, like an airplane that is going through misty clouds.[11] They could still hear his song:

> As the belt makes its way up the tree,
> Jumping, jumping,
> I climb and continue to weep,
> Jumping, jumping.

Then he disappeared completely, and the song was gone also. However, some of the leaves that his mother had used for wrapping his cassava fell to the ground, and they knew that he had stopped to eat.

The mother said, "I can't see him at all."

The mother and father stayed near the tree[12] and watched and waited. Two months passed,[13] and they accused Older Brother of killing Younger Brother.[14]

However, one day while they were watching, they heard his song:

> As the belt makes its way up the tree,
> Jumping, jumping,

> I climb and continue to weep,
> Jumping, jumping.

Then, soon they could just see him. He began to grow larger and larger as he descended from the tree, singing as he came.[15] They could see that his bag was full, so they supposed that he must have the bird.

When he reached the ground, his mother embraced him and said, "My son, I was sure you were dead. I couldn't see you." Then his father embraced him and the rest of the family.[16]

By then they were ready to hear his story.

When he had reached the top of the tree, a flock of birds came and roosted nearby. He was able to grab one. He took it and put it in his sack. Then he captured another and put it in his sack. "I heard all the birds sing together, and it was terrible.[17] Then I heard the very song[18] of Older Brother's bird and I knew I had found him. I grabbed him and put him in the sack with the others. Then I adjusted the belt again and climbed down out of the tree. I went up as a slave, but now I am free."[19]

After he had told his story, his mother gave him food.[20] Then they gathered to hear the birds. He took the two birds out of the sack and they sang,

> *Imbombe ika lonyanga*
> *Te tu.*
> *Njokwalimwa.*[21]

The people were more than pleased with the song. Then Older Brother took his bird and it sang,

> This is the way he acquired this bird:
> It flew down into the puddle,
> So he has me as his bird;
> It flew down into the puddle.

Everyone liked the song of Younger Brother's birds better than the song of Older Brother's bird. From then on, people came to hear Younger Brother's birds and refused to hear Older Brother's bird. Bokune became a very rich man, and Botomolo became a fool.[22]

Do not do evil to another lest the evil which you did will be seen.

Tale 86 and several others in the Ross collection (see especially Tales 32, 57, 84, and 85) focus on the demand of an individual—usually a person, but sometimes an antelope or other nonhuman animal—for the return of the *exact* object lent or lost. In each instance, an offer of substitution is made by the debtor or his family, but the offer is indignantly refused. Recovery of the missing item (a bird, a scarring instrument, a gourd carried away by the river, a wife drowned during an ordeal, or "truth test") in each case is at best difficult and dangerous, perhaps utterly impossible. Nonetheless, these samples from the oral tradition indicate that the demand must be met. In each of the tales cited, the demand *is* met, by one means or another (supernatural elements are included in most of these narratives), but in all except one story the creditor pays dearly for his stubborn insistence. All of these tales should fit within a single type (see below), but apparently in whatever tales found in other cultures that have involved such demands, the "demand" portion has been subordinated to some other factor, leading to classification that reflects the more dominant element.

Arewa's tale type 3485A offers limited help in classifying this tale: in Arewa's sample, a son allows his father's dove to escape; the father wants to kill the son for his misdeed; the boy recovers the dove at last; the father remains poor forever, though the son has become rich. Aarne-Thompson's types 467 and 468 offer "squinting" assistance, even more limited than that furnished by the Arewa sample. No single tale type found thus far adequately serves the needs of the present narrative.

Motifs:

T	B211.3.	Speaking bird.
T	H1132.	Task: recovering lost objects.
C	H1220.1.+.	Quest undertaken to pay debt.
T	H1280.	Quests to other realms.
T	F54.2.**.	Tree reaches sky.
T	N143.**.	Luck only with bird that is gained through courage.
T	L420.	Overweening ambition punished.

1. According to the narrator, the technique used by the mother and her sons for catching birds is common among the Nkundo.

2. *Botomolo*, the Lonkundo word for "older sibling of the same sex," and *Bokune*, the Lonkundo word for "younger sibling of the same sex," are used throughout this tale, as in many others, as the characters' proper names. For convenience, the boys have been termed "Older Brother" and "Younger Brother."

3. Most Nkundo households respect private ownership within the family, and Botomolo's family seemed to be no exception; both parents strongly discouraged Bokune from disregarding this custom. The expression used for their protests was the Lonkundo doubled form of "no": "*Nyo, nyo!*"

4. The bird's flying to higher and higher points from which he could sing what had become a taunting song clearly increases narrative suspense.

5. Both surprise and dismay are suggested in this particular use of *Mo!*

6. As the tale develops, the tree does have both branches and leaves, but they

are not visible from the ground. In this densely forested tropical area, competition for available sunlight and the resultant tall growth of the crowded trees had doubtless caused the loss of the lower branches.

7. Older Brother's concern for his bird was justified not only because the bird was his, but because it represented a source of income; supplementary income is highly valued by the Nkundo.

8. The narrator explained that the mother had cassava soaking in the swamp. She steamed this and wrapped it in leaves in small packages. The narrator does not mention Younger Brother's carrying a supply of water; the boy could probably catch dew or rain water on a leaf when he became thirsty.

9. The tree he was climbing must have had an exceptionally tall trunk, since Younger Brother was almost out of sight before he reached branches and had to leave the climbing belt behind, to be used when he descended.

10. Younger Brother's song serves here as a work song, to lighten the labor of climbing, as well as a means of expressing his grief and anxiety. As the sound of the song becomes fainter, suspense is increased, also; thus the song serves several functions in the narrative.

11. Inclusion of the airplane image seems anachronistic; actually, Bòlèngè has for several decades been within the flight pattern of various planes and, as narrators have always done, Amba here has drawn her image from an object in her environment familiar both to herself and to her listeners. In a nineteenth-century version of this tale, the narrator would probably have used some high-flying living creature (an eagle, a hawk) as a basis for the comparison, instead of an airplane. As the culture changes, the folktale mirrors these changes.

12. Younger Brother's parents, though they had sent him on what seemed an impossible mission, faithfully kept watch for his return. "I was sure you were dead," his mother greeted him—but she was there ready to receive him when he appeared. Blood ties—especially those between parent and child—are very close among the Nkundo. (See the concluding portion of Tale 87 for an instance where paternal love outweighs the marital tie, a choice quite in keeping with the Nkundo value system.)

13. It was not explained either in the tale or by the narrator where Younger Brother went during the two months of his absence or how he managed to live during that period. Perhaps this is a truncated version of a longer tale.

14. This accusation seems natural but unjust; both Younger Brother and his parents had sought the advice of the elders and had followed their counsel. The proverbial wisdom of the Nkundo, however, counsels against *unreasonable* insistence on matters of lost property.

15. Since this was among the tales erased to make room for those collected later, there is no means of determining whether the narrator repeated the song several times as she described Younger Brother's descent. Normally, a storyteller would repeat the song for suspense as well as for pleasure. (Interestingly, the "climbing" song is used without alteration, with clear disregard for the "facts"; logic here apparently yields to narrative unity, with the song serving as a signal that the one in the tree is truly Younger Brother.)

16. The formulaic greeting in common use among the Nkundo has been omitted by the narrator here, perhaps in the interest of satisfying the listeners' curiosity about Younger Brother's adventures.

17. Younger Brother's description of the birds' singing as "terrible" does not necessarily indicate that he had no feeling for bird songs; the volume alone (with birds so plentiful he could catch two and stuff them into his bag by hand) would have been sufficient cause to provoke such an observation. The listeners, aware of the countless sounds in the Nkundo-area forest—some beautiful and some with little charm—would accept his judgment merely from their own experience with the noisy and noisome *ndeke* birds, for example, which not only befoul the dwelling locations but rudely anticipate the dawn: *ndeke* birds are a communal breed, and their annoying predawn din *is* "terrible."

18. The Lonkundo reflexive form used here to add emphasis is translated as "the *very* song" rather than "the song *itself*." At this climax of Younger Brother's search, omission of emphasis would be unthinkable if the story were being told— as it was—by a committed narrator to a rapt audience.

19. Relief from the burden of fraternal and social debt is here expressed in a comparison (incorporated into various proverbs not only in Central but in West Africa—see Burton, *Wit and Wisdom of West Africa* [1865], *passim*, for samples) bitterly familiar to Nkundo listeners. As may be realized from even the limited survey of tales in this volume, slavery still exists in the oral tradition there, if less often in open practice than in former years. Its presence in the oral tradition in 1973 is of special interest in the light of the function of the folktale as a mirror of the culture in which it continues to survive.

20. If "food" had been mentioned in some other context, a mouth-watering description of each dish served would have been given here by the narrator. But the story Amba had set out to tell was feast enough to warrant eliminating the customary listing of foods. Besides, the telling blow—the superiority of Younger Brother's birds' song over that of Older Brother's bird—had yet to be delivered, and the storyteller herself could not be distracted by irrelevant details.

21. The literal translation of the first two songs in this tale presented only moderate difficulty for Mrs. Ross and her aides, perhaps because the content of each of the two was relatively familiar in Nkundo culture: snaring birds, climbing trees with a climbing belt, fear of the unknown. None of Mrs. Ross's translators, however, was able to provide a line-by-line translation of the song sung by Younger Brother's birds, although the interpreters agreed on the general import of the message: a song of joy telling how the birds liked to lie down and turn over and over.

In the interest of studies in diffusion, a mention of two different kinds of birds termed "roller birds" seems in order here. Both kinds winter in Rhodesia and are distinctive enough in their appearance and habits to have come to the attention of the Nkundo, either through observation of their annual migrations from the Mediterranean area (where they breed) or through hearsay. Of the two kinds, the Short-Tailed European Roller, or bluejay (*Coracias garrulus*), described in Cuthbertson's *Rhodesian Summer* ([1949] p. 7) as "a noisy bird, less shy than the Lilac-breasted Roller," fits more closely the brief description given of Bokune's birds than does the more beautiful specimen "first described as *Coracias caudatus* by Linnaeus in 1766, from a specimen taken in Angola" and long known as "Mzilikazi's Bird" because that Zulu chief had proscribed the use of its beautiful feathers by any but the royal family of the Matabele. For thirty years following the establishment of Mzilikazi's kingdom in 1837, the chief's name was one to reckon with, and none cared to dispute his claim to the "living jewel of green and blue" that is the Lilac-breasted Roller; the chief is reported on occasion to have given an ox to the man who could capture one of these shy birds for him. The term "roller" is derived from the rolling flight displayed by these birds during the mating season, descending from heights of more than 300 feet, "rolling from side to side in a sort of drunken flight. All the evolutions are accompanied by loud screams and calls. . . . " It is not unlikely that accounts of such unusual birds would have made their way into the oral tradition of Central Africa, to evidence their special traits in just such tales as this one that Amba told a hundred years and many hundreds of miles removed from Mzilikazi's kingdom.

The song sung by Bokune's birds is, appropriately, one of freedom, the kind of freedom Bokune himself expressed at being freed of his obligation [the Bantu-language proverb "Debts make slaves" is singularly appropriate here]; their song carries not at all the sense of helplessness and imprisonment conveyed by the song Botomolo's bird sang. Bokune obtained his birds by daring; Botomolo gained his bird by snaring: this narrative turn (reflection of the two diametrically opposed situations in the songs) is an arresting example of oral art.

22. Why Botomolo "became a fool" was not revealed by the narrator. The audience seemed to accept the statement readily. This expression may be interpreted literally; on the other hand, it may indicate that the rest of the community *regarded* him as a fool.

In any event, the juxtaposition of the two songs followed by a brief and satisfying conclusion, with a proverb to drive home the point, marks Amba as an accomplished storyteller indeed.

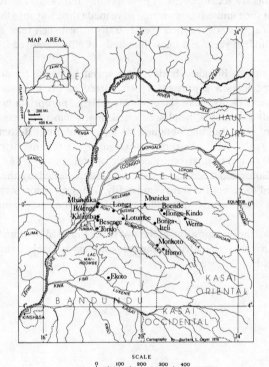

MAP AREA

EQUATEUR

HAUT-
ZAIRE

KASAI
ORIENTAL

BANDUNDU

KASAI
OCCIDENTAL

Mbandaka
Bolenge
Kalamba
Besenge
Tondo
Longa
Lotumbe
Monieka
Boende
Ilongo-Kindo
Bonga
Iteli
Wema
Monkoto
Ifomo
Ekoto
KINSHASA

Cartography by—Barbara L. Geyer 1978

SCALE

| 0 | 100 | 200 | 300 | 400 |
KILOMETERS

MILES
| 0 | 50 | 100 | 150 | 200 | 250 |

Part IV

ON-AND-ON

Cumulative and Dilemma Tales

Introduction

THE PRESENCE OF BUT ONE cumulative tale—"The Woman with One Loss After Another"—among more than seventy-five narratives collected by Mrs. Ross in the current Nkundo tradition posed more questions than answers. In an effort to discover whether contiguous oral traditions might offer more specimens than had been revealed by Mrs. Ross in her field collecting among the Nkundo, we examined various volumes by Badibanga, Mamet, Stappers, and de Bouveignes. A total of eight cumulative tales presented themselves: four told among the Luba, three among the Bolia, and one among the Lulua. The proportion of cumulative tales to those of other kinds was clearly exceedingly small; moreover, the emphasis in the bulk of this handful of tales lay more often in the "chain's" culmination in death by trickery than in the cumulative structure as a narrative device. We are therefore little closer today to a solution for the puzzle than we were when we first sought to unlock this mystery of the missing cumulatives.

Repetition is present in Nkundo tales in the patterns of expression used, so there is apparently no resistance to repetition as a device. Songs sung or chanted—almost a sine qua non in the cumulative tale—appear countless times in the Ross collection: the *cante fable* is a narrative staple. Why, then, is there such a paucity of cumulative tales among the Nkundo and their neighbors?

Perhaps the appearance of the white collector—whether missionary, teacher, priest, anthropologist, Peace Corps worker, or bilingual visitor—armed with tape recorder and notebook and interminable questions has discouraged the telling of such long, repetitive tales. The answer to the puzzle may eventually have to be uncovered by Nkundo anthropologists/folklorists dedicated to preserving their own culture and collecting solely among Nkundo audiences/narrators. With that hope, Mrs. Ross has entrusted to interested Nkundo teachers and narrators good recording equipment, including library-weight tape, inviting them to tape record all possible narratives (regardless of whether or not they consider the samples "good" or "complete" or "worthy") before Lonkundo falls out of use, carrying much, if not most, of the Nkundo oral art with it into oblivion. An excellent collection is underway presently in Lotumbe under the leadership of Ikolo, a medical student, and his wife, Mpiankita, both well educated and devoted to their traditional culture and to its preservation. In hand are the first two tapes of this collection, Ikolo's recorded in Lonkundo and Mpiankita's told in Lingala; the contents of these and subsequent tapes, translated into English, will surely widen the compass of the Ross-initiated study both of Nkundo cumulative tales and of other forms of narratives currently being told in the Cuvette of Zaïre and in contiguous areas.

As for dilemma tales, in the light of various scholarly studies—especially the helpful analysis by Bascom in Dorson's *African Folklore* —we had been prepared to find an ample supply of such narratives among those told to Mrs. Ross. Actually, of the tales she collected between November 1972 and May 1974, only three were handled entirely as dilemma tales: Tales 88, 93, and 94. A fourth narrative, Tale 95, translated from a Lonkundo school reader whose contents had been drawn from the Nkundo oral tradition current in the 1950s, qualifies as a dilemma tale only by virtue of its concluding with a question provocative of extended discussion in terms of conflicting social values.

A handful of additional tales in the Ross collection begin as dilemma tales might be expected to start, but undergo a transformation midcourse and end as *pourquoi* tales. One clear instance of this change occurs in Tale 88, which carries the palaver through to a decision by the chimpanzee and then has the chimpanzee suffer the consequence of his decision in favor of the oil palm: the raffia palm denies him and his kind the use of its fibers, and it is for that reason that he walks unclothed to this day. This variant has been included here with the dilemma tales because the major thrust appears to rest with the dilemma element. It is entirely possible that this variant, now in a state of flux, will gradually lose the details of the palaver and come to rest as a clear-cut *pourquoi*. On the other hand, it may lose the *pourquoi* ending (presently attached to many non-*pourquoi*-type tales for lagniappe) in versions told by other narrators, and be retained in the oral tradition as an out-and-out dilemma tale. Until that time, its position here among the dilemma tales seems justified.

There are undoubtedly a great number of dilemma tales present in the current Nkundo oral repertory. Evidence of their presence is afforded by Hulstaert and de Rop's treasury of more than forty dilemma tales (two in that collection are dilemma tales only by stretching the term somewhat: they are more markedly cumulative than "legalistic"), cited and summarized by Bascom in his *African Dilemma Tales* but not available presently in full in any languages other than the Lonkundo in which they were purportedly accumulated and the Flemish into which they were translated. To make a small sampling of these tales accessible to English-speaking readers, we offer here translations of the ones which are variants of those collected by Mrs. Ross; several other tales in the Hulstaert-de Rop volume are commented upon in the notes as they appear relevant. An English translation of the entire Hulstaert-de Rop collection is underway under the direction of Barbara K. Walker, but extensive use of the tales unrelated to those harvested by Mrs. Ross seems unwarranted in the present study. Another variant by de Rop *is* included here, however, drawn from his ... *woordkunst* ... because of the considerable contrast in style between this variant and the one of substantially the same tale presented in the Hulstaert-de Rop volume. Bascom's comparative analysis of almost 450 versions of dilemma and dilemma-like tales offers sufficiently detailed summaries of the versions to allow a reassessment of those tales in the Ross collection which we had considered to be in a state of flux and to remove from the state of limbo those which might not qualify within the Bascom rubric. The same test is being applied to the tales steadily being added by Nkundo collectors such as Ikolo and Mpiankita in an effort to determine whether or not the proportion of dilemma tales is decreasing in the face of alterations in the postcolonial methods of arriving at legal decisions.

Quite apart from information gained through the reading of scholarly studies and from the translation of collections from Lonkundo, Flemish, and French, one should have been prepared to find dilemma tales as a lively form of verbal art. A Lonkundo-speaking visitor who has spent even a few months among the Nkundo comes to share the Nkundo's delight in the seemingly endless public hearings, or palavers, at which, in the presence of the village elders as judges, both intra-family and extra-family squabbles are aired and decisions handed down. Wits are sharpened; skills in debate are honed; values are reweighed; balance is restored: the palaver is—or has been—an essential ingredient of Nkundo everyday legal practice.

Where, then, does the dilemma tale fit, and what is its cultural function? It is a skillfully abbreviated form of the palaver, a direct reflection of the palaver pared of peripheral arguments, with the kernel of the case and its conclusion carefully preserved. (Perhaps because of its intentional abbreviation, the dilemma tale lacks the "literary merit" which Bascom notes as a possible explanation for the relatively limited attention given by American folklorists to this characteristic African genre—see his *African Dilemma Tales*, p. 3.) There is—despite Hulstaert and de Rop's offering of "the decision" as "decision correct"—no "right" or "permanent" judgment. The same dilemma tale, offered to one audience after another, reaps widely varying judgments from the listeners-as-elders, with the differences in judgments accounted for both by the variations in audiences and in the narrators' skill in presenting the "case" and— subtly but unmistakably—by the gradual erosion of long-held values in the shifting currents of acculturation, both from African sources and from non-African influences. An objective multilingual study of changing patterns in the Nkundo dilemma tale could offer increased perspective on the evolution of the Nkundo value system.

Narrator: Tata Itofi
Location: Boende
Date: October 1973

87. *The Woman with One Loss after Another*

A woman had some edible roots[1] soaking in the swamp. When she went to get the roots, she met some blacksmiths.[2]

They said, "Give us some food. We are very hungry and want to eat. We will eat and be satisfied and then go on our way."

"I will give you some food. However, you must eat it all and not let any fall on the ground. That is wasteful and very bad."[3]

They gladly took the food and ate and ate. Some of the food fell to the ground, and the woman was quite disturbed. She sang,

> These blacksmiths ate my roots.
> They didn't steal them. They didn't steal them.
> They ate the cassava of my digging.

The blacksmiths gave her a spear that they had made. She took the spear and went on her way. Soon she met some men who had captured a wild pig and were trying to kill it by hitting it, *kao-kao-kao-kao*, with a heavy pole.[4]

When she saw them, she began to laugh. She said, "Ah! Ha! What do you have? How do you think you can kill a pig with a pole? Why don't you use my spear?"

They said, "The pole is not enough. You do have a spear. Give us the spear."

She said, "The spear which I am giving you is clean and new."

They took her spear and killed the pig. When they finished killing it, they threw the spear on the ground. She refused to take it because it hadn't been cleaned.

"I won't take the spear because it has blood and dirt from the pig, and you know that I can't clean up the things that are yours."[5] She sang,

> They killed the wild pig. They killed the wild pig.
> Look at the spear. Look at the spear
> Which the blacksmiths gave me.
> These blacksmiths ate my roots, my roots.

They didn't steal them. They didn't steal them.
They ate the cassava of my digging.

So they gave her some of the pig, and she put it in the basket she carried on her back.[6] She went on her way and found a mother and small child who had nothing to eat except the leaves from the cassava plant. They had no meat.

She asked, "Is it true that you have only cassava leaves to eat?"

"Yes, that's what we have."

"Very well. Cook the cassava leaves. We will eat them first and then we will cook the piece of wild pig that I have.[7] Then I will go. However, when you eat it, none must fall to the ground and be wasted." She agreed.

Since it was a large piece, they cut and cut in order to get it ready to cook, much, much, much. While it cooked, they ate the cassava leaves. Then they put some palm oil on the meat and ate it. They ate a little, a little, a little. However, the mother and child were not careful, and many bits fell to the ground. The woman was disturbed and sang,

> They ate the meat. They ate the meat.
> Bits of wild pig fell to the ground.
> Bits of wild pig fell to the ground.
> They killed the wild pig. They killed the wild pig.
> Look at the spear. Look at the spear
> Which the blacksmiths gave me.
> These blacksmiths ate my roots, my roots.
> They didn't steal them, steal them.
> They ate the cassava of my digging.

Then the mother gave her some plantains from her garden. The woman put these in her basket and went, *kao-kao*. Soon she came to a place where some men were pounding palm fruit in order to make palm oil.[8] As they worked, they sang, *"Toko-ki-o-ki-o-ki-o-ki-o-ki-o."*[9]

She realized that they had had no food. She said, "Eat my plantains. Then you will have strength to work. However, you must not let any bits fall to the ground."

They gladly took the plantains and cooked them in their palm oil. Then they ate and ate and ate until they no longer had hunger.[10] But they were careless, and crumbs fell to the ground. The woman was quite disturbed, and sang,

Those who pound the palm fruit swallow.
Those who pound the palm fruit swallow.
They eat the plantains; they eat the plantains
Which the mother gave me.
They ate that. They ate that.
Bits of wild pig fell to the ground.
Bits of wild pig fell to the ground.
They killed the wild pig. They killed the wild pig.
Look at the spear. Look at the spear
Which the blacksmiths gave me.
These blacksmiths ate my roots, my roots.
They didn't steal them, steal them.
They ate the cassava of my digging.

Then those who ate gave her a large bottle of very good palm oil. She put it in her basket and she went. She came to a rise in the path where it was very slick. She slipped and fell, *ba-kwa-a-a*.[11] The bottle of oil fell out and was broken. She was sad and felt much sorrow. She sang,

A high place in the path, a high place in the path
Broke my bottle of oil, broke my bottle of oil.
Those who pound the palm fruit swallow.
Those who pound the palm fruit swallow.
They eat the plantains; they eat the plantains
Which the mother gave me.
They ate that. They ate that.
Bits of wild pig fell to the ground.
Bits of wild pig fell to the ground.
They killed the wild pig. They killed the wild pig.
Look at the spear. Look at the spear
Which the blacksmiths gave me.
These blacksmiths ate my roots, my roots.
They didn't steal them, steal them.
They ate the cassava of my digging.

A witch doctor came by and heard her. He helped her find some large mushrooms, and they put them in her basket. She started on her way and soon came to the bank of the river. Then as she walked along the bank, the basket tipped and the mushrooms fell into the river, *bwu*.[12] She felt much sorrow. "The river took my mushrooms. Now what will I do?" She sang,

My mushrooms, my mushrooms
It has eaten, it has eaten.
A high place in the path, a high place in the path
Broke my bottle of oil, broke my bottle of oil.
Those who pound the palm fruit swallow.
Those who pound the palm fruit swallow.
They eat the plantains; they eat the plantains
Which the mother gave me.
They ate that; they ate that.
Bits of wild pig fell to the ground.
Bits of wild pig fell to the ground.
They killed the wild pig. They killed the wild pig.
Look at the spear. Look at the spear
Which the blacksmiths gave me.
These blacksmiths ate my roots, my roots.
They didn't steal them, steal them.
They ate the cassava of my digging.

Then the river gave her a very large fish, and she rejoiced. She put it in her basket. Then she went and went and went. A large hawk flew over and saw the fish. He flew back, grabbed it out of her basket, eating, eating, eating, and flew away with it. Ah-h-h. He went, *bwe.* Then once again she felt great sorrow. She sang,

The hawk took it. The hawk took it.
He carried it away. He carried it away.
My mushrooms, my mushrooms
It has eaten, it has eaten.
A high place in the path, a high place in the path
Broke my bottle of oil, broke my bottle of oil.
Those who pound the palm fruit swallow.
Those who pound the palm fruit swallow.
They eat the plantains; they eat the plantains
Which the mother gave me.
They ate that. They ate that.
Bits of wild pig fell to the ground.
Bits of wild pig fell to the ground.
They killed the wild pig. They killed the wild pig.
Look at the spear. Look at the spear
Which the blacksmiths gave me.
These blacksmiths ate my roots, my roots.
They didn't steal them, steal them.
They ate the cassava of my digging.[13]

Then the hawk saw her sorrow and gave her many feathers, feathers that were very beautiful. She went, *kao-kao*, and found many people dancing, both men and women.[14] They had large leaves on their heads, but when they saw her feathers, they were delighted and wanted some.

"I'll be glad to give them to you. However, you must put them in your hats. They must not fall to the ground and get dirty."

"Give them to us. We do not have anything so beautiful." She gave them the feathers and they went on with the dance, dancing, dancing. Soon the feathers were on the ground and getting dirty. She sang,

> The dance continues. The dance continues.
> Look at the feathers. Look at the feathers
> Which the hawk gave me, the hawk gave me.
> The hawk took it. The hawk took it.
> He carried it away. He carried it away.
> My mushrooms, my mushrooms
> It has eaten, it has eaten.
> A high place in the path, a high place in the path
> Broke my bottle of oil, broke my bottle of oil.
> Those who pound the palm fruit swallow.
> Those who pound the palm fruit swallow.
> They eat the plantains; they eat the plantains
> Which the mother gave me.
> They ate that. They ate that.
> Bits of wild pig fell to the ground.
> Bits of wild pig fell to the ground.
> They killed the wild pig. They killed the wild pig.
> Look at the spear. Look at the spear
> Which the blacksmiths gave me.
> These blacksmiths ate my roots, my roots.
> They didn't steal them, steal them.
> They ate the cassava of my digging.

Then those men gave her a bone from a monkey.[15] As she went, *kao*, she found some women in a swamp with a great many, many fish in baskets. They were trying to clean the fish, but were unable to clean even one. She offered the monkey bone, which could be used to clean them quickly and well.

"Have you one?"

"I have one."

"If you have one, give it to us."

They used it and then threw it down without cleaning it. The woman refused to take it back. She sang,

> This monkey bone, this monkey bone
> From the dancers of song.
> Regard the bone; regard the bone.
> The dance continues. The dance continues.
> Look at the feathers. Look at the feathers
> Which the hawk gave me, the hawk gave me.
> The hawk took it. The hawk took it.
> He carried it away. He carried it away.
> My mushrooms, my mushrooms
> It has eaten, it has eaten.
> A high place in the path, a high place in the path
> Broke my bottle of oil, broke my bottle of oil.
> Those who pound the palm fruit swallow.
> Those who pound the palm fruit swallow.
> They eat the plantains; they eat the plantains
> Which the mother gave me.
> They ate that. They ate that.
> Bits of wild pig fell to the ground.
> Bits of wild pig fell to the ground.
> They killed the wild pig. They killed the wild pig.
> Look at the spear. Look at the spear
> Which the blacksmiths gave me.
> These blacksmiths ate my roots, my roots.
> They didn't steal them, steal them.
> They ate the cassava of my digging.[16]

There some women had a very large *ntula* fish that they wanted to give her.

"I don't like it. It's too large."

"Do you like this one?"

"It's too large." They didn't give it to her.

They offered her many fish, giving, giving, giving. Each time, she refused. "No. I don't want a large fish. I want a very small one, one that is smallness itself."

They hunted through the fish, turning them over and turning them over. When she saw one that was smallness itself, she said, "Ah! That's the one I want."

It was very, very small, but she took it. They said, "Very good." They were surprised, but gave it to her.[17]

She took the fish home, *kao-kao*, and put it in a hole where she soaked cassava in the swamp nearby.

"I am going. I will return. When I call you like this, come and eat food."

She went and prepared and cooked and cooked food until her basket was very full, and she went to the swamp. She sang,

> Intswatswala Lolima,
> I play with a leopard.[18] I play with a leopard.
> I, your mother, call you.
> I play with a leopard. I play with a leopard.
> When I . . . . .
> I play with a leopard. I play with a leopard.
> From . . . . .
> I play with a leopard. I play with a leopard.
> From . . . . .
> I play with a leopard. I play with a leopard.

It came. Then she gave it food. The fish ate and ate and ate and ate and ate and ate. She left and went.

She filled her basket full, full, full, and went.

> Intswatswala Lolima.
> I play with a leopard. I play with a leopard.
> I, your mother, call you.
> I play with a leopard. I play with a leopard.
> When I . . . . .
> I play with a leopard. I play with a leopard.
> From . . . . .
> I play with a leopard. I play with a leopard.
> From . . . . .
> I play with a leopard. I play with a leopard.[19]

It came and ate until it was the size of her arm.[20]

Then she returned with much, much food. She would call it, *té-té-té*. It came and ate and ate.

Then she returned. She cooked and cooked and cooked much food. She called it, *té-é-té-é-té-é*. It came. It ate and ate.

Again she came with food. It was the size of her thigh.

She came again with food, and it was the size of her waist. She sang to it,

> Intswatswala Lolima.
> I play with a leopard. I play with a leopard.
> I, your mother, call you.

> I play with a leopard. I play with a leopard.
> When I . . . . .
> I play with a leopard. I play with a leopard.
> From . . . . .
> I play with a leopard. I play with a leopard.
> From . . . . .
> I play with a leopard. I play with a leopard.

It ate and ate and became the size of . . . largeness itself. *Të-ë-të-ë-të-ë*.

Then one day one of her children kept watching her carry off the basket of food, every day a basket of food. She finally said, "Father, our mother fills her basket with food and carries it off somewhere. I think I'll follow her and find out who eats all of this food."

That day when the mother left with her basket very full of food, *tò,*[21] the child followed her from a distance. Then the child hid nearby and heard her mother calling the fish,

> Intswatswala Lolima,
> I play with a leopard. I play with a leopard.
> I, your mother, call you.
> I play with a leopard. I play with a leopard.
> When I . . . . .
> I play with a leopard. I play with a leopard.
> From . . . . .
> I play with a leopard. I play with a leopard.
> From . . . . .
> I play with a leopard. I play with a leopard.

The child saw the large *ntula*. She slipped away home. She said, "Father, I have finished seeing what Mother is doing. Mother is feeding a huge *ntula* in the swamp. It is bigness itself."

"Is that really true?"

"Yes. That's the way it is."

No one told the mother that they knew about her fish. The next day, the mother left to go to her garden. The child and her father got a basket and a knife and went, *kao-kao-kao,* down the path to the swamp. They looked for the fish, but could not find it. The father called in a deep voice,

> Intswatswala Lolima.
> I play with a leopard. I play with a leopard.
> I, your mother, call you.
> I play with a leopard. I play with a leopard.

> When I . . . . .
> I play with a leopard. I play with a leopard.
> From . . . . .
> I play with a leopard. I play with a leopard.
> From . . . . .
> I play with a leopard. I play with a leopard.

The *ntula* fish didn't come. The child said, "We need to call as Mother does." She began in a higher voice.[22]

> Intswatswala Lolima.
> I play with a leopard. I play with a leopard.
> I, your mother, call you.
> I play with a leopard. I play with a leopard.
> When I . . . . .
> I play with a leopard. I play with a leopard.
> From . . . . .
> I play with a leopard. I play with a leopard.
> From . . . . .
> I play with a leopard. I play with a leopard.

The *ntula* came, and the father killed it with his knife. They cut it up and put the pieces in their basket. Then they took it home and cooked it.

The mother came home. She didn't know that the fish was dead. She filled her basket with food and went to the swamp.

> Intswatswala Lolima.
> I play with a leopard. I play with a leopard.
> I, your mother, call you.
> I play with a leopard. I play with a leopard.
> When I . . . . .
> I play with a leopard. I play with a leopard.
> From . . . . .
> I play with a leopard. I play with a leopard.
> From . . . . .
> I play with a leopard. I play with a leopard.

Wai-i-i. Quiet. Everything was very quiet; the fish did not come. A bird flew over and called her. The insides of the fish were hanging in a tree nearby, and he pointed them out to her.[23]

She went to see what the bird had. When she saw, she knew that it was her fish. She was very angry. However, she soon started down the path for home, crying for her lost child.

She said, "Up there is my own child."[24]

Tata Itofi brought seven or eight of the village elders with him when he came for this storytelling session, each eager to add to Tale 87 in progress, hoping eventually to hear his own voice on the machine that was "writing" them down. For a reasonably adequate approach to cultural appreciation, this particular cumulative tale needs to be read aloud, then heard as Tata Itofi recorded it on tape—comfortably, in his own tongue and relishing the audience's response—and then read silently, with the echoes of the two basic songs and the lively audience participation creating a sense of one's own presence in the group of listeners. Even then, the social and artistic functions of this tale may well elude the Western reader-listener.

Related ostensibly from a woman's point of view, Tale 87 was told by a male retired village school teacher (in his sixties) presently working in Boende as a part-time teacher of women in their teens and twenties, a number with small children of their own. The narrator could thus be assumed to be more empathetic with the concerns of women in a male-dominated society than would the usual Nkundo elder relating a tale.

Tata Itofi allows the woman's plight to speak for itself through a masterful handling of the dialogue and the songs, songs which in the local tongue reveal the high qualities of Nkundo poetry and music described at some length by de Rop in his solid study of Nkundo oral art, . . . *woordkunst* . . . . Note the interweaving of one line with another, poetry cumulative in its structure even as the tale itself is cumulative.

The narrator's skillful use of repetition was warmly received by the audience. Curiously, the primary response was that of laughter, largely at the "tall-tale-type" snowballing of the woman's losses, indicating not so much a lack of sympathy with the woman as an appreciation of the art and exaggeration of situational humor. The employing of dialogue throughout conveys the liveliness of the telling and the degree to which action and gesture accompanied voice in playing out the drama of the tale.

There are two basic "melodies," one (with a plaintive, narrow-range, ending-on-a-down-note tune) used for the song portions of the tale during which the woman shares and loses one item after another and the second (a cheerful, lively, optimistic-sounding, wider-range tune suggesting the woman's sense of happiness and growing contentment) used for the part of the tale in which she is nourishing her "child" to its full growth. The singing of the first song was done entirely by the narrator except for a subdued humming from the audience; the audience sang the "I play with a leopard" lines in the second song after Tata Itofi had sung the song once. In a large nighttime gathering including listeners of a wider age range there might well have been more verbal audience participation in the first song because of its highly repetitious character. An Nkundo-speaking specialist in poetry and an ethnomusicologist working together would find a study of the tape of this tale well worth while.

The emphasis throughout the tale on the need not to waste anything of value was ironically climaxed by the "wasting" of the "child," representative of the woman's well-intended but continually frustrated efforts to help those whom she met. Whether or not this cumulative tale reflects Nkundo values is open to debate: Read as a tale, the narrative carries one message, suggesting that pity might be engendered for the protagonist; heard on the tape, this tale presents an astonishingly different effect, one prompting amusement and—finally—shock and much dispute. Side by side, the two presentations suggest the misinterpretations which may more often than not have become attached to numerous African tale texts not accompanied by performance notes and other "live" evidence.

Aarne-Thompson's tale types 2034C and 2029 seem possible citations for this text; Klipple furnishes for tale type 2034*C a number of African samples that are relevant. Lambrecht's type 4464 fits the present tale in certain respects: a fish (the end-product of the series of loans) is hand-fed; the fish is killed; grief marks the end of the venture. These similarities, however, are outweighed by the introduction of several dramatic events which overshadow the elements mentioned: an ordeal, or water-test, is utilized to determine the identity of the destroyer of the fish; the guilty son, submerged, is netted by a fisherman and becomes a white woman; the white woman, courted by several animals, accepts the genet *nsimba*; the death of the latter provokes the bride to tears. Lack of performance data for the Lambrecht sample precludes a comparison of the audience's response. Perhaps Lambrecht's sample, too, drew from its auditors a less sympathetic response than the text would seem to suggest as "appropriate" for a Western reader. Are *both* tales provocative of a self-conscious, embarrassed laughter, a cover-up for a sympathy not considered proper or deserved from a male? On the other hand, might both tales be told purely for the amusement aroused by repetition and gross exaggeration?

Motifs:

T	J652.	Inattention to warnings.
T	N350.	Accidental loss of property.
T	Z41.5.	Lending and repaying: progressively worse (or better) bargain.
C	B569.+.**.	Helpful bird tells woman of child's death.

1. There are many tuberlike roots in Central Africa, only a few of which require soaking. Manioc (cassava) must be soaked for about six days before it is edible and was apparently the root the woman gave to the blacksmiths.

2. During the first few sentences of the tale, there was a good deal of noise and conversation in the audience.

Traveling craftsmen are not limited to early European and American history. The Nkundo blacksmith falls into this class, as well. His bellows are made with large leaves shaped like a small, fat wheel. From this wheel a tube passes directly to the fire. A stick standing in the center is pumped up and down by one of the local boys in order to blow the air into the embers. Usually there are three of these bellows. The blacksmith himself sits near the fire with his pieces of iron, which he hits with a homemade mallet into the required shape. Before the coming of the white man, the blacksmith found his iron ore in the ground and smelted it himself for his use. Since that time, every stray nail or other scrap of iron is carefully retrieved and used in the making of knives, spears, or whatever else his customers desire.

3. Many people, even in the deprived circumstances found among the Nkundo, tend to be careless and wasteful. The woman, aware of the time she had already spent in digging and soaking the roots, was trying to avoid the wasting of the result of her work.

It is interesting to note that in Tale 7 the dropping of bits of food is considered praiseworthy, whereas in the present tale on three occasions it provokes resentment and on two of those occasions outright complaint. We suspect that the Nkundo value system rests more nearly with the attitude taken toward waste in this cumulative tale than with that assumed by the animals in the *pourquoi* tale. Since the emphasis in the *pourquoi* lies on the Nkundo concern for sharing, however, "waste" becomes a virtue toward that end in Tale 7.

4. Since the wild pig is a ferocious animal and a fighter, the hunter armed with bow and arrows or other high-risk weapons must be wary about attacking him. (According to the song, the "pole" being used was a heavy tree branch.) The woman by tradition would not receive the choicest portions of the pig; they would be reserved for distribution in the time-honored Nkundo pattern of division of the spoils.

5. No one likes to clean up a mess made by others; this is especially true of the Nkundo. A nurse in an Nkundo-staffed hospital often refuses to take care of the bedpan of a patient or any bloody mess connected with that patient; some member of the patient's family is expected to do it. (Members of the patient's family live in or near the hospital compound, cook his food, wash his hospital linens and clothes, and care for various other personal needs.) This general reluctance to clean up after others outside the family explains why the woman refused her spear after it had been left uncleaned on the ground; later in the tale, she refused the monkey bone for the same reason.

An undercurrent of humming was furnished by the audience during the song, followed by hearty laughter at the end of the song. In each instance, laughter follows or accompanies the singing of the first song; the laughter subsides with a sliding-down-scale and diminishing-in-volume pattern.

6. Every female from the time she is five or six years old has a *yuka* to carry on her back. It is a long reed basket fastened to her body with shoulder straps. By leaning forward as she carries it and by walking pigeon-toed, she can carry a very heavy load. When it is loaded, she solicits any available help in order to lift it into place. If she is alone in the garden, she can set the basket on a tree stump and thus position it so that she can replace it herself in order to carry it home.

7. Cassava (or manioc) leaves when well prepared are quite good. However, the Nkundo feels that he is hungry unless he has had fish or meat. Since the mother was able to give the woman some plantains from her garden, she obviously had other food besides cassava leaves at hand to eat. Apparently the cassava leaves had already been thoroughly pounded and were thus more quickly prepared for eating than were the plantains.

8. To make palm oil, the men dig a cone-shaped pit. They put the palm fruit in the pit and pound it in rhythm with long poles. The fruit is then put over a slow fire with a funnel on the side of the container so that the oil can run off. In this way they can get an almost pure oil, used for frying many of their foods. (See note 5 on page 497 for further uses of this oil.)

9. The *ki-o* is stretched out by the narrator to suggest how hard the men were working while they were pounding.

In his . . . *woordkunst* . . . (pp. 16–19), de Rop furnishes a helpful introduction to the use of work songs by the Nkundo. Citing an extensive study by Prof. van Bulck (*Gesproken woordkunst in Afrika met toepassing op de Bakongo*, p. 31), de Rop points out that the work songs are used exclusively for the rhythm; in many songs used to lighten labor, there is no mention at all of the kind of work being done. (The Rosses observed that much comment was made in the songs about the employer.) The rhythm changes according to the character of the effort needed by the workers; the song leader sets the rhythm and then recites a line (improvised) which the laborers repeat after him in a continuous alternation, leader-workers-leader, with the line and chorus possessing to the Western ear almost no melody. [information summarized by BKW from a translation from the Flemish by Dr. Tinco E. A. van Hylckama]

10. "Had hunger" is a characteristic Lonkundo locution. (Again, as in every other instance, much laughter followed the singing of the song.)

11. The long-drawn-out sound of *kwa-a-a-a* emphasizes the sense of slipping.

12. Since the Nkundo live in a rain forest, there are many mushrooms to be found, a number of which are edible and highly desired. Children learn at an early age which ones are the good mushrooms.

It is quite unlikely that a woman would allow her basket to tip to the point where its contents would be spilled—especially a woman so concerned about waste. This incident provoked much laughter and comment.

13. The fish given to the woman is an *ntula*, a large, fatty member of the catfish family. In some areas it is considered a great delicacy; in others, it is thought to be good only for women to eat.

Much laughter and chatter followed the singing of this song; the sound ceased abruptly, without the descending subsiding quality noted at other points.

14. The Nkundo love of adornment has been noted in Tale 80. In the present instance, the feathers would be in great demand to enhance the dancers' appearance. Some sense of the degree of exaggeration in this tale may be conveyed by the unusual circumstance of men and women's dancing together, a departure from the customary Nkundo dance practice.

15. [Narrator's explanatory comment: "a special bone which is useful for many things."] The monkey bone has a knifelike edge; such bones are widely used for cleaning fish.

16. At this point in the storytelling, both the audience and the narrator were laughing with such abandon that the narrator could barely finish the song. To quiet the audience, the narrator finally said, "*Lokoza*" ["Listen"]. Upon that, one of the audience queried, "It's like that?"

17. Choice of the *smallest* fish is a direct departure from the expected Nkundo response; meat and fish are prized, and logic would dictate selection of the largest fish available. The choice made here is artistically in excellent keeping with the tall-tale character of the story; more significantly, it provides the keystone for the dénouement of the narrative, returns the action to the starting place (the swamp where the woman had been soaking the roots—unity of place), and narrows the focus to a dramatis personae for which a family-conscious audience is now ready. The subtlety of the shift suggests splendid narrative control.

18. The verses in Nkundo *cante fables* refused in many instances to yield gracefully to literal translation. "*Nsanya nkòi*" may certainly be literally translated as "I play with a leopard," but why the "mother" used this expression in her song is nowhere made clear. There may be a figurative purpose served by this term, a purpose

meaningful to Nkundo listeners but one which our translators hesitated to reveal. On the other hand, the combination of her repeated "I play with a leopard" with the inordinately large amounts of food the woman kept feeding a fish that had been chosen as one that was "smallness itself" may indicate merely that the song was intended to challenge the "child" to eat and to grow until he had indeed attained the size and strength of a leopard; a coaxing tone present in the singing tends to support the latter interpretation.

The portions of the song which remained unintelligible to Mrs. Ross and her translators, even after repeated listenings, are indicated by five spaced dots.

19. Heavy gulping sounds followed the song, sounds resembling those a pig makes when he keeps on eating even though his mouth is already full, mouthed with a full mouth. The gulping sounds followed every subsequent singing of the song except the one sung by the father.

Also, the audience served as a chorus in every singing of this song except the initial one: "I play with a leopard. I play with a leopard" was uniformly furnished by the audience of elders.

20. Among the Nkundo, measurements are often indicated in terms of the size of parts of the body. Narrators enjoy using the measurements of size, complete with appropriate gestures, both to indicate growth and to present an opportunity for repetition of the song. (Note the use of such measurements and gestures in all of the Nkundo tales involving ordeals by water.)

Much laughter and a suggestive pause (indicated by three spaced dots) accompanied by a gesture not interpreted for Mrs. Ross preceded the expression "largeness itself," on page 480.

21. *Tó* is an onomatopoetic term indicating that the basket was very full, perhaps overflowing. This expression is invariably accompanied by a gesture: the left hand forms a fist, with the thumb and forefinger uppermost, and the right hand is brought down, with the palm flat, against the top of the closed fist several times, to indicate that the contents of the basket had to be pressed down because the basket was so full.

22. The narrator's distinction between the two vocal pitches was only one of many evidences of storytelling art displayed for a highly responsive audience. It serves the additional function of allowing one more repetition of the song, prolonging suspense.

23. The "quietness" was emphasized by the narrator's sensitive use of pace and of pitch and volume.

In Nkundo narratives, as in tales told elsewhere in folk tradition, a bird often serves as an informer, especially where foul play has been an element of the action.

24. Beginning with "She went to see what the bird had," the narrator delivered the remaining few lines with such swiftness and economy and excitement that both he and his audience were caught up in a tumbling of words, a curiously unexpected conclusion for what had appeared a leisurely and rambling and laughter-provoking tale. Whether the ending would have been different for an audience of women is problematical; successive listenings to the tape failed to solve for us the mystery and piquancy of its cryptic ending. We should like to encounter an Nkundo variant

of this tale in order to discover how another narrator—particularly a female story-teller—would handle the dénouement.

A clue as to a poignant ending possible for such a tale was afforded us by a young woman from Botswana now doing her graduate work in the United States [she is herself a splendid narrator, sensitive to the value of the oral tradition within which she was nurtured]. In the Tswana tale, told in Setswana, a young woman develops an affection for a horse which she feeds secretly, and which she regularly visits. When she discovers that the horse has been removed, her grief is so great that she feels she *must* weep. Since her weeping will arouse questioning, she seeks a place at the evening fire where she will be in the path of the smoke; there she sits, with tears streaming down her cheeks. Offered a more "comfortable" seat, she chooses to remain where the smoke will allow her to cry without having to explain the real (and socially unacceptable) reason for her tears. The artistry shown in the Botswana narrator's conclusion suggests the wealth that lies in African oral narrative awaiting discovery and multilingual publication.

Similar poignancy is evidenced in a tale titled "The Fairy Tale of Mrile," credited to "the East African Bantus" by Lüthi (*Once Upon a Time: On the Nature of Fairy Tales* [1976], pp. 99–104), in which the oldest of three sons nourishes a Kolokasia tuber that has become a child; when the mother, told by the younger brothers about the hidden tuber-child, beats the tuber-child and kills it, the oldest weeps "with all his heart. Then they asked, 'Mrile, why are you crying?' But he answered, 'It is just the smoke in my eyes.'" (p. 100) Though they try to persuade him to sit "over here on the lower side," he continues to weep, inconsolable in his loss. In the tale of Mrile, the death of the tuber-child occurs early in the story, establishing the pattern for even more distressing losses; in the Ross-collected tale and in the one from Botswana, the loss of the "child" (or, perhaps, sweetheart) occurs at the end, providing an opportunity for a narrator, if he chooses, to furnish the bitter-sweet ending that the situation invites.

Narrator: Bokunge Jacques
Location: Bòlèngè
Date: March 1973

88.   *The Palaver between the Raffia Palm and the Oil Palm: Which Is More Valuable?* [1]

Lifeke (Raffia Palm) and Jiba (Oil Palm) had a big dispute. Raffia Palm said, "I am greater than you are, Oil Palm. I produce many things that give life to people. My raffia, *nkinga*, is used for making cloth. People pull my raffia, soak it and pound it until it is very thin, and then weave it together.[2] They take certain of my branches and make excellent bows.[3] In the crevices of my trunk a caterpillar[4] will leave her young. I cradle them and nourish them until they are fat. These caterpillars become a delicious and nourishing food for man. What do you produce that can give life to people?"

Oil Palm answered, "I can see that you produce much that adds to the living of man, but I produce more than you do. My very fruit, *mba*,[5] makes many nourishing dishes for man to eat. Then he can take the oil from my fruit and rub it on his body. This gives him comfort as well as beauty. Man takes my flower stalk and my palm fronds. He puts them in the fire and makes salt[6] for his food from them. He strips down to the center of my palm frond and makes an arrow[7] that will kill birds so that he can have meat. If he puts poison on this same arrow, he can kill small animals and have more meat. He can take this same center of my palm frond, strip it into narrow strips, and use this strong cord[8] for tying his house together. From my sap he can make excellent palm wine[9] that will give him happy dreams. When I am finally cut down, he takes the palm cabbage[10] from my heart and makes salad or cooks it for a vegetable. Further down in my heart he finds a gum[11] that is good for chewing. From this, you can see that I help man to live in many more ways than you do."

They argued for a long while until the argument became quite heated. Finally they went to the chimpanzee, Eza, who has the appearance of a man. "Come and settle this palaver that is between us," they called.

Chimpanzee agreed and listened to their stories. Raffia Palm told his story first, listing all the ways that he could help people. Then Oil Palm recited all his means of benefiting man.

When they had finished, Chimpanzee said, "You, Oil Palm, you win. You have a great many ways of helping man to live. But you, Raffia Palm, you lost the palaver. Even though you do have many ways of helping man to live, you do not have nearly as many as Oil Palm does."

Then Raffia Palm became very angry and he said to Chimpanzee, "You have always used my raffia for making your clothing. From now on, I will keep it for myself. You may never get it from me again."

Then Chimpanzee felt anger. Since now he no longer had clothes, he ran off into the forest. He has lived in the forest from that day to this.[12]

He who falls in a palaver does not like the judge who decided the case.

[Notes for Tale 88 follow Tale 92.]

Source:	Zaïrian school reader *Bekolo Bémò . . .* (in Lonkundo)
Translator:	Mabel Ross, with multilingual aides
Date of Translation:	July 1975

89. *The Palaver between the Raffia Palm and the Oil Palm: Which Is More Valuable?* (Variant I)

The raffia palm and the oil palm competed as peers. The oil palm said, "I am the older."[13]

The raffia palm that, "You do not have many works helping people. I have many works befriending people.

"I have raffia that helps people in killing animals.

"I have thread that helps people with cloth.

"I have branches that help people with brooms to clean their houses.[14]

"I have the desire that people have [to help people].

"I exceed you with works like that. Now you, what do you have?"

The oil palm answered, "I exceed you very much in the works for helping man.

"I have palm fruit.

"I help man with oil in many ways, in the way of eating, in the way of anointing their bodies, in baking in the fire.

"I have *njiika* which helps man with *bempenga* to have money.[15]

"I have flower stalks that man have salt.

"I have palm cabbage and people eat that, and my very trunk cut lengthwise in pieces, and people have salt again. Now, how do you say that you are my friend? I greatly exceed you in many things."

They called another person that he become their judge.

He heard their discussions, and he saw that the oil palm had won.

He said to the raffia palm that, "You lack many things like the oil palm; because of this the oil palm wins the palaver."

The raffia palm felt anger, and he snatched the clothing of the judge.

That person felt shame; and he departed to live in the place where no people were. And from that time he has been called "chimpanzee."[16]

[Notes for Tale 89 follow Tale 92.]

Source:	de Rop's ... *woordkunst* ...
	(in Flemish)
Translator:	Dr. Tinco E. A. van Hylckama
Date of Translation:	April 1975

90.   *The Palaver between the Raffia Palm and the Oil Palm: Which Is More Valuable?* (Variant II)

Once upon a time the oil palm and the raffia palm had an argument; they said, "Who of us two is the best?" The raffia palm said: "I am the best, because I produce raffia of which one weaves clothing. I produce fibers and one makes ropes of them from which the people make snares to catch animals. From my leaves one makes very good brushes and from my stems one makes very good couches to sleep upon."

The oil palm said: "Nonsense; the best things are mine, because I produce nuts and with nuts one makes oil and palm sauce. My flowers produce salt; my core is very tasty to eat; my wine is good and a stiff drink, which the people appreciate very much. My leaves are sold and one makes much money, and I have many other things on my side[.] ...[17] How dare you compare us?"

Then they called the chimpanzee, who looks like a human being, to settle their dispute. The chimpanzee came and told the raffia palm that he was wrong; he said: "The oil palm is the best, because the oil palm produces very many things that are necessary in the daily life of people."

When the raffia palm heard this he got angry and took away the raffia coat from the chimpanzee; the chimpanzee was ashamed[18] and fled into the jungle; he did not want to stay with people any more. But long ago the chimpanzee was somebody in a populated region.[19]

[Notes for Tale 90 follow Tale 92.]

Source:	Hulstaert and de Rop's *Rechtspraakfabels* . . . (in Flemish)
Translators:	Francien Muijen Wright and Dr. Tinco E. A. van Hylckama
Date of Translations:	April 1975

91. *The Palaver between the Raffia Palm and the Oil Palm: Which Is More Valuable?* (Variant III)[20]

On a certain day that the trees had gathered for a feast,[21] they had drunk a lot. When the beer was finished, the wives brought tasty food. This food was prepared with oil and really fine palm sauce. And the woman that brought the food had a really beautiful dress on.

When the oil-palm saw the woman come with the palm sauce and the oil in the food, he was really happy; he stood straight in the middle of all the people, made them stop the noise, and said to them: "Look at my use as oil-palm: I bring forth good oil, palm sauce, palm wine, really sharp salt, palm slats, brush nerves, palm nuts for oil; my flowers and my trunk bring grubs.[22] Who is better than I?"

The raffia-palm then stood very straight and spoke: "You say that no one is better than you; but I think that I surpass you. I give clothes to the people; I bring forth the fiber with which people kill the animals in snares; my leaf nerves are used to make brushes from, they are stronger than yours; with my nuts people make oil; I give to the people my palm stalks and they make cots; and I have also leaves which the people use to make houses; my salt is very good in your food; and when I die I bring forth fine grubs in my stem. In what do you think you outshine me?"

Thereupon they had a heavy dispute and told all the people about it. Then the people went into a secret meeting[23] to discuss the palaver. Who of the two surpasses his buddy?"[24]

Solution [Verdict]

In the dispute between the raffia- and the oil-palm, the raffia-palm wins. The raffia-palm wins because it covers the nakedness of people. Look here; either you do without palm-sauce, oil and palm-wine or for three or four days you sit there naked in the eyes of the people; is it not better to do without all that food from the palm tree? You can very well go hungry in the eyes of the people and of your family, but in the eyes of the people and of your family you cannot go naked.[25] Therefore in this dispute the raffia-palm is the most useful because he gives clothing.[26]

[Notes for Tale 91 follow Tale 92.]

Source:	Hulstaert and de Rop's *Rechtspraakfabels* ... (in Lonkundo)
Translators:	Mabel Ross and multilingual aides
Date of Translations:	August 1975

92. The Palaver between the Raffia Palm and the Oil Palm: Which Is More Valuable? (Variant IV)

One day when the trees met in their feast, they drank a great deal. Then the liquor was finished, and the women came with very good food. That food was made itself[27] with oil and palm sauce. And the woman who brought the food had a very beautiful dress on her body.

When the palm-oil tree saw the woman come with the palm sauce and oil in the food also, he felt much rejoicing itself,[28] he stood in the middle of the people and restrained the noise and told them that: "You see my own work: I bring good oil, palm sauce, liquor, salt with sharpness itself, split ribs of the palm frond, good brooms, the kernel for oil, and I bring caterpillars in my trunk. What person is equal to me?"

The raffia-palm stood there and said: "You say that no other person is like to you, but I think that I exceed you. I give people cloth, I bring forth the fibers that man may kill animals, my rib fibers make brooms which exceed yours in strength and my fruit makes oil; I give people my palm fronds in the making of beds, and I myself have *ndele*[29] for the building of people's houses, my salt is very good in food, then I bring caterpillars themselves. Now in what of these things do you exceed?"

Then their dispute became hard and they told it to the people. The people came in secret that they cut their palaver. Which of the two exceeds his friend?

*

*   *[30]

Raffia palm and oil palm, who excels truly raffia palm itself.[31] The raffia palm excels because he covers a person's nakedness. Regard a bit: you refuse oil, palm sauce, palm liquor, three days, maybe four, or you sit naked in the eyes of people; better to refuse all the food from the oil palm. You can go hungry in the eyes of people and all your family, but you cannot go naked in the eyes of the people and all your family. Therefore in the palaver of the two, who exceeds in usefulness itself is the raffia palm because he has clothing.[32]

Notes for Tales 88 through 92: Bokunge Jacques, the narrator of the Ross field-collected version of this dilemma tale, told Tale 88 to Mrs. Ross during a "rest break" in the arduous task of translating and transcribing tales previously recorded—both by himself and by various other informants—so that the tapes might be erased for the recording of further evidences of Nkundo verbal art. Like a number of other narratives recounted by Bokunge Jacques, this one is valued by the storyteller as a means of explaining how various creatures and customs originated. Perhaps more than any other of Mrs. Ross's informants, he was deeply concerned with preserving a record of how things were, of how they came to be so, both for the sake of his own grandchildren and for the understanding and appreciation of others who might never otherwise come to know and appreciate the range of Nkundo oral tradition. To "classify" this or any other narrative as a "dilemma tale" would not have occurred to him; even the term "story" was loosely used, both by Bokunge Jacques and by others among the Ross informants—among the present set of dilemma tales, the term "story" is used where others might have substituted "case" in the instances where the two trees present their respective claims for consideration by the judge of the palaver. The fact that Mrs. Ross was the sole listener for Tale 88 doubtless deprived the taped version of the lively discussion normally prompted by the dilemma tale as it is described in various scholarly studies; that it *has* continued in the Nkundo oral tradition as a dilemma tale is borne out by the accompanying variants.

Trees are personalized in this tale and its variants; in the animistic tradition everything has a spirit and can be readily personalized. Countless other instances of personalization could be cited from oral repertories in all parts of the world; an additional Nkundo example in Hulstaert and de Rop's *Rechtspraakfabels*... is found in the dilemma tale numbered 38, in which tree-borne fruits and ground-borne fruits dispute their relative values (in this palaver, the ground-borne fruits are concluded to be the more valuable).

Do today's Nkundo believe that once the chimpanzee wore clothes? In the Ross field tale and in Variants I and II, the chimpanzee is punished for his judicial verdict by being deprived of clothes; he appears to have felt man's sense of shame at being naked. This element of the dilemma tale may have been added because of acculturation: a century ago, the Nkundo wore full clothing only as protection from cold or other environmental factors (see note 25 below). Variants III and IV seem to us to reflect an earlier form of this particular tale, with the first three versions representing tales in a state of flux. The *pourquoi* element introduced by the chimpanzee's punishment may eventually dominate the story content and reduce the force of the narrative as a dilemma tale.

This particular short tale and its equally brief variants afford an exceptionally good opportunity for examination of narrative style, content, theme, and diction. All five of the forms have been taken from the Nkundo oral tradition; they clearly have the same core. But what has been done by the various narrators (and, to some degree, by the translators) is highly individual, an indication that these tales are by no means forever fixed in their wording or even in their structure, but are left free for the play of the narrator's imagination. Whatever extraneous materials may enter a given telling will live or die in accord with their appropriateness to the theme, to the cultural tradition from which the tale has sprung, and to changes which acculturation may produce in that tradition.

For the convenience of the users of the present volume, we have taken the liberty for Variant III of renumbering de Rop's footnotes (according to the Introduction, both the translation and the annotations in that joint work were furnished by de Rop), incorporating his footnotes within our own numbering system but identifying them [in translation by van Hylckama] as de Rop's.

It is interesting to observe that although de Rop does classify "The Chimpanzee" among "jurisprudence fables" (dilemma tales involving the handing down of decisions) in ... *woordkunst* ... , he offers for it no "*oplossing*" ["solution," or "verdict"], an item which follows several others of the dilemma tales he has included in that study of Nkundo verbal art. Perhaps the intrusion of the *pourquoi* element has caused this particular tale to sit uncomfortably under the dilemma-tale narrative form and thus rendered the palaver verdict anticlimactic. The further course of this tale in Nkundo oral tradition would be illuminating to follow; it might open a window on the close study of folktales in a state of flux and the various factors which determine their "final" narrative forms.

A variant not included in this volume but available in English may be found in Alice Cobble's *Wembi*. ... The "frame-story" structure within which the entire set of tales in this volume has been arranged and the moralistic tone of the intervening passages are features alien to traditional Nkundo storytelling; the tone stands between the tales and the reader who wishes to study Nkundo narrative style. "The Man Who Became a Chimpanzee," found on pages 34–36 of *Wembi* . . . , provides an interesting contrast to the five versions provided in the present collection.

The opening sentence describing Lambrecht's tale type 4206—"The Bashilele were quarreling about which was the most useful tree"—would appear to furnish an "umbrella" for Tale 88 and its variants. Further examination reveals, however, that the tale assigned Lambrecht's type number 4206 cannot qualify as a dilemma tale, at least in its present construction, but as a rather weak example among the accounts of "marriage tests," where it is presently classified by Lambrecht. It is suggested that, since the same sort of challenge of usefulness can be applied in a dilemma tale, some means of cross-referencing be provided to send the user of Lambrecht's "Tale Type Index for Central Africa" to the portion of the Index termed "IV Formula Tales," where this same challenge of relative usefulness might be explored in another oral-literature form.

Motifs:

L	H659.11.2.	What is the most useful tree?
C	B274.+.**.	Chimpanzee as judge in dispute between raffia palm and oil palm.
T	Q281.	Ingratitude punished.
T	Q430.	Abridgment of freedom as punishment.
T	Q595.	Loss or destruction of property as punishment.
C	D118.1.+.**.	Transformation: man to chimpanzee, by removal of clothing.

1. [Narrator's explanatory comment: "Lifeke is a palm tree that produces raffia. Men take this raffia and make cloth. Jiba is a palm tree that produces large bunches of palm fruit which are filled with a very delicious oil."]

2. Raffia is still commonly in use among the Nkundo for bed mats; the bed mat is flexible and thus can be rolled into a small ball and carried on a journey. Raffia is seldom used for clothing now that cotton cloth is available throughout Zaïre. If an elder from some bush village comes into the hospital wearing raffia cloth, the event is so unusual that not only the children but also the adults stare at him.

The strips of the raffia palm can be further reduced to long, fine, threadlike pieces that can be used for sewing clothing from raffia cloth or for any other purpose for which a coarse thread is needed. Strips of raffia of various thicknesses are also used in the construction of snares.

3. The center strip of the frond can be used as a flexible yet strong bow employed in killing birds and small animals.

4. Caterpillars are carefully nourished in the crevices of the tree where the old fronds have been cut away.

5. *Mba*, the fruit of the palm tree, is golden brown in color, with meaty pulp held around a nut by strands of fiber. The pulp separated from the fiber is used in a sauce with meat and vegetables in many Central African dishes, giving them much added nourishment as well as flavor. The fruit itself may be heated in water or baked

in the fire and then eaten with salt. It is very tasty, but also better eaten outdoors, since the oil continues to drip from it.

The oil from the pulp is extracted and used extensively for frying and cooking. It is also used by the Nkundo for anointing their bodies, giving their skins a gloss which is attractive to others and comfortable to them. Both the oil from the pulp and oil extracted from the kernel of the nut are used commercially in margarines, cooking oil, and soaps, and constitute one of the main exports of the Nkundo area.

6. These fronds and the flower stalks are put in the fire until they are reduced to ashes. After these ashes have been put in water and boiled, they are left to dry, and they become a very hard form of salt. The cook chips bits from this lump of salt and drops them into her food as she is cooking. When a tree is felled, the strips of the trunk are reduced to salt in this same manner.

The flower stalks, which make excellent fertilizer for almost any garden, are especially treasured by foreigners in the area.

7. These small arrows, effective only against birds, are used more often by young boys than by grown hunters.

8. After the poles are pounded into the ground where the walls are to be, the Nkundo weave these strips taken from the center of the palm frond back and forth between the poles. These strips support the mud which the women and children of the household daub on to finish the walls of the house.

9. In many Nkundo villages, one sees a gourd hung high in a palm tree close to the trunk. The sap of the tree drips slowly down a trough made by inserting a piece of split bamboo into a slit in the tree; the trough leads to the gourd. Palm wine, a common drink among the Nkundo, is potent enough to be poisonous to some who are exposed to it.

10. Right out of the heart of the palm tree, and available only when the tree is cut down, the palm cabbage serves as a pleasant addition to the diet. It is used in almost any way that regular cabbage can be used, but has a much more delicate flavor. Most non-Nkundo prefer it as a salad ingredient, since salad greens are scarce in an equatorial forest.

11. This makes a rather flavorless type of chewing gum which is normally of greater interest to children than to adults.

12. Even though this is basically a dilemma tale, the ending gives it the flavor of a *pourquoi* tale. Eza was "demoted" from the human state to the animal state. Being a judge is in numerous Nkundo tales a thankless service.

Undoubtedly this tale, with a number of others current in the oral tradition of the riverine peoples, serves as a means of venting the resentment of the listeners (and the narrator) against the injustices they themselves may have suffered at the hands of judges and various other administrators. Rattray in his *Akan-Ashanti Folk-Tales* (p. xi) has indicated this same usefulness of storytelling in allowing people in the Gold Coast area to laugh with impunity at matters or abuses they were not allowed to discuss or criticize in public.

13. To be older would give him more prestige; the older person requires more respect and is accepted as being wiser.

14. The frond of the raffia palm is long and can be used as a broom for sweeping

the dirt floors of the Nkundo houses. Foreigners like raffia-palm fronds for sweeping cobwebs from their ceilings.

15. In modern times, this use for the *njiika*, or kernel, is no longer practiced; now, the palm fruit is shipped to the factory, and the nut is cracked by machine. However, not so many years ago the palm nuts were carefully saved by the family. From time to time, the older people and the children would sit together, each with a couple of flat stones. With the stones they would crack the nuts and save the *njiika*, or kernels. These kernels would always bring ready cash for special things for the family. The word *bempenga* suggests an emergency or special need.

16. In the Zaïrian school reader, this tale carries the title "Eza èki Joso" ("The Chimpanzee Who Was First"), an indication that the compilers viewed it as a *pourquoi* narrative. The rather haphazard way in which each of the trees in turn states his case strengthens the assumption that the actual merits of the case were not as important to the narrator as was the punishment meted out to the judge of the palaver, a punishment accounting for the chimpanzee's origin (pp. 51–52).

17. The ellipses are de Rop's.

18. The suggestion that the chimpanzee was "ashamed" because he no longer had clothing is a further instance of the anthropomorphizing of animals in Nkundo —indeed, as in *many* African—folk narratives. To attribute to the chimpanzee a human feeling of shame because he is naked re-emphasizes the fine dividing line which these riverine people sense between themselves and both animate and inanimate sharers of their environment. Humanizing of yams, stews, mortars and pestles, and all kinds of birds and beasts allows the narrators and their audiences to air their grievances and concerns as people without exposing themselves to ridicule or to punishment. In this tale, the audience derives satisfaction from the humiliation of a judge, a figure who in Nkundo society wields a considerable amount of power and, since he has to decide *for* one litigant and *against* another, invariably arouses the resentment of those who lose in palavers.

19. In de Rop's volume . . . *woordkunst* . . . , the title of this tale, "De Chimpansee" ("The Chimpanzee"), reflects the unnamed narrator's interest in the plight of the judge. If one can assess the content and style of the original narrative from this English translation of the Flemish translation of the Lonkundo—a risky business, at best—one would doubtless concede that Variant II is a more artistic narration than is Variant I. We are reasonably confident of the accuracy of the English translation because of the care taken in double-checking all translations. De Rop's comments earlier in his own book make clear his awareness of narrative style and of the folktale as a form of narrative art, so his skill may well have contributed to the sentence variety and the pleasing balance of argument in this variant. Even the chimpanzee's judicial comment concerning the necessity of the oil palm's products "in the daily life of people" could be interpreted as a clue to de Rop's awareness of the function of the folktales as a mirror of the culture. The circumstances of this particular narration are not provided, so there is no way of determining whether the art of this piece lies with de Rop or with the Nkundo narrator. Clearly, one or the other was acutely aware of the poignancy of the chimpanzee's "fall from grace." And no reader of the tale can deny that the judge was faced with an exceedingly difficult decision, a characteristic feature of a well-developed dilemma tale.

20. [The footnote number originally followed the Flemish title; the footnote number assigned by de Rop was "2."] "The midrib of the leaf of the raffia palm is much stronger than that of the oil palm, and serves among other things to make couches to sleep upon. The leaves sewn together serve as roofing for a house. The leaves also provide raffia which can be woven and thus can serve as clothing or can be bundled together into a sort of short skirt. The male flowers of both palms are used to make salt: the flowers are burned and the remaining ashes are washed and then pressed together into cakes and dried."

21. The introduction of the idea that the trees had gathered for a feast indicates the freedom of the narrator for innovation in the telling of a traditional tale. The Nkundo themselves relish feasts, and enjoy listing the delicious dishes served, and they would see no irregularity in extending this pleasure to nonhuman features in their environment. If in the course of repeated tellings this innovation came to be regarded as extraneous, it would be eliminated by later narrators, who are as free to drop as to add improvisations. The fact that "women" served at the feast and that "men" were asked to judge the palaver furnishes another instance of the extremely narrow line that divides the Nkundo from the animals, vegetation, and inanimate objects of their environment. The observation of their respective products' actually being used by humans added fuel to the fire of the argument between the two palms. Unquestionably, this narrative device (a social situation's providing an occasion for the quarrel between the two palm trees) is an artistic one.

Whether the narrator—identified as P. Efeté—heard this introductory detail from some other narrator or developed it himself is not indicated; Hulstaert in his Introduction to the volume *Rechtspraakfabels* . . . says, "Most [of the] fables were written down by a few natives. . . . Especially fruitful work has been provided by P. Efeté of Wongata w'ajiko, who for many years has been a judge in the C.E.C. of Coq [Coquilhatville, long ago called Mbandaka and since Independence restored to its original name] who was thoroughly familiar with the native laws" (p. vii). If the narrator wrote down the version as it stands in Lonkundo [see Variant IV], he had ample opportunity to embellish what might originally have been a simpler narrative; if, in addition, he had been a judge himself, he would be careful to balance the "evidence" provided by both litigants so that the judge would truly be faced by a difficult decision, one demanding the reasoning power of someone of greater dignity than "a person" or "a chimpanzee." A "solution" or a "verdict" would of course be supplied by a narrator with judicial experience; the elegance of the handling of this particular verdict and the fact that the decision was given in favor of the raffia-palm might both be attributed to the narrator's imperative to enhance the position of the judge as a reasonable and impartial person well aware of the culture in which he lived and as a person of considerable dignity. The inclusion of the *pourquoi* element, present in the first three forms of the tale in the present "cluster," would not serve this particular narrator's purposes at all: the exposure of the judge to shame, ridicule, and isolation would be unthinkable. Thus the content and the style of this variant are strongly determined by the identity of the narrator-recorder and by his relationship with his intended audience.

22. [This footnote, de Rop's, was originally numbered "3."] "In the trunk of dead palms of both kinds are fat white grubs which are edible."

23. [This note, de Rop's, was originally numbered "1."] "If the decision in a lawsuit is unusually difficult or if the judges for other reasons are afraid openly to give their opinion in a dispute which is brought before them by influential persons, then they gather in secret. That is to say, the persons who brought up the lawsuit and also possible witnesses are sent away and the judges confer among themselves how to solve the dispute. After that, the persons involved in the lawsuit are called back and the chairman of the assembly speaks in the name of all the other assembled judges."

24. "Buddy" is the literal English translation of the Flemish word used by the narrator-recorder. To the Western reader, the term "buddy" appears out of keeping with the elegance of the rest of the wording; among the Nkundo, however, close friendships between males are highly valued, and terms indicating that closeness are perhaps more appropriately rendered in Lonkundo than in English. An age-mate is indeed a "buddy" among the Nkundo.

25. The image of the African as a "naked savage" has been overemphasized by various authors and photographers in magazines, in part for the goal of sensationalism. Actually, for centuries the African has covered his genitals and for a great number of years has covered his entire body [exceptions occur to the latter portion of the statement among the African Bushmen and other small nomadic groups long the subject of scholarly investigation]. In Zaïre a woman's bare breasts do not create the sense of embarrassment that such exposure might at one time have created in the Western world. On public occasions, the Nkundo woman wears a "cloth" that covers her completely and is draped gracefully about her.

26. The original Flemish title, "De raphia- en de elaeis-palm," is translated thus: "The Raffia- and the Oil-Palm" (the Flemish translation appears on pages 85 and 87 in the Hulstaert and de Rop collection, with the facing pages furnishing the tale in Lonkundo).

27. The use of "*ô*" ("itself") provides the additional emphasis usually furnished by the reflexive in Lonkundo: to emphasize the excellence, the very special quality, of that food.

28. Here the reflexive term "itself" is expressed in the Lonkundo by "*mongo*," used interchangeably with "*ô*," to add emphasis to the preceding word, "rejoicing." "*Mongo*" is the Lonkundo reflexive form used after "sharpness," also, in the palm-oil's description of the salt he produces. The reflexive form "*ô*" is used by the raffia palm to emphasize "I" in "I myself have *ndele* . . . ," to reinforce "raffia palm" in the first sentence of the "solution," and again in the concluding sentence to stress "usefulness."

It is interesting to observe that this use of the reflexive—common in everyday Lonkundo speech as well as in storytelling—has not been included in the Flemish translation. Omission of this flavorsome and characteristic bit of Lonkundo diction seems unfortunate. Other losses not noted here might well be explored by linguists in an effort to preserve the full force of this African tongue.

29. The fronds of the raffia palm are both longer and wider than those of the oil palm, and the former are preferred by the Nkundo as roofing material. A well-made *ndele* roof will last throughout several years of tropical heat and rain without requiring repair. Both the fronds themselves and the "strips" in which these raffia-palm fronds are bundled and sold in the market are called *ndele*.

30. Throughout the Hulstaert and de Rop volume, this pattern of asterisks separates the Lonkundo text of the dilemma tale from the paragraph in which a "solution" is provided for the dilemma. At no point does the Nkundo narrator label the final paragraph "solution" or "verdict," a wise decision in light of the fact that there can *be* no permanent, correct-without-a-doubt "solution" of any true dilemma.

What gives the dilemma tale special interest as a narrative form among the Nkundo is the opportunity it affords for the development of skill in debate and eloquent expression, both important in the art of legal oratory in a palaver, the means used for settling most of the disputes which arise in this largely oral society. The palaver serves both as the local court and as a source of entertainment and instruction, and these dilemma tales furnish examples for the handling of cases in real-life palavers.

The collection of dilemma tales compiled by Hulstaert and de Rop is curiously lacking in proverbs; whether this omission is a matter of oversight on the part of the compilers or whether it reflects a recognition of the difficulty in translating "the horse of conversation" (as the Yorubas describe the proverb) is a matter for conjecture. Proverbs do in a great many instances involve word play, as well as local or historical allusions; on the other hand, they are indispensable in the faithful presentation of the arguing-to-a-finish narrative structure termed a dilemma tale—by rights, the full presentation should include the discussion as well as the tale itself, though full transcripts of such discussions appear to be rare indeed.

One point in Hulstaert's Introduction was especially provocative: "... [O]ne should not consider these solutions as the only correct ones. *Although in most cases they are correct* [italics ours. B.K.W.], there still is room for dissenting points of view" (p. viii). The five versions in the present "cluster" indicate that diametrically opposed "solutions" have been furnished for the same basic dilemma. In truth, the "correct" solution to any given dilemma varies, dependent upon differences in legal knowledge, in sharpness of wit, in tribal traditions, in skill of argumentation, and in the relevance of the dilemma tale to some local problem or dispute. In a genuine dilemma, each "horn" has its points; various audiences determine their own preferences, and the dilemma tale will thus persist as a narrative form among primarily oral societies until there are no longer audiences to debate their "correct" conclusion.

31. In Lonkundo everyday speech as well as in the narrating of tales from the Nkundo oral tradition, the verb is frequently understood rather than stated. (Among other languages, Turkish shares this characteristic, particularly with respect to forms of the verb "to be.") Omission or truncation of various verbs in Lonkundo creates special problems in translation, offering distinct difficulties in the handling of poetry, songs, dialogue, and proverbs, as well as in the faithful rendition of prose narrative. In most instances, we have forgone the temptation to insert within brackets in the English translation the verb omitted in the Lonkundo, preferring to communicate as nearly as possible the flavor and diction of the original at the expense of smooth expression in English.

32. The original Lonkundo title, "Lifeke la liya," is translated "The Raffia Palm and the Oil Palm." The Lonkundo version appears on pages 84 and 86 of the Hulstaert and de Rop volume.

Narrator: Njoli Bombongo
Location: Tondo, but narrator's home
                    was in Kalamba
Date: June 1973

93. *The Palaver between the Hunter and the Leopard: Whose Goats?*

This is the story of Is'ea Njòkumbòyò (a hunter) and Male Nkòi (the leopard).[1] Hunter went into the forest to hunt. First he built a temporary shelter in the forest. He set some traps. The next day he went to see what he had caught and found that Esende (the squirrel) was entangled in the net. Squirrel said, "Respected Hunter, turn me loose and sometime I will help you to have life."

Hunter thought about this. He remembered that his wife and children were at home and hungry for lack of meat. Then he agreed. "No matter. I will untangle you. You are small and have very little meat on you for my family."

So Squirrel went on his way, and Hunter went home. There he found that his wife and children were still hungry, and he felt great sorrow.[2]

On another day, Leopard came and found Hunter in the yard with his goats. He watched him awhile and said, "Hunter! Hunter! I have come as a friend. I see that you have many female goats but that you have no male. I have a male goat. Let me bring my male to your yard and you can have more goats."

When they finished talking this way, Leopard went to the yard where he kept his goat[3] and brought it to the enclosure where Hunter kept his. Hunter had female goats, and Leopard had a male goat. Soon the goat family began to increase until the enclosure could hardly hold them all.

After that, Leopard came and looked at all the goats that were there. "Hunter!" he called out. "You are evil. Just look at all the goats that you have. *O soli e!*"[4]

Hunter answered, "I'm not bad. It must be you who are a demon."

"But look at all the goats you have in your yard. They are more than the yard will hold. This is because I brought my male goat here.

You couldn't have any goats without my goat. I'm going to take all of them because they are really mine."

Hunter wasn't willing to accept this. "How can you talk like that? They are all my goats."

Leopard responded, "No. You couldn't possibly have any goats if I hadn't brought my male. O your mother's vagina!"

The argument began to be heated until they called the families of each of them. They called people. Leopard called his family. Hunter called his family.[5]

Hunter explained, "Come and cut this palaver for us. I had female goats but no male. Leopard had a male goat which he brought to my goat enclosure. The goats increased very quickly. Leopard wants to take all the goats with him. He is strong and has strong claws and can dig them into me. He is very bad. *E-e-e-e*."

Just then, Squirrel came. He had been listening to the palaver. He said, "Look at me. I am pregnant."

Leopard looked at him. "How can you be pregnant? How can you be pregnant? How can you be pregnant?[6] You are a male."

Everyone got the teaching. If Squirrel couldn't be pregnant, then Leopard's goat couldn't be, either.

They laughed at Leopard. "You lose the palaver. Stop your talk. Take your goat home. He certainly didn't give birth to all of these goats that are in Hunter's yard any more than Squirrel is pregnant. O your mother's vagina!"

Leopard wanted to kill Squirrel, but he went into the forest.

The tale teaches this: If you have strength, you do not think that you have wisdom, because people with strength do not have wisdom. The squirrel is little; he exceeded the leopard with wisdom. He cut the palaver.[7]

It is finished.

Aarne-Thompson's tale type 75 furnishes the basic type for the core of this lively and entertaining Tale 93; Arewa's type 2578 provides an interesting variant from the Northern East African cattle area, and Lambrecht furnishes several variants of the-captured-animal-released-and-grateful pattern, all drawn from Central Africa, among them tale types 2410, 2426, and 2430. Klipple's sample for the Congo area is one taken from Weeks' *Jungle Life and Jungle Stories* (1923), pages 410ff., titled "How the Squirrel Repaid a Kindness," entered under tale type 75; the same tale, with the same title, appears also in Weeks' earlier *Congo Life and Folklore* (pp. 410–414), not indexed. All of the above examples are more helpful with respect to the earlier part of the present tale than for the latter portion. The false claim of ownership based on a male's producing young finds helpful type entries under Arewa's 1309 (1) and 1309 (2), with the latter the closest parallel we have found to the palaver that closes Njoli Bombongo's tale; "How the Squirrel Won a Verdict for the Gazelle," on pages 46–47 of Weeks' *Congo Life and Folklore*—not cited in any of the indexes —furnishes an admirable variant for the latter portion of the present tale, but the squirrel's act has not been preceded by his rescue: it is a voluntary act of kindness, as was the ape's rescue of the man in Tale 45. None of these citations even approximates the complexity of the situation presented in this narrator's skillful use of the rescued animal as the judge at the palaver.

Motifs:

T	B370.	Animal grateful to captor for release.
T	B364.1.	Animal grateful for rescue from trap (net).
T	Q40.	Kindness rewarded.
T	B274.	Animal as judge (voluntary).
C	H620.+.**.	To which one do the kids belong: owner of male goat or owner of ewe?
C	J1191.1.+.**.	Reductio ad absurdum: the decision about the kids.
T	J1191.1.	Reductio ad absurdum: the decision about the colt (kids).
T	J1179.**.	Clever judicial decisions—miscellaneous: rendered by ridiculous claim made by squirrel as witness.
T	J1533.	Absurdities concerning birth of animals, or men.
T	J1530.	One absurdity rebukes another.
T	J1250.	Clever verbal retorts—general.
T	B437.3.	Helpful squirrel.
C	B583.+.**.	Grateful squirrel solves dilemma, allowing hunter to keep all kids borne by his ewe.
C	J1171.1.+.**.	Judge of palaver, fearing reprisal from leopard, is prompted to award leopard the disputed goats despite patent absurdity of claim.

1. [Narrator's explanatory comment: "*Is'ea Njokumboyo* means 'Father of Njokumboyo.' It is always a sign of respect to refer to a man as the father of his oldest child or to a woman as the mother of her oldest child. 'Male' is often used when referring to an elder in the family, especially when it is an older brother. Nkòi is a leopard. This may refer to a leopard or be symbolic of it."] To facilitate reading, we have substituted "Hunter" and "Leopard" for the Nkundo terms. (Early in the telling, there were many interruptions by the houseboy.)

2. By tradition, whatever meat or fish has been caught by the man of the family is to be shared with his family. (See Tale 60 for a powerful instance of this point.)

Here, Hunter has had to make a choice between values held by his society—in effect, he faces a dilemma—and the palaver with which the tale closes is artistically a splendid sequel to the dilemma Hunter had earlier resolved. If this tale had been told in an Nkundo evening storytelling session, it might well have prompted the telling of one or more dilemma tales bearing on the same point, since Nkundo feelings run strong and deep concerning the matter of sharing.

3. The presentation of Leopard as living in a compound where he would have a yard for his goat is further reflection of the Nkundo's seeing animals as living in circumstances similar to their own; indeed, the "Leopard" is envisioned by the audience as any person strong enough to dominate others, rather than the four-legged creature who would eat a goat as soon as he had encountered it. In Nkundo tales as well as in those of the Bantu-speaking peoples generally (see Torrend, *Bantu Folk-Tales, passim*), animals are seen as people and people as animals.

4. The narrator here uses an expression which the Nkundo in Mrs. Ross's area call "swearing," but which has been identified by Philip Mayer (see "The Joking of 'Pals' in Gusii Age Sets," based on his fieldwork with a Bantu-speaking people in East Africa) as typical of a form of verbal insult-game prominent during adolescence but continued into old age; the exchange of pornographic references to one another's mothers was identified by Mrs. Ross in a storytelling situation on only this one instance. Loosely translated, *"O soli e"* (with the *"so"* heavily emphasized) says, "O your mother's vagina!" Subsequent uses of this expression by the narrator are furnished in English in the present translation; note that the expression is used both by Leopard and by members of the audience (presumably members of Leopard's family and of Hunter's family, as well as "people" called to hear the palaver). In the light of study by Abrahams and others of "Playing the Dozens," this use of pornographic insult in current Nkundo storytelling takes on special interest, and undoubtedly would repay investigation by a non-missionary collector, on the assumption that narrators in general might have felt constrained to temper their expressions in view of their mixed audience.

5. As is the practice in Nkundo villages, a heated argument here leads to the summoning of all interested parties for a palaver to settle the matter. (Note that in Tale 60 the same means of deciding a dispute was used.) Squirrel, as an interested party, really functioned as both judge and key witness in this instance, since it was he who demonstrated the ridiculous nature of Leopard's claim on the goats.

6. This portion of Leopard's argument was very loud and heated. Clearly, the narrator was relishing the fact that Leopard, in his stupidity, was in effect arguing against himself.

7. The narrator's identification of the squirrel as the one who "cut the palaver" singles Squirrel out as the judge, though "they"—the families of the leopard and the hunter—actually terminated the discussion.

Narrator: Bokunge Jacques
Location: Bólèngè
Date: March 1973

94.   The Palaver between the Eagle and the Leopard: How Many Porcupines Apiece?

On another day many years ago an eagle, Mpongo, went hunting with his dog.[1] Suddenly a leopard, Nkòi, met him and said, "It would be good if we went together for this hunt, the both of us." Eagle agreed that they go together, so they started out to hunt meat. After a while they had killed five porcupines, so they decided it was time to divide their catch.

Eagle gave Leopard two porcupines and he took three for himself. But Leopard objected. "That isn't a fair division. Why don't you take two porcupines, give one to the dog, and the two that are left will be mine?"

Eagle was not at all willing to accept this division. It wasn't long until they were arguing and had a real palaver to settle.

A wild pig, Nsombo, came along and heard the argument. He asked them, "What's your problem?"[2]

So they told Wild Pig all about the palaver, with each one telling his own story.

Wild Pig listened to each of them and finally said, "Come with me. Let us go to my yard and there I will cut the palaver so that it will suit both of you."

They agreed and went to the home of Wild Pig. Then Wild Pig called all the animals and all the birds to his yard and said to them, "Let those animals who live below on the ground sit together in one place. Then we will bring the palaver between Eagle and Leopard out in the open."

The animals divided, each to his kind. But the monkey went with the animals who lived on the ground and sat with them. Eagle said to him, "Nkema, you come to the place where the birds are, because you live above in the trees."[3]

But Monkey answered him, "I do not have wings such as birds have. How can I go with you? Can't you see the hairs on my skin?"

So Eagle let him alone, and they began to discuss the palaver.

However, because all of the animals feared Leopard, they wanted Leopard to win the palaver.

One little bird, Yokoke, felt sure that there was a plot of this sort among the animals. He went to Eagle and whispered to him,[4] "The animals are secretly plotting together. They very much hope that you will fall in the palaver and they want Leopard to win."

Because of that, Eagle made another plot to suit himself. He said, "Nkoiambe (Hawk), you pick up one of those porcupines; Ikete (Chicken Hawk), you pick up another porcupine; I will take what's left. Let us settle this palaver the way we want it settled."

So Chicken Hawk took one porcupine and flew away with it. Hawk picked up another porcupine and flew away. Then Eagle took up the porcupine that was left and followed them.

The gathering was completely broken up, *nyë.* Leopard grabbed Wild Pig and said, "I had planned to tie up Eagle and take the meat by force, but you interfered. You called all the animals and birds together. Eagle has friends who serve him. It is all your fault that things are as they are. Therefore you may not go free at all, *nyë.*" He killed Wild Pig until he was dead dead.

All of the animals disappeared from the yard and into the forest. Monkey returned to his place up in the trees. But soon Eagle came and said to Monkey, "Monkey, you refused to join the company of birds. You even showed me the hair on your body. How can you dare to return again up above in the trees?"

Before Monkey could give his reply, Eagle grabbed him, *bau,* and killed him completely dead, *ci.*

Even until this very day, the eagle and the monkey fight each other. Also, the wild pig will fight with the leopard. Their conflict is never finished.

The narrator, primarily interested in how things began, used Tale 94 ostensibly to explain why the eagle and the monkey are enemies and why the wild pig and the leopard are enemies. It may well be, however, that the *pourquoi* portion of the tale is a borrowing from other narratives to suit the storyteller's immediate purpose and that Tale 94 exists in the Nkundo oral tradition in a more stable and uncluttered form than the one furnished by Bokunge Jacques. Though this version has the trappings of two *pourquoi* tales, its central theme is the division of the spoils and its method of solution lies in the palaver, a feature of the dilemma tale.

This mingling of plot and subplots weakens the narrative structure and causes

the focus of the tale to be lost. It has been grouped with the dilemma tales because
the dilemma element, here underplayed, normally assumes center stage in the light
of Nkundo concern with justice, especially concerning sharing.

Lambrecht's tale type 547 provides the only coverage found for the basic plot
of Bokunge Jacques' narrative. Based on a tale translated into Bolia for Mamet's
Le Langage des Bolia by Gabriel Mbembe [Mamet credits the original fable, in the
ombo dialect, to Dr. Meeussen's book *Esquisse*], "L'antilope et la mouche" involves
only the antelope, the fly, and the catch of fish which they had gained by cooperating
in the emptying of a pond. When the antelope persists in dividing the catch unevenly,
the fly kills the antelope by flying into his nostril and appropriates all of the fish for
himself. There is no hint of a *pourquoi*; on the other hand, there is no palaver—the
tale is grouped not with the dilemma and other formula tales but with those involving
Death of Animals by Strategy. "Crop division" lies at the heart of both tales; either
or both could be made more complex by introducing other elements—as, indeed,
the Nkundo narrator has done, as nearly as can be determined.

Motifs:

C	B274.+.**.	Wild pig as judge in dispute between eagle and leopard.
T	J811.	Wisdom of concession to power.
T	J830.	Adaptability to overpowering force.
T	Q411.	Death as punishment.
L	Q382.	Punishment for helping.
T	A2494.	Why certain animals are enemies.

1. The eagle's use of a dog in his hunting evidences the Nkundo's attributing to
animals his own cultural patterns. Clearly, the eagle would have no need for a dog
in locating and securing his prey, nor would the dove and the crow need their dogs
and their guns and a huntsman in Weeks' *Congo Life and Folklore*, pages 401–402.

2. *Jói na?* is an often-used question difficult to translate with its full Lonkundo
flavor. Literally, it means "What word?" It approaches the Western query "What's
up?" or "What do you have to say?" or "What's the problem?" but it carries more
weight than these casual queries suggest.

3. "Each to his own kind" is an accepted way of life among the Nkundo;
consequently, the narrator would seize this opportunity to separate the animals
according to their kinds. The monkey seems to be neither bird, beast, nor fish, and
has thus been a popular subject for debate in "kingdom" determination, as has the
bat. Both the "bat" tales and the present "monkey" story may well reflect a human
concern with tribal identity and—since folktales mirror human concerns and values
—may thus gradually decrease in the African oral tradition with the de-emphasizing
of tribal loyalties in favor of national unity in the various rapidly developing nations.

4. The function of the bird as a carrier both of helpful messages and of gossip
is accepted by both narrator and audience. Interestingly, when an Nkundo woman
is asked where she learned a certain bit of news, she invariably answers, "I got it
from the birds."

Source:	Zaïrian school reader *Bekolo Bèmò . . .*
	(in Lonkundo)
Translators:	Mabel Ross, with multilingual aides
Date of Translation:	July 1975

95. *Whom Would You Scold?:*
Three Tests of Friendship

The mother of Bowane[1] was sick—in fact, nearly dead. But their village had no doctor for healing people.[2] The nearest doctor was in a very distant village.

All the family wanted Civet Cat to go and ask the doctor to come and heal the mother. Civet Cat agreed, and he called two of his friends to go with him, Nguma (the python) and Ulu (the tortoise).

When they reached a distant village, Civet Cat was very thirsty. He said, "Friends, I have a tabu[3] that I may not drink in another place except my very own. Now I will return home to get a drink of water. I will go. You wait right here. Then we will go on."

Even though they had gone a long way, Civet Cat returned home because of his tabu. He was gone a long time. Then he came back again. He said, "Stand up; let us go. I have already come."[4]

His friends did not approve of the way in which he had done. They scolded him considerably. They rose up and they went and went. But Python caught a small antelope and he swallowed all of it in one piece.[5] Then Python said, "Friends, do not forget my way. When I swallow an animal, I am not fit again for travel until the animal which I swallowed is digested in my stomach. Now we cannot go until the digestion is finished."

They had not forgotten that when Python swallows meat, he does not go on until the meat is digested. Because of that, they waited a very long time for him. Then Python said, "Arise and let us go; I have strength." So the three of them got up and went, going, going, into a very large forest. When they were near the village at the edge of the forest, they found the trunk of a tree fallen in the path.

Tortoise tried to cross that tree trunk, but he wasn't able—his legs were too short. He said, "Friends, I am your friend, and each person to his own way. You can cross the trunk, but I do not have long legs. I am not willing that one of you take me across because then I would be ashamed. Now we must sit here until the tree trunk rots, and then we can go."

Civet Cat said, "That's a real problem! When will we ever get there?"

Tortoise said, "Why do you complain? Do you think that this tree will stay here? Wait for me that I do not break my rules."

The friends did not forget that the tree trunk would take a long while to decay. So they stayed there for very many years. And the tree trunk rotted away. Tortoise said, "It is a thing of rejoicing because the tree trunk has decayed. Now the time for our journey has arrived. Arise; let us go quickly."

After they had gone a way, they entered the village of the doctor. They told the doctor why they had come. When the doctor there understood their problems, he said to them, "I do not have recent news for you, but you may as well return home. Your mother has been dead for many years. Why do you come to me?"

When they returned home, they found that the mourners had long since quit crying.[6] Those left in the village thought that the three who had gone had been taken by evil spirits. They were surprised when they saw them again.

And now whom would you scold?[7]

The attention drawn to Nkundo tales in Bascom's *African Dilemma Tales* prompts the inclusion of this particular sample, Tale 95, available presently only in Lonkundo and thus not tabulated in Bascom's overview. Although Mrs. Ross encountered no oral version of this tale in her field collecting in 1972–1974, Tale 14 of her harvest was similar in most respects to this one, and its popular reception suggests that there would be a ready audience for an oral telling of Tale 95 if a narrator were to tell it. The story was present in the Nkundo oral tradition in the early 1950s (as evidenced by its inclusion in *Bekolo Bèmò...*) and may well be uncovered by dedicated Nkundo collectors trained by Mrs. Ross and now at work in the field, especially in areas not tapped by Mrs. Ross in her fieldwork.

This dilemma tale carries to seemingly absurd lengths the traditional Nkundo respect for tabus, an exaggerated respect reflected also in Tale 14; in the latter tale, the emphasis rests on the *pourquoi* element. In neither tale, however, can the demands and obligations of friendship be ignored without serious consequences. The respect for tabus—absurd as the demands may seem to those outside the culture—reflects a continuing concern among the Nkundo for individual tabus; a number of other tales in this collection confirm the cultural emphasis on observance of such tabus.

Arewa's "Classification ..." lists dilemma tales as Type 4291, 4301, and 4311;

none of his samples seems close enough to the present tale to warrant its being listed among them. Lambrecht's tale type 4491 (4) [erroneously numbered, since it clearly continues Arewa's 4291 tabulation] and 4503 are the only two which would qualify as dilemma tales in the light of Bascom's analysis, and neither one of these offers as sound an "umbrella" as does Lambrecht's type 1030, though the latter is not treated as a dilemma tale. Aarne-Thompson's Index affords no parallel, nor does Bascom's sampling. Klipple offers two dilemma tales, both under Motif Z16., neither of which sheds light on the present tale.

Since the tale does not appear to bear the seriousness of tone present in a number of other dilemma tales we have examined, we are inclined to feel that it may fall within a special class of dilemma and dilemmalike tales of which both Bascom ("Folklore and Literature," in *The African World* . . . , p. 482) and Paul Goodman ("Introduction" to Jablow's *Yes and No* . . . , p. 21) have taken separate notice. Bascom comments, "Some African folktales combine the dilemma tale and the tall tale"; the "tall tale" flavor is certainly apparent in the present tale. Goodman observes, "The trick is to jabber about a dilemma until it turns into a comedy and vanishes into thin air, for the laughable is a big deal that comes to absolutely nothing. Now when a comedy collapses into the ridiculous, there is released a repressed energy of lust and malice, that used to be bound in the dilemma."

Whatever one might conclude concerning the social function of this particular tale in its own culture—either in a storytelling context or as an exercise in argument preparatory to successful palavers—one element deserves special attention. Extravagant as it may seem, the refusal of the tortoise to climb over the tree trunk is a staple in Nkundo oral tradition, and the reasoning behind that refusal can scarcely be faulted. (See the discussion of "Het Vuur" in the notes for Tale 3, providing an explanation for the origin of this tabu.)

Motifs:

T	H1558.	Test of friendship.
T	J230.	Choice: real and apparent values.
C	H1220.1.+.**.	Quest undertaken to fetch doctor for civet cat's dying mother.
T	H1110.	Tedious tasks.
T	J1511.	A rule must work both ways.
C	C640.+.**.	Tabu: tortoise's climbing over tree trunk.
C	J345.+.**.	Foolish messenger and friends neglect errand of fetching doctor while they indulge each other's appetites and tabus; patient dies before they reach the doctor.
T	J2137.	Death through lack of foresight.
T	H620.	The unsolved problem: enigmatic ending of tale.

1. The generic name in Lonkundo for the civet cat, a distant and somewhat less malodorous member of the family to which the skunk belongs.
2. Here again, animals live in villages and consult doctors, reflections of Nkundo cultural patterns.
3. Tabus vary widely in character, but violation of tabus is to be avoided at all costs.

The Nkundo themselves, as well as members of other African groups, have certain water sources more highly valued than others; in many instances, they will carry their own individual supply of water to a feast some distance away (see Tauxier, *Le Noir du Yatenga*, pp. 467 ff., "La vieille paivresse"; see also note 7 for Tale 18 in the present volume).

4. A common Lonkundo locution announcing one's own arrival. Normally— as is true among Bantu-speaking peoples in general (see Torrend, *Bantu Folk-Lore* ..., p. 109, fn. 28)—the first greeting ("You have come") is offered by the person being visited.

5. Tale 7 also reflects the Nkundo interest in the eating habits of snakes.

6. Mourning in an Nkundo village, expressed by rolling in the dirt (see Tale 61), pulling of clothes, and wailing, can last as long as six months. The mourning period is customarily followed by a fine feast. Here again, human patterns in an animal tale suggest the working out of human problems through animal "masks."

7. The Lonkundo version of this tale, titled "Nyang'ea Bowane" ("The Mother of the Civet Cat"), appears on pages 80–82 of *Bèkolo Bèmò*. ...

Appendixes

TALE TYPES CITED IN THE NOTES

All tale types cited have been included in the following list without indication as to their relative usefulness in classifying the Ross-collected tales and variants to which reference is made in the entries following the tale type numbers.

Aarne-Thompson Tale Types

9: 58–59, 60	280A: 71	785: 78
37: 29–30	291: 37	893: 15–17
60: 27–28	312C: 62–64	910A: 15–17
75: 43–45, 93	326: 5	949: 55
155: 34	336: 66	1030: 60
156: 43–45	467: 86	1074: 36
156A: 43–45	468: 86	1332: 15–17
211**: 47	480: 32 (n. 9)	1380: 83
220: 13, 42	780: 65	2029: 87
		2034C: 87

Arewa Tale Types

201: 51	855: 29–30	1157 (5): 36
479: 38	1001 (1): 27–28	1191: 18–20
550 (4): 18–20	1001 (2): 27–28	1309 (1): 93
550 (5): 18–20	1075: 9–10, 11–12	1309 (2): 93
670: 67–69 (n. 39)	1134: 37	1571 (1): 9–10, 11–12
762: 31	1157 (2): 36	1571 (2): 9–10, 11–12

Arewa Tale Types (continued)
1622: 67–69 (n. 39)
2086 (1): 33
2086 (2): 33
2421: 43–45, 46
2486: 43–45
2498: 43–45
2512: 46

2527 (1): 43–45
2540: 43–45, 46
2578: 43–45, 93
2751 (type and variants): 34
3017: 81
3485A: 86

3784: 79
3830: 84–85
3952B: 77
3979: 61
4291: 95
4301: 95
4311: 95

Klipple Tale Types

781*: 65
2034*C: 87
Variants A-T 9: 49–50, 58–59
37: 29–30
60: 27–28
75: 93
155: 34

156: 43–45
221: 42
249: 71
545: 47
780: 65
1074: 36
1119: 75–76

Variants Thompson Motifs:
A2491.1.: 6
C31.2.: 80
J2131.5.2.: 72–73
Z16.: 95

Lambrecht Tale Types

3: 3
5: 1
35: 3
65: 7
80 (1): 6
80 (2): 6
462: 21
547: 94
550 (6): 18–20
550 (7): 18–20
550 (8): 18–20
550 (9): 18–20
553: 58–59
579: 25–26
855 (8): 53
855 (9): 29–30
1001 (5): 27–28
1030: 95

1038: 14
1047: 82
1080: 22–24
1082: 22–24, 31
1157 (8): 36
1401C: 38
1462A: 35
1550 (variants): 37
1553 (1): 39–40
1571 (3): 9–10
1980: 84–85
2040: 60
2175: 56
2235: 41
2410: 43–45, 46, 93
2426: 43–45, 46, 93
2427: 43–45
2430: 93

2751 (variants): 34
3070: 72–73
3172: 78, 80
3221: 2 (n. 1)
3260: 2, 2 (n. 16)
3587: 75–76
3590 (3): 32
3650: 72–73
3705: 72–73
3740: 72–73
3752: 80
3831: 84–85
3952 (6): 77
3981: 61
4206: 88–92
4464: 87
4491 (4) [sic]: 95
4503: 95

Ross/Walker Tale Types

949**: 55

1332D: 15–17

1380B: 83

Motifs Cited in the Notes

Included in this listing, in single alphabetical order incorporating citations from the various indexes consulted, are all motifs provided throughout the present volume. The indexers are identified, as in the notes, by the surname initial preceding the motif number. Double asterisks in a motif entry indicate a Ross/Walker adaptation of the entry in the caption following the number. Figures following any given motif number cite the tales and tale clusters in which that motif has been discerned.

T A113.—4
T A220.—2
T A490.—4
T A524.2.**.—2
T A526.7.—2
T A527.3.1.**.—67–69
T A530.—2
T A1270.—1
L A1273.2.—1
T A1275.—1
T A1277.—1
T A1280.—1
T A1290.—1
T A1330.—1
T A1350.—1
T A1352.—1
T A1370.—1
T A1414.7.1.**.—3

T A1470.—1
T A1552.3.—1
T A1570.—1
T A1620.—2
C A1687.+.—84–85 (fn. 9)
T A2241.—31
C A2427.2.+.**.—14
C A2433.3.+.**.—7
C A2433.4.+.—8
T A2435.3.1.**.—15–17
L A2435.3.9.—34
C A2435.3.17.+.**.—11–12
T A2452.1.—14
T A2491.1.—6
T A2491.1.1.—6

C A2491.1.1.+.—6
A A2493.12.2.**.—22–24
T A2494.—94
C A2494.4.+.—15–17
L A2494.5.37.—27–28
C A2494.6.2.+.**.—29–30
L A2494.12.**.—6

T B131.2.—65
T B211.1.7.—14
T B211.2.**.—14
T B211.3.—25–26, 61, 86
T B211.3.**.—14
T B236.0.1.**.—7
T B236.1.**.—7

517

C D1318.+.**.—72–73
C D1318.17.+.**.—80
T D1347.**.—81
T D1389.2.**.—25–26
C D1444.+.**.—47
T D1602.2.2.**.—62–64, 75–76
T D1610.5.—72–73
T D1615.7.—72–73
T D1711.—62–64
C D1711.+.**.—62–64
C D1726.+.**.—62–64, 67–69
T D2161.3.1.1.**.—75–76

T E1.**.—48
T E50.—72–73
T E100.—6
C E225.+.**.—72–73
T E230.**.—65, 72–73
C E231.+.**.—65, 72–73
T E632.1.—72–73
T E761.7.**.—2

T F17.—2
T F54.2.**.—86
T F62.0.1.**.—2
C F253.1.+.**.—62–64, 65, 78
T F400.—62–64, 65
T F401.**.—66
C F401.2.+.**.—83
T F402.1.2.**.—65
T F402.1.4.—65
T F402.1.4.**.—65
C F402.1.4.+.**.—62–64, 65
T F405.**.—62–64, 67–69, 75–76
C F408.+.**.—67–69
T F420.**.—57, 62–64
T F441.**.—65
C F446.1.+.**.—79
T F500.**.—83
T F521.3.4.**.—83
C F529.+.**.—61
T F531.6.12.**.—62–64, 67–69

T F600.—80
C F628.1.0.1.+.**.—67–69
C F810.+.**.—62–64, 75–76
T F811.**.—75–76
T F838.**.—58–59
T F910.**.—67–69
T F911.—67–69
T F912.2.—77
T F912.2.**.—67–69
T F913.—77
T F915.**.—67–69
T F930.**.—57
T F940.—62–64, 78
C F949.+.**.—62–64
T F979.4.**.—75–76
C F988.3.+.**.—25–26

C G11.2.—79
C G11.15.+.**.—62–64, 77, 79
T G61.**.—18–20
C G80.+.**.—67–69
T G81.—61, 62–64
T G81.**.—62–64
T G84.**.—61, 62–64
T G88.**.—61
T G211.4.5.**.—75–76
C G261.+.**.—46
T G270.**.—75–76
T G275.2.—62–64
C G317.+.**.—62–64
T G351.1.—46
C G353.+.**.—75–76
C G361.+.**.—46, 77
T G400.—79
T G400.**.—62–64
T G440.—65
T G462.**.—75–76
T G500.—62–64, 67–69
T G501.—60, 75–76
T G501.**.—39–40 (fn. 4)
T G510.—75–76
T G510.**.—67–69
T G512.—67–69
T G512.**.—62–64
T G512.1.—77

T G512.1.**.—61, 84–85
T G512.3.—67–69
C G512.8.+.**.—61
T G512.9.1.—62–64
T G512.9.1.**.—46
T G519.**.—61
T G520.—39–40 (fn. 4), 67–69
T G520.**.—46
T G530.**.—61, 62–64
T G532.**.—62–64
T G551.—77
T G551.1.—61, 62–64
T G552.—62–64
T G555.—75–76
T G555.**.—75–76
T G560.—60
T G570.—60, 66
T G580.**.—60
T G582.1.**.—62–64, 66
T G630.—66

T H175.2.**.—81
C H175.2.+.**.—81
T H210.—57, 78
T H220.**.—62–64, 78
T H221.—25–26
T H223.**.—57
T H225.**.—57, 62–64
T H310.**.—51, 52
T H326.1.2.**.—51
T H331.4.1.—51
T H335.0.1.**.—51
T H479.**.—79
T H481.**.—81
T H506.—18–20, 72–73, 75–76
T H509.**.—49–50
T H620.—95
C H620.+.**.—93
L H659.11.2.—88–92
T H936.—2, 8
T H970.—36
T H1024.—27–28
T H1110.—8, 14, 95
T H1132.—32, 86
T H1149.—2
T H1219.**.—32

Selected Bibliography

With the exception of the few entries identified as "cited by ...," furnished within parentheses, all items listed in the Selected Bibliography have been consulted by us in the preparation of the present study.

AARNE, ANTTI, and STITH THOMPSON. *The Types of the Folktale: A Classification and Bibliography*. Folklore Fellows Communications No. 184, 2nd rev. Helsinki: Suomalainen Tiedeakatemia, 1961.

AREWA, E. OJO. "A Classification of the Folktales of the Northern East African Cattle Area by Types." Unpublished Ph.D. dissertation, University of California (Berkeley), 1966. Pp. 298. [available through University Microfilms, Ann Arbor, Michigan]

ASAMANI, J. O. *Index Africanus*. Stanford: Hoover Institution Press, 1975.

BADIBANGA. *L'Éléphant qui marche sur des oeufs*. Bruxelles: L'Eglantine, 1931.

BASCOM, WILLIAM. *African Dilemma Tales*. The Hague: Mouton, 1975.

—————. "African Dilemma Tales: An Introduction," in *African Folklore*, ed. Richard M. Dorson. Bloomington: Indiana University Press, 1972.

—————. "Folklore and Anthropology," *Journal of American Folklore*, 66 (1953), 283–290.

—————. "Folklore and Literature," in *The African World: A Survey of Social Research*. Ed. for the African Studies Association by Robert A. Lystad. New York: Frederick A. Praeger, 1965.

—————. "Folklore Research in Africa," *Journal of American Folklore*, 77 (1964), 12–31.

—————. "The Forms of Folklore: Prose Narratives," *Journal of American Folklore*, 78 (January–March 1965), 3–20.

—————. "Four Functions of Folklore," *Journal of American Folklore*, 67 (1954), 333–349.

—————. *Ifa Divination: Communication Between Gods and Men in West Africa*. Bloomington: Indiana University Press, 1969.

—————. "Verbal Art," *Journal of American Folklore*, 68 (1955), 245–252.

BATEMAN, MARTHA, LILLIAN BOYER HEDGES, AND WILMA JAGGARD, COMPS. *Bekolo Bèmò Bendemba Ba-Nkundo*. Bòlèngè, [Zaïre]: L'Imprimérie de la D.C.C.M., 1957.

BAYAKA, J., ET AL. "Politesse Mongo," *Aequatoria*, 8 (1945), 103–108.

BEN-AMOS, DAN. "Folklore in African Society," *Research in African Literatures*, 6 (1975), 165–198.

BERRY, JACK. "Oral Data Collecting and Linguistics in Africa," *Journal of the Folklore Institute*, 6, 2/3 (August/December 1969), 93–110.

BETTELHEIM, BRUNO. *The Uses of Enchantment: The Meaning and Importance of Fairy Tales*. New York: Alfred A. Knopf, 1976.

BIEBUYCK, DANIEL. "The Epic as a Genre in Congo Oral Literature," in *African Folklore*, ed. Richard M. Dorson. Bloomington: Indiana University Press, 1972.

BOELAERT, E. "De Elima der Nkundó," *Congo*, 1 (1936), 42–52.

—————. "Eloko, de boeman der Nkundó," *Zaïre*, 3 (1949), 129–137.

—————. *Lianja, het nationaal epos der Móngo*. Antwerp: De Sikkel, 1960.

—————. *Lianja—Verhalen I, Ekofo-versie*. Tervuren, 1957. [Pp. 244.]

—————. "Nsong'â Lianja," *Congo*, 1 (1934), 49–71, 197–216.

—————. "Nsong'â Lianja, L'Épopée nationale des Nkundó," *Aequatoria*, 12 (1949), 1–75.

—————. "La procession de Lianja," *Aequatoria*, 25 (1962), 1–9.

BREMOND, C. " 'The Impossible Restitution' as a Specifically African Theme," *The Conch*, 2 (September 1970), 54–58.

BURTON, RICHARD R. *Wit and Wisdom of West Africa*. London: Tinsley, 1865.

BURTON, W. F. P. "A Luba Folk-Tale," *Bantu Studies*, 9 (1935), 69–80.

—————. *The Magic Drum: Tales from Central Africa*. London: Methuen, 1961; New York: Criterion, 1961.

BUSTIN, EDOUARD. *A Study Guide for Congo—Kinshasa*. Boston: Boston University African Studies Center, 1970.

CHATELAIN, HELI. "African Folk-Life," *Journal of American Folklore*, 10 (1897), 21–34.

CLARKE, KENNETH W. "A Motif-Index of the Folktales of Culture-Area V, West Africa." Unpublished Ph.D. dissertation, Indiana University, 1958. Pp. vii + 589 + maps. [available through University Microfilms, Ann Arbor, Michigan]

COBBLE, ALICE. *Wembi, the Singer of Stories*. St. Louis: Bethany Press, 1959.

COMHAIRE-SYLVAIN, S. AND J. "Kinship Change in the Belgian Congo," *African Studies*, 16 (1957), 20–24.

COUGHLAN, MARGARET N., COMP. *Folklore from Africa to the United States*. Washington, D.C.: Library of Congress, 1976.

COURLANDER, HAROLD. *Tales of Yoruba Gods and Heroes: Myths, Legends and Heroic Tales of the Yoruba People of West Africa*. New York: Crown, 1973.

——————. *A Treasury of African Folklore*. New York: Crown, 1975.

CROWLEY, DANIEL J. "African Oral Literature [A Bibliography]," *African Studies Bulletin*, 5, ii (1962), 43–44.

——————. "The Dilemma of Congolese Folklore," *Journal of the Folklore Institute*, 4, 2/3 (June/December 1967), 162–170.

——————. "Extra-European Folktale Areas of the World: A Tabular Analysis," *Folklore Students Association Preprint Series* [Bloomington, Indiana], 1 (July 1973), 1–33.

——————. "The Uses of African Verbal Art," *Journal of the Folklore Institute*, 6, 2/3 (August/December 1969), 118–132.

CURTIN, PHILIP D. "Oral Traditions and African History," *Journal of the Folklore Institute*, 6, 2/3 (August/December 1969), 137–155.

CUTHBERTSON, MARGARET B. *Rhodesian Summer: Nature Notes from Veld & Vlei*. Bulawayo, Rhodesia: Rhodesian Printing & Publishing Company, Ltd., 1949.

DATHORNE, O. R. "African Folktales as Literature: Animals, Humans and Gods," *The Conch*, 2 (September 1970), 90–101.

DAYRELL, ELPHINSTONE. *Folk Stories from Southern Nigeria, West Africa*. London: Longmans, Green, 1910.

DE BOUVEIGNES, O[LIVIER] (pseudonym of Léon Guébels). *Ce que content les noirs*. Bruxelles: Collection Durendal, 1934. (cited in Lambrecht's index, p. 156)

——————. *En écoutant conter les noirs*. Collection Lavigerie, Grands Lacs, Namur, 1952.

——————. *Entendu dans la Brousse: Contes Congolaises*. Les Joyaux de l'Orient, X. Paris: Librairie Orientaliste Paul Geuthner, 1938.

——————. "La musique indigène au Congo Belge," *African Music*, 1950, 19–27.

——————. *Sur des levres Congolaises: Contes*. Collection Lavigerie, Grands Lacs, Namur, [n.d.].

DE ROP, A. *De gesproken woordkunst van de Nkundó.* Tervuren: Musée Royal du Congo Belge, 1956.

——————. *Lianja, L'Épopée des Móngo.* Bruxelles: Académie Royale des Sciences d'Outre-Mer, 1964.

DODGE, RALPH EDWARD. "Missions and Anthropology: A Program of Anthropological Research for Missionaries Working Among the Bantu Speaking Peoples of Central and Southern Africa." Unpublished Ph.D. dissertation, Hartford Seminary, 1944.

DONOHUGH, AGNES C. L., AND PRISCILLA BERRY. "A Luba Tribe in Katanga: Customs and Folklore," *Africa,* 5 (1932), 176–183.

DORSON, RICHARD M., ED. *African Folklore* [including the papers read at the Conference on African Folklore, Indiana University, July 16–18, 1970]. Bloomington: Indiana University Press, 1972.

ELLIOT, GERALDINE. *The Long Grass Whispers.* London: Routledge & Kegan Paul, Ltd., 1939.

——————. *Where the Leopard Passes: A Book of African Folk Tales.* London: Routledge & Kegan Paul, Ltd., 1949.

ENGELS, A. "Losáko et proverbes chez les Nkundo," *Bull. der zittingen K.B.K.I.,* 14 (1943), 556–570.

ESSER, JOSEPH. *Légende Africaine: Iyanza, Héros National Nkundo.* Paris: Presses de la Cité, 1957.

EVANS-PRITCHARD, E. E., ED. *The Zande Trickster.* Oxford: Clarendon Press, 1967.

FINNEGAN, RUTH. *Oral Literature in Africa.* Oxford: Clarendon Press, 1970.

FROBENIUS, LEO. "Mudima," in his *Atlantis: Volksmärchen und Volksdichtungen aus Afrika,* Vol. XII. 12 vols. Munich: Forschunginstitut für Kulturmorphologie, 1921–1928.

FUNKE, E. "De Familie im Spiegel der Afrikanischen Volksmärchen," *Zeitschrift für Kolonialsprachen,* 2 (1911–1912), 37–63.

GOETHEM, E. VAN. "Le Dieu des Nkundo," *Aequatoria,* 13 (1950), 1–6.

GOLDSCHMIDT, WALTER. "The Brideprice of the Sebei," *Scientific American,* 229 (July 1973), 74–85.

GÖRÖG, VERONIKA. "Toward a Method of Analysis of African Oral Literature: Introduction to a Selective Analytical Bibliography," *The Conch,* 2 (September 1970), 59–68.

HERSKOVITS, MELVILLE J. AND FRANCES S. *Dahomean Narrative: A Cross-Cultural Analysis.* Northwestern University African Studies, No. 1. Evanston: Northwestern University Press, 1958.

HIMMELHEBER, HANS. *Aura Poku, Volksdichtung aus Westafrika.* Eisenach, 1951. (cited in Clarke's index, p. 524)

HOSKYNS, CATHERINE. "Sources for a Study of the Congo since Independence," *Journal of Modern African Studies,* 1 (1963), 373–382.

HULSTAERT, G. "Chants de Portage," *Aequatoria*, 19 (1956), 53–64.

—————. "La clôture de chasse," *Aequatoria*, 25 (1962), 13–18.

—————. *Dictionnaire Français-Lomongo (Lonkundo)*. Tervuren: La Commission de Linguistique Africaine, 1952.

—————. "Les idées réligieuses des Nkundo," *Congo*, 2 (1936), 668–676.

—————. "Musique indigène et musique sacrée," *Aequatoria*, 12 (1949), 86–88.

—————. "Note sur les instruments de musique à l'Équateur," *Congo*, 2 (1935), 185–200, 354–375. (cited by de Rop in his *Lianja, L'Épopée* . . . , p. 59)

—————. "Que signifie le nom Batswa?" *Aequatoria*, 16 (1953), 101–104.

—————. "Style oral," *Aequatoria*, 8 (1945), 151–152.

—————, and A. de Rop, eds. *Rechtspraakfabels van de Nkundó*. Tervuren: La Commission de Linguistique Africaine, 1954.

JABLOW, ALTA. *Yes and No: The Intimate Folklore of Africa*. New York: Horizon Press, 1961.

JAHN, JANHEINZ. *Muntu: An Outline of Neo-African Culture*. Translated by Marjorie Grene. London: Faber and Faber, Ltd., 1961. [German edition published in 1958 by Eugen Diederichs Verlag]

JUNG, CARL G. "The Phenomenology of the Spirit in Fairytales" (first published in 1948), in *The Collected Works of C. G. Jung*, Vol. IX. Translated by R. F. C. Hull. New York, 1959.

KLIPPLE, MAY AUGUSTA. "African Folk Tales with Foreign Analogues." Unpublished Ph.D. dissertation, Indiana University, 1938. 2 vols. Pp. xxiv + 973. [available through University Microfilms, Ann Arbor, Michigan]

KNAPPERT, JAN. "The Epic in Africa." *Journal of the Folklore Institute*, 4, 2/3 (June/December 1967), 171–190.

LAMBRECHT, WINIFRED. "A Tale Type Index for Central Africa." Unpublished Ph.D. dissertation, University of California (Berkeley), 1967. Pp. 368. [available through University Microfilms, Ann Arbor, Michigan]

LÜTHI, MAX. *Once Upon a Time: On the Nature of Fairy Tales*. Translated by Lee Chadeayne and Paul Gottwald. Bloomington: Indiana University Press, 1976. [German edition: *Es war einmal—Vom Wesen des Volksmärchens*. Göttingen: Vandenhoeck & Ruprecht, 1962.]

M. V. "Valeurs culturelles," *Aequatoria*, 15 (1952), 146–147.

MCDONALD, GORDON C., ET AL. *Area Handbook for the Democratic Republic of the Congo (Congo Kinshasa)*. Washington, D.C.: The American University (Foreign Area Studies), 1971.

MAMET, M. "Les Idéophones du Lontómbá," *Anthropos*, 68, 5/6 (1973), 910–935.

——————. *Le Langage des Bolia*. Sciences de l'Homme, Linguistique. Tervuren: Musée Royal du Congo Belge, 1960.

MAQUET, J. J. "The Modern Evolution of African Populations in the Belgian Congo," *Africa*, 19 (1949), 265–271.

MAYER, PHILIP. "The Joking of 'Pals' in Gusii Age-Sets," *African Studies*, 10 (1951), 27–41

MINTZ, JEROME R. "Discussion of Daniel J. Crowley's Paper ['The Uses of African Verbal Art']," *Journal of the Folklore Institute*, 6, 2/3 (August/December 1969), 133–136.

OKEKE, UCHE. *Tales of Land of Death: Igbo Folk Tales*. New York: Doubleday (Zenith Books), 1971.

PARSONS, ELSIE CLEWS. *Folk-Lore of the Sea Islands, South Carolina*. Memoirs of the American Folk-Lore Society, Vol. XVI. Cambridge, Mass.: The American Folk-Lore Society, 1923.

PAULME, DENISE. "Littérature orale et comportements sociaux en Afrique," *L'Homme*, 1 (1961), 37–49.

——————. "Le thème des échanges successifs dans la littérature Africaine," *L'Homme*, 9 (1969), 5–22.

POSTMA, MINNIE. *Tales from the Basotho*. Translated by Susie McDermid. Memoirs of the American Folklore Society, Vol. 59. Austin: University of Texas Press, 1974.

RADIN, PAUL, ED. *African Folktales*. Bollingen Series. New Haven: Princeton University Press, 1952; rev. ed., 1964.

RATTRAY, R. S[UTHERLAND]. *Akan-Ashanti Folk-Tales*. Oxford: Clarendon Press, 1930.

RETEL-LAURENTIN, ANNE. "Structure and Symbolism: An Essay in Methodology for the Study of African Tales," *The Conch*, 2 (September 1970), 29–53.

RUSKIN, E. A. AND L. *The Dictionary of the Lomongo Language*. London: Christian Literature Society, [n.d.].

STAPPERS, L. *Textes Luba: Contes d'Animaux*. Tervuren: Annales, Musée Royal d'Afrique Centrale, 1962.

TALBOT, P. AMAURY. *In the Shadow of the Bush*. London: William Heinemann, 1912.

THOMPSON, LEONARD. "Discussion of Philip D. Curtin's Paper ['Oral Traditions and African History']," *Journal of the Folklore Institute*, 6, 2/3 (August/December 1969), 156–163.

THOMPSON, STITH. *The Folktale*. New York: Dryden Press, 1946.

——————. *Motif-Index of Folk-Literature*. 2nd ed. 6 vols. Bloomington: Indiana University Press, 1955–1958.

TORREND, J. *Specimens of Bantu Folk-Lore from Northern Rhodesia.* London: Kegan Paul, Trench, Trubner & Co., Ltd., 1921.

TRILLES, H. "Les légendes des Béna Kanioka et le folklore Bantou," *Anthropos*, 4 (1909), 945–971; 5 (1910), 163–180.

UNITED NATIONS ECONOMIC COMMISSION FOR AFRICA. *Africa's Food Producers: The Impact of Change on Rural Women.* A *Focus* pamphlet, 25 (January–February 1975), 16 pp. New York: American Geographical Society, 1975.

VUGTEVEEN, VERNA AARDEMA. "How Spider Sold a Big 'Dog,' " in *Laughing Together: Giggles and Grins from Around the Globe*, ed. Barbara K. Walker. New York: UNICEF/Four Winds Press, 1977.

WALKER, BARBARA K. AND WARREN S. *Nigerian Folk Tales.* New Brunswick: Rutgers University Press, 1961.

WEEKS, JOHN H. *Congo Life and Folklore.* London: Religious Tract Society, 1911.

——————. *Jungle Life and Jungle Stories.* London, 1923. (cited in Klipple's index, p. 134)

WERNER, ALICE. *African Mythology* (Vol. 7 of *The Mythology of All Races*, ed. L. H. Gray). New York: Cooper Square Publishers, 1964 [c. 1925].

WESTERMARCK, EDWARD. *Ritual and Belief in Morocco.* 2 vols. London: Macmillan and Co., Ltd., 1926.

WHITELEY, W. H. *A Selection of African Prose. 1. Traditional Oral Texts.* Oxford: Clarendon Press, 1964.

WOLFE, ALVIN W. *In the Ngombe Tradition: Continuity and Change in the Congo.* Evanston: Northwestern University Press, 1961.

Index

Numbers in **boldface** refer to tales or tale clusters; numbers in roman refer to pages. Nkundo personal names are alphabetized according to the initial letter of the African portion of the name, ignoring the honorific "Tata." Terms appearing in lists of motifs have not been indexed.

Aardema, Verna, 219
Aardvark, 390, 399n.14
Aarne, Antti. *See* Aarne-Thompson, *The Types of the Folktale*
Aarne-Thompson, *The Types of the Folktale*, 37; major divisions of, used in present volume, 38; method used in citing, 39; tale types cited from, 515
Abrahams, [Roger D.], 505n.4
Acculturation:
——effects of: on community life, 27, 28; on customs, 26, 101, 103n.8, 495, 500n.25; on family life, 26, 27, 28, 29, 102n.1, 133n.11; on storytelling, 30
——evidences of, 93n.21, 99, 103n.5, 110n.1, 119, 124, 125, 137n.5, 176, 185n.2,5, 205, 207n.3, 226, 247, 249n.5–6, 268n.6,12, 274, 287, 290–91n.2, 311n.9, 368n.35, 400, 404n.2, 413n.7, 448n.20, 456n.9, 463n.11, 495, 499
——resistance against, 109, 110n.7,

123n.2–3, 405n.9
Accusation, unjust, 53, 435–40, 460, 463n.14; in variants, 300–301, 342
Adia unen, in variant, 274
Adornment, 277, 278–79n.4, 426n.4, n.6–8, 485n.14
Adultery, 83, 447n.1
African, *passim*
"African Folk Tales with Foreign Analogues" (Klipple). *See* Klipple, May Augusta
Africa's Food Producers: The Impact of Change on Rural Women, 102n.1
Age: as measure of authority, 261, 404n.4; respect for, 28, 29, 196, 198n.4,6, 277, 278n.3, 279n.16, 295n.1, 296n.5, 300, 303, 311n.13, 337n.22, 404n.4, 457n.12, 497n.13, 504n.1; sets, 22, 255, 355, 367–68n.31
Agriculture: dependence of diet on, 24, 25
——labor involved in: by children, 295n.1; by men, 21, 23, 126n.3, 177n.2; by slaves, 340, 343n.6;

531

This book has been filmset in Times New Roman by Asco Trade Typesetting Ltd of Hong Kong. Times New Roman was designed and produced under the supervision of Stanley Morison for *The Times*, London, England, and was first used by that newspaper in 1932. Because it is an attractive and legible typeface, it is well adapted for use in books. Cushing-Malloy Inc of Ann Arbor, Michigan, has printed the book on a low-acid, long-lived paper. It has been bound at The Short Run Bindery Inc of Medford, New Jersey. All art is the work of Nkundo artists and reflects scenes and objects familiar to those who keep the tales alive today in Zaïre.